GUESTHOUSES
FARMHOUSES
& INNS
IN BRITAIN

GW00632314

Editor: Joan Fensome

Designers: Ashley Tilleard and Paul Fry

Gazetteer compiled by the Publications Research Unit

Maps by Cartographic Services Department

CONTENTS

Produced by the Publications Division of the Automobile Association, Fanum House, Basing View, Basingstoke, Hampshire RG21 2EA

Phototypeset by: Petty & Sons Ltd, Leeds

Printed and bound by: William Clowes (Beccles) Ltd

CONTENTS

Advertising: Peter Whitworth, Head of Advertisement Sales
Tel 0256 20123 (Ext 3061)

Advertisement Sales Representatives:

North England & Scotland:	Brian Nathaniel 061-338 6498
Wales & Midlands:	Arthur Williams 0222 60267
South West:	Bryan Thompson 027580 3296
South East & East Anglia:	Edward May 0256 20123 or 0256 67568

How we chose the Farmhouse of the Year

by Brian Langer, Head of Administration,
Hotel & Information Services

Off the beaten track Britain can still offer excellent value for money, and a friendliness and courtesy of which this country can be proud. It was as a result of the Automobile Association's quest for these qualities that it was decided to seek the best farmhouses from among those listed by the Association, with the purpose of choosing the 'Farmhouse of the Year' for 1980.

We followed the same procedure as for 'Inn of the Year' (1978) and 'Guesthouse of the Year' (1979). Our regional inspectors submitted candidates for the award, based on their own personal knowledge of farmhouses within their area. Subsequently your editor and I booked at, stayed in and assessed the comparative merits of the nominees. We were seeking an active farm, preferably with an especial welcome for families, with the proprietors providing the warmth and hospitality one hopes to find when holidaying in someone's home. Of course standards of cooking and domestic décor were taken into account, but the overall homeliness and genuineness of the experience tended to sway our judgement.

We quickly realised that we had to be sure what we were looking for. Some people treat farms as a form of relatively cheap accommodation *per se* – often oblivious to the wider opportunities such a holiday location can offer. Others seek the peace and solitude associated (rightly or wrongly) with country living, without wishing to take part in any of the activities usually connected with farm life. And some decide on a farm holiday partly because they like the country and want an inexpensive holiday, but also because they want to find out about, and participate in, the life of a farm. We agreed that our Farmhouse of the Year should appeal to the last of these groups and our overall winner combined all the qualities we sought. Other finalists excelled in one or more aspects – décor and furnishings, scenic location, or sophistication of menus – but we can assure you that our overall winner, Leworthy Farm near Holsworthy, Devon, will provide you with hospitable hosts in the persons of Eric and Marion Cornish; a relaxed atmosphere amidst the rolling landscape of the Devon-Cornwall border country; ample, honestly-presented food; opportunities for daytime activity on the farm; and plenty to do in the evenings. You will be able to choose the farm which most nearly suits your particular requirements when you have read about our Farmhouse of the Year and about the Regional Winners, in the special feature beginning on Page 17.

In general, if you are thinking of holidaying on a farm, remember that an arable farm may not have animals for children to see and (with the farmer's permission) make friends with; and activities, including harvesting, where machinery is involved, can be fraught with danger. Equally a small holding with numerous dogs, chickens, cows and horses may prove a bigger success with a family than a farm extending to hundreds of acres all of which are out of bounds to holidaymakers.

Leworthy was the only farm visited which made a point of organising a wide variety of evening entertainments on the farm itself. This may not be to everybody's taste but in an isolated location it can be a great asset to both parents and children. We felt it was one more instance of Eric and Marion Cornish's concern for their guests' wellbeing.

This attitude of caring for guests' happiness was less discernible at some of the other farms, and there was a noticeable variation in the 'availability' of hosts during the hours they were most likely to be needed. Nowhere did we find the hosts' presence intrusive, but in some their total absence for long periods made life a little lonely. A friendly enquiry during the evening, with perhaps the offer of a hot nightcap drink, would not have gone amiss and would have led one to feel that one was staying in someone's home, which happened to be a farm, rather than in an impersonal hotel, which happened to be in the country.

Food we found to be good throughout our journeyings, though we were a bit disappointed not to find more use made of home produce and local specialities. In addition the variety offered, both at dinner and breakfast, was not always in direct relation to the cost of the stay. The advantages to a housewife, catering for her own family as well as guests, of presenting a set meal to her visitors are obvious, but we felt it should be possible to tell guests in advance what the menu was to be, and to provide some simple alternative if required. This was done at some of the farms we visited. We found a welcome pride in the quality of the dishes presented and our farms lived up to the reputation of rural establishments for offering wholesome, honest cooking.

The quality of the bedroom accommodation surprised us both. Some of the owners had obviously gone to great trouble in providing very attractive furnishings and decorations, in addition to that increasingly-sought-after luxury, a private bath or shower and WC. Family rooms, too, were frequently available, so providing an economical holiday; and as the farms we visited were old and contained some spacious rooms ideally suited for the purpose, this accommodation was in no way cramped. One farm even provided a dimmer switch on the room's main light – helpful when settling a child down in a strange room.

If there is a general criticism to be made it has to be over the lack of explicit tariff details available with letters confirming bookings and on display in farms. A few of the farms visited appeared to abide by the statutory requirements to the letter, but regretfully this was not always the case. If anything is likely to upset a guest and ensure he never returns it is a hassle over the bill at the end of a holiday. So please, farmers, clearly show your accommodation and meal prices and whether they are subject to or inclusive of VAT so as to leave nobody in doubt as to the truly excellent value your accommodation offers, whether on a nightly or weekly basis.

We enjoyed our stays at a highly commendable selection of farms in Britain. If a holiday with comfortable accommodation, wholesome food, personal friendliness, good country air, and a chance to experience life on a farm, appeals to you, it can be yours at very low cost, as can be seen from the prices quoted in the gazetteer of farmhouses which begins on page 218.

CHILDREN WELCOME
by Patricia Kelly

Where can you go this year to give the kids a really good holiday, and have one yourselves at the same time? Here we turn the spotlight on a few guesthouses which not only provide pleasant surroundings, good food and all the modern facilities normally associated with AA-inspected accommodation, but do a whole lot more besides. The proprietors of these guesthouses go out of their way to ensure that families with young children will feel welcome. No stiff and starchy formalities, no strained looks at less-than-perfect table manners. Just a happy, healthy environment and the sort of attitude that so often brings out the best in children, making it possible for their parents to relax too.

These are our 'homes from home' for you to enjoy:

Invermoy House, Moy, nr Tomatin, Highland (Inverness-shire)

Invermoy House, set amid pinewoods and moorland, is centrally situated in the Scottish Highlands and is an ideal base for exploring the many places of interest in the area, including Aviemore and the Cairngorms, Culloden Moor and the Kyle of Lochalsh.

The house used to be a railway station, and the main Perth–Inverness line still runs outside the building, but the half-acre grounds are completely enclosed, making it quite safe for children at play. The station was converted in 1969 to form an unusual ranch-type house with bedrooms, lounge, dining room and bathroom all on one level.

The proprietors, Graham and Irene Zimbler, have three children of their own and so plenty of children's toys and outdoor games are available. There are no family rooms, but children are accommodated as near to their parents as possible. Cots and high chairs can be provided for smaller children, and special mealtimes for children can be arranged out of season in order to allow parents the utmost freedom.

Graham Zimbler says that if parents wish to go out in the evenings they will babysit and listen out for the children, and his wife adds that if any washing needs doing (she fully appreciates that children at play get dirty) then she will willingly do it herself.

Mrs Zimbler used to be an air hostess and speaks several languages. Non-English-speaking children are always pleased if they find they are understood, and enjoy their holiday all the more. In fact families from all over Europe are regular guests.

For detailed information, see gazetteer entry under Moy

Graham Zimbler (left) with Mr and Mrs Finkensieper, their young son and Korean daughters Mei-sook and Suyin. The little girl in the middle is Samantha Zimbler

Visitors comment:
'We so enjoyed our holiday at Invermoy House last year that we are going there again this. It is a nice, quiet and very friendly place. Mr and Mrs Zimbler . . . are able to create a special atmosphere to make you feel welcome. We have two Korean daughters and it's nice for them that there are other children to play with. Nearby we found a lot of lovely spots in the woods and the heather, close to little rivers and brooks where our children loved to play and picnic.'
Mr & Mrs S Finkensieper, Den Helder, Holland

Primrose Valley Hotel, St Ives, Cornwall

Situated only 100 yards from Porthminster beach in this popular resort with its ancient buildings, narrow cobbled streets and picturesque harbour, the Primrose Valley is a privately-owned hotel. Ken and Liz Butterworth, who personally supervise the hotel, say that because they have children of their own they are well aware of the needs of families. They do their utmost to create a homely, relaxed atmosphere – in fact relaxation (particularly for mums) is their main theme.

Family and double bedrooms are available, with reductions for children, and a radio/intercom/baby-listening service is provided.

For detailed information see gazetteer entry under St Ives, Cornwall

Ken and Liz Butterworth behind the bar

Woodpeckers Country Hotel, Womenswold, nr Canterbury, Kent

Built over 100 years ago as a rectory, Woodpeckers is ideally situated for those wishing to travel to or from the Continent via Dover, Folkestone or the Ramsgate Hoverport. Over 80 miles of beautiful and varied coastline is within easy reach by road, and a wealth of historical interest in towns and villages throughout East Kent is but a few minutes away.

Ted and Pat Millard took over Woodpeckers in June 1977. Having stayed at many hotels themselves, they knew exactly the pitfalls to avoid, particularly those concerned with dealing with young families. Their backgrounds, too, well equipped them for this type of life, which they took to immediately. Ted was Chairman of one of the largest boys' clubs in England for many years and he is now Life Honorary Vice-President. Pat, too, is much involved with people. She helps to care for the elderly, in association with the local Social Services Department, and regularly holds charity functions for the Kent blind and disabled.

Woodpeckers has acquired a reputation for serving well-cooked traditional English meals and Pat Millard takes overall responsibility for the cooking. She believes in using only the best cuts of meat and fresh vegetables, mostly grown in the garden.

Everything is provided for families, including cots, high chairs, baby-listening and simple washing, ironing and airing facilities. The staff are ready and willing to help in every way to ensure the satisfaction of guests.

In the grounds of over two acres are a swing, sandpit, pets' corner (look out for Edith, the goat) and a heated swimming pool with diving board and water slide. The two lounges provide adequate opportunity for indoor relaxation, one being equipped with television and a selection of children's games.

Ted believes that if the children are made to feel at home, then the parents have no option but to enjoy themselves too. This theory has been proved correct over the years – families return again and again to this popular hotel. He says 'as soon as families arrive, from the word go it is an outright attack on the children. They know when they are wanted . . .' Comments from happy visitors are given in a separate panel, but perhaps the last word should come from Ashley Alexander (aged 11) of Croydon, Surrey, who writes:

'I think Woodpeckers is good. I wish I was staying longer. Peter, the dog, is a good football player and the swimming pool is fantastic. The beds are warm and nice to sleep in. I hope to come back and stay again some day soon.'
What more is there to say?

For detailed information see gazetteer entry under Womenswold

---

Visitors comment:
'On all our visits to Woodpeckers both our children and ourselves have been made very welcome – we feel totally at home immediately. Ted and Pat spare no effort to make each visit enjoyable – our children being treated as if part of their family. Even at the busiest times they and their staff always have time to listen to guests' requests and to provide what is required. As each holiday draws to a close my wife and I are always in agreement with the children when they insist that we re-book for the following year.'

David and Carol Shepherd, Woodlesford, Leeds
'It is wonderful there. Mr & Mrs Millard like children.'

Walter & Barbara Kampe, Rheine, Germany
(writing on behalf of their family party of 6 adults and 10 children who have stayed at Woodpeckers 8 times)

HOW TO USE THE GAZETTEER

Arrangement of gazetteer

The first part of the gazetteer lists Guesthouses and Inns; the second part lists Farmhouses. Each section is arranged in alphabetical order by placename. The establishments are generally more modest in the way of facilities than the AA hotels classified by stars (listed in *AA Members' Handbook* and the AA guide *Hotels and Restaurants in Britain*).

At the back of the book is a 16-page atlas showing the location of establishments.

Reading a map reference

In the gazetteer section of this guide, the main place name is given a two-figure map reference to key with the location atlas. In the Farmhouse section six-figure references have also been given which can be used in conjunction with a larger scale Ordnance Survey map to pinpoint the exact position.

Example: Two-Figure Reference
Map 3 ST76: This is the map reference for Bath in the county of Avon. Turn to Map 3 in the atlas, refer to the group of squares, ST. Find sub-division 7 from *left* to *right* and sub-division 6 from *bottom* to *top*. While every effort has been made to ensure the correct gazetteering of establishments, in some cases the information received by us has been insufficient. In these instances the establishments have been marked at the nearest town.

Town Plans

A number of town plans have been included in the text to show the positions of establishments in some of the larger towns or cities. Included on these maps are the following: one-way streets, car parks, post offices, information centres, cathedrals, and castles. As the gazetteer information is continually being updated, some of the establishments shown on the town plans may have been deleted from the text; conversely some more recent gazetteer entries do not appear on the relevant town plans. The mileages at road exits are calculated from the border of the plan. A list of town plan symbols appears on page 16.

To find a guesthouse, farmhouse or inn

Look at the area you wish to visit in the atlas. *Towns with guesthouses or inns* are marked with a solid dot ●. *Towns with guesthouse/s and/or inn/s plus farmhouse/s* are marked with a dot in an open circle ☉. *Towns with farmhouses only* are marked with an open circle ○.

Remember that farmhouses are listed under the nearest identifiable town or village and may in fact be a few miles away. See also paragraph above *Reading a map reference*.

Gazetteer notes
A key to abbreviations and symbols in gazetteer entries appears on the inside covers.

Accommodation for under £6
Not all guesthouses or inns shown in this publication provide bed and breakfast for under £6 per person per night. Those which expect to do so during 1981 carry the appropriate symbol (⊢⊣).

Annexes
The number of bedrooms in an annexe is indicated by the abbreviation A followed by the number, both bracketed, eg (A6). It should be noted that annexes often used only during the season may lack some of the facilities available in the main building. It is advisable, therefore, that the exact nature of the accommodation and the charges should be checked before reservations are confirmed.

Bathrooms
The gazetteer entry indicates the number of rooms with private bath or shower and wcs where applicable.

Central Heating
Some establishments which are noted as having central heating (🔟🔟) may not have it operating – especially in bedrooms – during cold weather outside the normally recognised winter months. Central heating is indicated only where establishments have **full** central heating.

Cheques
Most establishments will accept cheques in payment of accounts only if notice is given and some form of identification (preferably banker's card) is produced.

Children
Guesthouses and farmhouses usually accommodate children of all ages unless a minimum age is given (eg nc8 – no children under eight), but it does not necessarily follow that they are able to provide special facilities. If you have very young children, enquire about the arrangements that can be made and the provision of any special amenities such as cots and high-chairs. In the gazetteer, establishments which do have special facilities for children are indicated by the symbol ♠. All the following amenities will be found at these establishments: baby-sitting service or baby intercom system, playroom or playground, laundry facilities, drying and ironing facilities, cots and high-chairs, and special meals. Before reserving accommodation it is advisable to ask about facilities and whether reductions are made for children.

Complaints
If you have any complaints you should inform the proprietor immediately so that the trouble can be dealt with promptly. If a personal approach fails, inform the AA using the report form at the back of the book, as soon as possible – within at most a week – so that we can make an investigation. State whether or not you want your name disclosed to the proprietor, and whether you took up the complaint with him/her at the time.

County Names & Postal Addresses

After the place name, the name of the administrative county is shown; it is not necessarily the correct postal address. For places in Scotland the region is given followed by the old county name in *italics*.

Deposits

Some establishments require a deposit before accepting a booking.

Disabled Persons

If the wheelchair symbol &. is shown in an establishment's entry it means that the disabled can be accommodated. This information has been supplied to the AA by the proprietor but it is advisable to check before making reservations. Details more relevant to disabled persons may be obtained from *The AA Guide for the Disabled* priced £1 from AA offices (free to members). Members with any form of disability should notify proprietors so that appropriate arrangements can be made to minimise difficulties, particularly in the event of an emergency.

Dogs

Establishments which do not accept dogs are indicated by the symbol ✖. There may be restrictions on dogs of certain sizes or the rooms into which they may be taken. The conditions under which pets are accepted should be confirmed with the management when making reservations.

Family bedrooms

In this edition, for the first time, we indicate whether family bedrooms are available by the abbreviation fb together with the relevant number of rooms, both appearing bracketed, eg (2fb).

Farms

Within each gazetteer entry is the six-figure reference to be used in conjunction with Ordnance Survey maps. This number follows the establishment name and is in *italics*.

The acreage of each establishment is shown in the body of each entry (*eg* 55 acres) followed by the type of farming that predominates in the relevant farm (*eg* dairy, arable etc). An innovation is that we now give the name/s of the proprietor/s of each farmhouse.

Although the AA lists working farms, some may have become 'non-working' before publication if, for instance, the farmer has sub-let or sold land. Potential guests should ascertain the true nature of the farm's activity before booking to ensure their requirements are met.

Fire Precautions

So far as can be ascertained at the time of going to press, every unit of accommodation listed in this publication, provided it is subject to the requirements of the Act, has applied for and not been refused a fire certificate. The Fire Precautions Act 1971 does not apply to the Channel Islands or the Isle of Man, both of which exercise their own rules with regard to fire precautions for accommodation units.

Gazetteer Entry

Establishment names shown in *italics* indicate that particulars have not been confirmed by the management in time for this 1981 edition.

Licences

An indication is given in each entry where a guesthouse is licensed. Most places in the guesthouse category do not hold a full licence but all inns do. Licensed premises are not obliged to remain open throughout the permitted hours and may do so only when they expect reasonable trade. Note that at establishments which have registered clubs, club membership does not come into effect — nor can a drink be bought — until 48 hours after joining. For further information refer to leaflet HH20 'The Law about Licensing Hours and Children/Young Persons on Licensed Premises' available from AA offices.

London

It is common knowledge that in London prices tend to be higher than in the provinces. For hotels, we have tried to select establishments where the accommodation is inexpensive and where bed and breakfast is normally provided. We have also included a few which provide a full meal service and whose charges are consequently higher.

Meals

In some parts of the country, high tea is generally served in guesthouses although dinner is often also available on request. The latest time that the evening meal can be **ordered** is indicated in the text. On Sundays, many establishments serve their main meal at midday and will charge accordingly. This may mean that only cold supper is available in the evening.

Prices

Prices are liable to fluctuation and it is advisable to check when you book. Also, make sure you know exactly what facilities are being offered when you are verifying charges, because there are variations in what an establishment may provide within inclusive terms. Weekly terms, for instance, vary from full board to bed and breakfast only. This is shown in the text by the symbol **Ł** (no lunches) and **M** (no main meals). Some establishments provide packed lunches, snacks or salads at extra cost — inns providing snacks are identified in entries by the abbreviation sn. All prices quoted normally include VAT and service, where applicable.

*1980 Prices

When proprietors have been unable to furnish us with their proposed 1981 prices, those for 1980 are quoted, prefixed by an asterisk (✳).

Requests for Information

If you are writing to an establishment requesting information it is important to enclose a stamped, addressed envelope. Please quote this publication in any enquiry.

13

Reservations
Please book as early as you possibly can or you may be disappointed. If you are delayed or have to change your plans, let the proprietor know at once. You may be held legally responsible if the room you booked cannot be re-let. Some establishments, especially those in short-season holiday centres, do not accept bookings for bed and breakfast only. Additionally, some guesthouses – particularly in seaside resorts – do not take bookings from midweek to midweek, and a number will not accept period bookings other than at full board rate, *ie* not at nightly bed and breakfast rate plus individual meals.

It is regretted that the AA cannot undertake to make any reservations.

The hotel industry's Voluntary Code of Booking Practice was introduced in June 1977. Its prime object is to ensure that the customer is clear about the precise services and facilities he or she is buying, and what price he will have to pay, before he commits himself to a contractually binding agreement. The guest should be handed a card at the time of registration, with a full tariff including the total obligatory charge, and details may also be displayed prominently at the reception office.

The Tourism (Sleeping Accommodation Price Display) Order 1977 was introduced in February 1978. It compels hotels, motels, guesthouses, inns and self-catering accommodation with four or more letting bedrooms to display in entrance halls the maximum and minimum prices charged for each category of room. This order complements the Voluntary Code of Booking Practice.

Every effort is being made by the AA to encourage the use of the Voluntary Code in appropriate establishments.

Restricted Service
Some establishments operate a restricted service during the less busy months. This is indicated by the prefix rs. For example, rs Nov–Mar indicates that a restricted service is operated from November to March. This may be a reduction in meals served and/or accommodation available.

Seasonal Openings

Unless otherwise stated establishments are open all year. Where dates are shown these are inclusive; eg *Apr–Oct* indicates that the establishment is open from the beginning of April to the end of October.

Telephone Numbers
In some areas telephone numbers are likely to be changed by the Post Office during the currency of this publication. If any difficulty is found when making a reservation it is advisable to check with the operator.

It is most important that the following note on telephone numbers is read and understood: Much confusion has arisen in the past by members not reading it and consequently misinterpreting numbers in the gazetteer entries.

IMPORTANT – Unless otherwise stated, the exchange is that of the place under which the entry is listed.

For instance, if an establishment is listed under Whitby and the telephone number is given as (☎12345), the exchange to dial is Whitby. In a case such as the Traddock Guest House, however, which is listed under Austwick, the number is given as (☎Clapham 224), and the exchange to dial is Clapham. For details of dialling codes, see Post Office *Telephone Dialling Codes*.

Television
If the gazetteer entry shows 'CTV' or 'TV', either colour or monochrome television is available in lounge.

VAT and Service Charge
In the United Kingdom and the Isle of Man, Value Added Tax is payable on both basic prices and any service. The symbol S% in the gazetteer indicates that the inclusive prices shown reflect any separate accounting for service made by the establishment. VAT does not apply in the Channel Islands. With this exception, prices quoted in the gazetteer are inclusive of VAT at 15%.

Explanation of a gazetteer entry
The example is fictitious

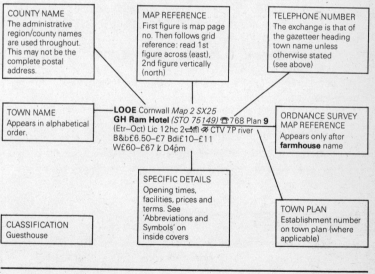

COUNTY NAME
The administrative region/county names are used throughout. This may not be the complete postal address.

MAP REFERENCE
First figure is map page no. Then follows grid reference: read 1st figure across (east), 2nd figure vertically (north)

TELEPHONE NUMBER
The exchange is that of the gazetteer heading town name unless otherwise stated (see above)

TOWN NAME
Appears in alphabetical order.

LOOE Cornwall Map 2 SX25
GH Ram Hotel *(STO 75149)* ☎768 Plan **9**
(Etr–Oct) Lic 12hc 2⇔🛏 ⊁ CTV 7P river
B&bf£6.50–£7 Bdif£10–£11
Wf£60–£67 ⚓ D4pm

ORDNANCE SURVEY MAP REFERENCE
Appears only after **farmhouse** name

SPECIFIC DETAILS
Opening times, facilities, prices and terms. See 'Abbreviations and Symbols' on inside covers

TOWN PLAN
Establishment number on town plan (where applicable)

CLASSIFICATION
Guesthouse

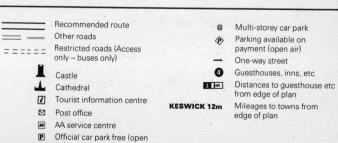

▬▬▬ Recommended route	⓪ Multi-storey car park
══ ══ Other roads	℗ Parking available on payment (open air)
═ ═ ═ ═ Restricted roads (Access only – buses only)	→ One-way street
♜ Castle	❹ Guesthouses, inns, etc
♆ Cathedral	🔲 Distances to guesthouse etc from edge of plan
🄘 Tourist information centre	**KESWICK 12m** Mileages to towns from edge of plan
✉ Post office	
Ⓜ AA service centre	
℗ Official car park free (open air)	

15

| **AA** | # Publications
| | ## Guides and Atlases for every occasion

SUPERGUIDES

Hotels and Restaurants in Britain

Impartially inspected and updated annually, this guide lists 5,000 AA approved places to stay or wine and dine in comfort.

Camping and Caravanning in Britain

1,000 sites around Britain, checked for quality and maintenance of facilities and graded accordingly A special colour feature describes a picturesque camping route to Lakeland.

Guesthouses, Farmhouses and Inns in Britain

Thousands of inexpensive places to stay, selected for comfortable accommodation, good food and friendly atmosphere. Special feature on the search for "Farmhouse of the Year"

Self Catering in Britain

A vast selection for the independent holiday-maker — thatched cottages, holiday flats, log cabins and many more, all vetted by AA inspectors.

Stately Homes, Museums, Castles and Gardens in Britain

An unlimited choice for all the family, including zoos, wildlife parks, miniature and steam railways, all listed with opening times, admission prices, restaurant facilities etc.

Motoring in Europe

Camping and Caravanning in Europe

Guesthouses, Farmhouses and Inns in Europe

ATLASES

Complete Atlas of Britain

Superb value for the modern motorist. Full colour maps at 4 miles to 1 inch scale. 25,000 place name index, town plans, 10 page Central London guide, distance chart and more.

Motorists' Atlas of Western Europe

Brand new AA atlas covering Europe at 16 miles to 1 inch scale. 10,000 place name index, route planning section, town plans of capital cities.

All these publications and many more are available from AA shops and major booksellers.

THE AA FARMHOUSE OF THE YEAR

and WINNER, SOUTH WEST ENGLAND

Leworthy Farm, Holsworthy, Devon (Mr and Mrs Eric Cornish)

Eric and Marion Cornish

Every year Eric Cornish writes a long newsy letter to old friends who have spent holidays at Leworthy Farm, and the same letter goes to people booking for the first time so that they will know a bit about the people, the animals and the place – and Eric's philosophy – before they arrive. 1980's letter made the point that if you can survive the first ten minutes you'll have joined the Leworthy club.

We arrived at about 6.15pm, smiled at the signpost near the farm gate which points north to England, south to France, west to Sunnybank and east to Leworthy (we found out later that France is the name of the next hamlet), parked the car, and exclaimed at the wellie-stand outside the door which accommodates a dozen or so pairs of boots upturned over little posts. Eric, who came out to meet us, pointed out a clematis coming into bloom, the lake beyond the home paddock where Canada geese have made their home, and the woods where deer can be seen if you are quiet. Indoors we stepped around a young Australian visitor who was sitting on the floor vigorously polishing a saddle, and were then taken into the lounge.

'I expect you'd like a cup of tea after your journey,' said Eric, 'make yourselves at home while I check with my wife which rooms you're to have.' The lounge is a pleasant room with comfortable settee and chairs, a piano in one corner, a sizeable bar facing it, and an ancient fire range and bread oven taking up almost the whole of one side. On the walls are an aerial photo of the farm and family pictures, including a child's drawing of Eric. We'd only just had time to take all this in when the subject of the drawing returned with a tea tray.

There were three cups and saucers and only two of us, but the arithmetic was explained when Eric sat down and we shared the really good hot brew between us. When it is remembered that Eric had no idea who we were, and that we had booked for only one night, his keenness to make us feel really welcome was quite remarkable.

So we – and he – got through the first ten minutes with flying colours. And the rest of the visit did not disappoint us.

Marion Cornish was putting the finishing touches to dinner, but she found time to show us to our rooms, which were clean and comfortable, and gave one all one needed in the way of equipment. We had washbasins in our rooms, with good bathrooms and toilets nearby, but two bedrooms have shower and WC *en suite*.

The large, airy dining room – converted from stables – can accommodate about fifty people and often does, for an annexe across the lane (not AA-listed) is used for additional guests. Shortly before our visit a party of disabled youngsters had taken the place over and had a marvellous time.

Because she was properly trained in catering and cooking – she has a degree from Bristol University – Marion makes no trouble of providing meals for a crowd. And what meals! Dinner started with a choice of soup or fruit juice, then came the main course which might well have been pre-pared by an old-fashioned mum for a special occasion. I doubt whether the succulent chicken had ever seen the inside of a freezer, and the stuffing which accompanied it tasted of fresh herbs. We each had a joint and slices carved from the breast, and freshly-cooked vegetables were left on the table for us to help ourselves. The sweet was a choice from various fruit and ice-cream or Devonshire cream combinations, including banana split and fresh strawberries and cream. Biscuits and a selection of cheeses were offered but by that time my hunger had been assuaged. However, my colleague Brian sampled them and we both enjoyed a cup of coffee to complete a very enjoyable meal. Wines, etc, are available with dinner, but Eric does not press them on his guests and water is placed on the tables.

Guests enjoy tea in the big garden

Later that evening I chatted to Eric at the bar and he told me how he and his wife had moved back to his native Devon in 1964, having first started farming in Buckinghamshire. At that time they had a dairy herd as well as sheep and beef cattle, but to help with finances they decided to do bed and breakfast. For some years they slept in a caravan during the season so as to have most of the rooms in the house available for letting. Now, of course, the house is much larger, farm buildings having been incorporated into the main house. Additional bedrooms have been constructed, and a big new living room for the family has been built on. An old barn nearby is currently being converted into self-catering units.

Eric says he was very shy when they first took guests – difficult to believe now! – but soon got over that and now really enjoys his job as 'front man'. Tourism has, in fact, taken over from farming to some extent; he has given up his dairy herd and his 240 acres are used for beef cattle and sheep. However, one of the things we most like about Leworthy is that it retains the feeling of a farm, and Eric is endlessly inventive in finding double uses for his buildings. The cattle are wintered in a new barn which, during the holiday season, becomes a badminton court, while the slurry pit is cleaned out and changes, in a few waves of a besom, into a tennis court. The floor of the big dining room is just right for dancing, but in season it also accommodates a snooker table, and a corner of the lounge has a little raised platform for the Country and Western guitarist who comes in on Sundays.

That gives an idea of the way Eric and Marion look after their guests, but the list is by no means finished. Horses are available (free) for anyone who wants to ride, provided they wear hard hats; you can't fish in the lake – Eric did stock it with trout but says cormorants have taken nearly all of them – but you may fish in the nearby river; there's a weekly show for children – a film or a conjuror usually; adults are catered for by a weekly grown-ups-only party, and live music for dancing is provided at least once a week. There is a TV lounge – evenings only – but not many people use it, there's so much else to do.

Morning tea was provided without extra charge, and a substantial break-fast consisted of fruit juice; cereal; bacon, sausage (locally made and very good), egg/s, fried bread (or just eggs, done anyway you like); toast and marmalade, and a pot of tea (coffee provided on request).

The coast, at Bude, is not far away, and there are many interesting places nearby, but with so many things on the farm to keep visitors occupied they don't always want to go out for the day so Marion will provide a snack lunch – ploughman's or pasty – if required. Eric tells me they use home-grown beef and lamb, and fruit, vegetables, cream, etc. are locally produced.

There's plenty for children to do

The main factors which ensured the winning position for Mr and Mrs Cornish were not furnishings and equipment (though these were good) or food (though they cater for healthy appetites with tasty meals in Devon tradition) but the welcome given to children as well as adults, the great enthusiasm shown by both Eric and Marion in making Leworthy a happy place to stay, and excellent value for money.

WINNER, SOUTH EAST ENGLAND

University Farm, Lew, Oxfordshire (Mrs Mary Rouse)

University Farm is built of mellow Cotswold stone, with farm buildings as attractive as the house itself; and a big garden (where many vegetables for use in the farm kitchen are grown) leads to fields where Donald Rouse's herd of Friesians graze. It's a peaceful rural scene, though the quiet is occasionally disturbed by aircraft from Brize Norton airfield. Mary Rouse tells us that most guests are interested in the planes, particularly Concorde; and anyway aircraft noise is hardly audible from indoors.

With Donald busy on the farm it falls to Mary to run the guesthouse side of the business and she does this almost single-handed and with great efficiency, always managing to look well-groomed herself however busy she may be. Because she is chef she cannot always spare time to be with her guests, which may make one's initial welcome seem a bit distant, but she is really a very warm and friendly person who takes an interest in her guests' well-being. She used to be a secretary, and then a teacher, but after helping out at a hotel belonging to friends and finding she enjoyed the work, she suggested selling the farm (which had been their home for 17 years) and buying a hotel. Donald was not at all in favour. 'Why not take guests here?' he asked, which seemed a sensible compromise. Over the four years since then they have converted, adapted and improved until they now have four letting rooms, three of them with bathroom *en suite*. All are attractively furnished, with a careful blend of pastel shades, have comfortable beds (with duvets) and are spotlessly clean.

Plants and flowers are much in evidence downstairs, adding to the pleasant décor of the public rooms. In the lounge are scrabble and other games, plenty of brochures about places of interest nearby, and colour television.

Donald and Mary Rouse

Basic terms here are for bed and breakfast only and by an oversight we had not ordered dinner. We arrived at about 6 o'clock, which was rather late for Mary to rustle up extra meals (especially out of season when only two other people were staying at the farm) but she coped most creditably. We had succulent smoked mackerel with salad garnish followed by *daube* of beef served on rice in individual dishes, with a superb side salad. Home-made wholemeal rolls were supplied, with plenty of fresh butter. Sweets were delicious and Mary obviously enjoys this part of the cooking for she says she likes having the house full so that she can offer a trolley with a good selection of sweets. We had the choice of three, from which I selected profiteroles and Brian had lemon chiffon, both of which were delicious. Biscuits and cheese followed, for anyone with a corner to fill. Romboults coffee was available as an extra.

Breakfast was another good meal, with cereal or fruit juice, sausage, bacon, egg, tomato and fried bread, toast with home-made marmalade, and tea or coffee.

Mary Rouse serves set meals but she takes the precaution of sending a list of her standard dishes to longer-term guests some weeks before they are due, inviting them to say if there is anything they dislike or are not allowed to eat.

Children are welcomed to University Farm, and there are plenty of fields for them to play in but they must be kept under supervision. At one end of the house is an old chapel, now headquarters of a weightlifting club. Table tennis is available and Don, who is interested in Country music, sometimes organises barn dances which guests are welcome to attend. There is a grass tennis court behind the house which was rather rough when we were there but is being improved.

Children will enjoy playing with the dogs, a rumbustious, friendly lot. Throw a stick and it will always be old Cindy who brings it back. If one of the younger dogs reaches it first he may pick it up and bring it half way, but will dutifully put it down again for the doyen of the pack to retrieve and return.

Lew is a very good centre for touring the Cotswolds and the upper Thames valley, and there are a number of stately homes and other places of interest, including Oxford and Stratford-on-Avon, not far away.

University Farm was nearly our over-all winner, but we decided that it is not quite so good for children as Leworthy Farm, and, although it offers good value for money, it is perhaps a little on the expensive side for a family holiday. However, we do recommend it highly for adults who want somewhere to stay, with beautifully appointed accommodation and excellent food, either for a restful break or as a touring centre.

WINNER, SCOTLAND

Rovie Farm, Rogart, Highland (Mrs Christine Moodie)

Rovie farm has a setting typical for a Scottish farm, securely placed in the centre of a valley through which runs the River Fleet, with hills rising to 1,000ft on either side.

For 23 years Stan and Christine Moodie have been farming at Rovie, both having been brought up in this part of the world. It was only after running several other farms that Stan finally decided to settle here. At present there are 120 arable acres on which oats, swedes and potatoes are grown, as well as 4,000 hill acres on which 450 lambing ewes graze. There are also cattle and sheep around the farm in addition to three collies, three Shetland ponies and the occasional pig. Stan is ably assisted around the farm by his son John, who can be seen at times scrambling around the farm on his motorbike. Stan is also a man of action and guests may see him literally swooping down upon his farm as he is a keen hang-glider pilot.

The needs of guests are ably catered for by Christine Moodie in her comfortably-furnished house which has one twin-bedded and two double letting bedrooms, all of which have wash basins. These bedrooms have the use of one bathroom, one shower room and two toilets.

On the ground floor the lounge accommodation is to a very high standard, reflecting the Moodies' personal tastes and providing space and comfort. In addition to the main lounge there is a small sun lounge to the rear of the house. The dining room is furnished with dark wood polished tables and Regency-striped chairs. Christine does her best to ensure that guests receive the best of local produce, with a regular rotation of menu ensuring no repetition, and in addition to dinner and breakfast she provides a late supper with home baking. She says she has a job to keep guests out of her kitchen as they enjoy being there so much.

Children will feel particularly welcome here, with plenty to do, from paddling and fishing in the gently-flowing River Fleet to assisting in general farm chores, which Stan really encourages. Guests may even be lucky enough to hitch a ride over some of the more rugged terrain in Stan's amphibious vehicle.

At Rovie you can enjoy good Highland hospitality in quiet secluded surroundings, yet the beach and town of Dornoch are only 14 miles away.

WINNER, NORTHERN ENGLAND

Parrock Head Farm, Slaidburn, Lancashire (Mrs Pat Holt)

You couldn't find a much quieter spot than Parrock Head Farm, surrounded by the Bowland Fells and far from road noise. Only the cattle and the clouds move, the former grazing their way across rich meadows, the latter making ever-changing patterns of light and shade across the land.

Yet this is the least typical farm of any we visited and could better be described as a select guesthouse in a rural setting.

Pat Holt started taking guests when left with two teenage children to bring up on her own. In 1977 she married Richard Holt, who has his own profession but is a great help to Pat when he is at home.

I was shown a photograph of the house taken, I would guess, about a hundred years ago. In the picture it looks somewhat dilapidated and poor, hardly recognisable as the beautifully appointed and tastefully furnished house as it exists now. Of course it has been extended, as well as being repaired and modernised. A new annexe contains four bedrooms with bathrooms *en suite*, excellently fitted up and with trolleys containing everything necessary for tea or coffee making, plus packets of biscuits. Tissues and cottonwool balls are other thoughtful extras. In the main house the bedrooms are larger, two of them being family rooms with separate single rooms *en suite* and private bathrooms.

We had rooms in the annexe, very well appointed and attractive. Brian thought that the tea and coffee-making facilities were a bit impersonal and not quite what one expected on a farm, but I was too thankful for the opportunity to have extra cuppas to be critical. On the other hand I found my bed hard – possibly just because it was very new – but Brian had no complaint on this score. Duvets are used, but the beds are made with top sheets as well, which I thought was a good idea. Walls are kept plain and pale, colour being provided in the soft furnishings.

This was the only farm where the menu was à la carte. Pat Holt reckons always to offer one reasonably cheap main course for those who prefer to spend their money on other things. Also one need not necessarily take all courses, or alternatively one could ask for extra dishes if a day's fell walking had produced an outsize appetite. Starters included soup at 50p with hot rolls, and hors d'oeuvre platter at £1.40 which sounds as though it would serve as main course for anyone on a diet. Meat pie at £2.50, and York ham or turbot at £3, were the main-course choices when we were there. Vegetables were not quite as well presented as at some of the other farms we visited but were quite acceptable. I chose apricots in cointreau at 65p for my sweet and very much enjoyed them. Cheese and biscuits were available, and good coffee with a piece of fudge and a chocolate peppermint cost 35p. From this it can be seen that one could have a good three-course meal with coffee from about £4. Wines, etc, are available from the pleasant little bar. In cold weather Pat puts Lancashire hotpot on the menu, and at the other end of the price range she offers casserole of venison in white wine. Breakfast was an excellent meal with the usual fruit juice, cereal, bacon and egg, etc, and toast and marmalade, with a pot of coffee or tea.

The dining room is well furnished, with individual tables seating two or four. Also downstairs is an attractive bar with comfortable chairs. The large lounge upstairs, known as the library, has a good selection of leaflets about places of interest in the North of England. There are some very interesting books on the shelves, but not much in the way of pass times is provided.

Richard and Pat Holt, with Pat's farmer son and friends

The farm is owned by Pat's son, who runs sheep and beef cattle and provides some meat for the farm kitchen. Bessy, the dog shown in our photograph, is a family pet, but the working dogs are kept away from the house. There is another dog which the family and one or two visitors have seen. It is a friendly white, long-muzzled dog which occasionally walks through the house as though on important business of its own — and disappears. Not a ghost to be afraid of, we are assured.

Pat says she does not encourage children because, although she is fond of children herself, she is afraid they will disturb the peace which is the main attraction to other visitors.

As a touring centre, or a base for fell-walking, or just as a quiet place away from the madding crowd, Parrock Head could hardly be bettered.

WINNER, WALES

Cilpost Farm, Whitland, Dyfed
(Mrs C M and Mrs I A Lewis)

Ann Lewis was on the step to greet us when we drove into Cilpost Farm, which she runs with her mother-in-law while husband Gwyn looks after the 160-acre dairy farm in lush Dyfed countryside. We had been held up on our way from Basingstoke and arrived tired and hungry – and rather late for dinner. But Ann made no trouble of that and gave us time to wash and change before we went down to the very attractive dining room which has a central Welsh stone archway and well-polished furniture including some antique pieces. Large tables are used, and a party of six already occupied one of these. Our places were laid at a second big dining table. Our meal started with excellent home-made soup followed by grilled brown trout, fresh from the river, firm and flavoursome, served with salad garnish and freshly-cooked chipped potatoes and peas. Home-made apple pie and cream followed, with ice-cream as an alternative. Cheese and biscuits were followed by coffee. Wines are available on request.

Three different cereals were offered at breakfast, or one could have fruit juice, and the cooked dish consisted of two rashers of bacon, egg, tomato and fried bread. Bread, toast, butter and marmalade were provided, and a good pot of tea. Coffee was available, too.

Ann looks after the guests while Mrs Lewis senior does most of the cooking, but both are ready to find time for a chat and to advise visitors about places to visit.

Gwyn's mother with Ann and Mair

Gwyn is only the second generation of the Lewis family to farm at Cilpost, which was built as a farmhouse about 300 years ago. He married Ann, who comes from the Tywi valley, five years ago. She had been brought up in a hotel and knew just what was needed to convert the house so that they could take visitors. We had pleasant rooms with bathrooms *en suite*. Furniture was purpose-built and the beds, with duvets, were comfortable. Five of the ten letting bedrooms have private bathrooms; the others have wash basins but share only one bathroom and WC between them.

Gwyn and Ann now have a little girl called Mair, who, when we were there, was just beginning to speak a few words of English. Amongst themselves the Lewises speak Welsh.

Colour TV and board games are provided in the comfortable lounge and plenty of informative leaflets are available – kept in a drawer nowadays, away from Mair's little hands. Visitors have the run of the farm, there is free trout fishing and some rough shooting in season. Children can help feed the young animals if there are any on the farm, and may watch the cows being milked. There is a games room in one of the barns, with table tennis, etc, but the favourite sport, especially for men, is playing on the full-sized snooker table housed in a separate building across the garden.

Ann does not provide lunches as most visitors go out during the day; the coast is only a half-hour drive away, and many places of interest in this corner of the Principality are within easy reach.

WINNER,
ENGLISH MIDLANDS

Wormbridge Court Farm, Wormbridge, Hereford & Worcester
(Mrs Mary Thomas)

Four generations of the Thomas family have lived at Wormbridge Court, but its history goes back further as it was built in the 15th Century as a manor house. To help with the upkeep of this fine old house Mary Thomas decided to take holiday guests, and says she enjoys the work and has made many good friends.

First love of the Thomases, though, is horses. They have just opened a riding school and employ a qualified instructor, so anyone keen to learn to ride would find this a good place for a holiday. All equipment needed, including hard hats, is available for hire.

Interior design is not Mary's and John's strongest point but one can forgive that as the old house is so interesting and is very comfortably furnished. It is a pity that the main Hereford–Abergavenny road has been taken through so close to the house, but there is not a lot of traffic at night and thick walls damp down the noise fairly effectively.

Mary and John Thomas

Notice the carving over the fireplace in the dining room. This dates back to the 14th Century and was in the nearby church until the Reformation, when it was removed to the Manor House for safety. The pulpit, still in use in the church, is carved in a similar style. There was a Herefordshire school of carving and anyone interested should be sure to visit Kilpeck church in the adjoining parish.

However, most people visit farms for open air pursuits, quiet comfort and good food. Here children are welcome to take an interest in the farm but must not get near machines; they may be allowed to collect the eggs, and there are fields to play in. There is a duck pond behind the house which, when we were there, seemed to be swarming with ducklings and goslings; twenty-six of them, in fact, the offspring of two pairs of mallards and a pair of domestic geese. The farm is surrounded by gentle countryside but it is near the Welsh border with rugged mountainous scenery a short drive away. In the lounge is a good selection of literature about the area.

You certainly won't go hungry at Wormbridge either. For dinner we were offered fruit juice or egg mayonnaise as starter; chicken with mushrooms and other vegetables was served to the table *en casserole* (one casserole to each table, and the two of us might have eaten two joints each had we been hungry enough) served with mashed potatoes and freshly-baked rolls and butter. Sweets included a chocolate gateau (second helpings were offered); cheese and biscuits were available, and we were given a choice of tea or coffee to round off the meal. At breakfast we were asked to help ourselves from a selection of fruit juices and cereals, and were then served a good fry-up of sausage, bacon, egg and fried bread. Toast and marmalade were on the table and both tea and coffee were available.

Mary Thomas aims to provide good nourishing food without anything very fancy, but says she often cooks in cider, a Herefordshire speciality of course, and in season she does pheasant in wine. Beef is home-grown and cream comes from the next door farm.

This is a pleasant place for an overnight stay and would make a good holiday centre, especially for anyone keen on horses.

Gazetteer

GUEST HOUSE AND INN SECTION

For details of AA-listed Farmhouses see separate section page 218

The gazetteer gives locations and details of AA-listed guest houses and Inns in England, Wales and Scotland, Channel Islands and Isle of Man.

Details for islands are shown under individual placenames; the gazetteer text also gives appropriate cross-references. A useful first point of reference is to consult the location maps which show where guesthouses or Inns are situated.

N.B. *There is no map for Isles of Scilly.*

ABERDARE Mid Glam *Map 3 SO00*
GH *Cae-Coed* Craig St ☎871190
Lic 5hc TV 5P 🛏 D7pm

ABERDEEN Grampian *Aberdeens*
Map 15 NJ90 **See Plan**
GH Broomfield Private Hotel
15 Balmoral Pl ☎28758 Plan:**1**
8rm 7hc (1fb) CTV 20P 🛏 S% B&bfr£7.50
Bdi fr£12 Wfr£75.60 ⊾ D5.30pm

GH *Carden Hotel* 44 Carden Pl ☎26813
Plan:**2** 7hc nc5 CTV 6P 🛏

GH Crown Private Hotel 10 Springbank
Ter ☎26842 Plan:**3** 9hc (2fb) ⊗ nc10
CTV S% B&b£7.50 Bdi£11 W£65.45
⊾ D4pm

GH Dunromin 75 Constitution St ☎56995
Plan:**4** 5hc (1fb) CTV P 🛏 S% ✳B&bfr£6

GH Klibreck 410 Great Western Rd
☎36115 Plan:**5** Closed Xmas & New Year
7hc (1fb) ⊗ CTV 3P 🛏 B&bfr£6.50
Bdi fr£9 50 Wfr£63 ⊾ D3pm

GH Mannofield Hotel 447 Great Western
Rd ☎35888 Plan:**6** Lic 10hc (2fb) CTV
14P 🛏 S% B&b£12.65 Bdi£18.40
W£128.80 ⊾ D4pm

⊷GH Urray House 429 Great Western Rd
☎35204 Plan:**7** 6hc nc5 CTV 5P
1🏠 🛏 S% B&b£5.50–£6 Bdi£8.50–£9
W£56 ⊾ D3pm

GH Western 193 Great Western Rd
☎56919 Plan:**8** 6hc (2fb) ⊗ CTV 10P
🛏 S% B&b£8

ABERDOVEY Gwynedd *Map 6 SN69*
⊷GH Cartref ☎273 6hc (1fb) ⊗ TV 7P
B&b£5.25 Bdi£7 D6.30pm

1 Broomfield Private Hotel
2 Carden Hotel
3 Crown Private Hotel
4 Dunromin
5 Klibreck
6 Mannofield Hotel
7 Urray House
8 Western

1 Four Seasons Hotel
2 Glan-Aber Hotel
3 Glyn-Garth
4 Shangrila
5 Swn-y-Don
6 Windsor Private Hotel

GH Maybank Private Hotel ☎500
Apr–Oct Lic 7hc 2⇔🏠 nc4 CTV 🍴 river
⊬ D9pm

ABERFELDY Tayside *Perths*
Map 14 NN84
GH Balnearn Private Hotel Crieff Rd
☎431 13hc (2fb) CTV 15P 2🏠 ♿
B&b£9.20–£10.50 Bdi£13.80–£14.80
W£78.75 ⊬ D7pm

GH Guinach House Urlar Rd ☎251
Apr–Oct Lic 8rm 7hc (3fb) CTV 8P S%
B&b£8–£9.50 Bdi£13–£15.50 W£80–£95
⊬ D6pm

GH Nessbank Private Hotel Crieff Rd
☎214 Mar–Nov rsDec–Feb Lic 7hc CTV
7P S% B&bfr£8.50 Bdi fr£12.50 Wfr£80
⊬ D6pm

⊢⊣**GH Tirinie** (4m W B846) ☎ Kenmore 362
5hc 1⇔🏠 (1fb) 10P 🍴 S%
B&bfr£5.75 Bdi fr£9.75 D7pm

ABERGAVENNY Gwent *Map 3 SO21*
GH Park 36 Hereford Rd ☎3715
Lic 6hc (1fb) CTV 8P S% B&bfr£6
Bdi fr£8.75 Wfr£58.75 ⊬ D5.30pm

INN Great George Hotel Cross St ☎4230
Lic 4hc CTV 11🏠 🍴 D9.30pm

ABERGELE Clwyd *Map 6 SH97*
⊢⊣**GH Coed Mor** Groes Lwyd
☎822261 6hc (2fb) TV 3P 🍴 S%
B&b£4.75–£5.75 Bdi£6.50–£7.25
W£45.50–£50.25 ⊬ D5pm

INN Bull Hotel Chapel St ☎822115
Lic 6hc ♿ CTV 10P 🚗 S% B&b£7–£8
Bdi£11–£13 W£77 ⊬ L£3–£6 &alc sn
D8pm£4–£7

ABERPORTH Dyfed *Map 2 SN25*
GH Ffynonwen Country ☎810312
12hc 1⇔🏠 (2fb) 30P 🍴 S% B&b£7.50–£8
Bdi£11.50–£12.50 W£80.50–£87.50 ⊬

ABERSOCH Gwynedd *Map 6 SH32*

GH Llysfor ☎2248
Etr–Oct Lic 8hc 1⇔🏠 (2fb) ♿ CTV 12P
river sea S% B&b£7 Bdi£11 D4pm

ABERYSTWYTH Dyfed *Map 6 SN58*
See Plan
GH Four Seasons Hotel 50–54 Portland St
☎612120 Plan:**1** Closed Xmas Lic 17hc
6⇔🏠 (3fb) ♿ nc5 CTV 12P 🍴 S%
B&b£9–£10 Bdi fr£14 Wfr£85 ⊬ D7.30pm

GH Glan-Aber Hotel Union St
☎617610 Plan:**2** Lic 14hc (A 3hc) (1fb)
CTV S% B&b£7.25 Bdi£10.50 Wfr£63
⊬ D6.30pm

GH Glyn-Garth South Rd ☎615050
Plan:**3** Closed 2wks Xmas rsOct–Apr
(no dinners) Lic 12hc 2⇔🏠 (2fb) ♿ nc7
CTV 🍴 sea S% B&b£6.50–£7.50
Bdi£10–£11.50 Wfr£65 ⊬ D4pm

GH Shangrila 36 Portland St ☎617659
Plan:**4** 5hc (1fb) CTV S% B&b£5
Bdi£7.50 W£52.50 ⊬ D4pm

GH Swn-y-Don 40–42 North Pde
☎615059 Plan:**5** Closed Xmas Lic
25hc (A 4hc) (4fb) CTV 7P 🍴 S%
B&b£8.05 Bdi£11.50 W£89.90 ⊬ D8.30pm

GH Windsor Private Hotel 41 Queens
Rd ☎612134 Plan:**6** 10hc ♿ CTV 7P
⊬ D5pm

ACASTER MALBIS N Yorks *Map 8 SE54*
INN Ship ☎ York 703888
Lic 5hc 27P 🍴 river S% B&b£6–£9 sn
L50p–£1.75 D9.30pm£4.50–£7.50 &alc

ACLE Norfolk *Map 9 TG41*
GH Fishley Manor Hotel & Country Club
South Walsham Rd ☎ Great Yarmouth
750377 Lic 12hc nc6 CTV 40P D9.30pm

AINSTABLE Cumbria *Map 11 NY54*
INN Heather Glen Country Hotel
☎ Croglin 329 Closed 1–17Mar Lic 3hc
1⇔🏠 nc8 50P 🍴 🚗 S% B&b£7.50–£11
W£50 Ⓜ D9pm£7.50alc

35

ALBRIGHTON *(Nr Wolverhampton)* Salop
Map 7 SJ80
INN *Crown Hotel* High St ☎2204
Lic 3hc ✿ 80P 🛏

ALDEBURGH Suffolk *Map 5 TM45*
GH Granville Hotel 243–247 High St
☎2708 Closed Xmas wk Lic 9hc 2⊸🖾
(2fb) ✿ CTV 1🔔 🛏 B&b£19.50–£23
Bdi£15–£16.50 D8.30pm

ALDERSHOT Hants *Map 4 SU85*
GH Glencoe Hotel 4 Eggars Hill ☎20801
Closed Xmas 10hc (2fb) ✿ nc7 CTV 12P 🛏
S% B&b£10 Bdi£15 Dam

ALMONDSBURY Avon *Map 3 ST58*
GH *Hill Farm* 6 Gloucester Rd ☎613206
11rm 10hc ✿ ⌂ CTV 10P D6.30pm

ALNMOUTH Northumb *Map 12 NU21*
GH Marine House Private Hotel
1 Marine Dr ☎349 Lic 8hc (4fb) ⌂ CTV
10P 🛏 sea S% B&b£8–£9.50
Bdi£12.50–£15 W£82–£100 ⅃
(W only July & Aug) D4pm

ALNWICK Northumb *Map 12 NU11*
GH Aln House South Rd ☎602265
Closed Xmas wk 7hc (3fb) ✿ nc5 CTV
7P B&bfr£6.38 Bdifr£9.58 Wfr£65 ⅃
D5.30pm

⊶⊷**GH Bondgate House Hotel** Bondgate
Without ☎602025 Lic 8hc 1⊸🖾(4fb)
CTV 7P 🛏 S% B&b£5.50–£8
Bdi£9.50–£12 W£56–£76 ⅃ D3pm

GH Eradell 1 Beaconsfield Ter, Upper
Hawick St ☎602619 7hc (4fb) nc5 .

TV 7P S% B&b£6.90–£7.44
Bdi£10.65–£11.19 W£67.06–£72.59
⅃ D6pm

⊶⊷**GH Georgian** 3–5 Hotspur St ☎603165
Apr–Oct 7hc (1fb) ✿ nc5 TV 7P 🛏 S%
B&b£5.75–£6.75 W£35–£42 M

⊶⊷**GH Hope Rise** The Dunterns ☎602930
Lic 7hc (2fb) ✿ nc5 CTV 12P 🛏 S%
B&b£5.50–£6 Bdi£8.50–£9 W£57–£60
⅃ D4pm

ALTRINCHAM Gt Manchester
Map 7 SJ78
GH Bollin Hotel 58 Manchester Rd
☎061-928 2390 10hc (3fb) CTV 12P
B&bfr£8.63

AMBLESIDE Cumbria *Map 7 NY30*
GH Compston House ☎2305
Lic 10hc (2fb) ✿ CTV ✳B&b£6–£6.50
Bdi£8.50–£9.95 W£58–£68 ⅃ Dnoon

GH Gables Church Walk, Compston Rd
☎3272 Mar–Oct Lic 15hc 2⊸🖾(5fb)
nc3 CTV 8P B&bfr£7 Bdifr£10.50 Wfr£70
D5.30pm

⊶⊷**GH Hillsdale Private Hotel** Church St
☎3174 7hc (3fb) ✿ CTV 🛏 S%
B&b£5.80–£6.80 Bdi£9.70–£10.70
W£63–£69 ⅃ D4pm

GH Horseshoe Rothay Rd ☎2000
Mar–Dec 6hc (5fb) CTV 10P 🛏 S%
✳B&bfr£6.50 Wfr£43.75 M

GH Norwood House Church St ☎3349
Closed Xmas 8hc (5fb) ✿ CTV 🛏 S%
✳B&b£5.50–£6 Bdi£8.50–£9 D4pm

GH Oaklands Country House Hotel
Millans Park ☎2525 Mar–Nov Lic 6hc

(3fb) ✣ CTV 8P 🍽 S% B&b£6–£7
Bdi£10–£11.50 W£65–£76 ⚓ D4pm

GH Riverside Hotel Gilbert Scar ☎2395
Closed Dec–Feb Lic 8hc (1fb) ✣ nc8 CTV
10P 🍽 river Bdi£14–£17.50 W£95–£115 ⚓

GH Rothay Garth Hotel Rothay Rd
☎2217 Lic 12hc 2⇌🛏 (2fb) CTV 13P 🍽
S% B&b£10.92–£12.94 Bdi£13.80–£17.25
W£89.70–£112.12 ⚓ D6pm

GH Smallwood Hotel Compston Rd
☎2330 Mar–Oct 13hc 1⇌🛏 5fb nc1
CTV 10P 🍽 S% B&bfr£7.50 Bdifr£12
Wfr£84 ⚓ D6pm

AMROTH Dyfed *Map 2 SN10*
GH *Sunnyridge* ☎ Saundersfoot 812335
May–Sep 8hc nc3 CTV 7P D5pm

ANCHOR Salop *Map 7 SO18*
INN Anchor ☎ Kerry 250
Lic 8hc 2⇌🛏 CTV 100P 🍽 🚗 S%
✳B&b£6.75–£7.75 sn Lunch£5alc
D9.30pm£5alc

ANNAN Dumfries & Galloway
Dumfriesshire Map 11 NY16
GH Ravenswood St Johns Rd ☎2158
Lic 11hc (3fb) CTV 3P S% B&bfr£6.25
Bdifr£8.75 Wfr£58 ⚓

APPLEBY Cumbria *Map 12 NY62*
GH Bongate House ☎51245
7hc 1⇌🛏 (2fb) CTV 4P 2🅰 🍽 S% B&b£6
Bdi£9 W£54 ⚓ D6pm

⊶GH Howgill House ☎51574
6hc (3fb) ✣ CTV 6P S% B&bfr£4.50

ARBROATH Tayside *Angus Map 12 NO64*
GH *Gladsheil* 38 Ogilvy Pl ☎73470
Closed Oct rs Nov–Apr (B&b only) 6hc
CTV 7P

GH Kingsley 29–31 Market Gate
☎73933 18hc (7fb) nc5 CTV 🍽 ✳B&b£5
Bdi£7 W£43.70 ⚓ D5pm

ARDROSSAN Strathclyde *Ayrs
Map 10 NS24*
GH Ellwood House 6 Arran Pl ☎61130
7hc (1fb) CTV sea S% B&b£6

ARNSIDE Cumbria *Map 7 SD47*
GH *Grosvenor Private Hotel*
The Promenade ☎761666 Mar–Oct Lic
13hc CTV 10P 🍽 ⚓ D5pm

ARRAN, ISLE OF Strathclyde *Bute Map 10*
See Blackwaterfoot, Corrie, Lamlash
Lochranza, Sannox, Whiting Bay

ARRETON Isle of Wight *Map 4 SZ58*
GH Stickworth Hall ☎233
May–Sep rs Apr & Oct Lic 25hc (3fb) ✣
nc5 CTV 45P 🍽 ✳B&b£8.30–£10.02
Bdi£13.80–£15.52 W£82.80–£91.85
⚓ D7pm

ARUNDEL W Sussex *Map 4 TQ00*
⊶GH Bridge House 18 Queen St
☎882142 Closed Xmas 9hc 2⇌🛏 (7fb)
🅰 CTV 2P 2🅰 🍽 river S% B&b£5–£11
W£30–£70 M

ASCOTT-UNDER-WYCHWOOD Oxon
Map 4 SP31
INN Wychwood Arms Hotel
☎ Shipton-under-Wychwood 830271 Lic
5⇌🛏 nc14 CTV 30P 🍽 🚗 B&b£10 Bdi£14
sn L£4.50alc D10pmfr£4.60&alc

ASHBURTON Devon *Map 3 SX76*
GH Clitheroe House St Lawrence Ln
☎53053 Mar–Oct 16hc 2⇌🛏 ✣ CTV
8P

GH Gages Mill Buckfastleigh Rd ☎52391
Lic 7hc 2⇌🛏 (1fb) ✣ nc5 CTV P 🍽 S%
✳B&b£6–£7 Bdi£9.50–£10.50
W£60–£62.50 ⚓ D7pm

ASHBY-DE-LA-ZOUCH Leics
Map 8 SK31
GH Fernleigh 37 Tamworth Rd ☎4755
6hc CTV 8P 🍽 D6.30pm

ASHFORD Kent *Map 5 TR04*
GH Croft Hotel Canterbury Rd, Kennington
☎22140 Closed Xmas Lic 15hc 3⇌🛏
(A 6⇌🛏) (3fb) ✣ CTV 22P 🍽 S%
✳B&b£8.80–£10 Bdi£10–£12
W£65–£75 ⚓ D8pm

GH Downsview Willesborough Rd,
Kennington ☎21953 Closed Xmas Lic
17hc 4⇌🛏 (1fb) CTV 20P 🍽 S%
B&b£8.85–£10 D9pm

ASHWELL Herts *Map 4 TL23*
INN Three Tuns Hotel 6 High St
☎2387 Lic 7hc nc3 CTV 25P 🍽 🚗
✳B&b£10–£15.50 Bar lunch£1.50alc
D10pm£5alc

AUCHNASAUL Strathclyde *Argyll
Map 10 NM71*
GH Old Clachan Farm House
☎ Balvicar 281 Closed Xmas 3hc 1⇌🛏
✣ CTV 3P S% ✳B&b£5–£7 W£31–£45 M

AUSTWICK N Yorks *Map 7 SD76*
GH Traddock ☎Clapham (N Yorks) 224

Apr–Oct Lic 12hc 6⇄🛏 (6fb) ⊗ nc5
CTV 12P 🍴 B&b£8–£9.20
Bdi£12.65–£13.80 W£82–£90 ⓀD4pm

AVIEMORE Highland *Inverness-shire*
Map 14 NH81
GH Aviemore Chalets Motel Aviemore
Centre ☎810618 Lic 72⇄🛏 (72fb) ⊗
CTV 288P 🍴 S% B&b£7.95–£9.35
Bdi£13.80–£15.75 D10pm

GH Corrour House Inverdruie ☎810220
Closed Nov Lic 11rm 9hc (5fb) CTV 12P
🍴 S% B&b£10.35–£12.07
Bdi£16.10–£17.82 W£108.68–£120.75
ⓀD6.30pm

GH Craiglea Grampian Rd ☎810210
12hc 1⇄🛏 (4fb) CTV 10P S% B&b£7–£8
W£45–£52.50 M

GH Ravenscraig ☎810278
4hc (1fb) ⚲ CTV 10P 🍴 S% B&b£6–£6.90
W£35–£42 M

AYR Strathclyde *Ayrs Map 10 NS32*
GH Clifton Hotel 19 Miller Rd ☎64521
rs Nov–Etr (no lunches) Lic 11hc (3fb)
⊗ nc5 CTV 16P B&b£6–£8 Bdi£9.50–£12
W£59.50–£70 (W only Jun–Aug) D5.30pm

╟╢**GH Inverlea** 42 Carrick Rd ☎61538
Jan–Sep 6hc (3fb) CTV 6P S% B&bfr£5.50

GH Kingsley Hotel 10 Alloway Pl
☎62853 6hc CTV 🍴 sea˙S%
✳B&b£8.05–£8.62 Bdi£10.92–£11.50
W£72.45–£77.05 Ⓚ

╟╢**GH Lochinver Hotel** ☎65086
Lic 8hc (3fb) CTV 8P 🍴 S% B&b£5–£5.25
Bdi£7–£7.50 W£49–£52.50 Ⓚ
(W only Jul & Aug) D5pm

AYTON, GREAT N Yorks *Map 8 NZ51*
INN Royal Oak Hotel High Gr ☎2361
Lic 5hc 1⇱🍴 CTV D9.15pm

BACTON Norfolk *Map 9 TG33*
GH Keswick Hotel Walcott Rd
☎Walcott 468 Lic 6hc 3⇱🍴 nc12 CTV
50P ✷ sea S% B&bfr£11 Bdifr£15 D10pm

BACUP Lancs *Map 7 SD82*
GH Burwood Todmorden Rd ☎3466
Lic 6rm 5hc (1fb) ✺ CTV 8P 🛏 S%
✳B&bf£6.50–£7.50 Bdif£8.50–£9.75
W£59 ⚓ D7pm

BAKEWELL Derbys *Map 8 SK26*
GH Merlin House Ashford Ln, Monsal Head
☎Great Longstone 475 Lic 7hc 1⇱🍴
(1fb) nc5 CTV 6P S% B&bf£8–£12
Bdif£13–£18 W£106–£120 ⚓

BALA Gwynedd *Map 6 SH93*
GH Frondderw Farm ☎520301
Closed 2wks Xmas Lic 7hc ✺ ♨ CTV
10P S% B&bf£7.50 Bdif£12.50 W£82
⚓ D6.30pm

GH Plas Teg Tegid St ☎520268
Closed Xmas Lic 8hc (4fb) CTV 10P lake
S% B&bfr£6.75 Bdifr£10.75 Wfr£69
⚓ D7pm

BALDOCK Herts *Map 4 TL23*
GH Butterfield House Hitchin St
☎892701 Lic 11⇱🍴(1fb) 🛏TV 12P 🛏
S% B&bf£13.08–£19.40 Bdif£17.68–£24
D8.30pm

BALLANTRAE Strathclyde *Ayrs
Map 10 NX08*
INN Ardstinchar Main St ☎383
Lic 3hc CTV sea 🛏 S% B&bf£6.50
Bdif£8.50–£9 Bar lunch 80p–£1.75
D10.30pm £1.95–£2.40

BALLATER Grampian *Aberdeens*
Map 15 NO39
GH Moorside Braemar Rd ☎492
Apr–Oct Lic 7hc (4fb) CTV 10P 🛏
S% B&bf£7 Bdif£10 Wfr£65 ⚓ D7pm

GH Morvada Braemar Rd ☎501
Mar–Oct Lic 6hc (2fb) CTV 6P S%
B&bf£6.50 Bdif£10 W£65 ⚓ D6pm

BALLOCH Strathclyde *Dunbartons
Map 10 NS48*
INN Lomond Park Hotel Balloch Rd
☎Alexandria 52494 Lic 7hc ✺ CTV 30P
🛏 D7.45pm

BALMAHA Central *Stirlings Map 10 NS49*

GH Arrochoile ☎231 Apr–Oct 6hc
(2fb) ✺ CTV· 12P 🛏 lake S% B&bf£5

BAMPTON Oxon *Map 4 SP30*
GH Bampton House Bushey Row
☎ Bampton Castle 850135 Closed Xmas wk
Lic 6rm 5hc 2⇱🍴(1fb) ♨ CTV 12P 🛏 S%
B&bf£8–£10 Bdif£14–£16 W£90–£100
⚓ D5pm

BANBURY Oxon *Map 4 SP44*
GH Lismore 61 Oxford Rd ☎2105
Closed Xmas wk 8hc (4fb) CTV 4P 2🏠 🛏
S% B&bf£9.50

GH Tredis 15 Broughton Rd ☎4632
5hc (1fb) CTV 🛏 S% B&bf£5.50–£6
W£38–£42 Ⓜ

BANFF Grampian *Banffs Map 15 NJ66*
GH Carmelite House Private Hotel
Low St ☎2152 Lic 8hc (4fb) ✺ CTV 6P S%
B&bf£5.50–£6.50 Bdif£7.50–£9 W£50–£60
⚓ D4pm

GH Ellerslie 45 Low St ☎5888
6hc CTV sea D4.30pm

BANGOR Gwynedd *Map 6 SH57*
GH Dilfan Garth Rd ☎53030 8hc CTV
6P 🛏 D6pm

GH Telford Hotel Holyhead Rd ☎52543
Lic 9hc 3⇱🍴(1fb) ✺ CTV P 🛏 sea
✳B&bf£9.50 Bdif£14 W£98 ⚓ D9pm

BANTHAM Devon *Map 3 SX64*
INN Sloop ☎ Thurlestone 489 Lic 6hc
1⇱🍴 nc14 30P D10pm

BARMOUTH Gwynedd *Map 6 SH61*
GH Belgrave Hotel Marine Pde
☎280369 Mar–Oct Lic 12hc (5fb) CTV
🛏 sea S% B&bf£8.62–£10.92
Bdif£12.65–£14.95 W£88–£100 ⚓ D6pm

GH Lawrenny Lodge ☎280466
Etr–Oct Lic 10hc CTV 15P sea B&bf£9.20
Bdif£13.22 W£92 ⚓

GH Morwendon Llanaber (1m N A496)
☎280566 Lic 7hc (3fb) ✺ nc5 CTV 10P
sea S% ✳B&bfr£6 Bdifr£9 Wfr£60
⚓ D5.30pm

BARNSTAPLE Devon *Map 2 SS53*
GH Cresta Sticklepath Hill ☎74022
Closed Xmas 5hc (A 1hc 1⇱🍴) (3fb) ✺
nc5 CTV 8P 🛏 S% B&bf£6.50–£8
Bdif£10–£11.50 W£66.50–£77 ⚓ Dnoon

GH Northcliff 8 Rhododendron Av
(Off A39) ☎2524 9hc ✺ CTV 9P 2🏠
D2pm

GH Yeo Dale Hotel Pilton Bridge ☎2954
Closed Xmas 10hc (4fb) CTV 5P S%
B&b£7 Bdi£9.75 W£68.50 ⊀ Dnoon

BARRY S Glam Map 3 ST16
GH Maytree 9 The Parade ☎734075
Closed Xmas Lic 5hc (2fb) CTV sea S%
B&b£6–£9

⊪⊲**GH Sheridan** 11 The Parade ☎738488
5hc (5fb) ⊗ CTV 〰 sea S% B&b£5–£6

BARTON-ON-SEA Hants Map 4 SZ29
GH Binley Hotel Beach Ave ☎ New
Milton 610460 Mar–Oct rs Nov–Mar Lic
9hc CTV 9P 〰 D7pm

GH Cliff House Hotel Marine Drive West
☎ New Milton 619333 Feb–Nov Lic 11hc
(1fb) CTV 20P ✱B&b£8.50–£9
Bdi£12.40–£13 W£75–£78 ⊀ D8pm

GH Dome Hotel Barton Court Ave ☎ New
Milton 616164 Lic 10hc 3⇆〰 (4fb) CTV
18P 1🏠 〰 sea S% ✱B&b£8.30 Bdi£10.80
W£64.40–£75.90 ⊀ D7.30pm

GH Gainsborough Hotel 39 Marine Drive
East ☎ New Milton 610541 9hc 1⇆〰
(2fb) ⊗ nc8 CTV 20P 5🏠 〰 sea S%
✱B&b£7.50–£9.65 Bdi£11.35–£13
W£79.45–£91 ⊀ D6.30pm

GH Old Coastguard Hotel 53 Marine
Drive East ☎ New Milton 612987 Lic 7hc
nc12 CTV 8P 〰 sea S% B&b£9.20–£9.78
Bdi£11.50–£13.80 W£76.48–£92.58
⊀ D7.30pm

BASINGSTOKE Hants.
see **Sherfield-on-Loddon**

BASSENTHWAITE Cumbria
Map 11 NY23
GH Bassenfell Manor Hotel
☎ Bassenthwaite Lake 366 Mar–Nov Lic
18hc 6⇆〰 (4fb) ⊗ CTV 20P 〰 lake
B&b£8.50 Bdi£14.50 W£91.35–£101.50
⊀ D8.15pm

BATH Avon Map 3 ST76 **see Plan**
GH Apsley Garden House Hotel
Newbridge Hill ☎21368 Plan:**1** Lic 11hc
1⇆〰 (3fb) CTV 9P 〰 S% B&b£9.75–£11
Bdi£15.50–£16.75 W£104 ⊀D7.45pm

GH Ashley Villa Hotel 26 Newbridge Rd
☎21683 Plan:**2** Lic 18hc 6⇆〰 (1fb) CTV
9P 〰 ⚸✱B&b£10–£13 W£91 ⋈ D9.30pm

GH Avon Hotel Bathwick St ☎22226
Plan:**3** 16hc 12⇆〰 (9fb) TV 20P 1🏠 〰
S% B&b£9–£15.50 W£63–£108.50 ⋈

GH Coningsby 20 Park Ln ☎21119
Plan:**4** Closed Xmas Lic 5hc (2fb) nc6
CTV 4P 〰 S% B&b£8–£13
W£50.40–£81.90 ⋈

⊪⊲**GH Dorset Villa** 14 Newbridge Rd
☎25975 Plan:**5** Mar–Nov 6hc (2fb) ⊗
nc10 CTV 6P 〰 S% B&b£5.50–£6

GH Eastfield House 57 Upper Oldfield Pk
☎314990 Plan:**6** Feb–20Dec Lic 10hc
1⇆〰 (3fb) ⊗ CTV 8P S% ✱B&b£6.50–£9.75
Bdi£10–£13.25 D6pm

GH Edgar Hotel 64 Gt Pulteney St
☎20619 Plan:**7** Lic 11hc 4⇆〰 (3fb) ⊗
CTV 〰 S% B&b£9–£13 Bdi£13–£17

GH Georgian 34 Henrietta St ☎24103
Plan:**9** 8hc CTV 2🏠

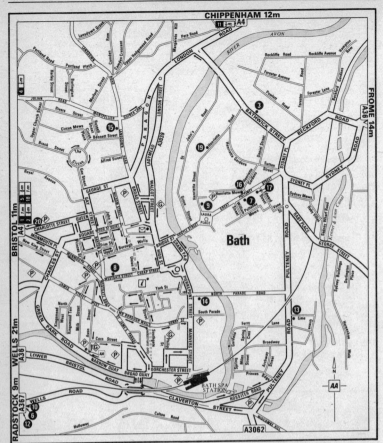

1 Apsley Garden House Hotel
2 Ashley Villa Hotel
3 Avon Hotel
4 Coningsby
5 Dorset Villa
6 Eastfield House
7 Edgar Hotel
8 Edwardian Hotel (*Inn*)
9 Georgian
10 Glenbeigh Hotel
11 Grove Lodge
12 Kingsley House Private Hotel
13 Lynwood
14 North Parade Hotel
15 Oxford Private Hotel
16 Richmond Hotel
17 St Monica's Hotel
18 Tacoma
19 Villa Magdala Private Hotel
20 Waltons

GH Glenbeigh Hotel 1 Upper Oldfield Pk
☎26336 Plan:**10** Closed Jan Lic 8hc
(2fb) CTV 10P 2🏠 🐾 S% B&bf6.50–£7.50

GH Grove Lodge 11 Lambridge, London Rd
☎310860 Plan:**11** Lic 8hc (2fb) ⊗ TV
S% B&bf8

GH *Kingsley House Private Hotel*
53 Upper Oldfield Park ☎25749 Plan:**12**
Feb–Dec Lic 6hc 4⊸🏠 ⊗ nc 6P 🐾

GH Lynwood 6 Pulteney Gdns ☎26410
Plan:**13** Closed Xmas 6hc (2fb) nc2 CTV
S% B&bf7–£7.50

GH North Parade Hotel North Pde
☎60007 Plan:**14** Feb–Nov Lic 17hc
(3fb) 🐾 S% B&bf8.80

⊷⊷**GH Oxford Private Hotel** 5 Oxford Row,
Lansdown Rd ☎314039 Plan:**15** 8hc
1⊸🏠 ⊗ CTV 1🏠 S% B&bf5.75–£6.90
W£41.40 M

GH Richmond Hotel 11 Gt Pulteney St
☎25560 Plan:**16** Lic 31hc 13⊸🏠 (3fb)
CTV 3P 🛠B&bf8.75–£9.75

Bdif12.25–£13.25 D4.30pm

GH *St Monica's Hotel* Gt Pulteney St
☎62092 Plan:**17** Lic 23hc 🐾 CTV 2🏠 🐾
D7.50pm

GH Tacoma 159 Newbridge Hill ☎310197
Plan:**18** Jan–20 Dec 8hc (3fb) 🐾 CTV 5P
🐾 S% B&bf7–£9

GH Villa Magdala Private Hotel
Henrietta Rd ☎25836 Plan:**19** 9⊸🏠
(2fb) 🐾 CTV 12P 3🏠 S% ✱B&bf14–£20

GH Waltons 17 Crescent Gdns
☎26528 Plan:**20** 20hc (3fb) CTV 🐾 S%
B&bf6.25 Bdif8.25 D8.30pm

INN *Edwardian Hotel* 38 Westgate St
☎61642 Plan:**8** Closed Xmas Day Lic
26hc 15⊸🏠 D11.15pm

BEAULY Highland *Inverness-shire*
Map 14 NH54
⊷⊷**GH Chrialdon** Station Rd ☎2336
Apr–Oct Lic 11hc (4fb) CTV 16P 🐾 S%
B&bf5.25–£5.75 Bdif9.25–£9.75
D7.45pm

GH Gruinard ☎2417 Apr–Oct 6hc (2fb)
TV 6P ✳B&b£4.75 W£32 M

BEAUMARIS Gwynedd *Map 6 SH67*
⊨⊨**GH Sea View** West End ☎810384
6hc nc10 TV 5P sea S% B&b£5 Bdi£8.50

BEAUMONT Jersey, Channel |slands
Map 16
GH Seawold Private Hotel St Aubin's Rd
☎ Jersey 20807 22hc 22⇌▥ ⊘ CTV 5P
▥ sea (W only May–Sep) D6.45pm

BECKERMET Cumbria *Map 11 NY00*
INN Royal Oak Hotel ☎84551 Lic
(A 8⇌▥) 20P ▥ S% ✳B&b£9–£11.50
Bar lunch £1.50 D10pm

BEDDGELERT Gwynedd *Map 6 SH54*

GH Sygyn Fawr ☎258 Lic 7hc CTV 25P
D7.30pm

BEDFORD Beds *Map 4 TL04*
GH Kimbolton Hotel 78 Clapham Rd
☎54854 Closed Xmas wk Lic 18hc CTV
24P ▥ D6.30pm

BEER Devon *Map3 SY28*
⊨⊨**GH Bay View** Fore St ☎ Seaton
(Devon) 20489 Etr–Oct 6hc (2fb) nc5
CTV sea B&b£5.50–£6.50 W£38 M

BENLLECH BAY Gwynedd *Map 6 SH58*
GH Rhostrefor ☎ Tyn-y-Gongl 2347
Etr–Oct Lic 4hc (A6hc) 10P (W only Jul
& Aug)

BENSON Oxon *Map 4 SU69*
INN White Hart Hotel ☎ Wallingford
35244 Lic 10hc nc3 TV 60P
B&bf£11–£14 Bar lunch 60p–£2.20
D9pm£4.75alc

BERRIEW Powys *Map 7 SJ10*
INN *Talbot Hotel* ☎260 Lic 8hc 1⇉🛏
CTV 40P D9.30pm

BERRYNARBOR Devon *Map 2 SS54*
GH Seacliffe Country Hotel ☎ Combe
Martin 3273 10hc (3fb) ⌘ CTV 12P 🍴
sea S% ✱B&bf£6.90 Bdi£10.35
Wf£56.92–£65.55 ⚡ D9pm

BETWS-Y-COED Gwynedd *Map 6 SH75*
⋈**GH Bod Hyfryd** Holyhead Rd ☎220
6hc (2fb) TV 7P river S% B&bfrf£5.50
Bdi fr£7.50 Wfr£52.50 ⚡ D6.30pm

GH *Fairy Glen Hotel* Dolwyddelan Rd
☎269 Lic 10hc 1⇉🛏 12P 1🏠 🍴 river
D7pm

GH Glenwood ☎508 Closed Xmas 6hc
1⇉🛏 (5fb) nc4 CTV 18P 🍴 S%
B&bf£6.50–£8 Bdi£9.50–£11.50 D8.30pm

GH Gwynant ☎372 Etr–Oct 5rm 4hc
(1fb) TV 5P S% ✱B&bfrf£5

GH Hafan ☎233 Lic 7hc 1⇉🛏 (3fb)
nc3 CTV 10P 🍴 S% B&bf£6–£6.50
Bdi£10–£12 Wfrf£65 ⚡

GH Henllys (Old Court) Private Hotel
☎534 Feb–Nov Lic 12hc 6⇉🛏 (1fb) nc6
CTV 14P river B&bf£6.50–£9
Bdi fr£10.50 Wf£70–£90 ⚡ (W only Jul
& Aug) D6pm

GH Mount Garmon Hotel ☎335

Mar–Oct Lic 6hc ⌘ nc5 CTV 6P 🍴 S%
✱B&bf£6.90 Bdi£12.65 Wf£88.55 ⚡ D5pm

BEXHILL-ON-SEA E Sussex *Map 5 TQ76*
GH Alexandra Hotel 2 Middlesex Rd
☎210202 Feb–Nov rs Dec & Jan Lic 9hc
(2fb) nc3 CTV 1P 🍴 S% B&bf£7–£8
Bdi£9.50–£11.50 Wf£60–£68 ⚡ D4pm
GH Dunselma Private Hotel 25 Marina
☎212988 Etr–10 Oct 11hc 2⇉🛏 (2fb) nc5
sea B&bf£8.63–£10.93 Bdi£12.65–£14.95
Wf£66.70–£79.35 ⚡ D7.30pm
GH Radclive Private Hotel 36 Woodville
Rd ☎212007 Lic 8hc (4fb) CTV 🍴
B&bf£6.50–£7.50 Bdi£9.50–£11.50
Wf£63–£70 ⚡ D8pm
GH Victoria House 1 Middlesex Rd
☎210382 Mar–Oct rs Dec & Feb (B&b
only) Lic 11hc (5fb) CTV 5P sea S%
✱B&bf£8.50–£9.50
Wf£43.50–£46 ⚡ D6.30pm.

BICKINGTON *(Nr Newton Abbot)* Devon
Map 3 SX77
⋈**GH Privet Cottage** ☎319 8hc (2fb) ⌘
CTV 8P S% B&bf£5 Bdi£9 Wf£63 ⚡
D6.30pm

BICKLEIGH *(Nr Tiverton)* Devon
Map 3 SS90
GH Bickleigh Cottage ☎Tiverton 230
May–Sep rs Apr & 1–15 Oct (B&b only)
11rm.9hc 2⇉🛏 (2fb) ⌘ TV 10P river
✱B&bf£6–£8 Bdi£10.25–£12.25
Wf£36–£48 Ⓜ D5pm

BIDEFORD Devon *Map 2 SS42*
GH Edelweiss 2 Buttgarden St ☎2676
Mar–Oct rs Nov–Mar (closed Xmas) Lic

11hc (5fb) CTV river S% B&bf£5.95–£6.60
Bdi£9.30–£10 Wf£54.50–£59.50 ⊻
D9.30pm

GH Mount Private Hotel Northdown Rd
☎3748 Lic 7hc (2fb) ✦ TV 1🏠 ⬛ S%
B&bf£6.75–£7.25 Bdi£10.25–£10.75
Wf£71.75–£75.25 ⊻ D8.30pm

GH Sonnenheim Private Hotel Heywood
Rd, Northam ☎4989 Lic 9hc 1⊏🚿 (4fb)
CTV 10P ⬛ & S% B&bf£7–£9
Bdi£10.50–£13 Wf£63–£77 ⊻ D6.30pm

BIGBURY-ON-SEA Devon *Map 3 SX64*
GH Easton House Private Hotel ☎296
Mar–Nov & Xmas Lic 15hc 9⊏🚿(9fb) ♨
CTV 20P ⬛ S% ✱B&bf£7.50–£10
Bdi£11.50–£14 (W only mid Jul–Aug)
D8.30pm

BILBROOK Somerset *Map 3 ST04*
GH Bilbrook Lawns Hotel ☎Washford
331 Lic 8hc 3⊏🚿 (6hc 2⊏🚿) (4fb) ✦
CTV 14P ⬛ S% B&Bf£6.50–£7.50
Bdi£10.50–£11.50 Wf£59–£65 ⊻
D6.30pm

GH Bilbrook Lodge Hotel ☎Washford
561 Mar–Oct 6hc (4fb) ✦ nc8 CTV 12P ⬛
S% ✱B&bf£5.50–£6 Bdi£7.50–£8.50
W fr £50 ⊻ D6.30pm

BIRMINGHAM W Midlands *Map 7 SP08*
(See Plan)
GH Alexander 44 Banbury Rd, Northfield
☎021-475 4341 Plan:**1** 12hc (2fb) CTV
12P ⬛ S% B&bf£7 Bdi£11 D6.30pm

GH Bridge House Hotel 49 Sherbourne
Rd, Acocks Gr ☎021-706 5900 Plan:**3**
Lic 9hc ✦ TV 10P ⬛ B&b fr £6.90

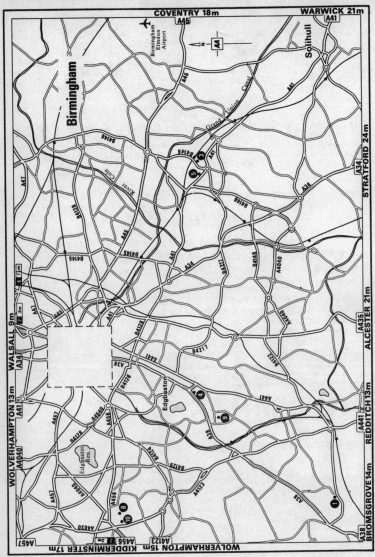

1 Alexander
2 Highfield House
(*see under Rowley Regis*)
3 Bridge House Hotel
4 Bristol Court Hotel
5 Kerry House Hotel
6 Lyndhurst Hotel
7 Stanbridge Hotel
(*see under Sutton Coldfield*)
8 Wellesley House
9 Wentsbury Hotel
10 Wentworth Hotel

Bdi fr £9.90 D7.30pm.
GH Bristol Court Hotel 250 Bristol Rd
☎021-472 0413 Plan :**4** Lic 30hc 3⇄🛉
(3fb) CTV 20P 2🏠 ⬛ ✳B&b£8.50
D8.30pm

GH Kerry House Hotel 946 Warwick Rd,
Acocks Green ☎021-707 0316 Plan :**5**
Lic 23hc 1⇄🛉 CTV 20P ⬛ S%
B&b£10.93–£12.65 Bdi£13.93–£17.65
D7.30pm

GH Lyndhurst Hotel 135 Kingsbury Rd,
Erdington ☎021-373 5695 Plan :**6**
Closed Etr & Xmas 18hc (1fb) ⊘ nc3 CTV
15P ⬛ S% B&b£8.50 Bdi£11 D6.30pm

GH Wellesley House 57 Wentworth Rd,
Harborne ☎021-427 1577 Plan :**8** Closed
Xmas 8hc (1fb) TV 6P ⬛ S% B&B£8

GH Wentsbury Hotel 21 Serpentine Rd,
Selly Park ☎021-472 1258 Plan :**9** Closed
Xmas 8hc (1fb) CTV 10P ⬛ S% B&b£7.25
Bdi£11 D6pm

GH Wentworth Hotel 103 Wentworth Rd
Harborne ☎021-427 2839 Plan :**10**
Closed Xmas wk 22hc 5⇄🛉 (2fb) CTV
14P 2🏠 ⬛ ♿ S% ✳B&b£7.50–£12
✳Bdi£11.50–£16 D7.30pm

BIRNAM Tayside *Perths Map 11 NO04*
⊢⊣**GH Waterbury House** Murthly Ter
☎ Dunkeld 324 6hc (2fb) TV 6P ⊞ S%
B&b£5.50 Bdi£9.50 W£57.50 ⚓ D5pm

BISHOP'S CLEEVE Glos *Map 3 SO92*
⊢⊣**GH Old Manor House** 43 Station Rd
☎4127 6hc (2fb) CTV 8P S%
B&b£5.50–£6.50 Bdi£10–£12

BISHOP WILTON Humberside
Map 8 SE75
INN Fleece ☎251 Lic 4hc ⊗ 20P ⊞
B&b£6.50 Bdi£12 Bar lunch 38p–£3
D9.30pm fr£5.25

BLACKPOOL Lancs *Map 27 SD33*
See Plan
GH Arandora Star Private Hotel 559

New South Prom ☎41528 Plan:**1**
Jan–Oct Lic 18hc (3fb) CTV 12P 4⚓ sea
S% ✱B&b£8.05–£8.63 W£56.35–£60.41
⚓ D5pm

GH Arosa Hotel 18–20 Empress Dr
☎52555 Plan:**2** Etr–Nov Lic 20hc 12⇆⊓
(6fb) ⊗ CTV 6P ⊞ S% B&b£7–£9
Bdi£9.20–£11.50 D3pm
See advertisement page 45

GH Beaucliffe Private Hotel 22 Holmfield
Rd, North Shore ☎51663 Plan:**3** Etr–Oct &
Xmas 12hc (2fb) ⊗ nc4 CTV 10P ⊞ S%
B&b£6.90 Bdi£8.16 W£54.32 ⚓ D3pm

⊢⊣**GH Channings** 557 New South Prom
☎41380 Plan:**5** Lic 21hc (5fb) CTV 12P ⊞
sea S% B&b£5.50–£7 Bdi£6.50–£8 D5pm

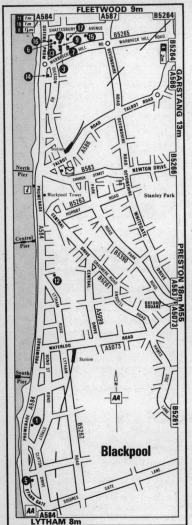

1 Arandora Star Private Hotel
2 Arosa Hotel
3 Beaucliffe Private Hotel
4 Breck Hotel (*see under Poulton-le-Fylde*)
5 Channings
6 Croydon Private Hotel
7 Denely Private Hotel
8 Garville Hotel
9 Lynstead Private Hotel
10 Manxonia Hotel
11 Mavern Private Hotel
12 Motel Mimosa
13 North Mount Private Hotel
14 Sunnycliff
15 Sunray Private Hotel
16 Surrey Hotel
17 Ventnor Private Hotel

GH Croydon Private Hotel 12 Empress Dr
☎52497 Plan:**6** Etr–Oct 11hc (6fb) ✠
CTV 7P S%✱B&b£5–£5.50
Bdi£5.75–£6.75 W only Jul–Aug D5pm

GH Denely Private Hotel 15 King
Edward Av ☎52757 Plan:**7** 8hc (2fb) ✠
CTV 5P ⌲ S% B&b£6.87–£7.10
Bdi£7.90–£815 W£54.30–£57.05 ⌿
D4.30pm

GH *Garville Hotel* 3 Beaufort Av, Bispham
(2m N) ☎51004 Plan:**8** Etr–Nov Lic 7hc
2⇱⅏ CTV 6P ⌲ D5.15pm

GH Lynstead Private Hotel 40 King
Edward Av ☎51050 Plan:**9** Lic 11hc (5fb)
✠ CTV S% B&b£6.50–£7.25
Bdi£7.50–£8.25 W£52.50–£57.75 ⌿
D3pm

GH Manxonia Hotel 248 Queens Prom,
Bispham (1m N A584) ☎51118 Plan:**10**
Xmas, Etr & Spring Bank Hol–Oct Lic 18hc
(5fb) CTV 9p ⌲ sea S% B&b£6.30–£7
Bdi£7.65–£8.50 W£53.55–£59.50 ⌿
(W only Jul & Aug) DNoon

GH Mavern Private Hotel 238 Queens
Prom, Bispham (1m N A584) ☎51409
Plan:**11** Lic 23hc (5fb) CTV 14P ⌲ sea S%
B&b£6.50–£8 D6pm

GH Motel Mimosa 24a Lonsdale Rd
☎41906 Plan:**12** Closed Xmas 15⇱⅏ ✠
nc11 CTV 12P 1🅰 ⌲ S% B&b£8.90–£9.75
W£62.30–£68.25 M

Ⓜ GH North Mount Private Hotel 22
King Edward Ave ☎55937 Plan:**13**
Apr–Oct Lic 8hc (2fb) ✠ CTV ⌲ S%
B&b£5–£5.25 Bdi£7–£7.25 D5pm

GH Sunnycliff 98 Queen's Prom ☎51155
Plan:**14** 12hc (4fb) CTV 12P S%
B&b£6.50–£8 Bdi£8.50–£10
W£59.50–£70 ⌿ D5pm

Ⓜ GH Sunray Private Hotel 42 Knowle
Av, Queen's Prom ☎51937 Plan:**15**
Apr–Oct 6hc (1fb) CTV 6P ⌲ S%

B&b£5.95–£7.80 Bdi£9.50–£11.95
W£66.50–£83.65 ⫩ D5pm

⊢⊣**GH Surrey House Hotel**
9 Northumberland Av ☎51743 Plan:**16**
Apr–Oct rs Mar & Nov 12hc 5⇌ঌ⋔ (2fb)
CTV 6P 1ଈ ⊪ S% B&b£5.20–£6.50
Bdi£6.90–£8.75 W£48.30–£61 ⫩ D5pm

GH Ventnor Private Hotel 57 Holmfield
Rd ☎51314 Plan:**17** Closed Xmas & New
Year 8hc (2fb) ⊗ CTV ⊪ S% B&b£6–£7
Bdi£7.50–£8.50 W£48–£54 ⫩ D3pm

BLACKWATERFOOT Isle of Arran
Strathclyde *Bute Map 10 NR92*
INN *Greannan Hotel* ☎Shiskine 200 Lic
12rm 11hc ঌ CTV 14P ⊪ sea D10pm

BLACKWOOD Gwent *Map 3 ST19*
INN Plas Gordon Rd ☎224674 Lic 6hc
TV 80P ⊪ S% B&b£11.50 W£80.50 M
Bar lunch £2.10alc D9.15pm£5alc

BLAENAU FFESTINIOG Gwynedd
Map 6 SH74
⊢⊣**GH Don Restaurant & Guest House**
147 High St ☎403 Lic 6hc (3fb) ⊗ CTV 2P
2ଈ ⊪ B&b£5–£5.50 D8.30pm

BLAIR ATHOLL Tayside *Perths*
Map 14 NN86
GH Invergarry The Terrace ☎255
Mar–Oct 7rm 6hc (4fb) ⊗ nc10 TV 12P ⊪
S% B&bfr£7 Bdifr£9.50 Wfr£65.50 ⫩

BLAIRGOWRIE Tayside *Perths*
Map 11 NO14
GH Kintrae House Hotel Balmoral Rd
☎2106 Lic 8hc (2fb) nc11 CTV 15P ⊪ S%
B&b£7.50 Bdi£11.50 W£77 ⫩ D8.30pm

BLANDFORD FORUM Dorset
Map 3 ST80
GH Portman Lodge Hotel Whitecliff,
Mill St ☎52842 Lic 8hc 3⇌ঌ⋔nc10 TV
10P ⊪ S% ✱B&b£4–£8.50
Bdi£6.25–£13 D6.30pm

BLEADNEY Somerset *Map 3 ST44*
**GH Threeway Country House Hotel &
Restaurant** ☎Wells 78870 Closed Xmas &
New Year Lic 10hc 2⇌ঌ⋔ (2fb) ⊗ CTV 30P
3ଈ ⊪ S% B&b£6–£7.50
W£37.80–£47.25 M D9.30pm

BLETCHINGLEY Surrey *Map 4 TQ35*
INN Whyte Harte ☎Godstone 843231
Lic 9hc 4⇌ঌ⋔ ⊗ CTV 100P ⊪ ⇘
B&b£10–£12 sn L£3.50–£5&alc
D10pmfr£8&alc

BLUE ANCHOR Somerset *Map 3 ST04*
GH Camelot ☎Dunster 348 Closed Xmas
8hc (2fb) ⊗ nc12 CTV 8P ⊪ sea S%
B&b£6–£7 Bdi£9–£10 W£53–£60 ⫩
D5pm

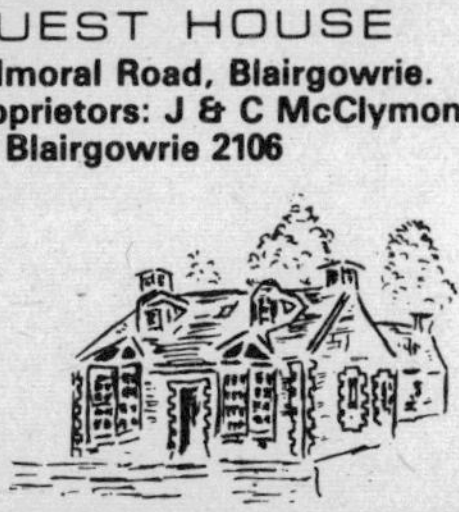

⊢⊣**GH Newlands** ☎Dunster 354 Lic 6hc
(1fb) CTV 7P ⊪ sea S% B&b£5–£7.50
Bdi£8–£10.50 W£48–£64 ⫩ D6pm

BLYTH Northumb *Map 12 NZ38*
INN Kitty Brewster 549 Cowpen Rd
☎2732 Lic 7hc ⊗ CTV 20P ⊪ S%
B&b£8.25 Bdi£12.25 W£82 ⫩ sn
L£1.50–£4.50 D9.30pm£3.50–£6.50

BODEDERN Gwynedd *Map 6 SS38*
INN Crown Hotel ☎Valley 740734 Lic
5hc ⊗ 60P ⊪ S% B&b£6 W£42 M
Bar lunch£1alc

BODIAM E Sussex *Map 5 TQ72*
GH Justins Hotel ☎Staplecross 372 Closed Nov Lic 10hc 8⇌🚿 (3fb) ♣ CTV 20P 🍴 S% B&b£11.73 Bdi£17.48 W£115.36 Ł D8pm

BODMIN Cornwall *Map 2 SX06*
GH Washaway Your Troubles Washaway ☎4951 Lic 5hc (A3rm 2hc) (1fb) ⊘ nc5 CTV 10P 🍴 S% B&b£8–£11 Bdi£14–£17 W£84–£102 Ł D5pm

BOGNOR REGIS W Sussex *Map 4 SZ99*
GH Homestead Private Hotel 90 Aldwick Rd ☎823443 Lic 7hc (A 2hc) (5fb) CTV 12P ✱B&b£5–£5.50 Bdi£6.50–£7.50 W£45–£50 Ł D7.30pm

GH Landsdowne Hotel 55–57 West St ☎865552 rs Xmas (no meals) Lic 10hc (6fb) CTV 3P 🍴 sea B&b£7–£9.50 Bdi£10.50–£13 W£65–£90 Ł D4.30pm

BOLLINGTON Cheshire *Map 7 SJ97*
INN *Turners Arms Hotel* 1 Ingersley Rd ☎73864 Lic 5rm 4hc TV 🍴 D10pm

BONAR BRIDGE Highland *Sutherland Map 14 NH69*
⟷ **GH Glengate** ☎Ardgay 318 Mar–Oct 3hc (2fb) nc5 CTV 4P 🍴 S% B&b£5–£5.50

BONTDDU Gwynedd *Map 6 SH61*
INN Halfway House Hotel ☎635 Etr–Dec Lic 4hc (A 1⇌🚿) ⊘ CTV 12P 3🏠 🚐 B&b£8 Bdi£14.50 W£101.50 Ł Bar lunch£2alc D9pm£6.50&alc

BONTNEWYDD Gwynedd *Map 6 SH46*
GH *Dwynfa* ☎Llanwnda 830414 Mar–Oct 12hc ⊘ nc10 CTV 15P river

BOOT Cumbria *Map 7 NY10*
GH Brook House ☎Eskdale 288 Lic 6hc (2fb) CTV 8P B&bfr£8 Bdifr£11 Wfr£70 Ł W mid Jul–10 Sep D6pm

BOSCASTLE Cornwall *Map 2 SX09*
GH St Christophers Country House Hotel ☎412 Mar–Nov Lic 6hc 1⇌🚿 (2fb) 6P 🍴 sea S% B&b£8–£9 Bdi£13–£14 W£84–£93 Ł

GH Tolcarne Private Hotel ☎252 Lic 9hc (A 5hc) (3fb) ♣ CTV 30P B&b£8–£8.75 Bdi£10.50–£11.50 W£68–£76 Ł D7.30pm

BOSWINGER Cornwall *Map 2 SW94*
GH Van Ruan House ☎Mevagissey 2425 Mar–Oct Lic 7hc (1fb) ⊘ nc7 CTV 10P 🍴 sea S% B&b£7–£8 Bdi£11–£12 W£70–£80 Ł (W only Jul–Aug) D4.30pm

BOURNEMOUTH AND BOSCOMBE
Dorset *Map 4 SZ09*
Telephone Exchange 'Bournemouth'
See Central and District Plans
For additional guesthouses see **Poole** and **Christchurch**

⟷ **GH Alcombe House** 37 Sea Rd, Boscombe ☎36206 Central plan:**1** Closed Xmas 12hc (4fb) CTV 6P S% B&b£5.75–£8 Bdi£8–£11.50 W£52–£76 Ł D4.30pm

GH Alum Bay Hotel 19 Burnaby Rd, Alum Chine ☎761034 District plan:**48** Etr–Oct & Xmas Lic 12hc (4fb) ⊘ CTV 10P 🍴 S% B&b£6.50–£8 Bdi£8.50–£11 W£50–£69 Ł (W only Jun–Aug)

GH Alumcliff Hotel 121 Alumhurst Rd, Westbourne ☎764777 District plan:**49** Etr–Oct Lic 18hc 11⇆🛏 (4fb) ⊗ nc7 CTV 14P 🍴 sea S% B&b£9–£9.50 Bdi£12.50 W£78–£89 ⊬ (W only Whitsun–mid Sep)

GH Alum Court Hotel 10 Studland Rd ☎761069 District plan:**50** Lic 12hc 1⇆🛏 CTV 9P 1🛁 🍴 sea D10pm

GH Alum Grange Hotel 1 Burnaby Rd, Alum Chine ☎761195 District plan:**51** Mar–Oct & Xmas Lic 14hc 4⇆🛏 (6fb) ⊗ nc3 CTV 8P S% B&b£8–£10 Bdi£10.50–£13 W£72–£85 ⊬ (W only last two wks in Jul, 1st two wks in Aug) D4.30pm

GH Anfield Private Hotel 12 Bradburne Rd ☎20749 Central plan:**2** Mar–Oct & Xmas 16hc (3fb) ⊗ nc5 CTV 12P S%

B&b£7.48–£9.78 Bdi£10.06–£12.08 W£59.50–£79.35 ⊬ D6pm

GH Arundale Hotel 38 Christchurch Rd ☎28088 Central plan:**3** Lic 42hc 1⇆🛏 (17fb) CTV 24P 🍴 ✳B&b£8.51 Bdi£12.60 (W only high season)

⊨GH Balmer Lodge Hotel 23 Irving Rd, Southbourne ☎424879 District plan:**53** May–Sep 8hc (7fb) CTV 6P 🍴 S% B&b£5.50–£6.50 Bdi£9–£10 W£56–£62 ⊬ (W only Jul & Aug) D4pm

GH Bay Tree Hotel 17 Burnaby Rd, Alum Chine ☎763807 District plan:**54** Lic 12hc (3fb) nc3 CTV 6P 🍴 sea S% B&b£6–£9 Bdi£7.50–£10.50 D4pm

⊨GH Blinkbonnie Heights Hotel 26 Clifton Rd, Southbourne ☎426512 District plan:**56** Mar–Nov 12hc 1⇆🛏

1 Alcombe Private Hotel
2 Anfield Hotel
3 Arundale
4 Braemar Private Hotel
5 Britannia Hotel
6 Bursledon Hotel
7 Carisbrooke Hotel
8 Carysfort Lodge Private Hotel
9 Hotel Cavendish
10 Charles Taylor Hotel
11 Chilterns Hotel
12 Cintra
13 Cliffside Hotel
14 Clock House Hotel
15 Crescent Grange Hotel
16 Dean Court Hotel
17 Derwent House
18 East Cliff Cottage Private Hotel
19 Eglan Court Hotel
20 Fallowfield Hotel
21 Farlow Private Hotel
22 Freshfields Touring Hotel
23 Gervis Court Hotel
24 Hamilton Hall Private Hotel
25 Hawaiian
26 Highlin Private Hotel
27 Hollyhurst Hotel
28 Kings Barton
29 Linwood House Hotel
29A Loddington Grange Hotel
30 Mae-Mar Private Hotel
31 Mon Bijou
32 Penmone Hotel
33 Pine Beach
34 St Ronans
35 Sandelheath
36 Sea Shells
37 Seastrole Private Hotel
38 Sea View Court Hotel
39 Hotel Sorrento
40 Southlea Hotel
41 Tower House Hotel
42 Tudor Grange Hotel
43 Wenmaur House
44 West Bay Hotel
45 Whitley Court Hotel
46 Windsor Court Hotel
47 Wood Lodge Hotel

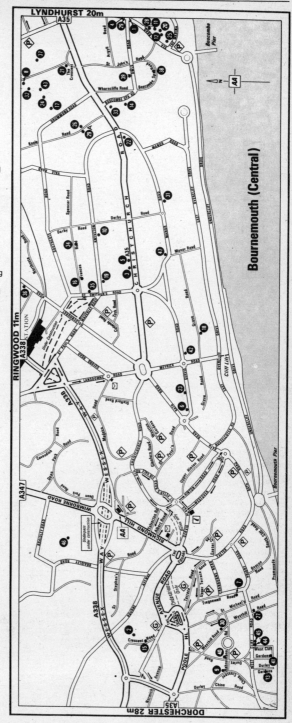

Bournemouth (Central)

(3fb) ♨ CTV 12P 🛏 & S%
B&bf5.75–£6.90 Bdif8.65–£10.35
Wf52–£70 ⓚ D6.15pm

GH Bracken Lodge Private Hotel
5 Bracken Rd, Southbourne ☎428777
District plan:**58** Apr–Oct 12hc ✗ nc1 CTV
12P 🛏 S% B&bf6.50–£9.50
Bdif10.50–£15 Wf50.50–£75 ⓚ
D6.30pm

⊮ **GH Braemar Private Hotel** 30 Glen Rd,
Boscombe ☎36054 District plan:**4**
Xmas, Etr–Oct Lic 11hc 1⇆🛏 (6fb) ✗ CTV
8P 🛏 S% B&bf5.70–£7 Bdif7–£9
Wf46–£58 ⓚ (W only Jul & Aug)

GH Britannia Hotel 40 Christchurch Rd
☎26700 Central plan:**5** Closed Xmas

GH Bursledon Hotel Gervis Rd ☎24622
Central plan:**6** 23hc 5⇆🛏 (4fb) nc3 CTV

12P 5🛍 🛏 S% ✲B&bf7.50–£11.50
Bdif9.20–£16.10 Wf62.10–£96.60
D6.30pm

GH Carisbrooke Hotel 42 Tregonwell Rd
☎20432 Central plan:**7** Apr–Oct Lic 25hc
(3fb) nc4 CTV 18P S% B&bf8.65–£11
Bdif12.15–£14.50 Wf63.25–£90 ⓚ
(W late Jun–mid Sep) D4pm

GH Carysfort Lodge Private Hotel
19 Carysfort Rd, Boscombe ☎36751
Central plan:**8** 10hc (4fb) ✗ nc3 CTV 10P
S% B&bf6.50 Bdif9 Wf52 ⓚ D4pm

GH Hotel Cavendish 20 Chine Cres,
West Cliff ☎20489 Central plan:**9**
Etr–Oct 18hc ✗ CTV 15P (W only last wk
Jun–first wk Sep) D6.30pm

GH Charles Taylor Hotel 40/44 Frances
Rd, Knyveton Gdns ☎22695 Central

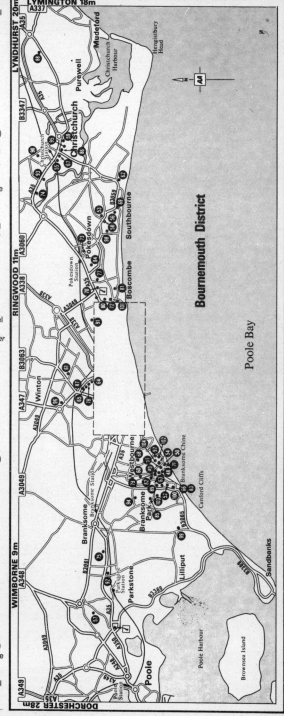

plan:**10** Etr–Nov Lic 29hc 11⟷📶 (9fb) ⊛
nc3 CTV 12P 🍴 B&b£6.50–£11
Bdi£9.50–£13.50 W£56–£82 ⫽ (W only
Jul–Sep) D5pm

⋈ **GH Chilterns Hotel** 44 Westby Rd
☎36539 Central plan:**11** Apr–Oct Lic
19hc (8fb) CTV 17P 2🏠 S%
B&b£5.75–£9.50 Bdi£9–£12.50
W£57.50–£82 ⫽ D5pm

GH Chine Cote Private Hotel 25 Studland
Rd, Alum Chine ☎764108 District plan:**60**
Etr–Oct 9hc (7fb) ⊛ CTV 4P S%
B&B£6.50–£7.50 Bdi£8.50–£9.50 D6pm

GH Cintra Hotel 10–12 Florence Rd,
Boscombe ☎36103 Central plan:**12**
mid Apr–1st wk Nov Lic 39hc 5⟷📶 (12fb)
⊛ CTV 12P S% B&b£6.90–£9.20
Bdi£8.50–£13.50 W£52–£80 D10am

GH Cliffside Hotel 7 Durley Gdns, West
Cliff ☎27833 Central plan:**13** Lic 21hc
(9fb) ⊛ nc3 CTV S% B&b£6.32–£10.92
Bdi£8.05–£13.47 W£48.30–£86.25 ⫽
(W only Jun–Sep) D9.30am

GH Clock House Hotel 13 Boscombe Spa
Rd ☎36988 Central plan:**14** Mar–Nov Lic
22hc (3fb) CTV 12P sea S% ✳B&b£6–£7
Bdi£7.50–£8.50 W£49.50–£58 ⫽

GH Collingdale Lodge 154 Richmond
Park Rd ☎514528 District plan:**61**
rs 22–28 Dec (B&b only) Lic 10rm 5hc
3⟷📶 (2fb) ⊛ nc8 CTV 10P B&bfr£9.20
Bdifr£13.80 Wfr£60.40 ⫽ D8pm

GH Crescent Grange Hotel 6–8 Crescent
Grange Rd, The Triangle ☎26959 Central
plan:**15** Jan–Oct & Xmas Lic 23hc 4⟷📶
(4fb) ⊛ nc3 CTV 20P 🍴
B&b£6.90–£10.43 Bdi£10.35–£13.80

W£71.30–£92 ⫽ (W only 4 Jul–5 Sep)
GH Crossroads Hotel 88 Belle Vue Rd,
Southbourne ☎426307 District plan:**62**
Closed Xmas 10hc (4fb) ⊛ nc5 CTV 10P
S% ✳B&b£4.60–£7.47 Bdi£6.90–£10.92
W£35–£63.25 ⫽ D4.30pm

⋈ **GH Dean Court Hotel** 4 Frances Rd
☎28165 Central plan:**16** Closed Nov Lic
11hc (4fb) ⊛ nc3 CTV 5P 🍴 S%
B&b£5.50–£9.Bdi£7.50–£11 W£44–£66
⫽ (W only Jul–Aug) D Noon

⋈ **GH Derwent House** 36 Hamilton Rd,
Boscombe ☎39102 Central plan:**17** Lic
11rm 10hc (4fb) ⊛ CTV 14P 🍴 S%
B&B£5.75–£6.90 Bdi£9.20–£10.35
W£46–£69 ⫽ (W only Jun–Sep) D4pm

GH Dorchester Hotel 64 Lansdowne Rd
North ☎21271 District plan:**64** Lic 15⟷📶
(11fb) ⊛ CTV 15P 🍴 ⅂ S% B&b£7–£11
Bdi£10–£16 W£50–£80 ⫽ (W only 5 Jul–
20 Sep) D5.30pm

⋈ **GH Dorset Westbury Hotel** 62
Lansdowne Rd ☎21811 District plan:**65**
Lic 21hc 3⟷📶 (3fb) nc6 CTV 20P 🍴 S%
B&b£5.80–£8.80 Bdi£8.80–£11.80
W£56.70–£76.90 ⫽

GH Earlham Lodge 91 Alumhurst Rd,
Alum Chine ☎761943 District plan:**66**
Feb–Nov & Xmas Lic 14hc 6⟷📶 (4fb) ⊛
CTV 9P 🍴 B&b£8.05–£11.50
Bdi£10.50–£14.95 W£80.50–£92 ⫽
D6pm

GH East Cliff Cottage Private Hotel
57 Grove Rd ☎22788 Central plan:**18**
Apr–Oct 10hc 4⟷📶 (1fb) nc5 CTV 8P S%
B&b£8.50–£12.50 Bdi£11.50–£16
W£62–£96 ⫽ D4pm

GH Eglan Court Hotel 7 Knyveton Rd
☎20093 Central plan:**19** May–Oct Lic
15hc 3⇨🛁 (4fb) ⊛ nc5 CTV 10P 🍴 S%
B&b£6.50–£7.50 Bdi£9–£10 W£55–£65
⅄ D10am

GH Fallowfield Hotel 25 Florence Rd,
Boscombe ☎37094 Central plan:**20**
Mar–Oct rs Jan & Feb Lic 12hc (6fb) CTV
12P 1🏠 S% B&b£8–£11.50
Bdi£10–£13.50 W£55–£80 ⅄ (W only
Jul & Aug) D6pm

GH Farlow Private Hotel 13 Walpole Rd,
Boscombe ☎35865 Central plan:**21**
Closed 1 wk spring, 2wks Oct 13hc (1fb) ⊛
4nc CTV 14P S% B&b£6.33–£7.48
Bdi£9.78–£10.93 W£57.50–£69 ⅄
(W only Jul & Aug) D4pm

GH Freshfields Touring Hotel
55 Christchurch Rd ☎34023 Central
plan:**22** Lic 15hc (2fb) ⊛ nc5 CTV 12P 🍴
S% B&b£8.05 Bdi£10.35 W£67.85 ⅄
D6pm

GH Gervis Court Hotel 38 Gervis Rd
☎26871 Central plan:**23** Etr–Oct Lic 18hc
(2fb) ⊛ ♨ CTV 20P 1🏠 S%
B&b£7.50–£12.25 Bdi£11.25–£15.75
W£63.25–£91.45 ⅄ D7pm

GH Gordons Hotel 84 West Cliff Rd
☎765844 District plan:**68** Etr–Oct rs Jan–
Mar (B&b only) Lic 17hc 1⇨🛁 (5fb) nc5
CTV 16P S% B&b£7–£8
Bdi£10.50–£11.50 W£65–£75

GH Grassmere 5 Pine Ave, Southbourne
☎428660 District plan:**69** Etr–Oct 10hc
(3fb) ⊛ 3nc CTV 10P S% B&b£6–£6.50
Bdi£7.50–£8 W£50–£60 ⅄ D5pm

GH Hamilton Hall Private Hotel
1 Carysfort Rd, Boscombe ☎35758

Central plan:**24** Lic 10hc 3⇨🛁 (3fb) CTV
10P 🍴 S% ✳B&b£5–£7 Bdi£8–£10
W£53.50–£66.50 ⅄ (W only Jul & Aug)
D Noon

GH Hawaiian Hotel 4 Glen Rd, Boscombe
☎33234 Central plan:**25** Mar–Oct 12hc
4⇨🛁 (3fb) ⊛ nc5 CTV 9P S%
B&b£6–£7 Bdi£8–£10 W£50–£60 ⅄

GH Heathcote Hotel 2 Heathcote Rd,
Boscombe ☎36185 District plan:**70**
Closed Xmas rs Nov–Etr (B&b only) Lic
16hc 3⇨🛁 (7fb) ⊛ CTV 15P S%
✳B&b£5.17–£8.62 Bdi£8.62–£12.07
W£51–£74 ⅄

GH Highlin Private Hotel 14 Knole Rd
☎33758 Central plan:**26** Lic 11hc (4fb) ⊛
nc10 CTV 7P 🍴 S% B&b£6 Bdi£9
W£50–£65 ⅄ D6.30pm

GH Hollyhurst Hotel West Hill Rd, West
Cliff ☎27137 Central plan:**27** Mar–Nov &
Xmas Lic 24hc 5⇨🛁 (10fb) CTV 21P sea
S% B&b£7.25–£9.75 Bdi£10.35–£13
(W only Mar–Nov) D6.15pm

GH Holmcroft Hotel 5 Earle Rd, Alum
Chine ☎761289 District plan:**71**
Apr–Oct Lic 22hc (8fb) ⊛ nc3 CTV 17P
S% B&b£8–£12 Bdi£12–£16 W£70–£90
⅄ D6pm

GH Holme Lacy Hotel Florence Rd
☎36933 District plan:**72** Etr & mid May–
early Oct 30hc 3⇨🛁 (7fb) 3nc CTV 16P ♿
S% ✳B&b£7.50 Bdi£9.75–£11 W£63–£68
⅄ D6pm

⊨GH Hurley Lodge 20 Castlemain Av,
Southbourne ☎427046 District plan:**73**
6hc (3fb) ⊛ nc6 CTV 6P 🍴 S%
B&b£5.50–£7 Bdi£8–£9.50 W£40–£50
⅄ (W only Jul–Aug) D4pm

GH Kings Barton 22 Hawkwood Rd, Boscombe ☎37794 Central plan:**28** Lic 15hc (6fb) ✲ CTV P 🛏 S% B&b£6.50–£7.50 Bdi£9–£10 W£60–£65 ⓚ

GH Linwood House Hotel 11 Wilfred Rd ☎37818 Central plan:**29** Mar–Nov, rs Jan & Feb (B&b only) Lic 10hc (4fb) nc5 CTV 7P 🛏 S% B&b£7–£9 Bdi£9–£11 W£68–£73 ⓚ D6pm

GH Loddington Grange Hotel 13 Knole Rd ☎36117 Central plan:**29A** 10hc (5fb) ✲ CTV 8P S% B&b£6.90–£9.20 Bdi£12.65–£14.95 W£51.75–£74.75 ⓚ

GH Mae-Mar Private Hotel 91–93 Westhill Rd, West Cliff ☎23167 Central plan:**30** Lic 28hc (7fb) CTV 🛏 lift S% W£46.30–£56.35 Ⓜ (W only Jul–Aug) D10am

GH Mariner's Hotel 22 Clifton Rd, Southbourne ☎420851 District plan:**77** Feb–Oct 15hc (2fb) ♨ CTV 20P 🛏 sea B&b£7.48–£8.05 Bdi£9.76–£10.93 W£62.10–£65.55 ⓚ D6.30pm

⊢⊣**GH Mon Bijou Hotel** 47 Manor Rd, East Cliff ☎21389 Central plan:**31** Feb–Oct rs Jan 10hc 2⇨🛁 ✲ 12nc CTV 8P 🛏 S% ✳B&b£6–£8 Bdi£7.50–£9.50 W£53–£65 ⓚ (W only Jun–Sep) D6.30pm

GH Moorings Hotel 66 Lansdowne Road North ☎22705 District plan:**78** Lic 18hc (2fb) nc10 CTV 18P 🛏 B&bfr£7 Bdifr£10 Wfr£70 ⓚ D7pm

GH Mount Lodge Hotel 19 Beaulieu Rd, Westbourne ☎761173 District plan:**79** Etr–7 Nov rs 24 Dec–Etr Lic 11hc (2fb) ♨ CTV 6P 🛏 S% B&b£6.50–£10 Bdi£9.85–£13 W£68–£85 ⓚ D7pm

⊢⊣**GH Myrtle House Hotel** 41 Hawkwood Rd, Boscombe ☎36579 District plan:**80** 10hc (5fb) ♨ CTV 9P 🛏 B&b£5.50–£7.50 Bdi£6.50–£9 W£42–£62 ⓚ D6pm

GH Naseby-Nye Hotel Byron Rd, Boscombe ☎34079 District plan:**81** Lic 13hc 3⇨🛁 nc4 CTV 10P 🛏 sea D6.30pm

GH Newfield Private Hotel 29 Burnaby Rd, Alum Chine ☎762724 District plan:**82** Lic 12hc 3⇨🛁 (2fb) ✲ CTV 6P 🛏 S% B&b£6–£9 Bdi£9–£12 D6pm

GH Northover Private Hotel 10 Earle Rd, Alum Chine ☎767349 District plan:**83** Apr–Oct 11hc 2⇨🛁 (3fb) nc3 CTV 10P sea S% B&b£8–£10 Bdi£10–£13 W£69–£90 ⓚ (W only mid Jun–Aug) D5.30pm

GH Oak Hall Private Hotel 9 Wilfred Rd, Boscombe ☎35062 District plan:**84** Mar–Oct Lic 12hc 2⇨🛁 (3fb) nc5 CTV 8P 🛏 (W only mid Jun–mid Sep) D6.30pm

GH Penmone Hotel 17 Carysfort Rd, Boscombe ☎35903 Central plan:**32** Lic 9hc CTV 10P 🛏 D6pm

⊢⊣ **GH Perran Court Hotel** 58 Lansdowne Rd ☎27881 District plan:**87** Lic 14hc 2⇨🛁 (4fb) ✲ nc7 CTV 14P 🛏 S% B&b£5–£7.50 Bdi£7.50–£10.50 (W only mid Jul–mid Aug) D6.30pm

GH Pine Beach Hotel 31 Boscombe Spa Rd ☎35902 Central plan:**33** Etr–Oct Lic 20hc ✲ nc8 CTV 17P sea D6.30pm

GH St Ronans Hotel 64–66 Frances Rd ☎23535 Central plan:**34** Mar–Oct Lic 13hc (5fb) CTV 8P 🛏 S% ✳B&b£6.50–£8 Bdi£7.50–£9.50 W£45–£60 ⓚ D4pm

GH St Wilfreds Private Hotel 15 Walpole Rd, Boscombe ☎36189 District plan:**91** 8hc (3fb) ⊗ CTV 3P B&b£6.30–£7 Bdi£7.50–£8 W£52–£56 ⌑D5.30pm

GH Sandelheath Hotel 1 Knyveton Rd, East Cliff ☎25428 Central plan:**35** Lic 15hc (4fb) ⊗ nc4 CTV 12P ⊠ S% B&b£7–£8.50 Bdi£9.50–£10.35 W£58.75–£68.50 ⌑D7pm

GH Sea Shells 201–205 Holdenhurst Rd ☎292542 Central plan:**36** 12hc (A6hc) (10fb) nc3 CTV 30P S% B&b£6.90–£9.20 W£46–£62.10 ⋈

⊢⊣ **GH Seastrole Private Hotel** 12 Campbell Rd, Boscombe ☎36996 Central plan:**37** 9hc (3fb) ⊗ 2nc CTV 8P S% B&b£4.50–£8 Bdi£6–£9.50 W£40–£60 ⌑ D Noon

GH Sea View Court Hotel 14 Boscombe Spa Rd ☎37197 Central plan:**38** Apr–Oct Lic 14hc 2⇥▥ (5fb) nc3 CTV 18P sea S% B&b£6–£10 Bdi£10–£15 W£50–£70 ⌑D2pm

GH Silver Trees Hotel 57 Wimborne Rd ☎26040 District plan:**96** 10hc (2fb) ⊗ nc5 CTV 10P S% B&b£7–£10 Bdi£10–£13 W£69–£84 ⌑D5pm

GH Hotel Sorrento 16 Owls Rd, **Boscombe** ☎34019 Central plan:**39** Mar–Oct 19hc 2⇥▥ (3fb) nc5 CTV 20P S% B&b£7.50–£8.75 Bdi£10.50–£12.65 W£57.50–£86.25 ⌑ D6pm

GH Hotel Sorrento 8 Studland Rd, **Alum Chine,** Westbourne ☎762116 District plan:**97** Lic 20hc 7⇥▥ (4fb) nc7 CTV 10P ⊠ sea B&b£7.50–£8.50 Bdi£10–£11:50 ⌑D6.30pm

GH Southlea Hotel Durley Rd, West Cliff ☎26075 Central plan:**40** Apr–Oct 20hc (6fb) 3nc CTV 16P B&b£8.05–£9.75 Bdi£9.75–£11.50 W£64.40–£75.90 ⌑ D6pm

GH Stratford Hotel 20 Grand Ave, Southbourne ☎424726 District plan:**98** Lic 14hc (8fb) ⊗ CTV 10P ⊠ S% *B&b£7.50–£9.50 Bdi£9–£11 W£60–£72 ⌑ D6pm

GH Tower House Hotel West Cliff Gdns ☎20742 Central plan:**41** Apr–Oct & Xmas Lic 34hc 12⇥▥ (17fb) nc5 CTV 20P ⊠ lift sea S% B&b£9–£11 Bdi£10.50–£14 W£66–£99.50 ⌑ D6.30pm

GH Tudor Grange Hotel 31 Gervis Rd ☎291472 Central plan:**42** Mar–mid Nov Lic 12hc 1⇥▥ (6fb) CTV 8P ⊠ S% B&b£7.50–£11.75 Bdi£11–£15.25 W£70–£99 ⌑ D7pm

⊢⊣ **GH Valberg Hotel** 1A Wollstonecraft Rd, Boscombe ☎34644 District plan:**101** 10hc 7⇥▥ (3fb) ⊗ 5nc CTV 8P ⊠ S% B&b£5–£7 W£29–£39 ⋈ (W only Jul & Aug)

GH Wenmaur House 14 Carysfort Rd, Boscombe ☎35081 Central plan:**43** Lic 12hc ⊗ CTV 10P S% B&b£6.90–£8.05 Bdi£10.35–£11.50 (W only Jul/Aug)

GH West Bay Hotel West Cliff Gdns ☎22261 Central plan:**44** Etr & mid May–early Oct 13hc (4fb) CTV 6P B&b£7.48–£10.10 Bdi£9.86–£12.40 W£60.95–£78.78 ⌑ (W only mid Jun–mid Sep) D6pm

GH West Dene Private Hotel 117 Alumhurst Rd, Westbourne ☎764843

District plan:**102** Mar–mid Oct & Xmas
Lic 17hc 6⇱🛁 (3fb) ⌖ CTV 17P sea S%
B&b£7–£9 Bdi£9–£12 W£64–£77 ⚹
(W only mid Jul–Aug) D6.15pm

GH Whitley Court Hotel West Cliff Gdns
☎21302 Central plan:**45** Closed Jan 16hc
nc3 CTV 10P 🛏 sea D5pm

GH Windsor Court Hotel 34 Bodorgan Rd
☎24637 Central plan:**46** Lic 37hc 16⇱🛁
(10fb) ⌕ CTV 22P 🛏 & ✱B&b£4.37–£15.87
Bdi£6.67–£18.17 W£40.25–£109.25 ⚹
D7.30pm

GH Woodford Court Hotel 19–21
Studland Rd, Alum Chine ☎764907
District plan:**104** Etr–Oct 12hc 4⇱🛁
(A10hc 4⇱🛁) (6fb) nc2 CTV 12P sea S%
B&b£7–£8.50 Bdi£8–£11 W£58–£72 ⚹
(W only Jun, Jul & Aug)

GH Wood Lodge Hotel 10 Manor Rd,
East Cliff ☎764907 **47** Etr–mid
Oct Lic 15hc 8⇱🛁 (3fb) CTV 12P 🛏 S%
B&b£10–£16 Bdi£12.50–£19.50
W£75–£117 ⚹ (W only high season) D4pm

BOURTON-ON-THE-WATER Glos
Map 4 SP12
INN *Mousetrap* ☎20579 Lic 3hc nc14
16P 🛏 ⇛ D9.30pm

BOVEY TRACEY Devon *Map 3 SX87*
GH *Kestor* Challabrook Ln ☎832277 6hc
⌕ CTV 6P 🛏 D7pm

BOWLAND BRIDGE Cumbria
Map 7 SD48
INN Hare & Hounds ☎Crosthwaite 333
Lic 4hc (A4⇱🛁) CTV 150P 🛏 S%
✱B&b£7.50–£8.50 Bdi£13–£14 sn
L£2–£2.50 D9.30pm£5.50

BOWNESS-ON-WINDERMERE Cumbria
Map 7 SD49 **Guesthouses are listed
under Windermere**

BRADFORD W Yorks *Map 7 SE13*
GH Belvedere Hotel 19 North Park Rd,
Manningham ☎492559 Closed Xmas &
New Year Lic 13hc 🛏 nc5 CTV 20P 🛏 S%
✱B&b£10.12 Bdi£13.27 D5.30pm

GH Maple Hill 3 Park Dr, Heaton ☎44061
10hc ⌖ CTV 10P 4🏠 🛏 S%
B&b£6.40–£6.90

GH Midway 218 Keighley Rd, Frizinghall
☎42667 6hc (1fb) CTV 🛏 S% ✱B&b£6.20

BRAEMAR Grampian *Aberdeens
Map 15 NO19*

GH Braemar Lodge ☎617 Lic 9hc
(2fb) CTV 20P B&b£6–£7 Bdi£11–£12
D8pm

GH Callater Lodge ☎275 Close mid Oct–
26 Dec Lic 9hc (1fb) 42P 2🏠 🛏 S%
B&b£8.70 Bdi£14.60 W£110.32 ⚹ D8pm

BRAUNTON Devon *Map 2 SS43*
GH *Brookdale Hotel* 62 South St
☎812075 Lic 10hc 1⇱🛁 ⌕ ⌖ CTV 10P
1🏠 🛏 D5pm

BREAGE Cornwall *Map 2 SW62*
GH Hilladale Hotel Polladras ☎Germoe
3334 Lic 9hc (7fb) ⌕ CTV 9P 🛏 S%
B&b£9.20–£11.50 Bdi£12.65–£14.95
W£57.50–£69 ⚹ D4pm

BREDE E Sussex *Map 5 TQ81*
GH Roselands Private Hotel ☎882338
10 Jan–10 Dec 16hc (2fb) CTV 20P 🛏 sea
S% ✱£7.75–£8.75 Bdi£11.65–£12.65
W£56–£76 ⚹ D6pm

BRENT KNOLL Somerset *Map 3 ST35*
GH Battleborough Grange Hotel
☎760208 Closed Xmas wk Lic 12hc (3fb)
CTV 30P 🛏 S% B&b£9 Bdi£12.50 W£85
⚹ D9pm

GH Woodlands Hill Lane ☎760232 Lic
10hc 3⇱🛁 (3fb) ⌕ CTV 20P 🛏 S%
✱B&b£8.50–£9.50 Bdi£10–£11.50
W£57.50–£62.50 ⚹ D Noon

BRIDFORD Devon *Map 3 SX88*
⊯ **GH Bridford** ☎Christow 52563
Mar–Nov rs Dec–Feb (closed Xmas) 6hc
(1fb) ⌖ CTV 6P 🛏 S% ✱B&b£5.50
Bdi£8.50 W£51 ⚹ D4.30pm

BRIDGNORTH Salop *Map 7 SO79*
GH Severn Arms Hotel Underhill St
☎4616 Lic 10hc CTV

INN Ball Hotel East Castle St ☎2478 Lic
5hc ⌖ CTV 10P 1🏠 🛏 ⇛ S%
B&b£8.50–£9.50 Bar lunch80p–£3

BRIDLINGTON Humberside *Map 8 TA16*
GH Shirley Private Hotel 47/48 South
Marine Dr ☎72539 Apr–Oct Lic 37hc
2⇱🛁 (14fb) CTV 14P lift sea B&b£8–£9
Bdi£11–£12 W£89–£94 D6pm

GH Southdowne Hotel South Marine Dr
☎73270 Apr–mid Oct Lic 10hc 1⇱🛁
(3fb) CTV 8P 🛏 sea B&b£6 Bdi£8.50
W£60 ⚹ (W only Jul–Aug) D6pm

BRIDPORT Dorset *Map 3 SY49*
GH Britmead House 154 West Bay Rd

☎22941 Lic 8hc 3⇔🏠 (3fb) CTV 15P 🖤
S% B&bf£7.80–£8.50 Bdif£11.40–£12.50
Wf£70–£77 ⚓D4.30pm

GH Roundham House Hotel West Bay Rd
☎22753 mid Jan–Nov Lic 8hc (3fb) CTV
6P 🖤 sea B&bf£8.50–£9 Bdif£12.50–£13
Wf£84–£88 ⚓D7pm

INN Railway Terminus 114 St Andrews Rd
☎22911 Lic 4hc ⊗ TV 8P 2🏠 S%
✱B&bfr£5 Bdifr£8 Wfr£50 ⚓
Bar lunch 50p–£3 D9pmf£2.50–£4.50

BRIGHTON E Sussex *Map 4 TQ30*
See also Hove
GH Ascott House 21 New Steine,
Marine Pd ☎688085 11hc (5fb) CTV sea
S% B&bf£6.50–£7.50 Wf£43–£50 M

▸◂**GH Downlands Private Hotel**
19 Charlotte St ☎601203 Closed Xmas
10hc (2fb) CTV S% B&bf£5.50–£6
Bdif£8–£8.50 Wf£54 ⚓Dam

GH Marina House Hotel 8 Charlotte St
☎605349 Closed Xmas Lic 11hc 6⇔🏠
(3fb) CTV 🖤 S% B&bf£6.90–£8.05
Bdif£9.75–£11.50 Wf£67–£79 ⚓D9am

GH Melford Hall Hotel 41 Marine Pde
☎681435 Lic 12hc 4⇔🏠 (5fb) CTV 6P
sea S%✱B&bf£8–£12.50 (W only Jul, Aug
& Sep)

GH Regency Hotel 28 Regency Sq
☎202690 Closed Jan Lic 13hc 5⇔🏠
CTV 🖤 D10.30pm

GH Rowland House 21 St George's Ter,
Kemp Town ☎603639 Lic 10hc (2fb) nc5
CTV 1P 🖤 B&bf£6.50–£8 Bdif£9.50–£11.50
Wf£57–£69 ⚓D5pm

GH Trouville 11 New Steine, Marine Pde

☎697384 9hc (3fb) ⊗ nc12 CTV S%
B&bf£6.50–£8.50 Wf£43.75–£57.75 M

GH Twenty One Hotel 21 Charlotte St,
Marine Pde ☎686450 Lic 6hc (2fb) ⊗
nc5 CTV 🖤 sea S% B&bf£9–£11
Bdif£13.50–£16 Wf£96.25–£113.75 ⚓
D1pm

GH Twenty Three 23 New Steine
☎684212 9hc (5fb) CTV S% B&bf£5–£7.50
Wf£31.50–£35 M

BRISTOL Avon *Map 3 ST57* **See Plan**
GH Birkdale Hotel 11 Ashgrove Rd,
Redland ☎33635 Plan:**1** Closed Xmas
& New Years Day Lic 18hc 4⇔🏠
(A 24hc 3⇔🏠) (5fb) CTV 10P 🖤 B&bf£10.06
Bdif£15.46 D7.30pm

▸◂**GH Burlington** 19 Henleaze Rd,
Henleaze ☎622078 Plan:**2** 4hc (2fb) CTV
2P 🖤 S% B&bf£5–£7 Bdif£7–£9 Wf£30
M D6pm

GH Cambridge Hotel 15 Iddesleigh Rd
☎36020 Not on plan Lic 13hc (4fb) CTV
🖤 S% B&bf£7.50 Bdif£11 Dnoon

GH Cavendish House Hotel 18 Cavendish
Rd, Henleaze ☎621017 Plan:**3** 6hc (3fb)
CTV 5P 🖤 S% B&bf£6.90

GH Chesterfield Hotel 3 Westbourne Pl,
Clifton ☎34606 Plan:**4** Closed Xmas wk
13hc 1⇔🏠 (4fb) CTV 🖤 S% B&bf£7.13

GH Hotel Clifton St Pauls Rd, Clifton
☎36882 Plan:**5** 65hc 24⇔🏠 (4fb) CTV
10P 🖤 lift S%✱B&bfr£7.13–£9.78 D10pm

GH Glenroy Hotel 30 Victoria Sq, Clifton
☎39058 Plan:**6** Closed Xmas wk Lic 32hc
4⇔🏠 (11fb) CTV 15P 🖤 ✱B&b£8.05–£9.20

Roundham House Hotel

West Bay Road, Bridport, Dorset.
Tel: Bridport 22753 (STD 0308)

Special commendation recommended by British Tourist Authority.

A fine old, mellowed stone house in lovely surroundings with every
comfort and convenience. Standing in its own grounds of three quarters
of an acre, overlooking Eype Down, cliffs and sea.

Full choice of interesting and varied menus daily with fresh homegrown
vegetables.

Hot, cold and shaving points in all rooms, colour television, library and bar.

Restaurant and residential licence.

Guests warmly welcomed with personal attention.

Inclusive terms: dinner, bed & breakfast — £13.00 daily and £88.00
weekly inclusive of Value Added Tax.

Telephone or write for brochure, tariff and sample menus.

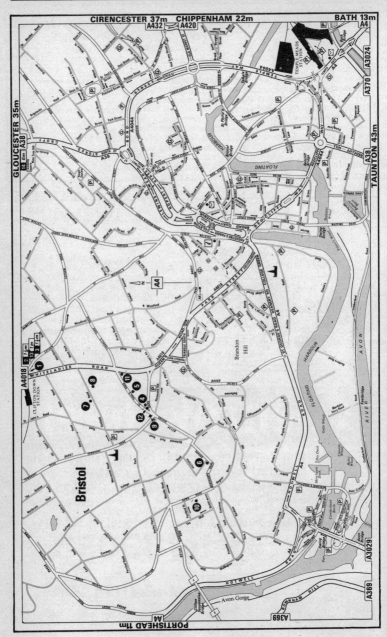

1	Birkdale Hotel	4	Chesterfield Hotel	8	Oakfield Hotel	12	Washington Hotel
2	Burlington	5	Hotel Clifton	9	Pembroke Hotel	13	Westbury Park
3	Cavendish House	6	Glenroy Hotel	10	Rodney Hotel		Hotel
	Hotel	7	Oakdene Hotel	11	Seeley's Hotel	14	Willow

GH Oakdene Hotel 45 Oakfield Rd
☎35900 Plan:**7** Closed Xmas 10hc (9fb)
⊘ nc5 TV ✱B&f£9.66 W£62.10 M

GH Oakfield Hotel 52–54 Oakfield Rd
☎35556 Plan:**8** 2Jan–23Dec 27hc (4fb)
CTV 10P 🛏 S% ✱B&b£7.48 Bdi£10.93
D7pm

⊨◀GH Pembroke Hotel 13 Arlington
Villas ☎35550 Plan:**9** Closed Xmas
15hc (2fb) CTV 🛏 S% B&bfr£6.78–£7.13

GH Rodney Hotel 4 Rodney Pl, Clifton
Down Rd ☎35422 Plan:**10** Closed Xmas
& New Year 30hc (5fb) ⊘ CTV 🛏 B&b£8.95

GH Seeleys Hotel 19–27 St Pauls Rd, Clifton ☎38544 Plan:**11** Closed Xmas Day Lic 40hc 26⇌🛏 (A 20hc 9⇌🛏) (35fb) 🅰 CTV 10P 18🏛 🎵 S% * B&b£7.32 Bdi£11.07 W£70.49 ⅃ D10.30pm

GH Washington Hotel 11–15 St Pauls Rd, Clifton ☎33980 Plan:**12** 32hc (3fb) CTV 13P 🎵 S% ✱B&b£7.13

GH Westbury Park Hotel 37 Westbury Rd, Westbury-on-Trym ☎620465 Plan:**13** Closed Xmas Lic 9hc CTV 5P 🎵 S% ✱B&b£6.90–£7.95 Bdi fr£10.50 D7pm

GH Willow 209 Gloucester Rd, Patchway ☎ Almondsbury 612276 Plan:**14** 6hc (3fb) CTV 8P 2🏛 🎵 S% B&b£7

BRIXHAM Devon *Map 3 SX95*
See Plan
GH Beverley Court Private Hotel Upper Manor Rd ☎3149 Plan:**1** May–Oct Lic 11hc (4fb) 🌣 CTV 18P 🎵 S% B&b£6.78–£9.20 Bdi£10.23–£12.66 W£56.35–£69 ⅃

⚭**GH Brioc Private Hotel** 11 Prospect Rd ☎3540 Plan:**2** Lic 10hc (2fb) CTV 🎵 sea S% B&b£5.75 Bdi£9.20 W£57.50–£58.25 ⅃

GH Cottage Hotel Mount Pleasant Rd ☎2123 Plan:**3** Whitsun–Sep Lic 10hc (2fb) nc3 CTV 5P sea B&b£6–£6.50 Bdi£8.50–£9.50 W£49.50–£68.50 ⅃ (W only Jul & Aug) D5pm

⚭**GH Harbour View Hotel** King St ☎3052 Plan:**4** 10hc (4fb) TV 2P sea S% B&b£5.65–£7.50 Bdi£10.15–£12 D5.30pm

GH *Holywell Villa* 119 New Rd ☎3496 Plan:**5** Closed late Oct 7hc nc4 CTV 10P

⚭**GH Orchard House** St Marys Rd ☎3590 Plan:**6** Closed Jan & Feb Lic 5hc (2fb) 🌣 CTV 12P S% B&b£5–£6 Bdi£8.25–£8.75 W£54–£58 ⅃ Dnoon

GH Parkway House Private Hotel 2 Greenswood Rd ☎2730 Plan:**7** Closed Xmas 7hc (3fb) CTV 6P 1🏛 S% ✱B&b£6 Bdi£7.50 W£52 ⅃ D6pm

GH *Pola* 63–65 Berry Head Rd ☎2019 Plan:**8** Closed 22–30Dec 12hc CTV sea D10am

GH Raddicombe Lodge 105 Kingswear Rd ☎2125 Plan:**9** 9hc (3fb) 🌣nc1 CTV 10P sea S% B&b£7.60 Bdi£11.40 W£79.80 ⅃ D5pm

BRIXTON Devon *Map 2 SX55*
⚭**GH Rosemount** ☎ Plymouth 880770 Lic 6hc (2fb) 🌣 CTV 10P S% B&b£6 Bdi£8.75–£9.75 W£32.25–£40.25 Ⓜ DNoon

BROADFORD Isle of Skye, Highland *Inverness-shire Map 13 NG62*
GH *Hilton* ☎322 Apr–Oct 10rm 9hc TV 10P 🎵

BROAD HAVEN *(Nr Haverfordwest)* Dyfed *Map 2 SM81*
GH Broad Haven Hotel ☎366 Closed Xmas Lic 40hc 24⇌🛏 (15fb) CTV 60P 🎵 B&b£6–£8 Bdi£9.50–£12.50 W£55.50–£85.50 ⅃ D7pm

BROADHEMPSTON Devon *Map 3 SX86*
GH Downe Manor ☎ Ipplepen 812239 Etr–Sep 8hc (1fb) CTV 5P 2🏛 S% ✱Bdi£6.75 W£45 ⅃ D6.30pm

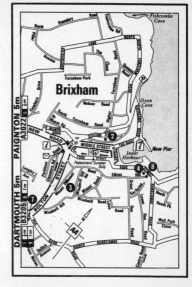

1 Beverley Court Hotel
2 Brioc Private Hotel
3 Cottage Hotel
4 Harbour View
5 Holwell Villa
6 Orchard House
7 Parkway House
  Private Hotel
8 Pola
9 Raddicombe Lodge

BROAD MARSTON Heref & Worcs *Map 4 SP14*
GH Broad Marston Manor ☎ Stratford-upon-Avon 720252 Mar–Nov 7hc 1⇌🛏 (1fb) 🌣 nc12 CTV 30P 🎵 S% B&b£8.25–£9.50

BROADSTAIRS Kent *Map 5 TR36*
GH Bay Tree Hotel 12 Eastern Esp ☎ Thanet 62502 Lic 9hc (3fb) CTV 9P 🎵 sea S% B&b£6–£7.50 Bdi£8–£10.50 W£45–£55 ⅃ D2pm

GH Corner Ways 49–51 West Cliff Rd ☎ Thanet 61612 Feb–Oct Lic 12hc (7fb) CTV 13P S% B&b£7.50–£10.85 Bdi£10.35–£12 W£57–£65 ⅃ D6.30pm

GH Denmead Hotel 13 Granville Rd ☎ Thanet 62580 Lic 8hc (4fb) 🌣 CTV 8P 🎵 B&b£8.05 Bdi£12.50 D10.30pm

GH Dutch House Hotel 30 North Foreland Rd ☎ Thanet 62824 Lic 10hc (4fb) 🌣 CTV 6P 🎵 sea S% ✱B&b£8–£8.50 Bdi£11–£12 W£58–£62.50 ⅃ D6.30pm

GH East Horndon Private Hotel 4 Eastern Esp ☎ Thanet 68306 9hc 1⇌🛏 (4fb) CTV P 2🏛 🎵 B&b£11.50 Bdi£14.50 W£67.20–£90 ⅃ D7.30pm

GH Keston Court Hotel 14 Ramsgate Rd ☎ Thanet 62401 Lic 9hc (3fb) 🌣 nc1 CTV 6P 🎵 S% B&b£7.50–£8 Bdi£10.50–£11 W£57–£63 ⅃ D8pm

GH Kingsmead Hotel Eastern Esp ☎ Thanet 61694 Lic 14hc (4fb) CTV 12P 🎵 sea S% B&b£6.50–£7 Bdi£10–£11 D6pm

GH St Augustines Private Hotel 19 Granville Rd ☎ Thanet 65017 Apr–Sep & Xmas rs Feb, Mar & Nov Lic 15hc 3⇌🛏 (5fb) TV 1P 🎵 B&b£7.50–£8.50 Bdi£11.50–£12.50 W£68–£82 ⅃ D7.15pm

GH Seapoint Private Hotel 76 West
Cliff Rd ☎ Thanet 62269 May–Oct
rs Mar–May Lic 10hc (4fb) CTV 10P 1🐾
🍴 sea S% B&b£7.50–£8.50
Bdi£8.50–£9.50 W£65–£70 ⚓ D6pm

BROCKENHURST Hants *Map 4 SU30*
GH Fern Lodge Hotel Sway Rd ☎3189
8hc 2⇆🖤 (3fb) CTV 15P 🍴 S%
B&b£6.50–£9 Bdi£11–£13.50
W£74.70–£91.35 ⚓ D6pm

BROMLEY Gt London *London plan 4
(page 266)*
GH Bromley Continental Hotel 56
Plaistow Ln ☎01-464 2415 Lic 13hc
(3fb) ⊗ CTV 14P 🍴 S% B&b£9.20
Bdi£13.75 W£90 ⚓ D1pm

GH Bromley Villa St Philomena Hotel
1–3 Lansdowne Rd ☎01-460 6311 Lic
20hc 5⇆🖤 (7fb) ⊗ CTV 6P 🍴 B&b£8.62

BUCKFASTLEIGH Devon *Map 3 SX76*
GH Black Rock Buckfast Rd, Dart Bridge
(At Buckfast 1m N) ☎2343 Closed Xmas
Lic 10hc (4fb) ⚓ CTV 25P 🍴 river S%
B&b£6.50–£7 Bdi£9.50–£10 W£63 ⚓
D5.30pm

GH *Furzeleigh Mill* ☎2245 Closed Xmas
& New Year Lic 16hc TV 20P

BUDE Cornwall *Map 2 SS20*
See Plan
GH Cliff Maer Down, Crooklets ☎3584
Plan:**7** Mar–Oct 12⇆🖤 (6fb) CTV 14P sea
S% B&b£6.50–£7.50 Bdi£9.50–£10.50
W£63–£70 ⚓ D8pm

GH *Dunridge* 30 Downs View ☎2589
Plan:**1** Etr–Oct 10hc CTV 9P D6pm

⋈GH Kisauni 4 Downs View ☎2653
Plan:**2** Etr–Sep 6hc (3fb) nc5 CTV 5P
S% B&b£5.50–£6.50 Bdi£8–£9
W£50–£55 ⚓ D5pm

GH Links View 13 Morwenna Ter ☎2561
Plan:**3** Closed Xmas Lic 7hc (2fb) ⊗ CTV 🍴
sea S% B&b£6–£6.50 Bdi£8.50–£9.50
W£56–£60 ⚓ D5.30pm

⋈GH Pencarrol 21 Downs View ☎2478
Plan:**4** Apr–Oct 7hc (3fb) 1🐾 S%
B&b£4.60–£6.90 Bdi£6.90–£9.20
W£42–£50 ⚓ D5.30pm

⋈GH Sandiways 35 Downs View ☎2073
Plan:**5** Mar–Oct Lic 11hc 1⇆🖤 (5fb) ⊗ nc5
CTV 8P S% B&b£5.50–£6 Bdi£7.50–£8
W£50–£55 ⚓ D6.30pm

GH *Surf Haven* 31 Downs View ☎2998
Plan:**6** Apr–Oct Lic 6hc ⚓ CTV 6P sea
D5pm

BUDLEIGH SALTERTON Devon
Map 3 SY08

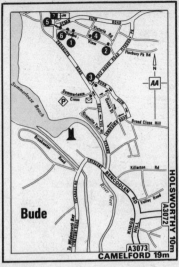

1   Dunridge   5   Sandiways
2   Kisauni   6   Surf Haven
3   Links View   7   Cliff
4   Pencarrol

GH Park House Hotel 7 Park Ln, Little
Knowle ☎3303 Etr–Oct Lic 10hc (5fb) ⊗
CTV 12P sea S% B&b£9–£11 Bdi£13–£15
W£78–£90 ⚓ D5.30pm

GH *Tidwell House* ☎2444 Closed Xmas
9hc ⚓ CTV 10P 2🐾 D5pm

GH Willowmead 12 Little Knowle ☎3115
6hc (1fb) CTV 8P 🍴 S% B&b£8–£9
Bdi£10.50–£11.50 W£55–£65 ⚓ D7pm

BUILTH WELLS Powys *Map 3 SO05*
INN Lion Hotel ☎3670 Lic 18hc 5⇆🖤
CTV 14P river B&b£6.50–£10
Bdi£10.50–£16 Wfr£80 sn L£4–£6.50
D8.30pm£4–£6.50

BURFORD Oxon *Map 4 SP21*
GH Corner House Hotel High St ☎3151
Mar–Dec Lic 10hc 1⇆🖤 (2fb) CTV 🍴
B&b£9–£10 Bdi£13–£14 D8pm

BURLEY Hants *Map 4 SU20*
GH Highcroft Hotel Highcroft Woods
☎2525 mid Jan–mid Dec Lic 11hc (3fb)
CTV 20P 🍴 S% ✳B&b£9.50–£10
Bdi£10–£15 W£70–£92.50 ⚓ D5pm

GH Tree House New Forest ☎3448 Lic
8hc (3fb) CTV 8P ▥ S% B&b£8–£10

BURNSALL N Yorks *Map 7 SE06*
GH Manor House ☎231 Mar–Nov
rs Oct–Feb (party bookings only) Lic 8hc
(2fb) CTV 6P river S% ✳B&b£6.50–£7
Bdi£10.25–£10.75 (W only Jul & Aug)

BURNT ISLAND Fife *Map 11 NT28*
⊷**GH Forthaven** 4 South View
Lammerlaws ☎872600 4hc (2fb) TV 4P
river S% B&b£4.50 W£28 M

BURROW BRIDGE Somerset
Map 3 ST33
GH Old Bakery ☎234 Lic 6hc CTV 12P
S% ✳B&bfr£5.75 Wfr£55 ⱡ D10.30pm

BURTON UPON TRENT Staffs
Map 8 SK22
GH Delter Hotel 5 Derby Rd ☎35115
Lic 5hc (2fb) ⊘ CTV 5P ▥ S% ✳B&b£8.05
Bdi£11.50–£12.65 W£80.50–£88.55 ⱡ
D7.30pm

BURWASH E Sussex *Map 5 TQ62*
INN Admiral Vernon ☎882230 Lic 5hc
1⇻🍴nc10 CTV 30P 1🏠 ▥ S%
B&b£9–£10 Bdi£12.50–£13.50 W£60 ⱡ
sn L£1.90–£3.90 D9.30pm£2.20–£4.20

INN Bell High St ☎882304 rs Xmas Lic
5hc 15P ▥ ⇻ ✳B&b£6.75–£8 Wfr£42 M
sn L£3alc D9pm£5alc

BURY ST EDMUNDS Suffolk *Map 5 TL86*
GH Swan 11 Northgate St ☎2678 Closed
Xmas 6hc (1fb) ⊘ CTV ▥ S%
B&b£7.75–£8.33 Bdi£10.63–£11.78
W£60.42–£68.40 ⱡ D2pm

BUTE, ISLE OF Strathclyde *Bute Map 10*
See Rothesay

BUTTERTON Staffs *Map 7 SK05*
INN *Black Lion* ☎Onecote 232 Lic 4hc ⊗
nc12 TV 14P ▥ D9pm

BUXTON Derbys *Map 7 SK07*
⊷**GH Fairhaven** 1 Dale Ter ☎4481
Closed Xmas Lic 6hc (2fb) CTV ▥ S%
B&b£5–£5.50 Bdi£7.50–£8 D4.30pm

⊷**GH Griff** 2 Compton Rd ☎3628 Closed
Xmas & New Year 6hc (1fb) CTV 5P ▥
B&b£5.50–£6 W£38–£40 M

GH *Hawthorn Farm* Fairfield Rd ☎3230
Closed Xmas rs Oct–Etr 6hc (A 8hc) TV 14P
2🏠 (W only May–Sep) D noon

⊷**GH Kingscroft** 10 Green Ln ☎2757
Lic 7hc (2fb) CTV 9P 2 ▥ S% B&b£5.50
Bdi£8 W£49 ⱡ D6pm

GH Old Manse 6 Clifton Rd, Silverlands
☎5638 Closed Xmas Lic 8hc (2fb) CTV 4P
▥ S% ✳B&bfr£5 Bdifr£8 Wfr£49 ⱡ

GH Roseleigh Private Hotel 19
Broadwalk ☎4904 Lic 14hc (2fb) nc7 CTV
12P S% B&b£7.48 Bdi£11.08 W£74 ⱡ
D5.30pm

GH Thorn Heyes Private Hotel 137
London Rd ☎3539 Lic 7hc 3⇻🍴 (2fb) nc3
CTV 7P ▥ S% B&b£9–£9.56
Bdi£14.30–£14.86 W£100.10–£104.02
ⱡ D7pm

GH Westminster Hotel 21 Broadwalk
☎3929 Lic 15hc (2fb) CTV 12P
B&bfr£7.50 Bdifr£11.50 Wfr£77.50 ⱡ

CAERNARFON Gwynedd *Map 6 SH46*
GH Bryn-Menai Llanbellig Rd ☎2120
Etr–mid Dec 7hc ⚘ CTV P sea D6.30pm

Black Boy Inn

**Northgate Street, Caernarfon, Gwynedd.
Telephone Reception: 3604**

(Free House). Situated within Caernarfon Castle walls is almost as old as the castle itself. Oak beams and inglenooks make a delightful setting for a restful holiday. Hot and cold water in all bedrooms. Plus six with private showers and bathrooms. Private car park at rear of hotel. Wine, dine and enjoy your stay in the olde worlde atmosphere of this lovely 14th century inn.

Reservation and SAE for tariff, telephone 3604, attention Mr & Mrs Williams.

Kinnell House

24 Main Street, Callander, Perthshire

Kinnel is an attractive Victorian Town House which backs onto the scenic beauty of the River Teith. It is convenient for the shops, bus service and other amenities. The house has a reputation for good food and comfortable accommodation. Facilities include a private car park, wash hand basins in all rooms, a colour TV in the lounge and electric blankets on all beds. Callander is set in the beautiful Trossachs area and is the ideal centre for those interested in sport, scenic beauty and history. Write, or telephone Callander (0877) 30181, for brochure.

Pendarves Lodge Guest House

PENDARVES, CAMBORNE, CORNWALL TR14 0RT

Situated in its own grounds with lawns secluded by trees and flowering shrubs. Large car park. We are noted for our high standard of food and wine list. Attractive dining room and lounge. Bright, comfortable bedrooms. Access to guest house at all times, key supplied. Within easy reach of both coasts.
Proprietors: Gwen & Harry Willis.

Enjoy a stay at Cambridge's premier Guest House. Situated in its own grounds with private car park. All rooms are fully carpeted with central heating, H & C, razor sockets, radio etc. Bath and shower facilities. Comfortable lounge with TV. Conveniently situated for colleges and city.

Member of EATB.

Suffolk House

69 Milton Road, Cambridge. Tel: 352016 STD (0223)

⊢⊣ **GH Caer Menai** 15 Church St ☎2612 Closed Nov 7hc (2fb) TV S% B&b£5–£5.50 W£35–£38.50 M

GH Menai View Hotel North Rd ☎4602 Mar–Oct 6hc (1fb) ⊘ TV sea B&b£7.15 W£80.85 ⱡ D8pm

INN Black Boy Northgate St ☎3604 Lic 16hc 6⇔🛁 CTV 8P S% B&b£6.90–£9 Bdi£11.40–£13.40 (W only Nov–Mar) sn L£3–£3.50 D9pm£4.50–£5

CALLANDER Central *Perths*
Map 11 NN60

GH Abbotsford Lodge Stirling Rd ☎30066 Lic 18hc (7fb) CTV 20P ♨ S% ✱B&b£6.25 Bdi£10.85 W£71.60 ⱡ D7pm

⊢⊣ **GH Annfield** 18 North Church St ☎30204 Apr–Oct 8hc (3fb) TV 8P S% B&b£5.50–£6

GH Ashlea House Hotel Bracklinn Rd ☎30325 Mar–Nov 20hc 2⇔🛁 (3fb) ⊘ CTV 17P ♨ B&b£8.50–£10.50 Bdi£11–£15.50 W£60–£92 ⱡ D7.15pm

GH *East Mains House* Bridgend ☎30080 Lic 8hc CTV 12P D6.30pm

⊢⊣ **GH Edina** 111 Main St ☎30004 8hc (2fb) CTV 8P S% B&b£4.89 Bdi£7.77 Wfr£49.95 ⱡ D7.30pm

GH Highland House Hotel South Church St ☎30269 Mar–Oct Lic 10hc 4⇔🛁 (1fb) ⊘ CTV ♨ B&bfr£7.50 Bdifr£11.25 Wfr£75 ⱡ D7.30pm

GH Kinnell 24 Main St ☎30181 Mar–Nov 8hc (2fb) CTV 8P ♨ B&b£6–£6.50 Bdi£10.50–£11 D7.15pm

GH *Lubnaig* Leny Feus ☎30376 Mar–14 Oct Lic 10hc 10⇔🛁 ⊘ nc7 CTV 14P ♨ (W only mid May–mid Sep) D8pm

⊢⊣ **GH Rock Villa** 1 Bracklinn Rd ☎30331 Etr–mid Oct 7hc (1fb) ⊘ 7P ♨ S% B&b£5–£5.50

GH *Tighnaldon Private Hotel* 156 Main St ☎30703 Lic 6hc TV D6pm

CALNE Wilts *Map 3 ST97*

GH Chilvester Lodge ☎812950 Mar–Dec 4⇔🛁 ⊘ nc10 CTV 3P 1🏠 ♨ S% B&b£10–£15 Bdi£17.50–£25 W£90–£125 ⱡ D9pm

INN White Hart Hotel 2 London Rd ☎812413 Lic 10hc 2⇔🛁 ⊘ TV 10P ♨ S% B&b£8.05 Bdi£13 sn L£1–£5&alc D8.30pm£5&alc

CAMBORNE Cornwall *Map 2 SW64*

GH Pendarves Lodge ☎712691 Closed Apr & Oct Lic 8hc (2fb) CTV 8P S% B&b£7.50 Bdi£11.50 W£80 ⱡ D8pm

GH Regal Hotel Church Ln ☎713131 Lic 13hc 2⇔🛁 (2fb) ⊘ CTV 13P ♨ S% ✱£7–£8 Bdi£11–£12 W£74–£81 ⱡ D8pm

GH St Clair Hotel Basset Rd ☎713289 Lic 12hc (2fb) ⊘ CTV 20P ♨ S% B&bfr£9.78 Bdifr£14.03 Wfr£73.50 ⱡ D9pm

CAMPBELTOWN Strathclyde *Argyll*
Map 10 NR72

GH *Westbank* Dell Rd ☎2452 Feb–Nov 7hc CTV

CAMBRIDGE Cambs *Map 5 TL45*

⊢⊣ **GH All Seasons** 219 Chesterton Rd ☎353386 10hc (3fb) TV 4P ♨ S% B&b£5.50–£6 Bdi£8–£9 W£52–£60 ⱡ D3pm

GH Belle Vue 33 Chesterton Rd ☎51859 Lic 8hc (2fb) 6P river S% B&b£6–£7

GH Guest House Hotel 139 Huntington Rd ☎352833 Closed Xmas 13hc (5fb) ⌂ CTV 13P ♨ S% B&b£10–£12 D7.15pm

GH *Helen's Hotel* 167–169 Hills Rd ☎46465 5Jan–5Dec Lic 19hc (A 6hc) CTV 20P ♨

GH Lensfield Hotel 53 Lensfield Rd ☎355017 Closed 18Dec–2Jan Lic 28rm 10hc 18⇔🛁 (8fb) ⊘ CTV 12P 4🏠 ♨ S% B&b£8–£15.50

GH Suffolk House 69 Milton Rd ☎352016 6hc (2fb) ⊘ CTV 7P ♨ D10am

CAMELFORD Cornwall *Map 2 SX18*
During the currency of this guide Camelford telephone numbers are liable to change

GH Sunnyside Hotel 7 Victoria Rd ☎2250 Lic 9hc (5fb) CTV 16P ♨ S% B&b£7.50–£9 Bdi£11–£13.25 W£62–£74 ⱡ D6.30pm

GH *Warmington House* 32 Market Pl ☎3380 Lic 7hc 2⇔🛁 ⌂ CTV 2P 3🏠 ♨ D9.30pm

CANONBIE Dumfries & Galloway
Dumfriesshire Map 11 NY37

INN *Riverside* ☎295 (Closed last 2wks Jan) Lic 7hc ⊘ CTV 25P ⛟ D8.30pm

CANTERBURY Kent *Map 5 TR15*
See plan

GH Abba Hotel Station Rd West ☎64771 Plan:**1** Lic 14hc (1fb) ⊘ CTV 6P ♨ S% B&b£8–£10 Bdi£12–£14 D11pm

GH *Barcroft* 56 New Dover Rd ☎69177 Plan:**2** 14hc CTV 16P ♨

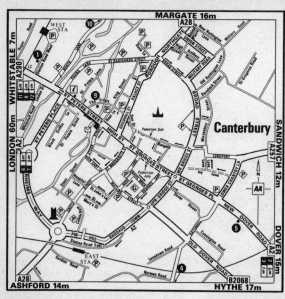

1 Abba
2 Barcroft
3 Canterbury Hotel
4 Carlton
5 Ersham Lodge
6 Harbledown Court
7 Highfield Hotel
8 Magnolia House
9 Pilgrims
10 St Stephens
11 Victoria
12 Wesley Manse

GH Canterbury Hotel 71 New Dover Rd
☎68750 Plan:**3** rs Sun (no evening meal)
Lic 8⇆🛏 (6fb) CTV 20P 🚻 ✲B&b£11–£13
(W only Oct–Jun) D9.30pm

GH Carlton 40 Nunneryfields ☎65900
Plan:**4** 11hc (3fb) TV 5P 🚻 S%
B&b£6–£7.50

GH Ersham Lodge 12 New Dover Rd
☎63174 Plan:**5** 15hc 5⇆🛏 (A 8hc 1⇆🛏)
(4fb) 17P 2🏠 🚻 S% B&b£7–£10.35

GH Harbledown Court 17 Summer Hill,
Harbledown ☎60659 Plan:**6** 7hc 1⇆🛏
CTV 8P 🚻

GH Highfield Hotel Summer Hill,
Harbledown ☎62772 Plan:**7** Closed Xmas
Lic 10hc 1⇆🛏 (A 1⇆🛏) (3fb) ✗ 3nc CTV
12P 🚻 B&b£7.50–£10

ᕻᕻ**GH Magnolia House** 36 St Dunstan's
Ter ☎65121 Plan:**8** Closed Xmas & New
Year 6P S% B&b£5–£6

GH Pilgrims 18 The Friars ☎64531
Plan:**9** Closed 4 days Xmas 14hc CTV 8P 🚻

GH Pointers 1 London Rd ☎56846
Not on plan Lic 15hc 7⇆🛏 (2fb) CTV 10P
🚻 S% ✲B&b£10–£12.50 Bdi£16–£18.50
D10pm

GH Red House Hotel London Rd,
Harbledown (1m W A2) ☎63578 Not on
plan Closed Xmas & New Year Lic 19hc
8⇆🛏 🛁 CTV 18P 🚻 D8pm

GH St Stephens 100 St Stephen's Rd
☎62167 Plan:**10** Lic 9hc 1⇆🛏 (1fb) ✗
CTV 8P 🚻 S% B&b£7.48–£8.05 D5pm

GH Victoria Hotel 59 London Rd
☎65447 Plan:**11** Lic 25hc 10⇆🛏 (4fb) 🛁
CTV 25P 🚻 S% B&b£9–£10 D8.30pm

ᕻᕻ**GH Wesley Manse** 71 Whitstable Rd
☎55164 Plan:**12** Lic 8hc (2fb) CTV 5P 🚻
S% B&b£4.75–£8.05 D5pm

CAPEL ISAAC Dyfed *Map 2 SN52*
**GH Maesteilo Mansion Country House
Hotel** ☎Dryslwyn 510 Lic 8rm 7hc 6⇆🛏
✗ nc14 CTV 20P 4🏠 🚻 B&b£8–£16
Bdi£16–£21 W£80–£120 ⃠ D7pm

CARDIFF S Glam *Map 3 ST17*
GH Ambassador 4 Oakfield St ☎33288
Closed Xmas Lic 16hc ✗ CTV 🚻 D3pm

GH Balkan Hotel 144 Newport Rd
☎491790 13hc 1⇆🛏 (4fb) ✗ CTV 16P 🚻
✲B&b£8.63 Dnoon

The ideal hotel for visiting south east Kent

- ★ Charming Victorian hotel
- ★ 6 miles Canterbury, 9 miles coast
- ★ 2½ acres including lawns, flower beds and vegetable garden
- ★ Childrens' play area including sandpit & swing

- ★ Happy atmosphere and good service
- ★ Horse riding, fishing, golf & tennis nearby
- ★ A wealth of historical places to visit just a short car ride away
- ★ **Farm Holiday Guide diploma winner for accommodation & food 1979**

The Woodpeckers Country Hotel Ltd.

Womenswold, Nr Canterbury, Kent
Barham 319 (STD 022782)

- ★ Heated swimming pool, water slide & diving board
- ★ Television lounge and quiet lounge
- ★ 16 comfortable rooms all with H/C water & tea & coffee-making facilities
- ★ **Four-poster, Georgian, brass bedstead, bridal bedrooms all en suite**

- ★ Warm air central heating
- ★ Highly recommended for traditional country home baking as reported in 'The Daily Express' 'The Guardian', the 'Dover Express' and 'The Telegraph'
- ★ Packed lunches
- ★ Licenced

'A Taste of England'
Prices from £9.00 bed & breakfast - reduced prices for children
£12.50 dinner bed & breakfast - all inclusive VAT service & tea/coffee

Personal attention from resident proprietors

GH Domus 201 Newport Rd ☎495785
Closed Xmas & New Year rs Jul & Aug
(no evening meals) Lic 10hc 2⇩📷 (2fb) ⊗
CTV 10P 🍴 S% B&b£6—£7 Bdi£9.75—£11
D3pm

GH Dorville Hotel 3 Ryder St ☎30951
·13hc (3fb) ⊗ nc3 CTV 🍴 S% B&b£7.50—£9

GH Ferrier's (Alva Hotel) 132 Cathedral Rd
☎23413 Closed 2wks Xmas Lic 27hc 1⇩📷
(3fb) ⊗ CTV 12P 🍴 S% B&b fr£9.75
Bdi fr£14.75 D6.30pm

GH Princes Princes St, Roath ☎491732
7hc (2fb) ⊗ CTV 3P 🍴 S% ✳B&b£5—£6
Bdi£8—£9 D4pm

GH *St Winnow's Hotel* Tygwyn Rd,
Penylan ☎45577 9hc 1⇩📷 (A 2hc) CTV
11P 🍴 D noon

GH Tane's Hotel 148 Newport Rd
☎491755 9hc CTV 8P 🍴 S%
✳B&B fr£6.90 Bdi fr£10.35

CAREY Heref & Worcs *Map 3 SO53*
INN Cottage of Content ☎242 Lic 3hc
nc14 CTV 30P 🍴 S% B&b£9—£10 sn
L£2—£5&alc D9.30pm£6.50alc

CARLISLE Cumbria *Map 11 NY35*
GH Angus Hotel 14 Scotland Rd
☎23546 Closed Xmas & New Year Lic
8hc (3fb) CTV 🍴 S% B&b£6—£6.50
Bdi£9—£9.75 D5pm

GH Cumbria Park Hotel 32 Scotland Rd
☎22887 Closed Xmas Lic 19hc 8⇩📷
(A 9hc 2⇩📷) (2fb) ⊗ CTV 22P 🍴 S%
✳B&b£8.50—£10 Bdi£13.10—£14.60
Wfr£59.50 Ⓜ D6.30pm

⊷⊷**GH East View** 110 Warwick Rd
☎22112 8hc 2⇩📷 (3fb) ⊗ TV 🍴 S%

B&b£5—£6 W only Sep—Jun Ⓜ

GH Kenilworth Hotel 24 Lazonby Ter
☎26179 6hc (2fb) CTV 5P 🍴 S%
✳B&b£5—£8

CARNFORTH Lancs *Map 7 SD47*
GH Holmere Hall Yealand Conyers
(2m N off A6) ☎2931 Closed Jan Lic 6hc
(2fb) ⊗ CTV 15P 5📷 🍴 S% B&b£7.25
D9pm

CARNOUSTIE Tayside *Angus*
Map 12 NO53
GH Dalhousie Hotel 47 High St
☎52907 Lic 6hc (1fb) ᗁ CTV 6P S%
B&bfr£6.75 Bdi fr£10.25 W£79 D8.30pm

CARRADALE Strathclyde *Argyll*
Map 10 NR83
⊷⊷**GH Drumfearne** ☎232 Apr—Sep 6rm
5hc (3fb) ⊗ TV P S% B&b£5—£6
Bdi£7.50—£9 Wfr£45.50 Ⅼ D6pm

GH *Duncrannag* ☎224 Apr—Sep Tem
11hc 8P

⊷⊷**GH** *Dunvalanree* Portrigh ☎226
Etr—Sep 12hc (3fb) TV 9P 🍴 S% B&b£5
Bdi£7 W£49 Ⅼ D5pm

CARRBRIDGE Highland *Inverness-shire*
Map 14 NH92
GH Ard-na-Coille Station Rd ☎239
6hc (1fb) TV 7P 🍴 S% B&b fr£6
Bdi fr£10 Wfr£70 Ⅼ D3pm

GH Dalrachney Lodge Private Hotel
☎252 7hc 1⇩📷 (2fb) ⊗ nc5 CTV 10P 🍴
S% B&b fr£7 Bdi fr£12 Wfr£75.90 Ⅼ
D6.30pm

GH Old Manse Private Hotel Duthil
(2m E A938) ☎278 Closed Nov 9hc (3fb)

CTV 10P 🛏 B&b£8 Bdi£10.50 W£70
⅃ D1pm

CASTLE DONINGTON Leics *Map 8 SK42*
GH Delven Hotel 12 Delven Ln ☎810153
Lic 7hc (1fb) ⊗ nc16 CTV 4P 4🏠 🛏 S%
B&b£9–£18 Bdi£14–£23 W£78–£112
⅃ D9.30pm

CASTLE DOUGLAS Dumfries & Galloway
Kirkcudbrights Map 11 NX76
⊢⊣**GH Rose Cottage** Gelston ☎2513
5rm 4hc (A 4hc) (1fb) ⊗ CTV 12P S%
B&b£5.50–£6.50 Bdi£7.50–£9.50
W£52.50–£66.50 ⅃

CATÈL Guernsey, Channel Islands Map 16
GH Lilyvale Private Hotel Hougue Du
Pommier, Route De Carteret
☎ Guernsey 56868 May–Oct Lic 13hc
5⊐🖩 (10fb) ⊗ nc2 CTV 12P S%
Bdi£8.50–£12.50 D6.30pm

CATON Lancs *Map 7 SD56*
INN Ship Hotel Lancaster Rd ☎770265
Lic 3hc ⊗ nc TV 20P 3🏠 🛏 ⇔ S%
B&b£7.50–£8.50 Bar lunch £2–£5

CAWOOD N Yorks *Map 8 SE53*
GH Compton Court Hotel ☎315
Closed Xmas & New Year Lic 7hc 1⊐🖩
(A 3hc 1⊐🖩) (2fb) CTV 12P
B&b£12.60–£16 Bdi£17.50–£21 D7pm

CHAGFORD Devon *Map 3 SX78*
GH Glendaragh ☎3270 Closed Nov Lic
8hc (1fb) CTV 9P 🛏 B&b£8.50–£9
Bdi£14–£14.50 W£98 ⅃ D7pm

CHALE Isle of Wight Map 4 SZ47
INN Clarendon Hotel & Wight Mouse
☎ Niton 730431 Lic 12hc 4⊐🖩 (4fb) ⚘
CTV 100P 🛏 B&b£10–£12.50
Bdi£13.50–£16 W£90–£102 ⅃ D10pm

CHALFONT ST PETER Bucks
Map 4 TQ09
INN Greyhound High St
☎ Gerrard Cross 83404 Lic 11hc ⊗ TV
30P 🛏 ⇔ S% Bar lunch 40p–£2.50

CHANNEL ISLANDS Map 16
**Information is shown under individual
place names. Refer first to Guernsey
or Jersey for details**

CHAPELHALL Strathclyde *Lanarks*
Map 11 NS76
GH Laurel House Hotel 101 Main St
☎ Airdrie 63230 Lic 6rm 5hc ⊗ CTV 6P 🛏

S% B&b£10 Bdi£13 D5pm

CHARD Somerset *Map 3 ST30*
⊢⊣**GH Watermead** 83 High St ☎2834
Lic 7hc (2fb) ⚘ CTV 8P 2🏠 🛏 S%
B&b£5.50 Bdi£8.50 W£56 ⅃ D10pm

CHARLTON W Sussex *Map 4 SU81*
GH Woodstock House Hotel
☎ Singleton 666 Mid Feb–Dec Lic 12hc
4⊐🖩 ⊗ nc9 CTV 12P 🛏 B&b£10.50–£14
Bdi£16–£20 W£105–£125 ⅃ D7.30pm

CHARLWOOD Surrey *Map 4 TQ74*
**For accommodation details see under
Gatwick Airport**

CHARMOUTH Dorset *Map 3 SY39*
GH Cottage High St ☎60407
Closed Xmas 5hc (A 1hc) (4fb) CTV 30P
S% B&bfr£7.50 Bdifr£11 D7.30pm

GH Newlands House Stonebarrow Ln
☎60212 Apr–Oct Lic 10hc 9⊐🖩 (2fb) ⊗
nc3 CTV 12P 🛏 S% B&b£6.90–£8.05
Bdi£10.35–£11.50 W£65.55–£72.45
D5.30pm

⊢⊣**GH White House** 2 Hillside ☎60411
Mar–Oct Lic 9hc 1⊐🖩 (5fb) ⊗ CTV 15P
🛏 lift B&b£5–£6 Bdi£8–£9 W£52–£59
⅃ D7pm

CHEDDAR Somerset *Map 3 ST45*
GH Gordon's Hotel Cliff St ☎742497
Mar–Oct rs Nov & Feb Lic 14hc (3fb) ⚘
CTV 10P lift S% B&b£6.50–£8 W£42–£55
M D8pm

CHELMSFORD Essex *Map 5 TL70*
GH Beechcroft Private Hotel 211 New
London Rd ☎352462 Closed Xmas & New
Year 26hc (2fb) CTV 15P 🛏 S% B&b£10.30
GH Tanunda Hotel 219 New London Rd
☎354295 Closed Xmas 21hc 7⊐🖩 ⊗
nc5 CTV 🛏 B&b£9–£11

CHELTENHAM Glos *Map 3 SO92*
GH Bowler Hat Hotel 130 London Rd
☎23614 Lic 6hc 1⊐🖩 (4fb) ⊗ CTV 8P 🛏
S% ✱B&b£6.50–£7 Bdi£10.50 W£45 M
D4pm
GH Brennan 21 St Lukes Rd ☎25904
5hc (1fb) CTV S% ✱B&b£5
GH Cotswold Grange Hotel Pittville Circus
Rd ☎515119 Lic 20hc 7⊐🖩 (5fb) CTV 18P
🛏 S% B&b£7.50–£9.50 D7pm
GH Hollington House Hotel 115 Hales
Rd ☎519718 Lic 6hc (2fb) CTV 10P 🛏
S% B&b£7.50–£8 Bdi£11.50–£12.50
W£52.50–£56 M D9am

GH *Ivy Dene* 145 Hewlett Rd ☎21726
7hc CTV 5P 1🏚 🍴

GH Micklinton Hotel 12 Montpellier Dr
☎20000 8hc 1⇨🛏 (3fb) nc4 CTV 8P 1🏚
🍴 B&b£6.90 Bdi£10.20 W£67.74 ⅄
Dam

GH North Hall Hotel Pittville Circus Rd
☎20589 rs Xmas (B&b only) Lic 21hc
(2fb) CTV 20P 🍴 B&B fr£8.05 Bdi fr£10.92
D5pm

GH Willoughby 1 Suffolk Sq ☎22798
Closed 2 wks Xmas 10hc (2fb) CTV 10P S%
B&b fr£7.48 Bdi fr£10.70 W fr£70.84 ⅄

CHESTER Cheshire Map 7 SJ46
GH Abbotsford Hotel 17–19 Victoria Rd
☎26118 Lic 16hc ⊗ TV 🍴

GH Brookside Private Hotel 12 Brook Ln
☎27279 (Number is liable to change to
381934 during currency of this guide)
Lic 21hc 7⇨🛏(6fb) CTV 12P 1🏚 🍴 ⅃
S% B&b£6.50–£7.50 Bdi£9.50–£10.50
D6pm

GH Buckingham Private Hotel 38 Hough
Green ☎673374 8hc (3fb) CTV 8P 🍴 S%
✱B&b£7.50 Bdi£11 W£77 ⅄ D7pm

GH Chester Court Hotel 48 Hoole Rd
☎20779 Closed Xmas wk Lic 15hc
10⇨🛏(5fb) CTV 15P 🍴 S% B&b£8–£9
Bdi£12–£13 D7pm

⊬⊣**GH Eversley Private Hotel** 9 Eversley
Pk ☎25620 (373744 from Oct 1980) Lic
7hc (3fb) ⊗ nc3 CTV 10P 🍴 S% B&b£6.85
Bdi£10.85 D10am

GH Gables 5 Vicarage Rd, Hoole ☎23969
Closed Xmas wk 6hc (2fb) CTV 5P S%
B&b£10.50–£12 W£70–£77 Ⓜ

GH Green Bough Hotel 60 Hoole Rd
☎26241 Closed 2 wks Xmas Lic 11hc
6⇨🛏(2fb) CTV 11P 🍴 B&b£8–£10
Bdi£11.50–£14 W£75–£95 ⅄ D6.30pm

GH Hamilton 5–7 Hamilton St ☎45387
Lic 10hc (4fb) CTV 4P 3🏚 🍴 S%
B&b£6.50–£7.50 Bdi£9–£10.50 D4pm

GH Malvern 21 Victoria Rd ☎41922
Closed Xmas & New Year 7hc (1fb) ⊗ nc2
CTV 2P S% B&b£6–£7

GH Redland Private Hotel 64 Hough Gr
☎671024 10hc (5fb) ⊗ CTV 10P 4🏚 S%
✱B&b£7–£9

GH Riverside Private Hotel 22 City
Walls, off Lower Bridge St ☎26580
Closed 2 wks Xmas Lic 16hc 8⇨🛏(3fb)
CTV 20P 🍴 river B&b£12–£15
Bdi£15–£18 D8pm

⊬⊣**GH Weston Hotel** 82 Hoole Rd
☎26735 Closed Xmas Lic 9hc (A 14⇨🛏)
⊗ nc5 CTV 50P 🍴 S% B&b£5.50–£12
D9pm

CHICKLADE Wilts Map 3 ST93
GH Old Rectory ☎Hindon 226 Closed
1st 2 wks May, Oct & 1 wk Xmas 8hc
(2fb) TV 8P 1🏚 S% B&b£7.20–£8.20
Bdi£10.70–£12 W£59–£68.50 ⅄ D2pm

CHIDEOCK Dorset Map 3 SY49
GH *Thatch Cottage* ☎473 Apr–Oct Lic
5hc ⊗ nc10 CTV 3P 2🏚 🍴 D8.30pm

CHILLINGTON Devon Map 3 SX74
GH Fairfield ☎Kingsbridge 580388 Lic
12hc 1⇨🛏(9fb) ⅌ TV 30P 3🏚 🍴 ⅃
B&b£8.05–£9.20 Bdi £10.92–£12.08
W£72.45–£80.50 ⅄ D7pm

CHIPPING SODBURY Avon Map 3 ST78
GH Moda Hotel 1 High St ☎312135
Closed Xmas Lic 7hc (A 3hc) (1fb) nc3
TV 🍴 S% ✱B&b£7.50–£8.50

INN Portcullis ☎312004 Lic 6hc ⊗ nc10
CTV 🍴 ⇦ S% B&b fr£11 sn L£3.50alc
D9.30pm£4.50alc

CHITTLEHAMOLT Devon Map 3 SS62
GH *Beares Farm* ☎523 Closed Xmas &
New Year Lic 6hc 12P 🍴 D9pm

CHRISTCHURCH Dorset Map 4 SZ19
For locations and additional guesthouses
see **Bournemouth**
GH Belvedere Hotel 59 Barrack Rd
☎485978 Bournemouth district plan:**55**
Lic 10hc TV 12P 🍴 D6.30pm

GH Broomway Hotel 46 Barrack Rd
☎483405 Bournemouth district plan:**59**
Lic 10hc (5fb) nc2 CTV 12P S%
B&b£8.05–£9.20 Bdi£12.65–£14.95
W£57.50–£74.75 ⅄

GH Ferndale 41 Stour Rd ☎482616
Bournemouth district plan:**67** 6hc (1fb) ⊗
CTV 6P 🍴 S% ✱B&b£5–£6 W£35–£38.50
Ⓜ W only Jul & Aug

⊬⊣**GH Laurels** 195 Barrack Rd ☎485530
Bournemouth district plan:**74** Closed
24–26 Dec Lic 14hc 3⇨🛏(3fb) CTV 12P
🍴 S% B&b£5.75–£8.50 Bdi£8.75–£12
W£52.50–£75 ⅄ D5.30pm

GH Park House Hotel 48 Barrack Rd
☎482124 Bournemouth district plan:**86**
Lic 10hc 1⇨🛏(4fb) ⊗ CTV 14P S%
B&b£9 Bdi£14 W£98 ⅄ D noon

GH Pines 39 Mudeford Rd ☎475121
Bournemouth district plan:**88** Lic 13hc
2⇨🛏(4fb) ⅌ CTV 14P 🍴 S%
B&b£6.50–£8 Bdi£8–£10 W£56–£70 ⅄
D6pm

⊬⊣**GH St Albans Hotel** 8 Avenue Rd
☎471096 Bournemouth district plan:**90**
Apr–Oct Lic 9hc (4fb) CTV 12P ⅃ S%
B&b£6.50–£7.50 Bdi£10–£11
£67–£74 ⅄ D2pm

⊬⊣**GH Sea Witch Hotel** 153–5 Barrack Rd
☎482846 Bournemouth district plan:**93**
Lic 9hc (2fb) ⊗ CTV 20P 🍴 B&b£5.50–£7
Bdi£7.50–£10 W£45–£60 ⅄ D5pm

GH Shortwood House Magdalen Ln
☎485223 Bournemouth district plan:**95**
7hc.(1⇨🛏)(3fb) ⊗ CTV 8P 🍴 S%
B&b£6–£9 Bdi£12–£14 W£60–£75 ⅄
D4pm

INN Somerford House Somerford
☎482610 Not on plan Lic 7hc 2⇨🛏 ⊗
CTV 150P S% ✱B&b fr£9.50 Bdi fr£19 sn
Lfr£2.95 D9.30pm fr£4.95

CHURCH STRETTON Salop Map 7 SO49
GH Mynd House Private Hotel Ludlow
Rd, Little Stretton (2m S B4370) ☎722212
Feb–Dec Lic 13hc 4⇨🛏(2fb) CTV 16P 🍴
S% B&b£5.15–£6.15 Bdi£8.65–£9.65
W£53.55–£60.55 ⅄ D6pm

CILIAU AERON Dyfed Map 2 SN55
GH Ty Lôn ☎Aeron 470726 Mar–Oct Lic
5hc (2fb) ⅌ TV 6P 🍴 S% ✱B&b£6–£6.50
W£40–£42 Ⓜ

CINDERFORD Glos Map 3 SO61
INN White Hart Hotel St Whites Rd,
Ruspidge (B4227) ☎23139 Lic 6hc 60P
S% B&b£6.50 W£42 Ⓜ sn L£2–£3.50&alc
D9.45pm£3–£5&alc

76

CIRENCESTER Glos Map 4 SP00
⊢⊣ **GH Raydon** 3 The Avenue ☎3485
10rm 8hc (2fb) CTV 6P S% B&b£5.75–£6

GH Rivercourt Beeches Rd ☎3998
Closed Xmas & New Year 6hc (2fb) (A 4hc)
⊛ TV 12P 11🏠 🍴 S% B&b£6–£7

GH La Ronde 52–54 Ashcroft Rd ☎4611
Lic 10hc (4fb) ⊛ CTV 🍴 S% B&b£7–£8
Bdi£12–£15 D8pm

GH Wimborne Victoria Rd ☎3890
Feb–Nov 6hc ⊛ nc5 CTV 6P B&b£7–£8.50
Bdi£11–£13 D noon

CLACTON-ON-SEA Essex Map 5 TM11
GH Argyll Private Hotel 8 Colne Rd
☎23227 Apr–Dec Lic 24hc 1⇔🍴 (9fb) ⊛
nc5 CTV 5P B&b£7.50–£9 Bdi£10–£14
W£75–£85 ⅃ D6pm

GH Sandrock Hotel 1 Penfold Rd
☎28215 Closed Jan Lic 6⇔🍴 ⊛ CTV 6P
🍴 sea S% B&b£9

GH York House 19 York Rd, Holland-on-
Sea (2m NE B1032) ☎814333 Closed Nov
rs Xmas, Dec–Mar (B&b only) Lic 6hc ♨
CTV 12P 2🏠 🍴 Dnoon

CLARE Suffolk Map 5 TL74
GH Old Bear & Crown Hotel
20 Market Hill ☎440 Lic 5hc (1fb) TV 5P
B&b£9–£11 Bdi£15.50–£17 W£105
⅃ D7pm

CLEARWELL Glos Map 3 SO50
INN Wyndham Arms ☎ Coleford 33666
Mon & Xmas Lic 3hc TV 30P 1🏠 🍴 🚗
B&b£6.90–£7.80 sn L£2.85&alc
D10pm£10alc

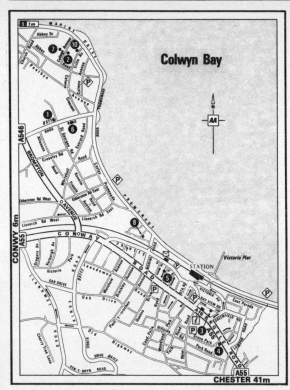

1 Brompton Lodge Hotel
2 Cabin Hill Private Hotel
3 Green Lawns
4 Grosvenor Hotel
5 Idaho Hotel
6 Northwood Hotel
7 St Luke's
8 Southlea
9 Sunny Downs Private Hotel
10 West Mains Private Hotel

Colwyn Bay

CHESTER 41m

CLIFTON *(Near Penrith)* Cumbria
Map 12 NY52
GH Whitrigg House ☎ Penrith 64851
Lic 5hc 1⇩🛏(2fb) ⊗ nc5 CTV 6P 3🏠 🛏
S% B&b£8–£9 Bdi£13–£14 W£130–£150
D7pm

CLITHEROE Lancs *Map 7 SD74*
⊢⊣**GH Fairway House** 48 King St ☎22025
Lic 10hc 4⇩🛏(5fb) ⊗ CTV S%
B&b£5–£12 Bdi£9.50–£16.50
W£75.60–£104.50 ⅃ D7.30pm

CLUN Salop *Map 7 SO38*
INN Sun ☎559 Lic 4hc ⊗ nc6 CTV 8P 🛏
⇌ S% ✱B&b£7–£10.50 Bdi£11.50–£15
W£70 ⅃ sn fr50p D9.30pm£4.50&alc

COCKERMOUTH Cumbria *Map 11 NY13*
GH Hundith Hill Hotel Lorton Valley
(2m SE B5292) ☎822092 Apr–Oct Lic
14hc 7⇩🛏(A 6hc 1⇩🛏)(4fb) CTV 30P 🛏
B&b£8.70–£11 Bdi£13.20–£15.50
W£84–£101.50 ⅃ D7pm

COLCHESTER Essex *Map 5 TM02*
GH Cloisters Hotel 94 Maldon Rd
☎73756 Feb–Nov Lic 9hc 1⇩🛏(2fb) ⊗
nc5 CTV 10P 🛏 S% ✱B&b£7.50–£8

COLDINGHAM Borders *Berwicks*
Map 12 NT96
INN Anchor ☎338 Lic 4rm 3hc ⊗ CTV P
🛏 ⇌ ✱B&bfr£6 D8pm£4

COLLYWESTON Northants *Map 4 TF00*
INN Cavalier Main St ☎ Duddington 288

Lic 6hc ⊗ TV 55P 🛏 ✱B&b£9 Bdi£9.50–£20
sn L£2–£3&alc D9.30pm£2–£3&alc

COLWYN BAY Clwyd *Map 6 SH87*
See Plan
GH Brompton Lodge Hotel Rhos Rd,
Rhos-on-Sea ☎44784 Plan:**1**
mid May–Sep Lic 15hc (4fb) CTV 12P
B&b£8–£9.50 Bdi£10.50–£12 W£70–£80
⅃ D6.30pm

GH Cabin Hill Private Hotel College Av,
Rhos-on-Sea ☎44568 Plan:**2** Mar–Oct
Lic 10hc 3⇩🛏(4fb) ⊗ nc3 CTV 5P 🛏 S%
B&bfr£8 Bdifr£10 D5.30pm

GH Green Lawns 14 Bay View Rd
☎2207 Plan:**3** Closed Nov Lic 16hc
(A 2hc) nc4 CTV 10P D6pm

GH Grosvenor Hotel 106–108 Abergele
Rd ☎31586 Plan:**4** Lic 16hc 2⇩🛏(8fb)
⊗ CTV 12P S% B&b£8.28–£9.28
Bdi£11.78–£12.78 W£82.46–£89.46 ⅃
D5.30pm

⊢⊣**GH Idaho Hotel** 19 Wynnstay Rd
☎30494 Plan:**5** Lic 7hc (3fb) ⊗ CTV 6P 🛏
S% B&b£5.75 Bdi£8.50 W£59.50 ⅃ D4pm

GH Northwood Hotel Rhos Rd,
Rhos-on-Sea ☎30800 Plan:**6** May–Oct
rs Nov–Apr Lic 14hc 4⇩🛏 nc3 CTV 12P
🛏 D7pm

GH St Luke's 20 College Av, Rhos-on-Sea
☎48035 Plan:**7** Lic 18hc (4fb) ⊗ CTV
20P 4🏠 🛏 lift S% B&b£6.50 Bdi£10.50
W£85 D6.30pm

GH Southlea 4 Upper Prom ☎2004
Plan:**8** Lic 12hc (3fb) CTV S% B&b£6.90

Bdi£9.78 W£56.35 ⊾ D6.30pm
GH Sunny Downs Private Hotel
66 Abbey Rd, Rhos-on-Sea ☎44256 Plan:**9**
Lic 17hc (7fb) CTV 10P 🎇 B&b£8.50
Bdi£11.50 W£77 ⊾ D5pm

GH West Mains Private Hotel Trillo Av,
Rhos-on-Sea ☎44664 Plan:**10**
May–Sep Lic 10hc CTV 15P sea D6.30pm

COLYFORD Devon *Map 3 SY29*
GH Elmwood Hotel Swanhill Rd
☎ Colyton 52750 Lic 9hc (A 3hc) ⊗ CTV
12P 1🏚 🎇 D7pm

GH St Edmunds ☎ Colyton 52431
md May–Sep & Etr 9rm 8hc CTV 10P 🎇
D7pm

COLYTON Devon *Map 3 SY29*
GH Old Bakehouse ☎52518 Mar–Nov
Lic 7⇔🏚 10P 🎇 B&b£15–£17 Bdi£25–£30
D8.30pm

COMBE MARTIN Devon *Map 2 SS54*
GH Britannia Private Hotel Moorey
Meadow, Seaside ☎2294 Lic 10hc (2fb)
⊗ CTV 14P 2🏚 🎇 sea S%
B&b£10.92–£12.07 Bdi£12.65–£14.66
W£86.25–£92 ⊾ D7.30pm

GH Coulsworthy House Hotel ☎2463
Lic 12hc 6⇔🏚 (5fb) CTV 20P 🎇
B&b£10.60–£11.60 Bdi£15–£16.50
W£99–£106 ⊾ D8pm

⊷⊶**GH Firs** Woodlands ☎3404 Lic 9hc
(7fb) ⊗ ⅏ CTV 10P 🎇 sea S% B&b£5.20
Bdi£9.25 D4pm

⊷⊶**GH Miramar Hotel** Victoria St ☎3558
Lic 11hc (5fb) ⅏ CTV 9P 2🏚 🎇 S%
B&b£5.10–£6.10 Bdi£7.40–£7.70
W£48.30–£56 ⊾ D5.30pm

GH Newberry Lodge Hotel Newberry Rd
☎3316 Mar–Oct & Xmas Lic 14hc 1⇔🏚
(4fb) nc3 CTV 14P sea S% B&b£7–£12
Bdi£9.50–£14.50 W£65.80 ⊾ D7pm

COMPTON Berks *Map 4 SU57*
INN Swan Hotel ☎269 Lic 4hc CTV 40P
S% B&b£8.50–£10 Bdi£14.50–£17.50
sn L£5.25alc D9pm£6alc

COMRIE Tayside *Perths Map 11 NN72*
GH Mossgiel ☎567 Mar–Oct rs Jan &
Feb (B&b only) 6hc nc5 CTV 6P 🎇
S% ✳B&b£5 Bdi£8 D5pm

CONGRESBURY Avon *Map 3 ST46*
GH Lyndhurst ☎ Yatton 832279 6hc ⊗
CTV 2P 3🏚 D1pm

CONISTON Cumbria *Map 7 SD39* ⁃
**GH Low Bank Ground Country House
Hotel** ☎525 Apr–Oct rs Nov–Dec &
Feb–Mar Lic 14hc (4fb) 🎇 ⅋ S%
B&b£12.65–£14.65 Bdi£19.60–£22.50
W£137.20–£157.50 ⊾ D7.30pm

CONNOR DOWNS Cornwall *Map 2 SW53*
GH Pine Trees ☎ Hayle 753249
rs Oct–Feb (B&b only) Lic 6hc (4fb) ⊗
CTV 10P S% B&b£6–£7 Bdi£8.50–£10
W£55–£68 ⊾ D noon

CONSTANTINE Cornwall *Map 2 SW72*
GH High Cross ☎373 Closed Xmas 5hc
⊗ CTV 6P D4pm

CONWY Gwynedd *Map 6 SH77*
GH Cyfnant Private Hotel Henryd Rd
☎2442 Etr–Oct Lic 6hc 4⇔🏚 (2fb) ⊗

CTV 6P ⏣ S% B&b£6.50–£8 Bdi£10–£12 D6.30pm

⊢⊣**GH Sunnybanks** Woodlands, Llanrwst Rd ☎3845 Etr–Sep 7hc (2fb) nc4 TV 6P ⏣S% B&bfr£5 Bdi fr£7.50 W£42 ⱔ D7pm

CORRIE Isle of Arran, Strathclyde *Bute Map 10 NS04*
GH Blackrock House ☎282 Mar–Oct 9hc (3fb) TV 7P ⏣ S% B&b£8 Bdi£10 W£70 ⱔ D6pm

CORWEN Clwyd *Map 6 SJ04*
GH Central Hotel ☎2462 Closed 24–26 Dec 10hc (6fb) CTV 20P 1🏠 ⏣ S% ✳B&b£6.50–£7.50 Bdi£9–£11 Wfr£77 ⱔ D9.30pm

COVENTRY W Midlands *Map 4 SP37*
GH Croft Hotel 23 Stoke Green,

(off Binley Rd) ☎457846 Lic 13hc (1fb) CTV 14P ⏣ S% B&bfr£9.50 Bdifr£13.50 D7pm

⊢⊣**GH Fairlight** 14 Regent St ☎24215 12hc (2fb) CTV 8P ⏣ S% B&b£5–£6 W£28–£35 Ⓜ

GH Mount 7–9 Coundon Rd ☎25998 10rm 9hc (1fb) CTV ⏣ S% B&b£6.50 W£45.50 Ⓜ

GH Northanger House 35 Westminster Rd ☎26780 Closed Xmas 7hc (2fb) ⊘ CTV 2P ⏣ S% B&b£6.50

CRAFTHOLE Cornwall *Map 2 SX35*
INN Finnygook ☎St Germans (Cornwall) 338 Lic 6hc ⊘ nc14 CTV 6P 🛏 sea B&b£9.20 L£1–£5.35&alc D9.30pm£3.20–£8.30&alc

---

CRAIL Fife Map 12 NO60
⊯ **GH Caiplie House** 51–53 High St
☎564 Apr–Sep Lic 7hc (2fb) CTV 20P
B&b£5.50

CRANBROOK Kent Map 5 TQ73
INN George Hotel Stone St ☎713348
Lic 13hc CTV 30P 2🏠 S% B&b£12 Bdi£16
sn L£6alc D9pm£6alc

CRANTOCK Cornwall Map 2 SW76
GH Crantock Cottage Private Hotel West
Pentire Rd ☎232 May–Sep Lic 11hc (2fb)
✿nc7 CTV sea S% B&b£7.50–£8
Bdi£9–£10.80 W£63.25–£69 ⅃ D5pm

CRAWLEY W Sussex Map 4 TQ23
**For accommodation details see under
Gatwick Airport**

CREETOWN Dumfries & Galloway
Kirkcudbrights Map 6 NX45
GH Creeton Arms ☎282 Lic 6hc (2fb)
CTV 15P S% B&b£7 Bdi£11 D9.30pm
⊯ **GH Mayburn** ☎317 Etr–Sep 5hc (2fb)
✿ TV 5P S% B&b£4.75–£5.50
Bdi£7.50–£8 D7.30pm

CRESSAGE Salop Map 7 SJ50
INN Cound Lodge ☎322 Lic 7hc ✿ CTV
45P 🍺 D9.30pm

CRIANLARICH Central Perths
Map 10 NN32
⊯ **GH Mountgreenan** ☎286 Closed Xmas
day 5hc (1fb) ✿ CTV 5P S% B&b£5
Bdi£7.50 D6pm

CRICCIETH Gwynedd Map 6 SH53
GH Min-y-Gaer Private Hotel Portmadoc
Rd ☎2151 Etr–Oct 10hc (4fb) CTV 12P
sea S% B&b£6.50–£7 Bdi£8.50–£9.50
Wfr£59.50 ⅃ D7.30pm

GH Moorings Marine Ter ☎2802
Mar–mid Oct 7hc (3fb) CTV S%
✱B&b£4.75–£5.75 Bdi£7.50–£8.50
W£48.50–£67 D6.30pm

GH Môr Heli Private Hotel Marine Ter
☎2794 Etr–Sep rs Oct Lic 16hc (6fb) CTV
24P sea S% B&bfr£6.50 Bdi fr£7.50
W£52–£58 ⅃ D6.30pm

GH Neptune Private Hotel Marine Ter
☎2794 Etr–Sep rs Oct Lic 14hc (6fb) CTV
24P sea S% ✱B&bfr£6.50 Bdi fr£7.50
W£56–£58 ⅃ D6.30pm

CRICKHOWELL Powys Map 3 SO21
GH Dragon Country House Private Hotel
High St ☎810362 Lic 11hc 2⇲🛁 (2fb) ✿
CTV 6P 2🏠 ✱B&bfr£6.90 Bdi fr£11.50
Wfr£66 ⅃ D8pm

INN Beaufort Arms Hotel ☎810402
Jun–Sep rs Oct–May (B&b only) Lic 6hc 🍺
D9pm

CRIEFF Tayside Perths Map 11 NN82
⊯ **GH Comely Bank** 32 Burrell St ☎3409
Apr–Sep rs Oct–Nov & Feb–Mar 6hc (2fb)
CTV S% B&b£5.50 Bdi£8 W£49 ⅃ D6pm

GH Heatherville 31 Burrell St ☎2825
5hc (1fb) ✿ CTV 5P S% B&b£6 Bdi£9.50
W£66.50 ⅃

GH Lockes Acre Hotel Comrie Rd ☎2526
Lic 7hc (2fb) CTV 5P 🍺 S% B&b£6.90
Bdi£12.08 D6pm

CROMER Norfolk Map 9 TG24
⊯ **GH Chellow Dene** 23 Macdonald Rd

☎513251 Closed Xmas wk Lic 7hc (2fb)
nc3 CTV 6P 🍺 S% B&bfr£5.50 Bdi fr£8
Wfr£49 ⅃ D6pm
⊯ **GH Coolhurst** 25 Macdonald Rd
☎512073 7hc (4fb) CTV 2P S%
B&b£4.75–£5.25 Bdi£6.75–£7.25
W£44–£48 ⅃ D5.30pm
GH Home Farm ☎511600 rs Xmas Lic
7hc (4fb) ✿ CTV 7P 🍺 S%
B&b£6.95–£8.95 Bdi£8.95–£10.95
W£62.65–£76.65 ⅃ (W only Aug) D10am
GH Westgate Lodge Private Hotel
10 Macdonald Rd ☎512840 Lic 12hc
(5fb) ✿ nc3 CTV 14P 🍺 S% B&bfr£7.20
Bdi fr£9.80 Wfr£59.80 ⅃ D6.30pm

CROSS GATES Powys Map 3 SO06
GH Guidfa ☎Penybont 241 mid May–Sep
Lic 5hc 2⇲🛁 (1fb) TV 6P 🍺
✱B&b£6.50–£7.50 Bdi£10–£11
W£60–£65 ⅃

CROSSWAY GREEN Heref & Worcs
Map 7 SO86
INN Mitre Oak ☎Hartlebury 352 Lic
7rm 6hc CTV 7P 🍺 S% B&b£7.75 sn
L£2.95–£3.50 D9.30pm£6alc

CROYDE BAY Devon Map 2 SS43
GH Seabirds Hotel Baggy Point
☎890224 Apr–Sep Lic 8hc (2fb) CTV 20P
🍺 sea S% ✱B&b£7.50–£10
W£83.45–£98.75 ⅃ D9pm

CROYDON Gt London
London plan 4 E4 (page 266)
GH Central Hotel 3–5 South Park Hill Rd
☎01-688 0840 Lic 27hc 7⇲🛁 (1fb) ✿
CTV 12P 🍺 S% B&b£13 Bdi£17 D7.30pm
GH Friends 50 Friends Rd ☎01-688 6215
10hc (3fb) ✿ nc4 5P S% B&b£8.50–£9.50
W only Nov–Feb
GH Markington Hotel 9 Haling Park Rd,
South Croydon ☎01-688 6530 Lic 16hc
7⇲🛁 (2fb) ✿ CTV 7P 1🏠 🍺 B&b£11–£15
Bdi£16–£20 W£112–£140 D6.30pm
GH Oakwood Hotel 69 Outram Rd
☎01-654 2835 Lic 9hc 2⇲🛁 (1fb) CTV 5P
3🏠 🍺 S% B&b£10.50 Bdi£14.50
D6.30pm

CULLEN Grampian Banffs Map 15 NJ56
⊯ **GH Wakes** Seafield Pl ☎40251
Apr–Oct Lic 23rm 22hc (3fb) CTV 16P ⅃
B&b£5.50–£7.50 Bdi£8–£10 W£45–£50
⅃ D6pm

CURY CROSS LANES Cornwall
Map 2 SW62
GH Pendragon Private Hotel ☎Mullion
240631 6hc (1fb) ✿ nc5 CTV 12P S%
B&b£6.25–£6.50 Bdi£9.50–£9.75
W£66.50–£68.25 ⅃ D5.30pm

DARLINGTON Co Durham Map 8 NZ21
GH Raydale Hotel Stanhope Road South
☎58993 Closed Xmas & New Year Lic
11hc (2fb) ✿ CTV 12P 🍺 S% B&b£10.35
Bdi£15.23 D3pm

DARTMOUTH Devon Map 3 SX84
GH Downderry 6 Church Rd ☎2788 6hc
(2fb) ✿ CTV 6P river S% ✱B&b£6–£7
Bdi£10–£11 W£64–£71 ⅃ D10am
GH Orleans 24 South Town ☎2967
Closed Xmas & New Year 5hc ✿ TV 🍺 S%
B&b£6–£9.50

DAWLISH Devon Map 3 SX97
GH Barton Grange Private Hotel
5 Barton Villas ☎863365 rs Nov–Apr 9hc

(1fb) nc5 CTV 7P 🖭 S% B&b£6–£7
Bdi£8.50–£9.50 W£54–£60 ⮕ D4.30pm

GH Brockington 139 Exeter Rd ☎863588
9hc nc10 CTV 8P 🖭 S% B&b£5–£5.75
Bdi£8–£8.75

⊢⊣GH Broxmore Private Hotel
20 Plantation Ter ☎863602 Mar–Dec Lic
8hc (4fb) ⊗ nc3 CTV 🖭 S% B&b£5.35–£7
Bdi£8.25–£11 W£56–£75 ⮕ D5pm

⊢⊣GH Lamorna Private Hotel 2 Barton Ter
☎862242 Lic 10hc (5fb) ⊗ CTV S%
B&b£5.50–£7 Bdi£8.50–£10 W£52–£65
⮕ D7pm

GH Lynbridge Private Hotel Barton Villas
☎862352 Etr–Oct 9hc (2fb) 🖭
S% B&b£6–£6.50 Bdi£8–£8.50 D4pm

⊢⊣GH Marldon House Hotel 6 Barton Villas
☎862721 8hc (3fb) nc10 CTV 6P 🖭 S%
B&b£5–£5.90 Bdi£8–£9 W£55–£59.50
⮕ D9am

⊢⊣GH Mimosa 11 Barton Ter ☎863283
Mar–Oct 9hc (4fb) ⊗ nc5 CTV 2P 🖭 sea
S% B&b£5.50–£6.50 Bdi£7–£8 W£37–£44
⮕ D2pm

GH Portland House 14 Marine Pde
☎864040 Etr–Oct 7hc (3fb) ⊗ CTV 6P sea
S% B&b£6–£8.50 Bdi£10–£12 W£60–£78
⮕ D8.30am

GH Radfords Dawlish Water ☎863322
Mar–Nov Lic 22hc 21⇆🖩 (A 5hc 1⇆🖩)
(27fb) ⮁ CTV 50P 🖭 S% B&b£9.20–£11.50
Bdi£13.80–£16.50 W£96–£115 ⮕
(W only Jun–Aug) D6.45pm

DEAL Kent Map 5 TR35
GH Pension Castle Lea 2 Gladstone Rd
☎2718 Mar–Oct 3⇆🖩🔥 nc5 CTV 🖭 sea
S% B&b£8 Bdi£12 W£84 ⮕ D6.30pm

GH *Winthorpe Private Hotel* Kingsdown
Rd.-Walmer ☎5788 Etr–Oct Lic 7hc ⊗
nc14 CTV 7P 🖭 sea D6.30pm

DENT Cumbria Map 7 SO78
INN George & Dragon ☎256 Lic 9hc
CTV 14P 🖭 🚍 S% B&b£9–£9.50
W£60–£63 ℳ Bar lunch £1.40alc
D8pm£4alc

DENTON Gt Manchester Map 7 SJ99
GH *Elsinore* 121 Town Ln ☎061-320
7606 Lic 12⇆🖩 CTV 18P 🖭 S% D8pm

DERBY Derbys Map 8 SK33
GH Ascot Hotel 724 Osmaston Rd
☎41916 Lic 18hc (2fb) CTV 12P 🖭 S%
✳B&b£7.47–£8.58 Bdi£10.47–£11.58
D4.30pm

GH Georgian House Hotel 34 Ashbourne
Rd ☎49806 17hc 1⇆🖩 (3fb) ⊗ CTV 20P
🖭 S% B&b£9.49 Bdi£13.29 D6pm

DERSINGHAM Norfolk Map 9 TF63
GH Westdene House Hotel 60 Hunstanton
Rd ☎40395 Lic 5hc (1fb) ⊗ CTV 15P 🖭
S% ✳B&b£7.25 D9pm

DEVIZES Wilts Map 4 SU06
INN *Castle Hotel* New Park St ☎2046
Lic 13hc CTV 8🔥 🖭 D9pm

DEVORAN Cornwall Map 2 SW73
GH *Driffold* 8 Devoran Ln ☎863314 Lic
7hc ⊗ CTV 6P 🖭 D noon

DINAS MAWDDWY Gwynedd
Map 6 SH81
INN Buckley Arms Hotel ☎261
Mar–Dec Lic 14hc 1⇆🖩 TV 60P 🖭 river

S% B&b£7.50 Bdi£12.50 W£82 ⱡ
Bar lunch £1–£2 D9pm£5–£6

DINORWIC Gwynedd *Map 6 SH50*
GH Hafodty ☎ Llanberis 548 Etr–Sep Lic 6hc (3fb) nc8 6P ♨ S% B&b£7.50–£8 Bdi£11–£12 W£66–£72 ⱡ (W only mid Jul–Aug) D6pm

DIRLETON Lothian *E Lothian Map 12 NT58*
INN Castle ☎221 Lic 5hc (A 4hc) CTV 12P ♨ ♿ B&b£9 Bdi£14 W£85 ⱡ
Bar lunch£1 D8.30pm£5

DODDISCOMBSLEIGH Devon *Map 3 SX88*
INN Nobody Inn ☎ Christow 52394 Lic 4hc ⊘ nc14 TV 50P ⛟ ✱B&b£7–£9
Bar lunch 50p–£2 D7.30pm£5.50alc

DOLWYDDELAN Gwynedd *Map 6 SH75*
INN Gwydyr ☎209 Lic 2hc ⊘ nc14 12P sn D9.30pm

DONCASTER S Yorks *Map 8 SE50*
GH Regent Hotel Regent Sq ☎64180 Lic 27⇌fl (2fb) ⊘ CTV 12P ♨ lift S% B&bfr£18 Bdi fr£21.50 D10pm

DONINGTON Lincs *Map 8 TF23*
INN *Red Cow* ☎298 Lic 7hc TV 30P sn

DORCHESTER Dorset *Map 3 SY69*
INN White Hart Hotel High East St ☎3545 Closed Xmas Lic 6hc TV 12P 6⌂ ♨ S% B&b£6.33–£6.90 sn L£1.70–£3.95 D9.30pm£1.70–£3.95

DOUGLAS Isle of Man *Map 6 SC37*
⊢⊣**GH Ainsdale** 2 Empire Ter, Central Prom ☎6695 May–Sep 19hc (8fb) ⌂ CTV sea S% B&b£5.75–£6.25 Bdi£6.50–£7

GH Rosslyn Private Hotel 3 Empire Ter, Central Prom ☎6056 19hc (7fb) ⊘ CTV S% B&b£7.19–£7.76 Bdi£7.76–£8.90 W£54.33–£62.38 ⱡ

GH *Rutland Hotel* Queens Prom ☎21218 Etr–Oct 93hc 13⇌fl ⊘ CTV lift D noon

DOVER Kent *Map 5 TR34*
GH Allwyn Cottage 337 Folkestone Rd ☎201126 Closed Xmas 6hc (2fb) ⊘ CTV 9P 1⌂ ♨ S% B&b£5.25–£6.50

GH Beulah House 94 Crabble Hill, London Rd ☎ Kearsney 4615 7hc (3fb) ⊘ 10P 2⌂ ♨ river S% B&b£7–£8

GH Dover Stop 45 London Rd, River (2m NW A256) ☎ Kearsney 2751 Lic 7hc 1⇌fl (A 5hc) (1fb) CTV 14P ♨ S% B&b£8.50 (W only out of season)

GH *Gordon House Hotel* 31–32 East Cliff ☎204459 Closed Dec Lic 18hc CTV ♨ D8.30pm

GH Number One 1 Castle St ☎202007 5hc 3⇌fl (3fb) TV 1P 2⌂ S% B&b£6–£7.50

GH St Brelade's 82 Buckland Av ☎206126 Mar–Nov, rs Dec–Feb (no meals) Lic 8hc (4fb) ⊘ TV 6P 1⌂ ♨ S% ✱B&b£7–£7.50 W£46–£49 M

GH Whitfield Hotel 107 Sandwich Rd ☎820236 Lic 9hc (2fb) ⊘ CTV 15P ♨ S% B&b£7 Bdi£11 W£45 M D9.30pm

INN Railway Bell Hotel London Rd ☎ Kearsney 2016 rs Nov–Mar Lic 6hc ⊘ nc14 50P ♨ ⛟ S% B&b£7.50 W£50 M L£1–£3.50alc D7.30pm£1–£3.50alc

DOWNTON Wilts *Map 4 SU12*
GH Warren High St ☎20263 6hc 1⇌fl (1fb) nc6 CTV 7P ♨ S% ✱B&b£6.50–£7.50

DRUMNADROCHIT Highland *Inverness-shire Map 14 NH53*
INN Lewiston Arms Hotel Lewiston ☎225 Lic 4rm 3hc (A 4hc) CTV 40P ⛟ river S% B&b£8 Bdi£13 W£91 ⱡ
Bar Lunch£1.50alc D8pm£5alc

DULOE Cornwall *Map 2 SX25*
GH Duloe Manor Hotel ☎Looe 2795 Etr–mid Oct Lic 11hc 10⇌fl (4fb) CTV 20P ♨ S% B&b£13–£15 Bdi£18.70–£20.70 W£128.50–£145 ⱡ D8pm

DUMFRIES Dumfries & Galloway *Dumfriesshire Map 11 NX97*
GH *Dalston Hotel* 5 Laurieknowe ☎4422 9hc ⊘ ⌂ CTV 10P ♨ D7pm

⊢⊣**GH Fullwood Private Hotel** 30 Lovers Walk ☎2262 5hc (2fb) TV S% B&b£5.25 W£34–£38 M

GH Newall House 22 Newall Ter ☎2676 Lic 7rm 6hc (3fb) CTV 7P ♨ S% B&b£7 Bdi£10 W£65 ⱡ D5pm

DUNBAR Lothian *E Lothian Map 12 NT67*
GH Cruachan East Links Rd ☎63595 6hc 1⇌fl (1fb) CTV sea S% B&b£6–£6.50 Bdi£9–£9.50 W£58–£60 ⱡ D5pm

⊢⊣ **GH Marine** 7 Marine Rd ☎63315 10hc (3fb) CTV ♨ sea S% B&b£5–£6 Bdi£7–£8 W£45–£50 ⱡ D6pm

GH St Laurence North Rd ☎62527 6hc ⊘ nc12 sea S% B&b£6.50 Bdi£10 W£63 ⱡ D6.30pm

GH Springfield House Edinburgh Rd
☎62502 Apr–Oct 6hc (2fb) CTV 9P ◫
S% B&bfr£7 Bdifr£12 Wfr£70 ⟁ D5pm

DUNBLANE Tayside *Perthshire*
Map 11 NN70
GH Altair Neuk Hotel Doune Rd
☎822562 Lic 9hc (2fb) CTV 10P ◫ S%
B&b£8.05–£9.20 Bdi£12.55–£13.70
W£80–£90 ⟁ D8.45pm

DUNOON Strathclyde *Argyll Map 10 NS17*
GH Cedars Private Hotel Alexandra Pde
☎2425 Feb–Nov Lic 14hc 2⇄◧ (2fb) CTV
◫ sea B&b£7.47–£8.90
Bdif£11.50–£12.93 W£72.45–£82.80 ⟁
D7pm

DUNSFORD Devon *Map 3 SX88*
INN *Royal Oak* ☎Christow 52256 Closed
Xmas Lic 3hc ⍉ nc10 TV 10P 2🏠
D9.30pm

DUNVEGAN Isle of Skye, Highland
Inverness-shire Map 13 NG24
⊨ **GH Argyll House** Kensalrog, Roskhill
(3m S A863) ☎230 Apr–Oct 6rm 5hc (1fb)
CTV 6P ◫ sea S% B&b£4.75 Bdi£7.25
D7.30pm

GH Roskhill Roskhill (3m S A863) ☎317
Mar–Dec 5hc (2fb) TV 6P ◫ river S%
B&b£6–£6.50 Bdi£9.25–£10 W only
Jun–Oct D6pm

DUXFORD Cambs *Map 5 TL44*
GH Highfield House 55 St Peter's Street
☎Cambridge 833160 Lic 8hc 3⇄◧ (1fb)
♨ CTV 12P 2🏠 S% B&b£10.35
Bdi£14.95 D7pm

EASTBOURNE E Sussex *Map 5 TV69*
See Plan

GH Aberfoyle Hotel 83 Royal Pde
☎22161 Plan:**1** Lic 8hc (2fb) ⍉ nc5 CTV
2P ◫ sea S% B&b£6.33–£11.50
Bdi£8.63–£13.80 W£52–£62 ⟁ D6pm

GH *Alfriston Hotel* Lushington Rd
☎25640 Plan:**2** Closed Xmas & 1st 3 wks
Nov rs last wk Nov–Mar Lic 10hc ⍉ nc5
CTV 1🏠 D10am

⊨ **GH Beachy Rise** Beachy Head Rd
☎639171 Plan:**3** Etr–Sep 6hc nc5 CTV ◫
S% B&b£5.50–£6.50 Bdi£7.50–£8.50
W£50–£57 ⟁ D4.30pm

⊨ **GH Cavendish** 1 Cavendish Pl ☎24284
Plan:**4** Closed Nov & Dec 11hc (3fb) nc3
TV sea S% B&b£5.75–£7.50
Bdi£8.62–£10.35 W£57.50–£69 ⟁
D4pm

GH Le Chalet 7 Marine Pde ☎20029
Plan:**5** 8hc (3fb) ⍉ nc10 CTV sea S%
B&b£8.05–£8.50 Bdi£11.27–£12
W£70–£75 ⟁ D6pm

GH Chesleigh Hotel 4 Marine Pde
☎20722 Plan:**6** May–Oct 7hc 2⇄◧ nc7
CTV sea S% B&b£7

GH Courtlands Hotel 68 Royal Pde
☎21068 Plan:**7** Lic 7hc (1fb) ⍉ CTV 1P
2🏠 sea S% B&bfr£11.50 Bdifr£13.80
Wfrf£86.25 ⟁ D6pm

GH *Downland Private Hotel* 37 Lewes Rd
☎32689 Plan:**8** Lic 14hc 10⇄◧ ⍉ nc3
CTV 14P ◫ D6.30pm

GH Edelweiss 10 Elms Av ☎32071
Plan:**9** Whit–Sep 6hc (1fb) ⍉ nc4 CTV ◫
B&b£8 W£42 M

⊨ **GH Edmar** 30 Hyde Gdns ☎33024
Plan:**10** Etr–Oct 9hc 1⇄◧ (1fb) ⍉ nc5

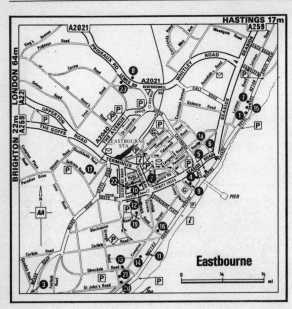

1. Aberfoyle Hotel
2. Alfriston Hotel
3. Beachy Rise
4. Cavendish House
5. Le Chalet
6. Chesleigh Hotel
7. Courtlands Hotel
8. Downland Private Hotel
9. Edelweiss
10. Edmar
11. Elmscroft Private
12. Hanburies Hotel
13. Little Crookham
14. Lynwood Hotel
15. Marina
16. Mowbray
17. Orchard House
18. St Clare
19. Somerville Private Hotel
20. South Cliff
21. Southcroft
22. Traquair Private Hotel
23. Wynstay Private Hotel

CTV S% B&b£5.70–£9.50 Bdi£7–£14 W£49–£97 ⚓ D5pm

GH Elmscroft Private Hotel 53 Jevington Gdns ☎21263 Plan:**11** 12hc (3fb) ⊗ CTV S% B&b£7–£8.50 Bdi£8–£11 W£46–£66 ⚓ D5pm

GH Hanburies Hotel 4 Hardwick Rd ☎30698 Plan:**12** Lic 14hc 9⇋ (2fb) CTV 4P 卿 B&b£9–£11.50 Bdi£10.80–£14.20 W£86–£99 D7pm

GH Little Crookham 16 Southcliffe Av ☎34160 Plan:**13** rs Oct–Apr (B&b only) 8hc (1fb) nc5 CTV 卿 S% B&B fr£7 Bdifr£10.50 Wfr£68 ⚓ D6pm

GH Lynwood Hotel Jevington Gdns ☎23982 Plan:**14** Lic 78hc 15⇋ (6fb) nc2 CTV 4P 4🏠 lift S% B&b£9.50–£14 Bdi£11.25–£22 W£80–£150 D7.45pm

GH Hotel Marina 86–87 Royal Pde ☎20297 Plan:**15** Etr–Oct Lic 18hc 1⇋ (4fb) CTV 卿 S% B&b£8–£10.50 Bdi£8.50–£12 D5.45pm

GH Mowbray Hotel Lascelles Ter ☎20012 Plan:**16** Etr–Oct 16hc 4⇋ (1fb) ⊗ nc7 CTV lift B&b£8.72–£9.60

W£52.17–£61.56 Ⓜ

GH Orchard House 10 Old Orchard Rd ☎23682 Plan:**17** 7hc 2⇋ (2fb) ⊗ nc4 CTV S% B&b£7.50–£8.50 Bdi£10.50–£11 W£55–£70 ⚓ D4pm

⊢⊣GH St Clare 70 Pevensey Rd ☎29483 Plan:**18** 8hc (4fb) ⊗ CTV S% B&b£5.50–£7 Bdi£8.50–£9.75 W£47.50–£57.50 ⚓ D4pm

GH Somerville Private Hotel 6 Blackwater Rd ☎29342 Plan:**19** Etr–Oct Lic 11 hc (1fb) ⊗ CTV S% B&b£8–£8.50 Bdi£10–£11 W£61–£66 ⚓ D2pm

GH *South Cliff House* 19 South Cliff Av ☎21019 Plan:**20** rs Xmas (B&b only) Lic 6hc CTV 卿 D6pm

GH Southcroft 15 South Cliff Av ☎29071 Plan:**21** Lic 6hc (3fb) nc3 CTV 卿 S% ✳B&bfr£7.50 Bdifr£9.50 Wfr£65 ⚓ D4pm

GH Traquair Private Hotel 25 Hyde Gdns ☎25198 Plan:**22** Lic 10hc 5⇋ (3fb) CTV B&b£8–£10.50 Bdi£13–£15.50 W£75–£98 ⚓ D6pm

GH Wynstay Private Hotel 13 Lewes Rd
☎21550 Plan:**23** rs Winter 7hc (1fb) ✿
CTV 7P S% B&bfr£6 Bdifr£9 Wfr£50 ⅃
D3pm

EAST COWTON N Yorks *Map 8 NZ30*
INN *Beeswing* ☎North Cowton 349 Lic
3hc ✿ P 🍴 D10pm

EASTLEIGH Devon *Map SS42*
GH Pines Farmhouse Hotel (2½m NE of
Bideford off A39) ☎Instow 860561
Etr–Oct Lic 7hc (2fb) ✿ nc2 CTV 10P 🍴
S% B&bfr£8 Bdifr£11 Wfr£69 ⅃ (W only
Jun–Aug) D5pm **See advertisement on
page 87**

EASTLEIGH Hants *Map 4 SU41*
GH *Lynden* 28 Romsey Rd ☎613054
9hc ✿ CTV 10P 🍴

EAST WITTERING W Sussex
Map 4 SZ79
GH Wittering Lodge Hotel Shore Rd
☎3207 Etr–mid Oct Lic 11hc 1⊸🛁 (2fb)
CTV 20P 2🏠 🍴 B&b£11 Bdi£15.50 W£92
⅃ D9.30pm

EBBERSTON N Yorks *Map 8 SE88*
GH Foxholm Hotel (on B1258)
☎Scarborough 85550 Mar–Nov Lic 10hc
3⊸🛁 (2fb) CTV 12P 🍴 B&b£7.50–£11
Bdi£11.50–£15 W£73–£95 ⅃ D7.30pm

EDINBURGH Lothian *Midlothian*
Map 11 NT27 **See Plan**
GH Adam Hotel 19 Lansdowne Cres
☎031-337 1148 Plan:**1** Lic 9hc (1fb) CTV
S% B&b£8–£9 Bdi£11.75–£13
W£75–£80 ⅃ D6pm

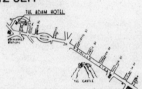

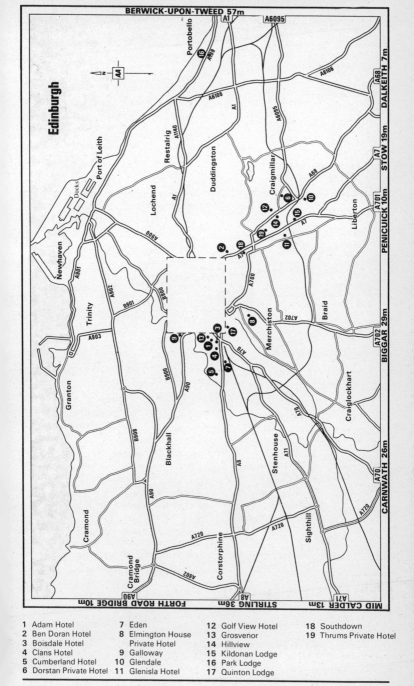

Edinburgh

1 Adam Hotel
2 Ben Doran Hotel
3 Boisdale Hotel
4 Clans Hotel
5 Cumberland Hotel
6 Dorstan Private Hotel
7 Eden
8 Elmington House
   Private Hotel
9 Galloway
10 Glendale
11 Glenisla Hotel
12 Golf View Hotel
13 Grosvenor
14 Hillview
15 Kildonan Lodge
16 Park Lodge
17 Quinton Lodge
18 Southdown
19 Thrums Private Hotel

GH *Albany Hotel* 39 Albany St
☎031-556 0397 Not on Plan Lic 10hc
CTV 🛏

GH Ben Doran Hotel 11 Mayfield Gdns
☎031-667 8488 Plan **2** 9hc (5fb) CTV
7P S%✱B&b£5–£7 Bdi£7.50–£8.50

(W only winter)

GH Boisdale Hotel 9 Coates Gdns
☎031-337 4392 Plan **3** 12⇌🛏 (4fb) CTV
🛏 B&b£5–£9 Bdi£7.50–£12 D7.30pm

GH *Clans Hotel* 4 Magdala Cres
☎031-337 6301 Plan **4** Lic 8hc ⊘ CTV 🛏

89

GH Cumberland Hotel 1 West Coates
☎031-337 1198 Plan:**5** 7hc (4fb) ✷ CTV
9P ﷽ S% B&bf9–£11 Wf60–£70 M

GH Dorstan Private Hotel 7 Priestfield Rd
☎031-667 6721 Plan:**6** Closed Xmas &
New Year rs Oct–Feb (B&b only) 14hc
4⇔f (2fb) CTV 9P ﷽ S% B&bf6.63–£7.84
Bdif11.23–£12.44 Wf77.05–£85.67 ⊬
D10am

GH Eden 12 Osbourne Ter ☎031-337 4185
Plan:**7** 6hc (2fb) ✷ 8P ﷽ S%
B&bf7.50–£8.50

GH Elmington House Private Hotel
45 Leamington Ter ☎031-229 1164
Plan:**8** Lic 7hc 3⇔f (4fb) ✷ nc5 CTV S%
✱B&bf6–£7.50 Bdif10.50–£12 Wf66.50
⊬ D6.30pm

⊢✕⊣**GH Galloway** 22 Dean Park Cres
☎031-332 3672 Plan:**9** 8hc 1⇔f (2fb)
CTV ﷽ B&bf5.50–£6.50 Bdif7.50–£8.50
D5pm

GH Glendale 5 Lady Rd ☎031-667 6588
Plan:**10** 7hc (1fb) ✷ CTV 8P ﷽ S%
B&bf6.50–£9

GH Glenisla Hotel 12 Lygon Rd
☎031-667 4098 Plan:**11** Closed 3 wks
Xmas & New Year 9hc (1fb) CTV 5P ﷽ S%
✱B&bfrf7 Bdifrf10.50 D4pm

GH *Golf View Hotel* 2 Marchall Rd,
(off Dalkeith Rd) ☎031-667 4812 Plan:**12**
Mar–Oct Lic 11hc 8⇔f CTV 12P ﷽

GH Greenside Hotel 9 Royal Ter
☎031-557 0022 Not on plan
Closed Xmas & New Year 12hc (3fb) ✷
nc5 CTV ﷽ S% B&bf8.63–£9.78

GH Grosvenor 1 Grosvenor Gdns,
Haymarket ☎031-337 4143 Plan:**13**
7hc 2⇔f (3fb) TV ﷽ S% B&bf6.50–£7.50

GH Halcyon Hotel 8 Royal Ter
☎031-556 1033 Not on plan Feb–Nov
16hc (5fb) CTV ﷽ S% B&bf7.48–£8.05

⊢✕⊣**GH Hillview** 92 Dalkeith Rd
☎031-667 1523 Plan:**14** 8hc nc3 CTV
2P ﷽ S% B&bf5.75–£6.50
Bdif9.20–£10.45 Wf64–£72.50 ⊬
D4.30pm

GH Kildonan Lodge Hotel 27 Craigmillar
Pk ☎031-667 2793 Plan:**15** Lic 8hc (5fb)
nc5 CTV 14P ﷽ S% B&bf8.05

⊢✕⊣**GH Kirkridge** 8 Kilmaurs Ter
☎031-667 6704 Not on plan 8hc (2fb)
TV ﷽ S% B&bf5–£6 Wf30–£39 M

GH Northesk Hotel 3 Pilrig St
☎031-554 4205 Not on Plan 11hc
(A 8hc 5⇔f) (6fb) TV 2✿ ﷽ S%
B&bf6–£8 Bdif9–£11 D6.30pm

GH Park Lodge 13–15 Abercorn Ter,
Portobella ☎031-669 9325 Plan:**16**
14rm 11hc 6⇔f (4fb) ✷ CTV 8P ﷽ S%
B&bf7–£8 Bdif9–£10 Wf60–£65 ⊬
D6pm

GH Quinton Lodge 24 Polwarth Ter
☎031-229 4100 Plan:**17** Closed Xmas &
New Year 6hc (2fb) ✷ CTV 8P ﷽ S%
B&bf6 Bdif9 D6.30pm

⊢✕⊣**GH Salisbury Hotel** 45 Salisbury Rd
☎031-667 1264 Not on Plan 15hc
2⇔f (4fb) CTV 12P ﷽ S%
B&bf5.50–£10 Wf35 M

⊢✕⊣**GH Southdown** 20 Craigmillar Pk
☎031-667 2410 Plan:**18** 8hc 1⇔f
(4fb) ✷ CTV 8P ﷽ S% B&bf5–£6
Bdif8.50–£9.50

GH Thrums Private Hotel 14 Minto St,
Newington ☎031-667 5545 Plan:**19**
Lic 7hc 1⇔f (2fb) CTV S% B&bf6–£7

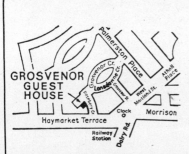

EGGLESTON Co Durham *Map 12 NY29*
INN Moorcock Hilltop ☎ Teesdale 50395
Lic 6hc 50P 🍴 S% B&b£7.50 sn
L£1.25–£1.95 D9.45£1.25–£1.95&alc

ELIE Fife *Map 12 NO40*
GH Elms Park Pl ☎330404 Lic 6hc (2fb)
⊗ CTV 8P 🍴 S% B&b£6.50–£7 Bdi£10–£11
W£66–£73 ⇖ D6pm

ELLESMERE Salop *Map 7 SJ33*
GH Grange Grange Rd ☎2735
Closed Xmas wk Lic 12hc 6⇖🛁 (3fb) ⋒
CTV 20P S% B&b£9.50–£12
Bdi£13.50–£16 W£90–£105 ⇖ D6.30pm

EMPINGHAM Leics *Map 4 SK90*
INN White Horse ☎221 Lic 3hc ⊗ 50P
6🛁 S% B&b£10 sn L£4.50alc
D9.30pm£5.75alc

EMSWORTH Hants *Map 4 SU70*
GH Jingles 77 Horndean Rd ☎3755
8hc (1fb) CTV 8P 🍴 S% B&b£7.50–£9.50
Bdi£9.50–£11.50 D8.30pm

GH Merry Hall Hotel 73 Horndean Rd
☎2424 Closed Xmas wk Lic 10hc 5⇖🛁
(3fb) ⊗ TV 12P 🍴 S% B&b£11.39
Bdi£15.04 D9.30pm

ESKDALE Cumbria *Map 7 SD19*
INN Bower House ☎244 Lic 6hc
(A 8⇖🛁) CTV 60P 4🛁 🍴 S%
B&b£12.50–£14.50 Bdi£19.40–£21.40
W£125 ⇖ sn Lfr£3.50 D9pmfr£6.90

EVESHAM Heref & Worcs *Map 4 SP04*
GH *Waterside Family Hotel*
56–59 Waterside ☎2420 Lic 10hc 7⇖🛁
(A 3hc 1⇖🛁) ⋒ CTV 14P 🍴 river D7.30pm

EXETER Devon *Map 3 SX99* **See Plan**
GH Brayside 21 New North Rd ☎56875
Plan:**1** 8hc (4fb) ⊗ TV S% B&b£6–£8

GH Hotel Gledhills 32 Alphington Rd
☎71439 Plan:**2** Closed Xmas wk 12hc
(5fb) ⊗ CTV 9P 3🛁 🍴 S% B&b£6.90
Bdi£9.78 W£57.50 ⇖ D5pm

GH Park View Hotel 8 Howell Rd
☎71772 Plan:**4** Closed 23Dec–1Jan
9hc 2⇖🛁 (A 4hc) (4fb) ⋒ CTV 6P 🍴
B&b£6.90–£7.48 Bdi£10.93–£11.50
D6pm

GH Radnor Hotel 79 St Davids Hill
☎72004 Plan:**5** Closed Xmas 9hc (2fb)
CTV 7P 🍴 S% B&b£6.50–£7.50
Bdi£10–£11.50 D4pm

GH Regents Park Hotel Polsloe Rd
☎59749 Plan:**6** Closed 2wks Xmas 11hc
(2fb) CTV 16P B&b£8 Bdi£12 W£84 ⇖

GH Sylvania House Hotel 64 Pennsylvania
Rd ☎75583 Plan:**7** Closed Xmas &
New Year 8hc 5⇖🛁 (2fb) CTV 4P 🍴
S% B&bfr£6.50–£7.50

GH Telstar Hotel 77 St David's Hill
☎72466 Plan:**8** 7hc 2⇖🛁 (2fb) ⊗ CTV
4P 🍴 S% ✱B&b£6.90 Bdi£9.78 D2pm

GH Trees Mini Hotel 2 Queens Cres,
York Rd ☎59531 Plan:**9** Closed 2wks Xmas
12hc (1fb) ⊗ nc18mths CTV 2P 3🛁 🍴
S% B&b£7–£7.50 Bdi£11–£12 D6.30pm

GH Trenance House Hotel 1 Queen's Cres,
York Rd ☎73277 Plan:**10** Closed Xmas wk
10hc 1⇖🛁 (4fb) CTV 7P 🍴 S%
B&b£6.50–£7.50 Bdi£10.50–£11.50
W£73.50–£80.50 D1pm

GH Westholme 85 Heavitree Rd ☎71878
Plan:**11** Closed 1wk Xmas 7hc (1fb) CTV

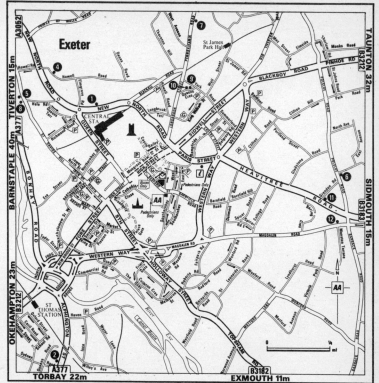

1 Brayside	6 Regent's Park Hotel	9 Trees Mini Hotel	12 Willowdene Hotel
2 Hotel Gledhills	7 Sylvania House	10 Trenance House	
4 Park View Hotel	Hotel	Hotel	
5 Radnor Hotel	8 Telstar House	11 Westholme Hotel	

8P S% B&bf6.90–£7.50 Bdif9.90 (not high season) Dnoon

GH Willowdene Hotel 161 Magdalen Rd
☎71925 Plan:**12** Closed Xmas 8hc
1⇌🛅(1fb) ⊛ CTV S% B&bf7

EXFORD Somerset *Map 3 SS83*
GH *Exmoor House* ☎304 Mar–Oct 5hc
(A 12hc) TV 18P 🍴 D6pm

EXMOUTH Devon *Map 3 SY08*
GH Anchoria 176 Exeter Rd ☎72368
Closed Xmas 8hc 2⇌🛅(2fb) ⊛ CTV 8P 1🏠
S% B&bf6–£7 Bdif9.50–£11
Wf59–£67.50 ƚ D3pm

GH Carlton Lodge Free House
Carlton Hill ☎3314 Lic 6hc 9P 🍴 sea S%
B&bf9 Bdif12.35 Wf75 ƚ D2.30pm

◄►**GH Clinton House** 41 Morton Rd
☎71969 Apr–Sep 8hc nc CTV B&bf5.25
Bdif7.50 Wf49 ƚ

◄►**GH Dawson's** 8 Morton Rd ☎72321
Etr–Oct 7hc (2fb) ⊛ CTV 2P 2🏠 S%
B&bf4.50–£4.75 Bdif6.75–£7
Wf43–£50 ƚ

GH Dolphin House 4 Morton Rd ☎3832
Lic 28hc 5⇌🛅(14fb) CTV 6P 🍴 S%
B&bf6–£7.50 Bdif7.50–£9.50
Wf44–£54 D7.30pm

GH Farthings Hotel 81 Salterton Rd
☎72161 Lic 7hc 1⇌🛅(3fb) ⊛ CTV 8P 🍴

S% B&bf6.50–£7.50 Bdif10.50–£11.50
Wf59–£65 ƚ D6pm

◄►**GH Morton Villa** 37 Morton Rd
☎73164 Etr–Sep Lic 7hc (3fb) ⊛ CTV 🍴
B&bf5–£5.50 Bdif7.50–£8.50
Wf45–£55 ƚ

FAIRBOURNE Gwynedd *Map 6 SH61*
GH Liety Heulog 2–4 Alyn Rd ☎250228
Mar–Oct rs Nov–Feb (Bookings only) Lic
12hc (5fb) CTV 12P sea S% B&bf6.90
Wf48.30 ƚ D8.30pm

FALMOUTH Cornwall *Map 2 SW83*
See Plan
GH Bedruthan 49 Castle Dr ☎311028
Plan:**1** Lic 6hc (2fb) ⊛ CTV 4P 🍴 sea S%
B&bf7–£8 Bdif10–£11 Wf64–£70 ƚ
D5pm

GH Collingbourne Hotel Melvill Rd
☎311259 Plan:**2** Mar—Oct Lic 16hc
9⇌🛅(10fb) ⊛ CTV 16P 🍴 S%
✱B&bf5.20–£8.05 Bdif7–£10.35
Wf48.30–£72.45 ƚ D9.30pm

GH Cotswold House Private Hotel
49 Melvill Rd ☎312077 Plan:**3** Closed
Xmas Lic 11hc 2⇌🛅 ⊛ nc13 CTV 12P sea
S% B&bf7.95–£9 Bdif10.95–£12.50
Wf75–£85 ƚ D5.45pm

GH Hotel Dracaena Dracaena Av
☎314470 Plan:**4** Lic 10hc (A 8hc) (6fb) 🛅
CTV 20P S% B&bf6.90–£8.05

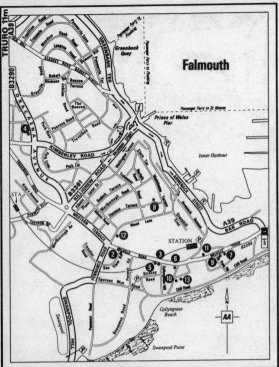

1 Bedruthan
2 Collingbourne Hotel
3 Cotswold House Private Hotel
4 Hotel Dracaena
5 Evendale Private Hotel
6 Gyllyngvase House
7 Homelea
8 Langton Leigh
9 Milton House
10 Rosemary Hotel
11 Tregenna
12 Trevone Hotel
13 Wickham

Bdi£8.50–£10.35 W£52.90–£69.50 ⊬ D6.30pm

GH Evendale Private Hotel 51 Melvill Rd ☎314164 Plan:**5** Mar–Oct 10hc 3⇩🏠 (4fb) CTV 10P S% ✱B&b£7–£8 Bdi£10–£11 W£55–£69 ⊬ D6.30pm

GH Gyllyngvase House Hotel Gyllyngvase Rd ☎312956 Plan:**6** early Mar–early Nov Lic 16hc 6⇩🏠 (2fb) ⊗ CTV 16P B&bfr£8.60 Bdifr£11.50 Wfr£75 ⊬ D7pm

GH Homelea 31 Melvill Rd ☎313489 Plan:**7** mid May–Sep 7hc ⊗ nc12 TV 4P B&b£6–£7.50 Bdi£8.50–£10 W£58–£66 ⊬ D5pm

⋈ GH Langton Leigh 11 Florence Pl ☎313684 Plan:**8** Apr–Oct 8hc (4fb) CTV 6P 🏠 🍺 sea S% B&b£5.75–£6.75 Bdi£7.75–£8.75 W£50.50–£59.50 ⊬

GH Milton House 33 Melvill Rd ☎314390 Plan:**9** rs Oct–Apr (booking only) 7hc ⊗ nc5 CTV 6P sea

GH Rosemary Hotel 22 Gyllyngvase Ter ☎314669 Plan:**10** Apr–mid Oct Lic 11hc (7fb) ⊗ CTV 4P sea S% ✱B&b£7.50–£9.75 Bdi£9.20–£10.35 W£52.90–£71.30 ⊬ D6.30pm

GH Tregenna 28 Melvill Rd ☎313881 Plan:**11** Lic 6hc (2fb) ⊗ CTV 4P sea S% ✱B&b£5 Bdi£7–£7.50 W£46.50–£50 ⊬

GH Trevone Hotel 33 Wood Ln ☎313123 Plan▸**12** Apr–Oct Lic 17hc 4⇩🏠 (4fb) nc2 CTV 12P sea S% ✱B&b£8.50–£9.50 Bdi£12.10–£14.25 W£74–£90 ⊬ D6.30pm

GH Wickham 21 Gyllyngvase Ter ☎311140 Plan:**13** Apr–Oct 11hc (2fb) ⊗

nc3 CTV 3P sea B&b£6.50–£7.50 Bdi£8.50–£10.50 W£55–£65 ⊬ D5pm

FAREHAM Hants *Map 4 SU50*
GH Carrick House 11–13 East St ☎234678 Lic 10hc (3fb) CTV 🍺 S% B&b£7.50

GH Maylings Manor Hotel 11A Highlands Rd ☎286451 Lic 28hc 20⇩🏠 (4fb) 65P 🍺 S% B&b£10.50–£17.50 D9.30pm

FARNHAM Surrey *Map 4 SU84 ·*
GH Eldon Hotel 43 Frensham Rd, Lower Bourne ☎Frensham 2745 Lic 14hc 9⇩🏠 CTV 🍺 S% B&b£11–£15 Bdi£14–£25 D9.30pm

GH Trevena House Hotel Alton Rd ☎716908 Lic 19hc nc5 CTV 40P 🍺 D7.30pm

FAZELEY Staffs *Map 4 SK20*
GH Buxton House Hotel 65 Coleshill St ☎Tamworth 4392 Lic 12rm 11hc 4⇩🏠 (3fb) CTV 15P 🍺 S% B&bfr£8.50 Bdifr£12 Wfr£72 ⊬ D5pm

FEATHERSTONE PARK Northumb *Map 12 NY66*
INN Wallace Arms Hotel ☎Haltwhistle 20375 Lic 3hc nc5 CTV 36P 🍺 S% ✱B&b£8 L£3.25alc D9pm£4.50alc

FENITON Devon *Map 3 ST19*
GH Colestocks House Colestocks (1m N unclass) ☎Honiton 850633 Mar–Oct Lic 6hc 4⇩🏠 (1fb) ⊗ nc12 CTV 6P S% B&b£7–£9.50 Bdi£9.50–£12.50 W£59.50–£80 ⊬ D7pm

FERNDOWN Dorset *Map 4 SU00*
GH Broadlands Hotel West Moors Rd
☎877884 Lic 12hc (2fb) CTV 15P
B&b£9.25 Bdi£12.50 W£84 ½ D6.30pm

FFESTINIOG Gwynedd *Map 6 SH64*
GH Newborough House Hotel Church Sq
☎2682 Lic 7hc (4fb) ♨ CTV 6P 洄 S%
B&b£6.50–£8.50 Bdi£10–£12.50
W£65–£80 ½ D6pm

FIDDLEFORD Dorset *Map 3 ST81*
INN Fiddleford ☎Sturminster Newton
72489 Closed Xmas day 4hc nc14 30P 洄
B&B£7.50–£10 Bar lunch85p–£4.10
D10pm85p–£4.10

FILEY N Yorks *Map 8 TA18*
GH Beach Hotel The Beach
☎Scarborough 513178 May–mid Oct
rs Mar & Nov Lic 21hc (11fb) CTV sea S%
B&b£7 Bdi£7.50 W£52.50–£63 ½
(W only Jul & Aug) D6pm

GH Downcliffe Hotel The Beach
☎Scarborough 513310 May–Sep rs Etr Lic
16hc 4⇥洄 (9fb) CTV 9P 1🏠 sea
✱£6.75–£7.30 Bdi£8.65–£91.0
W£60.55–£63.70 ½ D6pm

GH Southdown Hotel The Beach
☎Scarborough 513392 14 May–22 Sep
24hc (11fb) CTV 4P S% ✱B&b£6.21–£6.90
Bdi£7.76–£10.35 W£54.34–£72.54 ½
W only 19 Jul–Aug D6pm

FIVE LANES Cornwall *Map 2 SX28*
INN Kings Head Hotel ☎Pipers Pool 241
Lic 5hc ⊘ nc 45P 洄 S% B&b£7 D9.30pm

FLAX BOURTON Avon *Map 3 ST56*
INN Jubilee Farleigh Rd ☎2741 Lic 4hc
nc14 40P S% ✱B&b£7 sn L£2
D9.45pm£2.50–£3

FLEETWOOD Lancs *Map 7 SD34*
GH Southbrook Private Hotel 41 The
Esplanade ☎3944 Lic 10hc (2fb) CTV 4P
S% ✱B&b£7.50 D9pm

FLUSHING Cornwall *Map 2 SW83*
GH Nankersey Hotel St Peters Rd
☎ Penryn 74471 rs Xmas Lic 8hc 2⇥洄
(4fb) ⊗ CTV 4P 洄 sea S% ✱B&b£5.50–£8
Bdi£9–£10.50 W£63–£73.50 ½ D8pm

FOLKESTONE Kent *Map 5 TR23*
See Plan
GH Argos Private Hotel 6 Marine Ter
☎54309 Plan:**1** Lic 9hc (2fb) nc3 CTV 洄
S% B&b£6.90–£8.62 Bdi£10.35–£12.07
W£65–£75 ½ D10pm

GH Arundel Hotel 3 Clifton Rd ☎52442
Plan:**2** Lic 13hc (2fb) ⊗ CTV P 洄 S%
B&b£6.33–£7.47 Bdi£8.05–£9.02
W£44.85–£51.75 ½ D6.30pm

⊷GH Beaumont Private Hotel 5 Marine
Ter ☎52740 Plan:**3** Lic 8hc 1⇥洄 (4fb)
CTV 1🏠 洄 B&b£5.75–£6.90
Bdi£9.20–£10.35 D6pm

GH Belmonte Private Hotel 30 Castle
Hill Av ☎54470 Plan:**4** Apr–Sep 10hc
(A 4hc) (2fb) nc3 CTV 8P S%
B&b£6.50–£7.20 Bdi£8.90–£9.80
W£51.50–£57.50 ½ D6pm

GH Claremont Private Hotel 20–22
Claremont Rd ☎54897.Plan:**5** Lic 14hc

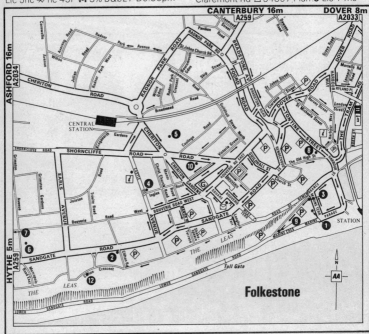

Folkestone

1	Argos Private Hotel	4	Belmonte Private Hotel	7	Kasfaret	11	Wearbay
2	Arundel Hotel	5	Claremont Private Hotel	8	Micheal's	12	Westward Ho! Private Hotel
3	Beaumont Private Hotel	6	Horseshoe Private Hotel	9	Pier Hotel		
				10	Shannon Private Hotel		

(4fb) ⊗ nc8 CTV 7P ▥ S% B&b fr£10.93 Bdi fr£14.50 Wfr£75.03 Ł D4pm

GH *Horseshoe Private Hotel* 29 Westbourne Gdns ☎52184 Plan:**6** Apr–Sep 10hc 1⇌fl ⊗ nc6 CTV 15P ▥

⊢⊣ **GH Kasfaret** 91 Bouverie Rd West ☎53705 Plan:**7** Etr–Oct 13hc (5fb) ⊗ nc3 CTV 9P ▥ S% B&b£5.75 Bdi£8.05 W£46 Ł (W only mid Jun–mid Sep) D12.30pm

GH Michael's 35 Tontine St ☎55961 Plan:**8** Mar–Dec Lic 12hc (2fb) ⊗ CTV ▥ S% ✱B£4 W£28 Ɱ D10.30pm

GH Pier Hotel 1 Marine Cres ☎54444 Plan:**9** Lic 28hc (7fb) CTV sea S% B&b£6.50–£8.50 Bdi£9–£11 W£50–£60 Ł D6pm

GH Shannon Private Hotel 59–61 Cheriton Rd ☎52138 Plan:**10** Apr–Sep Lic 24hc 2⇌fl CTV 11P B&b£6–£8.50 Bdi£8.50–£11.50 W£63–£68 Ł D7.15pm

GH Wearbay Hotel 25 Wearbay Cres ☎52586 Plan:**11** Lic 12hc 1⇌fl (1fb) CTV 1⌂ sea S% B&b£7–£12.10 Bdi£12–£17.95 W£72.50–£113.65 Ł D11pm

GH Westward Ho! Private Hotel 13 Clifton Cres ☎52663 Plan:**12** Lic 11hc (8fb) CTV ▥ lift sea S% B&b£10–£12 Bdi£11.50–£13 W£40–£62 Ł D5pm

FONTMELL MAGNA Dorset *Map 3 ST81*

GH Estyard House Hotel ☎811460 Closed Nov & Xmas 6hc nc10 8P ▥ S% B&b£7.50 Bdi£11 W£68 Ł D5pm

FORDINGBRIDGE Hants *Map 4 SU11*

GH Oakfield Lodge 1 Park Rd ☎52789 Mar–Oct 9hc (2fb) ⊗ CTV 10P B&b£6.50 W£41 Ɱ

GH St Ives & Seven Wives High St ☎52006 Restaurant closed Tue Lic 6hc (A 2⇌fl) (1fb) CTV S% ✱B&b£5.50–£6 Bdi£8–£10 W£48–£55 Ɱ D9pm

FORRES Grampian *Moray Map 14 NJ05*

⊢⊣ **GH Regency** 66 High St ☎72558 Lic 7hc CTV S% B&b fr£5.50 Bdi fr£8.50

FORT WILLIAM Highland *Inverness-shire Map 14 NN17*

⊢⊣ **GH Benview** Beford Rd ☎2966 Mar–Nov 15hc (2fb) CTV 20P ▥ S% B&b£5.75–£8.05 Bdi£10.30–£12.65 D6pm

GH Guisachan Alma Rd ☎3797 15hc (4fb) TV 14P ▥ lake S% B&b fr£6 Bdi fr£9 Wfr£63 Ł D5.30pm

⊢⊣ **GH Hillview** Achintore Rd ☎4349 Apr–Oct 9hc (3fb) CTV 9P ▥ lake S% B&b£4–£4.75 Bdi£7.75–£8.50 D6.30pm

GH Innseagan Achintore Rd ☎2452 Apr–Oct 20hc 6⇌fl (2fb) CTV 20P ▥ lake Bdi£9.50–£12 W£66.50–£84 Ł D7pm

⊢⊣ **GH Loch View** Heathercroft, off Argyll Ter ☎3149 Apr–7 Oct 7hc 1⇌fl (3fb) CTV 8P ▥ lake B&B fr£4.75

GH Rhu Mhor Alma Rd ☎2213 Mar–Oct 7hc (2fb) ⊗ CTV 9P lake S% B&b fr£6 Bdi fr£9 Wfr£60 Ł

⊢⊣ **GH Stronchreggan View** Achintore Rd ☎4644 Apr–Oct 7hc (5fb) ⊗ 7P ▥ lake S% B&b£5.50–£6 Bdi£8.50–£9 W£59.50–£63 Ł D6.30pm

FOVANT Wilts *Map 4 SU02*

INN *Cross Keys Hotel* ☎284 Closed Wed 2 wks, Oct & Xmas Lic 4hc ⊗ nc8 TV 14P ▥ ⛍ D9pm

FOWEY Cornwall *Map 2 SX15*

GH *Ashley House Hotel* 14 Esplanade ☎2310 Mar–Nov Lic 6hc D7pm

GH Carnethic House Lambs Barn ☎3336 Etr–Nov Lic 7hc 2⇌fl (2fb) ⊗ nc9 CTV 20P ▥ S% B&b£7.48–£8.63 Bdi£11.85–£13 W£82–£90 Ł D3pm

⊢⊣ **GH Polmear** 62 Esplanade ☎3464 6hc (2fb) ⊗ nc8 TV sea S% B&b£5–£6.50 Bdi£8–£10 W£49–£63 Ł D6pm

FOWNHOPE Heref & Worcs *Map 3 SO53*

GH Bowens Farm ☎430 Lic 6hc (1fb) nc10 CTV 6P 4⌂ ▥ B&B fr£8 Bdi fr£12.50 Wfr£48 Ɱ D8.30pm

FOYERS Highland *Inverness-shire Map 14 NH42*

GH Foyers Bay House Lower Foyers ☎Gorthleck 631 6hc CTV 15P 3⌂ ▥ lake S% B&b£6.25–£7.25 Bdi£11.50–£12.50 D10pm

FRADDON Cornwall *Map 2 SW95*

GH Denmar ☎860359 Lic 6hc (2fb) ⊗ CTV 6P ▥ S% B&b£6 Bdi£7.50–£8 Wfr£52.50 Ł W only last 2 wks Jul & Aug D6.30pm

GH St Margaret's Private Hotel ☎860375 Closed Xmas wk Lic 12hc (5fb) CTV 20P ▥ S% B&b£7–£9 Bdi£10–£12 W£45–£63 Ł (W only in season) D2pm

FRAMPTON Dorset *Map 3 SY69*

GH Wessex Barn ☎ Maiden Newton 20282 Lic 4hc ⊗ 4P 2⌂ ▥ S% B&b£6–£7 Bdi£12–£14 W£75–£80 Ł

FRESHWATER BAY Isle of Wight
Map 4 SZ38
GH Blenheim House Gate Ln
☎Freshwater 2858 May–Oct Lic 11hc
4⇩🛏 (4fb) nc5 CTV 6P 4🏠 🍴 sea S%
B&b£6.50–£7 Bdi£10–£10.50
Wf£65–£68 kD7pm

GH Saunders Hotel Coastguard Ln
☎Freshwater 2322 Apr–Oct Lic 13hc
(5fb) CTV 10P sea S% ✳B&b£6 Bdi£9.75
Wf£62 k D5pm

FRINTON-ON-SEA Essex *Map 5 TM21*
GH *Forde* 18 Queen's Rd ☎4758 6hc ⊗
nc5 TV 1P 🍴

GH Uplands 41 Hadleigh Rd ☎4889
29 Mar–3 Oct Lic 7hc (2fb) CTV 8P 🍴 S%
B&b£7.90–£8.28 Bdi£9.80–£10.20
Wf£60.90–£63 kD3.30pm

GAERWEN Gwynedd *Map 6 SH47*
INN Holland Arms ☎651 Lic 6hc CTV
40P 🍴 B&b£7.48 sn L£6alc D9pmf£6alc

GAIRLOCH Highland *Ross & Crom
Map 14 NG87*
GH Horisdale House Strath-Gairloch
☎2151 Apr–15 Oct rs 15 Oct–Mar
(Bookings only) 9hc (3fb) ⊗ nc7 20P 🍴
sea S% B&b£7–£8 Bdi£11–£12.50
Wf£73.50–£84 k D7pm

GARFORTH W Yorks *Map 8 SE43*
GH *Coach House Hotel* 58 Lidgett Ln
☎Leeds 862303 Closed Xmas–New Year
6hc (A 4hc) ⊗ CTV 8P 3🏠

GARGRAVE N Yorks *Map 7 SD95*
GH Kirke Syke 19 High St ☎356 Closed
Nov–15 Dec & Feb Lic 5hc (A 4⇩🛏) nc12
CTV 12P 🍴 S% B&b£7 Bdi£11 Wf£75 k
D noon

GARTMORE Central *Perths Map 11 NS59*
GH Baad Springs Farm ☎Aberfoyle 207
Etr–Oct Lic 3⇩🛏 (1fb) CTV 6P S% B&b£8
Bdi£14 D8pm

GARTOCHARN Strathclyde *Dunbartons
Map 10 NS48*
INN *Gartocharn Hotel* ☎204 Lic 5hc
CTV 35P 🍴 D8.25pm

GATWICK AIRPORT, LONDON
W Sussex *Map 4 TQ24*
GH Barfield Farm Stanhill, Charlwood
☎Norwood Hill 862545 Closed Xmas &
New Year 5hc (3fb) ⊗ nc5 CTV 10P 5🏠 🍴
S% B&b£9

GH Barnwood Hotel Balcombe Rd,
Crawley ☎Crawley 882709 Closed Xmas
Lic 29hc 28⇩🛏 (14fb) ⊗ CTV 35P 🍴 &
S% B&b£12.08–£17.25 D8.45pm

GH Gainsborough Lodge Massetts Rd,
Horley (2m NE of Airport adjacent A23)
☎Horley 3982 6hc 1⇩🛏 (1fb) ⊗ TV 10P
🍴 B&b£7.50–£9.50

GH *Frames Skylodge Motel* London Rd
County Oak, Crawley (2m S of airport on
A23) ☎Crawley 514341 Lic 21hc 21⇩🛏
⊗ CTV 45P 🍴

GH Trumbles Hotel and Restaurant
Stanhill, Charlwood ☎Crawley 862212
Closed Xmas & New Year Lic 5⇩🛏 nc9
CTV in bedrooms 20P 🍴 B&b£12.50
D8.45pm

GIFFORD Lothian *E Lothian Map 12 NT56*
GH *Cornerways* ☎238 4hc 4P

GIGGLESWICK N Yorks *Map 7 SD86*
GH Woodlands The Mains ☎Settle 2576
Closed Xmas & New Year Lic 6hc (2fb) ⊗
nc3 6P 🍴 S% B&b fr£9 Bdi fr£14 Wfr£82
k D noon

GLASGOW Strathclyde *Lanarks
Map 11 NS56*
See Plan
⊢⊣**GH Auld's** 8 Belgrave Ter, Hillhead
☎041-339 8668 Plan**:1** 4hc (1fb) TV 4P 🍴
S% B&b fr£5.50

GH Burnbank Hotel 67–85 West
Prince's St ☎041-332 4400 Not on plan
36hc 5⇩🛏 (4fb) CTV 🍴 S%
B&b£8.50–£10 Bdi£11.50–£13 D7pm

GH Chez Nous 33 Hillhead St, Hillhead
☎041-334 2977 Plan**:2** Lic 14rm 13hc
(3fb) CTV 9P 🍴 S% B&b£7.48–£8.05
Bdi£11.48–£12.50 Wf£75.36–£82.50 k
D9pm

GH Dalmeny Hotel 62 St Andrews Dr,
Nithsdale Cross ☎041-427 1106 Plan**:3**
Lic 10hc 4⇩🛏 (1fb) CTV 20P 🍴
B&b£10–£17

GH *Devonshire Hotel* 5 Devonshire Gdns,
Great Western Rd, Kelvinside ☎041-334
1308 Plan**:4** 15hc 2⇩🛏 CTV P D7pm

GH Kelvin Private Hotel 15 Buckingham
Ter, Hillhead ☎041-339 7143 Plan**:5**
15hc (3fb) CTV S% ✳B&b£5.75–£7

GH Linwood House 356 Albert Dr,
Pollokshields ☎041-427 1642 Plan**:6**
16hc (2fb) ⊗ CTV 6P 🍴 S% B&b£6.50–£7

GH *Marie Stuart Hotel* 46–48 Queen
Mary Av, Cathcart ☎041-423 6363 Plan**:7**

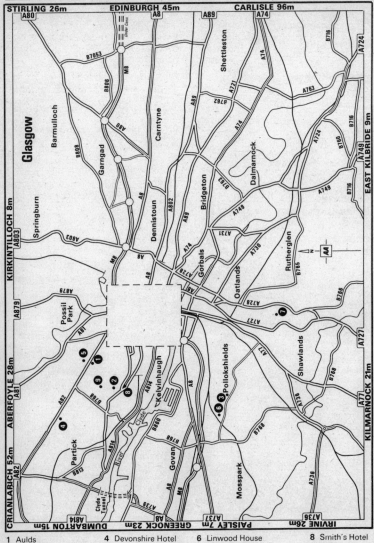

1 Aulds
2 Chez Nous
3 Dalmeny Hotel
4 Devonshire Hotel
5 Kelvin Private Hotel
6 Linwood House
7 Marie Stuart Hotel
8 Smith's Hotel
9 Wilkies

Closed Xmas Lic 24hc 1⊆🛏 CTV 50P 🍽
D6.30pm

GH Smith's Hotel 963 Sauchiehall St
☎041-339 7674 Plan **8** 28hc ⊗ CTV 🍽
S% B&b£7.20–£9.20

GH Wilkies 14–16 Hillhead St, Hillhead
☎041-339 6898 Plan **9** 10hc 1⊆🛏
(2fb) CTV 4P S% B&b£6–£6.50

GLASGOW AIRPORT Strathclyde
Renfrews Map 11 NS46
GH Ardgowan 92 Renfrew Rd, Paisley
☎041-889 4763 Closed 2 wks at Xmas &
New Year 5hc nc3 6P 🍽 S%
B&b£7.50–£8.50

GH Broadstones Private Hotel 17 High
Calside, Paisley ☎041-889 4055 8hc
(2fb) CTV 12P 🍽 S% B&b£7.50–£9.50

GLASTONBURY Somerset *Map 3 ST53*
GH Hawthorn House Hotel 8–10
Northload St ☎31255 10hc 2⊆🛏 (2fb) ⊗
TV 2🔥 🍽 B&b£6.90–£7.50 D9.30pm

GLENCOE Highland *Argyll Map 14 NN15*
⊷⊶ **GH Dunire** ☎Ballachulish 318 6hc
3⊆🛏 (4fb) CTV 10P 🍽 S%
B&b£5–£5.50 Bdi£7.50–£8
W£52.50–£57 ⅃ D7pm

⊷⊶ **GH Scorrybreac** ☎Ballachulish 354
Closed Nov 6hc (2fb) ⊗ nc4 TV 10P 🍽 S%
B&b fr£4.75 Bdi fr£7.75 W only Jan–May &
Oct–Nov D5.30pm

GLENRIDDING Cumbria *Map 11 NY31*
GH Bridge House ☎236 Mar–Nov 6hc
(4fb) 🍽 lake S% B&b fr£6

GLOSSOP Derbys *Map 7 SK09*
GH Hurst Lee Derbyshire Level, Sheffield
Rd ☎3354 Closed Xmas Lic 6hc (1fb) CTV
6P 🛏 S% B&b£6.50–£9.50 Bdi£10–£13
W£70–£91 ⅒ D4pm

GLOUCESTER Glos *Map 3 SO81*
GH Alma 49 Kingsholm Rd ☎20940 8hc
❀TV 6P 1🏠 🛏

GH Claremont 135 Stroud Rd ☎29540
6hc (2fb) ❀ TV 6P 🛏 S% ✱B&b£6–£6.50
W£38.50–£42 Ⓜ

**GH Hucclecote Garden Hotel &
Restaurant** 164 Hucclecote Rd ☎67374
Lic 11hc 2⇔🍴(1fb) ❀ CTV 20P 🛏 S%
B&b£8.95 Bdi£11.95 W£76.50 ⅒
D9.50pm

GH Monteith 127 Stroud Rd ☎25369
8hc (3fb) CTV 8P 🛏 S% ✱B&b£5.50–£6

GH New Bridge Hotel West End Ter
☎34792 Lic 9hc (3fb) CTV 8P S%
B&b£6.50–£7.50 Bdi£8.50–£10
W£60–£70 ⅒ D9.30pm

GH Stanley House Hotel 87 London Rd
☎20140 Lic 7hc 2⇔🍴(A 7hc 2⇔🍴)
(2fb) CTV 30P 🛏 S% B&b£7.65–£8.22
Bdi£10.65–£11.22 W£80–£90 D7.30pm

GODALMING Surrey *Map 4 SU94*
INN King's Arms Royal Hotel High St
☎21545 Lic 17hc ❀ CTV 50P D8.45pm

GOMSHALL Surrey *Map 4 TQ04*
INN Black Horse ☎Shere 2242 Lic 6hc
❀ nc12 CTV 60P 🐾 sn D9.30pm

GOONHAVERN Cornwall *Map 2 SW75*
GH Reen Cross Farm ☎Perranporth
3362 Closed Xmas wk Lic 9hc (2fb) CTV
15P S%✳B&bf£5–£6 Bdi f£7–£8 Wf£45–£50
⊾ D6.30pm

GOREY Jersey, Channel Islands *Map 16*
GH Lavender Villa Hotel Grouville
☎Jersey 54937 Apr–Sep rs Oct–Dec
(B&b only) Lic 17hc 15⇘🛁 (2fb) ⊗ nc6
CTV 12P 🛏 ⅋ S% B&bf£9–£10
Bdi f£12–£12.50 D6.30pm

GORRAN HAVEN Cornwall *Map 2 SX04*
GH Perhaver ☎Mevagissey 2471
Etr–mid Oct Lic 5hc ⊗ nc CTV 5P sea S%
B&bf£8.50 Bdi f£11–£11.50 Wf£66–£68.50
⊾ D5pm

GOSPORT Hants *Map 4 SZ69*
GH *Bridgemary Manor Hotel* Brewers Ln
☎Fareham 232946 Lic 16hc CTV 15P
D5.30pm

GOUROCK Strathclyde *Renfrews*
Map 10 NS27
GH Claremont 34 Victoria Rd ☎31687
6hc (2fb) CTV 🛏 S% B&b fr£6

GOVILON Gwent *Map 3 SO21*
GH Llanwenarth House ☎Gilwern
830289 rs Xmas & New Year (Restaurant
closed) Lic 4hc 4⇘🛁 (4fb) CTV 20P 🛏
B&bf£15.30–£17.80 Bdi f£24.80–£27.30
D7pm

GRAMPOUND ROAD Cornwall
Map 2 SW95
INN Midway ☎St Austell 882343 Lic
5hc ⊗ CTV 4P 6🏠 S% B&bf£9–£10
Bdi f£13.60–£14.30 Wf£85–£95 ⊾ sn
Lf£4.75alc D9.30pm£4.30–£4.60&alc

GRANGE *(in Borrowdale)* Cumbria
Map 11 NY21
GH Grange ☎Borrowdale 251 Mar–Oct
7hc 1⇘🛁 (1fb) TV 7P 🛏 S% B&b fr£7
Bdi fr£10.50 Wfr£80 ⊾ D4pm

GRANGE-OVER-SANDS Cumbria
Map 7 SD47
GH Elton Private Hotel Windermere Rd
☎2838 Closed Oct & Xmas 9hc (3fb) CTV
6P S% B&bf£6–£7 Bdi f£8.50–£9.50
Wf£55–£60 ⊾

GH Grayrigge Private Hotel Kents Bank Rd
☎2345 Lic 27hc 3⇘🛁 (A 12hc) (12fb)
CTV 60P sea B&bf£6.90 Bdi f£11.50
Wfr£62.10 ⊾ D7pm

GH Thornfield House Kents Bank Rd
☎2512 Etr–Oct 6hc (2fb) ⊗ nc5 CTV 6P
🛏 sea S%✳B&b fr£5 Bdi fr£7.80
Wfr£54.60 ⊾ D2pm

GRANSMOOR Humberside *Map 8 TA15*
GH Gransmoor Lodge Country House
☎Burton Agnes 340 Lic 6hc (3fb) ⊗ ⅋
CTV 12P S% B&bf£10–£12 D6.30pm

GRANTOWN-ON-SPEY Highland
Moray Map 14 NJ02
GH Braemoray Private Hotel Main St
☎2303 Feb–Nov Lic 7hc 3⇘🛁 (1fb) CTV
6P 🛏 S% B&bf£7–£9 Bdi f£12–£14
Wf£80–£98 ⊾ (W only Feb–Jun &
Oct–Nov) D7.30pm

GH Dar-il-Hena ☎2929 Etr–Oct 7hc
(3fb) CTV 10P 🛏 S% B&b fr£8.50
Bdi fr£12.75 D7pm

GH Dunachton Off Grant Rd ☎2098
Jan–Oct 8hc 1⇘🛁 (3fb) ⊗ CTV 9P 🛏
B&bf£6.25–£6.75 Bdi f£9.25–£9.75
Wf£60–£64.50 ⊾ D7pm

GH Kinross House Woodside Av ☎2042
Closed Xmas 6hc (2fb) 6P 🛏 D4pm

GH Pines Hotel Woodside Av ☎2092
Etr–Sep 10hc (2fb) ⅋ CTV 5P S%
B&b fr£7.48 Bdi fr£11.39 Wfr£70.84 ⊾
D5pm

GH Riversdale Grant Rd ☎2648 7hc
(2fb) ⅍ CTV 8P 🛏 S% B&bf£6.50–£7
Bdi f£9.50–£10 Wf£63–£66.50 ⊾ D6pm

GH Umaria Woodlands Ter ☎2104 8hc
(4fb) TV 8P S% B&b fr£6.50 Bdi fr£10
Wfr£67 ⊾ D5pm

GRASMERE Cumbria *Map 11 NY30*
GH Bridge House Hotel Stock Ln ☎425
Mar–Oct Lic 12hc 4⇘🛁 (1fb) 20P S%
Bdi f£17–£18.50 Wf£107–£116 ⊾ D4pm

🅸🅴🅸 **GH Chestnut Villa Private Hotel**
Keswick Rd ☎218 Closed Jan & Feb 8hc
(2fb) 10P 🛏 S% B&bf£5.50–£6.50

GH Dunmail Keswick Rd ☎256 6hc (2fb)
⊗ CTV 6P 🛏 S%✳B&bf£5.50 Bdi f£8.50
Wf£56 ⊾ D6.30pm

GH Lake View Lake View Dr ☎384
Mar–Oct 7hc CTV 11P lake B&bf£7.50–£8
Bdi f£12–£12.50 Wf£80–£82 ⊾

GH Meadow Brow ☎275 Mar–Nov Lic
6hc ⊗ 10P 🛏 S%✳B&bf£8.50 Bdi f£15.50
Wf£100 ⊾

GH Titteringdales Pye Ln ☎439
Apr–Oct Lic 6hc (2fb) TV 8P 🛏 S%
B&bf£7–£8.50 Bdi f£11.50–£13
Wf£80–£90 ⊾ D4pm

GREAT
Placenames incorporating the word 'Great'
such as Gt Malvern and Gt Yarmouth, will
be found under the actual placename,
ie Malvern, Yarmouth

GRETNA Dumfries & Galloway
Dumfriesshire Map 11 NY36
GH Surrone House Annan Rd ☎341 Lic
7⇔氚(5fb) ⚹ CTV P 🕮 ✳B&b£8.20–£9.20
Bdi££13.50–£14.50 W£51.66–£66·06 M
D7.30pm

GRETNA GREEN Dumfries & Galloway
Dumfriesshire Map 11 NY36
⊢⊣**GH Greenlaw** ☎361 Etr–Oct 8hc
(1fb) CTV 8P 🕮 S% B&b£5–£5.25

GRIMSBY Humberside *Map 8 TA20*
INN *Wheatsheaf Hotel* Bargate ☎54729
Closed Xmas Lic 4hc ⚹ nc10 TV 60P 🕮

GUERNSEY Channel Islands *Map 16*
See Câtel, St Martin, St Peter Port

GUILDFORD Surrey *Map 4 SU94*
GH Blanes Court Hotel Albury Rd ☎73171
Lic 15hc 3⇔氚(A 2hc) TV P 🕮 S%
✳B&bfr£10.35 Wfr£62.10 M D9.30pm

GUILDTOWN Tayside *Perthshire
Map 11 NO13*
INN Angler's Rest Main Rd ☎Balbeggie
329 Lic 5hc ⚹ nc3 CTV 40P 🐎 S%
B&b£9.50 sn L£3alc D9.30pm£4.50alc

GWBERT-ON-SEA Dyfed *Map 2 SN15*
GH *Anchor Hotel* ☎Cardigan 2638
Mar–Oct Lic 13hc CTV 12P 1🏠 🕮 D6pm

HALESWORTH Suffolk *Map 5 TM37*
INN *Angel Hotel* The Thoroughfare
☎3365 Lic 8hc 2⇔氚 CTV 100P 6🏠 sn
D9pm

HALFORD Warwicks *Map 4 SP24*
INN *Bell* ☎Stratford-on-Avon 740382 Lic
8hc CTV 50P 2🏠 sn D9pm

HALTWHISTLE Northumb *Map 12 NY76*
GH Ashcroft ☎20213 6hc (3fb) CTV 12P
S% ✳B&b£4.50 Bdi£6.50 W£39 ⚡ D8pm

HALWELL Devon *Map 3 SX75*
GH Stanborough Hundred Hotel ☎East
Allington 236 Lic 8hc (2fb) ⚹ nc5 CTV
10P S% B&b£7–£9.50 Bdi£11–£13.50
W£60–£75 ⚡ D9.30pm

HAMPTON COURT Gt London
London plan 4 D2 (page 266)

INN Cardinal Wolsey The Green
☎01-941 3781 Lic 19hc 1⇔氚 ⚹ 20P 🕮
S% B&bfr£12.50 Bdifr£17.15 sn
Lfr£4.65&alc D9pm fr£4.65&alc

HAMPTON HILL Gt London
London plan 4 D2 (page 266)
GH Jasmin House 88–94 High St
☎01-977 2117 9hc 4⇔氚(A 4hc) (5fb) ⚹
CTV 5P 🕮 S% B&b£10.35–£12.65

HARLECH Gwynedd *Map 6 SH53*
⊢⊣**GH Cemlyn** ☎780425 20 Mar–Oct Lic
7hc (6fb) CTV 🕮 sea S% B&b£5.95
Bdi£7.95 D9.30pm

INN Rum Hole Hotel ☎780477 Lic 8hc
4⇔氚 CTV 25P 🕮 S% B&b£7.50–£12
sn L£1–£3 D9.30pm£1–£3

HARLOW Essex *Map 5 TL41*
INN Green Man Hotel Mulberry Green
☎21342 Lic 6hc 50P 🐎 S%
✳B&b£11–£13.75 sn L£5.50alc
D9pm£6alc

HARPENDEN Herts *Map 4 TL11*
GH Milton Private Hotel 25 Milton Rd
☎2331 Lic 9hc (1fb) ⚹ CTV 9P 🕮 S%
B&b£9 Bdi£11.75 D8pm

HARROGATE N Yorks *Map 8 SE35*
GH Alexa House Hotel 26 Ripon Rd
☎501988 6hc (2fb) CTV 6P 3🏠 🕮 S%
✳B&b£7.25 Bdi£10.50 D6pm

GH *Boston Private Hotel* 3–7 Swan Rd
☎502918 Lic 19hc CTV 10P 🕮 D7pm

GH Carlton Hotel 98 Franklin Rd
☎64493 10hc (2fb) CTV 8P 🕮 B&b£7.50
Bdi£11 D7.30pm

GH Franklin Private Hotel 25 Franklin Rd
☎69028 Lic 6hc nc5 CTV 4P S%
B&b£6–£6.50 W£40–£43 M

GH Gillmore 98 King's Rd ☎503699 Lic
18hc 2⇔氚(4fb) CTV 18P 2🏠 🕮 S%
B&b£6.50–£7 Bdi£9–£10 D3pm

GH Hartington Franklin Mount ☎69534
2 wks Xmas & New Year 12hc (2fb) CTV
6P 🕮 S% B&b£7.20 Bdi£10.80–£11.20 W£74.22–£76.96 ⚡
D noon

GH Manor Hotel 3 Clarence Dr ☎503916
Lic 16hc (5fb) ⚹ CTV 6P 🕮
B&b£9.52–£10.50 Bdi£13.52–£15.50
W£87.58–£100.72 D8.15pm

GH Norman Hotel 41 Valley Dr ☎58416
Lic 18hc 4⇔氚(1fb) CTV 🕮 S%
B&b£9–£9.50 Bdi£14–£15 D7pm

⋈ **GH Oakbrae** 3 Springfield Av ☎67682
Closed Xmas 6hc (1fb) CTV P 🍴 S%
B&b£5.75–£6.25 Bdi£8.75–£9.25 W£38
Ⓜ D6pm

GH Roan 90 Kings Rd ☎503087 Closed
25 & 26 Dec 6hc (2fb) ⊗ CTV 🍴 S%
✱B&b£6 Bdi£9 D4.30pm

GH Shelbourne 78 Kings Rd ☎504390
Lic 7hc (2fb) nc3 CTV 🍴 S% B&b£8.50
Bdi£12.50 W£55–£80 ↳ D6.30pm

GH Springfield 80 Kings Rd ☎67166
Closed Xmas 6hc (2fb) ⊗ CTV 5P
B&b£7.75 W£54.25 Ⓜ

GH Strayend 56 Dragon View, Skipton Rd
☎61700 6hc (2fb) CTV 6P 🍴 S%
B&b£6–£7.50 Bdi£9–£11 W£63–£70 ↳
D5pm

GH Wessex 23 Harlow Moor Dr ☎65890
Lic 14hc 8⇔🛁 (3fb) CTV 🍴 S% B&b£9
Bdi£13.50 W£83.50 ↳ D7pm

GH Youngs Private Hotel 15 York Rd
☎67336 Closed Xmas wk & 1 Jan Lic
10hc 3⇔🛁 (3fb) CTV 12P 1🏠 🍴 S%
B&b£7–£11 Bdi£12–£16 W£80–£112 ↳
D7pm

HARROW Gt London
London plan 4 A2 (page 266)
GH Harrow Hotel 12–18 Pinner Rd
☎01-427 3435 rs Xmas Lic 81hc 41⇔🛁
(A 17hc 12⇔🛁) (16fb) CTV 48P 🍴 S%
B&b£16.10–£25.30 Bdi£22.15–£31.35
W£159.90–£213.10 D9pm

GH Hindes Hotel 8 Hindes Rd
☎01-427 7468 13hc 1⇔🛁 (3fb) ⊗ CTV
5P 🍴 S% B&b£9–£12 W£60–£80 Ⓜ

HARTLAND Devon *Map 2 SS22*
INN Anchor Fore St ☎414 Lic 11hc 5⇔🛁
⊗ CTV 16P 7🏠 B&b£8–£9 W£53–£60 Ⓜ
Bar Lunch£1–£2.50 D9.30pm£5.50alc

HARWICH Essex *Map 5 TM23*
GH Hotel Continental 28 Marine Pde,
Dovercourt Bay ☎3454 Lic 8hc (3fb) CTV
7P sea S% B&b£9–£10 Bdi£13–£14
W£84–£94 ↳ D10pm

HASTINGS & ST LEONARDS E Sussex
Map 5 TQ80
GH Bryn-y-Mor 12 Godwin Rd ☎441755
4hc 1⇔🛁 (A 2⇔🛁) (2fb) CTV 🍴 sea
B&b£8–£12 Bdi£12–£18 W£59.50–£90
↳ D8pm

GH Burlington Hotel 2 Robertson Ter
☎429656 Lic 15hc (2fb) CTV 🍴 sea S%
B&b£7.50–£15 Bdi£11.25–£18.75
W£77.75–£147.75 D8pm

GH Chimes Hotel 1 St Mathews Gdns
☎434041 Closed Nov Lic 11hc 2⇔🛁
(2fb) CTV 🍴 S% B&b£8–£11.50
Bdi£12.50–£16.50 W£75–£102 ↳
D5.30pm

GH Harbour Lights 20 Cambridge Gdns
☎423424 8hc (1fb) ⊗ CTV 🍴 S%
✱B&b£5.50 Bdi£8 W£56 ↳ D am

GH Russell Hotel 35 Warrior Sq ☎431990
Lic 10hc (5fb) CTV 1🏠 S% B&b£9–£12
Bdi£13–£16 W£65–£90 ↳ D2pm

GH Waldorf Hotel 4 Carlisle Pde
☎422185 Lic 12hc (3fb) ⊗ CTV S%
B&b£6.50–£8 Bdi£9–£11.50
W£60–£77.50 ↳ D noon

HATHERLEIGH Devon *Map 2 SS50*
INN Bridge Bridge St ☎357 Lic 4hc nc3
CTV 20P S% ✱B&b£6.90–£13
W£66–£125 ⊭ sn L90p–£3
D9.30pm£4&alc

HAVERFORDWEST Dyfed *Map 2 SM91*
GH Elliots Hill Hotel Camrose Rd ☎2383
Lic 21hc (4fb) ⊗ CTV 30P 🚿
B&b£6.50–£7.50 Bdi£10–£12
W£60–£70 ⊭ D8pm

HAWKSHEAD Cumbria *Map 7 SD39*
GH Highfield House Hawkshead Hill
☎344 Jan–Nov Lic 12hc 2⇌🛏 (4fb) nc2
12P 🚿 B&b£10.25–£12.30
Bdi£15.25–£17.30 W£100–£115 ⊭
D6.30pm

GH Ivy House ☎204 Mar–Nov Lic 6hc
1⇌🛏 (A 5hc) (3fb) CTV 12P 🚿 S%
✱B&b£7 Bdi£10.50 W£64–£69.50 ⊭
(W only 24 May–mid Sep) D5pm

GH Rough Close Country House ☎370
Apr–Oct 6hc (2fb) ⊗ CTV 12P 🚿 lake S%
B&B£6

INN Kings Arms Hotel ☎372 Lic 6hc
CTV 🚿 B&b£9 W£60 Ⓜ sn L£1.20alc
D10pm£2.50alc

HAWORTH W Yorks *Map 7 SE03*
GH 'Rough Nook' Residential Hotel
West Ln ☎43165 6hc 4⇌🛏 TV 6P 🚿

HAYFIELD Derbys *Map 7 SK08*
GH Hazel 1–2 Valley Rd ☎New Mills
43671 9hc 2⇌🛏 (2fb) CTV 10P 🚿 S%
B&b£7 D9pm

HAYLING ISLAND Hants *Map 4 SU70*
GH Avenue 5 Wheatlands Ave ☎3121
7hc (2fb) ⊗ CTV 8P 🎵 S%
B&b£6.50–£7.50 Bdi£10.50–£11.50
W£73.50–£80.50 ⊀ D noon

⊨⊨ **GH Dolphin Court Hotel** 37 St
Leonard's Ave ☎2910 8hc (4fb) CTV 6P 🎵
S% B&b£5.50–£6.50 Bdi£8–£9.50
W£49–£60 ⊀ D am

HAY-ON-WYE Powys *Map 3 SO24*
INN Old Black Lion Lion St ☎820841 Lic
6rm 2hc 4⇱🏛 CTV 20P 🎵 ⚐ S%
B&b£10.20–£12.80 W£64.26 M sn
L£6.50alc D9pm£7alc

HEASLEY MILL Devon *Map 3 SS73*
GH Heasley House ☎North Molton 213
Mar–Oct Lic 8hc (2fb) CTV 12P 1🏛
🎵 B&b£6.20 Bdi£10 W£65 ⊀ D7pm

HEATHFIELD E Sussex *Map 5 TQ52*
GH Broadhurst Swife Ln, Broad Oak
(3½m NE A265) ☎West Burwash 461 5hc
1⇱🏛 TV 15P

HEDDON'S MOUTH Devon *Map 3 SS64*
INN Hunters ☎Parracombe 230 Etr–Oct
Lic 11hc 5⇱🏛 CTV 200P S% B&b£11–£13
Bar lunch£1–£5 D9pm£5–£10&alc

HELENSBURGH Strathclyde *Dunbartons*
Map 10 NS28
⊨⊨ **GH Aveland** 91 East Princes St ☎3040
6hc (2fb) nc5 CTV 8P sea S% B&b£5–£6
Bdi£7.50–£8 W£47–£52 ⊀ D6pm

HELSBY Cheshire *Map 7 SJ47*
GH Poplars Private Hotel 130 Chester Rd

☎3433 Closed Xmas wk 7hc (2fb) ⊗ nc5
CTV 6P 🎵 S% ✳B&b£7 Bdi£10 W£43 M
D4pm

HELSTON Cornwall *Map 2 SW62*
GH Bona Vista 22 Meneage Rd ☎2579
Lic 6hc TV 10P D6pm

⊨⊨ **GH Hillside** Godolphin Rd ☎4788 Lic
7hc (2fb) ⊗ CTV 6P S% B&b£5–£6
Bdi£8.50–£9.50 W£58–£65 ⊀ D noon

HEMEL HEMPSTEAD Herts *Map 4 TL00*
GH South Lea Private Hotel 8 Charles St
☎3061 11hc ⊗ CTV 8P 1🏛 🎵 ✳B&b£7.50

GH Southville Private Hotel 9 Charles St
☎51387 12hc (2fb) ⊗ CTV 9P 🎵 S%
B&b£7–£8

HENLEY-ON-THAMES Oxon
Map 4 SU78
GH Sydney House Hotel Northfield Rd
☎3412 Lic 10hc 1⇱🏛 (4fb) ⊗ nc5 CTV
7P 🎵 S% ✳B&b£11.50

GH Thamesmead Remenham Ln ☎4745
7hc nc5 7P 🎵 B&b£8.40

HENSTEAD Suffolk *Map 5 TM48*
GH Henstead Hall Country Hotel
☎Lowestoft 740345 Lic 14hc (3fb) nc5
CTV 14P S% ✳B&b£8.50–£9
Bdi£13.50–£14 W£72.45–£76.40 ⊀
D6pm

HEREFORD Heref & Worcs *Map 3 SO54*
GH Ferncroft Hotel 144 Ledbury Rd
☎65538 Closed mid Dec–mid Jan Lic
10hc (2fb) ⊗ CTV 8P 🎵 S% ✳B&b£7.50
Bdi£11 W£75 ⊀ D7.30pm

GH Munstone House Munstone (2m N unclass off A49) ☎67122 Feb–Nov 6hc (3fb) ✇ TV 10P ⊞ S% B&b£6–£7.50

HERNE BAY Kent *Map 5 TR16*
⊯**GH Beauvalle** 92 Central Pde ☎5330 6hc (1fb) CTV ⊞ sea S% B&b£5–£7 D8.30pm

GH Northdown Hotel 14 Cecil Park ☎2051 Lic 5hc (A 2rm) (3fb) ⊛ CTV 8P ⊞ S% ✳B&b£7–£10 Bdi£10–£14 W£72–£78 ⊬ D9pm

HERSTMONCEUX E Sussex *Map 5 TQ61*
GH Cleavers Lyng Country Hotel ☎3131 Closed Xmas wk Lic 8hc CTV 12P 2🏠 ⊞ B&b£8.50 Bdi£11 W£72.50 ⊬ D6pm

HERTFORD Herts *Map 4 TL31*
GH Tower House Private Hotel 2 Warren Park Rd, Bengeo ☎53247 6hc 1⇨🛏 (1fb) 6P ⊞

HEWISH Avon *Map 3 ST46*
⊯**GH Kara** ☎ Yatton 834442 Closed Xmas 7hc (2fb) ✇nc5 TV 7P ⊞ S% B&b£4.50–£6.50 Bdi£7–£8.50

HEYSHAM Lancs *Map 7 SD46*
⊯**GH Carr-Garth** Bailey Ln ☎51175 2May–9Oct 10hc (6fb) ✇ CTV 7P B&bfr£5.58 Bdifr£7.19 W£fr56.35 (W only Spring Hol–Sep)

HIGH WRAY Cumbria *Map 7 SD39*
GH Balla Wray Country Hotel ☎ Ambleside 3308 Mar–Oct 8hc (3fb) ✇nc5 CTV 10P lake S% Bdi£10.93 W£69 ⊬

HIGH WYCOMBE Bucks *Map 4 SU89*
GH Clifton Lodge Private Hotel 210–212 West Wycombe Rd ☎29062 12hc 1⇨🛏 (A 3hc) (1fb) ✇nc5 CTV 16P ⊞ S% ✳B&b£8 Bdi£11

GH Drake Court Hotel London Rd ☎23639 Lic 19hc 2⇨🛏 (5fb) ✇ CTV 30P ⊞ S% B&b£8–£15 Bdi£12–£19 D7.30pm

HILLESLEY Avon *Map 3 ST78*
INN Fleece ☎ Wotton-under-Edge 3189 Lic 3hc nc10 TV 30P ⇛ S% ✳B&bfr£5.50 sn L£1–£5 D9pm£1–£5

HILL HEAD Hants *Map 4 SU50*
GH Seven Sevens Private Hotel Hill Head Rd ☎ Stubbington 2408 8hc 1⇨🛏 (1fb) CTV 10P ⅙ S% ✳B&b£6.50–£6.75 Bdi£9.50–£9.75 D4pm

HINCKLEY Leics *Map 4 SP49*
GH Cecilia's Private Hotel 13–19 Mount Rd ☎37193 Closed 1 wk Xmas Lic 8hc CTV 8P ⊞ ✳B&bfr£8.25

HINDON Wilts *Map 3 ST93*
INN Grosvenor Arms ☎253 Closed Xmas wk Lic 3hc 10P S% B&b£8.50 Bdi£12 W£70 ⊬ Bar lunch£1.50–£5.50&alc D9.30pm£3.50–£5.50&alc

HITCHIN Herts *Map 4 TL12*
GH Redcoats Farmhouse Hotel Little Wymondley ☎ Stevenage 3500 Closed 1wk Xmas Lic 7hc 1⇨🛏 (A 3⇨🛏) (2fb) CTV 20P S% B&b£16.50–£19.50 Bdi£24.50–£28.50 D9pm

HOLMROOK Cumbria *Map 6 SD09*
GH Carleton Green ☎608 Apr–Oct 6hc 1⇨🛏 (1fb) TV 6P ⊞ S% B&b£7.Bdi£10.50 W£69 ⊬ D7pm

HOLNE Devon *Map 3 SX76*
INN Church House ☎ Poundsgate 208 Lic 5hc nc14 TV 8P ⊞ ⇛ B&b£10.50 W£60 ⋈ sn L£5alc D10pm£5alc

HOLNEST Dorset *Map 3 ST61*
GH Manor Farm Country House Holnest Park ☎474 Apr–Oct Lic 10hc (2fb) CTV 20P ⊞ ✳B&b£7.20 Bdi£11.50 W£77 ⊬

HOLT Norfolk *Map 9 TG03*
GH *Lawns Private Hotel* Station Rd ☎3390 Lic 9hc 2⇨🛏 nc7 CTV 9P ⊞ D6pm

HONITON Devon *Map 3 ST10*
INN Monkton Court Monkton (2m E A30) ☎2309 Lic 5hc 1⇨🛏 TV 130P ⊞ S% B&bfr£11.50 D10.15pm

HOPE COVE Devon *Map 3 SX63*
⊯**GH Fern Lodge** ☎ Galmpton 326 Mar–Oct 5hc (A 2⇨🛏) (2fb) TV 4P 3🏠 ⊞ B&b£5.50–£7.50 Bdi£8.50–£9.50 W£57–£63 ⊬

GH Lantern Lodge Hotel ☎ Galmpton 280 Mar–Dec Lic 15⇨🛏 ✇ nc12 CTV 20P ⊞ sea S% Bdifr£17.50 D9pm

GH Sand Pebbles Hotel ☎ Galmpton 673 Apr–Nov Lic 6hc 4⇨🛏 (3fb) CTV 12P sea B&b£6.50–£10 Bdi£10–£17 W£70–£150 ⊬ D7.15pm

HOPTON CASTLE Salop *Map 7 SO37*
GH Lower House Country Lodge ☎ Bucknell 352 Mar–Dec Lic 4hc ✇ nc14

CTV 10P 2🏠 S% B&b£15 Bdi£23.25
W£150 ⚓ D6pm

HORNSEA Humberside *Map 8 TA24*
GH Promenade Hotel Marine Dr ☎2944
Closed Xmas & Oct 12hc (4fb) ⊗ CTV
17P 🍴 B&bfr£6 Bdifr£10 Wfr£60 ⚓ D6pm

GH Hotel Seaforth Esplanade ☎2616
7hc (3fb) CTV 5P 🍴 sea S% B&b£6
Bdi£9.50 W£63 ⚓ D4pm

HORRABRIDGE Devon *Map 2 SX56*
GH Overcombe ☎ Yelverton 3501
Lic 7hc 1⇔🍴 (2fb) ⇪ CTV 7P 1🏠 🍴
S% ✳£7.50 Bdi£12 W£77.28 ⚓ D7.15pm

HORSHAM W Sussex *Map 4 TQ13*
GH Wimblehurst Private Hotel
6 Wimblehurst Rd ☎62319 14hc 2⇔🍴
(3fb) ⊗ CTV 14P 4🏠 🍴 S% B&b£10–£15
Bdi£15–£20 D6pm

HORSHAM ST FAITH Norfolk
Map 9 TG21
GH Elm Farm Chalet Norwich Rd
☎ Norwich 898366 Closed 25 & 26 Dec
12hc 4⇔🍴 ⊗ CTV P 🍴 S% B&b£8–£12
Bdi£12.50–£16.50 W£85.75–£113.75
⚓ D6.30pm

HORTON Dorset *Map 4 SU00*
INN Horton ☎ Witchampton 252 Lic
7hc 3⇔🍴 CTV 75P 🍴 🐴 D10pm

HORTON-IN-RIBBLESDALE N Yorks
Map 7 SD87
INN Crown ☎209 Lic 10hc CTV 20P 🍴
🐴 B&b£7.50–£9 Bdi£12–£14
W£77.70–£90 ⚓

HOVE Sussex *Map 4 TQ20*
See also Brighton
GH Bigwood Lodge Hotel 40 Old Shoreham
Rd ☎ Brighton 737430 Lic 16hc 4⇔🍴
(1fb) CTV 4P 4🏠 ⊗ S% B&b£10–£17.50
Bdi£13.50–£21 W£85–£140 ⚓ D4pm

GH Croft 24 Palmeira Av ☎ Brighton
732860 Apr–Nov 12hc (4fb) CTV 🍴 S%
B&b£7.25–£8.50 W£49–£57.75 Ⓜ

GH Polonia Hotel 36–38 St Aubyns
☎ Brighton 733640 Lic 51hc ⊗ ⇪ CTV
28P lift 🍴 sea D8pm

GH Tatler Hotel 26 Holland Rd
☎ Brighton 736698 Lic 12hc (3fb) CTV S%
✳B&b£7.50 Bdi£11 Wfr£77 ⚓ D7pm

HOWEY Powys *Map 3 SO05*
GH Corven Hall Country ☎ Llandrindod
Wells 3368 Lic 6hc (2fb) CTV P 2🏠 S%

✳B&b£5.50–£6 Bdi£8.50–£9
W£47.50–£52.50 ⚓ D9pm

HOWMORE South Uist, Western Isles
Inverness-shire Map 13 NF73
GH Ben Mor ☎ Grogarry 283 8hc (2A)
9P D7pm

HOYLAKE Merseyside *Map 7 SJ28*
GH Sandtoft Hotel 70 Alderley Rd
☎051-632 2204 Lic 9hc CTV 10P 3🏠
🍴 D6pm

HUDDERSFIELD W Yorks *Map 7 SE11*
GH Cote Royd Hotel 7 Halifax Rd,
Edgerton ☎47588 Closed 3wks July,
1 wk Xmas, rs wknds (B&b only) Lic 10rm
7hc 3⇔🍴 ⊗ CTV 14P 4🏠 🍴 S%
✳B&b£12.50 Bdi£17 D7pm

GH Dryclough House Hotel Dryclough Rd,
Crossland Moor ☎651731 Closed Xmas
Lic 10hc 1⇔🍴 CTV 12P 3🏠 🍴
B&bfr£8.05 Bdifr£11.05 D1.30pm

HULL Humberside *Map 8 TA02*
GH Ashford 125 Park Av ☎492849 ⟍
Closed Xmas 6hc (2fb) ⊗ CTV 6P 🍴 S%
B&b£7.50 Bdi£11.50 W£133 ⚓ D5.30pm

INN Good Fellowship Cottingham Rd
☎ 42858 Lic 7hc CTV 200P 2🏠 🍴
✳B&bfr£9 Bdifr£12 Bar lunch
£1.20–£2.50 D7.30pm£2.50–£5

HUNDLETON Dyfed *Map 2 SM90*
INN Corston Guest House Axton Hill
☎ Castlemartin 242 Lic 12hc ⊗ TV 30P
🍴 🐴 D6pm

HUNSTANTON Norfolk *Map 9 TF64*
GH Dolphin Private Hotel 15 Cliff Ter
☎2583 Lic 10hc CTV sea D8pm

GH Lincoln Lodge Private Hotel
Cliff Pde ☎2948 Etr–Oct rs Nov–Etr
(Wknds only) Lic 14hc 2⇔🍴 (4fb) nc3
CTV 6P S% B&b£8–£9 Bdi£13 W£86
⚓ D8.45pm

GH Norfolk Private Hotel 32 Kings Lynn
Rd ☎2383 Lic 11hc 2⇔🍴 (6fb) CTV 14P
🍴 ⅄ S% B&b£7.50–£8.50
Bdi£10.50–£11.50 W£60–£64 ⚓ D6.30pm

GH Sutton House Hotel 24 Northgate
☎2552 Closed Nov Lic 10hc (2fb) ⊗
CTV 7P 🍴 sea S% B&b£7.50–£8.50
Bdi£10.50–£12 W£63–£69 ⚓ D10pm

GH Tolcarne Private Hotel 3 Boston Sq
☎2359 Apr–Oct rs Xmas Lic 11hc (2fb)
nc2 CTV 8P 🍴 sea B&b£7.50–£8.50
Bdi£11–£12.50 W£69.50–£79.50 ⚓
D6pm

INN Wash and Tope Le Strange Ter ☎2250 Lic 11hc CTV 14P ▥ ⛟ sea S% ✱B&b£7.50 sn L£3.75&alc D9.15pm£3.75&alc

HUNTINGDON Cambs *Map 4 TL27*
INN Black Bull Post St, Godmanchester (1m S B1043) ☎53310 Lic 8hc ⊘ CTV 30P 6⌂ ⛟ S% B&bfr£10.07 Bdifr£13.52 sn L£1.10–£2.50 D7pm£3.45

HURN Dorset *Map 4 SZ19*
INN *Avon Causeway Hotel*
☎ Christchurch 482714 Lic 9hc TV 50P

HUTTON-LE-HOLE N Yorks *Map 8 SE79*
GH Barn ☎ Lastingham 311 Mar–Oct 10rm 9hc (1fb) TV 15P ▥ S% B&b£7–£8.50

HYTHE Kent *Map 5 TR13*
GH Dolphin Lodge 16 Marine Pde ☎69656 6hc (2fb) ⊘ nc2 CTV 4P ▥ S% B&b£6–£7 Bdi£9–£10.50 W£47.50–£59 k

ICKENHAM Gt London
London plan 4 B1 (page 266)
GH *Woodlands* 84 Long Ln ☎ Ruislip 34830 Closed Xmas 9hc ⊘ nc5 CTV 9P ▥

ICKLESHAM E Sussex *Map 5 TQ81*
GH Snailham House Broad St ☎556 Mar–mid Oct Lic 7hc (1fb) ⊘ CTV 8P ▥ S% B&b£6.05–£8.25 Bdi£8.80–£11 W£57.20–£72.60 k D6pm

ILFORD Gt London *London plan 4 B6 (page 266)*

GH Blenheim House Hotel 2 Blenheim Av, Gants Hill ☎01-554 4138 Lic 8hc (2fb) ⊘ CTV 4P ▥ S% ✱B&b£12.65 Bdi£17.54 D4pm

GH Cranbrook Hotel 24 Coventry Rd ☎01-554 6544 Lic 16hc 11🛁 (7fb) CTV 12P 2⌂ ▥ S% B&b£9.95 Bdi£12.95 W£90.65 k D9pm

GH Park Hotel 327 Cranbrook Rd ☎01-554 9616 Lic 20hc 1🛁 (2fb) CTV 23P ▥ S% B&b£8.90 Bdi£12.50 D8.15pm

ILFRACOMBE Devon *Map 2 SS54*
See Plan
GH Avenue Private Hotel Greenclose Rd ☎63767 Plan:**1** Apr–Oct Lic 24hc (6fb) ⊘ CTV 15P B&b£6.90–£8.05 Bdi£9.70–£12.65 W£66.70–£79.35 k D7pm

GH Bickleighscombe House 41 St Brannocks Rd ☎63899 Plan:**2** Mar–Oct Lic 14hc (5fb) CTV 14P S% B&b£6.90–£9.20 Bdi£10.93–£13.23 W£73.60–£89.70 k D6pm

⋈**GH Blenheim** 5 St James Pl ☎63787 Plan:**3** Etr–Oct 11hc CTV S% B&b£5.75–£6.25 Bdi£8.50–£9.25 W£52–£59 D4.30pm

GH Carbis Private Hotel 50 St Brannocks Rd ☎62943 Plan:**4** Closed Dec Lic 10hc (6fb) ⊘ CTV 10P S% ✱B&b£5.25–£7 Bdi£7–£9.75 W£54–£65 k D6.30pm

⋈**GH Clutha Private Hotel** Hillsborough Ter ☎62798 Plan:**5** Feb–Oct Lic 10hc (4fb) CTV 4P sea S% B&b£5–£7.50 Bdi£8–£10.50 W£56–£73.50 k D6.30pm

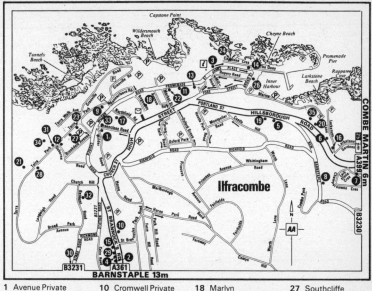

1 Avenue Private Hotel
2 Bickleighscombe House
3 Blenheim
4 Carbis
5 Clutha Private Hotel
6 Collingdale Hotel
7 Combe Lodge Hotel
8 Craigmillar
9 Cresta Private Hotel
10 Cromwell Private Hotel
11 Dèdés Hotel
12 Elmfield Hotel
13 Glendower
14 Headlands Hotel
15 Lantern House Hotel
16 Laston House Private Hotel
17 Lympstone Private Hotel
18 Marlyn
19 Merrydene Private Hotel
20 New Cavendish Hotel
21 Norbury
22 Queen's Court Hotel
23 Riversdale Hotel
24 Rockcliffe Hotel
25 Rosebank Hotel
26 Royal Britannia (*Inn*)
27 Southcliffe
28 South Tor Hotel
29 Strathmore Private Hotel
30 Sunny Hill
31 Torrs Private Hotel
32 Wentworth House Private Hotel
33 Westbourne Private Hotel
34 Westwell Hall Private Hotel
35 Wilson

GH Collingdale Hotel Larkstone Ter
☎63770 Plan:**6** Lic 9hc (4fb) CTV sea S%
B&b£6.50–£8 Bdi£9–£11 Wf£55–£70
ﬗ D5.30pm .

GH Combe Lodge Hotel Chambercombe Park Rd ☎64518 Plan:**7** Mar–Oct
rs Nov–Feb (restaurant only) Lic 9hc
(3fb) ♨ CTV 7P sea S% B&b£6.55–£7.28
Bdi£9.85–£12.28 Wf£68.95–£85.96 ﬗ
(W only mid Jul–1st wk Sep) D7.30pm

GH Craigmillar 22 Crofts Lea Pk (New
Barnstaple Rd) ☎62822 Plan:**8** Spr Bank
Hol–end Sep 8hc ⊘ nc1 CTV 5P sea D4pm

GH Cresta Private Hotel Torrs Park
☎63742 Plan:**9** mid May–Oct Lic 26hc

14⇔🚿 (14fb) CTV 34P 🚐 lift S%
B&b£8.62–£10.35 Bdi£11.21–£12
Wf£74.75–£80.50 ﬗ D6.30pm

⊨◄GH Cromwell Private Hotel 20–21
St Brannocks Rd ☎63829 Plan:**10**
Mar–Oct & Dec Lic 15hc 2⇔🚿 (4fb) CTV
30P 2🏠 S% B&b£5–£10.50
Bdi£7.50–£13 Wfr£55–£78 ﬗ D6.30pm

⊨◄GH Dèdés Hotel 1–2 The Promenade
☎62545 Plan:**11** Etr–mid Oct Lic 17hc
6⇔🚿 (A 5hc) (6fb) CTV sea
B&b£4.60–£9.20 Bdi£8.05–£12.65
Wf£56.35–£88.65 ﬗ D9.45pm

⊨◄GH Elmfield Hotel Torrs Park ☎63377
Plan:**12** Apr–Oct 6hc (4fb) ♨ CTV 12P S%

B&bf£4.25–£6.25 Bdi£6–£8 W£42–£56 ⱠD3pm

GH *Glendower* Sea Front, Wilder Rd ☎62121 Plan:**13** Lic 12hc CTV 22P 🍴 sea D7.30pm

GH Headlands Hotel Capstone Cres ☎62887 Plan:**14** Mar–Oct Lic 26hc (5fb) CTV 12🏠 sea S% B&bf£8–£9 Bdi£11–£12 W£65–£85 Ɫ D6.15pm

⊷GH Lantern House Hotel 62 St Brannocks Rd ☎64401 Plan:**15** Lic 10hc (4fb) CTV 9P 🍴 S% B&bf£5.95–£7.95 Bdi£8.20–£10.20 W£53–£73 Ɫ D5pm

GH Laston House Hotel Hillsborough Rd ☎62627 Plan:**16** Lic 12hc 5⇔🛏 (6fb) CTV 12P sea S% B&bf£8.05–£9.77 Bdi£10.70–£12.42 W£71.61–£86.94 Ɫ D5.30pm

GH Lympstone Private Hotel 14 Cross Park ☎63038 Plan:**17** Closed Xmas 17hc (6fb) CTV 5P S% B&bf£6 Bdi£9 W£50.60–£57.50 Ɫ D5pm

⊷GH Marlyn 7–8 Regent Pl ☎63785 Plan:**18** Etr–Oct Lic 12hc (3fb) CTV 6🏠 🍴 S% B&bf£5.50–£6.50 Bdi£7.50–£8.50 D5.30pm

GH Merrydene Private Hotel 10 Hillsborough Ter ☎62141 Plan:**19** May–Sep 12hc (2fb) nc5 CTV 4P 3🏠 sea S% B&bfr£7 Bdifr£9 Wfr£56 D6.30pm

GH New Cavendish Hotel 9–10 Larkstone Ter ☎63994 Plan:**20** Etr–Oct & Xmas Lic 21hc (9fb) 🐾 CTV 25P sea B&bf£6.90–£8.05 Bdi£9.75–£11.50

W£69–£80.50 (W only Jul & Aug) D6.30pm

GH *Norbury* Torrs Park ☎63888 Plan:**21** Apr–Oct Lic 8hc TV 8P sea D5pm

GH Queen's Court Hotel Wilder Rd ☎63789 Plan:**22** Apr–Oct Lic 17hc (7fb) CTV 17P sea S% B&bf£8.05–£9.20 Bdi£10.35–£11.50 W£72.45–£80.50 Ɫ (W only Jul & Aug) D6.30pm

GH *Riversdale Hotel* Torrs Park ☎62535 Plan:**23** Apr–Sep rs Oct–Mar Lic 12hc 🐾 CTV 18P D4pm

GH *Rockcliffe Hotel* Capstone Pde ☎62267 Plan:**24** Lic 16hc nc4 CTV 12P sea D10.30pm

GH Rosebank Hotel 26 Watermouth Rd, Hele Bay ☎62814 Plan:**25** Lic 7hc (4fb) CTV 🍴 S% B&bf£7.50–£8 Bdi£9.50–£12 W£64–£80 Ɫ (W only Jul & Aug) D6pm

⊷GH Southcliffe Hotel Torrs Park ☎62958 Plan:**27** Mar–Oct Lic 20hc 1⇔🛏 (12fb) 🐾 CTV 12P S% B&bfr£5.75 Bdifr£10.35 Wfr£80.50 D6.45pm

GH South Tor Hotel Torrs Park ☎63750 Plan:**28** May–Sep & Xmas Lic 15hc 6⇔🛏 (3fb) nc4 CTV 10P 2🏠 S% B&bf£7.50–£12 Bdi£11–£15 W£72.50–£89 Ɫ D5.30pm

GH Strathmore Private Hotel 57 St Brannocks Rd ☎62248 Plan:**29** Closed Xmas Lic 10hc 1⇔🛏 (5fb) 🐾 CTV 10P S% B&bf£6–£7 Bdi£8.78–£9.75 Wfr£57.80 D7pm

GH Sunny Hill Lincombe, Lee ☎62953 Plan:**30** Lic 8hc 2⇔🛏 (3fb) nc5 CTV 6P 🍴 sea S% ✱B&bf£6.75–£9 Bdi£10.17–£12.80 W£65.25–£83 Ɫ D7.30pm

GH Torrs Private Hotel Torrs Park
☎62334 Plan 31 Lic 16hc 2⇔🖭 (5fb) CTV
16P sea S% B&b£7.90–£10.98
Bdi£8.80–£11.88 W£52.90–£71.30 ⱡ
D8pm

⊷ **GH Wentworth House Private Hotel**
Belmont Rd ☎63048 Plan 32 Mar–Oct
11hc 1⇔🖭 (6fb) CTV 10P 2🏠 S%
B&b£5.25–£6 Bdi£8–£9 W£51–£56 ⱡ
D5pm

GH Westbourne Private Hotel Wilder Rd
☎62120 Plan 33 Closed Jan Lic 51hc
(7fb) CTV lift S% B&b£6.50–£8.50
Bdi£8–£10 W£52–£65 D7.30pm

GH Westwell Hall Private Hotel Torrs
Park ☎62792 Plan 34 Apr–Sep Lic 14hc
(7fb) nc3 CTV 15P S% B&b£6.32–£7.47
Bdi£9.77–£10.92 W£64.40–£72.50 ⱡ
D4pm

⊷ **GH Wilson** 16 Larkstone Ter ☎63921
Plan 35 Lic 9hc (5fb) ⊛ CTV sea S%
B&b£5.50–£6.50 Bdi£8–£9 W£49–£57
ⱡ D6pm

INN Royal Britannia The Quay ☎62939
Plan 26 Closed Xmas Lic 12hc CTV ⊅ S%
B&b£8.75–£11 Bdi£12.50–£14.75
W£83.75–£98.25 ⱡ Bar lunch£3.25alc
D2pm£3.75

ILKLEY W Yorks Map 7 SE14
GH Greystones Private Hotel Ben
Rhydding Rd ☎607408 Lic 10hc 8⇔🖭🕭
CTV 15P D8pm

INGHAM Suffolk Map 5 TL87
INN Cadogan Arms ☎Culford 226 Lic
5hc ⊛ nc3 CTV 50P 🍺 B&b£8.50

INGLETON N Yorks Map 7 SD67
GH Oakroyd Private Hotel Main St
☎41258 Feb–Nov Lic 8hc (3fb) CTV 4P S%
✳B&B£6 Bdi£8.90 W£59.50 ⱡ

GH Springfield Private Hotel Main St
☎41280 Closed Nov 6hc (4fb) CTV 12P
S% B&b£6.75–£7.25 Bdi£10–£12
W£62–£65 ⱡ D4.30pm

INSTOW Devon Map 2 SS43
GH Anchorage Hotel The Quay ☎860655
Apr–Oct Lic 10hc (6fb) ♨ CTV 9P sea S%
B&b£9.20 Bdi£12.80 W£78.70–£90.60
ⱡ (W only mid May–Sep) D6.30pm

GH Sandlea The Quay ☎860475
Etr–Oct Lic 8hc (4fb) ♨ CTV 8P sea S%
✳B&b£5.25–£7.25 Bdi£8.55–£10.25
W£48.50–£63 ⱡ D7pm

INVERGARRY Highland *Inverness-shire*
Map 14 NH30
GH Aberchalder Lodge (3m NE A82)
☎208 8hc 1⇔🖭 (1fb) nc10 TV 8P
B&b£7–£7.50 Bdi£12–£12.50 W£67–£80

GH Graigard ☎258 Apr–Oct Lic 7hc
(2fb) ⊛ nc5 6P B&b£6.45 Bdi£9.72
W£59.90 ⱡ D6.30pm

GH Lundie View Aberchalder (3m NE A82)
☎291 Lic 6hc (3fb) CTV 6P S% B&b£5
Bdi fr£8.50 Wfr£57 ⱡ D8pm

INVERMORISTON Highland *Inverness-
shire Map 14 NH41*
GH Tigh Na Bruach ☎Glenmoriston
51208 Apr–mid Oct 7rm 5hc (2fb) nc5
10P lake B&b fr£9.20 Bdi fr£12.65
Wfr£72.45 ⱡ D7pm

INVERNESS Highland *Inverness-shire
Map 14 NH64*
⊷ **GH Abermar** 25 Fairfield Rd ☎39019
11hc 3⇔🖭 (2fb) CTV 8P
B&b£5.50–£6 W£38.50–£42 Ⓜ

⊷ **GH Ardnacoille House** 1A Annfield Rd
☎33451 May–mid Oct 5hc (2fb) nc9 CTV
7P 🍺 S% B&b£5–£6 Bdi£8.50–£9.50
W£55–£63 ⱡ D3pm

⊷ **GH Arran** 42 Union St ☎32115 Closed
2 wks Apr & 2 wks Oct 7hc (2fb) TV S%
B&b£5–£5.50 W£35–£38.50 Ⓜ

GH Craigside 4 Gordon Ter ☎31576
Mar–Oct rs Dec–Feb (B&b only) 6hc 2⇔🖭
⊛ nc9 4P 🍺 S% B&b£6–£7.50
Bdi£11.50–£12.50 W£70–£75 ⱡ
D7.30pm

⊷ **GH Four Winds** 42 Old Edinburgh Rd
☎30397 Closed Xmas & New Year days
6hc (2fb) CTV 15P 🍺 S% B&b£5–£6 W£38
Ⓜ

⊷ **GH Glencairn** 19 Ardross St ☎32965
11hc (4fb) CTV 6P 🍺 👌 S%
B&b£5.50–£6.50

⊷ **GH Leinster Lodge** 27 Southside Rd
☎33311 Closed Xmas & New Year 6hc
(2fb) CTV 7P 🍺 S% B&b£5

⊷ **GH Lyndale** 2 Ballifeary Rd ☎31529
Mar–Nov 1hc TV 6P S% B&b£5–£6

GH Moray Park Hotel Island Bank Rd
☎33528 7hc (2fb) CTV 10P 🍺 S%
B&b£7.15 Bdi£12.60 W£81.65 ⱡ D5pm

GH Riverside Hotel 8 Ness Bank
☎31052 9hc (3fb) ⊛ CTV S%
B&b£6–£7.50 Bdi£10–£12.50 D7pm

GH *Tigh a' Mhuillinn* 2 Kingsmill Gdns
☎38257 6hc CTV 8P D2pm

IPPLEPEN Devon *Map 3 SX86*
INN Wellington Fore St ☎812375 Lic
5hc ⊘ CTV 40P S% B&b£6 Bdi£9.50
W£52 ⅃ D8pm

IPSWICH Suffolk *Map 5 TM14*
GH Gables Hotel 17 Park Rd ☎54252
Lic 12hc CTV 10P ⊞ S% B&b£8.62
Bdi£11.50 W£60.38 ℳ D6pm

ISLAY, ISLE OF Strathclyde *Argyll
Map 10*
See Port Ellen

ISLE OF MAN *Map 6*
Places with AA-listed guesthouses/inns
are indicated on location map 6. Full
details will be found under individual
placenames in the gazetteer section

ISLE OF SKYE Highland *Inverness-shire
Map 13 NG*
See Broadford, Dunvegan,
Isle Ornsay, Portree, Waterloo

ISLE OF WIGHT *Map 4*
Places with AA-listed accommodation
are indicated on location map 4. Full
details will be found under individual
placenames within the gazetteer

ISLE ORNSAY Isle of Skye, Highland
Inverness-shire Map 13 NG71
⋈ **GH Post Office House** ☎201 Feb–Nov
4rm 3hc (A 2hc) TV 10P sea S% B&b£5–£6
W£35–£42 ℳ

ISLES OF SCILLY (No map)
See St Marys

IVER HEATH Bucks *Map 4 TQ08*
⋈ **GH Bridgettine Convent** Fulmer
Common Rd ☎Fulmer 2073 22hc (3fb)
nc3 TV 15P ⊞ S% B&b£4.50–£6.50
Bdi£6.25–£8.50 Wfr£50 D2pm

IVYBRIDGE Devon *Map 2 SX65*
GH Sunnyside Western Rd ☎2561
Mar–Oct Lic 8hc (1fb) CTV 2P
B&b£6.33–£8.05 Bdi£9.48–£11.20
W£60–£65 ⅃ D6.30pm

JEDBURGH Borders *Roxburghs
Map 12 NT62*
⋈ **GH Kenmore Bank** Oxnam Rd ☎2369
Mar–Oct 6hc (2fb) ⊘ TV 5P 🏠 ⊞ S%
B&b£5–£5.50 D7pm

JERSEY Channel Islands *Map 16*
See Beaumont, Gorey, La Haule,
Rozel Bay, St Aubin, St Brelade,
St Clement, St Helier, St Martin,
St Peter's Valley, St Saviour, Trinity

KEITH Grampian *Banffs Map 15 NJ45*
⋈ **GH Aultgowrie** 124 Moss St ☎2052
5rm 4hc (1fb) ⊘ CTV 5P 🏠 ⊞ S%
B&b£5.50–£6 W£34.65–£37.80 ℳ

KELSO Borders *Roxburghs Map 12 NT73*
⋈ **GH Bellevue** Bowmont St ☎2588
Mar–Oct 8hc (2fb) ⊘ TV 6P S%
B&b fr£5.25 Bdi fr£8.75 D4pm

KENILWORTH Warwicks *Map 4 SP27*
GH Enderley 20 Queens Rd ☎55388
Closed mid Dec–mid Jan Lic 6rm 5hc CTV
⊞ S% ✱B&b£6–£6.50

⋈ **GH Ferndale** 45 Priory Rd ☎53214
Closed Xmas 7hc (1fb) CTV 8P ⊞ S%
B&b£5–£8 W£35–£42 ℳ

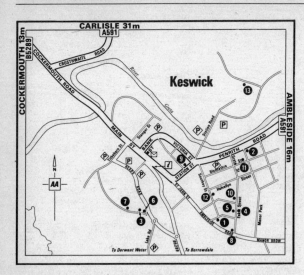

1 Acorn House
  Private Hotel
2 Bay Tree
3 Burleigh Mead
  Private Hotel
4 Clarence House
5 Foye House
6 Hazeldene Hotel
7 Highfields
8 Lynwood Private
  Hotel
9 Ravensworth
  Private Hotel
10 Richmond House
11 Silverdale Hotel
12 Sunnyside
13 Woodlands

GH Hollyhurst 47 Priory Rd ☎53882
Jan–Nov 9rm 8hc (2fb) nc3 CTV 10P S%
B&bf5

GH Nite Lite 95 Warwick Rd ☎53594
Lic 12hc (2fb) CTV 🛏 S%
B&bf6.33–£8.05 D10.30pm

KENTISBURY Devon Map 2 SS64
GH Homeside Kentisburyford
☎Combe Martin 3506 Mar–Oct 3hc (2fb)
⚭ nc8 CTV P S% B&bf5–£5.50
Bdif8.50–£9 Wf55–£60 ⚮ D5pm

KENTMERE Cumbria Map 12 NY40
GH Grove ☎Staveley (Cumbria) 821548
Mar–Sep rs New Year Lic 7hc CTV 🛏 river
D noon

KESWICK Cumbria Map 11 NY22
See Plan
GH Acorn House Private Hotel
Ambleside Rd ☎72553 Plan:1 Etr–Oct
9hc (4fb) CTV 8P 🛏 B&bf6–£7
Bdif10–£12 Wf68–£84 ⚮ D3pm

GH Bay Tree 1 Wordsworth St ☎73313
Plan:2 Lic 6hc (2fb) CTV 🛏 river B&bf6.95
Bdif8.95 Wf58 ⚮ D6.30pm

GH Burleigh Mead Private Hotel The
Heads ☎72750 Plan:3 10 Mar–10 Nov
Lic 8hc (A 6hc) (9fb) CTV 6P lake S%
B&bf7.50–£10 Bdif11.50–£14
Wf77–£90 ⚮ D5pm

GH Clarence House 14 Eskin St
☎73186 Plan:4 8hc (3fb) CTV 🛏 S%
B&bf5.50–£5.80 Bdif8.50–£8.80
Wf56–£59 ⚮ D6.15pm

GH Foye House 23 Eskin St ☎73288
Plan:5 Lic 6hc ⚭ nc5 TV 🛏 B&bfr5.50
Bdifr£9 Wfr£60 ⚮

GH Hazeldene Hotel The Heads
☎72106 Plan:6 10 Mar–10 Nov Lic 14hc
(14fb) CTV 12P 🛏 lake B&bf7.50–£10
Bdif11.50–£14 Wf77–£90 ⚮ D5pm

GH Highfields The Heads ☎72508 Plan:7
Etr–Oct Lic 10hc (3fb) nc3 CTV 🛏 lake
B&bf7.50 Bdif11.80 Wf82.60 ⚮

GH Lynwood Private Hotel 12 Ambleside
Rd ☎72081 Plan:8 Lic 8hc (4fb) ⚭ nc CTV
🛏 S% B&bf6 Bdif8.50 Wf58.50 ⚮ D5pm

GH Ravensworth Private Hotel Station
St ☎72476 Plan:9 Etr–Oct 9hc (4fb) nc
CTV 4P 🛏 S% B&bf6–£6.80

GH Richmond House 39 Eskin St
☎73965 Plan:10 Closed Nov Lic 11hc
2⇋🖿 (3fb) CTV 🛏 S% B&bf5.50 Bdif9
Wf60 ⚮ D6pm

GH Rickerby Grange Portinscale (1m W
A66) ☎72344 Not on plan Mar–Nov Lic
8hc 3⇋🖿 (1fb) CTV 10P 🛏 S%
✳B&bf6.60–£7.20 Bdif9.50–£10
Wf61–£65.50 ⚮ D6.30pm

GH Silverdale Hotel Blencathra St
☎72294 Plan:11 Lic 12hc (3fb) ⚭ CTV 8P
🛏 B&bf8 Bdif10 Wf65 ⚮ D5pm

GH Sunnyside 25 Southey St ☎72446
Plan:12 Mar–Oct 8hc (3fb) ⚭ nc8 CTV 7P
S% B&bf6.50 Bdif9.50 Wf64 ⚮ D3pm

GH Woodlands Brundholme Rd
☎72399 Plan:13 Etr–Oct 7hc (2fb) ⚭ nc6
CTV 9P 🛏 S% B&bf5.75 Bdif9 Wf56 ⚮
(W only Apr, May, Sep, Oct) D am

KEYNSHAM Avon Map 3 ST66
GH Uplands Farmhouse The Wellsway
☎5764 9hc (5fb) CTV 20P 🛏
✳B&bf7–£8 Bdif11.20–£12.20 D4pm

KIDLINGTON Oxon Map 4 SP41
GH Bowood House 238 Oxford Rd
☎2839 6hc 1⇋🖿 (2fb) ⚭ CTV 12P 🛏 S%
B&bf7.50–£10

KILKHAMPTON Cornwall Map 2 SS21
INN London ☎343 Lic 3hc nc CTV 6P 2🏠
⚘ B&bf7.50 Bdif10.50 Wf65 ⚮
Bar lunchf1.50–£2 D9pmf3alc

KILLIECRANKIE Tayside Perths
Map 14 NN96
GH Dalnasgadh House ☎237 Apr–Oct
6hc (2fb) ⚭ nc5 CTV 8P 🛏 S%
B&bf5.50–£6.50

KILMARTIN Strathclyde Argyll
Map 10 NR89
INN Kilmartin Hotel ☎250 Lic 5hc CTV
14P ⚘ S% B&bf7.05–£7.70
Bdif9.35–£13.20 Bar lunchf2.50alc
D9pmf5–£6&alc

KILNSEY N Yorks *Map 7 SD96*
GH Chapel House ☎Grassington 752654 Mar–Oct Lic 12hc 6🛁 (2fb) CTV 25P ♨ S% *Bdi£11.50 W£78.20 ⱡ

KILVE Somerset *Map 3 SS14*
INN Hood Arms ☎Holford 210 Lic 6hc 2🛁 nc CTV 12P 🚗 ♨ B&b£8 W£48 M Bar lunch£2.20alc D9.30pm£5alc

KINGHORN Fife *Map 11 NT28*
GH Odin Villa 107 Pettycur Rd ☎890625 Lic 6🛁 (1fb) CTV 20P ♨ sea B&b£6.50–£8.50 Bdi£10–£12 W£70–£84 ⱡ D9pm

KINGSBRIDGE Devon *Map 3 SX74*
GH Hotel Kildare Balkwill Rd ☎2451 Closed Xmas & New Year Lic 12hc (A 3hc) (6fb) ♣ CTV 12P S% *B&b£9.20 Bdi£14.26 W£68.71–£77.05 ⱡ D6.30pm

GH Westerlands Country Hotel Belle Cross Rd ☎2268 Lic 10hc 6🛁 (2fb) ⊘ CTV P 2🏠 ♨ *B&b£7–£10 Bdi£11.50–£14.50 W£77–£101.50 ⱡ D7pm

KINGSDOWN Kent *Map 5 TR34*
GH Blencathra Country Kingsdown Hill ☎Deal 3725 Etr–Oct Lic 5hc (3fb) ⊘ nc3 CTV 7P ♨ S% B&b£7.50 Bdi£11.50 W£69 ⱡ

KINGSKERSWELL Devon *Map 3 SX86*
⊷**GH Harewood** Torquay Rd ☎2228 Apr–Oct 6hc (3fb) CTV 10P ♨ S% B&b£5–£7 W£35–£49 M

KING'S LYNN Norfolk *Map 9 TF62*
GH Runcton House Hotel 53 Goodwins Rd ☎3098 Lic 9hc 1🛁 (2fb) CTV 12P ♨ B&b£7.50–£10.80 Bdi£11.45–£14.75 D7pm

KINGSTON Devon *Map 2 SX64*
GH Trebles Cottage ☎ Bigbury-on-Sea 268 Feb–Nov Lic 5hc 1🛁 ⊘ ♣ CTV 6P ♨ S% B&b£6–£8.50 Bdi£10–£12.50 W£58.50–£75 ⱡ D9am

KINGSTON UPON THAMES Gt London
London plan 4 D2 (page 266)
GH Hotel Antoinette 26 Beaufort Rd ☎01-546 1185 Lic 120hc 100🛁 (30fb) nc10 CTV 80P ♨ S% B&b£10.35–£11.75 Bdi£15.35–£16.75 D8.30pm

GH Lingfield House Hotel 29 Beaufort Rd ☎01-546 1988 7🛁 (3fb) ⊘ nc6 CTV 6P ♨ S% B&b£10–£11

KINGSWINFORD W Midlands
Map 7 SO88
INN *Swan Hotel* Stream Rd ☎3720 Lic 4hc ⊘ nc5 TV 50P ♨ 🚗 sn

KIRBY MUXLOE Leics *Map 4 SK50*
GH Forest Lodge Hotel Desford Rd ☎ Leicester 393125 Lic 29hc 5🛁 (4fb) CTV 60P ♨ S% *B&b£10.90 Bdi£14.95 D8pm

KIRKBEAN Dumfries & Galloway
Dumfriesshire Map 11 NX95
GH Cavens House ☎234 Closed Xmas Day Lic 6🛁 (1fb) ⊘ CTV P ♿ S% B&bfr£9 Bdi fr£15

Guesthouse of the Year 1979 Northern England Winner

. . . one of only six chosen from hundreds in Britain . . .

A Taste of Rural England in the peace of the Eden Valley.

Prospect Hill Hotel · Kirkoswald

Penrith · Cumbria · CA10 · 1ER
telephone Lazonby (std 076883) 500

. . . so far and yet so near . . .

Twenty minute drive from the M6 · Junctions 41 and 42

Quotes from the AA Guesthouse of the Year article
". . . a wider choice of dishes than the other guesthouses visited . . ."
". . . much of the food is delightfully different . . ."
". . . a syllabub was out of this world . . ."
". . . service by pleasant local girls, is quick and efficent . . ."
". . . it offers extremely good value for money
in a characterful building in a delightful part of the country . . ."

The illustration conveys the surroundings of the establishment.
It does not imply such close proximity of the river or the grounds of the hotel.

KIRKOSWALD Cumbria *Map 11 NY54*
GH Prospect Hill Hotel ☎ Lazonby 500
Closed Feb Lic 8hc 2⇨🛁 (2fb) ⊗ CTV
20P 1🅿 river B&bf£14.50–£17.60 Wf£88.88–£108 ⊬
D8.20pm

KIRKWALL Orkney *Map 16 HY41*
GH *Foveran* (½m SW A964) ☎2389
Closed Oct Lic 10hc CTV 12P 🅿 D9pm

KNAPTON Norfolk *Map 9 TG33*
GH Knapton Hall Hotel ☎ Mundesley
720405 mid Mar–Oct Lic 10hc (A 4hc)
(5fb) ⊗ CTV 14P S% B&bfr£6
Bdifr£8.50 Wfr£56 ⊬ D7pm

KNOWSTONE Devon *Map 3 SS82*
INN Masons Arms ☎ Anstey Mills 231
Lic 3hc nc12 TV 8P 🅿 🚗
✳B&bf£9.20–£13.20 Bar lunch60p–£2
D9pmf£5alc

KNUTSFORD Cheshire *Map 7 SJ77*
GH Longview Private Hotel
55 Manchester Rd ☎2119 Closed Xmas
Lic 10hc 1⇨🛁 (1fb) CTV 6P 🅿 S%
B&bf£9.50 Bdif£14.50 D6pm

KYLE OF LOCHALSH Highland
Ross & Crom Map 13 NG72
GH Retreat ☎ Kyle 4308 14hc (2fb) TV
12P 2🅿 S% B&bf£6.50–£6.75

LA HAULE Jersey, Channel Islands
Map 16
GH Au Caprice Private Hotel Route de
La Haule ☎ Jersey 22083 Etr–Dec Lic
14hc (3fb) ⊗ CTV sea S% B&bf£6–£7
Bdif£9–£11 Wf£63–£77 ⊬ (W only Jun–20
Sep) D6pm

LAIRG Highland *Sutherland Map 14 NC50*
⊶**GH Carnbren** ☎2259 Apr–Oct 3hc
TV 4P 🅿 lake S% B&bfr£5

LAMBERHURST Kent *Map 5 TQ63*
INN George & Dragon Hastings Rd
☎605 Lic 1hc 2⇨🛁 (A 3hc) ⊗ 80P 🅿
B&bf£15–£17 sn L£3.95&alc
D10pmf£5.50&alc

LAMLASH Isle of Arran, Strathclyde
Bute Map 10 NS03
GH Glenisle Hotel ☎258 Mar–Oct
3⇨🛁 (A 3rm) (6fb) CTV 16P sea
S% B&bf£6.50–£9.50 Bdif£9–£12.50
Wf£63–£87.50 ⊬ Dnoon

GH Marine House Hotel ☎298
Apr–Oct 20rm 13hc 6⇨🛁 (6fb) CTV 12P 🅿
sea S% ✳B&bf£6.04 Bdif£7.76 Wf£60.38

LANCASTER Lancs *Map 7 SD46*
⊶**GH Belle Vue** 1 Belle Vue Ter, Greaves
☎67751 Closed New Year 6hc (3fb) CTV
6P S% B&bf£5–£6 Wf£32–£40 ⊠

LANCING W Sussex *Map 4 TQ10*
GH Beach House 81 Brighton Rd ☎3368
Closed 18 Dec–6 Jan 6hc (2fb) CTV 6P 🅿
sea S% ✳B&bf£6.50–£7 Wf£42–£45

GH *Seaways* 83 Brighton Rd ☎2338
8rm 7hc CTV 6P 🅿 sea

INN Sussex Pad Hotel Old Shoreham Rd
☎ Shoreham 4647 Lic 6⇨🛁 (A 3hc) CTV P 🅿
river ✳B&b£11–£15 sn Lfr£5.60&alc
D10pmf£8.50alc

LANGDALE, GREAT Cumbria
Map 11 NY30
GH New Dungeon Ghyll Hotel ☎213

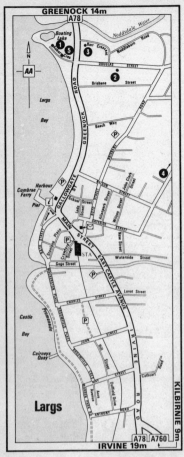

1 Aubery
2 Douglas House
3 Gleneldon Hotel
4 Holmesdale
5 Sunbury

Mar–Nov Lic 17hc (3fb) ⌖ TV 40P
✱B&b£9.84 Bdi£15.89 W£103.56 ⅃
D7pm

LANGLAND BAY W Glam *Map 2 SS68*
GH Wittemberg Hotel 2 Rotherslade Rd
☎ Swansea 69696 Closed Xmas Lic
12hc (2fb) ⌖ nc5 CTV 12P ⬜ S%
✱B&b£7–£8 Bdi£11–£12 W£60 ⅃ D6pm

LANGPORT Somerset *Map 3 ST42*
GH Ashley The Avenue ☎250386 Lic
8hc (2fb) ⌖ ⌖ CTV 12P ⬜ S%
B&bfr£6 Bdifr£9 W£58 ⅃

GH Brookside Ducks Hill, Huish Episcopi
☎250259 Lic 7hc 1⌖⬛ (3fb) ⌖ CTV
12P ⬜ S% B&b£7.50 Bdi£12 W£82 ⅃
D9.30pm

LARGS Strathclyde *Ayrs Map 10 NS25*
See Plan
⊦◅**GH Aubery** 22 Aubery Cres ☎672330
Plan:**1** Etr–Sep 6hc nc2 TV 6P sea S%
B&b£5.50 Bdi£7.50 W£49 ⅃ D5.30pm

GH Douglas House 42 Douglas St
☎672257 Plan:**2** Apr–Oct rs Dec Lic

14hc (2fb) CTV 12P ⬜ S% B&bfr£6.90
D6pm

GH Gleneldon Hotel 2 Barr Cres
☎673381 Plan:**3** Mar–Dec Lic 11hc
(2fb) ⌖ CTV 12P ⬜ B&bfr£9.25
Bdifr£14.75 Wfr£86 ⅃ D7.45pm

⊦◅**GH Holmesdale** 74 Moorburn Rd
☎674793 Plan:**4** Closed Oct, Xmas & New
Year 8hc (2fb) ⌖ CTV 5P ⬜ S% B&b£5.50
Bdi£8.50 W£59.50 ⅃

GH Sunbury 12 Aubery Cres ☎673086
Plan:**5** May–Oct 6hc (2fb) ⌖ CTV 8P sea
S%✱B&b£5 Bdi£8 D6pm

LAURENCEKIRK Grampian
Kincardineshire Map 15 NO77
GH Eastview Private Hotel ☎468 8rm
6hc (2fb) CTV 8P S% B&b£6–£8
Bdi£9–£11 W£40–£75 Ⓜ D7.30pm

LEAMINGTON SPA Warwicks
Map 4 SP36 **See Plan**
GH Beech Lodge Hotel 28 Warwick New
Rd ☎22227 Plan:**1** Closed Xmas & New
Year Lic 12hc 10⌖⬛ (1fb) CTV 8P 1🏠 ⬜
S% B&b£8.50–£9.50 Bdi£13.50–£14.50
D7.30pm

GH Buckland Lodge Hotel 35 Avenue Rd
☎23843 Plan:**2** 8hc (1fb) CTV 12P S%
B&b£7–£8 Bdi£11–£12 D2.30pm

GH Glendower 8 Warwick Pl ☎22784
Plan:**3** 8hc (2fb) CTV 7P 2🏠 ⬜ S%
B&b£7–£7.50

GH Poplars 1 Milverton Ter ☎28335
Plan:**5** Lic 11hc (5fb) ⌖ CTV 12P ⬜ S%
✱B&bfr£7.50 Bdifr£10.50 Wfr£49 Ⓜ
D4.30pm

GH *Veleta Hotel* 42 Warwick New Rd
☎21380 Plan **6** Lic 12hc 4⌖⬛ 15P ⬜
D8.30pm

GH Victoria Park 12 Adelaide Rd ☎24195
Plan:**7** 10hc (3fb) CTV 12P ✱B&b fr£6
Bdifr£8.50 D am

GH Westella Hotel 26 Leam Ter ☎22710
Plan:**8** Closed Xmas 10hc (2fb) CTV 12P
S% B&b£6.90–£7.50 Bdi£10.35–£12
W£58–£65 ⅃ D4pm

GH White House 22 Avenue Rd ☎21516
Plan:**9** 7hc (3fb) TV 10P 1🏠 ⬜ S%
✱B&bfr£6.50 Bdifr£10.50 D9am

GH York House 9 York Rd ☎24195
Plan:**10** 8hc (2fb) CTV 12P ✱B&bfr£6
Bdi fr£8.50 D am

INN Hintons Wine Bar Augusta Pl
☎37231 Plan:**4** Lic 13⌖⬛ ⌖ CTV ⬜ 🚗
S% ✱B&b£10–£12 sn L£1.20–£1.80
D10pm£4.50

LEEDS W Yorks *Map 8 SE33*
GH Anrosa House Hotel 47 Cliff Rd,
Hyde Park Corner ☎758856 Closed Xmas
& New Year Lic 14hc (1fb) nc2 CTV 8P S%
B&b£6.50 W£45.50 Ⓜ D8pm

GH Aragon Hotel 250 Stainbeck Ln,
Meanwood ☎759306 Closed Xmas Lic
12hc 2⌖⬛ (2fb) CTV 9P 1🏠 ⬜ S%
B&b£8–£16 Bdi£12–£20

GH *Ash Mount Hotel* 22 Wetherby Rd,
Roundhay ☎658164 Closed Xmas 14hc ⌖
CTV 12P ⬜

GH Budapest Private Hotel 14 Cardigan
Rd, Headingley ☎756637 Closed Xmas
13hc (2fb) ⌖ CTV 4P ⬜ B&b£7 Bdi£10
D6.30pm

GH Clock Hotel 317 Roundhay Rd,
Gipton Wood ☎490304 Lic 22hc (6fb) ⌖

Leamington Spa

KENILWORTH 4m
RUGBY 14m
A452
A445
B4453
WARWICK 2m
B4099
A445
WARWICK 2m
A425
BANBURY 19m
A452
NORTHAMPTON 29m
B4099
A425

1 Beech Lodge Hotel
2 Buckland Lodge Hotel
3 Glendower
4 Hintons Wine Bar (*Inn*)
5 Poplars
6 Veleta Hotel
7 Victoria Park
8 Westella Hotel
9 White House
10 York House

CTV 1OP S% ✳B&b£6.20–£7.94 Bdi£9.50–£11.22 D7.30pm

GH Highfield Hotel 79 Cardigan Rd, Headingley ☎752193 10hc (1fb) CTV 7P 🕮 S% B&b£9.20

GH Oak Villa Hotel 57 Cardigan Rd, Headingley ☎758439 Closed Xmas 10hc (2fb) CTV 8P 🕮 B&b£9.20

GH Trafford House Hotel 18 Cardigan Rd, Headingley ☎783222 9hc (2fb) ✍ CTV 6P 🕮 ✳B&b£7 Bdi£10 D10am

LEE-ON-THE-SOLENT Hants *Map 4 SU50*
GH Ash House Private Hotel 35 Marine Parade West ☎550240 6hc CTV 6P 🕮 sea S% B&b£6–£7

LEICESTER Leics *Map 4 SK50*
GH *Alexandra Hotel* 342 London Rd, Stoneygate ☎703056 Lic 25hc CTV 25P 🕮 D4.30pm

GH Daval Hotel 292 London Rd ☎708234 Closed Xmas wk Lic 13hc 1🛏🍴 (3fb) ✍ nc2 CTV 2OP 🕮 ✳B&b£9.50 Bdi£13.50 D7.30pm

GH Old Rectory Main St, Glenfield (3m W A50) ☎312214 14hc (3fb) nc3 CTV 30P 🕮 S% ✳B&bfr£8.05 Bdifr£11.50 D4pm

LELANT Cornwall *Map 2 SW53*
GH Ar-Lyn Private Hotel Vicarage Ln ☎Hayle 753330 Lic 11hc 2🛏🍴 (4fb) CTV 12P 🕮 sea S% B&b£6.50–£8.25 Bdi£10–£12 W£70–£84 ⚓ (W only Jul–Aug) D6.30pm

LERWICK Shetland *Map 16 HU44*
GH Carradale 36 King Harald St ☎2890 Closed Xmas & New Year 3hc (2fb) CTV 6P 🕮 S% ✳✳B&b£7 Bdi£11.50 D7.30pm

GH Glen Orchy Lee Knab Rd ☎2031 6hc (1fb) ✍ CTV sea S% B&b£7–£9 W£42 M

GH Solheim ☎3613 3hc (1fb) CTV S%
B&bfr£7 Bdifr£10.50 D7.30pm

LESLIE Fife *Map 11 NO20*
GH *Rescobie* ☎Glenrothes 742143 Lic
8hc 3⇨創 10P ㎜ D7.30pm

LEVISHAM N Yorks *Map 8 SE89*
GH *Moorlands* ☎Pickering 60247
Etr–Oct 5hc CTV 6P 1â D6.30pm

LEWIS, ISLE OF Western Isles
Ross & Cromarty Map 13
See Stornoway

LEYBURN N Yorks *Map 7 SE19*
GH Eastfield Lodge St Matthews Ter
☎Wensleydale 23196 Apr–Nov Lic 8hc
(2fb) CTV 10P ㎜ S% ✱B&bfr£6 Wfr£39
⚡D8.30pm

LEYSMILL Tayside *Angus Map 15 NO64*
GH Spynie ☎Friockheim 328 Closed Oct
Lic 5hc (2fb) TV 6P ㎜ S% B&b fr£6.90
Bdi fr£9.50 Wfr£60 ⚡D10pm

LICHFIELD Staffs *Map 7 SK10*
GH Oakleigh 25 St Chads Rd ☎22688
4hc (A 2hc) (2fb) CTV 20P ㎜ S%
B&bf£6.33–£9.20 Bdif£9.58–£12.65
D5.30pm

INN Old Crown Hotel Bore St ☎22879
7hc 10P 2â S% B&bf£9 Bar lunchf£1

LIFTON Devon *Map 2 SX38*
GH Mayfield House Hotel Tinhay ☎401
Lic 7rm 6hc (2fb) CTV 10P 2â lake
✱B&bfr£5 Bdifr£7

LINCOLN Lincs *Map 8 SK97*
GH Brierley House Hotel 54 South Pk
☎26945 Lic 7hc (1fb) CTV 8P ㎜
B&bf£8.63–£9.20 Bdif£12.36–£13.22
D6pm

GH D'Isney Place Hotel Eastgate
☎38629 12⇨創 (2fb) CTV 12P ㎜
B&bf£13.80–£20.70

LISKEARD Cornwall *Map 2 SX26*
GH *Hotel Nebula* 27 Higher Lux St
☎43989 Lic 10hc CTV 20P D5pm

LITTLEHAM Devon *Map 2 SS42*
INN Crealock Arms Shutta Farm
☎Bideford 2791 3hc ⌀ CTV 30P ⇔ S%
B&bfr£6 Bdifr£9

LITTLEHAMPTON W Sussex
Map 4 TQ00
GH Arun Hotel 42–44 New Rd ☎21206
Lic 10hc (4fb) ⌀ CTV 8P 2â ㎜ S%
B&bf£7.50 Bdif£10–£12 Wf£55–£63 ⚡
D5.30pm

GH *Braemar Private Hotel* Sea Front
☎5487 8hc CTV river

GH Burbridge Hotel 93 South Ter
☎21606 Lic 6hc (4fb) ⌀ nc4 CTV ㎜ S%
B&bf£8–£12 Bdif£12–£16 Wf£76–£90 ⚡
Dnoon

GH Harley House Hotel St Catherines Rd
☎5851 Lic 7hc (5fb) ⌀ CTV 4P ㎜ S%
B&bf£6.50–£7.50 Bdif£9.50–£11.50
Wf£66.50–£80.50 ⚡

GH Regency Hotel 85 South Ter
☎7707 Closed Xmas Lic 8hc (3fb) CTV
㎜ sea S% ✱B&bf£7 Bdif£10.50 Wf£57.50
⚡D4pm

GH The Rowers Hotel 42 South Ter

122

☎3940 Lic 9hc (2fb) CTV 3P 1â sea S%
✱B&b6.50 Bdif£9.50 Wf£59 ⚡D8pm

LITTLE HAVEN Dyfed *Map 2 SM81*
GH Pendyffryn Private Hotel
☎ Broad Haven 337 Apr–Oct Lic 7hc
(6fb) ⌀ nc4 CTV 6P ㎜ sea S%
✱B&b£5.75–£6.33 Bdif£9.78–£10.35
Wf£62.15 ⚡ (W only Jul–Aug) D5pm

LIZARD Cornwall *Map 2 SW71*
GH *Kynance Bay Hotel* ☎ The Lizard
290498 9hc CTV 9P sea D6.30pm

GH Mounts Bay Hotel Penmenner Rd
☎ The Lizard 290305 Mar–Nov Lic 10hc
(4fb) ⌀ CTV 10P sea S% ✱Bdif£10.35
Wf£66.70 ⚡ (W only Jul–Aug)

GH Parc Brawse House ☎ The Lizard
290446 Mar–Oct Lic 6hc nc7 TV 6P sea
B&bf£7.50–£8.50 Bdif£10–£11 Wf£67–£73
⚡D7pm

GH Penmenner House Private Hotel
Penmenner Rd ☎290370 Apr–Oct Lic
8hc (2fb) ⌀ CTV 12P ⌀ sea S% B&bfr£7
Bdi fr£9 Wfr£63 ⚡D6pm

LLANARTHNEY Dyfed *Map 2 SN52*
INN Golden Grove Arms Hotel
☎ Dryslwyn 551 Mar–Jan Lic 6hc 100P
㎜ S% B&bf£8 Bdif£12 Bar lunch
£1.50–£5 D10pmf£4–£5&alc

LLANBEDROG Gwynned *Map 6 SH33*
GH *Glyn Garth Hotel* ☎268
Etr–Oct rs Nov–Mar Lic 10hc 3⇨創 ⌀
CTV 20P D9.30pm

LLANBERIS Gwynedd *Map 6 SH56*
GH Lake View Tan-y-Pant (1m W A4086)
☎422 Lic 7hc (2fb) CTV 7P ㎜ S%
B&bf£6.61–£6.90 D9pm

LLANDDERFEL Gwynedd *Map 6 SH93*
INN *Bryntirion Hotel* ☎205 Lic 4hc
⌀ nc8 CTV 50P ㎜ river D10pm

LLANDOGO Gwent *Map 3 SO50*
GH Browns Hotel & Restaurant
☎ Dean 530262 Jan–Nov Lic 8hc
(A 3rm 2hc) 30P river S% B&bf£7–£7.50
D8pm

GH Craiglas ☎ Dean 530348
Mar–Oct 5hc (3fb) ⌀ TV 20P ㎜
B&bf£5–£5.50 Wf£32.50–£35.75 Ⓜ

LLANDOVERY Dyfed *Map 3 SN73*
GH Dyfri Hotel Market Sq ☎20297
13hc 1⇨創 (2fb) TV 10P ㎜ S% B&bf£7.50
GH Llwyncelyn ☎20566 6hc (3fb) ⌀
CTV 12P ㎜ S% B&bf£7.15–£8.30
Bdif£12.15–£13.30 Wf£80–£87 ⚡ D7.30pm

LLANDRINDOD WELLS Powys
Map 3 SO06
GH Griffin Lodge Hotel Temple St
☎2432 Lic 11hc (2fb) CTV 8P ㎜ S%
B&bf£8.50–£10 Bdif£13–£15 Wf£85–£100
⚡ D8pm

LLANDUDNO Gwynedd *Map 6 SH78*
See Plan
GH Bella Vista Private Hotel 72 Church
Walks ☎76855 Plan:**1** (mid Jan–mid Dec)
Lic 12hc (9fb) CTV 12P ㎜ sea S%
B&bf£6.90 Bdif£8.62 Wf£60.34 ⚡D5.30pm

GH Braemar Hotel 5 St David's Rd
☎76257 Plan:**2** rs Nov–Etr (B&b only)
6hc (4fb) CTV S% ✱B&bf£4.75 Bdif£6.25
Wf£42 ⚡D4pm

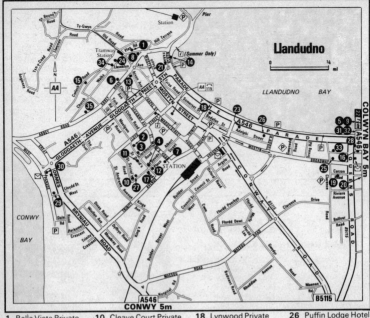

1	Bella Vista Private Hotel	10	Cleave Court Private Hotel
2	Braemar Hotel	11	Cliffbury Private Hotel
3	Brannock Private Hotel	12	Cornerways Private Hotel
4	Brigstock Private Hotel	13	Craig Ard Private Hotel
5	Britannia Hotel	14	Cumberland Private Hotel
6	Bryn Rosa	15	Cwlach Private Hotel
7	Buile Hill Private Hotel	16	Grafton Hotel
8	Capri Hotel	17	Heatherdale
9	Carmel Private Hotel		
18	Lynwood Private Hotel	26	Puffin Lodge Hotel
19	Mayfield Private Hotel	27	Rosaire Private Hotel
20	Minion Private Hotel	28	St Hilary Hotel
21	Montclare Hotel	29	Sandilands Private Hotel
22	Orotava Private Hotel	30	Sandringham Hotel
23	Penelope Private Hotel	31	Sun Ray Private Hotel
24	Plas Madoc Private Hotel	32	Tilstone Private Hotel
25	Prion Hotel	33	Victoria House
		34	Warwick Hotel
		35	Westdale Private Hotel

GH Brannock Private Hotel 36 St David's Rd ☎77483 Plan **3** Mar–Nov Lic 8hc (2fb) ⌧ nc6 CTV 5P 🚿 S% B&b£6.50–£7.50 Bdi£10.20–£10.75 W£71.75 ⌧

GH Brigstock Private Hotel 1 St David's Pl ☎76416 Plan **4** Mar–Nov rs Jan–Feb Lic 10hc 1⌧🛏(3fb) CTV 7P S% B&b£6.98–£8.05 Bdi£10.35–£10.93 W£65.55–£72.45 ⌧ D6pm

⋈GH Britannia Hotel 15 Craig-y-Don Pde ☎77185 Plan **5** 9hc (7fb) CTV sea S% B&b£5.25–£5.95 Bdi£7.75–£8.50 W£54.50–£59.50 ⌧

⋈GH Bryn Rosa 16 Abbey Rd ☎78215 Plan **6** Closed 2wks Oct 8hc (3fb) nc2 CTV 4P 🚿 sea S% B&b£4.75–£5.25 Bdi£6.25–£7 W£45–£49 ⌧ D6pm

GH Buile Hill Private Hotel St Mary's Rd ☎76972 Plan **7** Etr–Oct Lic 15hc 4⌧🛏 (1fb) ⌧ nc5 CTV 6P 🚿 B&bfr£8.60 Bdifr£14.42 Wfr£79 ⌧ D6.30pm

GH Capri Hotel 70 Church Walks ☎79177 Plan **8** Lic 10hc (7fb) CTV ✳B&bfr£5 Bdifr£7 D6pm

⋈GH Carmel Private Hotel 17 Craig-y-Don Pde, Promenade ☎77643 Plan **9** Etr–mid Oct 10hc 2⌧🛏(4fb) nc4 8P sea S% B&b£5.75–£6.75 Bdi£7.25–£8.75 D6.30pm

GH Cleave Court Private Hotel 1 St Seirol's Rd ☎77849 Plan **10** May–Oct 9hc (4fb) nc2 TV 9P sea S% B&b£6–£7 Bdi£7–£8 W£48–£55 ⌧

⋈GH Cliffbury Private Hotel 34 St David's Rd ☎77224 Plan **11** Etr–Oct 7hc (2fb) ⌧ nc6 CTV 4P sea S% B&b£5–£5.25 Bdi£6–£6.50 W£42–£42.50 ⌧ D5pm

GH Cornerways Private Hotel 2 St David's Pl ☎77334 Plan **12** Mar–Oct 7hc (4fb) nc5 CTV 6P 🚿 D4pm

GH Craig Ard Private Hotel Arvon Av ☎77318 Plan **13** Mar–Oct Lic 18hc CTV 11P D6pm

GH Cumberland Hotel North Pde ☎76379 Plan **14** Lic 18hc (9fb) ⌧ CTV 4P 🚿 sea S% B&b£7.50–£9 Bdi£8.50–£10 W£59.50–£70 ⌧ D6pm

⋈GH Cwlach Private Hotel Cwlach Rd ☎75587 Plan **15** Lic 9hc (4fb) ⌧ TV sea S% B&b£5.75–£8.25 Bdi£7.75–£10.25 W£49–£66.50 ⌧ D6pm

GH Grafton Hotel 13 Craig-y-Don Pde ☎76814 Plan **16** Apr–Oct Lic 21hc (6fb) CTV 14P 🚿 sea B&bfr£6.50 Bdifr£9.50 Wfr£60 ⌧ D6pm

Buile Hill Hotel

St Mary's Road, Llandudno
Tel: (0492) 76972

Well situated, detached and in own grounds. Only minutes' walk from two shores, rail and coach stations. First class service and every modern comfort. Lounge with colour TV, large dining room with separate tables. Good, wholesome food and varied menus. All bedrooms have every modern convenience. Hotel is open throughout the day with access to all rooms. Car park. We cater for bed, breakfast and dinner or just bed and breakfast.
Central Heating. Fire certificate.
Brochure on request — Joan and Tony Flint.

CORNERWAYS HOTEL

2 St David's Place, Llandudno
Telephone: (0492) 77334

Family-run 11-bedroomed hotel.
Centrally situated.
Close to the railway station.
Car park.
AA-listed.
Proprietors: Mr. & Mrs. D. Sedgwick.

Cumberland Hotel

North Promenade, Llandudno
Telephone (0492) 76379
Residential Licence

* Ideally situated overlooking Llandudno's beautiful bay
* Full fire Certificate
* Central heating throughout
* Colour TV Lounge
* Reduced terms for children sharing parents' bedroom
* Coach and private parties catered for at reduced terms during early & late season
* Ideal for all conference delegates

Send SAE for brochure & terms to:
Resident Proprietors Mr & Mrs J E Penrose-Williams

ROSAIRE PRIVATE HOTEL

2 St Seiriols Road, Llandudno, Gwynedd LL30 2YY
Tel: (0492) 77677 Proprietors: Mr and Mrs A Ross

* Excellent cuisine served in a pleasant dining room * Separate tables * Spacious lounge for your relaxation. Colour/B & W TV * Many single rooms available * Access to bedrooms and lounge at all times * Wall-to-wall carpeting throughout the hotel * Free private car park in own grounds * All bedrooms have H & C water, shaver sockets and lights, spring interior mattresses, infra-red fires * Full fire certificate * Modern decor and utmost cleanliness.

Situated in Llandudno's loveliest, select garden areas, yet convenient for both shores, entertainments and shops.
SAE for further details.

OPEN ALL YEAR

GH *Heatherdale* 30 St David's Rd
☎77362 Plan:**17** Mar–Oct 6hc CTV
D6pm

GH Lynwood Private Hotel Clonmel St
☎76613 Plan:**18** Closed Xmas Lic 12hc
(3fb) ⊘ CTV sea S% B&b£6.50–£9
Bdi£7.40–£10.50 W£51.80–£73.50 ⫽
D6pm

GH Mayfield Private Hotel 19 Curzon Rd
Craig-y-Don ☎77427 Plan:**19** Etr–Oct
8hc (5fb) CTV S% B&b£6 Bdi£8 Wfr£45
⫽ (W only end May–Aug)

⊷GH Minion Private Hotel 21–23
Carmen Sylva Rd, Craig-y-Don ☎77740
Plan:**20** Etr & 10 May–3 Oct Lic 14hc
(4fb) CTV 7P S% B&b£5.75–£6.32
Bdi£6.90–£8.05 D5pm

GH Montclare Hotel 4 North Pde
☎77061 Plan:**21** mid Mar–Oct Lic 16hc
(5fb) ⊘ CTV 4P sea ✳B&b£5–£7.18
Bdi£8–£10.05 D4.45pm

GH Orotava Private Hotel
105 Glan-y-Mor Rd, Penrhyn Bay ☎49780
Plan:**22** Etr–Oct 6hc (1fb) ⊘ nc5 CTV 6P
sea S% B&b£7 Bdi£10.25 W£71.75 ⫽
D6.30pm

GH Penelope Private Hotel Central Prom
☎76577 Plan:**23** Apr–Oct rs Nov–Mar
(advance bookings only) 12hc (9fb) ⊘
CTV 10P sea B&b£6.50–£7.50
Bdi£9.25–£11 W£62–£75 ⫽ (W only mid
Jun–mid Aug) D4pm

⊷GH Plas Madoc Private Hotel
60 Church Walks ☎76514 Plan:**24** Lic
8hc (3fb) ⊘ nc5 CTV 5P sea S% ✳B&b£6
Bdi£8 W£56 ⫽ D5pm

GH Prion Hotel 8 Mostyn Av,
Craig-y-Don ☎75050 Plan:**25** Mar–Oct

9hc (4fb) CTV 🕮 S% ✳B&b£4.25–£4.50
Bdi£6–£6.25 D6pm

GH Puffin Lodge Hotel ☎77713 Plan:**26**
Mar–Nov Lic 14hc (9fb) ⊘ CTV 15P sea S%
B&b£7–£8 Bdi£10–£11 W£65–£72 Ⓜ
D5pm

GH Rosaire Private Hotel 2 St Seiriol's Rd
☎77677 Plan:**27** 12hc (2fb) ⊘ nc5 CTV
7P 1🖾 S% B&b£5.90–£6.90
Bdi£8.10–£8.90 W£56–£60.50 ⫽ D6pm

⊷GH St Hilary Hotel Promenade
Craig-y-Don ☎75551 Plan:**28** Mar–Nov
11hc (6fb) CTV sea S% B&b£5.50–£5.75
W£38.50–£40.25 Ⓜ

GH Sandilands Private Hotel Dale Rd,
West Shore ☎75555 Plan:**29** Etr–Sept
rs Sept–Etr Lic 11hc (5fb) 11P 🕮 sea
B&b£6.50–£6.80 Bdi£9.45–£9.90
W£61.12–£64 ⫽ D5pm

GH Sandringham Hotel West Pde
☎76513 Plan:**30** Closed Jan Lic 18hc
3⊸🖾 (4fb) ⊘ CTV 8P 🕮 B&b£8–£10
Bdi£10.50–£12 W£84–£94 Ⓜ D7pm

GH Sun Ray Private Hotel 13 Carmen
Sylva Rd, Craig-y-don ☎77828 Plan:**31**
Lic 9hc (2fb) ⊘ nc5 CTV S%
B&b£6.25–£6.75 Bdi£8.50–£8.75
Wfr£58 ⫽ D5pm

GH Tilstone Private Hotel Carmen Sylva
Rd, Craig-y-Don ☎75588 Plan:**32** Lic
7hc (1fb) ⊘ nc5 CTV 🕮 S% ✳B&b£5.95
Bdi£7.95 W£55.65 ⫽ D5.30pm

GH Victoria House 4–5 Victoria St
☎79920 Plan:**33** 9hc (3fb) ⊘ CTV 3P
B&b£4.62–£5.75 Bdi£6.35–£7.48
W£44.70–£55.88 D7pm

GH Warwick Hotel 56 Church Walks
☎76823 Plan:**34** Etr–Oct Lic 17hc (9fb)

♨ CTV sea B&b£6.90–£7.48
Bdi£9.20–£9.78 W£62.10–£65.55 ⅃
D6.30pm

GH Westdale Private Hotel 37 Abbey Rd
☎77996 Plan:**35** Etr–Oct Lic 12hc (4fb) ⌀
nc5 CTV 7P sea S% B&b£6.50–£6.75
Bdi£8.25–£8.50 W£57–£58.50 ⅃ D6pm

LLANELLI Dyfed *Map 2 SN50*
GH Croft 89 Queen Victoria Rd ☎4539
Closed Etr & Xmas Lic 18hc (4fb) ⌀ CTV
20P 卿 S% B&b£8.40 Bdi£12.60 D6pm

LLANFAIRFECHAN Gwynedd
Map 6 SH67
GH Plas Menai Hotel Penmaenmawr Rd
☎680346 Mar Oct & Xmas Tem 29hc
2⊐卿 (7fb) ⌀ TV 12P S% Bdi£8–£11
W£56–£77 ⅃ (W only Aug) D am

⊢⊣**GH Queens House** ☎680509 8rm
7hc (3fb) ♨ CTV 20P S% B&b£4.50–£4.95

GH Rhiwiau Riding Centre Gorddinog
☎680094 Lic 3hc (A 4hc) (1fb) ⌀ CTV
12P sea S% B&b£7.50 Bdi£10 W£75

LLANGATTOCK Powys *Map 2 SO21*
GH *Park Place* The Legar ☎Crickhowell
810562 7hc ⌀ TV 8P 卿

LLANGORSE Powys *Map 3 SO12*
INN Red Lion Hotel ☎238 Lic 10⊐卿 ⌀
CTV 30P 2⋒ 卿 S% B&b£9.50–£10.50
Bdi£13–£15 D9.45pm

LLANSANTFFRAID YM MECHAIN
Powys *Map 7 SJ22*
GH *Bryn Tanat Hall Hotel* ☎Llansantffraid
259 mid May–Sep Lic 12hc ⌀ CTV 12P
2⋒ river D7pm

LLANYSTUMDWY Gwynedd
Map 6 SH43
⊢⊣**GH Gwyndy** ☎Criccieth 2720 Etr–Oct
Lic 6hc CTV 20P 卿 river B&b£6 Bdi£9
W£40 Ⓜ D8.30pm

LLWYNGWRIL Gwynedd *Map 6 SH50*
GH Gwelfor ☎Fairbourne 250343
Etr–Sep Lic 5hc (2fb) ⌀ nc4 CTV 8P 卿 sea
S% ✳B&b£5.50–£6.50 Bdi£8.50–£9.50
W£52 ⅃ D6pm

LOCHINVER Highland *Sutherland*
Map 14 NC02
⊢⊣**GH Ardglas** ☎257 8hc (3fb) CTV 20P
卿 sea S% B&b£5–£6

GH Hillcrest Badnaban (2m S on unclass
rd) ☎391 4hc ⌀ CTV 4P 卿 sea S%
✳B&b£5–£6 Bdi£9 W£63 ⅃ D7pm

GH Park House Hotel Main St ☎259 Lic
4hc CTV 15P 卿 river S% B&b£8–£10
D8pm

LOCHRANZA Isle of Arran, Strathclyde
Bute Map 10 NR95
GH Kincardine Lodge ☎267 Apr–Oct 8hc
(4fb) 6P sea S% B&b£8.62 Bdi£12.65
W£86.25 ⅃ D7pm

LOCKERBIE Dumfries & Galloway
Dumfriesshire Map 11 NY18
GH Rosehill Carlise Rd ☎2378 6hc
(3fb) CTV 4P 卿 S% ✳B&b£5

LONDON Greater London **See plans 1–4**
Small scale maps on atlas pages **4** & **5**
**A map of the London postal area
appears on pages 268 & 269**
Places within the London postal area are

listed below in postal district order commencing North, then South and West, with a brief indication of the area covered. Detailed plans **1–3** show the locations of AA-listed hotels within the Central London postal districts which are indicated by a number. Plan **4** highlights the districts covered within the outer area keyed by a grid reference eg A3. **Other places within the county of London are listed under their respective place names and are also keyed to this plan or the main map section**

N4 Finsbury Park *London plan 4 B4*
Redland Hotel 418 Seven Sisters Rd
☎01-800 1826 24rm 23hc (5fb) ✷ nc2
CTV 10P B&b£8–£9

N8 Hornsey *London plan 4 A4*
Aber Hotel 89 Crouch Hill ☎01-340 2847
9rm 8hc (4fb) ✷ TV ⏣ S% B&b£6.90

Highgate Lodge Hotel 9 Waverley Rd
☎01-340 5601 19hc 2⇦🛏 (2fb) CTV 5P
S% ✱B&b£7.62 W£44.08 Ⓜ

N10 Muswell Hill *London plan 4 A4*
Princes Hotel 36–38 Princes Av
☎01-883 5676 12hc (A 8hc) (4fb) ✷ TV
4P ⏣ S% B&b£5.75–£6.61
W£35.65–£40.25

N15 Tottenham *London plan 4 A5*
Granham House 97 Philip Ln
☎01-801 2244 Lic 15hc CTV 12P ⏣ S%
✱B&b£10.99–£15.53 D10.30pm

NW2 Cricklewood *London plan 4 B3*
Clearview House 161 Fordwych Rd
☎01-452 9773 Tem 7hc (1fb) ✷ CTV ⏣
S% B&b£5

GH Garth Hotel 72–76 Hendon Way
☎01-455 4742 Lic 36hc 23⇦🛏 (A 5hc)
(14fb) ✷ CTV 30P ⏣ S%
✱B&b£10–£16.95 D8pm

NW3 Hampstead and Swiss Cottage
London plan 4 B4
Langorf Hotel 20 Frognal ☎01-794 4483
32hc (2fb) CTV ⏣ S% B&b£8–£9

NW6 Kilburn, West Hampstead
London plan 4 B4
Dawson House Hotel 72 Canfield Gdns
☎01-624 0079 15hc ✷ nc7 CTV ⏣ S%
B&b£7–£8 W£47 Ⓜ (W only winter)

Hazlewood House Hotel 109 Broadhurst
Gdns ☎01-624 8443 13hc (4fb) nc3 TV ⏣
S% B&b£8.50–£9.50 W£30 Ⓜ (W only
Nov–Apr B&b only)

Mowbray House Hotel 5 Mowbray Rd
☎01-459 4481 10hc (7fb) CTV ⏣ S%
B&bfr£7.50

Mulroy 4–6 Burton Rd ☎01-624 0727
11hc (9fb) ✷ CTV 6P ⏣ & S% B&b£6–£7

NW11 Golders Green *London plan 4 A3*
Central Hotel 35–Hoop Ln
☎01-458 5636 18hc 3⇦🛏 (A 18hc
15⇦🛏) (4fb) ✷ CTV 10P ⏣ S%
B&b£12–£14 D6pm

Croft Court Hotel 44 Ravenscroft Ave
☎01-458 3331 20hc 5⇦🛏 (4fb) CTV 4P
⏣ S% B&b£11.50–£13.50
Bdi£15.50–£17.50 W£108.50–£115.50
Ⱡ D6pm

Ridgeway House Hotel 59 The Ridgeway
☎01-458 4146 6hc ✷ nc6 CTV 6P ⏣ S%
B&b£7–£8

SE3 Blackheath *London plan 4 C5*
Stonehall House Hotel 37 Westcombe
Park Rd ☎01-858 8706 23hc (A 2hc) CTV
🎱 S% B&bf8.05 Wf48.30 Ⓜ D7pm

SE9 Eltham *London plan 4 D6*
Yardley Court 18 Court Yard
☎01-850 1850 6hc 1⇦🛏 (2fb) ⊗ nc3
CTV 8P S% B&bf8.95

SE19 Norwood *London plan 4 D4*
Crystal Palace Tower Hotel 114 Church
Rd ☎01-653 0176 13hc ⊗ CTV 12P 🎱

SE25 South Norwood *London plan 4 D4*
Toscana 19 South Norwood Hill
☎01-653 3962 Lic 8hc ⊗ CTV 8P 🎱 S%
B&bf7.50–f9 Wf54 Ⓜ

SW1 West End–Westminster;
St James's Park, Victoria Station
Arden House 12 St Georges Dr
☎01-834 2988 Plan3**:1** 34hc 5⇦🛏
(A 14hc) (10fb) ⊗ CTV 🎱 S% B&bf9–f10

Beverley Towers Hotel 106–108 Belgrave
Rd ☎01-828 6767 Plan3**:2** Lic 53hc CTV
🎱 D9.30pm

Chesham House 64–66 Ebury St,
Belgravia ☎01-730 8513 Plan2**:3** Closed
Xmas 23hc (3fb) ⊗ CTV 🎱 S% B&bf9–f10

Chester House Hotel 134 Ebury St,
Belgravia ☎01-730 3632 Plan2**:2** 12hc
8⇦🛏 ⊗ CTV 🎱

Corbigoe Hotel 101 Belgrave Rd, Victoria
☎01-828 6873 Plan3**:5** 17hc 1⇦🛏 (6fb)
⊗ CTV 🎱 S% B&bf6–f9

Corona Hotel 87–89 Belgrave Rd, Victoria
☎01-828 9279 Plan3**:6** Closed Xmas Lic

32hc 14⇦🛏 (6fb) ⊗ CTV 🎱 S%
B&bf9–f12.50

Easton Hotel 36–40 Belgrave Rd, Victoria
☎01-834 5938 Plan3**:7** Lic 42hc 2⇦🛏
(A 12hc) (13fb) ⊗ CTV 🎱 S%
B&bf10–f11

Elizabeth Hotel 37 Eccleston Sq, Victoria
☎01-828 6812 Plan3**:8** 24hc 3⇦🛏 (6fb)
⊗ CTV 🎱 S% B&bf8–f16

Franterre Hotel 142 Warwick Way,
Victoria ☎01-834 5163 Plan3**:3** 8hc
4⇦🛏 (4fb) CTV 🎱 S% B&bf8.50 Wf40 Ⓜ
(W only Jan–Feb)

Hanover Hotel 30–32 St Georges Dr
☎01-834 0134 Plan3**:9** 34hc 10⇦🛏
CTV 🎱

Holly House 20 Hugh St ☎01-834 5671
Plan3**:10** 11hc (3fb) ⊗ 🎱 S% B&bf9–f10
W only Nov–Apr

Willet Hotel 32 Sloane Gdns, Sloane Sq
☎01-730 0634 Plan2**:12** 17hc 15⇦🛏
(9fb) ⊗ TV 🎱 B&bf10–f12.50

SW3 Chelsea
Blair House Hotel 34 Draycott Pl
☎01-581 2323 Plan2**:5** 17hc 10⇦🛏
(4fb) ⊗ CTV 🎱 S% ✱B&bf14.95 (W only
Nov–Mar)

Campden Court Hotel 28 Basil St
☎01-589 6286 Plan2**:7** 18hc 9⇦🛏 (1fb)
⊗ CTV 🎱 lift ✱B&bf13.38–f16.05

Culford Hall Hotel 7 Culford Gdns
☎01-581 2211 Plan2**:9** 29hc 12⇦🛏
(4fb) TV 🎱 S% B&bf9.78–f11.50

Eden House Hotel 111 Old Church St
☎01-352 3403 Plan2**:10** 14hc 6⇦🛏
(4fb) CTV 🎱 S% B&bf8.66–f13.80

Garden House Hotel 44–46 Egerton Gdns ☎01-584 2990 Plan2:**11** 30hc 10⇆⋔ (5fb) ⊗ ⋔ lift B&b£9–£13.50

Rutland Court Hotel 21–23 Draycott Pl ☎01-589 9691 Plan2:**21** 30hc 11⇆⋔ ⊗ nc8 CTV ⋔ lift

SW4 Clapham *London plan 4 D4*
Edwards 91 Abbeville Rd, Clapham Common ☎01-622 6347 8hc (3fb) ⊗ nc5 S% B&b£4.50–£7 W£30–£40 M

Regency Lodge Hotel 5 Crescent Gv, South Side, Clapham Common ☎01-622 2684 Lic 30hc nc4 CTV 6P ⋔ D7.30pm

SW5 Earls Court *London plan 4 C3*
Arlanda Hotel 17 Longridge Rd ☎01-370 5220 15hc 2⇆⋔ (3fb) ⊗ nc14 CTV ⋔ S% B&b£9–£11.50 W£45.50–£52.50 M

Burns Hotel 18–24 Barkston Gdns ☎01-373 3151 Plan2:**6** Lic 104hc (A 20hc) CTV lift ⋔ D9.45pm

Kensington Court Hotel 33–35 Nevern Pl ☎01-370 5151 Lic 35⇆⋔ (19fb) ⊗ CTV 10P 2🏠 ⋔ lift S% ✱B&b£14.50–£15 W£78 M

Manor Court Hotel 35 Courtfield Gdns ☎01-373 8585 Plan2:**14** Lic 88rm 20hc 53⇆⋔ (15fb) CTV ⋔ lift S% B&b£8.50–£11.50 Bdi£10.50 (W only mid Oct–mid Mar)

Merlyn Court Hotel 2 Barkston Gdns ☎01-370 1640 Plan2:**15** 18hc 2⇆⋔ (4fb) ⊗ CTV ⋔ S% B&b£7–£9

Nevern Hotel 29–31 Nevern Pl ☎01-370 4827 Lic 32hc 9⇆⋔ (11fb) ⊗ CTV ⋔ lift S% B&b£7.59–£11.96 (W only Nov–Feb)

SW6 Fulham *London plan 4 C3*
Seagrave Lodge Hotel 21–27 Seagrave Rd ☎01-385 7771 31⇆⋔ (31fb) ⊗ CTV 10🏠 ⋔ lift S% B&b£9–£16

SW7 South Kensington
Adelphi Hotel 127–129 Cromwell Rd ☎01-373 7177 Plan2:**1** Lic 57hc 54⇆⋔ (14fb) ⊗ CTV ⋔ lift S% B&b£14.90–£18.90

Ashburn Hotel 111 Cromwell Rd ☎01-370 3321 Plan2:**4** Lic 44rm 40⇆⋔ ⊗ CTV 50🏠 ⋔ lift

Hotel Lindsay 12 Ashburn Gdns ☎01-370 5294 Plan2:**13** 22hc (6fb) ⊗ CTV ⋔ ✱B&b£7.20–£11.50 W£50.40–£74.55 M

Milton Court Hotel 68–74 Cromwell Rd ☎01-584 7851 Plan2:**16** 105hc 17⇆⋔ CTV ⋔ lift

Queensberry Court Hotel 7–11 Queensberry Pl ☎01-589 3693 Plan2:**20** Lic 43hc 21⇆⋔ (4fb) CTV ⋔ lift S% B&b£15.50–£19.50

Tudor Court Hotel 58–66 Cromwell Rd ☎01-584 8273 Plan2:**24** 83hc 42⇆⋔ (9fb) CTV ⋔ lift S% B&b£11.65–£19

SW13 Barnes *London plan 4 C3*
Arundel Hotel Arundel Ter ☎01-748 8005 30hc 6⇆⋔ (4fb) CTV ⋔ S% B&b£6.25–£11.50 W£27.50–£43.50 M

SW15 Putney *London plan 4 C3*
GH Lodge Hotel 52 Upper Richmond Rd ☎01-874 1598 rs Xmas Lic 30hc 22⇆⋔ (4fb) CTV 14P ⅙ & S% ✱B&b£10–£14 Bdi£12–£16

Wilton House Hotel 2 Ravenna Rd,
☎01-789 3768 10hc nc6 CTV 2P ▦

SW19 Wimbledon *London plan 4 D3*
Hatherley Hotel 87 Worple Rd
☎01-946 5917 9hc (9fb) CTV 6P ▦ S%
B&b£12.75

Trochee 21 Malcolm Rd
☎01-946 1579 17hc (2fb) CTV 8P ▦ S%
B&b£8–£11.50 (W only Oct–Mar)

Wimbledon Hotel 78 Worple Rd
☎01-946 9265 9hc (3fb) CTV 9P ▦ S%
B&b£9.75–£12.50

Worcester House 38 Alwyne Rd
☎01-946 1300 7hc 4⇌🖩 (1fb) ⊘ CTV ▦
S% B&bfr£9–£19

W1 West End, Piccadilly Circus,
St Marylebone and Mayfair *London plan 4*

Concorde Hotel 50 Gt Cumberland Pl
☎01-402 6169 Plan1 **4** Lic 28⇌🖩 CTV ▦
lift S% ✳B&b£20–£27

Eros Hotel 67 Shaftesbury Ave
☎01-734 8781 60rm 37hc 23⇌🖩 (15fb)
⊘ CTV ▦ lift S% B&b£12.25–£15.50

Georgian House Hotel 87 Gloucester Pl,
Baker St ☎01-486 3151 Plan1 **8** Lic
19⇌🖩 (3fb) ⊘ nc5 CTV ▦ lift S%
B&b£10.50–£11.50 (W only Nov–Mar)

Hart House Hotel 51 Gloucester Pl,
Portman Sq ☎01-935 2288 Plan1 **9** 15hc
8⇌🖩 (4fb) ⊘ CTV ▦ S% B&b£8–£12

Milford House 31 York St ☎01-935 1935
8hc 2⇌🖩 (1fb) ⊘ CTV ▦ S% B&b£6–£8
(W only Nov–Mar)

Rose Court Hotel 35 Gt Cumberland Pl
☎01-262 7241 Plan1 **13** Lic 60hc CTV
lift ▦

W2 Bayswater, Paddington *London plan 4*
Ashley Hotel 15 Norfolk Sq, Hyde Park
☎01-723 3375 Plan1 **11** 16hc 2⇔📶
(1fb) ✗ CTV 📶 S% B&bf7.10–£7.20

Britannia Court Hotel 80 Inverness Ter
☎01-727 5918 Plan1 **1** 12hc 5⇔📶 (5fb)
✗ CTV 📶 (W only Oct–Mar)

Caring Hotel 24 Craven Hill Gdns,
Leinster Ter, Hyde Pk. ☎01-262 8708
Plan1 **2** 26hc 18⇔📶 (8fb) ✗ 📶 S%
B&bf10.80

Century Hotel 18–19 Craven Hill Gdns
☎01-262 6644 Plan1 **3** Lic 60hc 60⇔📶
✗ CTV 2P 📶 lift

Dylan Hotel 14 Devonshire Ter
☎01-723 3280 Plan1 **5** 15hc CTV

Edward Hotel 1A Spring St ☎01-262
2671 Plan1 **6** Lic 59hc CTV 12P 📶 lift

D9.30pm

Garden Court Hotel 30–31 Kensington
Gdns Sq ☎01-727 8304 Plan1 **7** Lic
37hc 10⇔📶 (4fb) ✗ CTV 📶 S%

King's Hotel 60–62 Queensborough Ter
☎01-229 7055 Plan1 **10** 29hc CTV 📶

Pembridge Court Hotel 34 Pembridge
Gdns ☎01-229 9977 Lic 35hc 34⇔📶
(2fb) CTV 2🛏 📶 S% B&bf13–£19.50
D11pm

Slavia Hotel 2 Pembridge Sq ☎01-727
1316 Lic 31⇔📶 (8fb) ✗ CTV 2P 📶 lift
B&bf10–£18 (W only Jan–Dec) D7pm

W5 Ealing *London plan 4 B2*
Grange Lodge 50 Grange Rd ☎01-567
1049 Lic 14hc 4⇔📶 (4fb) ✗ CTV 4P 📶
S% B&bfr£6–£8.50 Bdifr£9–£11.50 ⅃
D6.30pm

W8 Kensington *London plan* **4** *C3*
Alexa Hotel 71–75 Lexham Gdns
☎01-373 7272 49hc 6⇌🛏 ⊗ nc3 CTV 🍽
lift

Clearlake Hotel 18–19 Prince of Wales
Ter ☎01-937 3274 Plan2 **8** Lic 20⇌🛏
(6fb) CTV 🍽 lift S% B&bf£6.90–£16.10
(W only Nov–Mar)

Observatory House Hotel Observatory
Gdns ☎01-937 1577 23hc (1fb) ⊗ CTV
🍽 S% B&bf£16–£17 (W only in winter)

Prince's Lodge 6–8 Prince of Wales Ter
☎01-937 6306 Plan2 **19** Lic 36hc 24⇌🛏
(9fb) ⊗ CTV 🍽 lift S% B&bfr£8 Wfr£45 M

Silver Star Hotel 13 Lexham Gdns
☎01-373 9426 Plan2 **22** 20⇌🛏 (3fb)
CTV 🍽 S% B&bf£10–£15

Suncourt Hotel 57–67 Lexham Gdns
☎01-373 7242 Plan2 **23** 111hc 28⇌🛏
(11fb) CTV 🍽 lift S% B&bf£11.65–£19

WC1 Bloomsbury, Holborn *London plan* **4**
Mentone Hotel 54–55 Cartwright Gdns
☎01-387 3927 27hc (10fb) ⊗ CTV 🍽
S% B&bf£6.50–£11 W only Dec–Mar

Mount Pleasant Hotel 53 Calthorpe St
☎01-837 9781 Lic 465hc 60⇌🛏 (10fb)
CTV 🍽 lift S% ✻B&bf£9.60 Bdif£15.10
D10pm

LONGDOWNS Cornwall *Map 2 SW73*
GH Marrack House ☎ Stithians 860231
6rm 5hc CTV 6P S% ✻B&bf£4–£5
Bdif£7–£8 Wf£45–£49 ⚓

LONG EATON Derbys *Map 8 SK43*
GH Camden Hotel 85 Nottingham Rd
☎62901 rs wknds (continental breakfast
only) Lic 7hc (A 9hc) (2fb) CTV 16P 🍽 S%
B&bfr£11.04 Bdifr£14.95 D7.30pm

LONGFRAMLINGTON Northumb
Map 46 NU10
INN Granby ☎228 Lic 2hc 1⇌🛏 ⊗
nc12 TV⚓30P 🍽 D8.30pm

LOOE Cornwall *Map 2 SX25* **See Plan**
GH Annaclone Hotel Marine Dr,
Hannafore ☎4177 Plan:**1** Etr–end Oct
Lic 8hc 2⇌🛏 ⊗ nc12 CTV 2P sea S%
B&b£6–£7.50 Wf£40.25–£50.75 M

GH Deganwy Hotel Station Rd ☎2984
Plan:**2** Mar–Oct Lic 9hc 1⇌🛏 (3fb) ⊗
nc3 CTV 6P river S% B&b£6.90–£9
Bdif£10.93–£13 Wf£59.50–£80.50 ⚓
D5pm

GH Fieldhead Hotel Portuan Rd,

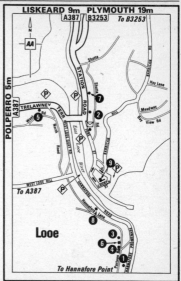

LISKEARD 9m   **PLYMOUTH** 19m

Looe

To Hannafore Point

1	Annaclone Hotel	6	Lemain Hotel
2	Deganwy Hotel	7	Riverside Hotel
3	Fieldhead Hotel	8	Rockwell Hotel
4	Hillingdon	9	Smugglers' House
5	Kantara		Hotel

Hannafore ☎2689 Plan:**3** Mar–Oct Lic 17hc
14⇌🛏 (4fb) ⊗ CTV 7P 5🚗 🍽 sea S%
✻B&b£7–£14 Bdif£11.50–£18.50
Wf£70–£119 ⚓ Dnoon

GH Hillingdon Portuan Rd, Hannafore
☎2906 Plan:**4** Mar–Oct 8hc (3fb) ⊗
CTV 2🚗 🍽 sea D5pm

⊢⊣**GH Kantara** 7 Trelawney Ter ☎2093
Plan:**5** Mar–Oct 6hc (2fb) ⊗ TV S%
B&b£5–£6 Wf£35–£42 M

GH Lemain Hotel Hannafore Ln,
Hannafore ☎2073 Plan:**6** Mar–Oct Lic
9hc (4fb) CTV 14P 🍽 sea S%
B&b£7.95–£11.25 Bdif£11.90–£15.22
Wf£68.10–£90.60 ⚓ D6pm

GH Riverside Hotel Station Rd ☎2100
Plan:**7** Etr–mid Oct Lic 13hc (5fb) ⊗ CTV
river B&b£7.60–£8.95 Bdif£11.75–£13.10
Wf£62.10–£82.80 ⚓ D4pm

GH Rockwell Hotel Hannafore Rd,
Hannafore ☎2123 Plan:**8** Mar–Nov &
Xmas Lic 12hc CTV 9P river sea

GH *Smugglers House Hotel* Middle Market St ☎2397 Plan:**9** Lic 7hc 3⇛⋔ (1fb) ⊗ CTV ⚹B&bf£9.78–£12.08 D10.30pm

LOSTWITHIEL Cornwall *Map 2 SX15*
GH Trevone Hotel ☎872528 Feb–Nov Lic 8hc (2fb) ⊗ CTV 20P 💷 S% B&bf£8.63–£10.93 Bdif£11.50–£13.80 Wf£74.75–£90.85 ⅄ D5pm

LOUGHBOROUGH Leics *Map 8 SK51*
GH De Montfort Hotel 88 Leicester Rd ☎216061 Closed Xmas wk Lic 9hc (1fb) CTV 💷 S% B&bfr£8 Bdifr£11.50 Wfr£70 ⅄ D4pm

GH Sunnyside Hotel The Coneries ☎216217 11hc ⊗ CTV 8P 3⋔ 💷 B&bfr£6.33 Bdifr£9 D6pm

LOUTH Lincs *Map 8 TF38*
INN King's Head ☎602965 rs Xmas (no accommodation) Lic 17hc 1⇛⋔ ⊗ CTV 30P 10⋔ 💷 S% ⚹B&bfr£9.50 Bdifr£13 sn L£1.40–£2.50&alc D10pm£3.50–£5&alc

INN Lincolnshire Poacher 211 Eastgate ☎603657 Lic 5hc ⊗ CTV 20P 💷 S% B&bf£6.90 Wf£48.30 ⋈ sn

LOWESTOFT Suffolk *Map 5 TM59*
⊬GH Amity 396 London Rd South ☎2586 Lic 6hc (4fb) ⊗ CTV 3P 💷 S% B&bf£5–£5.50 Bdif£6.75–£7 Wfrf£46 ⅄ D4pm

⊬GH Cleveland House 9 Cleveland Rd ☎62827 Closed Xmas 6hc (2fb) CTV 1P 💷 S% B&bf£5.50 Bdif£8.50 D6pm

GH *Kingsleigh* 44 Marine Pde ☎2513 Closed Xmas 6hc nc5 CTV 6P

GH Westview House Hotel Lyndhurst Rd ☎64616 Lic 13hc 4⇛⋔ (3fb) CTV 9P 💷 S% B&bf£6.90–£9.20 Bdif£10.35–£13.22 Wf£59.80–£74.75 D6pm

LUCKWELL BRIDGE Somerset *Map 3 SS93*
⊬GH Brook Farm Hotel ☎ Timberscombe 263 Closed Xmas Lic 6hc (2fb) ⊗ ⚖ CTV 6P 💷 S% B&bf£5.50–£6.50 Bdif£8.50–£10 Wf£53.25–£63 ⅄ (W only Aug) D9pm

LUDLOW Salop *Map 7 SO57*
GH Cecil Private Hotel Sheet Rd ☎2442 Lic 11hc (1fb) CTV 9P 💷 S% B&bfr£6.25 Bdifr£9.75 Wfrf£57.45 ⅄ D10am

GH *Croft* Dinham ☎2076 Lic 8hc river D noon

LULWORTH Dorset *Map 3 SY88*
GH Bishop's Cottage Hotel ☎West Lulworth 261 (A 3hc 2⇛⋔) (3fb) CTV 6P B&bf£7–£8 Bdif£12–£13 Wf£75–£85 ⅄ D9.30pm

GH Gatton House Hotel ☎West Lulworth 252 Closed Dec Lic 10hc (2fb) CTV 12P 💷 S% B&bf£6.50–£10 Bdif£10.50–£14 Wf£65–£90 ⅄ D7.30pm

GH *Lulworth Hotel* Main Rd ☎West Lulworth 230 Mar–Oct rs Nov–Feb Lic 12hc ⊗ nc5 CTV 12P

GH Shirley Hotel ☎West Lulworth 358 Mar–Oct rs Nov–Feb (booked parties only) Lic 16hc 7⇛⋔ (4fb) CTV 20P 💷 B&bf£7–£9.25 Bdif£10.25–£13.20 Wf£71.75–£92.40 ⅄

LUTON Beds *Map 4 TL02*
GH Albany House Hotel 9 Marsh Rd

☎591033 Lic 10hc (1fb) ⚭ CTV 12P 🏧 S% ✳B&b£8–£13.51 Bdi£11.50–£18.51 D6.30pm

GH Arlington Hotel 137 New Bedford Rd ☎419614 Lic 17hc (3fb) ⚭ 19P 🏧 S% ✳B&b£9.45 Bdi£14.45 W£85 ⚃ D6.30pm

GH Humberstone Hotel 618 Dunstable Rd ☎54399 10hc 5⇆🗏 (4fb) ⚭ nc9 CTV 11P 🏧 S% B&b£8.63–£9.78

GH Lansdowne Lodge Private Hotel 31 Lansdowne Rd ☎31411 Lic 12hc 2⇆🗏 (4fb) CTV 20P 🏧 S% ✳B&b£10–£16.95 Bdifr£15.95 D7.45pm

LYDFORD Devon *Map 2 SX58*
GH *Moor View* Vale Down ☎220 Apr–Oct 7hc TV 6P 1🏠 D4pm
INN Castle ☎242 Closed Xmas Day Lic 5hc nc5 10P 🏧 ⇌ S% B&b£8 Bar lunch fr 50p D9.30pm fr£2

LYME REGIS Dorset *Map 3 SY39*
⊶**GH Coverdale** Woodmead Rd ☎2882 Etr & May–Sep 9hc (3fb) CTV 11P 🏧 sea S% B&b£5.95–£7.95 Bdi£9–£11 W£54–66 ⚃ D5.15pm

GH *Kent House Hotel* Silver St ☎2020 Lic 10hc CTV 9P 🏧 lift D7pm

GH *Kersbrook Hotel* Pound Rd ☎2596 Apr–Nov 10hc 2⇆🗏 ⚭ CTV 10P sea D6.30pm

GH Old Monmouth Hotel Church St ☎2456 Lic 6hc 1⇆🗏 (2fb) ⚭ CTV sea S% ✳B&b£5–£7 Bdi£8.50–£10.50 W£53–£60 ⚃ D4pm

GH Rotherfield View Rd ☎2811 Apr–Oct 7hc (4fb) nc3 CTV 7P sea S%

B&b£6–£7.25 Bdi£8–£9.25 W£52.50–£63.50 ⚃ D6.50pm

GH White House 47 Silver St ☎3420 Mar–Oct Lic 6hc (4fb) nc3 CTV 🏧 sea S% B&b£6.75–£7.50 Bdi£9.25–£11.25 Wfr£57.50 ⚃ D noon

LYNDHURST Hants *Map 4 SU30*
GH Bench View Southampton Rd ☎2502 Closed Xmas 8rm 7hc (5fb) ⚭ CTV 8P S% B&b£6–£7 Bdi£9.50–£10.50 W£66.50–£73.50 ⚃

GH *Forest Gardens Hotel* 28–30 Romsey Rd ☎2367 Closed Jan Lic 16hc 9⇆🗏 CTV 28P 🏧 ⚃ D10pm

GH Ormonde House Hotel Southampton Rd ☎2806 Lic 17hc 4⇆🗏 ⚭ nc5 CTV P 🏧 D7pm *(see 'ad' on page 186)*

GH *Whitemoor House Hotel* Southampton Rd ☎2186 Lic 5hc ⚬ CTV 8P 🏧 D6pm

LYNMOUTH Devon *Map 3 SS74*
See Plan. See also Lynton
GH Bonnicott Hotel Watersmeet Rd ☎3346 Plan:**1** Mar–Dec Lic 9hc 1⇆🗏 (2fb) CTV sea S% B&b£8–£9 Bdi£12–£13.50 W£69–£80 ⚃ D7pm

GH Countisbury Lodge Hotel Countisbury Hill ☎Lynton 2388 Plan:**5** Feb–Nov Lic 8hc 2⇆🗏 (3fb) nc5 CTV 10P 🏧 river sea S% B&b£7.50–£8.85 Bdi£11.50–£13.30 W£75.90–£87.40 ⚃ W only Jul & Aug D6pm

⊶**GH East Lyn** Watersmeet Rd ☎Lynton 2540 Plan:**6** Mar–Nov rs Feb (limited accommodation) Lic 8hc (3fb) CTV 5P 3🏠 river sea S% B&b£5.75–£8.05 Bdi£8.50–£11 W£64.40–£74.75 ⚃ D4.45pm

1 Alford House (*see under Lynton*)
2 Bonnicott Hotel (*see under Lynmouth*)
3 Channel View (*see under Lynton*)
4 Conway Hotel (*see under Lynton*)
5 Countisbury Lodge (*see under Lynmouth*)
6 East Lyn (*see under Lynmouth*)
7 Gable Lodge Hotel (*see under Lynton*)
8 Glenville Hotel (*see under Lynmouth*)
9 Kingford House Private Hotel (*see under Lynton*)
10 Longmead House (*see under Lynton*)
11 Lyn Crest (*see under Lynton*)
12 Lynhurst (*see under Lynton*)
13 Mayfair Hotel (*see under Lynton*)
14 Neubia House (*see under Lynton*)

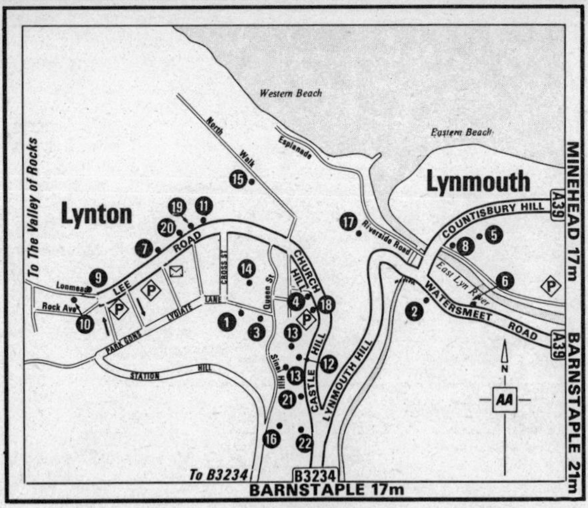

15 North Cliff Private Hotel (*see under Lynton*)
16 Pine Lodge (*see under Lynton*)
17 Rising Sun (*Inn*) (*see under Lynmouth*)
18 St Vincents (*see under Lynton*)
19 South View (*see under Lynton*)
20 Turret (*see under Lynton*)
21 Valley House Hotel (*see under Lynton*)
22 Woodlands Hotel (*see under Lynton*)

GH Glenville Hotel 2 Tors Rd ☎Lynton 2202 Plan:**8** Feb–mid Nov Lic 7hc 1🛁 (1fb) ⊘ nc5 CTV 8P river S% B&b£6.90–£8.05 Bdi£10.35–£11.50 W£69–£74.75 Ⱡ D9.30pm

INN Rising Sun Mars Hill, The Harbour ☎Lynton 3223 Plan:**17** Closed Jan Lic 15hc CTV 15P ⊞ ⊟ B&b£8.50–£9.50 Bdi£13.50–£15 W£87.50 Ⱡ sn L£3.50alc D9pm£5.50alc

LYNTON Devon *Map 3 SS74* **See Plan. See also Lynmouth**

GH Alford House 3 Alford Ter ☎2359 Plan:**1** Etr–mid Oct Lic 8hc (1fb) ⊘ nc5 CTV ⊞ sea S% Bdi£13–£15 W£80–£90 Ⱡ D6pm

GH Channel View 2 Alford Ter ☎3379 Plan:**3** Mar–Oct Lic 7hc ⊘ CTV sea D.645pm

GH Conway Hotel Castle Hill ☎2291 Plan:**4** Mar–Oct Lic 10hc (4fb) ⊘ CTV S% B&b£7–£9 Bdi£11––£13 W£70–£80 Ⱡ D6pm

GH Gable Lodge Hotel Lee Rd ☎2367 Plan:**7** Mar–Oct rs Nov–Feb (wknds only) Lic 9hc 6🛁 (2fb) CTV 4P 5⌂ ⊞ B&b£8–£11 Bdi£13–£16 W£87–£105 Ⱡ D6.30pm

GH Kingford House Private Hotel Longmead ☎2361 Plan:**9** Feb–end Nov Lic 8hc 2🛁 (3fb) ⊘ nc5 CTV 8P S% ✻B&b£5–£7 Bdi£7.50–£10 W£58–£63 Ⱡ D4.30pm

⟷ **GH Longmead House** 9 Longmead ☎2523 Plan:**10** Mar–mid Oct Lic 9hc 2🛁 (1fb) ⊘ nc5 CTV 11P ⊞ S% B&b£5.40–£6 Bdi£8.40–£9 D5pm

⟷ **GH Lyn Crest** Lee Rd ☎3269 Plan:**11** Closed Jan 7hc (1fb) nc5 TV 4P S% B&b£5.50–£6 Bdi£8.50–£9 W£51–£56 Ⱡ D7pm

GH Lynhurst Hotel Lynway ☎2241 Plan:**12** Mar–Oct Lic 7🛁 (1fb) CTV S% B&b£6–£7 Bdi£6.50–£8 W£48–£56 Ⱡ W only Mar–Oct D6pm

GH Mayfair Hotel Lynway ☎3227 Plan:**13** Lic 13hc 1🛁 (3fb) nc2 CTV 12P ⊞ sea S% B&b£7.48–£9.20 Bdi£9.43–£12.65 W£55.20–£77.05 Ⱡ W only Jul & Aug D6.30pm

GH Neubia House Lydiate Ln ☎2309

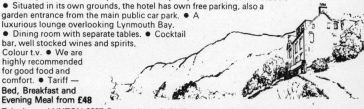

Plan:**14** Closed Nov Lic 12hc 6⇔🅷 (3fb)
CTV 12P 🏵 S% B&b£8.28–£9.11
Bdi£12.42–£14.08 W£82.80–£87.77 ⚓
D7.15pm

GH North Cliff Private Hotel North Walk
☎2357 Plan:**15** Etr–Oct 24hc (5fb) CTV
19P sea S% B&b£8–£9.50
Bdi£11.50–£13.50 W£60.50–£65.50 ⚓
D6.30pm

GH Pine Lodge Lynway ☎3230 Plan:**16**
Etr–Oct 10hc (1fb) nc5 TV 9P S%
B&b£8.05–£9.20 Bdi£10.64–£12.08
W£77.05–£82.80 ⚓

GH St Vincents Castle Hill ☎2244
Plan:**18** Apr–Oct & Dec Lic 6hc (2fb) CTV
5P S% B&b£7–£8 Bdi£10.25–£11.25
W£63 ⚓ D6.30pm

⊢⊣**GH South View** Lee Rd ☎2289

Plan:**19** Feb–Nov 8hc (2fb) ⊗ nc5 TV 6P
🏵 S% B&b£5.30–£5.60 W£36–£38 🅼

⊢⊣**GH Turret** Lee Rd ☎3284 Plan:**20**
Mar–Oct rs Nov & Feb (B&b only) 6hc
2⇔🅷 (1fb) ⊗ nc5 CTV 5🅰 S%
B&b£5–£5.75 Bdi£8.25–£9
W£52.50–£56 ⚓ D5pm

GH Valley House Hotel Lynbridge Rd
☎2285 Plan:**21** Lic 10hc (2fb) ⊗ CTV 9P
🏵 river sea S% B&b£8.75–£10
Bdi£12.50–£14 W£88–£98 ⚓ D6pm

GH Woodlands Hotel Lynbridge ☎2324
Plan:**22** Closed Nov Lic 10hc (4fb) ⊗ nc5
CTV 10P 🏵 river S% B&b fr£6.90
Bdi fr£9.20 Wfr£59.80 ⚓ D6.30pm

LYTHAM ST ANNES Lancs *Map 7 SD32*
**Telephone exchanges Lytham &
St Annes**

⊶**GH Beaumont Private Hotel** 11 All
Saints Rd, St Annes ☎723958 Lic 9hc
(4fb) ⊗ CTV 🍴 S% B&bf5.75—£6.90
Bdi£8.05 W£56.35 ⊮ D4.30pm

GH Gables Hotel 35 Orchard Rd, St Annes
☎729851 Apr—26 Oct Lic 17hc (8fb) ⊗
CTV 22P S% B&bf7.50 Bdi£8.50 W£59.50
⊮ W only Jul & Aug D5.45pm

⊶**GH Harcourt Hotel** 21 Richmond Rd,
St Annes ☎722299 Closed Xmas & New
Year Lic 10hc (1fb) ⊗CTV 6P 🍴
B&b£fr£5.50 Bdi fr£7 Wfr£49 ⊮

GH Heath House Private Hotel
4 Bromley Rd, St Annes ☎723109 6hc
(1fb) ⊗ CTV P S% B&b fr£6

GH Lyndhurst Private Hotel 338 Clifton
Drive North ☎724343 May—Oct 12hc
1⇥🛏 (4fb) CTV 11 P S%
B&b£6.50—£7.50 Bdi£8.50—£9.50
W£55—£65 ⊮ D6pm

GH Orchard Hotel 34—36 Orchard Rd, St
Annes ☎728840 Lic 18hc (5fb) CTV 8P S%
✱B&b£6.90 Bdi£9.20 W only Jul & Aug
D noon

GH Westbourne Hotel 10—12 Lake Rd,
Fairhaven, St Annes ☎734736 Closed
Xmas wk 19hc 1⇥🛏⊗ CTV 7P 🍴
B&b£7—£8.50 Bdi£9.75—£11.25
W£65—£75 ⊮ D6.30pm

MAIDSTONE Kent *Map 5 TQ75*
GH Rock House Hotel 102 Tonbridge Rd
☎51616 12hc (1fb) ⊗ CTV 8P 🍴 S%
B&b£8.50—£9.20 W£56—£60 🅜

MALDON Essex *Map 5 TL80*
INN Swan Hotel Maldon High St
☎53170 Lic 6hc ⊗ CTV 40P 🍴 ⇘ S%
✱B&bfr£9.20 Bdi fr£12.08 sn Lfr£1&alc
D8.30pmfr£2.50&alc

MALHAM N Yorks *Map 7 SD96*
GH Sparth House Hotel ☎ Airton 315
Lic 10rm 9hc 1⇥🛏 (3fb) ⊗ CTV 6P river
B&b£7.47—£8.62 Bdi£12—£13.16
W£69.57—£76.50 ⊮ D5pm

MALVERN, GT Heref & Worcs
Map 3 SO74
GH Bredon House 34 Worcester Rd
☎5323 Lic 9hc (2fb) CTV 10P 🍴 S%
B&b£7.50 W£52.50 ⊮ D5pm

MANCHESTER Gt Manchester
Map 7 SJ89
⊶**GH Kempton House Hotel** 400
Wilbraham Rd, Chorlton-cum-Hardy
☎061-881 8766 Closed Xmas—New Year

(2wks) Lic 14hc (1fb) ⊗ CTV 10P 🍴 S%
✱B&b£5.46—£6.90

GH Hotel Tara 10—12 Oswald Rd,
Chorlton-cum-Hardy ☎061-861 0385
Lic 12hc (4fb) ⊗ CTV 8P 🍴 S%
✱B&bfr£7.48 Bdi fr£10.93 D2pm
(bar meals till midnight)

GH White House Hotel 17 Whitelow Rd,
Chorlton-cum-Hardy ☎061-861 0890
Lic 15hc 3⇥🛏 (4fb) ⊗ CTV 15P 🍴 S%
B&b£8—£9 Bdi£11—£12 W£55—£60 🅜
D8.30pm

MAN, ISLE OF *Map 6*
**Places with AA-listed guesthouses/inns
are indicated on location map 6. Full
details will be found under individual
placenames in the gazetteer section.**

MARGATE Kent *Map 5 TR37*
⊶**GH Alice Springs Private Hotel**
6—8 Garfield Rd ☎ Thanet 23543 Lic
18hc (5fb) nc6 CTV 🍴 S% B&b£5—£6
Bdi£6.50—£8 W£30—£40 ⊮ Dnoon

GH Beachcomber Hotel 3—4 Royal
Esplanade, Westbrook ☎ Thanet 21616
Apr—Oct Lic 16hc (4fb) ⊗ CTV sea
B&b£8.05—£9.20 Bdi£10.35—£11.50
W£48.75—£63.25 ⊮

GH Charnwood 20 Canterbury Rd
☎ Thanet 24158 Lic 12hc (8fb) CTV S%
B&b£6.50—£8 Bdi£8—£10 W£42—£50
⊮ D6pm

GH *Lancelot* 39 Edgar Rd, Cliftonville
☎ Thanet 22944 Lic 8hc 1⇥🛏 ⊗ CTV 🍴
D4.30pm

GH Tyrella Private Hotel 19 Canterbury Rd
☎ Thanet 22746 Lic 9hc (3fb) ⊗ nc7
CTV 🍴 sea S% ✱B&b£5—£6.50
Bdi£7.40—£9 W£39—£54 ⊮ D6pm

MARLOW Bucks *Map 4 SU88*
GH Glade Nook 75 Glade Rd ☎4677
7hc 1⇥🛏 CTV 6P 1🏠 🍴 S%
B&b£11—£13.50

MARNHULL Dorset *Map 3 ST71*
INN Crown Hotel ☎820224 Lic 4hc ⊗ P
🍴 B&b£7—£8 Bdi£14—£15 sn L£4—£5&alc
D9.30pmf7

MARSDEN W Yorks *Map 7 SE01*
INN Coach & Horses Standedge
☎ Huddersfield 844241 Lic 10hc 1⇥🛏 TV
200P 5🏠 S% ✱B&b£10—£12
Bdi£15—£17 sn L£2.50—£4 D10pm£3—£7

MARSHBROOK Salop *Map 7 SO48*
INN Wayside ☎208 Lic 4hc nc10 30P 🍴
S% ✱B&b£5.75 W£40.25 🅜 sn L£11.50alc
D8.30pm£2alc

MARTINHOE Devon *Map 3 SS64*
GH The Old Rectory ☎ Parracombe 368
Apr–Oct Lic 11rm 7hc nc6 CTV 14P ⊞
B&b£6–£9 Bdi£10.50–£15 D7.30pm

MARYTAVY Devon *Map 2 SX57*
GH Moorland Hall ☎466 Mar–Nov Lic
10hc 2⇔▥(3fb) ♨ CTV 15P S%
B&b£9.50–£12 Bdi£13.50–£16
W£85–£105 ⊾ D8.30pm

MASHAM N Yorks *Map 8 SE28*
GH Bank Villa ☎605 Lic 7hc nc5 CTV
7P ⊞ S% ✳B&b£7.50–£9.50
Bdi£12.25–£14.25 W£77.50–£90 ⊾
Dnoon

GH Sutton Grange Country House Hotel
Leyburn Rd ☎400 Mar–Nov Lic 13hc
(3fb) nc4 CTV 20P ⊞ S% B&b£7–£8.50
Bdi£10–£12 W£60–£75 ⊾ D7pm

MATLOCK Derbys *Map 8 SK36*
GH Cavendish 26 Bank Rd ☎2443
7hc (3fb) CTV 2P D10am

MAWGAN PORTH Cornwall *Map 2 SW86*
⊩⊣**GH Pandora** Tredragon Rd ☎ St Mawgan
412 End May–Sep, rs mid Jul–mid Aug
(B&b only) Lic 7rm 6hc (1fb) ⊗ CTV 10P
sea S% B&b£5.50–£7 Bdi£7.50–£9
W£45.50–£61.50 ⊾ D4pm

GH Seavista Hotel ☎ St Mawgan 276
10hc (4fb) ♨ CTV 8P sea S% B&b£7–£9.25
Bdi£10.75–£12.75 W£60–£76 ⊾ D5pm

GH Surf Riders Hotel Tredragon Rd
☎ St Mawgan 383 Apr–Nov Lic 11hc
(5fb) ⊗ CTV 12P sea S% B&b£6.60–£7.80
Bdi£8.40–£10.20 W£54–£69 ⊾ D6pm

GH *Thorncliff Hotel* Trenance ☎ St
Mawgan 428 Lic 14hc CTV 18P sea D8pm

GH White Lodge Hotel ☎ St Mawgan 512
Etr–Sep Lic 20hc (8fb) nc4 CTV 19P Sea S%
B&b£8–£10 Bdi£11.50–£13.50
W£74–£88 ⊾ D7.15pm

MAYFIELD Staffs *Map 7 SK14*
INN Queens Arms ☎Ashbourne 2271
(changing to 42271 during the currency of
this guide) Lic 5hc TV 30P ⊞
B&b£6.43–£6.90 Bar lunch£1–£2

MELBOURNE Derbys *Map 8 SK32*
INN *Melbourne Hotel* ☎2134 Lic 8hc
CTV 50P ⊞ D10pm

MELKSHAM Wilts *Map 3 ST96*
GH Regency Hotel 10–12 Spa Rd
☎702971 12hc (1fb) CTV ⊞ S% ✳B&b£7
Bdi£11 W£77 ⊾ D6.30pm

GH York Church Walk ☎702063 10hc
(3fb) CTV S% B&bfr£6 Bdifr£9.50
Wfr£66.50 ⊾ D3pm

MELTON MOWBRAY Leics *Map 8 SK71*
GH Sysonby Knoll Hotel 225 Asfordby Rd
☎63563 Closed Xmas Lic 15hc 4⇔▥
(2fb) CTV 18P ⊞ river S% B&bfr£6.50
D8pm

GH Westbourne House 11A Nottingham
Rd ☎69456 17hc (3fb) CTV 18P ⊞ S%
B&b£6.50–£7.25 Bdi£8.50–£9.25
D7.30pm

MENHENIOT Cornwall *Map 2 SX26*
INN Sportsman's Arms Station Rd
☎ Widegates 249 Lic 5hc 4⇔▥ TV 60P S%
B&b£8–£9 Bdi£12–£13 Bar lunch48p–£3
D10pm£8alc

INN White Hart Hotel ☎ Liskeard 42245
Lic 6hc 3⇔▥ nc16 CTV 30P ⊞ S%

Sysonby Knoll Private Hotel

Asfordby Road, Melton Mowbray. Tel: Melton Mowbray 63563.

A small family hotel with outdoor swimming pool, set in two acres of ground. Our emphasis is on good food, pleasant and comfortably furnished bedrooms, with central heating, H&C. We have a residential licence and two lounges with colour TV. Facilities for children's cot, high chair. Dogs welcome.

The White Hart

Menheniot, Liskeard, Cornwall
Tel: Liskeard 42245
The White Hart is situated at the centre of the unspoilt Cornish village of Menheniot and yet is within easy reach of the coast at Looe and the modern city of Plymouth.

This 17th-century Free House offers superb accommodation, all rooms having colour T/V and either bathrooms en suite or showers, tea/coffee-making facilities and full central heating. Restaurant service available or bar food.

Proprietors
G P & G Crook, R C Hopgood

B&b£8–£10 Bar lunch 50p–£5alc
D9.30pm£6–£12alc

MERIDEN W Midlands *Map 4 SP28*
GH Meriden Hotel Main Rd ☎22005
8rm 6hc ⚲ CTV 20P 🚻 S%
✳B&b£10–£12.50 Bdi£13.75–£16.25
D7pm

MEVAGISSEY Cornwall *Map 2 SX04*
GH Headlands Hotel Polkirt Hill ☎3453
Mar–Nov & Xmas Lic 12hc 6⇱🛏 (2fb)
nc5 CTV 10P 🚻 sea B&b£7.99–£8.99
Bdi£11.45–£12.45 D7pm

GH Polhaun Hotel Polkirt Hill ☎3222
Etr–Oct Lic 8hc (1fb) ⚲ nc10 TV 10P 🚻
sea S% B&bfr£8 Bdifr£10.50 Wfr£72 ⚓
D6.30pm

GH Spa Private Hotel Polkirt Hill ☎2244
Etr–Oct Lic 12hc 6⇱🛏 ⚲ nc5 CTV
12P 1🏧 🚻 sea S% B&b£9.77–£11.27
Bdi£12.65–£14.09 W£79.29–£89.76 ⚓
D noon

GH Valley Park Tregoney Hill ☎2347
Closed Xmas & New Year Lic 8hc (2fb) ⚲
CTV 10P S% B&bfr£7 Bdifr£11 Wfr£75
⚓ D6pm

INN Ship ☎3324 Lic 5hc CTV 🚗 S%
✳B&b£7.50 W£45–£52.50 🅜 (W only
Jul–Sep) Bar lunch£1.75

MIDDLESBROUGH Cleveland
Map 8 NZ42
GH Chadwick Private Hotel 27 Clairville
Rd ☎245340 6hc (2fb) ⚲ CTV S%
B&b£6.50 Bdi£9 D4pm

GH Longlands Hotel 295 Marton Rd
☎244900 Lic 7hc (5fb) ⚲ CTV 5P 5🏧
🚻 S% B&b£7.50 Bdi£10 W£70 D6pm

MIDDLETON-ON-SEA W Sussex
Map 4 SU90
GH Ancton House Hotel Ancton Ln
☎2482 Lic 6hc 2⇱🛏 (2fb) ⚗ CTV 6P 4🏧
🚻 🕹 S% B&b£10–£11 Bdi£13.50
W£82–£90 ⚓ D6.30pm

MILFORD-ON-SEA Hants *Map 4 SZ29*
GH La Charmeuse 9 Hurst Rd ☎2646
Apr–Oct 4hc (1fb) ⚲ TV 8P 🚻 sea
B&b£7.50–£8.50

GH Kingsland Hotel Westover Rd ☎2670
Lic 18hc 7⇱🛏 (4fb) ⚲ nc6 CTV 14P 🚻 lift
S% B&b£8

MILLPOOL Cornwall *Map 2 SW53*
GH *Chyraise* ☎Germoe 3485 Mar–Sep
& Xmas Lic 9hc ⚲ CTV 10P D noon

MINCHINHAMPTON Glos *Map 3 SO80*
GH Sherrards ☎Brimscombe 2742
Closed Jan Lic 7hc 1⇱🛏 (1fb) ⚲ CTV 8P 🚻
S% B&b£8.50 Bdi£13 W£89.50 ⚓

MINEHEAD Somerset *Map 3 SS94*
See Plan
GH Carbery Western Lane, The Parks
☎2941 Plan **1** May–Oct Lic 6hc ⚲ nc CTV
6P 🚻 S% B&b£6–£7 Bdi£9.75–£10 D noon

GH Dorchester Hotel 38 The Avenue
☎2052 Plan **2** Lic 13hc (4fb) CTV 12P
S% B&b£6.75–£7 Bdi£9.75–£10
W£77–£80 D8.30pm

GH Gascony Hotel The Avenue ☎2817
Plan **3** Mar–Oct Lic 15hc 3⇱🛏 (6fb) ⚲ ⚗
CTV 10P S% B&b£8.50 Bdi£12
W£52–£69 ⚓ D8pm

KILBOL HOUSE

Tom and Carole Berry
Kilbol has a long history as a farm, and
has been converted to a luxurious hotel,
with extensive lawns and grounds.
Cornwall Tourist Board approved. Ideally
placed for touring Cornwall. Open all year.
Ample parking. Family rooms, double
rooms and single rooms, some with
bathrooms en suite, private bathrooms or
showers. Lounge and dining room. Also
16th Century lounge with bar. Central
heating. Bed and breakfast, optional
dinner — terms on request. Licensed.
Heated swimming pool. Kilbol has
exceptional peace and quiet, yet we are
located just 3-4 miles from 5 beaches.

Kilbol House, Polmassick, Nr. Mevagissey. Tel: Mevagissey 2481

AA Listed

Van Ruan House
Boswinger, Gorran, Nr. Mevagissey, Cornwall

"Van Ruan" is a select guest house set in peaceful
surroundings offering every comfort and good
food. Situated in its own grounds of over an acre,
overlooking the sea and a National Trust beauty
area. Six sandy beaches are within 2 miles, the
nearest is less than ½ mile.
Full central heating, most bedrooms have unrivalled
sea views, all with H&C. Some ground floor
bedrooms. Comfortable lounge with colour TV.
Licenced Bar. Own car park. Bed, Breakfast and
evening dinner. Stamp please for colour brochure
and terms to:—
Resident proprietors Mr & Mrs R Bulled
Telephone Mevagissey (072 684) 2425

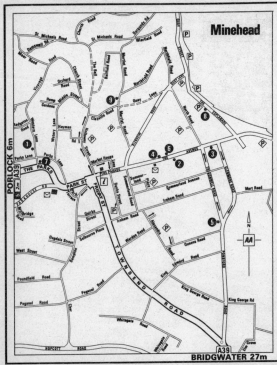

Minehead

1 Carbery
2 Dorchester Hotel
3 Gascony Hotel
4 Glen Rock Hotel
5 Higher Woodcombe Hotel
6 Mayfair Hotel
7 Mentone Hotel
8 Red Lion Hotel (*Inn*)
9 Wyndcott Hotel

GH Glen Rock Hotel 23 The Avenue
☎2245 Plan:**4** Mar–Nov Lic 12hc (2fb)
nc3 CTV 9P 1🏠 S% B&bf7.50–£9
Bdi£11–£12.50 Wf60–£68 ⅃ D7.30pm

GH Higher Woodcombe Hotel Bratton
Ln ☎2789 Plan:**5** Apr–Oct Lic 9hc (1fb)
nc9 CTV 9P 🚽 S% B&bf9–£9.50
Bdi£12.75–£13.50 Wf85–£90 ⅃
D6.30pm

GH Mayfair Hotel 25 The Avenue ☎2719
Plan **6** Mar–Sep Lic 18hc (5fb) CTV 14P
B&bf7–£7.80 Bdi£10.50–£11.25
Wf60–£64 ⅃ D6.45pm

GH Mentone Hotel The Parks ☎2549
Plan:**7** Mar–Oct Lic 12hc 5⊐🚽 (1fb) nc10
CTV 10P S% B&bf6.50–£8
Bdi£10.75–£13.25 Wf70–£89 ⅃ D6pm

GH *Wyndcott Hotel* Martlet Rd ☎4522
Plan:**9** Lic 13hc 4⊐🚽 CTV 13P 🚽 sea D7pm

INN *Red Lion Hotel* The Esplanade
☎2653 Plan:**8** Lic 7hc CTV 6P sea

MOFFAT Dumfries & Galloway
Dumfriesshire Map 11 NTOO
⊨⊣ **GH Arden House** High St ☎20220
Jan–Oct 7hc 4⊐🚽 (2fb) CTV 10P 🚽 S%
B&bf5–£6 Bdi£7.75–£8.50
Wf52.50–£59.50 D6.45pm

⊨⊣**GH Buchan House** 13 Beechgrove
☎20378 8hc 2⊐🚽 (3fb) TV 6P 🚽
S% B&bf4.50–£4.75 Bdi£7.50–£7.75
Wf50–£52.50 ⅃ (W only Oct–Apr) D7pm

GH *Craigieburn* 14 Selkirk Rd (2m E on
A708) ☎20229 mid Mar–mid Oct Lic 7hc
♨ TV 10P 🚽 D8.30pm

GH Hartfell House Hartfell Cres ☎20153
Closed Jan & Feb 9hc (2fb) TV 10P 🚽
B&bf6.20 Bdi£10.45 Wf67.25 ⅃ D7pm

GH Robin Hill Beechgrove ☎20050
Etr–Oct 6hc 5⊐🚽 TV 5P

GH Rockhill 14 Beechgrove ☎20283
Mar–Oct 10hc (3fb) CTV B&bfr£5 Bdi fr£8
Wfr£53 ⅃ D6.15pm

GH St Olaf Eastgate, off Dickson St
☎20001 Apr–Oct 7hc (3fb) ✳B&bf4.25
Bdi£7.25 D6.30pm

MONTROSE Tayside *Angus Map 15 NO75*
⊨⊣**GH Linksgate** 11 Dorward Rd ☎2273
6hc (3fb) CTV 6P S% B&bf5–£5.50
Bdi£7.30 Wf48 ⅃ D9am

MOODIESBURN Strathclyde *Lanarks
Map 11 NS67*
⊨⊣ **GH El Ranchero Western**
6 Cumbernauld Rd (on A80) ☎Glenboig
874769 rs 25 Dec–1 Jan (B&b only) 5hc
(2fb) CTV 30P S% B&bf5.95 Bdi£8.50
D6.45pm

MORECAMBE Lancs *Map 7 SD46*
GH Ashley Private Hotel 371 Marine Rd
East ☎412034 Closed Xmas Lic 14hc
(5fb) ⊗ CTV 4P 1🏠 ✳B&bf7.48–£8.63
Bdi£8.63–£9.78 Wf55.20–£63 ⅃ (W only
Jul & Aug) D4pm

GH Beach Mount 395 Marine Road East
☎420753 Nov–Mar Lic 26hc 10⊐🚽
(5fb) CTV 🚽 sea S% B&bf8–£9
Bdi£11–£12 Wf69–£72 D4pm

GH *Channings Private Hotel* 455 Marine
Road East ☎417925 Lic 24hc TV sea

⊨⊣**GH Ellesmere Private Hotel** 44
Westminster Rd ☎411881 Closed Xmas
6hc (2fb) ⊗ CTV S% B&bf4.50–£6
Bdi£5–£6.50 Wf36–£40 D5.30pm

GH *Elstead Private Hotel* 72 Regent Rd
☎412260 12hc ⊗ D3pm

GH Glendene 42 Westminster Rd
☎416358 Mar–20 Oct 6hc (1fb) ⊘ CTV ⊞
S% B&b£2.90–£3.50 Bdi£5.40–£6
W£36–£40 ⏽ D3pm

GH New Hazlemere Hotel 391 Marine
Rd, East ☎417876 Etr–Oct Lic 19hc (5fb)
CTV 2P sea S% ✱B&b£7–£8 Bdi£9–£10
W£50–£57.50 ⏽ D5.30pm

GH Hotel Prospect 363 Marine Rd East
☎417819 Etr–Sep Lic 15hc 8⇌⁄ (5fb)
CTV 6P ⊞ sea S% B&b£5–£6 Bdi£7–£8
W£48–£56 ⏽ D5pm

GH Rydal Mount Private Hotel 361
Marine Rd East ☎411858 Etr–Oct Lic
14hc (6fb) CTV 12P ⊞ sea S%
✱B&b£6.50–£7.50 Bdi£7.50–£8.50
W£59.80–£64.40 D3.30pm

GH Hotel Warwick 394 Marine Rd East
☎418151 Lic 20hc 1⇌⁄ (4fb) CTV ⊞ sea
S% B&b£6–£7 Bdi£8–£9 D5pm

GH Wilmslow Private Hotel 374 Marine
Rd East ☎417804 Mar–Oct Lic 15hc
(4fb) ⊘ CTV 4P ⊞ sea S%
B&b£6.50–£7.50 Bdi£8–£10 W£54 ⏽
D4.30pm

MORETONHAMPSTEAD Devon
Map 3 SX78
GH Cookshayes 33 Court St ☎374
Mar–Oct Lic 9hc 4⇌⁄ nc12 CTV 15P ⊞
S% ✱B&b fr£6.50 Bdi fr£10.50 Wfr£70 ⏽
D6.30pm

GH Elmfield Station Rd ☎327 Etr–Sep Lic
6hc (2fb) CTV 7P ⊞ S% B&b£6 Bdi£9.75
W£60 ⏽ D7pm

GH *Moreton House Hotel* 5 The Square
☎269 Lic 6hc CTV 4P ⊞ D9pm
GH *Wray Barton Manor* ☎246 Closed

Xmas 7hc ⊗ nc12 CTV P 2🏠 ⊞ river
D2.30pm
INN Ring of Bells North Bovey ☎375
rs Dec–Feb Lic 3⇌⁄ 6P 4🏠 ⊞ S%
✱B&b£12.94 Bdi£17.54 W£122.77 ⏽
Bar lunch95p–£1.95
D8.45pm£5.25–£5.75

MORFA NEFYN Gwynedd *Map 6 SH23*
GH Erw Goch ☎Nefyn 720539 Etr–Sep
Lic 15hc (5fb) ⚬ CTV 20P
✱B&b£5.25–£5.50 Bdi£8.25–£8.50
W£55.20 ⏽D5pm

MORTEHOE Devon *Map 2 SS44*
GH Baycliff Chapple Hill ☎Woolacombe
393 Mar–Oct Lic 10hc 1⇌⁄ (2fb) CTV 9P
sea S% B&b£9.20–£13.80
Bdi£13.80–£18.40 W£73.60–£100.20 ⏽
D7pm

GH Haven ☎Woolacombe 426. Mar–Oct
Lic 18rm 2hc 16⇌⁄ (12fb) ⚬ CTV 20P 2🏠
sea Bdi£10.50–£14 W£73–£98 ⏽
D7.45pm

GH Sunnycliffe Hotel ☎Woolacombe 597
(due to change to 870597 during the
currency of this guide) Lic 8⇌⁄ (2fb) nc10
CTV 11P ⊞ sea S% B&b£8 Bdi£11
D6.30pm

MOY Highland *Inverness-shire*
Map 14 NH73
GH Invermoy House Tomatin ☎271
Lic 7hc 1⇌⁄ ⊗ ⚬ CTV 10P ⊞ S%
B&b£5.75–£6.33 Bdi£8.63–£9.78
W£56.35–£63.25 ⏽ D6pm

MULL, ISLE OF Strathclyde *Argyll*
Map 10 & 13
See Salen, Tobermory

MULLION Cornwall *Map 2 SW61*
⊩⊣**GH Belle Vue** ☎240483 Etr–Sep 8hc
(1fb) ⊗ CTV 10P S% B&b£5–£6 Bdi£8–£9
W£55–£60 ⅃ D4pm

GH Henscath House Mullion Cove
☎240537 Feb–Nov Lic 6hc ⊗ nc5 CTV 6P
sea S% B&b£7.50 Bdi£11

GH *Trenowyth House Private Hotel*
Mullion Cove ☎240486 Lic 5hc CTV 10P
🍴 sea D6.30pm

⊩⊣**GH** *Trevelayan* ☎240378 Etr–Oct 5hc
(A 2rm 1hc) CTV 20P sea S% B&b£5.50
Bdi£9 W£60 ⅃

INN The Old Inn Church Town ☎240240
rs Xmas (no accommodation) Lic 7hc
4🛏⊗ nc14 TV 10P 🚗 sea ✻B&b£7–£8
Bar lunch60p–£2alc D9pm£5alc

MUMBLES W Glam *Map 2 SS68*
GH Carlton Hotel 654–656 Mumbles Rd,
Southend ☎Swansea 60450 Closed 2 wks
Xmas rs mid Nov–mid Feb (closed wknds)
Lic 19hc 3🛏 (2fb) CTV 🍴 sea S%
✻B&b fr£9.50 Bdi fr£14 W fr£75 ⅃ (W only
May–Oct)

GH Harbour Winds Private Hotel
Overland Rd, Langland ☎Swansea 69298
10 Jan–12 Dec 8hc 2🛏 (5fb) ⚿ CTV 15P
🍴 S% D6.30pm

GH *Southend Hotel* 724 Mumbles Rd
☎ Swansea 66329 Lic 11hc CTV 20P sea
D9.30pm

MUNDESLEY-ON-SEA Norfolk
Map 9 TG33
INN *Ingleside Hotel* Cromer Rd
☎720530 Lic 11hc TV 🍴 D9.30pm

MUNGRISDALE Cumbria *Map 11 NY33*
GH Mill Guest House ☎Threlkeld 659
mid Mar–Oct Lic 9hc (2fb) ⊗ CTV 12P
river S% B&b£8.50–£9 Bdi£11–£13.50
D5pm

INN Mill ☎Threlkeld 632 Mar–Oct Lic 8hc
⊗ 30P S% ✻B&b fr£6.50
Bar lunch40p–£1.80 D9pm

MUSBURY Devon *Map 3 SY29*
⊩⊣**GH Barley Close** ☎Colyton 52484 6hc
(2fb) ⊗ nc12 CTV 10P 🍴 S% B&b£5
Bdi£7.50 W£52.50 ⅃ D4pm

MUSSELBURGH Lothian *Midlothian
Map 11 NT37*
⊩⊣**GH Parsonage** 15 High St
☎031-665 4289 7hc (2fb) CTV 12P 🍴
S% B&b£5.50–£7.50

MYLOR BRIDGE Cornwall *Map 2 SW83*
⊩⊣ **GH Penmere** Rosehill ☎Penryn 74470
Etr–mid Oct 6hc (2fb) ⚿ CTV 6P 🍴 river S%
B&b£5.50 Bdi£9 W£49 ⅃ D5pm

NAILSWORTH Glos *Map 3 ST89*
GH Gables Private Hotel Tiltups End,
Bath Rd ☎2265 Lic 6rm 5hc (2fb) CTV
10P B&b£8 Bdi fr£11 D9pm

NAIRN Highland *Nairns Map 14 NH85*
GH Dun-Craig Glebe Rd, off Marine Rd
☎53345 May–Sep 10hc (5fb) CTV 12P S%
B&b£7 Bdi£9.75 W£63 D7pm

GH Glen Lyon Lodge Waverley Rd
☎52780 4hc (2fb) CTV 6P 🍴 S%
✻B&b£4.50 Bdi£7.50

GH Greenlawns 13 Seafield St ☎52738
Apr–Oct 6hc 2🛏 (3fb) CTV 8P S% B&b£6
Bdi£8.50 W£54 ⅃ D5pm

GH *Lothian House Private Hotel*
10 Crescent Rd ☎53555 Lic 9hc CTV 10P
sea D7pm

GH *Ramleh* ☎53551 Mar–Nov 9hc CTV
10P D noon

NARBERTH Dyfed *Map 2 SN11*
GH *Blaenmarlais* ☎860326 Spring Bank
Hol–Sep Lic 11hc 1⇔🅗 (A 3hc) (4fb) ⊗
CTV 30P 8🏠 B&b£7 Bdi£10 W£54–£56 ⊬
(W only Spring Bank Hol & mid Jul–Aug)
GH *Parc Glas Country House Hotel* Parc
Glas ☎860947 Etr–Oct Lic 6hc 2⇔🅗
(2fb) ⊗ CTV 10P 🎵 S% B&b£8–£9
Bdi£11–£12 W£70–£80 ⊬ D7pm

NEAR SAWREY Cumbria *Map 7 SD39*
GH *High Green Gate* ☎Hawkshead 296
Etr–Oct 7hc (1fb) CTV 8P 🎵 S%
✳B&b£6.33 Bdi£9.78 W£59.80 ⊬

GH *Sawrey House Private Hotel*
☎Hawkshead 387 Closed Xmas Lic 12hc
1⇔🅗 (4fb) nc1 CTV 20P 🎵 🅗 lake S%
B&b£7.50–£8 Bdi£11–£12.50
W£75–£85 ⊬ (W only Spring Hol–Aug)
D7pm

NEATISHEAD Norfolk *Map 9 TG32*
GH *Barton Angler Hotel* ☎Horning
630740 Mar–Oct rs Nov–Feb (wknds only)
Lic 8hc 2⇔🅗 (1fb) ⊗ nc7 CTV 12P 🎵
B&b£7.50 Bdi£11 D8.30pm

NESSCLIFF Salop *Map 7 SJ31*
INN *Nescliff Hotel* ☎253 Lic 5hc TV 75P
2🏠 ⇔ B&b£7 Bdi£8–£14 W£48 M sn
L£3–£3.50&alc D9.50pm£3–£3.50&alc

NEWBURY Berks *Map 4 SU46*
GH *The Guest House* 133 Andover Rd
☎41359 11hc (1fb) ⊗ nc10 12P 🎵 S%
B&b£6

NEWCASTLE-UNDER-LYME Staffs
Map 7 SJ84
GH *Grove Court Hotel* 100 Lancaster Rd
☎614406 Lic 11rm 10hc 4⇔🅗
(A 2hc) (1fb) CTV 12P 🎵 ✳B&b£8

NEWCASTLE UPON TYNE Tyne & Wear
Map 12 NZ26
GH *Chirton House Hotel* 46 Clifton Rd
☎730407 Closed Xmas–New Year Lic
12hc (1fb) ⊗ CTV 12P 🎵 S%
B&b£8.63–£9.78 Bdi£14.38 W£86 25 ⊬
D6.30pm

NEWHAVEN Derbys *Map 7 SK16*
INN *Newhaven Hotel* ☎Hartington 217
Lic 11rm CTV 200P 🎵 S% B&b£9.50 sn
L£5alc D1am£5alc

NEWLANDS (nr Keswick) Cumbria
Map 11 NY22
GH *Stoneycroft Hotel* ☎Braithwaite 240
Mar–Nov Lic 10hc 3⇔🅗 (2fb) nc5 CTV 20P
🎵 B&b£8–£9.25 Bdi£12–£14 W£79–£90
⊬

NEWNHAM-ON-SEVERN Glos
Map 3 SO61
INN *Victoria* ☎221 Lic 16hc 3⇔🅗 CTV
50P 3🏠 🎵 B&b£11.50 Bar lunch95p–£3.25
D9.30pm£3.50–£6.50&alc

NEWPORT Dyfed *Map 2 SNO3*
GH *Gellifawr* Pontfaen (4m S on unclass
rd) ☎820343 Etr–Oct Lic 8rm 7hc (3fb) ⊗

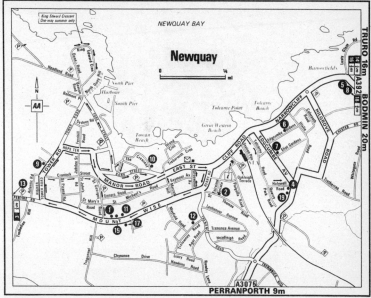

1 Arundell Hotel	**6** Gluvian Park Hotel	**11** Mount Wise Hotel	**15** Quies Hotel
2 Castaways Hotel	**7** Hepworth Hotel	**12** Ocean Hill Lodge	**16** Ranelagh Court
3 Cherington	**8** Kellesboro Hotel	Private Hotel	Hotel
4 Copper Beech Hotel	**9** Long Beach Hotel	**13** Philema	**17** Trevone Hotel
5 La Felica Hotel	**10** Minerva Hotel	**14** Pine Lodge	**18** Viewpoint Hotel
			19 Wheal Treasure

CTV P S% B&b£6 Bdi£9 W£60 ⚓ D7pm

INN Golden Lion Hotel East St ☎820321
Lic 10⇌🍴⚫ CTV 15P 🍲🍴
B&b£7.50–£8.50 W£42 M Bar lunch
35p–£2.75 D10pm£6alc

NEWPORT Gwent *Map 3 ST38*
GH Caerleon House Hotel Caerau Rd
☎64869 Lic 8hc (1fb) CTV 8P 🍲 S%
B&b£7.50–£8.50 Bdi£10.50–£12.50
D7.30pm

NEWPORT Isle of Wight *Map 4 SZ48*
GH Clatterford House Hotel Clatterford
Shute, Carrisbrooke (1m W B3323)
☎523969 rs Sun Lic 8hc 1⇌🍴 (2fb) nc5
TV 12P 🍲 river B&b£7–£8.50
Bdi£12.50–£14 W£75–£85 ⚓ D10.30pm

NEWPORT Salop *Map 7 SJ71*
INN Barley Mow Hotel High St ☎810146
Lic 5hc ⚫ CTV 12P 🍲 S% ✳B&b£8.05
Bdi£12–£15 sn L£2.50–£4 D8.30pm£4–£6

NEWQUAY Cornwall *Map 2 SW86*
See Plan
GH Arundell Hotel Mount Wise ☎2481
Plan:**1** Mav–Sep Lic 43hc 4⇌🍴 (8fb) CTV
27P sea S% B&b£7–£9.50 Bdi£8–£10.50
W£55–£72 ⚓ D6.45pm

GH *Castaways Hotel* 39 St Thomas Rd
☎5002 Plan:**2** Spring Bank Hol–Oct Lic
8hc ⚫ CTV 8P D5pm

⊢⊣**GH Cherington** 7 Pentire Av ☎3363
Plan:**3** Etr–Oct 22hc 1⇌🍴 (A 6hc) (4fb)
CTV 16P 🍲 sea S% B&b£6–£7
W£40–£60 ⚓ (W only Jul & Aug) D5.30pm

GH Copper Beech Hotel 70 Edgcumbe Av
☎3376 Plan:**4** Etr–Oct 16hc (5fb) ⚫ CTV

16P 🍲 S% B&b£5.75–£8.08
Bdi£8.05–£10.35 W£56.35–£72.45 ⚓
W only High Season D6.30pm

GH La Felica Hotel Henver Rd ☎2129
Plan:**5** Etr–Oct Lic 24hc (6fb) ⚫ CTV 15P
sea S% B&b£8.05–£14.95
Bdi£10.35–£17.25 W£63.25–£97.75 ⚓
(W only 27 Jun–5 Sep) D3pm

GH Gluvian Park Hotel 12 Edgcumbe Gdns
☎3133.Plan:**6** Lic 24hc 7⇌🍴 (8fb) ⚫
nc3 CTV 10P S% B&B£7.50–£10
Bdi£10.50–£13.50 W£65–£80 ⚓ D6.30pm

GH Hepworth Hotel 27 Edgcumbe Av
☎3686 Plan:**7** Etr–Sep Lic 13hc 4⇌🍴
(4fb) ⚫ CTV 10P 🍲 B&b£7–£12.05
Bdi£9.30–£14.35 W£56.85–£86.25 ⚓ .
(W only Jul & Aug) D6.30pm

GH Kellsboro Hotel 12 Henver Rd ☎4620
Plan:**8** Mar–Nov Lic 16hc 7⇌🍴
(6fb) CTV 16P 🍲 S% B&b£9–£10.50
Bdi£11.50–£13.80 W£80.50–£96.60 ⚓
D6.30pm

GH Long Beech Hotel 11 Trevose Av
☎4751 Plan:**9** Etr–Sep Lic 8hc (4fb) nc2
CTV 6P sea S% B&b£7–£11 Bdi£9–£11
(W only Jul & Aug) D6.15pm

GH Minerva Hotel The Crescent ☎3439
Plan:**10** Etr–mid Oct Lic 26hc 4⇌🍴 (11fb)
CTV 6P sea B&b£11.50–£16.10
Bdi£13.25–£17.83 W£56.93–£86.25
⚓ (W only Jul & Aug) D7pm

GH *Mount Wise Hotel* Mount Wise
☎3080 Plan:**11** Apr–Oct Lic 38hc 9⇌🍴
CTV 30P lift D7.30pm

⊢⊣**GH Ocean Hill Lodge Private Hotel**
4–6 Trelawney Rd ☎4595 Plan:**12**
May–Sep Lic 16hc (2fb) CTV 12P S%

B&b£5.50–£7.50 Bdi£7–£9 W£45–£60
ᵏ (W only Jul & Aug) Dnoon

GH Philema Hotel 1 Esplanade Rd,
Pentire ☎2571 Plan **13** Etr–mid Oct Lic
23hc 6⇨🛏(7fb) CTV 25P S% B&b£7–£11
Bdi£9–£13 W£49–£85 ᵏ (W only Jul &
Aug) D6.30pm

GH Pine Lodge Hotel 91 Henver Rd
☎2549 Plan **14** Lic 11hc 4⇨🛏(2fb) ⊗
nc7 CTV 20P 🍴 S% B&b£9.30–£16.85
Bdi£13.50–£18.90 D7.30pm

GH *Quies Hotel* 84 Mount Wise ☎2924
Plan **15** Etr–Oct Lic 10hc CTV 12P
W only 17Jun–16Sep

GH Ranelagh Court Hotel 101A Henver Rd
☎4922 Plan **16** Lic 8hc (1fb) nc8 CTV 12P
🍴 sea S% B&b£6–£6.50 Bdi£8–£10
D6.30pm

GH *Trevone Hotel* Mount Wise ☎3039
Plan **17** Apr–Sep Lic 34hc ⊗ CTV 28P
sea D7pm

GH *Viewpoint Hotel* 89 Henver Rd
☎2170 Plan **18** Lic 17hc 13⇨🛏⊗nc3
CTV 14P 🍴 sea D summer 8pm winter
7.30pm

GH Wheal Treasure 72 Edgcumbe Av
☎4136 Plan **19** Apr–Oct Lic 11hc (3fb)
⊗ nc4 CTV 11P 🍴 S% B&b£6
Bdi£8.50–£11.20 W£57.50–£72.50 ᵏ
(W only mid Jun–Aug) D5.30pm

NEW QUAY Dyfed *Map 2 SN35*
INN Queens Hotel Church St ☎560678
Mar–Oct Lic 8hc (2fb) Bdi£9.50–£12 W£84–£105
sn L£2.45–£2.95&alc D9.30pm
£2.45–£2.95&alc

NEWTON ABBOT Devon *Map 3 SS87*
GH Lamorna Exeter Rd, Coombe Cross,
Sandygate, (3m N A380) ☎5627 Lic 7hc
(3fb) ⊗ CTV 20P 🍴 S% ✳B&b£6–£7
Bdi£9.50–£10.50 W£66.50–£73.50 ᵏ
D9pm

NEWTONMORE Highland *Inverness-shire*
Map 14 NN79
GH Alder Lodge ☎376 Lic 7rm 6hc (1fb)
CTV 10P S% ✳B&b£7 Bdi£10 W£67
ᵏ D9pm

GH Alvey House Hotel Golf Course Rd
☎260 Dec–Oct Lic 7hc (2fb) CTV 12P S%
B&b£7.50 Bdi£10.50 W£70 ᵏ D7pm

GH Ard-na-Coille Hotel ☎214 May–Oct
Lic 13hc 5⇨🛏(3fb) CTV 20P S%
B&b£10.40–£11 Bdi£14.60–£16.60
D7.30pm

GH Cairn Dearg Station Rd ☎398 6hc
(2fb) ⚬ CTV 8P S% B&b£6–£6.90
Bdi£9–£10.25 W£61–£70 ᵏ D8pm

GH Coig-na-Shee Fort William Rd ☎216
Feb–mid Nov 6hc 1⇨🛏(1fb) ⚬ TV 8P 🍴 S%
B&b£7.50–£8.50 Bdi£12–£14 W£75–£88
ᵏ D6.30pm

NEWTON STEWART Dumfries &
Galloway *Wigtowns Map 10 NX46*
◄►**GH Duncree House Hotel** Girvan Rd
☎2001 Lic 6hc (5fb) CTV 25P S%
B&b£5.50 Bdi£8.50 W£59.50 ᵏ D6pm

NITON Isle of Wight *Map 4 SZ57*
GH Windcliffe House Hotel Sandrock Rd
☎730215 Etr–Oct Lic 12hc (7fb) CTV 18P
sea S% B&b£8.05–£11.50
Bdi£10.67–£13.96 W£74.75–£97.75

⚹ D6.15pm

NORTHALLERTON N Yorks *Map 8 SE39*
GH Windsor 56 South Parade ☎774100
Closed Xmas & New Year 6hc (3fb) CTV ⊞
S% B&bfr£6.50

INN Station Hotel 2 Boroughbridge Rd
☎2053 Lic 9hc CTV 30P ⊞ S%
B&b£6.50–£7.50 Bdi£8.50–£9.50 sn
L60p–£2 D6pm£2–£2.50

NORTHAMPTON Northants *Map 4 SP76*
GH Langham 4 Langham Pl, Barrack Rd
☎39917 Lic 15⇐🛏(8fb) ⚿ CTV 30P
3🏠 ⊞ S% B&b£8.05 Bdi£10.93 D6.45pm

GH Poplars Hotel Cross St, Moulton
☎43983 Lic 22hc 7⇐🛏(4fb) CTV 22P ⊞
S% B&bfr£7.50 Bdifr£11 D6.30pm

NORTH BERWICK Lothian *E Lothian
Map 12 NT58*

GH Belhaven Private Hotel Westgate
☎2573 mid Mar–Sep 6hc (2fb) sea
S% B&b£8 Bdi£11.50 W£67.85 ⚹

GH Cragside Private Hotel 16 Marine Pde
☎2879 Apr–mid Oct 6hc (1fb) CTV ⊞
sea S% B&b£7 Bdi£10.50 W£65 ⚹
D6.30pm

NORTH HYKEHAM Lincs *Map 8 SK96*
GH Loudor Hotel 37 Newark Rd ☎ Lincoln
680333 Lic 9hc (A 3hc) (1fb) ⚿ CTV 14P ⊞
S% B&b£9.20–£10.35 Bdi£13.23–£14.95
W£90 ⚹ D7.30pm

NORTH WALSHAM Norfolk *Map 9 TG23*
GH Beechwood Private Hotel 20 Cromer
Rd ☎3231 Closed 4 days Xmas Lic 11hc
2⇐🛏(8fb) ⚹ CTV 12P ⊞ B&b£9.75
Bdi£13.80 W£74–£91 ⚹ (W only
18 Jul–29 Aug) D6pm

ARD-NA-COILLE HOTEL

Formerly a millionaire's shooting
lodge standing in its own grounds
with magnificent views over
Strathspey to the Cairngorms,
Ard-na-Coille provides the perfect
base from which to explore the
beautiful and historic Scottish
Highlands. Special facilities for skiers.
Games room. Residential and table
licence.

Ard-na-Coille, Newtonmore, Inverness-shire. Tel: Newtonmore 214.

The Poplars Hotel

**MOULTON, NORTHAMPTON
NN3 1RZ**

Tel: Northampton (0604) 43983

This is a small country hotel of character, situated in a quiet village only four
miles from the centre of Northampton.
We welcome families, and children of all ages can be catered for.
There is a large car park and garden.
Personal attention is given to guests by the Proprietors — Peter and Rosemary
Gillies.

BEECHWOOD HOTEL

NORTH WALSHAM, NORFOLK

Sandy beaches 5 miles. Broads 7 miles.
Highly recommended for:
Good food — licensed
Two lounges — colour TV
Central heating
Games room
Comfortable beds
Some rooms with private bath/wc
Large attractive gardens
Children's playground
Free parking
Friendly personal service

Ring Ernest and Jenny Townsend North Walsham 3231

NORTHWOOD Salop Map 7 SJ43
⊢⊣**GH Woodlands Country House**
(1m S off B5063) ☎ Wem 33268
Closed Xmas Lic 8hc 3⇌🛉(3fb) ✍ CTV
12P 🍺 S% B&b£5.50–£6.75
Bdi£8.50–£9.75 W£57–£67 ⊬ D5pm

NORWICH Norfolk Map 5 TG20
GH Argyle House Hotel 10 Stracey Rd
☎27493 11hc ✍ nc CTV 🍺 S%
B&b£6.50–£8.50 Bdi£9.50–£11.50
W£67.50–£80.50 ⊬ D4pm

GH Gables 240 Thorpe Rd ☎34475 12hc
(A 4hc) (3fb) CTV 11P 🍺 ⅄S%
B&b£6.50–£7.50

GH Grange Hotel 230 Thorpe Rd
☎34734 24 Dec–6 Jan Lic 32hc 30⇌🛉
(4fb) CTV 38P 🍺 ⅄ river S% B&b£9–£12
Bdi£13–£17 D8pm

GH Marlborough House Hotel
22 Stracey Rd, Thorpe Rd ☎28005 Lic
11hc 3⇌🛉 CTV 5P 🏠 🍺

NOTTINGHAM Notts Map 8 SK53
GH Rufford Hotel Melton Rd, West
Bridgford (1m S on A52) ☎814202 Lic
33hc 30⇌🛉(6fb) CTV 40P 🍺 S%
B&b£10–£12 Bdi£14.50–£16.50
D7.30pm

⊢⊣**GH Waverley** 107 Portland Rd,
Waverley St ☎786707 Closed 2 wks Xmas
& New Year 18hc (2fb) CTV 1🏠 S%
B&b fr£5 Bdi fr£7.50 D4pm

GH Windsor 4 Watcombe Circus
☎621317 Closed Xmas 8hc (1fb) CTV 6P
🍺 S% B&b£6.50

GH Windsor Lodge Hotel 116 Radcliffe
Rd, West Bridgford (1m S on A52)

☎813773 Lic 40hc 12⇌🛉(5fb) ✍ CTV
48P 4🏠 🍺 S% B&b£8.50 Bdi£12.50
D7.15pm

NUNEATON Warwicks Map 4 SP39
GH Abbey Grange Hotel 100 Manor
Court Rd ☎348177 Closed Xmas Lic 9hc
3⇌🛉 ✍ 25P 🍺 S% ✳B&b£12.65–£14.54
D9pm

INN Bull Hotel Market Pl ☎386599 Lic
12hc CTV 18P 2🏠 🍺 D8pm

NUNNEY Somerset Map 3 ST74
INN George Church St ☎458 Lic 6rm 1hc
3⇌🛉 CTV 20P S% ✳B&b£15–£20 sn
L£6alc D9.30pm£6alc

OAKS, THE, Charnwood Forest Leics
Map 8 SK31
INN Belfry Hotel Oaks Rd ☎Shepshed
3247 Lic 10hc CTV 200P 🍺 D10pm

OBAN Strathclyde Argyll Map 10 NM83
See Plan
⊢⊣**GH Ardblair** Dalriach Rd ☎2668
Plan:**1** 6 May–28 Sep 15hc (A 7hc) (4fb) ✍
CTV 12P sea B&b£5.31–£6.25
Bdi£8.95–£9.89

⊢⊣**GH Barriemore Private Hotel**
Esplanade ☎2197 Plan:**2** Apr–mid Oct
14hc (2fb) CTV 16P B&b£5.50–£7
Bdi£8.50–£9

GH Corremar Hotel Corran Esp ☎2476
Plan:**3** Apr–Oct Lic 17hc 4⇌🛉(4fb) CTV
10P sea B&b£8–£12 Bdi£15–£19
W£80–£120 ⊬ D6.30pm

GH Crathie Duncraggen Rd ☎2619
Plan:**4** May–Oct 9hc nc3 CTV 12P sea

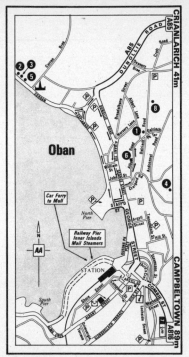

1 Ardblair	**5** Glenburnie Private
2 Barriemore Private	Hotel
Hotel	**6** Heatherfield Private
3 Corremar Hotel	Hotel
4 Crathie	**7** Kenmore
	8 Roseneath

GH Glenburnie Private Hotel Esplanade
☎2089 Plan:**5** May–Oct 13hc (3fb) ✆ nc8
TV 13P 1🏠 sea S% B&b£6.96–£9.49

GH Heatherfield Private Hotel Albert Rd
☎2681 Plan:**6** Apr–Oct 10hc (3fb) nc5 TV
10P sea S% ✳B&b£6.33 Bdi£10.30
W£65–£68 ⅃ D6.30pm

⊢⊣**GH Kenmore** Soraba Rd ☎3592
Plan:**7** 7hc (4fb) ✆ CTV 20P 🍴 S%
B&b£5–£5.50

GH Roseneath Dalriach Rd ☎2929
Plan:**8** 10hc (5fb) CTV 9P 🍴 S%
✳B&b£5.46–£6.32 Bdi£8.34–£9.48
W£62.10–£64.40 ⅃ D6.30pm

ODDINGTON Glos *Map 4 SP22*
INN Fox ☎Stow-on-the-Wold 30446 Lic
4hc ✆ TV 20P 🍴 sn D9pm

ODIHAM Hants·*Map 4 TQ75*
INN Kings Arms Hotel High St ☎2559
Lic 4hc CTV 4P S% ✳B&b£10 sn L£6alc
D9.30pm£6alc

OKEHAMPTON Devon·*Map 2 SX59*
INN *Fountain* Fore St ☎2828 Etr–Sep
Lic 6hc ✆ nc11 TV 6P 4🏠 🚗 D7pm

ONICH Highland *Inverness-shire
Map 14 NN06*
GH Glenmorven House ☎247 Mar–Oct
7rm 6hc (2fb) 20P 🍴 S% Bdi£11.78 W£80
⅃ D7pm

⊢⊣**GH Tigh-a-Righ** ☎255 Closed
22 Dec–7 Jan Lic 5hc (2fb) CTV 20P 🍴
B&b£4.89 Bdi£7.76 D8.30pm

ORFORD Suffolk *Map 5 TM44*
INN Kings Head Front St ☎271 Lic 5hc
✆ 100P 2🏠 🚗 B&b£11 sn L£6alc
D9pm£6alc

ORKNEY *Map 16*
See Kirkwall, Stromness

OSWESTRY Salop *Map 7 SJ22*
GH *Ashfield Country House* Llwyn-y-
Maen, Trefonen Rd ☎5200 Mar–Nov Lic
9hc 3⊣🍴 ✆ 15P 🍴

OXFORD Oxford *Map 4 SP50*
GH Ascot 283 Iffley Rd ☎40259 6hc
(3fb) ✆ CTV 2P 🍴 S% B&b£6–£7

⊢⊣**GH Brown's** 281 Iffley Rd ☎46822
6hc (2fb) CTV 3P 🍴 S% B&b£5–£6.50

⊢⊣**GH Combermere** 11 Polstead Rd
☎56971 6hc (2fb) ✆ nc8 CTV S% .
B&b£5.50–£6.50

GH Conifer 116 The Slade, Headington
☎63055 6hc (2fb) ✆ CTV 8P 🍴 S%
B&b£6–£6.50

⊢⊣**GH Earlmont** 322–324 Cowley Rd
☎40236 4hc (A 6hc) (2fb) ✆ CTV 10P 1🏠
🍴 S% B&b£5.50–£6.50

⊢⊣**GH Falcon** 88–90 Abingdon Rd
☎722995 12rm 10hc (3fb) ✆ TV 10P 🍴
S% B&b£5.75–£6.50 W£32–£38 M

GH Galaxie Private Hotel 180 Banbury
Rd ☎55688 20hc 2⊣🍴 (6fb) CTV 25P 🍴
S% B&b£7–£11

⊢⊣**GH Melcombe House** 227 Iffley Rd
☎49520 Closed Xmas 7hc (3fb) nc3 CTV
4P S% B&b£5.50–£7 (W only Nov–Mar)

⊢⊣GH Micklewood 331 Cowley Rd
☎47328 6hc (2fb) ⊗ CTV 6P 🎜 S%
B&b£5.50–£6.50

⊢⊣GH Pine Castle 290 Iffley Rd ☎41497
7hc (3fb) ⊗ CTV 4P 🎜 S% B&b£5–£6.50
Bdi£7.50–£8.50

GH *St Giles Hotel* 86 St Giles ☎54620
10hc ⊗ CTV

GH Victoria Hotel 180 Abingdon Rd
☎724536 Lic 20hc 5⇌🛁 (2fb) CTV 20P 🎜
& S% B&b£8.50–£10.50 D8.30pm

GH Westwood Country Hotel Hinksey
Hill Top ☎735408 Lic 16⇌🛁 (4fb) ⊗ CTV
19P 1🏚 🎜 S% B&b£9.49–£15.53
Bdi£12.37–£21.28 D2pm

GH Willow Reaches Private Hotel
1 Wytham St ☎43767 Lic 9hc 4⇌🛁 (3fb)

CTV 4P 2🏚 🎜 S% B&b£8–£10.50
Bdi£12.50–£14.50 W£87.50–£101.50 ⅃
D7.45pm

OXWICH W Glam *Map 2 SS58*
GH Oxwich Bay Hotel Gower ☎Gower
329 Etr–Sep rs Oct–mid Apr Lic 19hc
(2fb) ⊗ CTV 40P 🎜 sea S%
✳B&b£7–£8.18 D10pm

PADSTOW Cornwall *Map 2 SW97*
GH Cross House Church St ☎532391
Mar–Nov 9hc (4fb) ⊗ CTV 🎜 river
B&b£6.90 Bdi£9.20 W£62.10 ⅃ D6pm

GH Duke House 48–50 Duke St ☎532372
rs winter 10hc (6fb) TV S%
✳B&b£5.50–£7.50 W£37.50–£50 Ⓜ

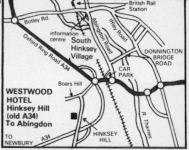

WILLOW REACHES

PRIVATE HOTEL
OXFORD

Residential licence

Comfortable accommodation with plenty of character. 5 bedrooms with bathroom en suite. Hot and cold water in all rooms. Colour TV lounge. 4 course evening meals. One mile only from city centre in quiet position off main road. Garden for use of guests. Five minute walk from lake, parks and swimming pools Garage accommodation.

**1 Wytham Street, Oxford.
Telephone; 721545**

CORNERWAYS HOTEL

16 Manor Road, Paignton

Telephone: 551207

★ LICENSED ★ First class catering
★ Ample free parking in Hotel grounds
★ Luxury bedrooms with private bathroom suites available ★ Bathing from Hotel ★ H&C and shaving points in all rooms ★ Dancing ★ Bar meals available NO RESTRICTIONS

REDUCED RATES FOR CHILDREN SHARING
SPECIAL TERMS FOR PARTIES EARLY AND LATE SEASON

Under the personal supervision of the Resident Proprietors: **Jennifer and Len Tyrell**

Residential licence.

Orange Tubs Hotel

Fire certificate.

**Manor Road, Paignton, Devon, TQ3 2HS
Telephone: 0803 551541**

The hotel is ideally situated in the centre of Torbay and on the level, yet only 100 yards from the sea front. Comfortable TV lounge. Sun lounge. Attractive bar. Excellent varied cuisine. Full central heating. Free parking at rear. Resident proprietors: Lynn and Ken Roughley.

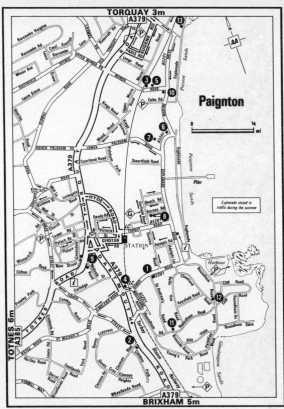

1 Amaryllis Hotel
2 Clennon Valley Hotel
3 Cornerways Hotel
4 Nevada Private Hotel
5 Orange Tubs
6 Redcliffe Lodge Hotel
7 Roseville Private Hotel
8 St Weonard Private Hotel
9 San Remo Hotel
10 Sea Verge Hotel
11 Shorton House
12 Sunnybank Private Hotelfi
13 Torbay Sands Hotel

GH Nook Fentonluna Ln ☎532317 mid Mar–Oct Lic 10hc (3fb) nc5 CTV 10P 🛏 S% ✱B&b£6–£7.60 Bdi£10–£11.60 W£34–£40 ℳ D6.15pm

GH Tregea High St ☎532455 Etr–Sep 8hc CTV 8P 🛏 S% B&b£8.34 Bdi£11.50 W£80.50 ⟁

PAIGNTON Devon Map 3 SX86 **See Plan**
GH Amaryllis Hotel 14 Sands Rd ☎559552 Plan:**1** 10hc ⊗ CTV 10P W only Jul–Aug

GH Clennon Valley Hotel 1 Clennon Rise ☎557736 Plan:**2** Closed Xmas Lic 12hc (5fb) CTV 12P 🛏 S% B&b£6.33–£6.90 Bdi£10.35–£11.50 W£69–£71.30 ⟁ D5pm

GH Cornerways Hotel 16 Manor Rd ☎551207 Plan:**3** Apr–Oct Lic 22hc 13⇄🍴 (8fb) CTV 22P sea S% B&b£6–£8.50 Bdi£9.50–£12.50 (W only Jul–Aug) D6pm

GH Nevada Private Hotel 61 Dartmouth Rd ☎558317 Plan:**4** Closed Xmas Lic 12hc (3fb) ⊗ CTV 12P 🛏 S% B&b£7–£8 Bdi£10–£11 W£63–£70 ⟁ D6pm

GH Orange Tubs Hotel 14 Manor Rd, Preston ☎551541 Plan:**5** Etr–Oct Lic 11hc 2⇄🍴(3fb) ⊗ CTV 8P 🛏 sea S% B&b£6–£10 Bdi£8–£12 D6.30pm

GH Redcliffe Lodge Hotel 1 Marine Dr ☎551394 Plan:**6** Mar–Oct Lic 16hc 4⇄🍴 CTV 24P

155

GH *Roseville Private Hotel* Marine Gdns ☎550530 Plan:**7** Lic 11hc CTV 12P

GH St Weonard Private Hotel 12 Kernou Rd ☎558842 Plan:**8** Lic 9hc (4fb) ⊘ CTV 2P S% B&b£7.50–£9.50 Bdi£9.50–£11.50 W£65–£72 ⱶ W only Jul–Aug D4.30pm

⊢⊣**GH *San Remo*** 35 Totnes Rd ☎557855 Plan:**9** Lic 18hc (A 4rm 3hc) ⊘ CTV 12P 1🏠

GH Sea Verge Hotel Marine Dr, Preston ☎557795 Plan:**10** Mar–Nov Lic 12hc 2🛁 (5fb) ⊘ CTV 18P sea S% B&b£6–£7.50 Bdi£9.50–£11 W£64.40–£70.15 ⱶ

GH Shorton House 17 Roundham Rd ☎557722 Plan:**11** Mar–Aug Lic 18hc (8fb) CTV 20P ♿ S% B&b£7–£9.50 Bdi£8.50–£11.50 Wfr£65 ⱶ D6pm

GH Sunnybank Private Hotel 2 Cleaveland Rd ☎559153 Plan:**12** Mar–Oct Lic 12hc 2🛁 (5fb) ⊘ CTV 12P S% B&b£7.20–£10 W£48–£59 ⱶ

GH Torbay Sands Hotel Sea Front, 16 Marine Pde ☎522012 Plan:**13** 13hc (4fb) CTV 6P sea S% B&b£6–£7.60 Bdi£8–£9.60 W£46–£60 ⱶ D4.30pm

PAISLEY Stratclyde *Renfrews Map 11 NS46* **For accommodation details see under Glasgow Airport**

PEACEHAVEN E Sussex *Map 5 TQ40*
INN Peacehaven Hotel South Coast Rd ☎4555 Lic 12hc 3🛁 CTV 50P ♨ ♿ B&b£12.50 W£160 L£1.65–£5.50&alc D9.45fr£6.60&alc

PEASMARSH E Sussex *Map 5 TQ82*
GH Flackley Ash Hotel & Restaurant ☎381 15Jan–23Dec Lic 17🛁 (4fb) ♣ CTV 40P 2🏠 ♨ S% B&b£12–£16 Bdi£18–£23 W£110–£125 ⱶ D10pm

PEEBLES Borders *Peebles Map 11 NT24*
⊢⊣**GH Lindores** Old Town ☎20441 Closed Nov 5hc (2fb) CTV 3P ♨ S% B&b£5.50–£6 W£38.50–£42 M

PEMBROKE Dyfed *Map 2 SM90*
GH Camrose House 106 St Michaels Sq ☎5383 7hc (2fb) CTV ♨ S% B&b£6–£7.50 Bdi£8.50–£10 D6.30pm

PENARTH S Glam *Map 3 ST17*
GH Alanleigh Hotel 14 Victoria Rd ☎Cardiff 701242 Lic 9hc 1🛁 CTV 8P ♨ S% B&b£8.05–£9.20 Bdi£12.08–£13.80 W£84.56–£96.60 ⱶ D6.30pm

GH Westbourne Hotel 8 Victoria Rd ☎707268 Lic 11hc (1fb) ⊘ CTV 6P ♨ S% B&b£9.78 D10pm

PENRITH Cumbria *Map 12 NY53*
GH Brandelhow 1 Portland Pl ☎64470 7rm 6hc (3fb) CTV 1P S% B&b£6–£7 Bdi£9.25–£10.25 W£64.75–£71.75 ⱶ D8pm

GH *Kinsale* 24 Wordsworth St ☎63265 6hc ⊘ CTV

GH Pategill Villas Carleton Rd ☎63153 Lic 12hc (4fb) ♣ CTV 16P ♨ S% B&b£6–£7 W£70–£80 ⱶ D6pm

GH *Waverley Hotel* Crown Sq ☎63962 Lic 7hc 1🛁 CTV 30P 2🏠

GH Woodland House Private Hotel Wordsworth St ☎64177 rs Xmas Day (B&b only) Lic 8hc (2fb) CTV 12P 1🏠 ♨ S% B&b£6–£6.50 Bdi£9.75–£10.25 W£68.25–£71.75 ⱶ D7pm

PENZANCE Cornwall *Map 2 SW43*
See Plan
GH Alverton Court Hotel Alverton Rd ☎2306 Plan:**1** Apr–Oct Lic 15hc 6🛁 (3fb) ⊘ nc5 CTV 12P 1🏠 sea S% B&b£6.50–£10.50 Bdi£12–£16 ⱶ D6pm

⊢⊣**GH Bella-Vista Private Hotel** 7 Alexandra Ter, Larrigan ☎2409 Plan:**2** 28Mar–17Oct 10hc (4fb) ⊘ nc3 CTV 8P sea S% B&b£5.50–£7.50 Bdi£8.75–£10.75 W£47–£61 ⱶ D5pm

⊢⊣**GH Camilla Hotel** Regent Ter ☎3771 Plan:**3** Closed Dec–Jan 10hc 2fb CTV 3P ♨ sea S% B&b£5–£6 Bdi£7–£8 W£45–£52 ⱶ

GH Carlton Private Hotel ☎2081 Plan:**4** Mar–Oct rs Jan–Feb (B&b only) Lic 12hc 3🛁 (3fb) ⊘ nc10 CTV sea S% B&b£7.50–£8.50 Bdi£12.50–£14 ⱶ D5pm

GH Dunedin Alexandra Rd ☎2652 Plan:**5** Mar–Nov Lic 9hc (5fb) nc3 CTV ♨ *B&b£6.50–£8 Bdi£10–£11.50 W£63–£75 ⱶ D4pm

GH Duporth Private Hotel 1 Mennaye Rd ☎2689 Plan:**6** Apr–Oct 9hc CTV sea B&b£6.50–£7.50 Bdi£10–£11 W£58–£70 ⱶ

GH Essex 23 Lannoweth Rd ☎5129 Plan:**7** May–Oct rs Mar–Apr (B&b only) Lic 11hc ⊘ nc12 CTV 6P sea S% B&b£6–£7 Bdi£8–£10 D4pm

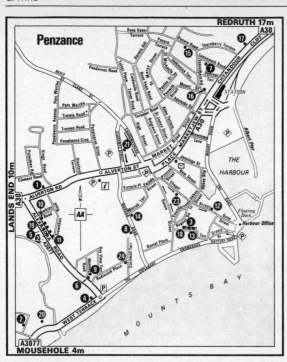

1	Alverton Court Hotel
2	Bella-Vista Private Hotel
3	Camilla Hotel
4	Carlton Private Hotel
5	Dunedin
6	Duporth Private Hotel
7	Essex
8	Estoril Private Hotel
9	Glancree Private Hotel
10	Hansord Private Hotel
11	Holbein Hotel
12	Hopedale
13	Kilindini Private Hotel
14	Kimberley House
15	Kirkstowe
16	The Longboat (*Inn*)
17	Mount Royal Hotel
18	Old Manor House Private Hotel
19	Penmorvah Hotel
20	Sea & Horses Hotel
21	Tarbert Hotel
22	Trenant Private Hotel
23	Trevelyan Hotel
24	Willows

GH Estoril Private Hotel 46 Morrab Rd ☎2468 Plan:**8** Lic 10⇄🛏(1fb) CTV 5P 🍴 B&b£11 Bdi£14.95–£15.52 W£89–£103.50 ⨭ D7pm

GH Glencree Private Hotel 2 Mennaye Rd ☎2026 Plan:**9** Mar–Oct 9hc (3fb) ⊗ CTV sea S% B&b£6.50–£7 Bdi£8.75–£9.25 W£60–£65 ⨭

GH Hansord Private Hotel Alexandra Rd ☎3311 Plan:**10** Mar–Oct rs Jan–Feb Lic 12hc (2fb) nc3 CTV 🍴 S% B&b£6.50–£7 Bdi£10–£11 W£60–£67 ⨭ D4pm

GH Holbein House Alexandra Rd ☎5008 Plan:**11** Lic 8hc 1⇄🛏(2fb) ⊗ nc3 CTV 🍴 S% B&b£6–£8 Bdi£9–£11 W£55–£70 ⨭ D5.30pm

GH Hopedale 29 Chapel St ☎3277 Plan:**12** 6hc (2fb) ⊗ CTV sea S% ✷B&b£6.50–£8

GH Kilindini Private Hotel 13 Regent Ter ☎4744 Plan:**13** Feb–Nov 11hc (3fb) ⊗ nc3 CTV 12P sea S% B&b£6.32–£8.05 Bdi£8.62–£10.35 W£55.20–£64.40 ⨭ D3pm

GH Kimberley House 10 Morrab Rd ☎2727 Plan:**14** Jan–Oct Lic 9hc ⊗ nc5 CTV 4P 🍴 S% B&b£7.75–£8.75 Bdi£12–£13 W£75–£84 ⨭ D6pm

GH Kirkstowe Penare Rd ☎3115 Plan:**15** Lic 9hc (2fb) ⊗ nc7 CTV 5P 🍴 S% B&b£7 Bdi£10 W£57–£62 ⨭ D4pm

GH Mount Royal Hotel Chyandour Cliff ☎2233 Plan:**17** Mar–Oct 9hc 1⇄🛏(1fb) CTV 12P 4🏠 🍴 sea S% B&b£7.50–£9 Bdi£12.50–£14 W£49–£59.50 Ⓜ D7pm

GH Old Manor House Private Hotel Regent Ter ☎3742 Plan:**18** Lic 12hc (6fb) ⊗ CTV 10P 🍴 sea S% B&b£7.80–£8.75 Bdi£10.80–£11.75 W£60–£75 ⨭ D6.30pm

GH Penmorvah Hotel Alexandra Rd
☎3711 Plan:**19** Lic 10hc 2⇔🏠 (4fb) CTV
2P 🛏 S% B&b£6–£9 Bdi£9–£12
W£50–£74 ⊾ D6.20pm

GH Sea & Horses Hotel 6 Alexandra Ter
☎61961 Plan:**20** Apr–Oct Lic 11hc
(4fb) ✦ CTV 9P 🛏 sea S% B&bfr£7.48
Bdi fr£10.93 Wfr£74.75 ⊾

GH Tarbert Hotel 11 Clarence St ☎3758
Plan:**21** Lic 9hc (4fb) ✦ CTV 🛏 S%
B&b£6.90–£8.05 Bdi£10.07–£10.93
W£69–£75.90 ⊾ D4pm

↣GH Trenant Private Hotel Alexandra Rd
☎2005 May–6Oct 7hc nc9 TV S%
B&b£5.40–£5.90 Bdi£8.20–£9
W£51.50–£58 ⊾ D5pm

↣GH Trevelyan Hotel 16 Chapel St
☎2494 Plan:**23** Lic 7hc (4fb) CTV 9P sea
S% B&b£5–£6 Bdi£7.50–£9
W£52.50–£63 ⊾ Dnoon

GH Willows Cornwall Ter ☎3744 Plan:**24**
6hc (1fb) nc5 CTV 6P 🛏 S%
B&b£6.65–£7.70 Bdi£9.35–£10.50
W£59–£66 ⊾ D3pm

INN Longboat Market Jew St ☎4137
Plan:**16** Lic 15hc 2⇔🏠 ✦ CTV 4🏠 🛏 S%
B&b£7–£10 W£42–£63 M sn L£3alc
D9pm£3.50alc

PERRANPORTH Cornwall *Map 2 SW75*
GH Beach Dunes Hotel Ramoth Way,
Reen Sands ☎2263 Apr–Oct Lic 8hc
1⇔🏠 (2⇔🏠) (3fb) ⚘ CTV 14P 🛏 sea S%
B&b£11.50–£13.50 Bdi£14.50–£16.50
W£101.50–£115.50 ⊾ D6pm

GH *Boscawen Private Hotel* ☎3472
Etr–5Oct Lic 15hc CTV 10P 1🏠

GH Cellar Cove Hotel Droskyn Point
☎2110 Lic 14hc (2hc 1⇔🏠) (5fb) CTV 18P
sea S% D6.30pm

GH Fairview Hotel Tywarnhayle Rd
☎2278 May–Oct Lic 15hc (6fb) ✦ CTV
3P 🛏 sea S% ✱B&b£6.32–£6.90
Bdi£8.62–£9.75 (W only Jul–Aug) D4pm

GH Lake House Private Hotel
Perrancombe ☎3202 Late Mar–early Oct
Lic 10hc (3fb) ✦ CTV 🛏 S%
B&b£6.90–£10.35 Bdi£8.05–£11.50
W£52.90–£75.90 ⊾ (W only Jul–Aug)
D6.30pm

GH Lamorna Private Hotel Tywarnhayle Rd
☎3398 Closed Xmas Lic 9hc (4fb) CTV 3P
S% B&b£7.48–£8.63 Bdi£9.78–£10.93
W£64.40–£74.75 ⊾ (W only Jun–Sep)
D6pm

↣GH Lynton Cliff Rd ☎3457 Lic 7hc
(3fb) ✦ CTV 6P 🛏 sea S% B&b£4.75–£6.25
Bdi£7.50–£9 W£44–£58 ⊾ D6pm

GH Park View Private Hotel 42
Tywarnhayle Rd ☎3009 Mar–Oct Lic 10hc
(4fb) CTV 10P S% B&b£6–£7.50
Bdi£8–£9.75 W£56.50–£64.50 ⊾ D4pm

PERRANUTHNOE Cornwall *Map 2 SW52*
GH Ednovean House ☎Marazion
711071 Closed Nov Lic 8hc 3⇔🏠 (1fb) ✦
nc7 CTV 12P 🛏 sea S% B&b£6–£10
Bdi£10.50–£15 W£70–£95 ⊾ D5pm

PERTH Tayside *Perths Map 11 NO12*
↣GH Clunie 12 Pitcullen Cres ☎23625
7hc 2⇔🏠 (3fb) ✦ CTV 8P 🛏 S%
B&b£5.50–£6.50 Bdi£8–£9
W£52.50–£59.50 ⊾ D6pm

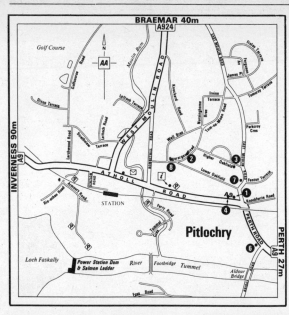

1 Acarsaid Hotel
2 Adderley Private Hotel
3 Balrobin Private Hotel
4 Craig Urrard Hotel
6 Fasganeoin Hotel
7 Poplars Private Hotel
8 Well House Private Hotel

⊨⊨ **GH The Darroch** 9 Pitcullen Cres
☎36893 7hc 1⊶🛋 (3fb) TV 10P 🛏 ⅋
S% B&b£5.50–£6 Bdi£8.50 D8.15pm

GH *Garth* Dundee Rd ☎22368 6hc CTV
8P 🛏

⊨⊨ **GH Pitcullen** 17 Pitcullen Cres
☎26506 8hc (2fb) CTV 10P 🛏 S%
B&b£5–£6 Bdi£8–£10 D6pm

PETERSFIELD Hants *Map 4 SU72*
GH *Malva Hotel* 3 Church Rd, Steep
(2m NW unclass) ☎2657 Lic 5hc ⅋ CTV
12P

PICKERING N Yorks *Map 8 SE88*
GH Bramwood 19 Hall Garth ☎74066
6hc (2fb) ⅋ nc6 CTV 6P 🛏 S%
B&b£7.20–£10.20 Bdi£9.30–£13.20
D6pm

PILTON Somerset *Map 3 ST54*
GH Long House ☎283 Lic 7hc 4⊶🛋
(1fb) 10P 2🏠 🛏 S% B&b£7.80–£9.75
Bdi£13.15–£15.10 W£93.25–£114.25 ⅃
D6.30pm

PITLOCHRY Tayside *Perths Map 14 NN95*
See Plan
GH Acarsaid Hotel 8 Atholl Rd ☎2389
Plan:**1** Lic 21hc ⅋ TV 20P

GH Adderley Private Hotel 23Toberargan
Rd ☎2433 Plan:**2** 20 Apr–5 Oct 10hc (2fb)
⅋ nc9 CTV 9P S% Bdi£10.75–£11.60
W£69.80–£77.20 ⅃ D6.30pm

GH Balrobin Private Hotel Higher
Oakfield ☎2901 Plan:**3** May–Sep 7hc
2⊶🛋 (2fb) 8P S% B&b£10 Bdi£15
W£90–£100 ⅃ D6.45pm

GH Craig Urrard Hotel 10 Atholl Rd
☎2346 Plan:**4** Mar–Nov Lic 10hc 2⊶🛋
(A 2hc) (4fb) CTV 16P B&b£9–£10
Bdi£13.50–£14.30 W£88.50–£95 ⅃
D7pm

GH Fasganeoin Hotel.Perth Rd ☎2387
Plan:**6** Apr–Sep Lic 9hc (4fb) ⅋ TV 20P 🛏
S% Bdi£13.50–£14.50 W£92–£99 ⅃
D7.30pm

GH *Poplars Private Hotel* Lower Oakfield
☎2129 Plan:**7** Mar–Oct Tem 8hc 3⊶🛋
CTV 10P 🛏

GH Well House Private Hotel
Toberargan Rd ☎2239 Plan.**8**
mid Apr–mid Oct Lic 8hc (3fb) ⅋ nc10 CTV
10P S% B&b£6.25–£6.50 W£42–£43.75
Ⓜ (W only)

PLOCKTON Highland *Ross & Crom
Map 14 NG83*
GH Haven ☎223 Closed Xmas 15hc 1⊶🛋
(4fb) CTV 9P 🛏 B&b fr£7.50 Bdi fr£12
W£80.50 ⅃ D8pm

PLYMOUTH Devon *Map 2 SX45*
See Plan
During the currency of this guide, all
Plymouth five figure telephone numbers
starting with 6, are liable to be prefixed with
a further 6

GH *Bowling Green Hotel* Lockyer St, The
Hoe ☎67485 Plan:**1** Tem 12hc CTV P 4🏠
🛏

⊨⊨ **GH Burgoyne Villa** 70 Alma Rd, Mile
House ☎62624 Plan:**2** 10hc (3fb) CTV
10P 🛏 S% B&b£5–£5.50

⊨⊨ **GH Cadleigh** 36 Queens Rd ☎65909
Plan:**3** 10rm 9hc (4fb) CTV 🛏 S%
B&b£5.50–£6 Bdi£8.50–£9 D am

⊨⊨ **GH Chester** 54 Stuart Rd,
Pennycomequick ☎63706 Plan.**4** 7hc
(2fb) nc6 CTV 7P 1🏠 🛏 S% B&b£5.50

⊨⊨ **GH Dudley** 42 Sutherland Rd, Mutley
☎68322 Plan:**5** 7hc (3fb) CTV 3P 🛏 S%
B&b£5.50–£6.50 Bdi£9.50–£10.50
D noon

GH Eddystone 16 Woodland Ter,
Greenbank ☎68672 Plan:**6** Closed Xmas
wk Lic 7hc (3fb) CTV 4P S% ✱B&b£5
Bdi£8 W£56 ⅃ D4.30pm

GH Gables End 6 Sutherland Rd, Mutley
☎20803 Plan:**7** 6hc CTV 🛏 S% ✱B&b£6
Bdi£10 W£65 ⅃ D3pm

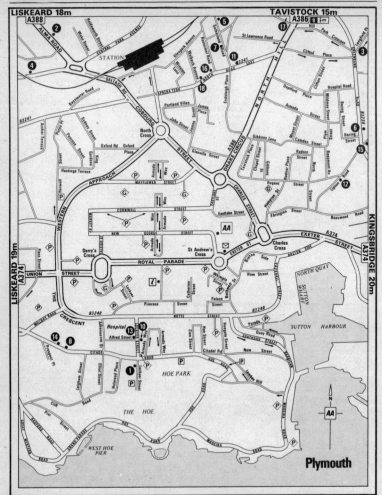

1	Bowling Green Hotel	6	Eddystone	11	Kildare	16	Welbeck House
2	Burgoyne Villa	7	Gables End Hotel	12	Lagos Hotel	17	York
3	Cadleigh	8	Georgian House Hotel	13	Lockyer House Hotel	18	Yorkshireman Hotel
4	Chester	9	Glendevon Hotel	14	St James Hotel		
5	Dudley	10	Imperial Hotel	15	Trenant House		

GH Georgian House Hotel 51 Citadel Rd, The Hoe ☎63237 Plan:**8** Lic 10hc 2⇌🛏 (1fb) CTV 1P 🚿 S% B&b£10—£12 D9pm

GH Glendevon Hotel 20 Ford Park Rd, Mutley ☎63655 Plan:**9** rs Xmas day & Boxing day Lic 8hc (2fb) ⚓ CTV 🚿 S% B&b£6.32—£7.50 Bdi£9.80—£11.60 W£68.60—£81.20 ⅄ D9pm

GH Imperial Hotel 3 Windsor Villas, Lockyer St, The Hoe ☎27311 Plan:**10** Closed Xmas Lic 24hc 11⇌🛏 (5fb) ⚓ CTV 20P 1🛏 🚿 S% B&b£10—£12.50 Bdi£15—£17 W£80—£125 ⅄ D7.30pm

⊢⊣GH Kildare 82 North Road East ☎29375 Plan:**11** Closed Xmas wk 9hc 1⇌🛏 (2fb) 🚿 CTV 🚿 S% B&b£5.75—£7

GH Lagos Hotel 46 Lipson Rd ☎69145 Plan:**12** Closed Xmas Lic 8hc (4fb) CTV ✳B&b£5.20—£6 Bdi£8.50—£9.30

W£36.40—£42 ⅄ D noon

GH Lockyer House Hotel 2 Alfred St, The Hoe ☎65755 Plan:**13** Lic 6hc (1fb) CTV 🚿 ✳B&b£6—£6.50 Bdi£9.50—£10 D am

⊢⊣GH Norway 70 Normandy Way, St Budeaux ☎361979 Not on plan 6hc (1fb) 🚿 CTV river S% B&b£4.75—£5.25 Bdi£7.25—£8 W£50—£53 ⅄D7.30pm

GH St James Hotel 49 Citadel Rd, The Hoe ☎61950 Plan:**14** Lic 9hc 6⇌🛏 (3fb) nc8 CTV S% ✳B&b fr£8.25 Bdi fr£11.75 Wfr£82.25 ⅄ D6pm

GH Trenant House Queens Rd, Lipson ☎63879 Plan:**15** Lic 21hc (2fb) CTV 20P 🚿 river S% B&b£8—£9 Bdi£12—£13.50 W£47—£56 M D4pm

⊢⊣GH Welbeck Hotel North Rd East ☎61350 Plan:**16** Closed Xmas wk 7hc 1⇌🛏 (2fb) CTV S% B&b fr£5

⊢⊣GH York 23 Wilderness Rd,
Mannamead ☎266129 Plan:**17** 6hc (2fb)
CTV sea S% B&b£5–£6 Bdi£7.50–£8.50
W(5dys)£37.50–£40.50 ⚊ D4pm

GH Yorkshireman Hotel 64 North
Road East ☎68133 Plan:**18** Closed Xmas
13hc (5fb) ⊗ CTV 7P

POLBATHIC Cornwall *Map 2 SX35*
GH *Tredis House Hotel* ☎St Germans
669 Lic 5hc ⚘ CTV 20P ⊞

POLMASSICK Cornwall *Map 2 SW94*
GH Kilbol House ☎Mevagissey 2481
Closed Xmas Lic 7hc 1⇔⋔(2fb) ⊗ nc5 CTV
15P ⊞ S% B&b£7.50–£8 Bdi£11.50–£12
W£80–£83 ⚊ W only mid Jun–Aug
D5.30pm

POLPERRO Cornwall *Map 2 SX25*

GH Atlantis Hotel Polperro Rd ☎72243
Lic 9hc 3⇔⋔(2fb) ⊗ CTV 12P S%
B&b£7.50–£8.50 Bdi£11–£12
W£60–£85 ⚊

⊢⊣GH Kit Hill Talland Hill ☎72369
Closed Xmas & New Year Lic 5rm 4hc
(1fb) ⊗ nc6 CTV 10P ⊞ S% B&b£5.50–£9
Bdi£10.50–£14 W£73.50–£98 ⚊ D5pm

GH Landaviddy Manor Landaviddy Ln
☎72210 Mar–Oct Lic 11hc 2⇔⋔⊗ nc12
TV 12P ⊞ sea B&b£8–£11
Bdi£13.75–£16.75 W£83–£93 ⚊ D10am

⊢⊣GH Sleepy Hollow Private Hotel
Brentfields ☎72288 Mar–Sep 7hc 2⇔⋔
(1fb) nc12 CTV 7P sea S%
B&b£5.50–£7.50 Bdi£8–£11
W£56–£77 ⚊ D4.30pm

POLRUAN Cornwall *Map 2 SX15*
GH Florizel Fore St ☎208 Mar–Oct 12hc
2⇄▥ nc8 CTV 4P 10▥ sea S%
B&b£8–£10 Bdi£12–£14 W£80–£90 ⅃
D7pm

POLYPHANT Cornwall *Map 2 SX28*
GH Bowden Derra Country House
☎Pipers Pool 230 Closed Xmas day Lic
7hc 2⇄▥ (2fb) ⌑ CTV P ▥ S%
✳B&b£8.05–£9.20 Bdi£13.23–£14.57
W£81.07–£94.87 ⅃ D9pm

POLZEATH Cornwall *Map 2 SW97*
⋈ **GH White Lodge** Old Polzeath
☎Trebetherick 2370 Lic 8hc (A 4hc) (2fb)
CTV 9P ▥ ⅋ S% B&b£5–£6
Bdi£8.50–£9.50 W£49.50–£62 ⅃ D4pm

PONTLYFNI Gwynedd *Map 6 SH45*
GH Bron Dirion Hotel ☎Clynnogfawr
346 Mar–Oct Lic 9hc (4fb) CTV 12P ▥ sea
S% ✳B&b£6.50–£7 Bdi£8–£8.50
W£50–£55 ⅃ (W only Jun–Aug) D6.30pm

POOLE Dorset *Map 4 SZ09*
For locations and additional guesthouses
see **Bournemouth**
GH Avalon Private Hotel 14 Pinewood
Rd, Branksome Park ☎760917
Bournemouth district plan:**52** Lic 14hc
5⇄▥ nc CTV 14P ▥ S% B&b£6.50–£7.50
Bdi£8.50–£10 D3pm

GH Blue Shutters Hotel 109 North Rd,
Lower Parkstone ☎748129 Bournemouth
district plan:**57** Lic 11hc (1fb) ⅋ CTV 10P
▥ B&B£9.66–£10.35 Bdi£13.45–£14.37
W£88.32–£92 ⅃ W only 24 Jul–Aug
D10pm

GH Dene Hotel 16 Pinewood Rd,
Branksome Park ☎761143 Bournemouth
district plan:**63** Jan–Oct & Dec Lic 16hc
6⇄▥ (5fb) CTV 19P ▥ S% B&b£8.50
Bdi£12.50 W£67.50 ⅃ D9pm

GH Lewina 225 Bournemouth Rd,
Parkstone ☎742295 Bournemouth district
plan:**75** 6hc (2fb) TV 8P S%
✳B&b£4.50–£5.50 Wfr£26 M

GH Ormonde House 18 Ormonde Rd,
Branksome Park ☎761093 Bournemouth
district plan:**85** Etr–mid Oct Lic 8hc (2fb)
⌑ CTV 5P S% B&b£7.59–£9.66
Bdi£10.35–£12.42 W£68.95–£83.44 ⅃
W only Jul–Aug D6pm

GH Redcroft Private Hotel 20 Pinewood
Rd, Branksome Park ☎763959
Bournemouth district plan:**89** 9hc (5fb) ⌑

nc5 CTV 12P S% B&b£7–£9 Bdi£10–£12
W£76–£86 D4pm

GH Sandbourne Hotel 1 Sandecotes Rd,
Parkstone ☎747704 Bournemouth district
plan:**92** 7hc 3⇄▥ (3fb) 8P ▥ S%
B&b£6.50 Bdi£9 Wfr£56 ⅃ D6pm

GH Sheldon Lodge 22 Forest Rd,
Branksome Park ☎761186 Bournemouth
district plan:**94** Xmas & Etr–Oct Lic 15hc
5⇄▥ (3fb) ⌑ CTV 15P 3▥ S%
B&b£9.08–£12.07 Bdi£12.07–£13.80
W£79.92–£89.70 ⅃ D6pm

GH Teesdale Hotel 3 De Maulley Rd,
Canford Cliffs ☎708707 Bournemouth
district plan:**99** Lic 15hc 5⇄▥ (3fb) ⅋ CTV
8P ▥ B&b£11–£12.50 Bdi£13.50–£15
W£74.50–£90.25 ⅃ (W only Jul–Aug)
D7pm

GH Twin Cedars Hotel 2 Pinewood Rd,
Branksome Park ☎761339 Bournemouth
district plan:**100** Lic 11hc 3⇄▥ (3fb) nc5
⅋ CTV 15P S% B&b£7–£10
Bdi£10–£13 W£65–£80 ⅃ D5pm

GH *Westminster Cottage Hotel*
3 Westminster Rd East, Branksome Park
☎76526b Bournemouth distric plan:**103**
Lic 12hc 4⇄▥ CTV 14P

PORLOCK Somerset *Map 3 SS84*
GH *Gables* ☎862552 Etr–Oct 8hc ⌑
nc12 CTV 9P D4pm

GH Lorna Doone Hotel ☎862404
Mar–mid Jan Lic 10hc 2⇄▥ (1fb) ⌑ CTV
8P ▥ ✳B&b£7–£8.50 Bdi£10.50–£12
W£45.50–£81.50 ⅃ D8pm

GH Overstream Parson St ☎862421
Closed Xmas 7hc (3fb) nc3 10P lift S%
✳B&b£6.50 Bdi£9.50 W£62 ⅃ D3pm

PORT ELLEN Isle of Islay, Strathclyde
Argyll Map 10 NR34
GH Tighcargaman ☎2345 Lic 3hc 1⇄▥
(A 6rm 4hc 1⇄▥) (2fb) ⅋ 9P ▥ sea S%
✳B&b£10.05 Bdi£16.70 W£110.75 ⅃
D8pm

PORT ERIN Isle of Man *Map 6 SC26*
GH *Golf Links Hotel* ☎832270
May–29 Sep Lic 64hc ⌑ ⅋ CTV 35P sea
D8pm

GH Regent Hotel ☎833454 Apr–Sep
12hc 1⇄▥ (3fb) ⌑ CTV sea S%
B&b£6–£6.50 Bdi£7–£7.50
W£49–£52.50 ⅃ D noon

GH *Snaefell* The Promenade ☎832273
May–Sep Lic 54hc ⅋ CTV 40P sea D7pm

PORTHCAWL Mid Glam *Map 3 SS87*
GH Collingwood Hotel 40 Mary St
☎2899 Lic 6hc (3fb) ⌘ CTV ⊕ S% B&b£6
Bdi£8.50 W£56 ⥼ D4pm

⤛ **GH Craig-Y-Don Private Hotel** 30 The
Esplanade ☎3259 9hc (2fb) ⌘ CTV ⊕ S%
B&b£5.50–£6 Bdi£7.50–£8 Wfr£50 ⥼
D7.30pm

⤛ **GH Gwalia Private Hotel** 40 Esplanade
Ave ☎2751 Closed Xmas wk 7hc (2fb) ⌘
TV ⊕ S% B&b£5.50

GH Seaways Hotel 28 Mary St ☎3510
Lic 12hc (3fb) ⌘ CTV B&b£12–£15
Bdi£18–£20 W£75 Ⓜ (W only Jun–Sep)
D8.30pm

PORTHCOTHAN BAY Cornwall
Map 2 SW87
GH Bay House ☎St Merryn 520472
Etr–Sep Lic 17hc (2fb) CTV 20P sea
✱B&b£6–£7.80 Bdi£8–£10.30
W£53–£69 ⥼ D noon

PORTHCURNO Cornwall *Map 2 SW32*
GH Corniche Trebehor Farm ☎Sennen
424 Closed Xmas Lic 6hc (1fb) ⌘ nc7 CTV
8P ⊕ B&b£6–£6.50 Bdi£9.50–£10
W£67–£70 ⥼ (W only Jul–Aug) D6pm

GH Mariners Lodge ☎St Buryan 236
Feb–Nov Lic 7hc 3⇔🛁 (2fb) nc5 CTV
15P ⊕ sea S% B&b£6–£11.50
Bdi£11–£17.50 D7.30pm

PORTHMADOG Gwynedd *Map 6 SH53*
GH Oakleys The Harbour ☎2482
Apr–Nov Lic 8hc 2⇔🛁 (2fb) ⌘ CTV 12P
S% B&b£7.50–£8.50 Bdi£11–£12
W£70–£80 ⥼ D6pm

GH Owen's Hotel High St ☎2098 Closed
Xmas Lic 12hc 1⇔🛁 (4fb) CTV 3P 5🏠 ⊕
S% B&b£8–£8.50 Bdi£12.50–£13
W£80–£86 ⥼D7pm

GH Tan-yr-Onnen Hotel Penamser Rd
☎2443 Closed Dec rs Nov & Feb Lic 11hc
1⇔🛁 (1fb) ⌘ CTV 10P ⊕ B&b£7–£7.50
Bdi£11–£11.50 W£75–£80 ⥼ D9am

PORT ISAAC Cornwall *Map 2 SW98*
GH Archer Farm Trewetha (1m E B3267)
☎522 Apr–Dec Lic 9rm 8hc 3⇔🛁 (1fb)
nc3 CTV 8P ⊕ S% ✱B&b£5.50–£6.50
Bdi£9.50–£10.50 W£64–£71 ⥼ (W only
end Jun–early Sep) D7.30pm

GH *Fairholme* 30 Trewetha Ln ☎323
Apr–mid Oct 7hc CTV 8P

GH *Trethoway Hotel* 98 Fore St ☎214
Lic 12hc ⌀ CTV 1🏠 ⅙ sea

PORTPATRICK Dumfries & Galloway
Wigtowns Map 10 NX05
⤛ **GH Blinkbonnie** School Brae ☎282
Feb–Nov 6hc (1fb) CTV 8P ⊕ B&b£5–£6
Bdi£8.50–£9.60 W£58–£66.20 ⥼ D6pm

GH Carlton 21 South Cres ☎253
Etr–Oct 8hc nc CTV ⊕ sea B&b£6–£7
Bdi£10–£11 W£55–£60 ⥼ D6.30pm

GH Melvin Lodge Dunskey St ☎238
Apr–Sep 13hc (4fb) CTV 9P sea
✱B&b£7 Bdi£9 W£56 ⥼ D6pm

GH South Cliff House Hotel ☎411 Lic
6hc (2fb) CTV 8P ⊕ sea S% B&b£10 Bdi£13
W£91 ⥼ D9pm

PORTREE Isle of Skye, Highland
Inverness-shire Map 13 NG44
GH Bosville Hotel Bosville Ter ☎2846

Corniche Farmhouse

Trebehor Farm, Porthcurno, Penzance, Cornwall
Tel: Sennen 424

Corniche is situated near the beautiful sandy beaches of Porthcurno and Sennen. There are many coves and cliff paths for those who like walking, and surfing at Sennen. The Farmhouse offers a high standard of comfort with a lounge/dining room commanding panoramic views of the sea. The bedrooms are well appointed. Much of the food served is provided by the farm.

THE OAKLEYS GUEST HOUSE

The Harbour, Porthmadog Telephone: Porthmadog 2482 (STD 0766)

Proprietors: Mr & Mrs A H Biddle.
H & C in bedrooms, electric shaver points.
Licensed. Spacious free car park. No undue restrictions. Informal atmosphere. Personal attention.
Comfortable lounge. Interior sprung beds. Teas and snacks obtainable during the day. Excellent facilities for salmon and trout fishing. Also some excellent sea fishing. Comparatively close to an excellent golf course.

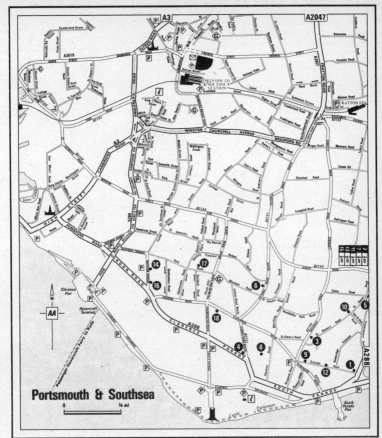

Portsmouth & Southsea

0   ¼ ml

1	Averano	7	Embell Hotel	10	Harwood Hotel	15	Salisbury Hotel
2	Beaufort Hotel	8	Gainsborough	11	Homeleigh	16	Somerset Private
3	Birchwood		House	12	Jesamine		Hotel
4	Bristol Hotel	9	Grosvenor Court	13	Lyndhurst	17	Tudor Court Hotel
5	Chequers Hotel		Hotel	14	Ryde View	18	Upper Mount House
6	Elms						

May–Sep 13hc 1⇌🛏 (3fb) CTV 8P ⏰ sea
S% B&b£7 Bdi£10 D7.45pm

GH Craiglockhart Beaumont Cres ☎2233
Mar–Nov 4hc (A 4hc) (3fb) TV 6P ⏰ sea
S% B&b fr£6.90 Bdi fr£10.36 Wfr£72.50
𝐤 D7pm

PORTSMOUTH & SOUTHSEA Hants
Map 4 SZ69
Telephone Exchange 'Portsmouth'
See Plan
GH Averano 65 Granada Rd, Southsea
☎20079 Plan:**1** 13hc (3fb) CTV 10P
2🛏 S% B&b£6.90–£8.05 Bdi£9.20–£11.50
W£49.45–£55.20 𝐤 D2pm

GH Beaufort Hotel 71 Festing Rd,
Southsea ☎23707 Plan:**2** 15hc (3fb) CTV
8P S% B&b£7–£8 Bdi£10–£11
W£46–£53 𝐤 D6pm

⊶ **GH Birchwood** 44 Waverley Rd,
Southsea ☎811337 Plan:**3** Closed 2wks
Xmas 6hc (4fb) ⊗ nc3 CTV B&b£5.50–£7
Bdi£7.50–£9.50 W£43–£49 𝐤 D2pm

GH Bristol Hotel 55 Clarence Pde,
Southsea ☎21815 Plan:**4** May–Nov Lic

14hc 4⇌🛏 (4fb) ⊗ CTV 7P
B&b£8.50–£9.75 Bdi£12.50–£13.75
W£60–£75 𝐤 D5pm

GH Chequers Hotel Salisbury Rd,
Southsea ☎735277 Plan:**5** Lic 13hc
2⇌🛏 (10fb) CTV 14P ⏰ B&b£9–£11
Bdi£14–£15 D6pm

GH Elms 48 Victoria Rd South, Southsea
☎23924 Plan:**6** Closed Xmas 7hc (2fb)
⊗ nc CTV 2P S% ✳B&b£5.50–£6
Bdi£7.50–£8 W£42–£47 𝐤 D4pm

GH Embell Hotel 31 Festing Rd,
Southsea ☎25678 Plan:**7** Closed Xmas wk
8hc (1fb) TV S% ✳B&b£5 W£35 M

GH Gainsborough House 9 Malvern Rd,
Southsea ☎22604 Plan:**8** Closed Xmas
7hc (2fb) nc2 CTV ⏰ S% ✳B&b£5
Bdi£7.50 Wfr£45 𝐤 D4pm

GH Grosvenor Court Hotel 37 Granada
Rd, Southsea ☎21653 Plan:**9** Mar–Oct
Lic 15hc (4fb) ⊗ nc2 CTV 10P S% B&b£8.50–£9
Bdi fr£10 W£56–£58 𝐤 (W only Mar–Oct)
D2.30pm.

167

Mariners Lodge

Porthcurno, Nr Penzance, Cornwall
Tel: St Buryan 236 (STD 073 672)

★ Centrally heated ★ Private car park ★ Garden
★ Comfortable lounge with colour TV
★ Licensed ★ Uninterrupted sea views.

Within a circle of ten miles of Mariners Lodge
you can visit the quaint fishing village of
Mousehole, the romantic Lamorna Cove, the
rugged coast of Land's End, Sennen Cove for
excellent surfing and Penzance with its shops.

We would like to welcome you to our small
private hotel and ask you to enjoy with us a
holiday in a superb, peaceful situation.
Resident proprietors: Trevor & Margaret Phipps.

SOUTHSEA

Rydeview

On the sea front overlooking
Southsea Common. The Solent, and
opposite the terminal for the Isle of
Wight Hovercraft. Close to Portsmouth
Naval Dockyard and main Southsea
shopping centre. Front door and bedroom
keys provided. H & C and razor points.
Spacious dining room with separate
tables. Spacious lounge bar with colour
TV. Centrally heated throughout. Open
all year round, except Xmas. Free
parking opposite.
Resident proprietors.

9 Western Parade, Southsea, Portsmouth, Hants. PO5 3JF. Tel: Portsmouth
(STD 0705) 20865

The Grange

Mrs M Butler

Raglan, Gwent NP5 2YA
Tel: Raglan 690260 (STD code 0291)

Elegant Victorian country-house
surrounded by 1½ acres of lawns and
trees. Ideally situated for Wye Valley,
Forest of Dean, Black Mountains,
Brecon Beacons. Within easy reach of
Abergavenny, Monmouth and
St Pierre golf courses.
Licensed. Open all the year. All meals
served; home-grown vegetables and
home-baked bread. Spacious,
comfortable bedrooms. Log fires and
central heating.
Small private and wedding parties arranged.
Collections of local artists' paintings on display.

Aeron Private Hotel & Guesthouse

191 Kentwood Hill,
Tilehurst, Reading.
Tel: Reception Reading 24119
      Visitors Reading 27654

Full central heating. Fire certificate awarded.
18 bedrooms with hot & cold water. Most
bedrooms with colour TV. Colour TV lounge.
Tea-making facilities. Personal supervision by
the proprietors.
Proprietors: M. K. Berry.
Please send for brochure.

GH Harwood Hotel 47–49 St Ronans Rd, Southsea ☎23104 Plan:**10** Lic 13hc (5fb) ✱ CTV ⊶ S% B&bf8.05–£9.20 Bdi£11.50–£12.65 W£51.75–£59.80

⊶**GH** *Homeleigh* 42–44 Festing Gv, Southsea ☎23706 Plan:**11** 10hc CTV

⊶**GH Jesamine** 57 Granada Rd, Southsea ☎734388 Plan:**12** Jan–Nov 5hc (2fb) ✿ nc5 TV 4P ⊶ S% B&bf4.50–£5.50 W£31.50–£38.50 M

GH Lyndhurst 8 Festing Gv, Southsea ☎735239 Plan:**13** Closed Xmas wk 7hc (2fb) CTV ⊶ S% ✱B&bf6 Bdi£7.20 W£45.50 ⱡ Dnoon

GH Ryde View 9 Western Pde, Southsea ☎20865 Plan:**14** Closed Xmas Lic 15hc (8fb) CTV ⊶ S% B&bf7–£7.50 Bdi£10.50–£11 D2pm

GH Salisbury Hotel 57–59 Festing Rd, Southsea ☎23606 Plan:**15** Lic 25hc (6fb) CTV 50P S% B&b9.20–£11.50 Bdi£12.65–£14.95 W£50–£55 ⱡ D5pm

GH Somerset Private Hotel 16 Western Pde, Southsea ☎22495 Plan:**16** Closed Xmas 16hc (7fb) nc3 CTV ⊶ S% B&bf7.50–£9 W£48.72–£59.71 M

GH Tudor Court Hotel 1 Queens Gv, Southsea ☎20174 Plan:**17** Lic 9hc (4fb) nc3 CTV 9P S% B&bf8 Bdi£12 W£72 ⱡ D3pm

GH *Upper Mount House* The Vale, Clarendon Rd, Southsea ☎20456 Plan:**18** Lic 12hc 4⇄▥ ✿ CTV 7P 1⌂ ⊶

PORT ST MARY Isle of Man
Map 6 SC26
GH *Mallmore Private Hotel* The Promenade ☎833179 Etr–1st wk Oct 47hc CTV P sea D8pm

POSTBRIDGE Devon *Map 3 SX67*
GH Lydgate House Hotel ☎88209 Closed Xmas Lic 9hc (1fb) CTV 11P ⊶ river S% ✱B&bf8.55 Bdi£11.50 W£72.45 ⱡ D7.30pm

POTTER HEIGHAM Norfolk *Map 9 TG41*
⊶ **GH** *Broadland House* Bridge Rd ☎401 9hc CTV 30P

POULTON-LE-FYLDE Lancs *Map 7 SD33*
For location see Blackpool Plan
GH *Breck Hotel* 28A Breck Rd ☎885702 Blackpool plan:**4** Lic 12hc ✿ nc10 CTV 10P ⊶ D1pm

POUNDSGATE Devon *Map 3 SX77*
GH Leusdon Lodge ☎304 Etr–Sep rs Oct–Etr Lic 7hc 1⇄▥ (2fb) CTV 25P ⊶ ✱B&bf5–£9.60 Bdi£11.95–£14.10 W£77.45–£98 ⱡ D9pm

PRAA SANDS Cornwall *Map 2 SW52*
GH La Connings ☎ Germoe 2380 Etr–Oct Lic 8hc (3fb) TV 12P ⊶ sea S% B&bf5–£8 Bdi£8–£9.50 W£56–£66 ⱡ D6.30pm

PRESTATYN Clwyd *Map 6 SJ08*
GH Bryn Gwalia Hotel 17 Gronant Rd ☎2442 Lic 9hc (1fb) TV 15P S% ✱B&bf8 Bdi£11.50 W£75 ⱡ D8.30pm

PRESTON Lancs *Map 7 SD52*
GH Beech Grove Hotel 12 Beech Gv, Ashton ☎729969 Closed Xmas Lic 7hc 1⇄▥ (3fb) ✿ nc4 CTV 6P ⊶ S% ✱B&bf10 Bdi£14 W£85 ⱡ D5pm

GH Fulwood Park Hotel 49 Watling Street Rd ☎718067 rs Xmas Lic 22hc 9⇄▥(A 4hc 1⇄▥) (1fb) CTV 20P ⊶ S% ✱B&bf8.25–£9 Bdi£12.50–£14 D7.15pm (except Sun)

GH Lauderdale Hotel 29 Fishergate Hill ☎55460 Closed Xmas Lic 18hc (3fb) CTV 10P 6⌂ ⊶ S% B&bfr£7.50 Bdifr£10 D5pm

GH Withy Trees 175 Garstang Rd, Fullwood (2m N on A6) ☎717693 10hc (2fb) ✿ CTV 20P ⊶ S% B&bf6–£8 W£42–£56

PRESTWICH Gt Manchester *Map 7 SD80*
GH Oak Lodge Hotel 514 Bury New Rd ☎061-773 1329 13hc 10⇄▥ (13fb) ✿ CTV 15P ⊶ S% ✱B&bf12–£17.25

PRESTWICK Strathclyde *Ayrs Map 10 NS32*
⊶ **GH Kincraig Private Hotel** 39 Ayr Rd ☎79480 Lic 7hc (1fb) ✿ CTV 8P ⊶ S% B&bf5.50 Bdif9 W£58 ⱡ D6pm

PWLLHELI Gwynedd *Map 6 SH33*
GH Seahaven Hotel West End Pde ☎2572 Etr–Sep Lic 10hc (8fb) CTV ⊶ sea S% B&bf6–£9.50 Bdi£8.50–£12 W£55–£69 ⱡ D7pm

QUEEN CAMEL Somerset *Map 3 ST52*
INN Mildmay Arms ☎ Yeovil 850456 Lic 3hc ✿ nc10 P ✱B&bf7–£8.50 Bar lunch £1.20alc D10.15pm£5alc

QUORNDON Leics *Map 8 SK51*
INN *Hurst Hotel* 23 Loughborough Rd ☎ Quorn 42541 Lic 7hc 1⇄▥ CTV P D7.30pm

RAGLAN Gwent *Map 3 SO40*
GH Grange Abergavenny Rd ☎690260 Closed Xmas Lic 5hc 1⇄▥ (1fb) CTV 10P ⊶ S% B&bfr£14 Bdifr£20 D9.30pm

RAMSGATE Kent *Map 5 TR36*
⊶ **GH Abbeygail** 17 Penshurst Rd ☎ Thanet 54154 Closed Xmas 10hc (3fb) ✿ nc2 CTV 1P S% B&bf5.50–£7 Bdi£8–£9.50 W£40–£54 ⱡ D2pm

GH Jalna Hotel 49 Vale Sq ☎ Thanet 53848 Lic 9hc 2⇄▥(8fb) ✿ CTV 4P 1⌂ ⊶ S% ✱B&bf6–£8 Bdi£9.50–£11.50 W£38–£49 ⱡ D4pm

GH St Hilary Private Hotel 21 Crescent Rd ☎ Thanet 51427 Closed Oct Lic 7hc (4fb) ✿ nc4 CTV 10P ⊶ B&bf6–£7.50 Bdi£9–£10.50 W£35–£56 ⱡ D3.30pm

GH *Sylvan Hotel* 160–162 High St ☎ Thanet 53026 Apr–Oct rs Xmas Lic 23hc ✿ CTV 12P ⊶

GH Westcliff Hotel 9 Grange Rd ☎ Thanet 581222 Closed Nov Lic 10hc (3fb) nc5 CTV 13P 1⌂ ⊶ sea S% B&bf8.50–£10

RAVENSTONEDALE Cumbria *Map 12 NY70*
INN Fat Lamb ☎Newbiggin-on-Lune 242 Lic 6hc CTV 50P ⊶ S% B&bf6.50–£7 Bdi£10–£11 W£70 ⱡ sn L£3.25alc D10pm£3.25alc

READING Berks *Map 4 SU77*
GH Aeron 191 Kentwood Hill, Tilehurst (3m W off A329) ☎24119 Closed Xmas 8hc (A 10hc 1⇄▥) (2fb) CTV 18P ⊶ S% B&bfr£9.50

GH Private House Hotel 98 Kendrick Rd
☎84142 Closed Xmas 7hc ⊘ nc12 CTV
5P ⬛ S% B&b£8–£9 Bdi£13–£14 D noon

REDCAR Cleveland *Map 8 NZ62*
GH Claxton House Private Hotel
196 High St ☎486745 Closed Xmas–
2 Jan 14hc 5⇔🚿 (1fb) ⊘ CTV 6P ⬛ sea S%
✱B&b£5.50–£6.50 Bdi£8–£9 D4pm

REDHILL Surrey *Map 4 TQ25*
GH Ashleigh House Hotel 39 Redstone
Hill ☎64763 10hc 2⇔🚿 (1fb) ⊘ CTV 10P
⬛ S% B&b£9.50–£10.50

REDRUTH Cornwall *Map 2 SW64*
⤝GH Foundry House 21 Foundry Row,
Chapel St ☎215143 Closed Etr & Xmas
6hc (2fb) nc3 CTV 5P 1🏠 S% B&b£5
Bdi£6.50 W£45.50 D4pm

⤝GH Lyndhurst 80 Agar Rd ☎215146
8hc (2fb) CTV 8P S% B&b£4.50 Bdi£7
W£45–£49 ⅃ D4pm

REIGATE Surrey *Map 4 TQ25*
GH Cranleigh Hotel 41 West St ☎40600
Lic 12hc 4⇔🚿 (3fb) ⏚ CTV 5P ⬛ S%
B&b£15.50–£18.50 D10pm

GH Priors Mead Blanford Rd ☎48776
9hc 1⇔🚿 (2fb) CTV 6P 1🏠 ⬛ S%
B&b£9–£9.50 Bdi£13–£13.50 W£85 ⅃
D3pm

RHES-Y-CAE Clwyd *Map 7 SJ17*
INN *Miners Arms* ☎Halkyn 780567 Lic
8hc 150P 3🏠 ⬛ D10pm

RHOS-ON-SEA Clwyd *Map 6 SH88*
See Colwyn Bay

RHUALLT Clwyd *Map 6 SJ07*
INN White House ☎St Asaph 582155
Lic 5hc CTV 100P S% B&b£5.50–£7
Bdi£8–£10 W£80–£110 ⅃ sn
L£2.20–£2.80&alc D10.30pm fr£4

RHYL Clwyd *Map 6 SJ08*
⤝GH Ashurst Private Hotel 7 Seabank
Rd ☎50417 Closed Oct–Jun Lic 7hc (3fb)
⊘ nc5 TV S% B&b£5.50 Bdi£7 W£40 ⅃

GH Ingledene Hotel 6 Bath St ☎4872
Closed Xmas & New Year Lic 11hc (4fb)
CTV S% B&b£6.50–£7 Bdi£8.50–£9
W£50–£56 ⅃ (W only Jul–Aug) D6pm

⤝GH Pier Hotel 23 East Pde ☎50280
Jan–Nov Lic 12hc 3⇔🚿 (3fb) CTV 2P ⬛
sea S% B&b£5.50–£6.50 Bdi£9–£10.50
W£44–£50 ⅃

GH Toomargoed Private Hotel 31–33
John St ☎4103 Etr–Sep Lic 15hc (8fb) ⊘
CTV S% B&b£6.90–£8.50 Bdi£9–£11
W£45–£55 ⅃

RIPON N Yorks *Map 8 SE37*
GH Crescent Lodge 42–42A North St
☎2331 12hc (3fb) ⏚ CTV 10P 1🏠 S%
B&b£6.25–£6.75 Bdi£10–£10.50 D7pm

GH Nordale 2 North Pde ☎3557 13hc
(4fb) CTV 12P B&b£6.30 Bdi£10
W£44.10–£60 ⅃ D5pm

⤝GH Old Country 1 The Crescent
☎2162 7hc (4fb) ⊘ TV 10P 2🏠 ⬛ S%
B&b fr£5.50

ROBIN HOOD'S BAY N Yorks
Map 8 NZ90
GH Storra Lee ☎Whitby 880593
Feb–Nov 6hc (1fb) ⊘ P sea S%
✱B&b£5–£6 Bdi£9–£10 D5pm

ROCHESTER Kent *Map 5 TQ76*
GH Greystones 25 Watts Av ☎Medway
47545 Closed Xmas 6hc (4fb) ⊘ CTV 4P
⬛ S% B&b£6.50–£7

ROEWEN Gwynedd *Map 6 SH77*
GH Tir-y-Coed Country House Hotel
☎Tyn-y-Groes 219 Mar–Dec Lic 8hc 7⇔🚿
(1fb) ⊘ CTV 10P B&b fr£9–£16
Bdi fr£13–£20 W£65–£85 M 8pm

ROMFORD Gt London *Map 5 TQ58*
GH Repton Private Hotel 18 Repton Dr
Gidea Park ☎45253 8hc ⊘ CTV S%
B&b£12.50–£15.50

ROMSEY Hants *Map 4 SU32*
GH Adelaide House 45 Winchester Rd
☎512322 6hc (1fb) ⊘ TV 6P ⬛ S%
✱£5.75–£6.50 W£38–£42 M

GH Chalet Botley Rd, Whitenap ☎514909
5hc (2fb) ⊘ CTV 6P ⬛ S% B&b£6 W£40 M

ROSSETT Clwyd *Map 7 SJ35*
INN *Golden Lion* ☎Chester 570316 Lic
4hc ⊘ CTV 50P ⬛ D9.15pm

ROSS-ON-WYE Heref & Worcs
Map 3 SO52
GH Bridge House ☎2655 Lic 9hc (2fb) ⊘
CTV 15P ⬛ river S% B&b£7.76–£8.75
Bdi£12.36–£14.20 W£92–£110 ⅃
D9.15pm

GH *Orles Barn Hotel* ☎2155 Lic 6hc CTV
12P ⬛

GH Ryefield House Gloucester Rd ☎3030

Lic 7hc 1⇄🛏 (3fb) CTV 8P 🍴 S% B&b£7
Bdi£11.20 W£70.50 ⚹ D4pm

ROTHERFIELD E Sussex *Map 5 TQ52*
INN Kings Arms ☎2465 Lic 4hc ⊗ nc14
CTV 50P 🍴 ⇔ B&b£8.50 Bar lunch
75p–£1.95 D9.15pm£6alc

ROTHESAY Isle of Bute, Strathclyde
Bute Map 10 NS06
⇥◀GH Alva House Private Hotel
24 Mountstuart Rd ☎2328 May–Sep 6hc
(1fb) ⊗ CTV sea S% B&b£5.50 Bdi£7
W£49 ⚹ D4pm

GH Morningside Mount Pleasant Rd
☎3526 Apr–Oct 6hc (A 3hc) (2fb) CTV
lake sea S% B&b£6–£6.50
Bdi£8.50–£9.50 W£54–£58 ⚹ D6.30pm
⇥◀GH St Fillans 36 Mountstuart Rd
☎2784 Apr–Oct 6hc (2fb) ⊗ nc2 CTV 6P
🍴 lake sea B&b£5 Bdi£6.75 W£45 ⚹
D6.30pm

ROTHLEY Leics *Map 8 SK51*
GH Rothley 35 Mountsorrel Ln
☎Leicester 302531 Closed Xmas Lic 9hc
⊗ CTV 9P 🍴 S% B&b£7–£7.50
Bdi£11.25–£11.75 D noon

ROTTINGDEAN E Sussex *Map 5 TQ30*
GH Braemar House Steyning Rd
☎Brighton 34263 15hc (4fb) CTV sea
S% B&b£6.90–£7.48

GH Corner House Steyning Rd
☎Brighton 34533 6hc (1fb) nc 🍴 S%
B&b£7.50

ROWLEY REGIS W Midlands
Map 7 SO98 **For location see
Birmingham Plan**
GH Highfield House Hotel Waterfall Ln
☎021-559 1066 Birmingham plan:**2**
Lic 12hc ⊗ nc12 CTV 12P 🍴 S%
✱B&b£7.50 Bdi£10 D10pm

ROZEL BAY Jersey, Channel Islands
Map 16
GH *Chateau la Chaire* ☎ Jersey 63354
Mar–Oct Lic 17hc 9⇄🛏 20P 🍴

RUGBY Warwicks *Map 4 SP57*
GH Grosvenor House Hotel 81 Clifton Rd
☎3437 Lic 9hc (1fb) CTV 6P 3🏠 🍴 S%
B&bfr£8.50 Bdifr£12

GH Mound Hotel 17–19 Lawford Rd
☎3486 Closed Xmas Lic 18hc 4⇄🛏
(5fb) CTV 17P 🍴 S% B&b£8.30–£16
Bdi£12.80–£20.50 D6.30pm

RUISLIP Gt London *London plan 4 A1*
(page 266)
GH 17th Century Barn Hotel West End Rd
☎36057 Lic 56hc 44⇄🛏 (6fb) CTV 60P
🍴 ✱B&bfr£14.90 D8.20pm

RUSTINGTON W Sussex *Map 4 TQ00*
GH Kenmore Claigmar Rd ☎4634
5hc 1⇄🛏 (3fb) TV 6P 🍴 B&b£5.75–£7.75
W£36.75–£48.25 ⓜ

GH Mayday Hotel 12 Broadmark Ln
☎71198 8hc (2fb) ⊗ nc6 CTV 12P 🍴 S%
B&b£10–£12 Bdi£15–£17 W£80–£95
⚹ D7.50pm

RUTHIN Clwyd *Map 6 SJ15*
INN Wynnstay Arms Hotel Well St ☎3147
Lic 8hc 2⇄🛏 ⊗ CTV 12P 🍴 ⇔ S%
B&b£6.50–£7.50 Bdi£8.50 D8.30pm

RYDAL Cumbria *Map 11 NY30*
GH Rydal Lodge Hotel ☎ Ambleside 3208
Apr–Oct Lic 8hc (1fb) CTV 12P river
B&b£8.80 Bdi£14.80 W£97 ⚹ D2pm

RYDE Isle of Wight *Map 4 SZ59*
GH Dorset Hotel Dover St ☎64327
mid Apr–mid Oct Lic 26hc 8⇄🛏 (7fb)
⊗ nc5 CTV 25P S% B&b£8–£9.50
Bdi£11–£12 W£52–£55 ⚹ D6.30pm

GH Teneriffe 36 The Strand ☎63841
Lic 16hc 2⇄🛏 (5fb) ⊗ CTV S%
✱B&bfr£5.75 Bdifr£8.05 Wfr£53.48 ⚹
(W only Jun–Sep) D11am

RYE E Sussex *Map 5 TQ92*
GH Little Saltcote 22 Military Rd ☎3210
Closed Xmas wk 6hc 2⇄🛏 (2fb) TV 3P 🍴
river S% B&b£6–£7 W£40–£45 ⓜ

GH *Mariner's Hotel* High St ☎3480
Lic 16hc 8⇄🛏 CTV 🍴 ⚹&.

GH Monastery Hotel & Restaurant
6 High St ☎3272 Lic 7hc ⊗ nc8 CTV 🍴
S% B&b£8.50–£9.50 D9.15am

GH Old Borough Arms The Strand ☎2128
9⇄🛏 (3fb) TV 2🏠 S% B&b£9.20–£10.50

ST ALBANS Herts *Map 4 TL10*
GH Grange Hotel 276 London Rd
☎51232 Lic 15hc 2⇄🛏 (2fb) ⊗ nc3 CTV
20P 🍴 B&bfr£10.35 D9pm

GH Melford 24 Woodstock Rd North
☎53642 Lic 12hc (2fb) CTV 12P 🍴 S%
B&b£9.20–£11.50
See advertisement overleaf

ST ANDREWS Fife *Map 12 NO51*
GH Argyle Hotel 127 North St ☎73387

Apr–Oct Lic 18hc (4fb) CTV 🍴 S%
B&b£6–£9 Bdi£10–£13 W£75–£85 ⚓
D6pm

GH Beachway House 4–6 Murray Park
☎73319 Mar–Nov rs Mar–Nov 11hc
(4fb) CTV 🍴 B&b£4.95–£6.95
Bdi£8.45–£10.70 W£57–£71 ⚓
(W only Jul–Aug) D2pm

⊶ **GH Cleveden House** 3 Murray Pl
☎74212 6hc (1fb) ⊗ CTV 20P S%
B&b£5.50–£6

GH Craigmore House 3–5 Murray Park
☎72142 Closed Dec rs Oct–Mar (B&b
only) 12hc (4fb) CTV 🍴 B&bfr£6.50
Bdifr£10.45 Wfr£68.50 ⚓ D4pm

GH *Hazelbank Private Hotel* The
Scores ☎72466 Mar–Nov 10hc ⊗ CTV
🍴 sea

GH Lorimer House 19 Murray Park
☎76599 Apr–Oct 4hc (3fb) nc2 CTV 🍴
B&b£6–£7 W£40–£45 M

GH *Nithsdale Hotel* The Scores
☎75977 Mar–Nov Lic 9hc CTV 🍴 sea

⊶**GH Number Ten** 10 Hope St ☎74601
9hc (3fb) CTV 🍴 S% B&b£5.25–£7
Bdi£8.75–£10.50 W£56–£70 ⚓ D6.15pm

⊶ **GH Yorkston Hotel** 68–70 Argyle St
☎72019 Lic 12hc (2fb) CTV 🍴
B&b£5.50–£7.50 Bdi£9–£11.50
W£55–£75 ⚓ D6.30pm

ST AUBIN Jersey, Channel Islands *Map 16*
GH *Panorama Private Hotel* High St
☎ Jersey 42429 17hc 1⊕🛏 ⊗ nc5 CTV
sea

ST AUSTELL Cornwall *Map 2 SX05*
GH Alexandra Hotel 52–54 Alexandra Rd
☎4242 Lic 14hc 4⊕🛏 (2fb) CTV 20P 🍴
S% B&b£6–£6.65 Bdi£9–£9.65
W£57.50–£63.25 ⚓ D5pm

GH *Copper Beeches* Truro Rd, Trevarrick
☎4024 Lic 8hc 1⊕🛏 CTV 8P 🍴

GH Cornerways Penwinnick Rd ☎61579
Closed Xmas wk Lic 6hc (2fb) ⊗ nc2 CTV
8P 🍴 S% B&bfr£6.75 W£43 M D6.30pm

⊶**GH Lynton House Hotel** 48 Bodmin Rd
☎3787 Lic 6hc (3fb) ⊗ CTV 6P S%
B&b£5.75–£6.50 Bdi£8.25–£9.25
W£52–£60 ⚓ Dnoon

⊶ **GH Treskillon** 26 Woodland Rd
☎2920 Lic 9hc (2fb) ⊗ CTV 10P 🍴 S%
B&b£5.60–£6.90 Bdi£8.80–£10.20
W£49–£60.50 ⚓ D6.15pm

GH *Wimereux* 1 Trevanion Rd ☎2187
Lic 14hc 5⊕🛏 ⊗ nc2 CTV 14P 🍴

INN Holmbush 101 Holmbush Rd ☎3217
Lic 3hc S% W£35 M Bar lunch50p–£1.50

ST BLAZEY Cornwall *Map 2 SX05*
⊶ **GH Moorshill House Hotel** Rosehill
☎ Par 2368 Lic 5hc (2fb) ⊗ CTV 6P 🍴
S% B&b£5.75–£6.25 Bdi£8–£9
W£48–£52 ⚓ D8.30pm

ST BRELADE Jersey, Channel Islands
Map 16
⊶**GH Arnewood Lodge** Route Des Genets
☎ Jersey 41516 Apr–Oct Lic 14hc 8⊕🛏
(2fb) ⊗ nc3 CTV S% B&b£5–£7
Bdi£10–£11.50 W£70–£80.50 ⚓
(W only mid Jun–mid Sep)

ST CATHERINE'S Strathclyde *Argyll*
Map 10 NN00
GH Thistle House ☎209 Etr–Sep 6hc
(1fb) 8P 🍴 B&bfr£6.50 D7pm

ST CLEMENT Jersey, Channel Islands
Map 16
GH *Linden* Jambart Ln, Pontac ☎ Jersey
51115 Closed Dec 6hc (A 2hc) 🐾 CTV
8P D6.30pm

ST DAVIDS Dyfed *Map 2 SM72*
GH Pen-y-Daith 12 Millard Park ☎720
Lic 8hc (3fb) ⊗ CTV 8P 🍴 ✳B&bfr£6
Bdifr£9

GH Y Glennydd 51 Nun St ☎576
Feb–Nov Lic 8hc (2fb) ⊗ CTV 🍴 S%
B&b£6–£6.90 Bdi£9.50–£11 W£62–£72
⚓ D6.30pm

ST DOGMAELS Dyfed *Map 2 SN14*
GH Glanteifi ☎ Cardigan 2353 (liable to
change to 612353 during the currency of
this guide) Mar–Oct Lic 11hc 3⊕🛏 (2fb)
CTV 20P 🍴 sea S% B&b£8.62–£11.50
Bdi£13.22–£17.82 W£87.92–£118.57
⚓ D5pm

ST FLORENCE Dyfed *Map 2 SN00*
⊶ **GH Flemish Court** ☎Manorbier 413
5hc (3fb) CTV 6P 🍴 S% B&b£5.25–£7.50
Bdi£8.25–£10.50 W£43–£48.50 ⚓
D7.30pm

GH Greenhills Hotel ☎Manorbier 291
Lic 11hc (7fb) CTV 30P ✳B&bfr£7.25
Bdifr£9.75 Wfr£60 ⚓ D9pm

GH Ponterosa Eastern Ln ☎Manorbier
378 May–Sep Lic 6hc (2fb) ⊗ CTV 6P S%
B&b£6–£8.50 Bdi£10.50–£13
W£50–£80 ⚓ (W only mid Jun–Aug)

INN *Parsonage Farm* ☎Manorbier 436
Mar–Oct, Xmas & New Year Lic 11hc CTV
25P 🍴 D9pm

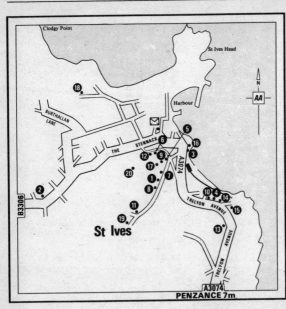

1 Channings Private
    Hotel
2 Chy-An-Creet
    Private Hotel
3 Cortina
4 Dean Court Hotel
5 Hollies Hotel
6 Island View
7 Longships
8 Lyonesse Hotel
9 Pondarosa
10 Primrose Valley
    Hotel
11 Rosemorran Private
    Hotel
12 St Margarets
13 St Merryn Hotel
14 Shun Lee Private
    Hotel
15 Skidden House
    Hotel
16 Sunrise
17 Trelissick
18 Verbena
19 Woodside Hotel
20 York Hotel

ST HELIER Jersey, Channel Islands *Map 16*
GH Almorah Hotel La Pouquelaye
☎Jersey 21648 Apr–Oct Lic 16hc 11⇌🖩
(5fb) ⊗ nc5 TV 10P 🛏 S%
B&b£7.50–£11 Bdi£8.50–£13 D6.30pm

GH *Runnymede Court Hotel* 48 Roseville
St ☎Jersey 20044 Mar–Nov 45hc 23⇌🖩
⊗ CTV

ST ISSEY Cornwall *Map 2 SW97*
INN Ring O'Bells ☎Rumford (Bodmin)
251, Lic 3hc CTV 40P S% B&b£8
Bar lunch50p–£4 D10pm

ST IVES Cambs *Map 4 TL37*
GH Firs Hotel 50 Needingworth Rd
☎63252 rs Sun & Mon (no restaurant
evenings) Lic 6rm 5hc (2fb) ⊗ nc5 CTV
14P 2🏠 🛏 B&b£9 Bdi£13.75 W£63 ᴹ
D9.30pm

ST IVES Cornwall *Map 2 SW54* **See Plan**
GH Boskerris Lodge Carbis Bay ☎797700
Not on plan Etr–Oct 7hc (2fb) CTV 8P sea
S% ✳B&b£5–£5.50 Bdi£7.50–£8.50
D6pm

GH Channings Private Hotel 3 Talland Rd
☎795681 Plan:**1** Apr–Oct Lic 12hc 4⇌🖩
(6fb) ⊗ CTV 12P sea S% B&b£7–£10
Bdi£10–£13 W£85 ⱪ (W only Jul–Aug)

⊶⊶ **GH Chy-An-Creet Private Hotel**
Higher Stennack ☎795381 Plan:**2**
Feb–Nov Lic 12hc (3fb) ⊗ CTV 12P S%
B&b£5.50–£7.50 Bdi£7.50–£9.50
W£55–£75 ⱪ D4.30pm

⊶⊶**GH Cortina & Kandahar** The Warren
☎796183 Plan:**3** Closed Xmas 11hc (1fb)
CTV 6P 🛏 sea S% B&b£5.75–£7

GH *Cottage Hotel* Cardis Bay ☎796351
Not on plan mid May–Sep Lic 52hc
(A 10hc) ⊗ CTV 100P lift 🛏 sea D7pm

GH Dean Court Hotel Trelyon Ave
☎796023 Plan:**4** Lic 12hc 10⇌🖩 ⊗ nc

CTV 12P 🛏 sea S% B&b£9.10–£13.50
Bdi£13–£15.50 W£85–£98 ⱪ D6pm

⊶⊶ **GH Grey Tyles** Carbis Bay ☎796408
Not on plan Apr–Oct Lic 17hc (7fb) CTV
12P sea S% B&b£5–£8 Bdi£9.50–£11
D5pm

GH Hollies Hotel Talland Rd ☎796605
Plan:**5** Lic 12hc (6fb) ⊗ 🐾 CTV 13P 🛏 sea
B&b£8.34–£12.08 Bdi£10.93–£14.66
W£52.90–£89.70 ⱪ (W only Jul–Aug)
D6pm

GH *Island View* 2 Park Av ☎795363
Plan:**6** Whit–Sep 9hc ⊗ nc12 D6pm

GH Longships 2 Talland Rd ☎798180
Plan:**7** Apr–Oct Lic 24hc 15⇌🖩 (10fb) 🐾
CTV 16P sea S% ✳B&b£5.50–£8
Bdi£8.75–£11.25 W£45–£80 D6pm

GH Lyonesse Hotel 5 Talland Rd
☎796315 Plan:**8** Mar–Oct Lic 15hc 5⇌🖩
(4fb) ⊗ CTV 4P 🛏 sea B&b£6.90–£10
Bdi£10.35–£14.95 W£77.05–£89.70 ⱪ
D6.30pm

GH Monowai Private Hotel Headland Rd,
Carbis Bay ☎796313 Plan:**9** not on plan
mid May–Sep Lic 10hc (2fb) nc5 CTV 7P
sea S% ✳B&b£6.33–£7.48
Bdi£8.63–£10.93 D6.30pm

⊶⊶ **GH Pondarosa** 10 Porthminster Ter
☎795875 Plan:**9** 10hc 1⇌🖩 (2fb) ⊗ nc3
CTV 8P S% B&b£5–£7
Bdi£7.50–£10.50 W£51–£72 ⱪ D5pm

⊶⊶ **GH Primrose Valley Hotel** Primrose
Valley ☎795564 Plan:**10** Etr–Oct Lic
11hc 4⇌🖩 (5fb) ⊗ CTV 10P sea
B&b£5.75–£11.50 Bdi£8.25–£15.18
W£57.50–£104.88 ⱪ D6pm

GH Rosemorran Private Hotel The
Belyars ☎796359 Plan:**11** Mar–Oct Lic
12hc (5fb) 🐾 CTV 10P sea S%
B&b£9.36–£9.81 Bdi£11.84–£13

GH Hotel Rotorua Trencrom Ln, Carbis
Bay ☎795419 Not on plan Etr–Oct Lic
14hc (7fb) CTV 14P ✳B&b£6.61–£8.91
Bdi£9.20–£11.50 W£64.40–£80.50 ⱪ
D7pm

GH *St Margarets* 3 Park Av ☎795785
Plan:**12** Closed Xmas Lic 8hc CTV sea

GH St Merryn Hotel Trelyon ☎795767
Plan:**13** Lic 12rm 2⊟▥ (A 3rm) ⊛ CTV 15P
▥ S% B&b£7.50–£8.50
Bdi£10.50–£11.50 (W only Jul & Aug)

GH Sherwell St Ives Rd, Carbis Bay
☎796142 Not on plan 8hc (2fb) ⊛ CTV 7P
▥ sea S% ✻B&b£5–£5.50
Bdi£7.25–£8.25 W£50.75–£56.50 ⌴
D6.30pm

GH Shun Lee Private Hotel Trelyon Ave
☎796284 Plan:**14** Mar–19 Oct Lic 11hc
1⊟▥ (2fb) ⊛ nc5 CTV 13P ▥ sea S%
B&b£8.25–£8.75 Bdi£12.75–£13.25
W£65–£85 ⌴ D6.30pm

GH Skidden House Hotel Skidden Hill
☎796899 Plan:**15** Lic 7hc ⊛ CTV 4P ▥
S% ✻B&b£6.90–£9.20 Bdi£11.50–£13.80
W£74.75–£89.70 ⌴ D noon

GH *Sunrise* 22 The Warren ☎795407
Plan:**16** 6hc (A 2hc) ⊛ nc3 CTV 4P sea

GH Trelissick Hotel Bishops Rd
☎795035 Plan:**17** wk before Etr–Oct
Lic 15hc 4⊟▥ (3fb) ⊛ CTV 11P sea S%
B&b£7.75–£11.75 Bdi£10.50–£14.25
W£65–£85 ⌴ D6.45pm

⤝ **GH Verbena** Orange Lane ☎796396
Plan:**18** Etr–Oct 7hc 2⊟▥ (2fb) nc6 CTV
8P sea S% B&b fr£5.50 Bdi fr£8 Wfr£50 ⌴
(W only Jun, Jul & Aug) D4pm

GH Woodside Hotel The Belyars
☎796282 Plan:**19** Lic 11hc (4fb) ⊛ ⌁
CTV 20P sea S% W£65–£75 ⌴ (W only
Jun–Aug) D6.30pm

GH York Hotel ☎796856 Plan:**20** Lic
29hc 19⊟▥ (4fb) CTV 28P 18🏠 ▥ sea
D10pm

ST IVES Dorset *Map 4 SU10*
GH Foxes Moon Hotel 40 Ringwood Rd,
☎Ringwood 4347 Jan–Oct Lic 6hc (1fb)
CTV 9P ▥ S% B&b£6.95–£7.50
Bdi£9.95–£10.50 W£47.50–£51 Ⓜ
D6.30pm

ST JUST Cornwall *Map 2 SW33*
GH Boscean House ☎788748 Lic 9hc
(3fb) ⊛ nc10 CTV 10P sea S%
B&b£8.63–£9.78 Bdi£13.23–£14.38
W£72.50–£77.60 ⌴ D11am

GH Boswedden House Private Hotel
Cape Cornwall ☎788733 Mar–Oct Lic
8rm 7hc 2⊟▥ (5fb) ⊛ nc3 CTV 7P 2🏠 ▥
sea S% ✻B&b£5.75–£8.27
Bdi£9.20–£12.36 W£63.25–£85.10 ⌴
(W only school hols) D7.30pm

ST JUST-IN-ROSELAND Cornwall
Map 2 SW83
GH Rose-Da-Mar Hotel ☎St Mawes 450
Etr–Oct Lic 9hc 5⊟▥ (2fb) ⊛ nc7 CTV 10P
▥ river S% ✻Bdi£13.80–£16.67
W£96.60–£116.69 ⌴ D7pm

ST KEYNE Cornwall *Map 2 SX26*
GH Old Rectory Hotel ☎Liskeard 42617
Etr–Oct rs Xmas (full board only) Lic 10rm
5hc 5⊟▥ (4fb) ⌁ CTV 10P ▥
B&b£11–£15.50 Bdi£16–£22
W£103–£120 ⌴ D7pm

ST LAWRENCE Isle of Wight
Map 4 SZ57
GH Woody Bank Hotel Undercliff Dr
☎ Ventnor 852610 Etr–Oct Lic 10hc
(3fb) CTV 10P sea S% B&b£8.05–£11.50
Bdi£11.50–£14.95 W£75.90–£97.75
⌴ D7.30pm

ST MARTIN Guernsey, Channel Islands
Map 16
GH Triton Private Hotel Les Hubits
☎38017 Apr–Sep 14hc 5⇨🛏 (2fb) ⊗
nc4 CTV 12P S% B&b£6.25–£7.25
Bdi£9–£10.50 W£63–£73.50 ⤶ D6.30pm

ST MARTIN Jersey, Channel Islands
Map 16
GH St Martin's House ☎ Jersey 53271
Closed Dec Lic 11hc 4⇨🛏 (2fb) ⊗ ⚬
CTV 11P 🍴&✱B&b£6.50–£7.50
Bdi£9–£10.50 D6.30pm

ST MARY CRAY Gt London *Map 5 TQ46*
GH *Sheepcote Farmhouse* Sheepcote Ln
☎ Orpington 70498 Apr–Oct 4hc ⊗ CTV
P 🍴 D7.30pm

ST MARY'S Isles of Scilly *(No map)*
GH Evergreen Cottage ☎ Scillonia 22711
Feb–Oct 5hc (1fb) ⊗ nc6 CTV 🍴
✱B&b£6.25–£6.50 Bdi£10.75 Dnoon

GH Hanjague ☎ Scillonia 22531
May–Sep Lic 5hc ⊗ nc10 CTV 🍴 sea
B&b£9 Bdi£15 D6.15pm

GH Tremellyn Private Hotel ☎ Scillonia
22656 Mar–Oct Lic 7hc (5hc) (2fb) ⊗
CTV sea S% B&b£10.80
Bdi£14.40–£14.90 W£100.80–£104.30 ⤶
(W only 14May–14Sep) D7pm

ST MAWES Cornwall *Map 2 SW83*
GH Waterloo House Upper Castle Rd
☎570 Mar–Oct Lic 5hc (2fb) nc6 CTV 8P
sea S% ✱B&b£9.20–£10.35
Bdi£12.08–£13.23 W£76.48–£84.53 ⤶

ST NEWLYN EAST Cornwall
Map 2 SW85
GH Trewerry Mill Trerice (2m W of
A3058 midway between Summercourt and
Quintrell Downs) ☎ Mitchell 345
Etr–Oct Lic 6hc (2fb) ⊗ CTV 12P S%
B&b£7–£8 Bdi£8–£10 W£50–£70 ⤶
(W only Jul & Aug) D6pm

ST PETER PORT Guernsey, Channel
Islands *Map 16*
GH Changi Lodge Private Hotel Les
Baissieres ☎ Guernsey 56446 Lic 14hc
2⇨🛏 (8fb) ⊗ nc7 CTV 20P 🍴 S%
B&b£8.50–£9.50 Bdi£9.75–£12.75
Dnoon

GH *Maison Du Guet Private Hotel*
Amhurst ☎ Guernsey 22007 Feb–Nov
Lic 18hc 3⇨🛏 ⊗ CTV 10P 🍴

ST PETER'S VALLEY Jersey, Channel
Islands *Map 16*
✻✻ **GH Midvale Private Hotel** ☎ Jersey
42498 Etr–Oct Lic 21hc 7⇨🛏 (3fb) ⊗
CTV 18P B&b£5.50 Bdi£7–£9.50
W£49–£69.50 ⤶ (W only High Season)
D6.30pm

ST SAVIOUR Jersey, Channel Islands
Map 16
GH Redwood Private Hotel Five Oaks
☎ Jersey 26370 Dec–Oct Lic 22hc
10⇨🛏 (8fb) ⊗ CTV 22P B&b£7–£12
Bdi£8–£13 D9.30pm

GH Talana Private Hotel Bagot Rd
☎ Jersey 30317 Lic 36hc 17⇨🛏 (3fb) ⊗
CTV 18P 🍴 S% B&b£9.50–£11.50
Bdi£10–£14 W£70–£98 ⤶ (W only
May–Sep) D7pm

SALCOMBE Devon *Map 3 SX73*
GH Bay View Hotel Bennett Rd ☎2238
Apr–Oct Lic 11hc 1⇨🛏 (2fb) ⊗ nc6 CTV
8P 🍴 sea B&b£8–£9 Bdi£11.50–£12.50
Wfr£80 ⤶ D7.30pm

GH Charborough House Hotel Devon Rd
☎2260 Mid Mar–Oct Lic 10hc 2⇨🛏
(1fb) ⊗ nc4 CTV 🍴 sea S% B&b£8.50
Bdi£13 W£81.50 ⤶ D5pm

GH Lyndhurst Hotel Bonaventure Rd
☎2481 Lic 8hc 2⇨🛏 (3fb) ⊗ nc7 CTV 8P
🍴 sea S% B&b£7.50–£8
Bdi£12.50–£14.40 W£64–£72 ⤶ D7pm

GH Melbury Hotel Devon Rd ☎2883
Etr & Spring Bank Hol–Sep Lic 14hc
4⇨🛏 (5fb) ⊗ nc5 CTV 14P sea
B&b£10.20–£13.20 Bdi£12–£15
W£72–£88.80 ⤶ D7.30pm

GH Stoneycroft Hotel Devon Rd ☎2218
Etr–Oct Lic 10hc (5fb) nc5 CTV 15P 1🏠
🍴 sea S% B&b£8.63 Bdi£13.23
W£74.75–£78.20 ⤶ (W only Jul–Aug)
D8pm

GH Trennels Private Hotel Herbert Rd
☎2500 Apr–Oct 11hc ⊗ nc12 CTV 8P
1🏠 🍴 sea S% ✱B&b£8–£9 Bdi£11–£12
W£62–£67 ⤶ Dnoon

GH Woodgrange Private Hotel Devon Rd
☎2439 Etr–Sep Lic 11hc 5⇨🛏 (3fb) ⚬
CTV 11P 🍴 sea B&b£7.10–£9.70
Bdi£11.15–£13.75 W£72–£92.80 ⤶
D5pm

SALEN Isle of Mull, Strathclyde
Argyll Map 10 NM54
GH Craig Hotel ☎Aros 347 Lic 7hc ⚬
8P sea S% B&b£10–£12.50
Bdi£13–£16.50

SALISBURY Wilts *Map 4 SU12*
GH Byways House 31 Fowlers Rd
☎28364 10hc (4fb) CTV 10P 🍴 S%
B&b£7–£8 W£45.50–£52.50 Ⓜ

⊷ **GH Holmhurst** Downtown Rd ☎23164
8hc nc5 7P 🍴 S% B&b£5–£6

INN *White Horse Hotel* Castle St
☎27844 Lic 12hc CTV 4P 6🛌 🚲 D8.45pm

SALTDEAN E Sussex *Map 5 TQ30*
GH Linbrook Lodge 74 Lenham Av
☎ Brighton 33775 Lic 7hc (1fb) CTV 6P
🍴 sea B&b£6.50–£8 Bdi£9.50–£11
W£49–£56 ⚿ D4pm

SANDOWN Isle of Wight *Map 4 SZ58*
GH Cliff House Hotel Cliff Rd ☎3656
Mar–Oct Lic 16hc 8⊣🛁 (5fb) CTV 20P
🍴 & sea B&b£9.60–£10.50 Bdi£14–£15
W£86.25–£91.27 ⚿ D6.30pm

GH Rostrevor Private Hotel
96 Sandown Rd ☎402775 Etr–Sep Lic
17hc (4fb) ⊗ nc2 CTV 14P S% sea
✻B&b£5.75–£8.63 Bdi£7.48–£9.70
W£46–£63.25 ⚿ D6pm

GH St Catherine's Hotel 1 Winchester
Park Rd ☎402392 Closed Xmas Lic 18hc
7⊣🛁 (2fb) ⊗ nc5 CTV 8P 🍴 S%
B&b£10–£13.50 Bdi£12.50–£17
W£80.50–£119 ⚿ D7pm

GH Trevallyn 32 Broadway ☎402373
Etr–Oct Lic 25hc (5fb) ⊗ CTV 20P S%
B&b£8 Bdi£12 W£56–£66 ⚿ D6.30pm

SANDPLACE Cornwall *Map 2 SX25*
GH Polraen Country House Hotel
☎ Looe 3956 Feb–mid Dec Lic 7hc

4⊣🛁 (1fb) ⊗ CTV 12P 🍴 S% B&b£11–£15
Bdi£14–£17.50 W£92–£115 ⚿ D7pm

SANDWICH Kent *Map 5 TR35*
INN Fleur de Lis Delf St ☎611131 Lic
5hc TV 3P 🍴 B&b£8–£10.50 sn
L£2.25–£4.15 D10.15pm£5alc

SANDY Beds *Map 4 TL14*
GH Fairlawn Hotel 70 Bedford Rd
☎80336 rs Sun & Public Hols (B&b only)
Lic 10hc (1fb) ⊗ CTV 10P 🍴 B&b£11.50
D8.30pm

SANNOX Isle of Arran, Strathclyde *Bute*
Map 10 NS04
⊷ **GH Cliffdene** ☎ Corrie 224 Closed Oct
& Nov 5hc (3fb) ⊗ TV 6P sea S%
B&b£4.93 Bdi£7.23 W£50.60 ⚿ D6.30pm

SANQUHAR Dumfries & Galloway
Dumfriesshire Map 11 NS71
INN Nithsdale Hotel High St ☎506
Lic 6hc CTV 🍴 S% B&b£6.50–£7
Bdi£10.50–£11 sn L£2.75–£5
D8.30pm£4–£7

SAUNDERSFOOT Dyfed *Map 2 SN10*
GH Harbour Lights Private Hotel 2 High
St ☎813496 Mar–Nov rs Dec–Feb Lic
12hc (5fb) ⊗ CTV 8P sea S%
B&b£7–£8.50 Bdi£9.50–£11
W£70–£73 ⚿ D4.30pm

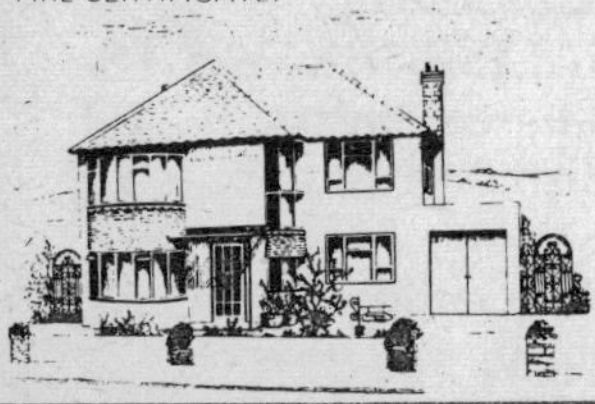

GH *Jalna Hotel* Stammers Rd ☎812282
Etr–Oct Lic 14hc 6⊣🛁 ⚙ CTV 16P 🍴

GH Malin House Hotel St Bride's Hill
☎812344 Etr–Sep Lic 13hc 8⊣🛁 (5fb)
⊗ CTV 60P 🍴 sea ✻B&b£9.20–£11.50
Bdi£10.92–£13.23 W£77.05–£92.57 ⚿
(W only Jul–Aug) D7pm

St Catherines Hotel

1 Winchester Park Road, Sandown, Isle of Wight Tel: 0983 402392
Resident Proprietors: Jim and Maureen Hitchcock

Relaxed, friendly atmosphere, comfortable furnishing, ample portions of quality food with full choice of varied menu are offered in this fully centrally heated, licensed hotel. Situated five minutes from the seafront and town centre. All bedrooms have radio/room call and free tea/coffee making facilities. Many have bath or shower and toilet en suite. Lounge with colour television.

Fleur de Lis Hotel

Delf Street, Sandwich, Kent. Tel: (03046) 611131

The hotel is situated in the centre of Sandwich, which is an old town and Cinque Port. Fully licensed with 3 bars. Good home-made food is provided, real ale served and there are coal fires in the winter. Part of the hotel is olde worlde with beams etc. in bedrooms. One bedroom, known as the Earl of Sandwich Bedchamber, has a half-tester bed.

Car parking facilities. Just 10 minutes from golf course and Ramsgate Hoverport. 30 minutes from Dover Car Ferry. 20 minutes from Canterbury.

JALNA HOTEL

**Resident Proprietors:
Mr. & Mrs. Frank Williams**

**Stammers Road, Saundersfoot, Dyfed.
Tel: Saundersfoot 812282**

Purpose built and situated on the flat just two minutes walk from sea front and harbour.

Overlooking bowling green and tennis courts.

Food of the best quality. Bar and TV lounge.

Ample car parking. Laundry room.

Small dogs by arrangement.

Double, twin-bedded and family rooms, some with private bathrooms.

TV and tea making facilities in all bedrooms.

MALIN HOUSE HOTEL

St. Brides Hill, Saundersfoot

Telephone Saundersfoot 812344

Malin is a house of character, Situated in peaceful surroundings 400 yards from the beach and shopping centre with ample car parking. Residentially licensed with a high standard of accommodation, food and wine. Some rooms with private shower or bath, H and C in all rooms. Malin, now under the same management as the Merlewood Hotel next door; who aim to maintain their high standard of service. Guests may make full use of all the facilities at Merlewood: — Heated swimming pool ect.

Send stamp to Dennis, Irene and Janet Williams for brochure and tariff.

➤⊣**GH Rhodewood House Hotel** St Bride's
Hill ☎812200 Lic 24hc 7⇌🛁 (7fb) CTV
30P sea S% B&b£5.50–£7.50
Bdi£8–£10 W£56–£70 ⅒ D7.30pm

SCARBOROUGH N Yorks *Map 8 TA08*
See Plan
GH Avoncroft Hotel Crown Ter ☎72737
Plan:**1** Closed Nov Lic 31hc 1⇌🛁 (9fb)
CTV 🍴 S% ✹B&b£6.21–£8.51
Bdi£7.36–£10.12 D6pm

GH Bay Hotel 67 Esplanade, South Cliff
☎73926 Plan:**2** Lic 19hc (2fb) ⊘ CTV 12P
sea S% B&b£9.78–£11.50
Bdi£13.23–£14.95 W£92.61–£104.65 ⅒
D6pm

GH Burghcliffe Hotel 28 Esplanade,
South Cliff ☎61524 Plan:**3** Mar–Nov
Lic 15hc (10fb) CTV sea S% ✹B&b£8.50
Bdi£10.35

GH Church Hills Private Hotel St Martins
Av, South Cliff ☎63148 Plan:**4** Jan–Oct
Lic 16hc (1fb) CTV 🍴 sea S%
B&b£9.78–£10.93 Bdi£10.93–£12.08
W£76.51–£84.56 ⅒ D6pm

GH *Green Park Hotel* 15 Prince of Wales
Ter, South Cliff ☎65770 Plan:**5** Etr–Oct
Lic 20hc 7⇌🛁 CTV lift

GH Ridbech Private Hotel 8 The Crescent
☎61683 Plan:**6** May–Oct 25hc (3fb) CTV
sea ✹B&b£6.90–£9.80 Bdi£7.50–£10.35
D5.45pm

GH Sefton Hotel 18 Prince of Wales Ter
☎72310 Plan:**7** Closed Nov, Jan, Feb Lic
16hc (10fb) nc4 CTV 🍴 lift S%
B&b£7–£8 Bdi£9–£11 W£72.45–£88.55

SCILLY, ISLES OF *(No map)*
See St Mary's

SEAFORD E Sussex *Map 5 TV49*
GH Avondale Hotel Avondale Rd
☎890008 Feb–Oct & Xmas 8hc (1fb) ⊘
nc4 CTV P 🍴 S% B&b£7.25–£8.50
Bdi£10.25–£11.65 W£63.50–£71.50 ⅒
D4.30pm

SEAMILL Strathclyde *Ayrs Map 10 NS24*
INN *Galleon* Ardrossan Rd ☎West Kilbride
822121 Closed New Year's Day Lic 7hc ⊘
CTV 24P 🍴 sea D8.30pm

SEATON Devon *Map 3 SY29*
GH Eyre House Queen St ☎21455
Mar–Oct Lic 8hc (3fb) CTV 8P S%
✹B&b£6.50–£7

GH Glendare Fore St ☎20542 Closed
Xmas Lic 6hc (3fb) ⊘ nc5 CTV 🍴 S%

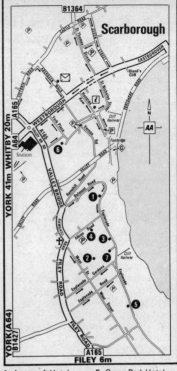

Scarborough

1	Avoncroft Hotel	**5**	Green Park Hotel
2	Bay Hotel	**6**	Ridbech Private Hotel
3	Burghcliffe Hotel	**7**	Sefton Hotel
4	Church Hills Private Hotel		

B&b£6.50–£7.50 Bdi£9.50–£10.50
W£63–£66.50 ⅒ D4pm

GH Harbourside 2 Trevelyan Rd ☎20785
6hc (2fb) CTV 6P 🍴 sea S% ✹B&b£5 Bdi£8
W£56 ⅒ D9am

GH Mariners Homestead Esplanade
☎20560 Lic 11hc (1fb) ⊘ nc3 CTV 11P 🍴
sea S% ✹B&b£8.35 Bdi£12.10 W£79.35
⅒ D4pm

GH Netherhayes Fore St ☎21646
Etr–Oct Lic 10hc (3fb) ⊘ nc3 CTV 10P
B&b£7–£7.50 Bdi£9–£10.50 W£65–£75
⅒ D5pm

GH St Margarets 5 Seafield Rd ☎21134
Etr–Oct Lic 9hc (5fb) ♨CTV 7P 🛏 sea S%
B&bf6.50–£8.50 Bdi£11.95–£13.25
Wf76.65–£85.35 ⓚ D6.30pm

GH Thornfield 87 Scalwell Ln ☎20039
Feb–Oct Lic 8hc (A 3hc) (3fb) CTV 12P
S% ✳B&bf5–£6.50 Bdi£8–£9.50
Wf48–£58 ⓚ D6.30pm

SEAVIEW Isle of Wight Map 4 SZ69
GH Northbank Hotel ☎2227 Etr–Oct Lic
18hc (9fb) ♨CTV 6P 2🛏 sea B&bf8–£10
Bdi£12–£14 Wf77–£95 D8pm

SELBY N Yorks Map 8 SE63
GH Hazeldene 34 Brook St ☎704809
7hc (2fb) ⊗CTV 5P S% B&bf6–£7

SELSEY W Sussex Map 4 SZ89
⊶⊷**GH Fairbrook** 71 Hillfield Rd ☎2914
Lic 6hc (5fb) ⊗ nc7 TV 6P S%
B&bf5.85–£6 Wf40 Ⓜ

GH White Waves Private Hotel Seal Rd
☎2379 Lic 7hc (A 2hc) (1fb) ⊗ CTV 3P
🛏 sea S% B&bf7–£8.50 Bdi£11–£12.50
Wf70–£85 ⓚ D noon

SEMLEY Wilts Map 3 ST82
INN Bennett Arms ☎East Knoyle 221 Lic
A 3🛏 CTV P 🛏 ⇔ S% ✳B&bf9.50–£11.50
D10pm

SEVENOAKS Kent Map 5 TQ55
GH Moorings Hotel 97 Hitchen Hatch Ln
☎52589 Lic 9hc 1🛏🛏 (A 2🛏🛏) (1fb) CTV
25P 🛏 S% ✳B&bf9–£19.55

GH Sevenoaks Park Hotel 4 Seal Hollow
Rd ☎54245 Lic 15hc 4🛏🛏 (A 3hc 1🛏🛏)
25P 3🛏 🛏

SHANKLIN Isle of Wight Map 4 SZ58
See Plan
GH Afton Hotel Clarence Gdns ☎3075
Plan:**1** Mar–Oct Lic 9hc 4🛏🛏 (A4hc)
(5fb) ⊗ nc5 CTV 8P 🛏 S%
B&bf11.23–£13.22 Bdi£12.95–£14.95
Wf80.04–£91.54 ⓚ D6pm

GH Aqua Hotel The Esplanade ☎3024
Plan:**2** Mar–Oct Lic 23hc 2🛏🛏 (7fb) ⊗
nc2 CTV 1P sea B&bf9.20–£10.35
Bdi£12.08–£14.38 Wf70.15–£92 ⓚ
D7pm

GH Berry Brow Hotel Popham Rd
☎2825 Plan:**3** Etr–Oct Lic 21hc ⊗ CTV
16P

GH Culham Private Hotel 31 Landguard
Manor Rd ☎2880 Plan:**4** Closed Xmas
10hc 1🛏🛏 ⊗ nc12 CTV 5P S%

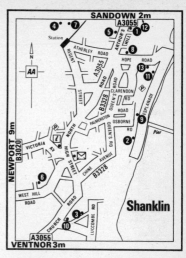

SANDOWN 2m

Shanklin

1 Afton Hotel
2 Aqua Hotel
3 Berry Brow Hotel
4 Culham Private Hotel
5 Cumberland Hotel
6 Fern Bank
7 Langthorne Private Hotel
8 Leslie House Hotel
9 Meyrick Cliffs
10 Monteagle Hotel
11 Ocean View
12 Overstrand Hotel
13 Sandringham Hotel

B&bf7.60–£8.30 Bdi£9.75–£10.45
Wf58–£62 ⓚ D4pm

GH Cumberland Private Hotel
26 Arthur's Hill ☎3000 Plan:**5** May–Sep
Lic 17hc ⊗ nc5 CTV 12P D5.30pm

GH Fern Bank Highfield Rd ☎2790
Plan:**6** Closed Xmas Lic 18hc 4🛏🛏 (3fb)
nc3 CTV 10P S% B&bf6.65–£7.75
Bdi£9.95–£11.50 Wf69.50–£80.50 ⓚ
D6.30pm

⊶⊷ **GH Langthorne Private Hotel**
3 Witbank Gdns ☎2980 Plan:**7** Apr–Oct
12hc 2🛏🛏 (3fb) ⊗ nc5 CTV 12P 🛏 S%
B&bf5.15–£6.15 Bdi£7.25–£8.25
Wf36.80–£53.13 ⓚ (W only Jun–Aug)
D8pm

GH Leslie House Hotel 10 Hope Rd
☎2798 Plan:**8** Jan–Oct Lic 10hc (2fb) ⊗
nc5 CTV 8P 🛏 sea S% ✳B&bf5–£7.50
Bdi£9.47–£11.49 Wfr£66.24–£80.40 ⓚ
D3pm

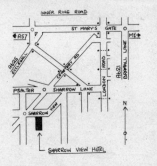

GH Meyrick Cliffs The Esplanade ☎2691
Plan:**9** May–Sep Lic 20hc 1⇔▥(6fb) ⊛ nc5
CTV 5P sea B&b£7–£7.50 Bdi£10–£10.50
Wfr£60 ⫝̸ (W only Jul–Aug) D6.30pm

GH Monteagle Hotel Priory Rd ☎2854
Plan:**10** Apr–Oct rs Mar Lic 40hc 18⇔▥
(3fb) ⊛ nc7 CTV 25P ⑭ S% B&b£10–£14
Bdi£13–£18 W£56–£76 ⫝̸ D7.30pm

GH Ocean View Hotel 38 The Esplanade
☎2602 Plan:**11** Feb–Nov Lic 36hc 13⇔▥
(17fb) CTV 25P sea S% B&b£8.65–£11
Bdi£12.65–£14.85 W£83–£103.50 ⫝̸
D7.45pm

GH Overstrand Private Hotel Howard Rd
☎2100 Plan:**12** 11 Apr–3 Oct Lic 14hc
4⇔▥(6fb) ⊛ CTV 18P ⑭ sea
B&b£8–£12 Bdi£9.70–£13.80
W£67.85–£96.60 ⫝̸ D6pm

GH *Sandringham Hotel* Hope Rd ☎3189
Plan:**13** Etr–mid Oct Lic 28hc TV P sea

SHAP Cumbria *Map 12 NY51*
GH Brookfield ☎397 Feb–Dec Lic 5hc
(3fb) ⊛ CTV 25P 5🚗 ⑭ S% B&b£6.30–£7
Bdi£12–£13 D7.30pm

SHAW Wilts *Map 3 ST86*
GH Shaw Farm ☎Melksham 702836 Lic
12hc 1⇔▥(4fb) ⊛ CTV 12P ⑭
B&b£8.25–£9 Bdi£12.25–£13
W£80–£85 ⫝̸ D7pm

SHEERNESS Kent *Map 5 TQ97*
⊶⊷**GH Victoriana** 107 Alma Rd ☎5555
12hc (2fb) CTV 5P 2🚗 ⑭ S%
B&b£5.95–£8.95 W£41.65–£62.65 Ⓜ

SHEFFIELD S Yorks *Map 8 SK38*
GH Millingtons 70 Broomgrove Rd (off
A625 Eccleshall Rd)☎669549 Closed
New Year 7hc 3⇔▥ CTV 4P ⑭ S%
B&bfr£7

GH Sharrow View Hotel 13 Sharrow
View ☎51542 Lic 15hc (A 5hc) (2fb) CTV
22P ⑭ S% B&b£10.25 Bdi£15 D6.30pm

SHEPTON MALLET Somerset
Map 3 ST64
INN *Bell Hotel* 3 High St ☎2166 Lic 4hc
TV 4🚗 D10pm

SHERFIELD ON LODDON Hants
Map 4 SU65
GH Wessex House Hotel ☎Turgis Green
243 Closed Xmas wk Lic 8⇔▥ CTV 12P ⑭
B&B£16 Bdi£21 D9.30pm

SHERINGHAM Norfolk *Map 9 TG14*
GH Beacon Hotel Nelson Rd ☎822019

Apr–Oct Lic 8hc (1fb) nc5 CTV 10P ⑭ sea
S% B&b£9–£10 Bdi£12–£13 W£76–£82
⫝̸ D5pm

GH Beeston Hills Lodge 64 Cliff Rd
☎822615 May–Sep 7hc 2⇔▥(1fb) ⊛
nc8 CTV 10P ⑭ sea S% B&bfr£6.60
Bdi fr£8.80 W£60 ⫝̸

GH Camberley House Hotel 62 Cliff Rd
☎823101 9May–10Oct 9⇔▥(3fb) ⚲
CTV 12P ⑭ sea S% B&b£6.50–£11
Bdi£8–£13.25 W£40–£60 ⫝̸ (W only
Jul–Aug) D7pm

GH Melrose Hotel 9 Holway Rd
☎823299 Mar–Nov rs Nov–Mar 10hc
(1fb) nc9 TV 10P S% B&b£6.50–£7.50
Bdi£8.50–£9 W£54–£56 ⫝̸

SHETLAND *Map 16* **See Lerwick**

SHIPSTON-ON-STOUR Warwicks
Map 4 SP24
INN Ye Olde White Bear Hotel High St
☎61558 Lic 7hc 19P S% B&b£8 W£90
Ⓜ sn L£5alc D9pm£6alc

SHOREHAM-BY-SEA West Sussex
Map 4 TQ20
GH Pende-Shore Hotel 416 Upper
Shoreham Rd ☎2905 Closed Xmas wk
Lic 14hc 1⇔▥(3fb) ⊛ CTV 8P ⑭ S%
B&b£7.96–£10.70 Bdi£12.36–£15.10
W£91.14–£97.65 ⫝̸ D6.30pm

SHOTTENDEN Kent *Map 5 TR05*
GH Cona Goldups Ln ☎ Chilham 405
Lic 10hc 4⇔▥(2fb) CTV 14P ⑭ S%
✳B&b£8.05–£8.65 Bdi£12.70–£13.25
W£60.90–£82.75 ⫝̸

SHOTTLE Derbys *Map 8 SK34*
GH Shottle Hall Farm ☎ Cowers Lane 276
Closed Xmas Lic 8hc 12P ⑭

SHREWSBURY Salop *Map 7 SJ41*
⊶⊷**GH Cannock House Private Hotel**
182A Abbey Foregate ☎56043 7hc (2fb)
nc5 CTV 4P 2🚗 ⑭ S% B&b£5.50–£6.50

GH Leagrove Hotel 29 Hereford Rd
☎52078 Lic 7hc 1⇔▥(4fb) CTV 8P S%
B&b£7.50 Bdi£11 W£70 ⫝̸ D5.30pm

GH *Shelton Hall Hotel* ☎3982 Lic 15hc
6⇔▥ CTV 50P ⑭

SIDMOUTH Devon *Map 3 SY18*
⊶⊷**GH Canterbury** Salcombe Rd ☎3373
6hc 4⇔▥(2fb) ⊛ nc6 CTV 5P S%
B&b£5.50–£7 Bdi£7.50–£9 W£50–£59
⫝̸ D7pm

The Beacon Hotel

**Nelson Road, Sheringham
Norfolk NR26 8BT
Tel: (0263) 822019**

The Beacon is a small comfortable licensed Hotel conveniently situated 2 minutes from the sea, and near the town and golf course. The bedrooms are on the first floor, all with hot and cold water, razor points, central heating, fitted carpets and interior sprung mattresses. Private car park and pleasant grounds. Over the years it has gained a reputation for excellent food and a cosy, friendly atmosphere.

Mount Pleasant Private Hotel

**Salcombe Road, Sidmouth, Devon.
Telephone: Sidmouth (STD 03955) 4694**

An early Georgian residence standing in ¾ acre of garden. The delightful lounge with colour TV overlooks the lawn which contains a nine-hole putting green. The hotel is only a short walking distance from the sea and shopping centre and it is also conveniently situated for interesting country walks. All bedrooms have hot and cold water and shaver point and are heated and comfortably furnished, a number of which have private toilet and shower. The menu is varied daily and provides good wholesome food served at separate tables in the licensed dining room. Ample free car parking. Fire Certificate is held.
Resident Proprietors: Mr and Mrs D J Morgan.

Southernhay Hotel

Fortfield Terrace, Sidmouth, Devon EX10 8NT. Tel: 3189 (STD 03955)

The Hotel is part of a regency terrace built in 1790. Situated in an excellent position overlooking cricket field, tennis courts and the sea front. A few yards from bus terminus, town and public gardens. A family run hotel with plenty of good food. All rooms have H & C, electric fires and tea making facilities. SAE for brochure to Ann Forth.

The Crown Inn

Fifteenth century

**SNAPE SAXMUNDHAM
SUFFOLK
Tel: Snape 324**

**Local fish and game in season
Crab & Lobster. Pheasant. Guinea Fowl etc. Wide range of hot and cold snacks.**

**Hosts: Louise and Stuart Pakes.
Pleasant Inn type accommodation.**

**Hot and Cold water. Central Heating. Razor points.
Television in all rooms.**

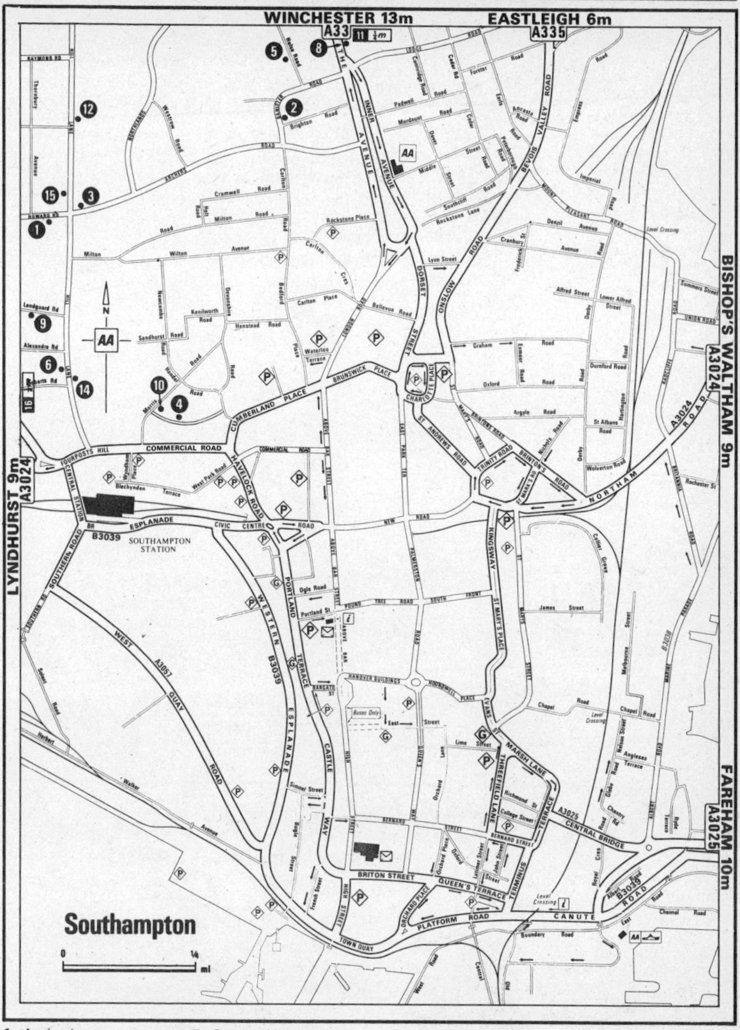

1 Amberley
2 Banister
3 Beacon
4 Claremont
5 County Hotel
6 Eaton Court Hotel
8 Elizabeth House Hotel
9 Hunters Lodge Hotel
10 Linden
11 Lodge
12 Madison House
14 Rosida Hotel
15 St Andrews
16 La Valle

GH Mount Pleasant Hotel Salcombe Rd ☎4694 Etr–mid Oct Lic 13hc 6⇌⋒ (3fb) CTV 15P ⅏ ✱B&bfr£9.75 Bdi fr£11.50 Wfr£73 D6.30pm

⋈**GH *Ryton House*** 52–54 Winslade Rd ☎3981 8hc CTV 8P ⅏

GH Southernhay 3–4 Fortfield Ter ☎3189 18hc (3fb) CTV sea S% B&b£7.84 Bdi£11.47 W£78.48 Ł D5pm

GH Westbourne Hotel Manor Rd ☎3774 Closed Oct–Mar Lic 14hc 8⇌⋒ (A 3hc 1⇌⋒) (3fb) CTV 15P ⅏ sea Bdi£15–£19 W£90 Ł (W only Jun–Aug) D7pm

SKIPTON N Yorks *Map 7 SD95*
GH Highfield Hotel 58 Keighley Rd ☎3182 Closed Xmas & New Year Lic 10hc 2⇌⋒ CTV S% B&bfr£7 Bdi fr£11.50 D7.15pm

SKYE, ISLE OF Highland *Inverness-shire Map 13 NG* **See Broadford, Dunvegan, Isle Ornsay, Portree, Waterloo**

SNAPE Suffolk *Map 5 TM35*
INN *Crown* ☎324 Lic 4hc nc12 TV 50P ⅏ D8.45pm

SOMERTON Somerset *Map 3 ST42*
GH Church Farm School Ln, Compton Dundon ☎72927 Closed last 2wks Oct Lic 3hc (A 2hc) (2fb) ⚘ CTV 6P B&b£8–£10 Bdi£13.50–£15.50 W£81–£93 Ł Dnoon

SOUTHAMPTON Hants *Map 4 SU41*
See Plan
⋈**GH Amberley** 1 Howard Rd ☎23789 Plan:**1** 8hc nc6 CTV 8P ⅏ S% B&b£5.50–£6.50 W£38.50–£45.50 M

GH Banister 11 Brighton Rd ☎21279
Plan:**2** Closed 10 days Xmas Lic 20hc (2fb)
CTV 12P 🎵 S% B&bfr£8.50 D7.30pm

GH Beacon 49 Archers Rd ☎25910
Plan:**3** 6hc (2fb) CTV 4P 🎵 S% B&b£5.50
Bdi£9 D1pm

GH Claremont 33 The Polygon
☎23112 Plan:**4** 12hc (4fb) CTV 10P 🎵
S% B&b£5–£6

GH County Hotel Hulse Rd ☎24236
Plan:**5** 15hc CTV 10P

GH Eaton Court Hotel 32 Hill Ln
☎23081 Plan:**6** Lic 15hc 2≤🗋 (8fb) ⊘
CTV 18P 🎵 S% B&b£9.25–£11.25 D6pm

GH Elizabeth House Hotel 43–44 The
Avenue ☎24327 Plan:**8** Closed last wk
Nov–1st wk Dec Lic 28hc 16≤🗋 (2fb)
CTV 28P 🎵 S% B&b£8.60 Bdi£12.39
Wfr£78.14 ⫽ D9pm

GH Hunters Lodge Hotel 25 Landguard
Rd, Shirley ☎27919 Plan:**9** Lic 16hc ⊘
CTV 14P 4🏠 🎵

GH Linden 51 The Polygon ☎25653
Plan:**10** Closed Xmas wk 10hc ⊘ CTV 6P
🎵

GH Lodge 1 Winn Rd, The Avenue
☎557537 Plan:**11** 8hc (1fb) ⊘ CTV
10P 🎵 B&b£8.25–£8.75 Bdi£12.25–£13
W£90–£154 ⫽ D8.30pm

GH Madison House 137 Hill Ln ☎22374
Plan:**12** 9hc (2fb) TV 15P 🎵 S%
✳B&b£4.50–£6.50

GH Rosida Hotel 25–27 Hill Ln ☎28501
Plan:**14** Closed 10 days Xmas Lic 36hc
(5fb) CTV 32P 🎵 B&b£10–£11 D7.30pm

GH St Andrews 128 Hill Ln ☎21140
Plan:**15** Lic 11hc (4fb) ⊘ nc7 CTV 7P 🎵
S% B&b£6 £6.50 Bdi£9.50–£10 D7pm

GH La Valle 111 Millbrook Rd ☎27821
Plan:**16** Closed Xmas 6hc (2fb) CTV 7P 🎵
S% B&b£4.50

SOUTHEND-ON-SEA Essex *Map 5 TQ88*
GH Camelia Hotel 178 Eastern Esplanade,
Thorpe Bay ☎587917 Lic 12hc 1≤🗋 ⊘
CTV 🎵 sea S% ✳B&b£10–£27 Bdi fr£14
W£102–£120 Ⓜ D10pm

GH Cobham Lodge Hotel 2 Cobham Rd,
Westcliff-on-Sea ☎46438 Lic 17hc (2fb)
⚓ CTV 🎵 S% B&bfr£8.25 Bdi fr£11.75
W£55–£65 ⫽ D9pm

GH Ferndown Hotel 136 York Rd
☎68614 Lic 14hc CTV 12P 🎵

GH Gladstone Hotel 40 Hartington Rd
☎62776 Lic 7hc (2fb) ⊘ nc3 CTV 🎵
B&b£6–£7 Bdi£8.50–£10 W£40–£47
Ⓜ D4pm

GH Haven Private Hotel 32–34 Burgess
Rd, Thorpe Bay ☎585085 Lic 16hc (3fb)
CTV 12P 🎵 ⚅ S% B&bfr£11.42 Bdi fr£17.02
D9pm

GH Maple Leaf Private Hotel 9–11
Trinity Av, Westcliff-on-Sea ☎46904
Lic 16hc (2fb) CTV 🎵 B&b£9–£9.50
Bdi£12.75–£13.50 W£76.50–£81 ⫽
D6pm

GH Marine View 4 Trinity Av,
Westcliff-on-Sea ☎44104 6hc (2fb) nc5
CTV 🎵 S% B&b£6–£7 W£36–£40 Ⓜ

GH Mayfair 52 Crownstone Av,
Westcliff-on-Sea ☎40693 Closed Xmas
6hc (1fb) ⊘ nc5 CTV 4P 🎵 S%

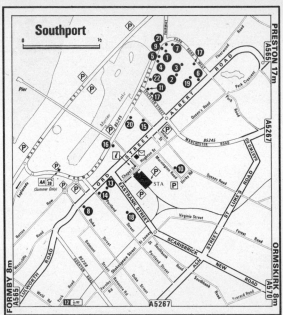

1 Abbey Hotel
2 Crimond Hotel
3 Fairway Private Hotel
4 Fernley Private Hotel
5 Franklyn Hotel
6 Fulwood Private Hotel
7 Garden Hotel
8 Glenwood Private Hotel
9 Golf Links Hotel
10 Hollies Private Hotel
11 Knowsley Private Hotel
12 Lockerbie House Hotel
13 Newholme
14 Oakwood Private Hotel
15 Ocean Bank
16 Richmond Hotel
17 Savoia Hotel
18 Sidbrook Hotel
19 Sunningdale Hotel
20 Westhaven
21 Whitworth Falls Hotel
22 Windsor Lodge Hotel

B&b£5–£5.50 Bdi£7–£7.50 W£35–£39.50 ⚓ D4pm

GH Miramare Hotel 84 Station Rd, Westcliff-on-Sea ☎44022 Lic 8hc 2⌂📺 (2fb) ✸ ⚓ CTV 2P 1🎪 🍴 sea S% B&b£8–£9 Bdi£11–£12 W£68 ⚓ D4.30pm

GH Pavilion 1 Trinity Av, Westcliff-on-Sea ☎41007 Closed Xmas 8hc (1fb) CTV 🍴 S% B&b£6.75 Bdi£9.25 Wfr£55 ⚓ D6.15pm

GH Terrace Hotel 8 Royal Ter ☎48143 Mid Jan–mid Dec Lic 9hc (4fb) nc10 CTV sea ✱B&b£6.50

GH Trinity Lodge Hotel 6–8 Trinity Av, Westcliff-on-Sea ☎46007 Lic 16hc (1fb) ✸ CTV 🍴 sea ✱B&b fr£8.62 Bdi fr£10.92 W£51.75–£69 ⚓

GH West Park Private Hotel 11 Park Rd, Westcliff-on-Sea ☎330729 Closed Xmas & New Year Lic 12hc 7⌂📺 (2fb) CTV 10P 🍴 S% B&b£11.50 Bdi£15.50 D4pm

SOUTH ERRADALE Highland *Ross & Crom Map 13 NG77*
GH Glendale ☎Badachro 256 Lic 9hc 5⌂📺 CTV 15P 🍴

SOUTH LAGGAN Highland *Inverness-shire Map 14 NN29*
GH Forest Lodge ☎Invergarry 219 Apr–Oct 6hc ✸ nc3 CTV 8P 🍴 lake

SOUTH LUFFENHAM Leics *Map 4 SK90*
INN Boot & Shoe ☎Stamford 720177 Lic 4rm 3hc ✸ TV 20P 🍴 sn D9.30pm

SOUTHPORT Merseyside *Map 7 SD31*
See Plan
⊯ **GH Abbey Hotel** 6 Latham Rd ☎38430 Plan:**1** 11hc (3fb) ✸ CTV 11P 🍴 ⚓ lake sea S% B&b£5.50–£7 Bdi£7.50–£9 W£50–£60 ⚓ D4pm

GH Crimond Hotel 28 Knowsley Rd ☎36456 Plan:**2** Lic 12hc (4fb) CTV 12P S% B&b£7–£10 Bdi£9.75–£12.75 W£65.25–£80 ⚓ D6pm

GH Fairway Private Hotel 106 Leyland Rd ☎42069 Plan:**3** Mar–Oct Lic 9hc 2⌂📺 (4fb) ✸ nc2 CTV 18P 🍴 S% B&b£6–£7 Bdi£8.50–£9.50 D4pm

GH Fernley Private Hotel 69 The Promenade ☎35610 Plan:**4** Lic 22hc (4fb) CTV 16P 🍴 sea D4pm

GH Franklyn Hotel 65 The Promenade ☎40290 Plan:**5** Lic 28hc (6fb) CTV 20P 🍴 sea ✱B&b fr£6 Bdi fr£8.25 Wfr£43.50 Ⓜ D6.30pm

⊯ **GH Fulwood Private Hotel** 82 Leyland Rd ☎30993 Plan:**6** Lic 12hc (1fb) CTV 8P 🍴 B&b£5.75 Bdi£8.63 W£54.63–£57.50 ⚓ D2pm

GH Garden Hotel 19 Latham Rd ☎30244 Plan:**7** Lic 10hc CTV 2P 1🎪 🍴 D6pm

GH Glenwood Private Hotel 98–102 King St ☎35068 Plan:**8** Lic 14hc (2fb) CTV 8P 🍴 B&b£6.33 Bdi£8.60 W£54.63–£57.50 ⚓ D2pm

GH Golf Links Hotel 85 The Promenade ☎30405 Plan:**9** Mar–Dec Lic 12hc (3fb) nc5 CTV 11P S% ✱B&b£5.50–£6 Bdi£7.50–£8 W£38–£50 ⚓ D10pm

GH Hollies Private Hotel 7 Mornington Rd ☎30054 Plan:**10** 17hc 4⌂📺 (3fb) ✸ CTV 17P 🍴 S% B&b£7.20–£8 Bdi£9.70–£11.50 W£64.50–£76.60 ⚓ D1pm

⊯ **GH Knowsley Private Hotel** Promenade, 2 Knowsley Rd ☎30190 Plan:**11** Closed Oct Lic 14hc TV 14P 🍴

GH Lockerbie House Hotel 11 Trafalgar Rd, Birkdale ☎65298 Plan:**12** Lic 12hc 10⌂📺 nc12 CTV 8P 🍴 S% ✱B&b£7–£8.50 Bdi£11–£12.50 W£77–£87.50 ⚓ D8pm

GH Newholme 51 King St ☎30425 Plan:**13** 6hc (2fb) CTV 2P 🍴 S%

B&b£6–£7 Bdi£8–£8.50 W£48–£51.50
⅃ D5pm

GH Oakwood Private Hotel 7 Portland St
☎31858 Plan:**14** Etr–Sep 8hc (2fb) ✹ nc5
CTV 6P ▥ S% B&b£6.50 Bdi£9.50 D6pm

⋈**GH Ocean Bank** 16 Bank Sq, Central
Promenade ☎30637 Plan:**15** 9hc (2fb) ✹
CTV 2P ▥ S% B&b£4–£4.50 Bdi£5.50–£6
W£40 ⅃ D5pm

GH Richmond Hotel 31 The Promenade
☎30799 Plan:**16** Lic 10hc (3fb) CTV 9P ▥
river ✱B&b£5.17–£6.32 Bdi£6.90–£8.05
W£47.15–£50.60 ⅃

GH Savoia Hotel 37 Leicester St ☎30559
Plan:**17** Lic 14hc (4fb) nc3 CTV 8P ▥ sea
B&b£7–£8 Bdi£9–£10 Wfr£60 ⅃ (W only
Jun–Sep) D3pm

GH Sidbrook 14 Talbot St ☎30608
Plan:**18** Lic 10hc (5fb) ♨ CTV 10P
✱B&b£6.32–£8.63 Bdi£9.77–£11.57
D6pm

GH Sunningdale Hotel 85 Leyland Rd
☎30042 Plan:**19** Lic 15rm 14hc 5⇆▥
(4fb) ✹ CTV 10P ▥ S% B&b£6.61–£7.76
Bdi£10.06–£11.21 W£66.99–£76.19 ⅃
D4pm

⋈**GH Westhaven** 22 Bank Sq ☎30219
Plan:**20** Lic 7hc (1fb) ✹ nc5 CTV 2P sea
S% B&b£5–£6 Bdi£6–£7.50 Wfr£52 ⅃
(W only fr last wk of May)

GH Whitworth Falls Hotel 16 Lathom Rd
☎30074 Plan:**21** Lic 14hc (3fb) ✹ CTV 9P
▥ S% B&b£7.45 Bdi£10.35 W£63.25 ⅃
D6pm

GH Windsor Lodge Hotel 37 Saunders St
☎30070 Plan:**22** Closed 2wks late Nov
Lic 12hc 1⇆▥ ✹ CTV 9P

SOUTHSEA Hants see **Portsmouth & Southsea**

SOUTH TAWTON Devon Map 3 SX69
INN Seven Stars ☎Sticklepath 292 Lic
4hc CTV ▥ S% ✱B&b£6.50–£7.50
Bar lunch£1.80alc D10.15pm£3.75alc

SOUTHWOLD Suffolk Map 5 TM57
GH Mount North Parade ☎722292 Closed
Xmas 7hc (5fb) ✹ TV ▥ B&b£6.33–£7.59
W£40.25–£49.13 Ⓜ

SOUTH ZEAL Devon Map 3 SX69
GH Poltimore ☎Sticklepath 209 Lic 7hc
(2fb) nc7 CTV 20P ▥ S% B&b£8.50–£9
Bdi£13–£13.80 W£89–£93 ⅃ (W only
Jun–Aug) D2pm

SPEAN BRIDGE Highland
Inverness-shire Map 14 NN28
⋈**GH Coire Glas** ☎272 Nov–Feb Lic 15hc
(3fb) TV 20P ▥ S% B&b fr£4.75 Bdi fr£8.50
D8pm

GH Druimandarroch ☎335 Feb–Dec Lic
7hc (3fb) TV 8P 3🏠 ✱B&b£5.92 Bdi£9.77
D7.45pm

⋈**GH Lesanne** ☎231 5hc (1fb) ✹ nc2
CTV 8P S% B&b£5.50 Bdi£9 D7.30pm

STAFFORD Staffs Map 7 SJ92
⋈**GH Abbey** 65–68 Lichfield Rd ☎58531
Closed Xmas & New Yr 6hc (A 4hc) (4fb) ✹
CTV 10P ▥ S% B&b£5.75 Bdi£7.70
D noon

⋈**GH Leonards Croft Hotel** 80 Lichfield
Rd ☎3676 12hc (A 6hc) (1fb) CTV 16P ▥
S% B&b£5.75

INN Royal Oak Rising Brook ☎58402 Lic
10hc CTV 200P ▦ B&b£8.50 sn
L£3–£4.25&alc D10pm£3–£4.25&alc

STAINTON Cumbria *Map 12 NY42*
⊷**GH Limes Country Hotel** Redhills
☎Penrith 63343 8hc (3fb) ⊗ CTV 12P ▦
B&bfr£5.75 Bdi£8.62 D6pm

STAMFORD Lincs *Map 4 TF00*
GH St Martins ☎3359 Closed Xmas Lic
10hc 1⇗🛏 (3fb) ⊗ CTV 4P 7🛏 ▦
✳B&b£7.50 D9pm

STANFORD LE HOPE Essex *Map 5 TQ68*
GH Homesteads 216 Southend Rd
☎2372 rs Xmas Lic 11hc (2fb) ◬ CTV 8P
▦ S% B&b£7 Bdi£9 W£63 ⱢD6pm

STEPASIDE Dyfed *Map 2 SN10*
GH Bay View Pleasant Valley
☎Saundersfoot 813417 Lic 12hc ⊗ ◬
CTV 20P ▦ W only Spring Bank Hol–Sep

STITHIANS Cornwall *Map 2 SW73*
GH Crellow Country House Hotel
☎860523 Etr–Oct Lic 9hc CTV 15P

STOCKBRIDGE Hants *Map 4 SU33*
GH Carbery Salisbury Hill ☎771 Closed
2wks Xmas Lic 11hc (3fb) ⊗ CTV 11P ▦
S% B&b£8.63 Bdi£12.65 W£57.50 Ⓜ
D6pm

STOKEINTEIGNHEAD Devon
Map 3 SX97
⊷**GH Bailey's Farm** ☎Shaldon 3361
Apr–Sep 10hc TV 8P

⊷**GH Santa Rosa** ☎Shaldon 2607 6hc
CTV 10P ▦ S% B&b£5–£6 Bdi£9–£10
W£54–£60 Ⱡ

STOKE ST GREGORY Somerset
Map 3 ST32
GH Meare Green ☎ North Curry 490250
Mar–Oct Lic 6hc ⊗ TV 6P 2🏠 S%
✳B&bfr£5.50–£10.50 Bdi£7.75

STONE Glos *Map 3 ST69*
GH Elms ☎ Falfield 260279 Lic 10hc
(3fb) CTV 20P 2🏠 ▦ S% ✳B&b£8.62
Bdi£12.07 D2.30pm

STONETHWAITE *(Borrowdale)* Cumbria
Map 11 NY21
GH Langstrath Hotel Borrowdale
☎ Borrowdale 239 mid Mar–Oct & Xmas/
New Year Lic 14hc (3fb) ◬ 20P ▦ S%
B&b£9 Bdi£13 W£85 ⱢDnoon

STORNOWAY Isle of Lewis, Western Isles
Ross & Crom Map 13 NB43
⊷**GH Ardlonan** 29 Francis St ☎3482
5rm 3hc (1fb) ⊗ CTV P ▦ S% B&b£5.50

GH Hebridean 61 Bayhead ☎2268 6hc
TV D2pm (Sun only)

GH Park 30 James St ☎2485 6rm 5hc
(A 2hc) CTV ▦ S% ✳B&bfr£6

STOURBRIDGE W Midlands *Map 7 SO98*
GH Limes 260 Hagley Rd, Pedmore
☎ Hagley 882689 10hc ⊗ CTV 12P ▦ ⅃

STOURPORT-ON-SEVERN Heref &
Worcs *Map 7 SO87*
INN Angel Hotel Severnside ☎2661
Lic 5hc CTV 40P ▦ river D9pm

STOW-ON-THE-WOLD Glos *Map 4 SP12*
GH Old Farmhouse Hotel Lower Swell
(1m W A436) ☎30232 Closed Xmas Lic
5hc 1⇗🛏 (1fb) ⊗ TV 15P ▦ S%
B&bfr£12.65 Bdifr£20.50 Wfr£142.30
Ⱡ D9pm

GH Parkdene Hotel Sheep St ☎30344
Closed Jan Lic 11hc 2⇗🛏 (1fb) ◬ CTV ▦
B&b£9.75 Bdi£9–£14.75
W£73–£103.25 Ⱡ D8.30pm

STRANRAER Dumfries & Galloway
Wigtowns Map 10 NX05
⊷**GH Lochview** 52 Agnew Gres ☎3837
6hc (2fb) CTV 6P S% B&b£5–£5.50
Bdi£8–£8.50 W£53–£56.50 Ⱡ Dnoon

STRATFORD-UPON-AVON Warwicks
Map 4 SP25 **See Plan**
GH Argos Hotel 5 Arden St ☎4321
Plan:**1** Closed Dec 9hc (1fb) ⊗ nc10
CTV ▦ S% B&b£6–£6.50

⊷**GH Avon House** 8 Evesham Pl
☎293328 Plan:**2** 9hc (2fb) ⊗ CTV ▦
B&b£5–£6 Bdi£8.50–£9.50 Dam

GH Glenavon Private Hotel Chestnut
Walk ☎292588 Plan:**3** 11hc (3fb) TV ▦
S% B&b£6–£7.50

⊷**GH Hunters Moon** 150 Alcester Rd
☎292888 Plan:**4** 7hc (2fb) CTV 6P S%
B&b£5.25–£7

GH Hylands Hotel Warwick Rd
☎297962 Plan:**5** Lic 12hc 3⇗🛏 (3fb)
⊗ CTV 20P ▦ S% ✳B&b£7.50–£10.75
Bdi£13–£16.50 D7.30pm

⊷**GH Marlyn** 3 Chestnut Walk ☎293752
Plan:**6** Closed Xmas 8hc (2fb) ⊗ TV ▦ S%
B&b££4.98–£8.75 W£29.70–£52.50

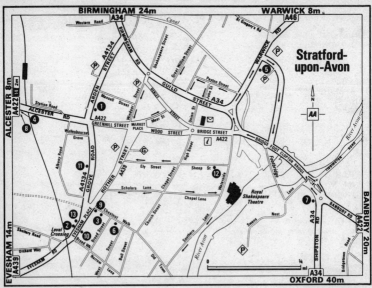

1 Argos Hotel
2 Avon House
3 Glenavon Private Hotel
4 Hunter's Moon
5 Hylands Hotel
6 Marlyn
7 Melita
8 Moonraker House
9 Nando's
10 Penshurst
11 Salamander
12 Stratford House Hotel
13 Virginia Lodge
14 Wildmoor

GH Melita 37 Shipston Rd ☎292432 Plan:**7** Closed Xmas rs Feb Lic 11hc 3⇨🛏️(4fb) ❀ CTV 12P 2🏠 🍴 S% B&b£7–£9 W£45–£60

GH Moonraker House 40 Alcester Rd ☎67115 Plan:**8** 7hc 6⇨🛏️(3fb) CTV 7P 🍴 S% B&b£5–£6.50 Bdi£8.50–£10 D3pm

GH Nando's 18–19 Eversham Pl ☎4907 Plan:**9** 12hc (4fb) ❀ CTV 🍴 S% B&b£6–£7.50 W£38–£45 M

GH Penshurst 34 Eversham Pl ☎5259 Plan:**10** 8hc (2fb) ❀ CTV 🍴 S% ✱B&b£5–£6 W£35–£40 M

GH Salamander 40 Grove Rd ☎5728 Plan:**11** 7hc (1fb) CTV 🍴 S% B&b£5.75–£6.75

GH Stratford House Hotel Sheep St ☎68288 Plan:**12** Lic 9hc 7⇨🛏️(1fb) ❀nc7 CTV 🍴 ৬ B&b£12.75–£17.25

GH Virginia Lodge 12 Eversham Pl ☎292157 Plan:**13** Closed Xmas Lic 6hc

(1fb) ⏀ CTV 5P 🍴 B&b£5–£6 W£30–£37 M

INN Wildmoor Alcester Rd ☎67063 Plan:**14** Lic 7hc 1⇨🛏️ CTV 50P sn D10pm

STRATHAVEN Strathclyde *Lanarks* *Map 11 NS74*
GH Springvale Hotel 18 Letham Rd ☎21131 Lic 5hc (A 6hc) CTV 6P 🍴 D7.30pm

STRATHPEFFER Highland *Ross & Crom* *Map 14 NH45*
GH Kilvannie Manor Fodderty ☎389 Lic 8hc (2fb) ❀ CTV 15P S% B&b£6–£8 Bdi£9.50–£11.50 W£66.50–£80.50 ৬ D7pm

GH Rosslyn Lodge Private Hotel ☎281 Feb–Nov 15rm 14hc (5fb) ⏀ CTV 15P 🍴 B&b£7.50–£8 Bdi£12–£12.50 W£78–£83 ৬ D6.30pm

PENSHURST GUEST HOUSE

34 Evesham Place, Stratford-upon-Avon
Tel: Stratford-upon-Avon 5259

Ideally situated for the Theatre and for touring the Cotswolds.
Penshurst offers friendly and comfortable accommodation with a first
class, full English breakfast.
Also included are colour TV lounge; dining room with separate tables;
bath and showers and private parking.
Full central heating. H & C all rooms.

"Salamander"
Guest House

**40 Grove Road, Stratford-upon-Avon, Warwickshire
Tel: Stratford-upon-Avon 5728**

Bed and breakfast. Hot and cold all rooms. Full Central
heating. TV lounge. Shower room.

Few minutes from theatre and historic buildings.

Proprietress: Mrs J Copestick.

THE INN
STRATHYRE

This 18th Century Inn has been tastefully
modernised to a very high standard, and is
set amongst some of Scotland's most
magnificent scenery. All the bedrooms
have private bathrooms. The bars and
dining room are finished in natural pine
wood, and have much character.

Golf, fishing, sailing, canoeing, hill and
forest walks are all available locally.

Tel: 087 74 660 or 224.

Resident Proprietors —
Mr & Mrs Bert Ramsay

TREGARE HOTEL

**9 Sketty Road, Uplands, Swansea
Tel: Reception 0792 56608**

Comfortable, fully centrally-heated hotel on
main road (A4118) to the Gower Peninsula, yet
within easy reach of the City Centre. Car Park.
Fire Certificate. Bed, Breakfast and Evening
Meal. Licensed Cocktail Bar. Separate Lounge
with Colour TV (TV sets in all bedrooms).
Most bedrooms have private bath or shower
with w/c. All bedrooms have radio, shaver
sockets and h/c water.

STRATHYRE Central *Perths Map 11 NN51*
INN Strathyre ☎224 Lic 7⇔🛆 CTV 50P
1🛆 ⠇⠇ ⇌ B&b£8.50–£9.75 W£90 M
sn`L£4alc D9.30pm£4alc

STRETE Devon *Map 3 SX84*
GH Highcliff ☎ Stoke Fleming 307
Etr–Oct Lic 10hc 1⇔🛆(3fb) 🛆 CTV 10P
sea S% B&b£6.50 Bdi£9.20 W£64.40
⠇ D7pm

GH *Tallis Rock Private Hotel* ☎ Stoke
Fleming 370 May–Sep 9hc CTV 6P 1🛆 sea

STRETTON Leics *Map 8 SK91*
INN Olde Greetham ☎ Castle Bytham 365
Lic 5hc 60P 🛆 S% B&bfr£8.10 Bdifr£12.10
sn L£2.95–£4.75 D9.30pm£4&alc

STROMNESS Orkney *Map 16 HY20*
GH Oakleigh Private Hotel Victoria St
☎850447 Lic 18hc 1⇔🛆(A 1hc)
(3fb) 🛆 CTV 2P ✱B&b£8.75 Bdi£12.50
W£84 ⠇ (W only Jun–Aug) D5pm

STROUD Glos *Map 3 SO80*
GH Downfield Private Hotel Caincross Rd
☎4496 Lic 18rm 13hc 6⇔🛆(2fb) CTV
25P 🛆 S% B&b£9–£9.50 Bdi£10–£13.50
W£55 M D8pm

STUKELEY, GREAT Cambs *Map 4 TL27*
GH The Stukeleys ☎ Huntingdon 56927
rs Sun (Restaurant closed) Lic 8hc (4fb)
CTV 20P 🛆 B&b£9–£11 D9.30pm

SUDBURY Suffolk *Map 5 TL84*
GH Oriel Lodge Hotel 21 King's Hill,
Cornard Rd ☎72456 Lic 11hc (3fb) CTV
20P 1🛆 🛆 S% B&b£7.47–£8.75
Bdi£9.97–£11.25 D9pm

SUNDERLAND Tyne & Wear
Map 12 NZ35
GH St Annes Private Hotel 1 Northcliff,
Roker Ter ☎ Closed 2wks Xmas &
New Year Lic 12hc (2fb) 🛆 CTV 12P S%
B&b£8.50–£9.50 D9pm

SURBITON Gt London *London plan 4 E2
(page 266)*
GH Dalton Private Hotel 317 Ewell Rd,
Tolworth ☎01-399 8663 18hc 12⇔🛆
(4fb) nc10 CTV 10P 🛆 S%
B&b£10.35–£11.75

GH Holmdene 23 Cranes Dr
☎01-399 9992 6hc (1fb) nc5 CTV 2P 🛆
S% B&b£7–£9.50

GH *Villiers Lodge* 1 Cranes Pk ☎01-399
6000 6hc 🛆 CTV 6P

GH Warwick 321 Ewell Rd ☎01-399
5837 9hc 1⇔🛆(3fb) CTV 5P 🛆 S%
B&b£8.63–£11.50 W£56.35–£80.50 M

SUTTON Gt London *London plan 4 E3
(page 266)*
GH Dene Private Hotel 39 Cheam Rd
☎01-642 3170 17rm 14hc 2⇔🛆(3fb) 🛆
nc5 TV 8P 🛆 S% B&b£9.20–£20.70

GH Eaton Court Hotel 49 Eaton Rd
☎01-642 4580 Closed 25–30 Dec Lic
12hc (3fb) CTV 8P 🛆 S% B&b£11.38

GH Thatched House Hotel 135 Cheam
Rd ☎01-642 3131 Lic 18hc 7⇔🛆 CTV
12P 🛆 ⠇ S% B&bfr£12 Bdifr£17
D6.30pm

SUTTON COLDFIELD W Midlands
Map 7 SP19
For location see Birmingham Plan

GH Cloverley Hotel 17 Anchorage Rd
☎021-354 5181 Not on plan Closed 2 wks
Xmas & New Year Lic 16⇔🛆 (A 1⇔🛆)
(2fb) 🛆 CTV 14P 🛆 S% ✱B&b fr£13.75
Wfr£96.25 D8pm

GH Standbridge Hotel 138 Birmingham
Rd ☎021-354 3007 Birmingham plan:**7**
Lic 8hc 2⇔🛆 (A 1rm 1hc) CTV 11P 🛆 S%
✱B&b£9.75–£11.25 Bdi£13.05–£14.55
D noon

SWANAGE Dorset *Map 4 SZ07*
GH Boyne Hotel Cliff Av ☎2939
Mar–Oct Lic 15hc 1⇔🛆(3fb) CTV 7P
B&b£6.90–£9.50 Bdi£8.59–£11.70
W£54.22–£70.10 ⠇ (W only Jul & Aug)
D5.30pm

GH Byways 5 Ulwell Rd ☎2322
mid May–mid Sep 11hc (4fb) nc5 CTV 4P
S% ✱B&b£5.50–£6.50 Bdi£7.50–£8.50
W£46.50–£49 ⠇ D6.30pm

GH Castleton Private Hotel Highcliff Rd
☎3972 Feb–Oct Lic 12hc (5fb) 🛆 nc3
CTV 8P 🛆 S% B&b£6.90–£8.63
Bdi£9.78–£11.50 W£57.50–£69.00 ⠇
D5pm

GH *Eversden Private Hotel* Victoria Rd
☎3276 Lic 10hc 3⇔🛆 🛆 nc3 CTV 10P 🛆

GH Golden Sands Private Hotel
10 Ulwell Rd ☎2093 5 Jan–20 Dec Lic
11hc 6⇔🛆(8fb) 🛆 🛆 CTV 14P 🛆 S%
B&b£7–£8.50 Bdi£9–£12 W£60–£80 ⠇
D6.30pm

GH Havenhurst Hotel 3 Cranbourne Rd
☎4224 Mar–Oct Lic 16hc 1⇔🛆(6fb) 🛆
CTV 16P 🛆 B&b£7.50–£9.50
Bdi£10.50–£13 W£68–£82.50 ⠇
D6.30pm

GH Horseshoe House Hotel Cliff Av
☎2194 May–Sep 10hc nc10 CTV 5P 🛆
S% B&b£6.90–£9.20 Bdi£11.50–£13.80
W£69–£86.25 ⠇ D9pm

GH Ingleston Private Hotel 2 Victoria Rd
☎2391 Apr–Oct Lic 8hc (4fb) 🛆 nc3 🛆
CTV 10P 🛆 S% B&b£6–£7.50
Bdi£9–£10.50 W£53–£56 ⠇ D4pm

GH Kingsley Hall Hotel 8 Ulwell Rd
☎2872 rs Winter Lic 16hc 2⇔🛆(7fb) 🛆
CTV 20P 🛆 sea ✱B&bfr£5 Bdi fr£6.50
Wfr£45.50 ⠇ (W Jul & Aug) D6.30pm

GH Oxford Hotel 3 & 5 Park Rd ☎2247
Closed Xmas Lic 14hc (5fb) 🛆 nc2 CTV S%
✱B&bfr£6.50 Bdi fr£9.50 Wfr£65 ⠇
D6.30pm

GH Tower Lodge Private Hotel 17 Ulwell
Rd ☎2887 Mar–Nov Lic 11hc (7fb) 🛆
CTV 9P S% B&b£8.22–£12.60
Bdi£11.09–£13.75 W£71.76–£83.03 ⠇
D5pm

GH *Westbury Hotel* 6 Rempstone Rd
☎2345 Etr–Oct Lic 20hc CTV 12P sea

SWANSEA W Glam *Map 3 SS69*
⊨⊨**GH '57' Bed & Breakfast** Bryn Rd,
Brynmill ☎466948 7hc (1fb) 🛆 CTV 🛆 sea
S% B&b£5.50–£6.50 (W only Apr–mid Jun)

GH Mount Vernon 18 Uplands Cres
☎466790 5hc 1⇔🛆(1fb) CTV 🛆 S%
B&b£6.50–£7.50

GH Parkway Hotel 253 Gower Rd,
Sketty ☎21632 Lic 13hc (A 1hc) CTV 30P
🛆 B&b£7–£9.20 Bdi£13.25 W£57.50 M
D5pm

GH St Anne's Hotel 6 Gore Ter ☎50914
8hc (1fb) 🛆 CTV S% ✱B&b£4.50–£5

GH Tregare Hotel 9 Sketty Rd,
Uplands ☎56608 Lic 11hc 8⊣🛏 (3fb)
CTV 6P 🕮 S% B&b£7–£8.40
Bdi£10.50–£12.60 W£63–£75.60 ⊬
D4.30pm

GH Uplands Court 134 Eaton Cres
☎59046 Lic 8hc (2fb) ⊛ nc3 CTV 6P 2🏠
🕮 S% B&bf6 Bdif9.50 W£57 ⊬ D4pm

⟷**GH Westlands** 34 Bryn Rd, Brynmill
☎466654 6hc (1fb) CTV B&b£5–£5.50
Bdif7.50–£8 W£44–£47.50

SWINTON Borders *Berwicks*
Map 12 NT84
INN Wheatsheaf Hotel Main St ☎257
Lic 4hc CTV 15P D9.30pm

SWYNNERTON Staffs *Map 7 SJ83*
INN Fitzherbert Arms ☎241 Lic 9hc
6⊣🛏 (A 5hc) CTV 100P 7🏠 🕮 B&b£10 sn
L£3.25–£3.75&alc D9.30pm£5.25&alc

SYMONDS YAT, EAST Heref & Worcs
Map 3 SO51
GH Garth Cottage Hotel ☎890364
9 Jan–1 Nov 7hc 2⊣🛏 (1fb) CTV 9P 🕮
river S% B&b£8–£9.20 Bdif£12.25–£13.95
W£82–£92 ⊬ D7pm

SYMONDS YAT, WEST nr Ross-on-Wye
Heref & Worcs *Map 3 SO51*
GH Woodlea ☎890206 Lic 10hc 1⊣🛏
(4fb) CTV 8P 🕮 river ✽B&b£7 Bdif£11.50
W£75–£77 ⊬ D6pm

TADCASTER N Yorks *Map 8 SE44*
GH Shann House 47 Kirkgate ☎833931
rs 24, 25 & 31 Dec 8⊣🛏 (1fb) CTV 8P 🕮
S% B&bf9.50

TAL-Y-LLYN Gwynedd *Map 6 SH70*
GH Minffordd Hotel (2m E on A487)
☎Corris 665 Mar–Oct rs Nov–Xmas &
2 Jan–Feb Lic 6hc (2fb) ⊛ nc3 15P 🕮 S%
B&b£10.30–£12.90 Bdi£15.90–£19.90
W£128.80 ⊬ D8.30pm

TARBET Strathclyde *Dunbartons
Map 10 NN30*
GH Edendarroch ☎Arrochar 223
Mar–Oct 7hc CTV 20P 🕮

TARPORLEY Cheshire *Map 7 SJ56*
GH Perth Hotel High St ☎2514 Closed
Jan Lic 9hc 2⊣🛏 (1fb) CTV 10P 1🏠 🕮
B&b£11 Bdif£16 W£65.50 M D9pm

TAUNTON Somerset *Map 3 ST22*
GH Brookfield House 16 Wellington Rd
☎72786 8hc (1fb) ⊛ CTV 8P 🕮 S%
B&b£8–£10 Bdif£12–£14 W£75–£85
⊬ D5pm

GH Meryan House Hotel Bishops Hull
☎87445 Lic 8hc (3fb) CTV 20P 🕮 S%
✽B&b£7–£8 Bdif£10–£11 W£55–£65 ⊬
D6.30pm

GH White Lodge Hotel 81 Bridgwater Rd
☎73287 10hc (3fb) ⊛ CTV 12P 🕮 S%
B&b£10.50 Bdif£15 W£90 ⊬ D7.45pm

TAVISTOCK Devon *Map 2 SX47*
GH Cherrytrees 40 Plymouth Rd ☎3070
5hc (1fb) ⊛ TV 1P 4🏠 river S%
B&b£6–£7.50

GH Dulverton 13 Plymouth Rd ☎2964
Lic 7hc (3fb) CTV 8P 🕮 ✽B&b£6.50–£7.50
Bdif£10.50–£11.50 W£65–£75 ⊬
D8.30pm

TEIGNMOUTH Devon *Map 3 SX97*
GH Bay Cottage Hotel 7 Marine Pde, Shaldon ☎ Shaldon 2394 Mar–Nov Lic 8hc (2fb) ⊘ CTV 4P Ⅲ river sea B&b£8 Bdi£12.50 W£82 ⱡ D5pm

GH Bay Hotel Sea Front ☎4123 Etr–Oct & Xmas Lic 20hc (4fb) CTV 14P B&b£8–£10 Bdi£11–£13.50 W£58–£75 ⱡ D6.30pm

⊢⊣**GH Glen Devon** 3 Carlton Pl ☎2895 Lic 8hc (4fb) ⊘ CTV 6P Ⅲ S% B&b£5–£7 Bdi£6–£8 W£50–£65 ⱡ D5pm

GH Hillsley Upper Hermonsa Rd ☎3878 May–Sep Lic 8hc (4fb) nc3 CTV 10P river sea S% B&b£7.47–£8.05 Bdi£10–£11.50 D6pm

⊢⊣**GH Leafield** 61 Dawlish Rd ☎2986 May–Sep 6hc (2fb) nc5 CTV 6P Ⅲ S% B&b£4.50–£6 W£28–£38 M

GH *New Strathearn Hotel* Bitton Park Rd ☎2796 Closed Xmas Lic 11hc ⊘ CTV 10P sea S% D6.30pm

GH *Overstowey Hotel* Dawlish Rd ☎4251 rs Oct–Apr (B&b only) Lic 10hc ⊘ CTV 10P Ⅲ

GH Thornhill Hotel Sea Front ☎3460 Etr–mid Oct Lic 14hc (3fb) nc2 CTV 4P Ⅲ sea S% B&b£7.50–£8.75 Bdi£9.75–£11 W£53.25–£66.50 ⱡ D6.30pm

GH Westlands Hotel Reed Vale ☎3007 Lic 16hc 5⇆ⓕ (3fb) ⊘ CTV 16P river D7pm

TENBY Dyfed *Map 2 SN10*
GH Belvedere Private Hotel Serpentine Rd ☎2549 Apr–Oct Lic 16hc 1⇆ⓕ (11fb) CTV 20P B&b£6.50–£9 Bdi£9–£11 D6.30pm

GH *Buckingham Hotel* Esplanade ☎2622 Dec & Jan Lic 25hc 8⇆ⓕ nc5 CTV

GH Hotel Doneva The Norton ☎2460 Apr–Oct Lic 14hc 3⇆ⓕ (5fb) CTV 18P S% B&b£7.50–£8.50 Bdi£9.50–£10 W£59–£70 ⱡ(W only Jul–Aug)

GH Harbour Heights Hotel 11 The Croft ☎2264 Etr–mid Oct Lic 11hc 3⇆ⓕ (6fb) ⊘ nc3 TV S% ✻B&b£7.50 Bdi£11.50 W£60–£73 ⱡ D7.30pm

GH Heywood Lodge Heywood Ln ☎2684 Etr–Oct Lic 14hc 3⇆ⓕ (4fb) ⌂ CTV 20P Ⅲ S% B&b£6.90 Bdi£10.92 W£65–£72 ⱡ D8.30pm

GH Myrtle House Hotel St Mary's St ☎2508 mid Mar–mid Oct Lic 9hc CTV Ⅲ B&b£6–£8.75 Bdi£8.75–£11.25 W£59–£76 ⱡ D6.30pm

GH Pembroke Hotel Warren St ☎3670 Closed Xmas & New Year Lic 15hc (6fb) CTV 5P Ⅲ ✻B&b£5–£5.75 Bdi£7.50–£8.25 W£52.50–£57.75 ⱡ D6.30pm

GH Sea Breezes Hotel 18 The Norton ☎2753 Etr–Oct Lic 18hc 4⇆ⓕ (3fb) ⊘ nc3 CTV Ⅲ sea B&b£6–£8 Bdi£10–£12.50 W£62–£80 ⱡ

TEWKESBURY Glos *Map 3 SO83*
GH South End House 67 Church St ☎294097 Lic 8hc (2fb) CTV 3P Ⅲ S% B&b£9.20 Bdi£14.95

THORNTHWAITE *(Nr Keswick)* Cumbria *Map 11 NY22*
GH Ladstock Country House Hotel ☎ Braithwaite 210 Mar–Oct Lic 17hc 1⇆ⓕ (2fb) ⊘ CTV 20P Ⅲ S% B&b£9 Bdi£14 W£85 ⱡ D6pm

THORNTON CLEVELEYS Lancs *Map 7 SD34*
GH Lyndhope 2 Stockdove Way, Cleveleys ☎ Cleveleys 852531 6hc (2fb) ⊘ nc3 CTV 10P Ⅲ S% ✻B&b£4.50–£5.50 Bdi£6–£6.50 W£42–£45.50 ⱡ D3pm

THORNTON HEATH Gt London *London plan 4 E4 (page 266)*
GH Clock House Hotel 47 Brigstock Rd ☎01-684 8480 12hc CTV 7P Ⅲ S% ✻B&b£6

THORPE BAY Essex
see **Southend-on-Sea**

THORVERTON Devon *Map 3 SS90*
GH Berribridge House ☎ Exeter 860259 Lic 6hc 1⇆ⓕ (1fb) CTV 6P 1⌂ ✻B&b£8.50–£9.50 D8.30pm

THURLESTONE SANDS Devon *Map 3 SX64*
GH La Mer ☎ Galmpton 207 24May–14Sep Lic 10hc (6fb) nc4 CTV 12P sea B&b£6.50–£9.50 Bdi£12–£14 W£82–£92 ⱡ D7pm

TICEHURST E Sussex *Map 5 TQ63*
INN Bell Hotel The Square ☎200234 Lic 3hc ⊘ nc4 30P Ⅲ ⇌ B&b£7.50 sn L£3.50alc D9.30pm£3.50alc

TICKENHAM Avon *Map 3 ST47*
INN Star ☎ Nailsea 2071 Lic 4hc nc5 CTV 80P S% B&bfr£8 Bdifr£10 sn L£1.60–£3 D£2–£4.50

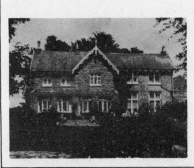

TIMSBURY Avon *Map 3 ST65*
GH Old Malt House ☎70106 Lic 7hc
3⇔🛏 (1fb) ❄ nc3 CTV 16P 🍴 river S%
B&b£9.20–£9.77 Bdi£14.95–£15.53
W£90.56–£94.59 ⌂

TINTAGEL Cornwall *Map 2 SX08*
GH Halgabron House ☎667 Etr–mid Sep
Lic 4hc (3fb) CTV 5P sea S% ✱B&b6.90
Bdi£11.50 W£57.50–£69 ⌂ (W only mid
Jul–Aug) D3pm
GH Penallick Hotel Treknow ☎296 Lic
10hc 1⇔🛏 (3fb) CTV 12P 🍴 sea S%
B&b£7.50–£9 Bdi£9–£11 W£59–£69
⌂ D6pm
GH Trebrea Lodge Trenale ☎410
Apr–Oct Lic 7hc (3fb) CTV 10P 🍴 sea S%
✱B&b£8.05 Bdi£11.50 W£63.25–£69 ⌂
(W only mid Jun–mid Sep) D6.30pm

TINTERN Gwent *Map 3 SO50*
GH Parva Farmhouse ☎411 Lic 7rm 5hc
(3fb) CTV P 🍴 river S% ✱B&b£6–£7
Bdi£10.50–£11.50 W£38–£48 M D6pm

TIVETSHALL ST MARGARET Norfolk
Map 5 TM18
GH Glenhaven ☎238 4hc (1fb) TV 8P 🍴
S% B&bfr£7 Bdifr£9.50

TOBERMORY Isle of Mull, Strathclyde
Argyll Map 13 NM55
GH Suidhe Hotel 59 Main St ☎2209
Apr–Oct Lic 9hc 1⇔🛏 (2fb) ❄ CTV 🍴 sea
S% B&b£8–£9 Bdi£13–£14
W£87.50–£94.50 ⌂ D7pm

GH Tobermory 53 Main St ☎2091
Closed Xmas & New Year Lic 11hc (1fb)

CTV 🍴 B&b£8.63–£9.78
Bdi£12.08–£13.22
W£74.75–£86.25 ⌂ D6.30pm

TORBAY Devon **See under Brixham,
Paignton and Torquay.**

TORCROSS Devon *Map 3 SX84*
GH Cove House ☎ Kingsbridge 580448
Mar–Nov Lic 12hc 5⇔🛏 (2fb) ❄ nc10
TV 12P sea S% B&b£8.05–£9.20
Bdi£11.50–£14.95 W£80.50–£92 ⌂
(W only Jul–Sep) D11am

GH Shingle ☎ Kingsbridge 580782
Mar–Oct Lic 6hc 1⇔🛏 ❄ nc5 TV 5P
sea S% B&b£7.20–£8 Bdi£10–£11.50
W£67.50–£75 ⌂ D6pm

TORMARTON Avon *Map 3 ST77*
INN Compass ☎ Badminton 242 Lic 6hc
2⇔🛏 TV 100P 🍴 S% B&b£11.90–£14.25
Bar lunch50p–£4.50 D10pmf£4.50

TORPOINT Cornwall *Map 2 SX45*
GH Elms 16 St James Rd ☎ Plymouth
812612 Lic 7rm 6hc (4fb) CTV 5P 🍴 S%
✱B&b£7 Bdi£11 W£73 ⌂ D7pm

TORQUAY Devon *Map 3 SX96*
See Central & District plan
GH Albaston House Hotel 27 St
Marychurch Rd ☎26758 Central plan:**1**
Closed mid Dec–mid Jan Lic 13hc 6⇔🛏
(7fb) CTV 12P S% B&b£6.50–£7.25
Bdi£11.50–£12.75 W£69–£79 ⌂ D9pm

GH Braddon Hall Hotel Braddons Hill
Road East ☎23908 Central plan:**2** Lic
13hc 1⇔🛏 (5fb) ❄ CTV 9P 1🚗 🍴 S%
B&b£6.50–£9.50 Bdi£8.50–£11.50
W£54–£79.50 ⌂ (W only Jul–Aug) Dnoon

Trebrea Lodge
Tel: Tintagel 410

Trenale, North Cornwall

Dating from 1300 AD with a fascinating
history and in the ownership of one family
for 600 years, Trebrea stands in three acres
looking out across fields to the sea with
swimming and surfing close by. Really
good food and drink is served in an
informal, friendly atmosphere. There is a
games room for children in the grounds.
We offer reductions for children and dogs
are welcome too. Previous guests' written
comments are available to be sent with
our brochure: they can't all be wrong!
Stamp for brochure, please, to Ann and
Guy Murray.

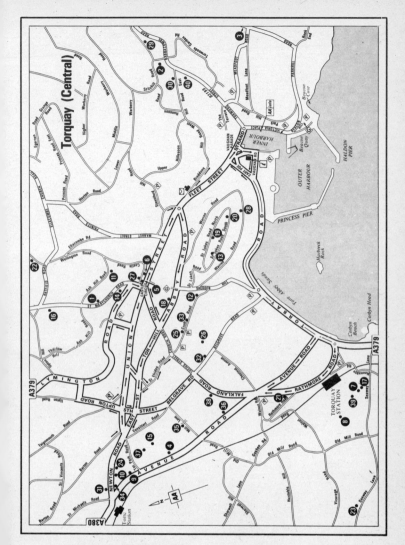

1	Albaston House Hotel	**10**	Hotel Concorde	**22**	Pencarrow Hotel	**33** Torcroft Hotel
2	Braddon Hall Hotel	**11**	Craig Court Hotel	**23**	Rawlyn House Hotel	**34** Tormohun Hotel
3	Brookesby Hall	**12**	Devon Court Hotel	**24**	Richwood Hotel	**35** Trafalgar House Hotel
4	Carn Brea	**13**	Fretherne Hotel	**25**	Riva Lodge	**36** Tregantle Hotel
5	Castle Mount	**14**	Glendon Hotel	**26**	Rothesay Hotel	**37** Tregenna Hotel
6	Castleton Private Hotel	**15**	Glenorleigh Hotel	**27**	St Bernard's Private Hotel	**38** Westgate Hotel
7	Chelston House Hotel	**16**	Hatherleigh Hotel	**28**	Seacliff Hotel	**39** Westowe Hotel
8	Chelston Tower Hotel	**17**	Ingoldsby Hotel	**29**	Sea Point Hotel	**40** Four Seasons Hotel (*Inn*)
9	Clovelly Hotel	**18**	Lindum Hotel	**30**	Shirley Hotel	
		19	Mapleton Hotel	**31**	Silverlands Hotel	
		20	Mount Nessing Hotel	**32**	Southbank Hotel	
		21	Normanhurst Hotel			

GH Brookesby Hall Hotel Hesketh Rd
☎22194 Central plan:**3** 12hc (3fb) CTV
12P ⬚ sea S% B&b£6.90–£8.63
Bdi£10.64–£12.65 W£73.60–£82.80 ⚓
D4pm

GH *Burley Court Hotel* Wheatridge Ln,
Livermead ☎607879 District plan:**41**
Apr–Sep Lic 22hc 10⬚⬚ ⬚ CTV 30P sea

GH Carn Brea 21 Avenue Rd ☎22002
Central plan:**4** Closed 10–27 Apr Lic 22rm
21hc 3⬚⬚⬚ (5fb) CTV 11P S%
✳B&b£6.32–£8.62 Bdi£10.35–£13.22
W£60.83–£78.02 ⚓ D6.30pm

GH Casey's Court Motel 127 Newton Rd
☎63909 District plan:**42** 6hc (2fb) ⬚ 6P
1⬚ ⬚ S% ✳B&b£4.25–£5.50

GH Castle Mount Hotel 7 Castle Rd
☎22130 Central Plan **5** rs Nov–Etr 9hc
(3fb) nc7 CTV 6P S% B&b fr£5.75
Bdi fr£8.05 Wfr£54.05 ⊁ D6pm

GH Castleton Private Hotel Castle Rd
☎24976 Central plan **6** 17Mar–Dec Lic
13hc ⊗ nc3 CTV 7P ⊗ sea D5pm

GH Chelston House Hotel Chelston Rd
☎605200 Central plan **7** Etr–Sep Lic 18hc
(3fb) ⊗ CTV 16P ⊗ S% B&b£7–£9.50
Bdi£9–£12.50 W£63–£85 ⊁ D5pm

GH Chelston Tower Hotel Rawlyn Rd
☎607351 Central plan **8** Closed Nov &
Dec Lic 24hc 9⊆⊪(9fb) CTV 30P sea S%
B&b£8.40–£11.20 Bdi£13.15–£15.95
W£70–£97.75 ⊁ D7.30pm

GH Clevedon Private Hotel Meadfoot Sea
Rd ☎24260 District plan **43** Apr–Oct Lic
16hc (4fb) nc6 CTV 10P B&b£9–£9.50
Bdi£12.50–£13.50 W£86–£91 ⊁ D7pm

GH Clovelly Hotel 89 Avenue Rd ☎22286
Central plan **9** Lic 14hc (7fb) ⊗ CTV 7P ⊗
✳B&b£5–£6 Bdi£7.50–£9.25
W£51.50–£64 ⊁

GH Hotel Concorde 26 Newton Rd
☎22330 Central plan **10** Jan 30Oct Lic
17hc ⊗ nc2 CTV 16P

GH Craig Court Hotel 10 Ash Hill Rd,
Castle Circus ☎24400 Central plan **11**
Mar–Oct Lic 10hc 2⊆⊪(3fb) ⊗ CTV 8P
sea S% B&b£5–£7 Bdi£7–£9 W£40–£60
⊁ (W only Jul–Aug) D5pm

GH Devon Court Hotel Croft Rd ☎23603
Central plan **12** Etr–Oct rs Xmas Lic 15hc
2⊆⊪(3fb) ⊗ CTV 15P ⊗ sea S%
B&b£10.35–£14.95 Bdi£12.65–£17.25
W£77.50–£106.95 ⊁

GH Exmouth View Hotel Bedford Rd,
Babbacombe Downs ☎37307 District
plan **44** Etr–Oct Lic 18hc 4⊆⊪(4fb) CTV
12P S% ✳B&b£7.50–£9.30
Bdi£9.80–£11.60 W£69–£81.10 ⊁
D5.30pm

GH Fairmount House Herbert Rd,
Chelston ☎605446 District plan **45** 8hc
(4fb) CTV 10P 1⌂ ⊗ sea S%
B&b£6.50–£8 Bdi£10–£12.50
W£70–£85 ⊁ D7pm

GH Forest Hotel Haldon Rd ☎24842
District plan **46** Etr & mid May–Oct Lic
34hc 12⊆⊪(5fb) CTV 20P sea S%
B&b£6.38–£10.35 Bdi£8.21–£14.95
W£57.50–£103.50 ⊁ D7.30pm

GH Fretherne Hotel St Lukes Rd South
☎22594 Central plan **15** Etr–Oct Lic
24hc (6fb) CTV 20P sea S% B&b fr£6.90
Bdi fr£10.06 Wfr£69 ⊁ D6pm

GH Glendon Hotel St Marychurch Rd
☎23117 Central plan **14** Lic 12hc 6⊆⊪
(5fb) ⊗ CTV 14P sea S% B&b£6–£8
Bdi£8–£10 W£50–£70 ⊁ D7pm

GH Glenorleigh Hotel 26 Cleveland Rd
☎22135 Central plan **15** Apr–Oct & Xmas
Lic 15hc (6fb) CTV 14P S% B&b£8–£10
Bdi£9–£12.50 W£57.50–£86.25 ⊁ (W only
Jun–Aug) D6pm

GH Hatherleigh Hotel 56 St Marychurch
Rd ☎25762 Central plan **16** Apr–Oct Lic
19hc (4fb) nc3 CTV 16P S%
B&b£7.28–£8.60 Bdi£9.25–£11.50
W£58–£80 ⊁ D2pm

GH Holly House Hotel York Rd ☎311333
District plan **47** Whit–Sep Lic 14hc 2⊆⊪
(4fb) ⊗ CTV 14P 2⌂ ⊗ B&b£7.47–£12.07

Bdi£9.78–£14.38 W£65–£97 k (W only mid Jul–mid Aug) D6.30pm

GH *Ilsham Valley* Ilsham Marine Dr ☎22075 District plan:**48** Mar–Oct rs Feb Lic 19hc (A 3hc) CTV 20P 3⋔ ⛗ D6pm

GH Ingoldsby Hotel 1 Chelston Rd ☎607497 Central plan:**17** Mar–Oct Lic 16hc (5fb) CTV 15P sea S% B&b£7–£11 Bdi£9.50–£13.50 W£63–£86 k D4.50pm

GH Kilworthy Hotel Westhill Rd, Babbacombe ☎37236 District plan:**49** Mar–Oct Lic 14hc (4fb) CTV 10P S% B&b fr£6.50 Bdi fr£10 Wfr£50 k D6.30pm

GH *Lindum Hotel* Abbey Rd ☎22795 Central plan:**18** 29Mar–Oct 21hc 4⤢🍽 nc3 CTV 17P

GH Mapleton Hotel St Lukes Rd North ☎22389 Central plan:**19** Apr–Oct Lic 9hc (3fb) ⚤ CTV 7P S% B&b£7.50–£10 Bdi£10–£12.50 W£62–£79 k (W only 23 May–5 Sep) D5pm

GH Mount Nessing Hotel St Lukes Rd North ☎22970 Central plan:**20** Mar–Oct & Xmas Lic 12hc (6fb) CTV 12P sea S% B&b£7–£9 Bdi£10–£13.25 W£62–£79.50 k D4.30pm

GH Normanhurst Hotel Rathmore Rd ☎22420 Central plan:**21** Mar–Oct Lic 14hc (7fb) CTV 8P S% ✳B&b£5.75–£6.90 Bdi£8.25–£9.50 W£57.52–£66.12 k D4.30pm

GH Overdale Hotel Great Hill, Barton ☎311280 District plan:**50** mid Apr–mid Oct Lic 11hc (3fb) CTV 20P sea S% B&b£7–£10 Bdi£10–£12.50 W£60–£80 k D5pm

GH Pembroke Hotel Meadfoot Sea Rd ☎22837 District plan:**51** Mar–Oct Lic 19hc 2⤢🍽 (14fb) ⚤ CTV 12P 3⋔ S% B&b£7–£11 Bdi£11.50–£14.50 (W only Jul & Aug) D10pm

⇥⇤**GH Pencarrow Hotel** 64 Windsor Rd ☎23080 Central plan:**22** Etr–mid Oct Lic 13hc (3fb) CTV 8P S% B&b£4.50–£5.50 Bdi£7–£8 W£48–£55 k (W only peak periods) D am

GH Pines Hotel St Marychurch Rd ☎38384 District plan:**52** Apr–Oct Lic 23hc (6fb) CTV 25P S% B&b£6.33–£9.20 Bdi£10.35–£12.65 W£57.50–£79.35 k D6.30pm

GH Rawlyn House Hotel Rawlyn Road, Chelston ☎605208 Central plan:**23** Lic 12hc 5⤢🍽 (A 4hc) (5fb) ⚤ CTV 15P S% B&b£6.15–£10.65 Bdi£8.65–£13.36 W£60.50–£93 k D7pm

GH Richwood Hotel 20 Newton Rd ☎23729 Central plan:**24** Etr–Oct Lic 23hc (6fb) CTV 12P S% ✳B&b fr£4.60 Bdi£7–£11 W£55–£75 k (W only Jul–Aug) Dnoon

GH Riva Lodge Croft Rd ☎22614 Central plan:**25** Mar–Oct Lic 18hc 7⤢🍽 (5fb) ⚤ nc10 CTV 18P S% B&b£8.50–£10.50 Bdi£11–£14.50 W£72–£85 k D6.30pm

GH Rosewood Teignmouth Rd, Maidencombe ☎38178 District plan:**53** Closed mid Dec–mid Jan 8hc 1⤢🍽 ⚤ nc10 CTV 14P sea S% B&b£5–£7 Bdi£7.95–£10 W£53–£65 k (W only Jun–Sep) D4pm

GH Rothesay Hotel Scarborough Rd ☎23161 Central plan:**26** Etr–Oct Lic 18hc

---

𝔐ount 𝔑essing 𝔥otel

St Lukes Road North, Torquay, TQ2 5PD.
Telephone: 0803 22970

A small, friendly hotel standing on Waldon Hill in quiet position facing south with panoramic views over the bay and town. Steps from hotel to promenade and town (approx 600 yds). Bar, TV and sun lounges. Car park.

Resident proprietors (7 years) have a reputation for good food and service as well as comfort. Inspection of kitchen welcomed. No service charge. Summer bus service. Fire Certificate granted. OPEN CHRISTMAS:

PENCARROW HOTEL
64 WINDSOR ROAD, TORQUAY.

Mr & Mrs Templeman are often complimented on the excellence of the food and the cleanliness of the hotel. Conveniently situated for town centre, beaches and all places of interest. All rooms have teasmades, most have showers. Near tennis courts, bowls, swimming pool. Free car park at rear. Sun-trap patios in front. Our terms are very moderate.
Send for brochure or telephone: Torquay (0803) 23080.

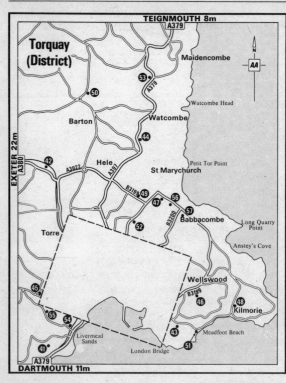

41   Burley Court Hotel
42   Casey's Court
43   Clevedon Private Hotel
44   Exmouth View Hotel
45   Fairmount
46   Forest Hotel
47   Holly House Hotel
48   Ilsham Valley
49   Kilworthy Hotel
50   Overdale Hotel
51   Pembroke Hotel
52   Pines Hotel
53   Rosewood
54   Sunleigh Hotel
55   Villa Marina Hotel
56   Watcombe View Hotel
57   Rose Grange Hotel (*Inn*)

(6fb) ॐ CTV 12P sea S% B&b£6.40–£10 Bdi£9.50–£13.20 W£63.50–£90 ⊬ D5pm

GH St Bernard's Private Hotel Castle Rd ☎22508 Central plan·**27** Lic 12hc (3fb) CTV 8P 🎵 sea S% B&b£7 Bdi£9 D6pm

GH Seacliff Hotel Warren Rd ☎24975 Central plan·**28** Apr–Oct Lic 22hc (8fb) CTV 🎵 S% B&b£6–£8 Bdi£8–£10 W£56–£70 ⊬ D6.30pm

GH Sea Point Hotel 5 Clifton Gv ☎28012 Central plan·**29** Lic 8hc (3fb) CTV 2P S% ✱B&b£4.90 Bdi£7–£9.50 W£42–£65 ⊬ (W only Jul–Aug) Dnoon

GH Shirley Hotel Braddons Hill Rd East ☎23016 Central plan·**30** Lic 13hc CTV 4P sea S% B&b£6–£8.50 Bdi£7.86–£10.29 W£55–£72 ⊬

GH Silverlands Hotel 27 Newton Rd ☎22013 Central plan·**31** Closed Xmas 12hc (1fb) nc2 CTV 12P ✱B&b£4.60–£6.32

GH Southbank Hotel 15–17 Belgrave Rd ☎26701 Central plan·**32** Mar–Nov Lic 20hc (5fb) ॐ CTV 14P S% B&b£7–£10 Bdi£8–£13.50 W£69.65–£91 ⊬ (W only Jul–Aug) D9pm

GH Sunleigh Hotel Livermead Hill ☎607137 District plan·**54** Etr–Sep Lic 19hc 9♨️🎵(6fb) ॐ CTV 16P 🎵 sea S% B&b£7.25–£11.75 Bdi£10.50–£13.25 W£57.60–£84 ⊬ (W only mid Jun–last wk Aug)

GH Torcroft Hotel Croft Rd ☎28292 Central plan·**33** Etr–Sep Lic 21hc 6♨️🎵 (5fb) CTV 21P sea B&b£6–£10 Bdi£8.50–£13 W£58–£85 ⊬ D6.45pm

GH Tormohun Hotel 28 Newton Rd ☎23681 Central plan·**34** Lic 22hc 9♨️🎵 (6fb) ॐ CTV 18P 🎵 S% B&b£6.33–£9.20 Bdi£10–£13 W£57.50–£85.85 ⊬ D7.30pm

GH Trafalgar House Hotel Bridge Rd ☎22486 Central plan·**35** Apr–Oct Lic 11hc (2fb) ॐ CTV 6P S% B&b£6–£8 Bdi£8.05–£10.35 W£56.35–£72.45 ⊬ D7.30pm

GH Tregantle Hotel 64 Bampfylde Rd ☎27494 Central plan·**36** Lic 11hc (3fb) CTV 10P 🎵 S% ✱B&b£5.50–£7 Bdi£7–£8.50 W£45–£59 ⊬ D4pm

GH Tregenna Hotel 20 Cleaveland Rd ☎23578 Central plan·**37** Closed Xmas Lic 11hc (3fb) ॐ CTV 8P sea S% B&b£7.50–£10.50 Bdi£9.50–£12.50 W£58–£75 ⊬ (W only Jul–mid Sep) D5pm

GH *Villa Marina Hotel* Cockington Ln, Livermead ☎605440 District plan·**55** Apr–Oct 26hc 19♨️🎵CTV 23P 🎵

GH Watcombe View Hotel St Albans Rd, Babbacombe ☎39967 District plan·**56** Etr–Sep Lic 18hc 5♨️🎵(3fb) ॐ CTV 10P 🎵 sea ✱B&b£6.50–£9.50 Bdi£8.50–£11.50 W£56–£83 ⊬ (W only Jul–Aug)

GH Westgate Hotel Falkland Rd ☎25350 Central plan·**38** Etr–mid Oct Lic 14hc (7fb) CTV 12P S% B&b£6.50–£8.50 Bdi£9–£12.50 W£63–£90 ⊬ (W only mid Jul–mid Aug) D6.30pm

GH Westowe Hotel Chelston Rd ☎605207 Central plan·**39** Mar–Sep Lic 13hc (1fb) ॐ nc5 CTV 8P sea S% B&b£8.20–£9.50 Bdi£10.20–£11.50

INN *Four Seasons Hotel* 547 Babbacombe Rd ☎25292 Central plan:**40** Lic 34hc ⚡ TV 10P

INN *Rose Grange Hotel* Babbacombe Rd ☎37074 District plan:**57** Lic 19hc TV 20P 6🛏 sn D10pm

TORRINGTON, GREAT Devon
Map 2 SS41
GH Smytham ☎2110 rs Oct–May (B&b only) Lic 12hc (2fb) CTV 12P S% B&b£6.50 Bdi£10 W£70 ⱪ D10am

TOTLAND BAY Isle of Wight *Map 4 SZ38*
GH Garrow Hotel Church Hill ☎ Freshwater 3174 Apr–Sep Lic 18hc 2🛏(7fb) nc3 CTV 18P 🚗 sea B&b£8 Bdi£10 W£68 ⱪ D7pm

GH Hermitage Hotel Cliff Rd ☎ Freshwater 2518 Apr–Oct Lic 12hc (2fb) ⚘ CTV 12P S% B&b£8–£10 Bdi£12.75–£14.25 W£85–£95 ⱪ D7pm

⨝**GH Lismore Private Hotel** 23 The Avenue ☎ Freshwater 2025 Closed Dec 8hc (5fb) ⚡ nc3 CTV 8P S% B&b£5.50–£6 Bdi£8–£8.50 W£51 ⱪ

GH Randolph Private Hotel Granville Rd ☎ Freshwater 2411 May–Sep 8hc (2fb) CTV 6P 🚽 S% ✳B&b£8.50–£9 W£54.62–£58.65 ⱪ D6.50pm

GH Sandy Lane Colwell Common Rd, Colwell Bay ☎ Freshwater 3330 Lic 9hc (5fb) CTV 5P river S% B&b£6.35–£6.76 Bdi£8.96–£9.18 W£57.13–£60.30 ⱪ D4pm

TOTTENHILL Norfolk *Map 9 TF61*
GH Oakwood House Private Hotel
☎ King's Lynn 810256 Closed Xmas Lic
9hc (2fb) ⊗ CTV 30P 🍴 S% B&b£9–£11
Bdi£13–£16.50 W£78–£107 ⌿ D7.30pm

TOWCESTER Northants *Map 4 SP64*
INN Brave Old Oak Watling St ☎50533
Lic 9hc 1⇌🛏 CTV 10P ✱B&b£8.50–£10.50
sn Lfr£2.85&alc D9.30pm£6alc

TREARDDUR BAY Gwynedd *Map 6 SH27*
GH Fairway Private Hotel ☎860255 Lic
7hc (2fb) ⊗ CTV 7P 🍴 sea S% B&bfr£8.05
Bdifr£11.50 Wfr£72.45 ⌿ (W only
Jul & Aug) D6pm

GH High Ground Lon Penrhvn Garw.
Ravenspoint Rd. ☎860078 8hc (3fb) ⚙
CTV 15P 🍴 sea S% B&b£6 Bdi£10
(W only Aug)

TREBARWITH Cornwall *Map 2 SX08*
INN Mill House ☎ Tintagel 200 Lic
5⇌🛏nc6 CTV 50P 🍴 ♨
✱B&b£9.20–£12.19 Bdi£14.09–£17.08
W£98.63–£119.56 ⌿ Bar lunch50p–£3.50
D8.30pm£4.89–£8.63&alc

TREGARON Dyfed *Map 3 SN65*
GH *Aberdwr* Abergwesyn Rd ☎255
Mar–Oct 8hc ⊗ TV 12P river

TREGONY *(Nr Truro)* Cornwall
Map 2 SW94
GH Tregony House 15 Fore St ☎671
Etr–Oct Lic 7hc (1fb) ⊗ nc7 CTV 6P 🍴 S%

✱B&b£6.50–£7 Bdi£9.50–£10 W£65–£68
⌿ D6pm

TRESILLIAN Cornwall *Map 2 SW84*
GH Manor Cottage ☎212 Mar–Oct Lic
7hc (1fb) nc2 CTV 10P 🍴 river S%
B&b£7.50–£8.50 W£49–£56 Ⓜ

TRETOWER Powys *Map 3 SO12*
INN Tretower Court ☎ Bwlch 730204
Lic 5hc ⊗ CTV 90P 🍴 B&b£6.50
Bar lunch65p–£2.60 D10pm£5.50alc

TREVONE Cornwall *Map 2 SW87*
⊢⊣**GH Bowen House Hotel** ☎ Padstow
520389 Etr–Oct Lic 15hc (3fb) nc4 15P sea
B&b£5.55–£7.82 Bdi£6.55–£8.97
W£43–£59.80 ⌿

GH Coimbatore Hotel ☎ Padstow
520390 May–Sep 11hc (4fb) ⊗ CTV 6P
8🏠 🍴 sea S% ✱B&b£6 Bdi£8.50
W£50.03–£54.63 ⌿

⊢⊣**GH** *Green Waves Private Hotel*
☎ Padstow 520114 Mar–Sep 14hc
(A 7hc) CTV 15P 5🏠

GH Newlands Hotel ☎ Padstow 520469
mid May–mid Sep Lic 12hc nc4 CTV 15P
S% ✱B&b£6–£8 Bdi£8–£10 W£48–£60
⌿ (W only Jun–Aug)

GH Sea Spray Hotel Trevone Bay
☎ Padstow 520491 Mar–Nov Lic 6⇌🛏
(3fb) nc3 CTV 8P sea S% ✱B&b£6–£6.75
Bdi£9.50–£11.50 (W only May23–Aug)

TREWARMETT Cornwall *Map 2 SX08*
GH Trevervan Hotel ☎ Tintagel 486 Lic
6hc (4fb) CTV 8P sea S% B&b£6.90–£7.50
Bdi£9.80–£11.50 W£59.80–£69 ⌿
D7.30pm

TRINITY Jersey, Channel Islands *Map 16*
GH Highfield Country Hotel Route Du
Ebenezer ☎Jersey 62194 Lic 26hc 14⇔🛏
(4fb) 🎱 CTV 20P 1🏠 sea S% ✱B&b£9–£13
Bdi£9.50–£14.75 W£66.50–£103.25 ⅃
(W only Low Season)

TROON Strathclyde *Ayrs Map 10 NS33*
⊨⊨**GH Glenside** Bentinck Dr ☎313677
6hc (2fb) CTV 6P 🍺 S% B&b£5.75–£6.25
Wfr£38 M

TRURO Cornwall *Map 2 SW84*
⊨⊨**GH Colthrop** Tregolls Rd ☎2920
7rm 6hc (3fb) nc7 CTV 8P 🍺 S%
B&b£5.50–£7.50 Bdi£9–£10 W£63–£68
⅃ D6pm

GH *Farley Hotel* Falmouth Rd ☎3680
Closed Xmas 23hc CTV 23P D6pm
⊨⊨**GH Pencowl** 12 Ferris Town ☎74946
Closed Xmas Lic 15hc (3fb) CTV 6🏠 🍺
S% B&b£5.75–£8 Bdi£9–£11.25
W£57–£71 ⅃ D7pm

INN Globe Frances St ☎3869 Lic 4hc
🎱 nc12 CTV 🚗 S% B&b£6.50–£7
Bdi£9–£9.50 W£56 ⅃ Bar lunch60p–f 1.50

TUNBRIDGE WELLS (ROYAL) Kent
Map 5 TQ53
GH *The Guest House* 89 Frant Rd
☎25596 Closed Jan 6hc 2⇔🛏CTV 10P 🍺
GH Marlborough Hotel 57 Mount Ephraim
☎21328 Lic 25hc 7⇔🛏 (3fb) CTV 6P S%
B&b£14.50–£15.50 Bdi£20.50–£21.50
W£100 M D7.30pm

TURVEY Beds *Map 4 SP95*
INN Three Cranes ☎305 rs Xmas

(no accommodation) Lic 3hc 🎱 nc14 20P 🚗
S% B&b£9.77–£11.50 Bdi£12.50–£14.20
W£58 M L£3alc D9.30pm£5alc

TWO BRIDGES Devon *Map 2 SX67*
GH Cherrybrook Hotel ☎Tavistock
88260 Closed Xmas & New Year Lic
8hc 3⇔🛏(2fb) 15P 🍺 S% B&b£9–£9.50
Bdi£13–£13.50 W£91–£95 ⅃ D7.30pm

TYWYN Gwynedd *Map 6 SH50*
GH Greenfield Private Hotel High St
☎710255 rs Nov–Etr Lic 9hc (2fb) 🎱 CTV
B&b£6.50–£7.25 Bdi£9.25–£10.25
W£62–£69.50 ⅃ D8.30pm

GH Min-y-Mon Marine Pde ☎710139
Lic 6hc 2⇔🛏(4fb) 🎱 🎱 CTV sea S%
✱B&b£6 Bdi£9.50 D5pm

GH Monfa Pier Rd ☎710858 rs Nov–Mar
8hc 4⇔🛏(3fb) 🎱 🎱 CTV 2P 🍺 lake sea S%
B&b£7.50–£8.50 Bdi£10.50–£11.50
W£70–£77 ⅃ D5pm

UIST (SOUTH), ISLE OF Western Isles
Inverness-shire Map 13
See Howmore

ULVERSTON Cumbria *Map 7 SD27*
GH Sefton House Hotel Queen St
☎52190 Lic 8hc (2fb) 🎱 CTV 3P 2🏠 🍺
B&b£9.60–£10.60 Bdi£13.20–£14.55
W£85.20–£93.45 ⅃ D8.30pm

UPLYME Devon *Map 3 SY39*
INN Black Dog Hotel Lyme Rd ☎Lyme
Regis 2634 rs Nov–Mar (no
accommodation) Lic 4hc CTV 19P 2🏠 🚗
S% ✱B&b£7.50 W£45 M Bar lunch£2alc

The Farley Hotel

Falmouth Road, Truro, Cornwall Tel: Truro 3680 (STD 0872)

Comfortable, family and commercial
private hotel. Open all year except at
Christmas. Excellent food and
friendly service. 23 Bedrooms. Radio,
electric blankets in rooms. Some
double rooms with showers. AMPLE
CAR PARKING. Ideal centre for
touring. Brochure on request.

VENN OTTERY Devon *Map 3 SY09*
GH Venn Ottery Barton ☎Ottery St Mary
2733 15 Mar–Oct Lic 11hc 2⇌訊 (2fb)
CTV 14P ⑩ B&b£9.50–£11.50
Bdi£11–£13.50 W£73–£89 ⫪ D7.30pm

VENTNOR Isle of Wight *Map 4 SZ57*
GH Channel View Hotel Hambrough Rd
☎852230 Mar–Nov Lic 14hc 2⇌訊 (4fb)
CTV 6P sea S% B&b£8.50–£10.50
Bdi£11.75–£13.75 W£63–£77 ⫪
D6.30pm

GH Delamere Bellevue Rd ☎852322
Apr–Oct 8hc (4fb) CTV 8P sea S%
B&b£6–£7 Bdi£7.50–£8.50 W£48–£55
⫪ D4pm

GH Kings Bay Hotel Kings Bay Rd
☎852815 Etr–Oct Lic 6hc ⊗ nc2 CTV
10P ⑩ sea

GH Macrocarpa Mitchell Ave ☎852428
Etr–Oct & Xmas Lic 20hc 11⇌訊(A 3hc)
(8fb) ⚲ CTV 20P sea S% B&b£7.50–£9
Bdi£12–£13.50 W£65–£95 ⫪ D7.30pm

GH Picardie Hotel Esplanade ☎852647
Apr–Oct Lic 15hc (3fb) ⊗ CTV sea S%
✱B&b£7–£9 Bdi£8.50–£10.50 D2pm

GH Richmond Private Hotel Esplanade
☎852496 Apr–Oct Lic 12hc 2⇌訊(2fb)
CTV 8P sea S% ✱B&b£7.50 Bdi£10
W£65–£70 ⫪

GH St Maur Hotel Castle Rd ☎852570
Lic 16hc (6fb) ⊗ nc2 CTV 12P ⑩ sea S%
B&b£7–£8.50 Bdi£9–£10.50 W£60–£65
⫪ D6.45pm

GH Under Rock Hotel Shore Rd,
Bonchurch (1m E) ☎852714 Apr–Oct Lic
9hc ⊗ nc10 12P ⑩ S% B&b£10.35
Bdi£13.50 W£96.60 ⫪ D4.30pm

WADHURST E Sussex *Map 5 TQ63*
INN Fourkeys Station Rd ☎2252 Lic 8hc
CTV 25P ⑩ B&b£6.33–£8.97
Bdi£8–£12.42 W£56.60–£75.60 ⫪
D11pm

WALLASEY Merseyside *Map 7 SJ29*
GH Divonne Private Hotel 71 Wellington
Rd, New Brighton ☎051-639 4727 Lic
15hc 5⇌訊 CTV 8P ⑩

GH Sandpiper Private Hotel 22 Dudley
Rd, New Brighton ☎051-639 7870 7hc
(2fb) ⊗ CTV 7P ⑩ S% B&b£6.50–£7.50
Bdi£9.15–£10.40 D4.30pm

WALL HEATH W Midlands *Map 7 SO88*
INN Prince Albert Hotel High St
☎Kingswinford 3905 Lic 5hc ⊗ TV 200P⤹
⑩ sn

WALTON-ON-THE-NAZE Essex
Map 5 TM22
GH Blenheim House Hotel 39 Kirby Rd
☎Frinton-on-Sea 5548 Closed Xmas Lic
7hc 1⇌訊 ⊗ TV 16P B&b£8–£9
W£50–£60 Ⓜ

WAMPHRAY Dumfries & Galloway
Dumfriesshire Map 11 NY19
GH Manse Country ☎Johnstone Bridge
367 Apr–Sep 6hc (2fb) TV 20P ⑩ S%
B&b£6.75 Bdi£12.50 W£87.50 ⫪ D7pm

WANSFORD Cambs *Map 3 TL09*
INN Cross Keys ☎Stamford 782266 Lic
3⇌訊(A 3⇌訊) ⊗ CTV P ⑩ ⇛ S%
✱B&b£15 D9.45pm

WAREHAM Dorset *Map 3 SY98*
GH Golden Acre Hotel East Stoke
(2m W on A352) ☎Bindon Abbey 462563
Apr–Sep Lic 6hc CTV 12P ⑩

WARWICK Warwicks *Map 4 SP26*
⊶⊷**GH Avon** 7 Emscote Rd ☎41367 7hc
(4fb) ⊗ CTV 5P 1🏠 ⑩ S% B&b£5

⊶⊷**GH Cambridge Villa** 20A Emscote Rd
☎41169 10hc (3fb) ⊗ CTV 12P ⑩ S%
B&b£5–£6

INN Wheatsheaf Hotel 54 West St
☎42817 Lic 6hc CTV 12P ⑩ S%
B&b£11.50 sn L75p–£7 D9.30pm

WASHFORD Somerset *Map 3 ST04*
⊶⊷**GH Washford House** ☎484 6hc (2fb)
⊗ CTV 8P ⑩ S% B&b£5–£5.50
Bdi£8–£8.50 W£52.50–£56 ⫪ D4pm

WATERBEACH Cambs *Map 5 TL46*
INN Bridge Hotel Clayhithe ☎Cambridge
860252 Lic 30hc (15⇌訊) CTV 60P ⑩
river S% B&b£11–£22 sn L£1.50–£2.50
D9pmf£2.50–£5.50&alc

WATERLOO Isle of Skye, Highland
Inverness-shire Map 13 NG62
GH Ceol-na-Mara ☎Broadford 323
Etr–Sep rs Oct 5hc (1fb) CTV 6P sea S%
✱B&b£5.50–£6.50 Bdi£9.50–£10.50
D9pm

WATERLOOVILLE Hants *Map 4 SU60*
GH Far End Private Hotel 31 Queens Rd
☎3242 Closed Xmas Lic 10hc 1⇌訊(2fb)
CTV 20P 5🏠 ⑩ S% B&b£14–£16
Bdi£18–£20 W£96–£110 ⫪ D4pm

WATERMILLOCK Cumbria *Map 12 NY42*
GH Knotts Mill Country House
☎Pooley Bridge 328 Etr–Oct Lic 5hc ⊗
TV 5P ⑩

205

WATERROW Somerset *Map 3 ST02*
INN Rock ☎Wiveliscombe 23293 Lic
7⬧🛏 CTV 12P 🍴 S% ✳B&b£8.50–£10.50
Bdi£13.50–£15.50 W£87–£94 ⚡ sn
L£5alc D9.30pm£6alc

WATFORD Herts *Map 4 TQ19*
GH White House Hotel 29 Upton Rd
☎37316 Lic 39hc 33⬧🛏 (A 26hc 16⬧🛏)
(5fb) CTV 36P 🍴 ⌖ S% B&b£9–£20
Bdi£14.50–£24.50 W£54–£120 Ⓜ
D8.30pm

WEEK ST MARY Cornwall *Map 2 SX29*
GH Lambley Park ☎368 Apr–Oct Lic 6hc
1⬧🛏 (2fb) CTV 8P sea S%
✳B&b£4.50–£5.75 Bdi£8.50–£9.75
W£55–£66.50 ⚡ D10.30am

WELLINGTON Somerset *Map 3 ST12*
GH Blue Mantle Hotel 2 Mantle St
☎2000 Lic 9rm 8hc (3fb) ⌖ CTV 🍴 S%
B&b£8–£8.50 Bdi£12–£12.50
W£80–£85 ⚡ D7.30pm

WELLS Somerset *Map 3 ST54*
GH Tor 20 Tor St ☎72322 9hc (7fb) CTV
10P S% B&b£6.60–£7.60
Bdi£10.05–£11.55 W£70.35–£80.85 ⚡
D4pm

WELLS-NEXT-THE-SEA Norfolk
Map 9 TF94
GH Arch House 50 Mill Rd ☎Fakenham
710696 Mar–Jul & Sep–Oct rs Aug & on
any Fri (no evening meals) Lic 5hc (1fb) ⌖
TV 5P 🍴 B&b£6–£6.50 Bdi£10.50–£11
W£71.50–£75 ⚡ D noon

WELSHPOOL Powys *Map 7 SJ20*
GH Garth Derwen Buttington (2½m NE
A458) ☎Trewern 238 mid Jan–mid Dec
Lic 8hc (2fb) ♨ CTV 20P 2🏠 S%
B&b£8.65–£9.25 Bdi£13.25–£14.75
W£81.50–£92.90 ⚡ D7.30pm

WEST CHARLETON Devon *Map 3 SX74*
INN Ashburton Arms ☎Frogmore 242
Closed late Oct–early Nov & Xmas Lic 5hc
⌖ nc7 TV 20P 🍴 S% B&b£8–£8.50
W£52.50–£56 Ⓜ sn Bar lunch40p–£3

WESTCLIFF-ON-SEA Essex
See Southend-on-Sea

WESTGATE-ON-SEA Kent *Map 5 TR36*
GH Edgewater Private Hotel 99 Sea Rd
☎Thanet 31933 Lic 9hc (4fb) ⌖ CTV 6P 🍴
sea S% B&b£7.70–£8.80 Bdi£10.45–£11
W£60.50–£66 Ⓜ D8pm

WEST LINTON Borders *Peebleshire
Map 11 NT15*
GH Rutherford Coaching House ☎231
6hc (2fb) CTV 12P 1🏠 🍴 S%
B&b£6–£7.50 Bdi£8.75–£10.75
W£58–£72 ⚡ D9pm

WEST LULWORTH Dorset
See Lulworth

WESTON-SUPER-MARE Avon
Map 3 ST36 **See Plan**
GH Beachlands Hotel 17 Uphill Road
North ☎21401 Plan:**1** Closed Xmas & Jan,
rs Feb (B&b only) Lic 20hc 1⬧🛏 (4fb) CTV
12P 2🏠 🍴 ✳B&b£8.50–£9.78
Bdi£12.08–£13.23 W£68.70–£77.90 ⚡
D6.30pm

GH Fourways 2 Ashcombe Rd ☎23827
Plan:**2** May–Sep rs Oct, Nov & Mar
(B&b only) 6hc (A 3hc) ⌖ nc10 TV 9P 🍴
S% ✳B&b£4.50–£5.50 Bdi£6.50–£7.50
W£46 ⚡ D6.30pm

GH Glenelg 24 Ellenborough Park South
☎20521 Plan:**3** Mar–Oct Lic 15hc (4fb)
CTV 12P 🍴 S% ✳B&b£7–£8.50
Bdi£8–£10.50 W£50–£58 ⚡ D5.30pm

GH Inwood Hotel 59 South Rd ☎29756
Plan:**4** rs Nov–Mar (B&b only) Lic 15hc
2⬧🛏 (A 2⬧🛏) (5fb) ♨ CTV 18P sea S%
✳B&b£6.90–£8.62 Bdi£9.77–£10.92
W£57.50–£74.75 ⚡ D6.30pm

📧**GH Kew Dee** 6 Neva Rd ☎29041
Plan:**5** 6hc (3fb) CTV 5P 🍴 S%
B&b£4.50–£5.50 Bdi£6.50–£7.50
W£42–£49 ⚡ D4pm

📧**GH Lockaine** 45 Locking Rd ☎29906
Plan:**6** 9hc (5fb) CTV 3P 🍴 S%
B&b£5.50–£6.50 Bdi£7–£8 W£53.90 ⚡
D4.30pm

📧**GH Lydia** 78 Locking Rd ☎417693
Plan:**7** Closed last wk Oct 6hc (2fb) CTV 4P
🍴 S% B&b£4.50–£5.50 Bdi£6.50–£8
W£45–£56 ⚡ D5pm

📧**GH Oaklands** 26 Severn Rd ☎25253
Plan:**8** Etr–Oct Lic 10hc (1fb) ⌖ nc12 CTV
6P 🍴 S% B&b£5.50–£7.50 Bdi£8–£10
W£52.50–£65 ⚡ D4.30pm

GH Owl's Nest Hotel Kewstoke ☎417672
Plan:**9** Mar–Nov & Xmas Lic 7hc (1fb) ⌖
nc6 CTV 10P 🍴 S% B&b£6.50 Bdi£9.75
W£61.25–£65 ⚡ D7.15pm

GH Russell Hotel 15–17 Clevedon Rd
☎20195 Plan:**10** Lic 23hc (5⬧🛏) (2fb) ⌖
nc5 CTV 20P 🍴 B&b£8.50 Bdi£11.50
W£88.55 ⚡ D7.30pm

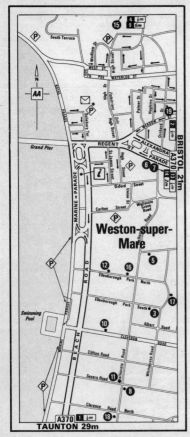

1 Beachlands Hotel
2 Fourways
3 Glenelg
4 Inwood Hotel
5 Kew Dee
6 Lockaine
7 Lydia
8 Oaklands Hotel
9 Owl's Nest Hotel
10 Russell Hotel
11 St Anne's Hotel
12 Scottsdale Hotel
13 Shire Elms
14 Southmead
15 Stanton Lodge Hotel
16 Tower House Hotel
17 Westgate Private Hotel
18 Willow
19 Wychwood

GH St Annes Hotel 35 Severn Rd
☎20487 Plan **11** Apr–Sep rs 23 Oct–Mar
(B&b only) Lic 12hc ⌘ CTV 8P S%
B&b£6.33–£7.20 Bdi£9.20–£10.35
W£54.05–£69 ⌫ D4.30pm

GH Scottsdale Hotel 3 Ellenborough Park
North ☎26489 Plan **12** Apr–Oct 13hc ⌘
nc14 CTV 13P ⌘ S% B&b£8 Bdi£10
W£65–£69 ⌫ D5pm

GH Shire Elms 71 Locking Rd ☎28605
Plan **13** Closed Dec Lic 11hc 1⌘ (3fb) ⌘
CTV 12P ⌘ S% ✳B&bfr£6.25 Bdifr£9
Wfr£55 ⌫ D5.30pm

⌦**GH Southmead** 435 Locking Road East
☎29351 Plan **14** Closed Xmas 6hc (2fb)
CTV 7P ⌘ S% B&b£4.50–£5.50
Bdi£7.50–£8.50 W£48–£55 ⌫ D5.30pm

GH Stanton Lodge Hotel Kew Rd
☎22261 Plan **15** May–Sep Lic 14hc ⌘

nc9 CTV 12P ⌘ S% ✳B&b£5.50–£6.50
Bdi£8–£9 Wf40–£50 ⌫ (W only Jun–Aug)

GH Tower House Hotel Ellenborough Park
North ☎21393 Plan **16** Jun–Oct rs Apr,
May & Nov (B&b only) 14hc 2⌘ (3fb)
CTV 10P ⌘ ✳B&b£6.50–£7.50
Bdi£8.75–£9.75 W£58–£65 ⌫ D3pm

GH Westgate Private Hotel
5 Ellenborough Cres ☎21952 Plan **17**
Apr–Oct rs Apr Lic 8hc nc8 CTV

GH Willow 3 Clarence Road East
☎413736 Plan **18** Etr–Oct 9hc (4fb) ⌘
CTV 8P ⌘ S% ✳B&b£4.50–£6
Bdi£6–£7.50 W£36–£45 ⌫

GH Wychwood Hotel 148 Milton Rd
☎27793 Plan **19** Lic 10hc (4fb) CTV 14P
S% B&b£6.33–£8.63 Bdi£9.20–£11.50
W£55.20–£69 ⌫

WEST PENNARD Somerset *Map 3 ST53*
INN *Red Lion* ☎Glastonbury 32941 Lic
7hc 100P 4⌘ ⌘ D9.30pm

WESTWARD HO! Devon *Map 2 SS42*
⌦**GH** *Culverkeys* Buckleigh Rd
☎Bideford 4218 Apr–Oct Lic 6hc (3fb) ⌘
CTV 8P ⌘ S% B&b£4.50–£5.50
Bdi£6.75–£7.25 W£45–£55 ⌫
(W only Jul & Aug) D3pm

WETHERBY W Yorks *Map 8 SE44*
GH Prospect House 8 Caxton St ☎62428
6hc (1fb) CTV 6P ⌘ S% B&b£6.90–£7.50

WEYMOUTH Dorset *Map 3 SY67*
GH Beechcroft Private Hotel 128–129
Esplande ☎786608 Mar–Oct Lic 34hc
10⌘ (15fb) ⌘ CTV 8P sea B&b£8–£9
Bdi£12–£13.50 W£60–£64 ⌫ D5pm

GH Dorincourt Hotel 183 Dorchester Rd
☎786460 Etr–Oct rs Nov–Etr Lic 11hc
2⌘ (1fb) ⌘ nc5 TV 16P ⌘
B&b£8.05–£9.77 Bdi£11.50–£13.80
W£67.27–£77.62 ⌫ D5pm

GH Ellendale Private Hotel 88 Rodwell
Av ☎786650 Lic 11hc (4fb) ⌘ CTV 16P
3⌘ ⌘ S% B&b fr£7.50 Bdi fr£10 D10pm

⌦**GH Greenhill Hotel** 8 Greenhill
☎786026 Lic 18hc 5⌘ (4fb) nc3 CTV
10P sea S% B&b£4.50–£8.50
Bdi£7–£10 W£43.70–£69 ⌫
(W only Jul–Aug)

⌦**GH Hazeldene** 16 Abbotsbury Rd.
Westham ☎782579 Feb–Nov Lic 8hc
(4fb) ⌘ nc5 CTV 7P ⌘ S% B&b£5–£6.50
Bdi£7.50–£8.50 W£45–£55 ⌫ (W only
mid Jun–Aug) D5pm

GH Kenora 5 Stavordale Rd ☎71215
Etr, May–Sep Lic 18hc (6fb) ⌘ CTV 12P
B&b£7–£7.60 Bdi£9.50–£10.20
W£55–£66 ⌫ D6pm

GH Kings Acre Hotel 140 The Esplanade
☎782534 Mar–Nov Lic 14hc (7fb) ⌘
CTV 9P ⌘ sea S% B&b£8–£10
Bdi£8.50–£12.50 W£50–£70 ⌫ D6pm

GH Kingsley Hotel 10 Kirtleton Av
☎785676 Mar–Oct Lic 7hc (3fb) CTV 7P
⌘ S% B&b£6–£8 Bdi£7.25–£10
W£42–£62 ⌫ D6pm

GH *Marina Court Hotel* 142 The
Esplanade ☎782146 Lic 14hc CTV 10P

GH *Redlands* 14–16 Carlton Road
South ☎786204 May–Sep Lic 14hc nc2
CTV 10P ⌘

GH Richmoor Hotel 146 The Esplanade
☎785087 Lic 22hc 2⇨📺 (9fb) ≫ CTV 9P
🍴 sea S% B&b£7–£11 Bdi£10–£14
£65–£80 ⌀ D5pm

GH Rosedene 1 Carlton Rd North
☎784021 Apr–Sep 6hc (4fb) ≫ nc3 CTV
8P S% ✳B&b£5 Bdi£6.85 W£47.50 ⌀

GH Southdene Hotel 24 Carlton Rd South
☎784621 Lic 17hc (3fb) ≫ nc3 CTV 12P
B&b£7–£9 Bdi£9–£11 W£48–£67 ⌀
D6.15pm

GH Sou'west Lodge Hotel Rodwell Rd
☎783749 Closed Xmas Lic 10hc (3fb) ≫
nc3 CTV 14P 🍴 S% B&b£7.50–£8.50
Bdi£10–£11 W£62.50–£67.50 ⌀
D6.30pm

GH Sunningdale Private Hotel 52 Preston
Rd, Overcombe ☎ Preston (Dorset) 832179
Etr–Xmas Lic 20hc 8⇨📺 (5fb) CTV 17P 3🏠
🍴 S% B&b£8.60–£10.60
Bdi£11.60–£13.50 W£75–£86 ⌀

GH Tamarisk Hotel 12 Stavordale Rd,
Westham ☎786514 Apr–Oct Lic 18hc
(7fb) ≫ CTV 18P 🍴 S% B&b£6.90–£8.05
Bdi£8.74–£9.78 W£58.65–£69 ⌀

GH Treverbyn Court Hotel 65 Dorchester
Rd ☎786170 rs Nov–Dec Lic 14hc (8fb)
CTV 14P 🍴 B&b£7–£10 Bdi£10–£13
W£55–£88 ⌀ D9.30pm

WHIMPLE Devon *Map 3 SY09*
GH Woodhayes ☎822237 Lic 6rm 4hc
2⇨📺 CTV 16P 2🏠 🍴 S% B&b£9.60–£11.20
Bdi£14–£16.50 W£62–£72.50 ⌀ D9pm

WHITBY North Yorks *Map 8 NZ81*
During the currency of this guide some
Whitby telephone numbers are liable to

be prefixed by 60.

GH Beach Cliff Hotel North Prom, West
Cliff ☎2886 Lic 12hc 1⇨📺 ≫ nc5 CTV 5P
🍴 sea S% ✳B&b£7.50–£8 Bdi£11
W£73.50 ⌀ D4.30pm

GH Europa Private Hotel 20 Hudson St
☎2251 Closed 20Dec–6Jan 8hc ≫ nc5
CTV D4pm

GH Hudsons Hotel 24 Hudson St ☎5277
6hc (2fb) CTV 🍴 ✳B&b£6.90–£9.20
Bdi£9.78–£12.65 D6pm

GH Prospect of Whitby 12 Esplanade
☎3026 Mar–Sep rs Oct (no evening meals)
Lic 16hc 4⇨📺 (6fb) CTV 🍴 sea
B&b£8.45–£8.95 Bdi£11.90–£12.40
W£55–£60 Ⓜ D4.30pm

GH Seacliffe Hotel North Promenade,
West Cliff ☎3139 Lic 19hc 1⇨📺 (3fb)
≫ CTV 8P sea ✳B&b£7.50–£8.50
Bdi£11–£12 W£74–£80 ⌀

WHITCHURCH Heref & Worcs
Map 3 SO51
GH Portland ☎ Symonds Yat 890757 Lic
8hc (2fb) ⚬ CTV 12P 🍴 S% B&b£7–£9

WHITFORD Devon *Map 3 SY29*
GH Chantry House ☎ Colyton 52359
Etr–Oct 7hc ≫ TV 12P

WHITING BAY Isle of Arran, Strathclyde
Bute *Map 10 NS02*
GH Trareoch Hotel Largiebeg ☎226
Apr–Sep Lic 8hc (2fb) ≫ TV 12P sea
B&b£9 Bdi£12.50 W£82 ⌀ D7.30pm

WHITLEY BAY Tyne & Wear
Map 12 NZ37

GH Croglin Hotel 35–41 South Pde
☎523317 rs Xmas day Lic 41hc 15⇔🛁
(15fb) ⚛ CTV 16P ▥ S% B&b£6–£19
Bdi£9.50–£26 (W only Jun–Aug) D9.30pm

WHITNEY-ON-WYE Heref & Worcs
Map 3 SO24
INN Rhydspence ☎ Clifford 262
Closed 25Dec Lic 2hc 1⇔🛁 ⊗ nc10 CTV
60P ▥ S% B&b£13–£20 Bdi£20–£27
W£77–£87.50 M sn Bar lunch£2alc
D9.30pm£7alc

WICKFORD Essex *Map 5 TQ79*
GH Wickford Lodge 26 Ethelred Gdns
☎62663 6hc (2fb) ⊗ CTV 6P ▥ S%
B&b£10 W£60 M

WICKHAM Berks *Map 4 SU47*
INN Five Bells ☎ Boxford 242 4hc CTV P
▥ S% ✳B&b£9.50 sn L£2–£3.50
D10pm£3.50&alc

WIDEGATES Cornwall *Map 2 SX25*
⊢◉GH Coombe Farm ☎223 Lic 8hc (7fb)
⚛ CTV 15P ▥ S% B&b£5.75–£6.90
Bdi£8.75–£9.90 W£56–£63 ⅄ D9pm

WIDEMOUTH BAY Cornwall *Map 2 SS20*
GH *Beach House Hotel* ☎256 May–Sep
Lic 8hc ⊗ CTV 20P sea D7pm

WIGHT, ISLE OF *Map 4*
Places with AA-listed accommodation
are indicated on location map 4.
Full details will be found under
individual placenames within the
appropriate gazetteer sections.

WILLITON Somerset *Map 3 ST04*
GH Fairfield House 51 Long St ☎32636
Lic 6hc (4fb) CTV 6P ▥ S% B&b£7.50
Bdi£11 D9pm

GH Old Rectory Nettlecombe (2m SW on
B3188, 1m E of junc with B3190)
☎Washford 444 Apr–Oct 6hc (1fb) ⊗ nc12
CTV 8P 1🎔 ▥ B&b£8.50–£9
Bdi£14.50–£15 W£95–£100 ⅄ D5pm

WILMINGTON E Sussex *Map 5 TQ50*
GH Crossways Hotel ☎ Polegate 2455
Lic 10hc 2⇔🛁 (2fb) nc2 CTV P 6🎔 ▥ S%
B&b£7.50–£8

WILSHAMSTEAD (WILSTEAD) Beds
Map 4 TL04
GH Old Manor House Hotel Cotton End Rd
☎ Bedford 740262 Lic 9hc CTV 10P ▥
S% B&b£10.35 Bdi£14.95 D6.45

WINCHESTER Hants *Map 4 SU42*
GH Clownstown Sleepers Hill ☎63990
Closed Xmas 6hc 1⇔🛁 ⊗ nc10 CTV 8P ▥
S% B&bfr£7 Bdi fr£13 Wfr£80 ⅄

WINDERMERE Cumbria *Map 7 SD49*
See Plan
⊢◉GH Archway ☎5613 Plan:**1** 6hc (3fb)
⊗ CTV 2P ▥ S% B&b£5.50–£6
Bdi£8.50–£9.50 D5pm

GH *Clifton House* Ellerthwaite Rd
☎4896 Plan:**3** Lic 6hc nc12 CTV 5P 1🎔 ▥

GH Craig Foot Hotel Lake Rd ☎3902
Plan:**4** Apr–Nov Lic 11hc 1⇔🛁(A 1⇔🛁) ⊗
nc CTV 16P ▥ S% B&b£10.35–£13.80

GH Elim Bank Hotel Lake Rd,
Bowness-on-Windermere ☎4810 Plan:**5**

211

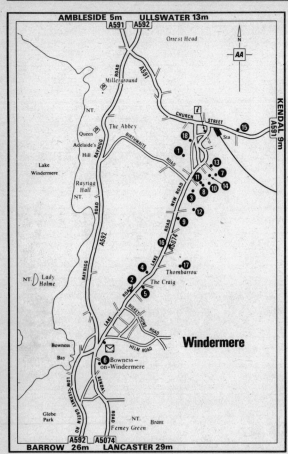

1 Archway
3 Clifton House
4 Craig Foot Hotel
5 Elim Bank Hotel
6 Fairfield Country
  House Hotel
7 Green Riggs
8 Haisthorpe
9 Hilton House Hotel
10 Hollythwaite
11 Kenilworth
12 Mylne Bridge
13 Oakfield
14 Orotava House
15 Orrest Head House
16 Rosemount
17 Thornleigh
18 Waverley Hotel
2 White Lodge Hotel

Jan–Nov Lic 7hc (2fb) ⊗ CTV 7P ⏣ S%
B&b£9.78 Bdi£14.95 W£94.19 ⫽ D5.30pm

GH Fairfield Country House Hotel
Brantfell Rd, Bowness-on-Windermere
☎3772 Plan:**6** Mar–Nov Lic 8rm 3hc
5⊣▥(5fb) nc5 CTV 12P ⏣ S%
B&b£9.50–£11.50 Bdi£14.50–£18.50
W£98–£120 ⫽ D5pm

⊷**GH Green Riggs** 8 Upper Oak St
☎2265 Plan:**7** Mar–Oct 6hc (2fb) CTV 3P
⏣ S% B&b£5 Bdi£8.50 W£55 ⫽ D5.30pm

GH Haisthorpe Holly Rd ☎3445 Plan:**8**
Etr–Oct 7hc nc4 CTV ⏣ S% B&b£6
Bdi£9.60 W£64 ⫽ D2pm

GH Hilton House Hotel New Rd ☎3934
Plan:**9** Lic 7hc 3⊣▥(2fb) ⊗ CTV 15P ⏣
S% B&b£7–£8.50 Bdi£12–£14
W£75–£88 ⫽

GH Hollythwaite Holly Rd ☎2219 Plan:**10**
7hc (2fb) CTV S% B&b£6.90 Bdi£10.35
W£48.30–£72.45 ⫽ D5pm

GH Kenilworth Holly Rd ☎4004 Plan:**11**
Mar–Oct 7hc (1fb) ⊗ CTV ⏣ S% ✳B&b£5
Bdi£8 Wfr£53 ⫽ D2.30pm

GH Mylne Bridge Brookside ☎3314
Plan:**12** Mar–Dec Lic 14hc (2fb) ⊗ nc7
CTV 14P ⏣ S% B&b£6.95–£7.95
Bdi£11.50–£12.50 W£70–£83 ⫽ D5pm

⊷**GH Oakfield** 46 Oak St ☎5692 Plan:**13**
rs Xmas (B&b only) 5hc (4fb) CTV ⏣ S%
B&b£5–£5.50 Bdi£7.50–£8.50
W£50–£56 ⫽ D6.30pm

GH Orotava House Broad St ☎5180
Plan:**14** mid Feb–early Nov 6hc (3fb) CTV P
🏠 ⏣ S% ✳B&b£5–£5.50 Bdi£7.50–£8.50
W£50–£52 ⫽ D5pm

GH Orrest Head House Kendal Rd ☎4315
Plan:**15** mid Mar–Oct Lic 9hc ⊗ nc5 CTV
10P S% B&b£7–£8 Bdi£11–£12.50
W£72.50–£80 ⫽

GH Rosemount Lake Rd ☎3739 Plan:**16**
Lic 8hc 2⊣▥(2fb) CTV 6P 2 🏠 ⏣ S%
B&b£6.50–£8 Bdi£11–£13 W£42–£87
⫽ D3pm

GH Thornleigh Thornbarrow Rd,
Bowness-on-Windermere ☎4203 Plan:**17**
Mar–Nov Lic 6hc (4fb) ⊗ CTV 6P ⏣ S%
B&b£6–£8 Bdi£10–£12 W£70–£84 ⫽

GH Waverly Hotel College Rd ☎3546
Plan:**18** Apr–Oct Lic 11hc (4fb) ⊗ CTV 8P
B&b£8.50 Bdi£13.28 W£92.58 ⫽ D6pm

GH White Lodge Hotel Lake Rd,
Bowness-on-Windermere ☎3624 Plan:**2**
Mar–15 Nov Lic 9hc (2fb) CTV 12P lake S%
✳B&b£9–£10 Bdi£13.80–£15
W£86.94–£94.50 ⫽ D8.30pm

WINTERBOURNE ABBAS Dorset
Map 3 SY69
GH Church View ☎Martinstown 296 Lic
8hc (3fb) CTV 7P ₩ S% ✻B&b£5.50
Bdi£8.50 W£56 ⚓

GH *Whitefriars* ☎Martinstown 206
Mar–Oct Lic 7hc ⚓ CTV 18P ₩

WINTHORPE Notts *Map 8 SK85*
INN *Lord Nelson* The Green ☎Newark
703578 Lic 3hc nc14 20P ₩ sn

WISBECH Cambs *Map 5 TF40*
GH Glendon Sutton Rd ☎4812
Mar–Oct Lic 18hc 1⇔🛏(3fb) CTV 50P ⚓
S% B&b£8–£9

WITHYPOOL Somerset *Map 3 SS83*
INN Royal Oak ☎Exford 236 Lic 8hc
4⇔🛏TV 20P ₩ ✻B&b£9.50 Bdi£15.25
W£115.11–£129.03 ⚓ Bar lunch
£1.95–£3.95 D8.30pm£5.75&alc

WITNEY Oxon *Map 4 SP30*
INN *Red Lion* Corn St ☎3149 Lic 6hc
CTV 2P 1🏠 D9pm

WIVELISCOMBE Somerset *Map 3 ST02*
INN Bear 10 North St ☎23537 Lic 5rm
4hc CTV 5P S% B&b£7–£7.50
Bdi£9.50–£10 W£62.50 ⚓ sn L£1alc
D9.30pm£3alc

WOMENSWOLD Kent *Map 5 TR25*
GH Woodpeckers Country Hotel
☎Barham 319 Jan–Nov Lic 12hc 4⇔🛏
(A 4hc 2⇔🛏) nc4 CTV 30P 2🏠 ₩ ⚓ S%
B&b£9.50–£12 Bdi£13–£15
W£91–£91.50 D8.30pm

WOODSTOCK Oxon *Map 4 SP41*
INN *Star* 22 Market Pl ☎811209 Closed
Xmas Day Lic 3hc nc14 CTV 6P D2pm

WOODY BAY Devon *Map 3 SS64*
◄►**GH Red House** ☎Parracombe 255
Mar–Oct 6hc (2fb) nc4 CTV 8P S%
B&b£5.50–£7.50 Bdi£9.50–£11.50
W£60–£74 ⚓ D5pm

WOOLACOMBE Devon *Map 2 SS44*
During the currency of this guide
Woolacombe telephone numbers are
liable to change. All 3 figure numbers
will change to 6 figure numbers by
prefixing with 870
GH Barton House Hotel Barton Rd ☎548
May–Oct Lic 12hc 6⇔🛏(5fb) CTV 12P S%
B&b£6.70–£9.96 Bdi£9.45–£12.71
W£66.13–£89 ⚓ D6pm

GH Combe Ridge Hotel The Esplanade
☎321 Etr–Sep 8hc (3fb) ⚓ nc3 CTV 9P sea
S% ✻B&b£6.33–£6.90 Bdi£9.20–£9.78
W£56.35–£66.70 ⚓ (W only mid Jun–Aug)
D4.30pm

GH *Holmesdale Hotel* Bay View Rd
☎335 Lic 15hc ⚓ CTV 10P ₩ sea

GH Seawards Beach Rd ☎249
Etr–early Oct 6hc (2fb) nc2 TV 6P sea S%
B&b£6–£6.60 Bdi£8.90–£9.75
W£51–£57.50 ⚓ (W only Spring Bank
Hol–Aug) D4.30pm

◄►**GH Wave Crest** Sunnyside Rd ☎334
May–mid Sep 6hc (1fb) nc3 CTV 6P sea S%
B&b£5–£6.50 Bdi£7–£8 W£50–£56 ⚓
D6pm

GH White Rose Hotel The Esplanade
☎406 May–Sep Lic 15hc 11⇔🛏(10fb)

CTV 12P ₩ sea S% B&b£9–£10
Bdi£13–£14.50 W£87.50–£96 ⚓
(W only Jul–Aug) D6.45pm

WORCESTER Herefs & Worcs
Map 3 SO85
GH Loch Ryan Hotel 119 Sidbury
☎351143 13hc (A 5hc 1⇔🛏) ⚓ nc8 CTV
₩ S% ✻B&b£8.05

INN Five Ways Hotel 14 Angel Pl
☎23129 Closed Xmas Lic 7hc ⚓ TV ₩
✻B&b fr£7.50 D11pm

WORKINGTON Cumbria *Map 11 NY02*
GH Morven Siddick ☎2118 Lic 6hc 2⇔🛏
(A 2hc) (2fb) ⚓ ⚓ CTV 18P ₩ sea S%
B&b£6–£6.50 Bdi£8–£8.50 W£56–£59
⚓ D4pm

WORTHING W Sussex *Map 4 TQ10*
GH Belmont Private Hotel 211 Brighton
Rd ☎202678 Lic 6hc (2fb) nc2 CTV 3P 6🏠
₩ sea S% ✻B&b£5.50–£6 Bdi£7.50–£8
W£40–£50 ⚓ D8.30pm

GH Blair House 11 St Georges Rd
☎34071 Lic 6hc (2fb) CTV 6P ₩ S%
B&b£6–£8 Bdi£9–£11 W£63–£77 ⚓
D6.30pm

◄►**GH** *Burcott* 6 Windsor Rd ☎35163
5hc ⚓ CTV 4P ₩

◄►**GH Camelot House** 20 Gannon Rd
☎204334 Lic 6hc (1fb) ⚓ 3P ₩ S%
B&b£4.50–£7.50 Bdi£6.75–£11
W£42–£73 ⚓ D noon

GH *Eleanor Lodge* 9–11 Alexandra Rd
☎33788 Closed Xmas 11hc CTV ₩

GH Meldrum House 8 Windsor Rd
☎33808 Mar–Oct 6hc (2fb) ⚓ CTV ₩ sea
S% B&b£6–£7

GH Pleasington 2 Wyke Av ☎30834
Closed Xmas 8hc ⚓ nc5 CTV 1P ₩ S%
B&b£6–£8 Bdi£9–£11 W£fr£50 ⚓ D noon

GH St Georges Lodge Hotel Chesswood
Rd ☎32621 Lic 9hc 2⇔🛏(2fb) ⚓ ⚓ CTV
10P 2🏠 ₩ S% B&b£8–£10.25
Bdi£11–£12.75 W£75–£88.50 ⚓ D7pm

GH Southdene 41 Warwick Gdns
☎32909 Lic 6hc (2fb) ⚓ nc12 CTV ₩ S%
B&b£6.50–£7.50 Bdi£9–£10 W£60–£65
⚓ D5pm

GH Wansfell Hotel 49 Chesswood Rd
☎30612 11hc 1⇔🛏(2fb) ⚓ nc5 CTV 8P
₩ B&b£8.50–£10 Bdi£12–£13.50
W£84–£89 D7.30pm

GH Williton 10 Windsor Rd ☎37974
6hc (3fb) ⚓ TV S% ✻B&b£5–£7
W£30–£45 Ⓜ

GH Windsor House 16–20 Windsor Rd
☎39655 Lic 12hc 3⇔🛏(6fb) CTV 16P ₩
B&b£6–£12 Bdi£9–£15.50 W£48–£95
⚓ D4.30pm

GH Windsor Lodge 3 Windsor Rd
☎200056 6hc nc5 CTV 2P ₩ sea S%
B&b£8–£9.50 Bdi£11–£12.50 W£72–£82
⚓ D1pm

GH Wolsey Hotel 179–181 Brighton Rd
☎36149 Lic 14hc (3fb) CTV ₩ S%
B&b£8.50 Bdi£12.65 W£88.50 ⚓ D5pm

WROTHAM Kent *Map 5 TQ65*
INN Moat Hotel London Rd ☎ Borough
Green 882263 Lic 8hc 2⇔🛏300P ₩ 🚗
S% B&b£12–£15 sn L£3.50–£4.50&alc
D10.20pm£5&alc

214

YARCOMBE Devon *Map 3 ST20*
GH Belfry ☎ Upottery 234 Closed Xmas
& 1st 3wks Jan Lic 6⇌🏠⊘ nc14 CTV 10P
🍴 S%✳B&b£13–£16.50 W£70 M

YARMOUTH, GT Norfolk *Map 5 TG50*
⊷⊣**GH Frandor** 120 Lowestoft Rd,
Gorleston-on-Sea (2m S A12) ☎62112
Apr–Oct Lic 8hc (4fb) CTV 8P S%
B&b£5.25–£6.75 Bdi£7.25–£8.75
W£43–£53 ⱡ D4pm

GH Georgian House Private Hotel 16–17
North Dr ☎2623 Closed Xmas Lic 22hc
8⇌🏠(4fb) ⊘ CTV 10P 🍴 sea S%
B&b£7–£16 W£40–£80 M

GH Palm Court Hotel 10 North Dr
☎4568 Apr–Oct Lic 46hc 24⇌🏠(10fb)
CTV 40P lift S% B&b£11–£17 Bdi£16–£22
W£65–£94 M D8pm

GH Porthole 52 Avondale Rd,
Gorleston-on-Sea (2m S A12) ☎61451
Apr–Sep rs Xmas 6hc (2fb) CTV 🍴 S%
B&b£7–£8 Bdi£9–£10 W£50–£55 ⱡ

YATTON Avon *Map 3 ST46*
INN Prince of Orange High St ☎832193
Lic 8hc 5⇌🏠 TV 40P ♿ B&b£10.48–£12.23
Bdi£14.56–£16.31 Bar lunch£1.50alc
D9.30pm£3.50&alc

YEOVIL Somerset *Map 3 ST51*
GH Pickett Witch House Hotel 100
Ilchester Rd ☎4317 Closed Xmas 10hc
1⇌🏠(A 6hc 1⇌🏠) (3fb) nc2 CTV 16P 2🏠
🍴 B&b£10 W£45 M

⊷⊣**GH Wyndham** 142 Sherborne Rd
☎21468 Closed Xmas Lic 6hc (2fb) CTV
6P S% B&b£5.50 Bdi£8.50 W£56 ⱡ D5pm

YORK N Yorks *Map 8 SE65*

GH Acomb Road 128 Acomb Rd ☎792321
Jan–Nov 14hc (4fb) CTV 15P 🛏 S%
B&bf£6 Bdif£10 D4pm

GH Alhambra Court Hotel 31 St Marys
☎28474 Lic 25hc 7⇔🛁 (3fb) CTV 18P
🛏 S% B&bf£8.50 Bdif£12 Wf£80 ⅃ Dnoon

GH Avenue 6 The Avenue, Clifton ☎20575
Jan–Nov 6hc (2fb) CTV S% B&bf£6–£7
Bdif£9–£10 Wf£60–£77 ⅃ D4pm

GH Beech 6–7 Longfield Ter, Bootham
☎34581 Lic 7hc (1fb) 🕸 CTV 4P S%
B&bf£6.33–£7.48 Bdif£9.78–£11.50
Wf£65–£76.30 ⅃ D4pm

GH Bootham Bar Hotel 4 High Petergate
☎58516 Closed Xmas 10hc (2fb) 🕸 CTV
🛏 lift S% ✳B&bf£7.18

GH Clifton Bridge Hotel Water End
☎53609 Lic 10hc (1fb) CTV 12P 🛏 S%
B&bf£10.50–£11.50 D7.30pm

GH Coach House Hotel Marygate
☎52780 Lic 12hc CTV 10P 🛏

GH Crescent 77 Bootham ☎23216 8hc
(2fb) 🕸 nc2 CTV 4P S% B&bf£6–£7
Wf£42–£49 Ⓜ

GH Croft Hotel 103 Mount Rd ☎22747
10hc 1⇔ (1fb) 🕸 nc2 CTV 3P 1🏠 🛏
✳B&bf£8–£10 Bdif£12–£14 D4pm

GH Fairmount Hotel 230 Tadcaster Rd
☎38298 Jan–Nov 7hc 1⇔🛁 (2fb) 🕸 CTV
6P 🛏 S% B&bf£7–£10 D4pm

GH Grasmead House Hotel 1 Scarcroft
Hill, The Mount ☎29996 Lic 6⇔🛁 (1fb)
CTV 🛏 S% ✳B&bf£11 Bdif£15 D5pm

GH Hobbits Hotel 9 St Peter's Gv ☎24538
Closed Xmas 2wks Lic 8hc 1⇔🛁 🕸 CTV

5P 🛏 S% ✳B&bf£9.49 Bdif£13.51 Wf£94.59
⅃

GH Inglewood 7 Clifton Gn ☎53523
6hc (2fb) 🕸 CTV 4P 1🏠 🛏 S% B&bf£6–£7

GH Jorvik Hotel 52 Marygate, Bootham
☎53511 Closed Xmas Lic 16hc 7⇔🛁 CTV
20P 🛏

GH Linden Lodge Nunthorpe Av, Scarcroft
Rd ☎20107 Closed Xmas Lic 8hc 1⇔🛁
(3fb) 🕸 nc7 CTV 🛏 S% B&bf£6–£6.50
Bdif£12–£12.50 (W only Jan–Mar &
Oct–Dec)

GH Mayfield Hotel 75 Scarcroft Rd
☎54834 Jan–Nov Lic 7hc (2fb) 🕸 nc5
CTV 🛏 S% B&bf£8–£12 Bdif£13.50–£18
Wf£94.50–£126 ⅃ D4.30pm

GH Moat Hotel Nunnery Ln ☎52926
9hc 🕸 CTV 10P

GH Old Vic 2 Wenlock Ter, Fulford Rd
☎37888 Lic 6hc (4fb) 🕸 CTV 4P 🛏 S%
B&bf£6.50–£7.50 Bdif£12–£13 Wf£84–£91
⅃ D5pm

GH Orchard Court Hotel 4 St Peter's Gv
☎53964 Lic 10hc 🕸 CTV 8P

GH Priory Hotel 126–128 Fulford Rd
☎25280 Closed Xmas 19hc 3⇔🛁 (4fb)
🕸 CTV 18P 🛏 S% B&bf£8

GH St Raphael 44 Queen Ann's Rd,
Bootham ☎54187 7hc (1fb) 🕸 nc7 CTV
🛏 S% B&bf£6.50–£7.50

GH Sycamore Hotel 19 Sycamore Pl
☎24712 Lic 6hc (2fb) 🕸 CTV 3P 🛏 S%
B&bf£6–£7 Bdif£9–£11 Wf£60–£75 Ⓜ
Dnoon

FARMHOUSE SECTION

The gazetteer gives details of AA-listed farmhouses in England, Wales and Scotland. Listed in alphabetical order of placenames. (*Note: there are no AA-listed farmhouses within the Channel Islands, Isle of Man, or Isles of Scilly*).

Details for islands are shown under individual placenames; the gazetteer text also gives appropriate cross-references. A useful first point of reference is to consult the location maps which show where farmhouses are situated.

ABBERTON Essex *Map 5 TM01*
Mr S. Miller **Oxley Hill** *(TM002194)*
Layer Rd ☎ Colchester 66422
Modern bungalow farmhouse with its own private nature reserve. Beautiful countryside views.
Feb–20 Dec rs Jan (B&b only) 6hc (2fb) ⊗
nc5 CTV 12P 3⋒ 📺 55acres arable S%
B&b£7.50–£10.50 D8pm

ABBEY CWMHIR Powys *Map 6 SO07*
Home *(SO091724)* ☎ Penybont 66
Smart, stone-built house in the village. Small trout stream passes through the farm.
2hc ⊗ TV 4P 1⋒ 450acres mixed

ABBOTS BICKINGTON Devon
Map 2 SS31
Mrs E. Bellew **Courtbarton** *(SS385133)*
☎ Milton Damerel 214
Stone-built farmhouse in an area of great natural beauty. Panoramic views from most windows. Rough shooting, fishing and riding available.
Whitsun–Sep 4rm 3hc (1fb) ⊗ nc4 TV
6P 600acres mixed S% ✱B&b£5–£7
Bdi£7–£9 D5pm

ABBOTS BROMLEY Staffs *Map 7 SK02*
Mrs M.K. Hollins **Marsh** *(SK069261)*
☎ Burton-on-Trent 840323
Large two-storey, cement rendered farmhouse set in open countryside 1 mile from village.
2rm (1fb) TV 6P 📺 43acres dairy S%
B&b£5 Bdi£7 D6.30pm

ABEREDW Powys *Map 3 SO04*
M.M. Evans **Danycoed** *(SO079476)*
☎ Erwood 298
Stone-built, two-storey farmhouse. Pleasant situation on edge of River Wye.
Etr–Oct 4rm 2hc 6P river 235acres mixed
S% B&b£5.25–£5.75 Bdi£7–£7.75
W£45–£50 ⥥ D5pm

ABERFELDY Tayside *Perths*
Map 14 NN84
Mr A. Kennedy **Tom of Cluny** *(NN875515)*
☎477
Small hillside farmhouse reached by long steep tarmac/rough drive. Magnificent views southward across the River Tay and Aberfeldy.
3rm (1fb) CTV 3P river 165acres arable
beef sheep S% B&b£5.50–£6
Bdi£6.50–£7.50 D6pm

ABERGAVENNY Gwent *Map 3 SO21*
Mrs V. Nicholls **Newcourt** *(SO317165)*
Mardy ☎3734
16th-century, stone-built farmhouse with views of Sugar Loaf Mountain.
3hc (1fb) ⊗ nc5 P ⋒ 85acres dairy
B&bfr£6

ABERHOSAN Powys *Map 6 SN89*
Mr A. Lewis **Bacheiddon** *(SN825980)*
☎ Machynlleth 2229

From the windows there are lovely views of the surrounding mountains and countryside. Off unclassified road linking Machynlleth and Dyliffe/Staylittle (B4518).
3rm 3⋒📶 ⊗ CTV P 850acres mixed S% ✱
B&b£5–£6 Bdi£8–£9 W£55–£62 ⥥ D7pm

ABERMULE Powys *Map 7 SO19*
Mr J.E. Wigley **Upper Brytalch** *(SO172961)*
☎252
1m NE of Abermule off B4386.
Mar–Oct 3hc (1fb) TV P 📺 200acres dairy
mixed S% B&b£5–£6 Bdi£7–£8
W£45–£50 ⥥ D9pm

ABINGTON Strathclyde *Lanarks*
Map 11 NS92
Mr G. Hodge **Craighead** *(NS914236)*
☎ Crawford 356
Large farm building in courtyard design. Set amid rolling hills on the banks of the River Duneaton. Main building dates from 1780. Off unclassified Crawfordjohn road. 1m N of A74/A73 junc.
May–Sep 3rm (1fb) ♨ CTV 6P 3⋒ river
800acres mixed S% B&bfr£4.50 Bdi fr£7.50
D6pm
Mrs D. Wilson **Crawfordjohn Mill** *(NS897242)* Crawfordjohn ☎ Crawfordjohn 248
Two-storey, brown-brick farmhouse. Set in its own land. Off A74 1m SE of Crawfordjohn on unclassified rd.
May–Oct 3rm TV 4P 📺 180acres arable
dairy S% B&b£5 Bdi£7.50 W£49 ⥥ D7pm

ACHARACLE Highland *Argyll*
Map 13 NM66
Mrs M. Macaulay **Dalilea House** *(NM735693)* ☎ Salen 253
A splendid turreted house with surrounding grounds giving excellent views over farmland, hills and Loch Shiel. A blend of the ancient and modern.
Mar–Oct 6hc (1fb) ⊗ 8P lake 14,000acres
beef sheep S% B&bfr£7.47 Bdi fr£10.92
Wfr£72.45 ⥥ D7pm

ALDWARK Derbys *Map 8 SK25*
J.N. Lomas **Lydgate** *(SK228577)*
☎ Carsington 250
Stone-built traditional farmhouse, about 300 years old, in quiet rural setting.
3rm (1fb) ⊗ CTV 3P 📺 300 acres dairy
sheep S% B&b£7 Bdi£10 Dnoon

ALFRISTON E Sussex *Map 5 TQ50*
Mrs D.Y. Savage **Pleasant Rise** *(TQ516027)* ☎870545
Attractive farm set in typical Sussex downland. Adjacent to B2108 Seaford road.
Etr–Oct 3hc (1fb) ⊗ TV 6P 95acres non-working S% B&b£6.50–£7 £42–£45.50 M

ALLENSMOOR Heref & Worcs
Map 3 SO43
Mrs O.I. Griffiths **Mawfield** *(SO453366)*
☎ Belmont (Hereford) 266
Large farmhouse set in narrow lane off the

beaten track, but close enough for Hereford's amenities.
Etr–Oct 3rm 2hc ⊗ nc8 CTV P 176acres arable S% B&b£4–£5.50 Bdi£7.50–£9

ALVERDISCOTT Devon Map 2 SS52
C.M. Tremeer **Garnacott** (SS516240)
☎ Newton Tracey 282
Farmhouse standing in small garden surrounded by open fields. Traditional farmhouse furnishings. Facilities nearby include fishing, golf and bathing.
Etr–Oct 3rm 1hc (2fb) ⊗ TV 3P 85acres mixed S% B&b£4.25–£5.50 Bdi£7.50–£8 W£49–£52.50 ⊬

ANNAN Dumfries & Galloway Dumfriesshire Map 11 NY16
Beechgrove (NY213652) ☎2220

Attractive redstone house with attractive garden, surrounded by pastureland. Views of Solway Firth.
3hc TV 12P sea 78acres beef D7pm

APPLEBY Cumbria Map 12 NY62
Mrs M. Wood **Gale House** (NY695206)
☎51380
Comfortable, quiet farmhouse with friendly atmosphere. Situated in delightful position 1m from centre of Appleby.
Apr–Sep 2rm (1fb) ⊗ nc5 3P 167acres dairy S% B&b£5.50 Bdi£8 W£52.50 ⊬ D3.30pm

ARDBRECKNISH Strathclyde Argyll Map 10 NN02
Mrs H.F. Hodge **Rockhill** (NNO72219)
☎Kilchrenan 218

*Loch-shore farm. Trout and perch fishing,
(free) and on the farm's private loch, by
arrangement.*
Apr–Sep 6hc (4fb) nc5 TV 8P 📺 lake
200acres sheep horses S% B&bfr£8
Bdi fr£11 Wfr£70 ⅃ (W only Jul–Aug) D7pm

ARDEN Strathclyde *Dunbartons
Map 10 NS38*
Mrs R. Keith **Mid Ross** *(NS359859)*
☎655
*Farmhouse pleasantly located 6 miles
from Helensburgh. E off A82.*
May–Oct 3hc (2fb) CTV P 📺 lake 32acres
arable mixed S% B&b£5–£6

ARDERSIER Highland *Inverness-shire
Map 14 NH75*
Mrs L. E. MacBean **Milton-of-Gollanfield**
(NH809534) ☎2207
*Stone farmhouse set on north side of A96
5 miles west of Nairn.*
Apr–Oct 3rm 2hc (1fb) ⚘ CTV P 365acres
mixed B&b£6–£10

ARDFERN Strathclyde *Argyll
Map 10 NM80*
Mrs G. McKinlay **Corranbeg** *(NM801045)*
☎Barbreck 207
*Large rambling farmhouse in quiet spot.
Surrounded by beautiful scenery.*
Etr–Sep 3rm (1fb) ⚘ P 208acres mixed S%
B&b£4.50 Bdi£8.50 W£59.50 D5pm

Mrs M.C. Peterson **Traighmhor**
(NM800039) ☎Barbreck 228
*Farmhouse offering magnificent views
towards Loch Craignish.*
Mar–Oct 4rm (1fb) ⚘ CTV 8P sea mixed
S% B&b£5 Bdi£10 D8pm

ASHBURTON Devon *Map 3 SX77*
Brembridge *(SX785701)* ☎52426
*Clean and brightly decorated farmhouse,
parts of which date back to early 16th-
century.*
3rm 2hc ⚘ ⚘ CTV 3P 📺 8acres mixed
Mrs S.I. Cundy **Parkfield** *(SX764882)*
☎52318
*Comfortable farmhouse in beautiful
countryside on south east edge of Dartmoor,
also within easy reach of South Devon.*
Etr–Sep 2rm 1hc (1fb) ⚘ ⚘ CTV 4P 1🏠 📺
400acres arable S% B&b£6.50–£7
W£42–£48 M

ASHFORD *(Nr Barnstaple)* Devon
Map 2 SS53
Mrs G. Hannington **Fair Oak** *(SS530348)*
☎Barnstaple 73698
*Modern farmhouse, arranged as mini-farm
specially catering for children, with pets*

*corner and aviaries with mixed birds.
Overlooks River Taw Estuary.*
May–Oct 5rm 4hc (4fb) ⚘ ⚘ CTV 6P 📺
river 89acres mixed S% B&b£5–£6
Bdi£7.50–£9 W£50–£60 ⅃ D4pm

ASH MILL Devon *Map 3 SS72*
Mr J.C. Blackmore **West Ford** *(SS789229)*
☎Bishops Nympton 231.
*Georgian farmhouse of architectural
interest within easy reach of Exmoor and
Dartmoor. Market town of South Molton
5 miles.*
Closed Nov Lic 4rm 3hc (3fb) ⚘ TV 6P
📺 32acres mixed S% B&b£7.50 Bdi£12
W£80 ⅃ D7.30pm

ASPATRIA Cumbria *Map 11 NY14*
Mr J. Mashiter **Scales Demesne**
(NY183461) ☎20847
*Comfortably furnished accommodation.
Two separate staircases and front doors
offer independence. Within easy reach of
sea and Lake District.*
Jun–Aug 3rm (1fb) ⚘ nc2 CTV 3P 1🏠 📺
231acres arable beef dairy S% B&b£5
Bdi£8 D5pm

ATCHAM Salop *Map 7 SJ50*
Chilton Grove *(SJ526090)* ☎Cross
Houses 215
*Large Georgian mansion with Tudor wing.
Elizabethan dovecote in grounds. Linked
with National Trust. Secluded and quiet
with 10 mile views.*
3rm 1⌀🏠 6P 2🏠 📺 34acres beef

AUCHENCAIRN Dumfries & Galloway
Kirkcudbrights Map 11 NX75
Mrs D. Cannon **Bluehill** *(NX786515)*
☎228
*Farm offers panoramic views overlooking
the Solway Firth and the English lakeland
hills.*
Etr–Sep 4hc (2fb) ⚘ nc10 CTV P 📺 sea
120acres diary B&bfr£5.50

AUSTWICK N Yorks *Map 7 SD76*
Mrs M. Hird **Rawlinshaw** *(SD781673)*
☎Settle 3214
*200-year-old farmhouse with attractive
views to the front of the house.*
Etr–Sep 2hc (2fb) ⚘ CTV 5P 📺 206acres
dairy mixed sheep S% B&b£4.50–£5
W£31–£35 M

AVONWICK Devon *Map 3 SX75*.
Mrs C. Scott **Sopers Horsebrook**
(SX711587) ☎South Brent 3235
*Old farmhouse situated in quiet valley
overlooking brook.*

May–Sep 2hc (2fb) CTV 2P 120acres mixed
S% B&b£5–£6 Bdi£8–£9.50 W£33–£40
M (W only mid Jul–Aug) D9am

AXBRIDGE Somerset *Map 3 ST45*
L. Dimmock **Manor** *(ST420549)* Cross
(on A38) ☎732577
*400-year-old farmhouse, formerly a coaching
inn. Farm offers horse riding facilities.*
9rm 3hc (3fb) CTV P 250acres mixed S%
✱B&b£5.98 Bdi£9.49 W£66.13 ✗
(W only Aug) D5pm

AXMINSTER Devon *Map 3 SY39*
Mrs S. Clist **Annings** *(SY299966)* Wyke
☎33294
*Large secluded farmhouse with modern
furnishings. Situated in elevated position
with fine views. Coast nearby. S of town on
unclassified road between A35 & A358.*
Apr–Oct 4rm 3hc (1fb) ⊗ CTV P 54acres
dairy S% B&b£7–£8.50 Bdi£9–£10.50
W£63–£73.50 ✗ D5pm

AYLESBEARE Devon *Map 3 SY09*
Mrs E.A. Slade **Rosamondford** *(SY027918)*
☎Woodbury 32448
*Old thatch and cob farmhouse with large
front garden. Conveniently placed for
Exeter, the airport and East Devon.*
Etr–Oct 2hc (1fb) ⊗ CTV 6P 125acres dairy
S% B&bfr£5.50 Bdi fr£8.50 Wfr£56 ✗
D noon

AYR Strathclyde *Ayrs Map 10 NS32*
Mr & Mrs A. Stevenson **Trees** *(NS386186)*
☎Joppa 270
*Comfortable accommodation in a quiet
location. 4m E on unclassified road,
between A70 and A713.*
Etr–Sep 3rm (1fb) ⊗ CTV 5P 125acres
beef S% B&b£5.50 Bdi£8.50–£9

BABELL Clwyd *Map 7 SJ17*
Mrs M.L. Williams **Bryn Glas** *(SJ155737)*
☎Caerwys 493
May–Sep 2rm (2fb) CTV 2P 40acres
mixed S% (W only May–Sep)

BALA Gwynedd *Map 6 SH93*
Tytandderwen *(SH944345)* ☎520273
*Two-storey manor house-style farmhouse
in open country. Stone-built and modernised
in parts. Borders on River Dee.*
Closed Xmas & New Year 6rm 3hc TV 6P
40acres 🍴 mixed

BALFRON STATION Central *Stirlings
Map 11 NS58*
Clachanry *(NS512888)* ☎Balfron 335

*Pleasant little hillside farmhouse with
reasonable access from the main road.*
Apr–Sep 3rm ⊗ TV 3P 🍴 135acres mixed

BALNAGUARD Tayside *Perthshire
Map 14 NN95*
Balmacneil *(NN979507)* ☎Ballinluig 213
*Modern bungalow on hillside of west bank
of River Tay. Good views of South Down &
Tay Valley.*
Mar–Nov 2hc CTV 2P 1🏠 🍴 river
2.600acres arable, beef, mixed & sheep
D6pm

BAMPTON Devon *Map 3 SS92*
Mr & Mrs R.A. Fleming **Holwell**
(SS966233) ☎452
*14th-century farmhouse with thatched roof,
studded oak front door and many oak beams
inside. Attractive gardens.*
3hc 1⇔🍴 ⊗ nc CTV 6P 1🏠 🍴 25acres
mixed S% B&b£6.50 Bdi£10 W£65 ✗
D4pm

R. Cole **Hukeley** *(SS972237)* ☎267
*16th-century farmhouse, on the edge of
Exmoor. Fine old beams. Rooms are
comfortable and well decorated.*
Etr–Oct 2hc (2fb) ⊗ CTV 4P 200acres
mixed S% B&bfr£5.75 Bdi fr£7.76
Wfr£57.75 ✗ D4pm

Mrs A. Campbell **Valeridge** *(SS918220)*
Oakfordbridge ☎Oakford 346
*A centuries old farmhouse in elevated
position with superb view of the Exe Valley.
3m W of Bampton on A361.*
3rm 2hc nc14 CTV 4P 🍴 17½acres mixed
S% B&bfr£6.50 Bdi fr£10 Wfr£65 ✗ D noon

BANAVIE Highland *Inverness-shire
Map 14 NN17*
Mrs A.C. MacDonald **Burnside** *(NN138805)*
Muirshearlich ☎Corpach 275
*Small, stone-built farmhouse with open
views over Caledonian Canal, loch and
north face of Ben Nevis. 3m NE off B8004.*
Apr–Sep 3hc (1fb) CTV 3P 🍴 lake 75acres
mixed S% B&b£4.50 Bdi£7 W£49 ✗ D5pm

BARBRECK Strathclyde *Argyll
Map 10 NM80*
Glenview *(NM841079)* Turnalt Farm
☎277
Apr–Oct 4rm ⊗ CTV 4P 3,500acres sheep
D6pm

BARNSTAPLE Devon *Map 2 SS53*
Mrs M. Lethaby **Home** *(SS555360)*
Lower Blakewell, Muddiford ☎2955

221

Farmhouse situated in peaceful North Devon countryside. Pony, many pets and Wendy House available for children.
Mar–Oct 4hc (3fb) ⚓ CTV 4P 40acres mixed
S% B&b£5–£8 Bdi£7.50–£10 W£45–£65
ⓚ D4pm

BARRA, ISLE OF Western Isles
Inverness-shire Map 13 **See Borve**

BASSENTHWAITE Cumbria
Map 11 NY23
Mrs P. Trafford **Bassenthwaite Hall**
(NY231322) ☎ Bassenthwaite Lake 393
Fully modernised 17th-century farmhouse in picturesque village close to quiet stream.
Etr–Oct rs Nov–Feb 2hc (2fb) ⚘ TV 3P
200acres beef sheep S% B&b£5–£6

BEESWING Dumfries & Galloway
Kircudbrights Map 11 NX86
Garloff *(NX912702)* ☎ Lochfoot 225
Pleasant farmhouse set at end of farm road on south east side of A711 6m west of Dumfries.
6hc TV 12P ⍟ 220acres dairy D5pm

BERRIEW Powys Map 7 SJ10
Mrs E.G.M. Jones **Upper Pandy**
(SJ149995) ☎338
Isolated, black and white timbered farmhouse. Berriew 1½ miles.
Etr–Oct 3rm 2hc (1fb) TV P 140acres beef mixed sheep S% B&b£5.50 Bdi£7.50
W£49 ⓚ D5pm

BETWS-YN-RHOS Clwyd Map 6 SH97
Mrs A. Jones **Pen-y-Bryn** *(SH914732)*
☎ Dolwen 223 2rm (1fb) ⚘ TV P 130acres
mixed S% ✳B&b£4.50 Bdi£6.50 W£42 ⓚ
D6pm

BICKINGTON *(Nr Ashburton)* Devon
Map 3 SX77
B.E. Heath **West Downe** *(SX794705)*
☎258
Modernised, 16th-century farmhouse situated on edge of Dartmoor. Ponies available for riding from the farm.
Etr–Oct 2hc (2fb) ⚓ CTV P 64acres mixed
S% B&b£4 Bdi£7 W£45 ⓚ D6pm

BIRCHER Heref & Worcs Map 7 SO46
Mrs P.P. Powell **Leys** *(SO471673)* Leys Ln
☎ Yarpole 367
17th-century farmhouse in rural setting with pleasant grounds. Close to Croft Castle and Bircher Common with its magnificent views.
4rm 1hc (1fb) CTV 110acres dairy S%
B&b£5 Bdi£7 W£49 ⓚ D8pm

BISSOE Cornwall Map 2 SW74
Holly Tree *(SW763416)* Fernsplatt
☎ Devoran 862126
Isolated farmhouse in beautiful countryside. Large garden with putting, pets' corner and pony rides.
May–Oct 5hc CTV 10P 10acres mixed

BLACK CROSS Cornwall Map 2 SW96
Mrs E.P. Edwards **Homestake** *(SW910606)*
☎ St Austell 860423
Pleasant house with garden on main village road. In central position for touring Cornwall.
Etr–Oct 8hc (4fb) CTV 10P 82acres dairy
S% B&b£4–£5.50 Bdi£5.50–£7 (W only
Whitsun–12Sep) D5pm

BLACK DOG Devon Map 3 SS80
Mr & Mrs D.J. Maunder **Lewdon**
(SS776105) ☎ Tiverton 860766
Lewdon farm is a very old Devon farmhouse which has been in the Maunder family since 1856. Situated in a picturesque and peaceful position. Access from south side B3042 ¾m W of Thelbridge Arms Inn (not in Black Dog Village).
Jan–Nov 3hc (1fb) ⚘ ⚓ CTV P 2🏠 220acres
arable beef sheep S% B&b£6.50 Bdi£9.50

BLEADON Avon Map 3 ST35
R.H. House **Purn House** *(ST334571)*
☎812324
Pleasantly situated amid open fields with views of the Mendip and Quantock Hills and Brent Knoll.
⚘ nc3 CTV 6P ⍟ river 400acres mixed S%
B&b£5–£6.50 Bdi£7.50–£9 W£50–£60
ⓚ (W only Jul & Aug) D6.30pm

BLEATHWOOD Heref & Worcs
Map 7 SO57
Bleathwood Manor *(SO560696)*
☎ Tenbury Wells 810446
Imposing manor house dating back over 600 years. Mixture of architectural designs. Large lounge with open fireplace. Country views.
5hc ⚘ TV 10P 114acres mixed D7pm

BLORE Staffs Map 7 SK14
K.W. Griffin **Coldwall** *(SK144494)* Okeover
☎ Thorpe Cloud 249
Stone-built farmhouse approximately 200 years old. Good views of the surrounding hills. 4 miles NW of Ashbourne.
Etr–Nov 2hc (2fb) ⚘ TV 6P 230acres mixed
S% B&bfr£5 Bdi fr£6.50 D6pm

BOGHEAD Strathclyde *Lanarks*
Map 11 NS74
I.A. McInally **Dykehead** *(NS772417)*
☎ Lesmahagow 892226
*Rough cast, two-storey farmhouse just fifty
yards from Strathaven/Lesmahagow road.*
15Mar–Oct 2rm CTV 6P 🚿 200acres dairy
sheep S% ✳B&b£4.50

BORELAND Dumfries & Galloway
Dumfriesshire Map 11 NY19
Mrs I. Maxwell **Gall** *(NY172901)* ☎229
*Situated on a hill looking towards the
Moffat hills.*
May–Sep 2hc (1fb) 🕸 ♨ CTV 2P 1066acres
beef sheep S% B&b£5.50–£6 W£38–£40 M

BORVE Isle of Barra, Western Isles
Inverness-shire Map 13 NF60
Mrs M. MacNeil **Ocean View** *(NF655014)*
☎ Castlebay 397
*Detached bungalow standing in natural
farmland facing west over Atlantic Ocean.*
3rm (2fb) 🕸 nc10 TV 12P sea 2¾acres
sheep B&bfr£6.50 Bdi fr£9 D8pm

BOTALLACK Cornwall *Map 2 SW33*
Mrs J. Cargeeg **Manor** *(SW368331)*
☎ Penzance 788525
*Previously known as 'Nanparra; home of
Ross Poldark from the television series
filmed here. Area steeped in history.*
4hc 🕸 CTV 4P 🚿 150acres mixed S%
B&bfr£5.50 Bdi fr£9

BOVEY TRACEY Devon *Map 3 SX87*
A.R. Roberts **Willmead** *(SX795812)*
☎ Lustleigh 214
*Farmhouse dating from 1327 situated on
edge of Dartmoor National Park in a
delightful valley.*
Closed Xmas 3hc nc10 CTV 10P 31acres
beef B&b£9.50 Bdi£14.50 D7.30pm

BOW Devon *Map 3 SX70*
Mrs V. Hill **East Hillerton House**
(SX725981) Spreyton (3m S unclass)
☎393
Farm is located 2m NE of Spreyton village.
Closed Xmas 2hc (1fb) 🕸 CTV P 340acres
mixed S% B&bfr£4 Bdifr£7

BRADNINCH Devon *Map 3 SS90*
Mrs. J. Cole **White Heathfield**
(ST012029) ☎ Hele 300
*Farmhouse in typical East Devon scenery.
Off southside of B3181.*
Apr–Sep 3rm (2fb) TV 3P 127acres mixed
S% B&b£4.50–£5 Bdi£6.50–£7
W£30–£42 ⱡ (W only Apr–Sep) D6pm

BRADWORTHY Devon *Map 2 SS31*
Dinworthy *(SS311156)* ☎297
*Farmhouse set in secluded locality. Fishing
and rough shooting available.*
Apr–Sep 3hc 🕸 TV 3P 105acres beef
dairy & mixed Dnoon

Lew *(SS326140)* ☎404
*Stone-built farmhouse on the outskirts of
the village.*
Jun–Sep 3rm 2hc 🕸 nc5 CTV 2P 60acres
mixed D4pm

BRANSCOMBE Devon *Map 3 SY28*
Higher Bulstone *(SY176898)* ☎391
*Fully modernised farmhouse dating from
1450. Situated about 2 miles from
Branscombe Beach.*
Etr–Sep 6hc 🕸 CTV 10P 100acres
dairy & mixed D5pm

BRAUNTON Devon *Map 2 SS43*
J. & T. Barnes **Denham Farm Holidays**
(SS480404) North Buckland ☎ Croyde
890297
*Large farmhouse, parts of which date from
the 18th-century, set in lovely countryside.
2 miles from Croyde and within easy
reach of Barnstaple and Ilfracombe.*
8hc (5fb) 🕸 CTV 1P 7🚿 160acres mixed
S% B&b£5–£6 Bdi£8–£9.50
W£52.90–£58.65 ⱡ (W only end Jun–Aug)
D6pm

J.E.J. Tucker **Middle Spreacombe**
(SS479421) ☎ Woolacombe 370
*Well-decorated, comfortable farmhouse
3m N of A361. Good location for country
walks, fishing and bathing.*
May–Sep 3hc 🕸 TV 3P 200acres mixed
S% W£40 ⱡ D6.30pm

BREAGE Cornwall *Map 32 SW62*
Sethnow *(SW614286)* ☎ Helston 3603
*Long, low, 17th-century granite farmhouse
with oak panelling. Fully modernised.
Picturesque setting.*
Apr–Oct 3hc TV 4P 110acres mixed

BRECHIN Tayside *Angus Map 15 NO56*
Mrs J. Stewart **Wood of Auldbar**
(NO554556) ☎ Aberlemno 218
*Fairly large farmhouse well back from
road amid farmland and woods 5m SW on
unclassified road, between B9134 and
A932.*
3rm (1fb) TV 3P 🚿 187acres arable
S% B&b£4.25–£4.50 Bdi£6.50–£7

BRENDON Devon *Map 3 SS74*
Mrs C.A. South **Farley Water** *(SS744464)*
☎272

Comfortable farmhouse adjoining the
moors. Good home cooking and freedom
for children.
mid May–Oct 5rm 4hc (2fb) TV P 223acres
beef sheep S% ✳B&b£4.03 Bdi£6.90
W£46 ⱡ

Mrs M.A. Phipps **Wingate** (SS780490)
☎285
This 18th-century stone-built farmhouse is
set 1,000ft up on Exmoor. The farm of 198
acres, runs down to the edge of the
Countisbury cliffs—giving marvellous
views of sea. 1½m NE off A39.
May–Sep 7hc (3fb) ⌀ CTV 7P sea 198acres
beef sheep S% B&b£7–£7.50 W£49 Ⓜ

BRENTELEIGH Suffolk Map 5 TL94
J.P. Gage **Street** (TL945476)
☎ Lavenham 247271
A most beautiful period house, tastefully
furnished to a high standard.
Apr–Oct 2hc ⌀ 🛏 142acres
arable S% B&b£6.50–£7.50
W£45.50–£52.50 Ⓜ

BRIDESTOWE Devon Map 2 SX58
Ebsleigh (SX510903) ☎225
Beautifully situated in 24 acres of ground
overlooking Dartmoor.
5rm 4hc nc14 CTV 20P 24acres mixed

W.H. Down **Little Bidlake** (SX494887)
☎233
Neat, clean and efficient farmhouse adjacent
to A30 between Bridestowe and
Launceston.
Whit–Sep 2hc ⌀ ⌀ CTV P 150acres beef
dairy

Mrs Ponsford **Stone** (SX503890) ☎253
mid May–mid Sep 7hc (3fb) ⌀ CTV 7P 🛏
260acres beef sheep S% B&bfr£6 Bdi fr£8
Wfr£50 ⱡ D6pm

Mrs J. Northcott **Town** (SX504905) ☎226
Tile-hung farmhouse with a pleasant,
homely atmosphere.
Etr–Oct 3hc (1fb) CTV 4P 150acres dairy
S% B&b£6–£6.50 Bdi£7–£8 W£48–£50
ⱡ D6.30pm

Mrs M. Hockridge **Week** (SX519913)
☎221
Farm is situated east of Bridestowe and
signposted from A30.
6hc (4fb) CTV 10P 160acres mixed S%
B&b£5–£6 Bdi£7–£8 D6pm

BRIDGERULE Devon Map 2 SS20
Buttsbeer Cross (SS266043) ☎210
Modernised farmhouse dating from
15th-century. Within easy reach of Bude
and North Cornish coast.

Etr–Oct 3rm 2hc ⌀ nc11 CTV 3P 143acres
mixed D5.30pm

BROMPTON REGIS Devon Map 3 SS93
Mrs G. Payne **Lower Holworthy**
(SS978308) ☎244
Small 18th-century hill farm on hill side
overlooking and bordering the Wimbleball
Lake in Exmoor National Park.
Closed Xmas 3rm 2hc ⌀ TV 4P 🛏 lake
160acres beef sheep S% B&b£7.50
Bdi£12 W£72 ⱡ Dnoon

BROUGH Cumbria Map 12 NY71
Mrs J. Atkinson **Augill House** (NY814148)
☎305
Stone-built Victorian farmhouse 1 mile
from village. Quiet, clean and comfortable.
Closed Xmas 3hc (1fb) TV 6P 🛏 40acres
dairy S% B&b£5.50 Bdi£8.50 D4pm

BRUTON Somerset Map 3 ST63
Gilcombe (ST696364) ☎3378
Small, well furnished farmhouse surrounded
by countryside, one mile from Bruton.
Apr–Oct 2hc ⌀ nc3 TV 4P 2🏠 400acres
dairy

BRYNGWYN Powys Map 3 SO14
Mrs H.E.A. Nicholls **Newhouse**
(SO191497) ☎ Painscastle 671
200-year-old, two-storey, stone-built
farmhouse set in 150acres of mixed
farmland.
2hc ⌀ CTV 2P 🛏 150acres mixed B&b£5
Bdi£8

BUCHLYVIE Central Stirlings
Map 11 NS59
Balwill (NS548927) ☎239
White-painted farmhouse and buildings set
off main road in the upper Forth Valley.
Etr–Oct 4rm 1hc ⌀ TV 4P 200acres beef &
sheep D6pm

BUCKIE Grampian Banffs Map 15 JN46
M. McLean **Mill of Rathven** (NJ446657)
☎31132
Farmhouse with attractive garden. On edge
of village of Rathven and surrounded by
arable land and several outbuildings.
3rm CTV 3P 2🏠 arable sheep S%
B&b£6.50–£8 Bdi£9–£10.50 D5pm

BUCKLAND BREWER Devon
Map 2 SS42
Mrs M. Brown **Holwell** (SS424159)
☎ Langtree 288
16th-century farmhouse with a friendly
and homely atmosphere.

May–Oct rs Nov–Apr 5hc (2fb) CTV P
310acres mixed S% B&b£5 Bdi£7 W£45
⫽ (W only mid Jul–Aug) D7pm

BUDOCK Cornwall *Map 2 SW73*
A.J. Dunstan **Menehay** *(SW787322)*
Bilckland Rd. ☎ Penryn 72550
*Pleasant farmhouse with good standard of
furnishings and decoration, convenient
for beach.*
Mar–Oct 3hc P 69acres mixed

BULKWORTHY Devon *Map 2 SS31*
Mrs K.P. Hockridge **Blakes** *(SS395143)*
☎ Milton Damerel 249
*Pleasant, comfortable and well-decorated
house in peaceful setting close to the
River Torridge.*
May–Sep 2hc (1fb) ⊗ nc12 CTV 4P mixed

BURNHOUSE Strathclyde *Ayrs
Map 10 NS35*
Burnhouse Manor *(NS383503)*
☎ Dunlop 406
*Large farmhouse in own grounds. Visible
and well signposted from main Paisley/
Irvine road. Off B706.*
Closed Sun, Mon (Oct–Feb) & Mon
(Mar–Sep) 7hc CTV 40P 🍴 160acres beef
D8.30pm

BURNISTON N Yorks *Map 8 TA09*
Mrs D. Muir **Beaconsfield House**
(NZ014928) South End ☎ Scarborough
870439
*Well-furnished and decorated farmhouse
in village.*
Spring Bank Hol–Sep 3rm ⊗ nc5 TV P
1🛏 🍴 50acres dairy S% ✳B&b£4.50

BUTE, ISLE OF Strathclyde *Bute Map 10*
See Rothesay

BUTTERLEIGH Devon *Map 3 SS90*
Mrs B.J. Hill **Sunnyside** *(ST975088)*
☎ Bickleigh 322
*The farmhouse, built about 1700, is situated
in heart of the Devonshire countryside
3 miles west of Cullompton.*
Closed Xmas 5hc (4fb) CTV 5P 110acres
mixed B&bfr£4.75 Bdi fr£7.50 Wfr£49 ⫽

BUXTON Derbys *Map 7 SK07*
Mrs J. Taylor **Priory Lea Guest House**
(SK059719) 50 White Knowle Rd. ☎3737
*Situated in quiet cul-de-sac surrounded by
wooded countryside. Fine views across
open fields to Grin Low Tower.*
Mar–Oct 10hc (4fb) ♨ CTV 11P 78acres
mixed S% B&b£5.50–£6.50 Bdi£9–£10
W£56–£63 ⫽

CABUS Lancs *Map 7 SD44*
T.&E. Cornthwaite **Wildings** *(SO489479)*
☎ Garstang 3321
*Modernised Victorian farmhouse on A6.
Clean and pleasant with plenty of home
produce used in cooking.*
3hc ⊗ nc12 TV 8P 60acres dairy S%
B&b£5.50

CADELEIGH Devon *Map 3 SS90*
Mrs I. Crimp **West Ridge** *(SS904093)*
☎ Bickleigh 295
*Part 16th-century farmhouse set in a
secluded, wooded valley. Farmhouse fare is
home-produced.*
Apr–Sep 3rm 1hc (1fb) ⊗ nc12 TV 4P
120acres dairy S% B&b£6 Bdi£8 Wfr£48
⫽ D6pm

CADNAM Hants *Map 4 SU21*
Mrs M. Garrett **Copythorne Lodge**
(SU308148) ☎2127
*Two-storey Victorian house set back from
the main road in wooded and rural
surroundings.*
4rm 1🚿🍴 (1fb) TV 6P 🍴 30acres dairy
S% B&bfr£5

Mr & Mrs R.D.L. Dawe **Kents** Winsor Rd,
Winsor ☎3497
*Picturesque thatched farmhouse,
recently renovated. Accommodation of high
standard. 2m NE unclass.*
Etr–Sep 2rm 1🚿🍴 (1fb) CTV 6P 3🛏 🍴
130acres dairy S% B&b£5.75–£6
W£38–£40 Ⓜ

CALDBECK Cumbria *Map 11 NY33*
Mrs D.H. Coulthard **Friar Hall** *(NY324399)*
☎633
*Modernised two-storey stone-built
farmhouse. Well-decorated and contains
good quality furniture. Overlooks river and
village church.*
Apr–Oct 3rm 2hc (1fb) ⊗ CTV 3P river
140acres mixed S% B&b£5.50–£6
Bdi fr£9 D4pm

CAMELFORD Cornwall *Map 2 SX18*
Melorne *(SX099856)* Camelford Station
☎3200
*Situated approximately 1m N of village
near site of old railway station. Fishing and
rough shooting available to guests.*
Etr–Oct 7rm 6hc CTV 10P 100acres dairy

CAPEL BANGOR Dyfed *Map 6 SN68*
Fron *(SN663804)* ☎221
*Elevated, stone-built farmhouse with
splendid views of the Rheidol Valley.*
4hc 5P 100acres mixed

CAPEL GARMON Gwynedd *Map 6 SH85*
Maes y Garnedd *(SH816548)*
☎Betws-y-Coed 428
Isolated farmhouse in elevated position.
2rm ⊗ nc TV P 150acres mixed

CAPEL SEION Dyfed *Map 6 SN67*
L. Davies **Rhoslawdden** *(SN628794)*
Moriah ☎ Aberystwyth 612585
Comfortable farmhouse overlooking fields.
Apr–Oct 3rm 1hc ⊗ CTV 3P 112acres
dairy S% B&b£4.50–£5.50 Bdi£7–£8

CAPUTH Tayside *Perths Map 11 NO04*
Mrs R. Smith **Stralochy** *(NO086413)*
☎250
*Situated in lovely spot looking down a
valley, trees merging in Sidlaw hills.*
May–Oct 3rm ⊗ TV 3P 🚗 239acres
arable S% Bdi fr£6.50 Wfr£45.50 ⫽ D4pm

CAREY Heref & Worcs *Map 3 SO53*
Mrs B. Davidson **Pear Tree** *(SO561306)*
☎201 Closed Xmas 3rm 1hc nc10 CTV
4P 🍴 23½acres mixed S% ✳B&bfr£6.50
Bdi fr£10.50

CARKEEL Cornwall *Map 2 SX46*
Eales *(SX414605)* ☎ Saltash 2865
*Clean and well decorated farmhouse.
Saltash 2 miles.*
4rm TV 6P 11acres dairy

CARNO Powys *Map 6 SN99*
R.G. & P.M. Lewis **Y Grofftydd**
(SN98 1965) ☎274
*Farmhouse is situated off A470 overlooking
typical mid-Wales scenery. Ideal centre*

for walking. Sporting clay-pigeon shoot on premises.
4hc 1🛏(1fb) ❀ CTV 4P 180acres sheep S% B&b£6 Bdi£9 D6pm

CARRONBRIDGE Central *Stirlings Map 11 NS78*
Mr A. Morton **Lochend** *(NS759856)*
☎ Denny 822778
Modernised, 18th-century hill farm. Pleasant farmyard with rose garden in centre. Set in quiet, isolated position.
1½m off unclass rd towards Bannockburn.
2rm 1hc ❀ nc3 TV P 🚗 380acres beef sheep S% B&b£4.75 Bdi£7

CARRUTHERSTOWN Dumfries & Galloway *Dumfriesshire Map 11 NY17*
Mrs J.S. Brown **Domaru** *(NYO93716)*
☎260
Modern, detached, two-storey farmhouse built at side of farm road. About 300 yards from farm buildings. Carrutherstown ½ mile.
3rm 2hc nc10 TV 3P 🚗 150acres dairy S% B&bfr£4.75 Bdifr£7.50 Wfr£42 ⅃ D8pm

CASTLE CARROCK Cumbria *Map 12 NY55*
B.W. Robinson **Gelt Hall** *(NY542554)*
☎Hayton 260
An old-world farmhouse built around a courtyard directly off the main street of this tiny village.
3rm CTV P ♨ 86acres dairy S%
✱B&hfr£4.50 Bdi fr£7 Wfr£49 ⅃ D8pm

CATLOWDY Cumbria *Map 12 NY47*
J.&M. Sisson **Bessiestown** *(NY457768)*
☎ Nicholforest 219
Neat farmhouse, tastefully furnished and

comfortable. Visitors welcome to stroll around farm buildings.
5hc CTV 12P 🚗 53acres sheep S% B&b£5.50–£6 Bdi£10 D1pm

CAWDOR Highland *Nairns Map 14 NH85*
Little Budgate *(NH834503)* ☎267
Small, cottage style farmhouse set amid fields. Cawdor 1 mile.
May–Sep 2rm (A 2hc) ❀ P 50acres arable

CEMMAES Powys *Map 6 SH80*
Mrs D. Evans-Breese **Rhydygwiel** *(SH826056)* ☎ Cemmaes Road 541
Remote, detached, stone-built farmhouse on north side of Dovey Valley. Attractive gardens at back of house.
2rm (1fb) P river 200acres mixed S%
✱B&bfr£4.50

CERNE ABBAS Dorset *Map 3 ST60*
R.&M. Paul **Giants Head** *(ST675029)*
Old Sherborne Rd ☎242
A modernised, detached farmhouse in elevated position at the head of the famous Cerne Giant. Open rural views.
Apr–Oct 5rm 4hc ❀ nc10 TV 10P 4acres sheep S% B&b£5–£5.50 Bdi£8–£8.50 W£45.50–£50 ⅃ D3pm

CHAGFORD Devon *Map 3 SX78*
D.G.&S.A. Bennie **Beechlands** *(SX694877)*
☎3313
Views of Dartmoor, Meldon and Nattadon Common. Also views of Castle Drogo and surrounding countryside.
Closed Xmas wk.3hc (1fb) (A 1🛏) CTV 10P 30acres mixed S% B&b£8 W£50 🅜

CHAPELTOWN Strathclyde *Lanarks Map 11 NS64*

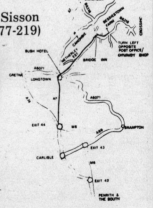

Mr R. Hamilton **East Drumloch**
(NS678521) ☎236
*Large stone-built farmhouse with a modern,
well-furnished interior.*
4rm 2hc (2fb) CTV 10P 260acres beef
mixed S% B&b£5 D6pm

Mrs E. Taylor **Millwell** *(NS653496)*
☎ East Kilbride 43248
*Small, 18th-century farm set in
tree-studded land.*
3rm CTV wk 3hc 94acres dairy S% B&b£4
Bdi£5.50 D5pm

CHAPMANSLADE Wilts *Map 3 ST84*
Mrs M. Hoskins **Spinney** *(ST839480)*
☎412
*Two-storey stone-built farmhouse
surrounded by fields and woodland with
farm buildings at rear.*
Closed Xmas wk 3hc (2fb) CTV 12P ▥
4acres sheep goats S% B&b£5.50–£6
W£33–£38 Ⓜ

CHAWLEIGH Devon *Map 3 SS71*
Toatley *(SS710108)* ☎ Lapford 206
*15th-century farmhouse in mid Devon
within easy reach of the north and south
coasts.*
5rm 4hc CTV 20P 160acres mixed D7pm

CHELVEY Avon *Map 3 ST46*
Midgell *(ST461680)* ☎ Flax Bourton 2213
*A pleasant old farmhouse in a peaceful,
rural setting. Garden with lawns.*
Etr–Sep 3rm 2hc ⊗ TV P ▥ 160acres
arable & beef D7.30pm

CHERITON FITZPAINE Devon
Map 3 SS80
D. M. Tricks **Brindiwell** *(SS896079)*
☎357
*Farmhouse situated on the side of a valley
with views of Exe Valley and Dartmoor.*
4rm (2fb) ⊗ CTV 4P 120acres mixed S%
B&b£5–£6 Bdi£8–£10 W£45–£50 ⌇
D8pm

CHILSWORTHY Devon *Map 2 SS30*
East Youldon *(SS322087)*
☎Bradworthy 322
*Farm located midway between Bradworthy
and Holsworthy.*
mid May–Sep 3hc ⊗ CTV 135acres dairy

CHURCHILL Avon *Map 3 ST45*
Primrose *(ST456609)* ☎852358
*Attractive two-storey, stone-built farmhouse
with a pretty, landscape garden.*
6rm nc5 CTV 6P ▥ 12acres non-working
D6.30pm

CHURCHINFORD Somerset *Map 3 ST21*
M. Palmer **Hunter Lodge** *(ST212144)*
☎Churchstanton 253
*Detached, two-storey farmhouse with slate
roof and large garden.*
4rm 3hc (1fb) CTV 6P 30acres mixed S%
B&b£5–£6 Bdi£7–£8 W£49–£56 ⌇ D5pm

CHURCH STRETTON Shropshire
Map 7 SO49
Mrs Inglis **The Hall** *(SO478925)* Hope
Bowdler (1m E B4371) ☎722041
*The Hall is an old farmhouse which has
recently been completely modernised. It is
set on the edge of the tiny peaceful village
of Hope Bowdler, and surrounded by
beautiful hills.*
Mar–Oct 3hc 1⛌🍴 nc10 4P ▥ 22acres
sheep S% B&b£5–£6

CLACHAN Isle of Skye, Highland
Inverness-shire Map 13 NG46
Mr & Mrs C. MacDonald **Windyridge**
(NG492666) ☎Staffin 222
*Small, white-painted croft with blue-tiled
roof. At north end of Island in a very
pleasant situation.*
May–mid Oct 3⛌🍴 (1fb) ⊗ nc6 TV 10P
10acres mixed S% ✳B&b£4.75–£5
Bdi£6.75–£7.20 D7pm

CLARENCEFIELD Dumfries & Galloway
Dumfriesshire Map 11 NY06
Mrs S. C. Hogg **Kirkbeck** *(NY083705)*
☎284
*Attractive farmhouse with a high standard of
décor. Near to Solway coast. Fishing and
golf. N on A724.*
Apr–Oct 3hc ⊗ CTV 3P ▥ 106acres arable
pigs S% B&b£4.50 Bdi£7 W£45 ⌇ D7pm

CLAVERHAM Avon *Map 3 ST46*
K. Dee-Shapland **Green** *(ST454662)*
☎Yatton 833180
*Long, low farm cottage located in a 'picture
postcard' setting.*
Closed Dec 4rm 3hc (2fb) CTV P 2🏠
5acres non-working S% B&b£6.50

CLAWDDNEWYDD Clwyd *Map 6 SJ05*
G. Williams **Maestyddyw Isa** *(SJ054535)*
☎289
*Old farmhouse filled with antiques. In rural
setting on the outskirts of Cleanog Forest.*
3hc ⊗ nc2 CTV P ▥ 365acres mixed
B&b£5.25–£5.50 Bdi£8–£8.50 Wfr£53 ⌇

CLOVELLY Devon *Map 2 SS32*
Burnstone *(SS325233)* Higher Clovelly
☎219

227

Large, comfortably furnished farmhouse
with open fire in spacious lounge. Good
farmhouse fare.
Etr–Sep 4hc ⊗ nc8 CTV 4P 🚽 240acres
arable & dairy

CLUN Salop *Map 7 SO38*
Llanhedric *(SO283841)* ☎203
Large and well furnished farmhouse with
oak beams and antique furniture.
May–Oct 2rm 1hc ⊗ ⚹ CTV 2P 400acres
dairy & mixed

CLUNTON Salop *Map 7 SO38*
Mrs J. Williams **Hurst Mill** *(SO318811)*
☎Clun 224
Small stone-built farmhouse in picturesque
setting, surrounded by tree-clad hills.
Friendly atmosphere.
4rm ⚹ TV 6P 100acres mixed S%
B&b fr£6 Bdi fr£8.50

CLYRO Powys *Map 3 SO24*
Mrs J. Harris **Crossways** *(SO216459)*
☎Hay-on-Wye 820567
Small farm situated in the hills. Quiet and
peaceful surroundings. Clyro village 1¾
miles.
Apr–Oct 2rm (1fb) ⊗ TV 4P 50acres mixed
S% B&b£4 Bdi£6 W£40 ⚹ D3pm

CLYST ST MARY Devon *Map 3 SX99*
Mrs L. Freemantle **Ivington** *(SX985912)*
☎Topsham 3290
Large brick-built farmhouse surrounded by
lawns and gardens, situated 200yds from
A3052.
Closed Xmas 3hc (2fb) CTV 4P 200acres
dairy S% B&b£4.50–£5 W£31.50 Ⓜ

COLEFORD Devon *Map 3 SS70*
Mrs M. Hockridge **Butsford Barton**
(SS764004) ☎Copplestone 353
New brick-built farmhouse with fine
pastoral views over Devonshire countryside.
Etr–Sep 3rm 2hc (1fb) ⊗ CTV P 156acres
mixed S% B&b£5 Bdi£7.50 W£45 ⚹ D4pm

COMBE MARTIN Devon *Map 2 SS54*
Mr & Mrs M. Stephens **Longlands**
(SS614451) ☎3522
Farmhouse and unspoilt woods and valleys
with fine views.
Etr–mid Oct 6hc (2fb) TV 15P 🚽 25acres
mixed S% ✱B&b£4.20 Bdi£6.56–£7.09
W£44.10–£48.30 ⚹

COMRIE Tayside *Perths Map 11 NN72*
Mrs J. H. Rimmer **West Ballindalloch**
(NN744262) ☎282

Cosy, small farmhouse with neat garden set
amid hills in secluded glen. Comrie 4 miles.
Apr–Sep 2rm (1fb) CTV 3P 1500acres
sheep S% B&b£4.50–£5

COOKLEY Suffolk *Map 5 TM37*
Mr & Mrs A. T. Veasy **Green** *(TM337772)*
☎Linstead 209
17th-century farmhouse with exposed
timbers in an area of rural peace and quiet.
Friendly atmosphere.
Mar–Nov 3hc ⊗ nc8 TV 4P 45acres mixed
S% B&b£6 Bdi£9 W£63 ⚹ D2pm

COOMBE Cornwall *Map 2 SW95*
Mrs J. Scott **Treway** *(SW945505)*
☎St Austell 882236
Pleasant, comfortable farmhouse in
isolated rural setting about 8 miles from
St Austell.
Etr–Oct 3rm 2hc (2fb) CTV 4P 🚽 160acres
dairy S% B&b fr£5 Wfr£35 Ⓜ

COTLEIGH Devon *Map 3 ST20*
Mrs J. Boyland **Barn Park** *(ST218050)*
☎Upottery 297
Comfortably furnished farmhouse offering
tasty country fare.
Mar–Sep 2rm (2fb) ⊗ CTV 3P 80acres
beef dairy S% B&bfr£4.50 Bdi fr£8 Wfr£45
⚹ D5pm

COVERACK BRIDGES *(Nr Helston)*
Cornwall *Map 2 SW63*
Mr & Mrs E. Lawrence **Boscadjack**
(SW673311) (2½m N of Helston, off B3207)
☎Helston 2086
Modernised farmhouse set in 52 acres of
dairy farmland, situated in the Cober Valley
amidst delightful, unspoiled countryside
2 miles from Helston.
Etr–Oct 4hc (2fb) ⊗ CTV P 🚽 52acres dairy
S% ✱B&b£4.60–£5.18 Bdi£8.34–£9.15
W£57.50–£63.25 ⚹ (W only end Jul–Aug)

CRACKINGTON HAVEN Cornwall
Map 2 SX19
Mrs M. Knight **Manor** *(SX159962)*
☎St Gennys 304
Attractive gardens with beautiful view in
secluded position 1 mile from beach. Most
sports in area, bathing, fishing, golf, gliding,
riding, walking, bird watching, pleasure boat
trips, museums.
2rm 1hc ⊗ nc TV 6P 180acres arable
mixed S% B&b£6 Bdi£8 W£70

CREDITON Devon *Map 3 SS80*
Mr & Mrs M. Pennington **Woolsgrove**

(SS793028) ☎Copplestone 246
17th-century farmhouse overlooking acres of grassland.
Feb–Nov 3rm 2hc (1fb) ⌁ TV 4P 160acres
mixed S% ✳B&b£4.75–£5 Bdi£7 D8pm

CROESGOCH Dyfed *Map 2 SM83*
Mr & Mrs A. Charles **Torbant**
(SM845307) ☎276
Well-kept farmhouse, tastefully furnished. Situated in pleasant spot overlooking open country.
23 May–19 Sep rs Etr–22 May &
20–30 Sep (B&b only) 11hc (A 2⇌🍴)
(5fb) ⌁ CTV 30P 🛏 150acres arable beef sheep S% B&b£6.50–£7.50
Bdi£11.50–£13 W£75–£82 ⌿ D8pm

Mrs M. B. Jenkins **Trerarched**
(SM831306) ☎310
Farm overlooks St George's Channel. Ideal for touring south-west Wales and coast.
8hc (3fb) CTV 20P 🛏 sea 139acres arable
S% ✳B&b£5.25 Bdi£9.20 D6.45pm

CROIK Highland *Ross & Crom Map 14 NH49*
Mrs K. M. Moffat **Forest** *(NH454914)*
☎The Craigs 322
Two-into-one 1870 farmhouse. Beautiful location but very isolated. 10 miles off single track road from Ardgay.
Apr–Oct 4rm (1fb) ⌁ TV 4P 3000acres
sheep B&b£3.50–£3.75 Bdifr£7 D9pm

CROMHALL Avon *Map 3 ST69*
Mrs S. Scolding **Varley** *(ST699905)*
Talbot End ☎Wickwar 292
Spacious, two-storey, stone-built farmhouse with garden. Well maintained and neatly decorated throughout.
Etr–Sep 4hc (4fb) ⌁ CTV 6P 🛏 75acres
dairy S% B&b£6 Bdi£8.50 W£57 ⌿
(W only Aug) D3.30pm

CROOK Cumbria *Map 7 SD49*
Mrs I. D. Scales **Greenbank**
(SD 462953) ☎Staveley 821216
Attractive farmhouse near village centre. Pleasant gardens. Mainly dairy plus small mushroom farm.
2 Jan–20 Dec 5hc (2fb) nc10 CTV 6P 🛏
14½acres non-working S% B&b£5–£6
Bdi£9–£10 D5pm

M. Clarke **Warriner Yeat** *(SD438950)*
☎Windermere 3828
Large, attractive house in small garden. Pleasant setting with fine views.
May–Sep 3rm 2hc ⌁ 6P 75acres mixed
B&b£3.50–£4.50

CRUCKTON Salop *Map 7 SJ41*
Woodfield *(SJ432108)* ☎Hanwood 249
Large, modern, detached farmhouse with neat gardens.
3rm ⌁ nc7 CTV 3P 83acres

CRYMYCH Dyfed *Map 2 SN13*
Mr & Mrs Hazelden **Felin Tŷgwyn**
(SN162355) ☎Crosswell 603
Approximately 2 miles from Crymych, at the foot of the Preseli Mountains, surrounded by farmland. Within easy reach of Newport beach, Cardigan, Carmarthen and Haverfordwest.
6rm 5hc (A 1hc) (2fb) ⌂ CTV 8P 🛏
8acres beef dairy poultry B&b£5.75–£7
Bdi£8.75–£10 W£57.42–£65.22 ⌿
(W only Jun–Aug)

CUBERT Cornwall *Map 2 SW75*
Mrs F. Whybrow **Treworgans**
(SW787589) ☎Crantock 200
Detached bungalow, situated approximately 1m from the village of Cubert.
Closed Xmas 5hc CTV 6P 72acres mixed
S% ✳B&b£4 Bdi£6.50 W£45 ⌿ D5pm

CULLODEN MOOR Highland *Inverness-shire Map 14 NH74*
Mrs E. M. C. Alexander **Culdoich**
(NH755435) ☎268
18th-century, two-storey farmhouse in isolated position near Culloden battlefield and Clava standing stones.
Etr–Oct 2rm (1fb) TV P 200acres mixed S%
B&b£4.50–£5 Bdi£6.50–£7 W£45 –£50
⌿ D7pm

CULLOMPTON Devon *Map 3 ST00*
Mrs A. C. Cole **Five Bridges** *(ST026095)*
☎33453
Well-maintained, brick-built farmhouse. Clean and well decorated.
Closed Xmas 5rm 4hc (3fb) CTV 6P 1🏠
22acres non-working S% B&b£4.50
Bdi£7 W£46 ⌿ D noon

CURRY RIVEL Somerset *Map 3 ST32*
Mrs M. Ribbons **Hillards** *(ST385249)*
☎Langport 251737
Well-furnished farmhouse, private tennis court and sometimes horse-riding available.
4hc nc3 CTV 20P 🛏 8acres calf rearing S%
B&b£6

CURY Cornwall *Map 2 SW62*
Mrs R. E. U. Benney **Nanplough**
(SW687215) ☎Mullion 240232
Attractive, comfortable farmhouse. Access via ½ mile gravel lane.

229

Etr–Sep 5rm 4hc (1fb) ✍ nc5 CTV 4P 🍴
51acres mixed S% B&b£5–£5.50 Bdi£10
W£50 ⅃ D4.30pm

CURY CROSS LANES Cornwall
Map 2 SW62
Mrs M. F. Osborne **Polglase** (SW286213)
☎Mullion 240469
5 miles from Helston.
Etr–Sep 6rm 5hc (2fb) ✍ CTV 4P 70acres
mixed

CUSHNIE Grampian Aberdeens
Map 15 NJ51
Brae Smithy Croft (NJ520108)
☎Muir of Fowlis 215
Approach from A980 (3m) W or B9119
(3m) N.
Apr–Sep 3rm CTV P 🍴 20acres arable

CYNWYD Clwyd Map 6 SJ04
B. E. Williams **Ceamawr** (SJ048419)
☎Corwen 2421
Pleasant, two-storey, stone-built farmhouse
in an elevated position.
5hc (1fb) ✍ CTV P 🍴 60acres dairy

DALGUISE Tayside Perths Map 14 NN94
Easter Dalguise (NN994470)
☎Dunkeld 206
18th century farmhouse set on hillside
overlooking valley of the Tay and hills
beyond.
May–Sep 2rm ✍ nc3 4P 🍴 river 130acres
mixed D6pm

DALWOOD (Nr Axminster) Devon
Map 3 ST20
Mrs S. W. Cobley **Elford** (ST258004)
☎Axminster 32415
17th-century farmhouse in country setting.
Panoramic, pastoral views.
Mar–Oct 5rm 4hc 2⇔🖩 (2fb) ✍ TV 8P
37acres beef dairy sheep S% B&b£6–£7
Bdi£8.50–£10.50 W£56–£70 ⅃ D6pm

DIDDLEBURY Shropshire Map 7 SO58
Mrs E Wilkes **Glebe** (SO507856)
☎Munslow 221 Mar–Nov 3rm 2hc ✍
nc12 TV 6P 2🏠 123acres beef sheep S%
B&b£8 Bdi£12 W£86 Ⅿ Dnoon

DILWYN Heref & Worcs Map 3 SO45
Mrs J. Anthony **Bedford House**
(SO435536) ☎Pembridge 260 Etr–Oct
3hc (2fb) TV 3P 🍴 17acres mixed
B&b£6–£6.50 Bdi£9–£9.50 W£56 ⅃
D6.30pm

DOCKLOW Heref & Worcs Map 3 SO55
West End (SO558578) ☎Steens
Bridge 256
Large, three-storey 17th-century farmhouse.
Solid oak floors and huge doors. A listed
building with large garden and coarse
fishing pool.
May–Oct 4rm ✍ TV 6P 91acres beef sheep
D5pm

DOLGELLAU Gwynedd Map 6 SH71
Mr & Mrs T. Price **Glyn** (SH704178)
☎422286
Stone-built farmhouse of historical interest
with oak beams, floors and doors. Well
situated for coastal resorts.
Mar–Nov rs Aug–Nov (B&b only) 5rm 4hc
(1fb) CTV P 140acres mixed S%
B&b£5–£5.50 Bdi£7.50–£8 W£40–£45 ⅃

DORNIE Highland Ross & Crom
Map 14 NG82

M. Macrae **Bungalow** (NG871272) ☎231
Farmhouse situated on main A87.
May–Oct 3hc (1fb) ✍ nc5 5P lake mixed
S% B&b£5–£5.50

DOUNBY Orkney Map 16 HY22
Chinyan (HY307200) ☎Harray 372
Small farm cottage overlooking Loch
Harray. Free loch fishing.
2rm ✍ ᐁ TV P lake 342acres arable beef
D2pm

DRIMPTON Dorset Map 3 ST40
Mr G.W. Johnson **Axe** (ST415061)
☎Crewkerne 72422
Stone-built, detached, double-fronted
farmhouse standing in isolated rural
position.
3hc ✍ nc12 TV 6P 🍴 160acres arable
dairy S% B&b£6.50–£7.50

DULFORD Devon Map 3 ST00
Mrs M. Broom **Nap** (ST069065)
☎Kentisbeare 287
Well-appointed farmhouse set in hamlet of
Dulford on main road to Cullompton.
Closed Xmas 5hc (2fb) TV 4P 🍴 36acres
mixed S% B&b£4.50 Bdi£6.50 W£40
Ⅿ Dnoon

DULVERTON Somerset Map 3 SS92
Warmor (SS944259) ☎23479
Very old farmhouse with a lot of character.
Parts are 400 years old.
May–Sep 3hc ✍ CTV 4🏠 70acres mixed
D5pm

DUNLOP Strathclyde Ayrs Map 10 NS44
Old Struther (NS412496) ☎346
Large farmhouse in its own gardens.
On edge of Dunlop village.
6hc TV 6P 50acres non-working

DUNSYRE Strathclyde Lanarks
Map 11 NT04
Mr Armstrong **Dunsyre Mains** (NT074482)
☎251 Mar–Oct 3rm 2hc (1fb) ✍ CTV P
400acres beef sheep S% B&bfr£4.75
Bdi fr£8.25 Wfr£57 ⅃ D7pm

DUNVEGAN Isle of Skye, Highland
Inverness-shire Map 13 NG24
Mr A. Munro **Feorlig House** (NG297422)
☎232
Two-storey, white-painted farmhouse dating
from 1820. Situated off main road looking
on to Loch Cavoy.
Jun–Oct 3rm TV 3P sea 1112acres beef
sheep S% B&b£5 Bdi£8 W£56 ⅃

EAGLESFIELD Dumfries & Galloway
Dumfriesshire Map 11 NY27
Mrs S. Johnstone **Newlands** (NY240741)
☎Kirtlebridge 269
Attractive white-faced farmhouse in
secluded position at end of ½ mile drive.
May–Oct 2hc (1fb) ✍ 2P 🍴 200acres
mixed S% B&b£5 Bdi£7.50

EAST CALDER Lothian Midlothian
Map 11 NT06
Mr & Mrs D.R. Scott **Whitecroft**
(NT095682) 7 Raw Holdings ☎Mid
Calder 881810
Surrounded by farmland and only ½ mile
from Almondell Country Park. Good views
of Pentlands to the south and Ochils and
Forth road bridge to the north.
3rm (1fb) ✍ 4P 🍴 5acres S% B&b£5 W£35

EAST MEON Hants *Map 4 SU62*
Mrs P.M. Berry **Giants** *(SU696207)*
Harvesting Ln ☎205
*Modern farmhouse, set in ½acre. Views -
from all rooms of the surrounding
countryside. Queen Elizabeth Country Park
of 1,400acres, with facilities for pony-
trekking and grass skiing, is nearby.*
Mar–Oct 3rm 2hc 1⇦🍴(1fb) ⊗ CTV 4P
🍴 55acres arable mixed S% B&b£4.50–£6
Bdi£8–£9.50 W£52–£63 ⅄ D4pm

EAST MEY Highland *Caithness
Map 15 ND37*
Mrs M. Morrison **Glenearn** *(ND307739)*
☎ Barrock 608
*Small croft situated on the main coast
road. Thurso 15 miles.*
Apr–Oct 4rm 2hc 2⇦🍴(2fb) CTV 6P 🍴
sea 7½acres arable sheep S% B&b£4.75–£5
Bdi£7.50–£8 Dnoon

EDINBURGH Lothian *Midlothian
Map 11 NT27*
Mrs Jack **Tower Mains** *(NT267693)*
Liberton Brae ☎031-664 1765
*Farmhouse in its own grounds within
residential area, but backed by farmland.
Overlooks golf course, city centre at
Arthur's Seat.*
5hc (2fb) CTV 20P 🍴 200acres arable
non-working S% B&b£4.80–£5.50

EDLINGHAM Northumb *Map 12 NU10*
M. Oates **Lumbylaw** *(NU115096)*
☎ Whittingham 277
*Modernised stone-built farmhouse in rural
surroundings.*
May–Oct 3hc (1fb) ⚭ CTV 4P 4🏠 🍴
900acres S% ✳B&b£5.50–£6.50
Bdi£8.50–£9.50 W£56–£60 ⅄
(W only Jul & Aug) D6.30pm

EGERTON Kent *Map 5 TQ94*
Mr & Mrs J.T. Lamb **Mundy Bois House**
(TQ906456) ☎ Pluckley 436
*Mundy Bois is a 15th-century half-timbered
farmhouse with beamed sitting room and
an open fire. Views from the bedrooms are
of the hills behind the house.*
2rm 1hc (1fb) TV 3P 🍴 12acres mixed
S% ✳B&b£7 Bdi£10 W£70 ⅄ D9am

EGLINGHAM Northumb *Map 12 NU11*
A.I. Easton **West Ditchburn** *(NU131207)*
☎ Powburn 337
*Comfortable farmhouse with garden
available to guests. Overlooking unspoilt
countryside.*
Feb–Nov 4rm 3hc (2fb) ⚭ CTV 10P 🍴

mixed S% B&b£6–£6.50 Bdi£9.50–£10
D7.30pm

EGLOSHAYLE Cornwall *Map 2 SX07*
F. D. Acocks **Croanford** *(SX034715)* Ford
☎ St Mabyn 349
*Small, compact farmhouse in pleasant
countryside. Stream in side garden.
Wadebridge 2½ mile.*
May–Oct 3rm ⊗ nc3 CTV 2P 1🏠 113acres
mixed S% B&b£5.50 Bdi£7.50 W£50
⅄ D5pm

ELLESMERE Salop *Map 7 SJ33*
Mereside *(SJ408343)* ☎2404
*Three-storey farmhouse 17th-century in
parts. Close to local beauty spot, The Mere.
Bird Sanctuary and abundant wild life.*
5hc TV 🏠 55acres dairy

ELSDON Northumb *Map 12 NY99*
Mr & Mrs T. Carruthers **Dunns**
(NY937969) ☎ Rothbury 40219
*Old farmhouse in quiet position amongst
the Cheviot Hills and Coquet Valley.*
3rm 2hc ⊗ CTV P 1,000acres mixed S%
B&bfr£5.50

Mr C. Armstrong **Raylees** *(NY926915)*
☎ Otterburn 20287
Comfortable, well-furnished farmhouse.
4rm 1hc (1fb) ⊗ nc3 CTV 4P 🍴 706acres
beef sheep S% B&b£5–£5.50

ETTINGTON Warwicks *Map 4 SP24*
Mr & Mrs B. Wakeham **Whitfield**
(SP265506) Warwick Rd
☎ Stratford-on-Avon 740260
*Pleasant house set in active farm with a
wide variety of animals for interest.*
Apr–Aug 3hc ⊗ CTV 3P 220acres mixed
S% B&b£4.25–£4.75

ETTRICK Borders *Selkirks Map 11 NT21*
Mrs E. Hall **Thirlestane Hope** *(NT285167)*
☎ Ettrick Valley 229.
*Quaint, white-painted farm in border hill
country. Small burn flows through farmland.
Good access by ¾-mile track.*
Feb–Nov 2⇦🍴(2fb) CTV 2P 900acres
sheep S% B&b£5.50–£6 Bdi£8.50–£9
D6.30pm

EXETER Devon *Map 3 SX99*
Hill Barton *(SX956932)* 133 Hill Barton Rd
☎67630
*Attractive, well built farmhouse with small,
trim garden and lawn. Situated on Exeter
bypass (A30).*
Closed Xmas 7hc TV 15P 80acres mixed

EXMOUTH Devon *Map 3 SY08*
Mrs A.J. Skinner **Maer** *(SY018803)*
Maer Ln ☎3651
*In large garden which has views of sea and
Haldon Hills. Approximately 5 min walk to
beach and 20 min walk to town.*
3rm (2fb) ❀ TV 3P ⊞ 300acres arable
beef dairy S% B&b£5

Mrs J. Reddaway **Quentance** *(SY037812)*
Salterton Rd ☎ Budleigh Salterton 2733
*Superior-style farmhouse. Bedrooms
overlook south-east Devon coastline.*
Apr–Nov 3hc (1fb) ❀ nc4 CTV P sea
230acres mixed S% B&b£5.50 Bdi£8
D6.30pm

FALFIELD Avon *Map 3 ST69*
Mrs D. S. E. Wood **Green** *(ST687943)*
☎260319
*A two-storey, colour-washed, stone-built
farmhouse. Lawns, hard tennis court and
swimming pool in the grounds.*
Closed Xmas 6hc (2fb) CTV 10P
non-working S% B&b£5.50–£7
Bdi£9.50–£11 W£60–£70 ⱡ D3pm

FARRINGTON GURNEY Avon
Map 3 ST65
Mrs D. H. Davis **Hayboro** *(ST628555)*
☎Temple Cloud 52342
*Small farmhouse adjacent to the Farrington
Inn. Garden adjoining the farm and fields.*
Closed Dec–14 Jan 3rm (1fb) 5P 78acres
dairy S% B&b£6–£7.50 Bdi£10–£11.50
W£40–£51 M D10am

FELMINGHAM Norfolk *Map 9 TG22*
Felmingham Hall *(TG245275)*
☎Swanton Abbot 228
*Large, interesting old manor house.
Remote but near North Walsham. Big
rooms comfortably appointed.*
11hc 5⇩⊞ nc15 CTV 100P 2🏠 ⊞
60acres sheep D6pm

FINTRY Central *Stirlings Map 11 NS68*
Mrs M. Mitchell **Nether Glinns**
(NS606883) ☎207
*Well-maintained farmhouse situated among
rolling hills. Access via signposted ½-mile
gravel drive.*
May–Sep 3rm (1fb) CTV P 2🏠 150acres
mixed S% B&bfr£4.50

FLASH (Buxton, Derbys) Staffs
Map 7 SK06
Mrs C. M. Povey **Far Brook** *(SK017670)*
Quarnford ☎Buxton 3085
*Old stone-built farmhouse situated in
picturesque and peaceful surroundings in
upper reaches of Dane Valley.*
Etr–Oct 3rm 2hc (1fb) nc5 P 2🏠 65acres
beef S% B&bfr£5.65 Bdifr£8.50 Wfr£58 ⱡ

FORDEN Powys *Map 7 SJ20*
Mrs K. Owens **Llettygynfach** *(SJ255022)*
☎272
*Views of Shropshire Hills and Powys Valley
from farmhouse.*
2rm 1hc (1fb) CTV P ⊞ 220acres dairy
sheep S% B&bfr£5 Bdifr£8

FORDOUN Grampian *Kincardines
Map 15 NO77*
Mrs M. Anderson **Ringwood** *(NO743774)*
(2m N on A966) ☎Auchenblae 313
*Small modernised villa in open setting
amidst farmland and with its own neat
garden and outhouse. Very high standard of
décor and furnishings. 1 mile north-west of*

village on B966.
Closed Nov–Mar 4hc (1fb) ❀ CTV 4P ⊞
17acres arable croft S% B&b£6 Bdi£9
W£60 ⱡ D6pm

FOWEY Cornwall *Map 2 SX15*
Mrs M. Dunn **Trezare** *(SX112538)* ☎3485
*Farmhouse conveniently situated 1 mile
from Fowey. Pleasant atmosphere and good
farmhouse fare.*
Jun–Oct 3rm 2hc ❀ CTV 4P sea 230acres
mixed S% B&b£6.50–£7 W£45.50–£49 M

FRESSINGFIELD Suffolk *Map 5 TM27*
Mrs R. Willis **Priory House** *(TM256770)*
Priory Rd ☎254
*Attractive 400-year-old brick-built
farmhouse with beamed interior. Quality
furniture. Secluded garden. Ideal touring
centre.*
Closed Xmas 4rm 3hc ❀ nc8 CTV 6P ⊞
2acres pig breeding S% B&b fr£10
Bdifr£12.50 Wfr£80 ⱡ

FYVIE Grampian *Aberdeens
Map 15 NJ73*
Mrs A. Runcie **Macterry** *(NJ786424)*
☎555
*Two-storey farmhouse with adjoining farm
buildings in rural setting.*
May–Oct 2hc (2fb) ❀ nc3 CTV 3P
105acres mixed S% B&b£5 Bdi£10
W£35–£52.50 ⱡ D am

GARTHMYL Powys *Map 7 SO19*
P. L. Jones **Trwstllewelyn** *(SO189984)*
☎Berriew 295
*Spacious 17th-century farmhouse,
traditionally furnished with some antiques
and open fires in the recently-discovered
and restored inglenook fireplace.*
Apr–Oct 5rm 4hc (1fb) ❀ TV 6P
300acres mixed S% B&b£6 Bdi£10 W£60
ⱡ D5pm

GATEHEAD Strathclyde *Ayrshire
Map 10 NS33*
Mrs R. Elliot **Old Rome** *(NS393360)*
☎Drybridge 850265
*Situated in a completely rural setting
300 yards off the A759 to Troon (5 miles)
Farmhouse has charm and character and
dates from 17th-century.*
Closed Oct 4hc (1fb) ❀🏠 CTV 14P 4🏠 ⊞
12acres non-working S% ✱B&b£5–£6.50
Bdi£7–£10 D9pm

GATE HELMSLEY N Yorks *Map 8 SE65*
Mrs K. M. Sykes **Lime Field** *(SE693534)*
Scoreby ☎York 489224
*Comfortably-furnished farmhouse with big
garden, set in the largely agricultural
Yorkshire Wolds.*
Mar–Oct 4rm 2hc (3fb) ❀ nc3 CTV 4P
125acres arable beef S%
✱B&b£5.50–£6.50

GEDNEY HILL Lincs *Map 8 TF31*
Mrs C. Cave **Sycamore** *(TF336108)*
☎Whaplode Drove 445
*Situated on the edge of the village
overlooking open countryside and
surrounded by trees.*
Closed Xmas 3rm (2fb) CTV 6P 1🏠 ⊞
75acres mixed S% B&b£7 Bdi£10.50
D4pm

GIGGLESWICK N Yorks *Map 7 SD86*
Mrs Bessie T. Hargreaves **Close House**

(SD801634) ☎Settle 3540
*17th-century farmhouse with tree-lined
private drive. Well-kept gardens. River
bathing and fishing nearby.*
May–mid Sep 4hc ⊗ nc 6P 230acres dairy
B&b£11.50 Bdi£19.55 W£126 ⌇

GLAN CONWY Gwynedd *Map 6 SH87*
Mrs C. Williams **Plas Ucha** *(SH818752)*
☎276
*Elizabethan farmhouse of historical interest
with oak beams, floors and doors. Well
situated for coastal resorts.*
Jul–Aug 3rm ⊗ nc 6P 250acres beef sheep

GLAN-YR-AFON Gwynedd *Map 6 SJO4*
Mr J. G. Jones **Llawr-Bettws** *(SJO16424)*
Bala Rd ⌂Maerdy (Clwyd) 224
Rambling, stone-built farmhouse with

*pleasant, homely atmosphere. At Druid
traffic lights on A5 follow A494 Bala road
for 2m.*
4rm 3hc (A 2rm 1hc 1⇨🛁) (2fb) ⊗ CTV
6P 2🏠 ♨ 72acres mixed sheep S%
B&b£5 Bdi£6.50–£7.50 W£40–£52 ⌇
D9.30pm

GLASBURY Powys *Map 3 SO13*
Mrs B. Eekley **Ffordd Fawr** *(SO192398)*
☎Glasbury 332
*1m E of Glasbury-on-Wye on B4350
towards Hay-on-Wye.*
Feb–Nov 2hc ⊗ TV 4P ♨ 280acres mixed
S% ✳B&b£5 Bdi£9 D8pm

GLASTONBURY Somerset *Map 3 ST53*
Mrs H. Tinney **Cradlebridge** *(ST477385)*
☎31827

*Large, renovated farmhouse with vegetable
and fruit gardens.*
Closed Xmas 4hc (1fb) TV 6P ⅏ 165acres
dairy S% B&b£5.50–£6.50 Bdi£10–£12
W£60–£72 ⱇ D noon

GLENMAVIS Strathclyde *Lanarks
Map 11 NS76*
Mrs P. Dunbar **Braidenhill** *(NS742673)*
☎Glenboig 872319
*300-year-old farmhouse on the outskirts of
Coatbridge. About ½ mile from town
boundary N off B803.*
3hc (1fb) CTV 4P ⅏ 50acres arable S%
B&b£6

GRAMPOUND Cornwall *Map 2 SW94*
Mrs L. M. Wade **Tregidgeo** *(SW960473)*
☎St Austell 882450
*Tregidgeo is a comfortably-furnished
farmhouse in a beautiful secluded and
peaceful setting.*
Mid May–Sep 4rm 3hc (2fb) ⊗ TV 4P
216acres mixed ✳B&b fr£5 Bdi fr£8
W fr£53 ⱇ D 10am

Mrs M. H. Thomas **Ventonwyn**
(SW957501) ☎St Austell 882349
*Well preserved, 13th-century farmhouse
¾ mile from the main St Austell to Truro
road.*
Etr–Oct 4rm 2hc (2fb) ⊗ CTV 6P 177acres
mixed S% ✳B&b£4

GULVAL Cornwall *Map 2 SW43*
Mrs J Osborne **Kenegie Home**
(SW481327) ☎Penzance 2515
*15th-century, 'olde-worlde' farmhouse
1 mile from Penzance. Accent on good
farmhouse food.*
May–Sep rs Apr & Oct (B&b only) 3hc
(1fb) ⊗ CTV 3P 200acres arable beef S%
B&b£7–£10 Bdi£10–£12 W£60–£75 ⱇ
D noon

GUNNISLAKE Cornwall *Map 2 SX47*
Cmdr W. R. Fowler RN **Whimple**
(SX428708) ☎Tavistock 832526
*Attractive 17th-century farmhouse. Oak
beams and panelling in lounge. On banks
of River Tamar.*
Closed Xmas 3hc ⊗ TV 6P river 50acres
dairy S% B&b£7.50 Bdi£10 W£60 ⱇ D5pm

GWEEK Cornwall *Map 2 SW72*
Tregoon *(SW699271)* ☎Mawgan
(Helston) 286
*Recently built bungalow in a convenient
location about 1 mile west of the village.*
Apr–Sep 4rm 3hc ⊗ CTV 6P river 54acres
arable & beef D5pm

GWINEAR Cornwall *Map 2 SW53*
Mrs R. Rapson **Chycoose** *(SW608367)*
33 Wall Rd ☎Leedstown 357
*Modern farmhouse situated in old Cornish
village. Small front garden. Home-produced
farmhouse meals.*
Mar–Oct 3rm 2hc ⊗ nc10 TV 3P ⅏
40acres mixed ✳B&b fr£5 Bdi fr£7 W fr£45 ⱇ

GWYDDELWERN Clwyd *Map 6 SJ04*
Mrs E. M. Lloyd **Bryngwenalt**
(SJ067473) ☎Corwen 2312
*Situated in a rural setting with excellent
views of countryside.*
Spring Bank Hol–Sep 3rm ⊗ nc5 CTV 3P
110acres mixed S% B&b£4.25 W£28 Ⓜ

GWYSTRE Powys *Map 3 SO06*
Mrs C. Drew **Gwystre** *(SO070656)*
☎Penybont 316

*Typical Welsh hill farm near to Elan Valley
reservoir.*
Mar–Oct 2rm (1fb) ⚭ TV P 150acres mixed
S% B&b£5–£5.50 Bdi£7–£8 D5pm

HABBERLEY Salop *Map 7 SJ40*
P. J. Madely **Hall** *(SJ397036)*
☎Pontesbury 689
*Farmhouse reputed to be 16th-century.
Large comfortable rooms with antique
furniture.*
Closed Dec 3rm 1hc (1fb) ⊗ 4P 138acres
mixed S% B&b£4 Bdi£7 W£45 ⱇ

HAILSHAM E Sussex *Map 5 TQ50*
Mr & Mrs S. A.'L. Rose **Chicheley**
(TQ576103) Hempstead Ln ☎841253
*Large house divided in two; set in typical
Sussex countryside.*
3hc (2fb) ⊗ nc3 TV 6P 5½acres poultry S%
B&b£6

HALFWAY HOUSE Salop *Map 7 SJ31*
Mrs E. Morgan **Willows** *(SJ342115)*
☎233
*Small farm cottage well situated for those
travelling to Wales. Cottage surrounded by
Long Mountain and Middlebar Hills.*
Mar–Oct 3rm 1hc (1fb) nc8 CTV 10P
35acres beef dairy S% B&b£4.50–£5.50
Bdi£6.50–£7.50 D4pm

HALSTOCK Dorset *Map 3 ST50*
Mrs M. A. Champion **New Inn**
(ST532036) ☎Corscombe 256
*17th-century farmhouse, previously an inn,
in quiet situation.*
Apr–Oct 3rm (1fb) ⊗ TV 5P 55½acres
mixed S% B&b£5.50–£6.50

HALTWHISTLE Northumb *Map 12 NY76*
Mrs J. W. Laidlow **White Craig**
(NY713649) Shield Hill ☎20565
*Stone-built Georgian-style bungalow in an
elevated position, providing excellent views.
Within walking distance of Hadrian's Wall.*
Closed Xmas 3hc ⊗ nc10 CTV 3P ⅏
17acres mixed S% B&b fr£5.25

HANMER Clwyd *Map 7 SJ44*
C. Sumner & F. Williams-Lee **Buck**
(SJ435424) (on A525 Whitchurch (7m)–
Wrexham (9m) road ☎339 4hc ⊗ CTV 10P
⅏ 7acres small holding S% B&b£5.40–£69
Bdi£8.10–£9 W£56.70–£63 ⱇ

HARBERTON Devon *Map 3 SX75*
Mrs I. P. Steer **Preston** *(SX777587)*
☎Totnes 862235
*Old farmhouse on outskirts of quaint and
attractive village. Totnes about 2½ miles.*
Apr–Sep 3hc (1fb) ⊗ nc3 CTV 2P 200acres
dairy mixed B&b£5.50 Bdi£8 W£50 ⱇ

R. Rose **Tristford** *(SX780594)* ☎Totnes
862418
*Charming house with 'olde-worlde'
atmosphere. Good centre for touring the
coast between Plymouth and Torbay.*
3hc ⊗ nc CTV 5🅿 ⅏ 150acres mixed S%
B&b£4.50 Bdi£7.50 D6pm

HARMER HILL Salop *Map 7 SJ52*
Mrs M. Williams **Hill** *(SJ487232)*
Newton-on-the-Hill ☎Clive 273
*Two-storey, red-brick house in quiet rural
situation.*
Etr–Oct 2rm ⊗ nc3 TV P 76acres mixed
S% B&b£4.50–£5.50 Bdi£6.50–£7.50

HARRIS, ISLE OF Western Isles
Inverness-shire
See Scarista

HARROP FOLD Lancs *Map 7 SD74*
Mr & Mrs P. Wood **Harrop Fold**
(SD746492) ☎Bolton-By-Bowland 600
*Lancashire longhouse built around 17th
century. Nestling in pleasant quiet valley.
Excellent accommodation, interesting
meals.*
3⇦🛏 (A 2⇦🛏) ⊛ nc12 CTV 10P 🍴
280acres beef sheep S% B&b£8.25–£9
Bd£14.25–£16 W£96–£103 ⨰ D5pm

HARTLAND Devon *Map 2 SS22*
Edistone *(SS249219)* ☎212
*Isolated farmhouse offering wholesome
country fare.*
mid May–mid Sep 3rm ⊛ CTV 3P
80acres mixed

Holloford *(SS289236)* ☎275
*Two-storey, stone-built Devonshire
farmhouse in rather isolated countryside.
Oak beams in bedrooms. Near Hartland
Point.*
Spring Bank Hol–mid Sep 3hc CTV P
200acres arable & dairy

Mettaford *(SS284245)* ☎249
*Attractive Georgian farmhouse, 2 miles
from the village of Hartland. In woodland
setting with panoramic views of coastline
and Lundy.*
5rm ⚭ CTV 10P 17acres mixed D8.30pm

HATHERSAGE Derbys *Map 8 SK28*
Mr & Mrs T. C. Wain **Highlow Hall**
(SK219802) ☎Hope Valley 50393
16th-century house of character. Well-
*furnished interior containing several
antiques. Isolated position south of
Hathersage.*
Etr–Oct 6hc (2fb) CTV 12P 200acres beef
sheep S% ✳B&b£8 Bd£12.50 W£80 ⨰
D6pm

HAUGH OF URR Dumfries & Galloway
Kirkcudbrights Map 11 NX86
Mrs G. Macfarlane **Markfast** *(NX817682)*
☎220
*Typical modernised farmhouse. Situated at
the gateway to Galloway's historical and
picturesque scenery with wide choice of
beaches, fishing, etc.*
(3fb) ⊛ TV 3P 140acres beef S% B&b£5
Bd£7 W£49 ⨰ D4pm

HAVERFORDWEST Dyfed *Map 2 SM91*
Mrs J. H. Evans **Cuckoo Grove**
(SM928162) ☎2429
*Comfortable accommodation for non-
smokers only, in recently refurbished
farmhouse. Swimming pool in grounds and
views of the distant Prescelly Mountains.*
Apr–Oct 5hc ⊛ CTV P 🍴 206acres dairy S%
B&b£5–£5.50 W£33–£37 Ⓜ

HELENSBURGH Strathclyde *Dunbartons
Map 10 NS28*
Duirland *(NS299872)* Glen Fruin ☎3370
*A comfortably-sized farmhouse situated
away from main road.*
Jun–15 Sep 3hc ⊛ nc5 CTV 5P 2🏠
775acres mixed

HELSTON Cornwall *Map 2 SW62*
*Within a short radius of this town there are
several AA-listed farmhouses at the*

following locations (see appropriate gazetteer entry for full details):
Coverack Bridges, Laity, Trenear, Trevenen Bal.

HENFIELD W Sussex *Map 4 TQ21*
Mrs E. Wilkin **Great Wapses** *(TQ243192)*
Wineham (3m NE off B2116) ☎2544
Part-16th-century and part-Georgian farmhouse set in rural surroundings.
3rm (1fb) TV 7P 1🏠 33acres mixed S%
B&b£6—£8

HENSTRIDGE Somerset *Map 3 ST71*
Mrs I. Pickford **Manor** *(ST692206)*
Bowden ☎Templecombe 70213
16th-century, stone-built farmhouse with lattice, windows. Surrounded by grassland and wooded areas.
May—Oct 2rm CTV P 1🏠 🛅 250acres arable dairy S% B&b£6 W£38 **M**

HETHERSETT Norfolk *Map 5 TG10*
Mr & Mrs P. G. Gowing **Park** *(TG148037)*
☎Norwich 810264
Modernised Georgian farmhouse. Interestingly furnished; part modern, part antique. Well situated for excursions to Norfolk Broads.
16hc 9⇱🈁 (3fb) 🛏 nc5 (Jul & Aug) 🐕 CTV
20P 4🏠🛅 200acres arable B&bfr£7.50
Bdifr£11 Wfr£70 ⅃ (W only Whitsun, Jul & Aug) D9.30pm

HOLBETON Devon *Map 2 SX65*
Mrs J. A. Baskerville **Keaton** *(SX595480)*
☎255
Large, stone-built and well-maintained farmhouse. Some walls 18in thick. Isolated rural position. Yachting at Newton Ferrers 3 miles away.
Apr—Sep 2rm (2fb) 🛏 nc5 TV 2P 117acres beef S% B&b£5—£6

HOLLYBUSH Strathclyde *Ayrs Map 10 NS31*
Mr A. Woodburn **Boreland** *(NS400139)*
☎Patna 228
Two-storey farmhouse with roughcast exterior, situated on the banks of the River Doon. West off A713 south of village.
Jun—Sep 3rm (2fb) 🛏🐕 TV P 150acres dairy non-working S% B&b£4.75—£5.25

HOLNE Devon *Map 3 SX76*
S Townsend **Wellpritton** *(SX716704)*
☎Poundsgate 273
Tastefully modernised farmhouse in Dartmoor National Park. There are panoramic views and the farm has its own swimming pool.
Closed Xmas 3hc (2fb) 🛏 nc7 🐕 CTV 4P 🛅
15acres mixed B&b£6 Bdi£9 W£49—£51
⅃ (W only Jul & Aug)

HOLSWORTHY Devon *Map 2 SS30*
Mr & Mrs E. Cornish **Leworthy** *(SS323012)* ☎253488
Low, white-fronted farmhouse with attractive garden facing open country. Pleasantly situated. **See colour section.**
Closed Xmas 12rm 11hc 2⇱🈁 (7fb) 🛏 nc4
🐕 CTV 20P 2🏠 240acres beef sheep S%
B&b£8—£10.50 Bdi£10.50—£12.50
W£65—£80 ⅃ (W only Whitsun—mid Sep)
D6pm

HOLT Clwyd *Map 7 SJ35*
Mrs G. M. Evans **New Farm** *(SJ394538)*
Commonwood ☎Farndon 270358
Small, comfortable and cosy farm.
rs Oct—Apr (B&b only) 2rm 🛏 CTV 4P

92acres dairy S% ✳B&b£4.50—£5
Bdi£6—£6.50 Wfr£42 ⅃ D10am

HOLYWELL Clwyd *Map 7 SJ17*
Mr & Mrs H. Kendrick **Garneddwen Fawr** *(SJ173707)* Lixwm ☎Halkyn 780298
16th-century, stone-built farmhouse with oak beams.
Apr—Oct 2rm 1hc 1⇱🈁 (1fb) 🛏 nc5 CTV 4P
66acres non-working S% B&b£5—£5.50

HONITON Devon *Map 3 ST10*
Mrs I. J. Underdown **Roebuck** *(ST147001)* Weston ☎2225
Modern farm on western end of Honiton bypass. 8 miles from the coast.
4rm 3hc (2fb) 🛏 CTV P 180acres dairy mixed S% B&b£5—£5.50

HORNS CROSS Devon *Map 2 SS32*
Mrs B. Furse **Swanton** *(SS355227)*
☎Clovelly 241
Modern, dormer-style bungalow pleasantly situated overlooking Bristol Channel.
Closed Xmas 3rm 2hc (2fb) 🛏 TV P sea
42acres dairy S% B&b£5.50 Bdi£7.50
W£48 ⅃ D am

HOWEY Powys *Map 3 SO05*
Mrs C. Nixon **Brynhir** *(SJO67586)* (1m E on unclass rd) ☎Llandrindod Wells 2425
Remote 17th-century hill farm, traditionally furnished. Good walks and views. Pony for children to ride.
Apr—Nov 4rm 2hc (3fb) 6P 150acres mixed S% B&b£5.50—£6 Bdi£7.50—£8.50
W£52—£58 ⅃ D5.30pm

Mrs R. Jones **Holly** *(SJO45593)*
☎Llandrindod Wells 2402 Apr—Nov 3rm
(1fb) CTV 6P 70acres mixed S%
✳B&bfr£4.50 Bdifr£7 Wfr£49 ⅃ D5.30pm

Mr & Mrs R. Bufton **Three Wells** *(SO062586)* ☎Llandrindod Wells 2484
7hc (3fb) CTV 20P 🛅 50acres beef sheep
S% B&b£5—£6 Bdi£7—£8 W£45—£50 ⅃
D6pm

HUNDRED HOUSE Powys *Map 3 SO15*
Mrs D. Kinsey **Box** *(SO129531)* ☎240
Two-storey, 17th-century stone farmhouse. In elevated position with good views of the Edw Valley.
Mar—Oct 2rm 🛏 nc CTV P sheep B&bfr£5

IDOLE Dyfed *Map 2 SN41*
Mr & Mrs A. Bowen **Pantgwyn** *(SN419157)* ☎Carmarthen 5859
Spacious rebuilt farmhouse. 3 miles south of Carmarthen.
3rm 🛏 CTV P 35acres dairy
✳B&b£5—£5.50

ILAM Staffs *Map 7 SK15*
J Fortnam **Beechenhill** *(SK129525)*
☎Alstonefield 274
Two-storey, stone-built farmhouse with exposed beams. Built about 1720. Unspoilt rural area with panoramic views.
May—Sep 2rm (1fb) CTV 2P 92acres dairy
S% B&b£6 W£42 **M**

INGLETON N Yorks *Map 7 SD67*
G. W. & M. Bell **Langber** *(SD689709)*
☎41587
A large detached property in open countryside in an elevated position on a 7-acre smallholding situated on a quiet country lane about 1 mile south of Ingleton village.
5hc 🛏 TV 6P 7acres sheep ponies

INVERGARRY Highland *Inverness-shire*
Map 14 NH30
Mrs G. Swann **Ardgarry** *(NH286015)*
Faichem ☎226.
*Farmhouse with converted outbuildings in a
quiet position off A87.*
1hc (A 3hc) (2fb) CTV 10P 10acres mixed
S% B&bf5–£6 Bdif8.50–£10
Wf59.50–£70 ⨍ D4pm

Mrs L. Brown **Faichem Lodge**
(NH286014) ☎314
*Beautiful modernised old stone house, with
cosy bedrooms and lounge. All bedrooms
overlook superb highland scenery.*
3hc (1fb) 5P 🚲 7½acres mixed S%
B&bfr£5 Bdifr£8 D7pm

INVERURIE Grampian *Aberdeens*
Map 15 NJ72
Mrs F. Cowie **Auchencleith** *(NJ760264)*
☎Wartle 232
*Small, pleasant farmhouse with several
outbuildings. 4 miles north of Inverurie off
B9001.*
Apr–Oct 2rm 1hc (2fb) TV 2P 100acres
mixed S% B&bf3.50–£4.50 Bdif5–£6
D6pm

IPSTONES Staffs Map 7 SK04
J. M. Brindley **Glenwood House**
(SK006488) ☎294
*Large house about 100 years old built of
dressed sandstone blocks in very
picturesque and peaceful rural surroundings.*
Closed Xmas & New Year 2rm CTV 4P 🚲
58acres beef S% B&bf5–£6 Bdif8–£9
Wf55–£62 ⨍ D4.30pm

IRTHINGTON Cumbria Map 12 NY46
Seat Hill *(NY483634)* ☎Kirklinton 226
*Sandstone building dating from 1726.
Interior fully modernised. Attractive flower
garden and lawn. On A6071.*
Mar–Oct 3rm 1hc CTV P 2🏠 217acres
mixed

ISLE OF SKYE Highland *Inverness-shire*
Map 13
See Clachan, Dunvegan, Portree, Uig

ISLE OF WIGHT Map 4
See Ryde

IVYBRIDGE Devon Map 2 SX65
Mr P. M. Dempsey **White Oaks**
(SX654562) Filham ☎2207
*Large bungalow with well-kept gardens and
lawns. 1m E on B3213.*
4hc (1fb) CTV 10P 🚲 3acres mixed S%
B&bf6.50 Bdif9.50 Wf66.50 ⨍ D8pm

JACOBSTOWE Devon Map 2 SS50
Mrs J King **Higher Cadham** *(SS585026)*
☎Exbourne 647
*Well-decorated and comfortably-furnished
16th-century farmhouse. Ideal base for
touring.*
Apr–Oct 4hc (1fb) 🐾 nc3 CTV 12P
139acres beef sheep B&bf4.50 Bdif7.50
Wf45 ⨍ (W only Jul & Aug) D5pm

KEA Cornwall Map 2 SW84
N Wenning Hobbs **Higher Lanner**
(SW831414) ☎Truro 3037
*Farmhouse 3 miles west of Truro on
unclassified road. Overlooks River Fal.*
Etr–Oct 3hc TV 6P river 150acres dairy S%
B&bf4.50–£5 Bdif6.50–£8 Wf45–£56
⨍ D2.30pm

KEITH Grampian *Banffs* Map 15 NJ45
Mrs J. Jackson **Haughs** *(NJ416515)*
☎2238
*Attractively decorated farmhouse. 1 mile
from Keith off A96.*
15 May–10 Oct 4hc (1fb) 🐾 CTV 8P 2🏠
220acres mixed S% B&bf4.50–£4.75
Wf31.50 Ⓜ

Mr & Mrs G. A. Farquhar **Mains of
Tarrycroys** *(NJ404537)* Aultmore ☎2586
*Attractive stone farmhouse with large
farmyard and several outbuildings
surrounded by arable land.*
4rm 2hc (1fb) 🐾 nc5 TV 8P 43acres arable
beef S% ✳B&bf4.50 Bdif7 Wf42 ⨍
D5.30pm

Mrs E. C. Leith **Montgrew** *(NJ453517)*
☎2852
*Farmhouse with several outbuildings and
pleasant views. 2m E off A95.*
Closed Oct–Apr 4rm 1hc (1fb) CTV 4P
211acres arable beef S% B&bfr£4
Bdifr£5.50 D6.30pm

Mrs G. Murphy **Tarnash House**
(NJ442490) ☎2728
*Two-storey, stone farmhouse with well-
maintained garden to the front. Surrounded
by farmland 1m S off A96.*
May–Oct 4hc (1fb) CTV 10P 1🏠 🚲
100acres arable S% B&bf5

KENDAL Cumbria Map 7 SD59
Mrs D. Atkinson **Bank Head** *(SD496926)*
Underbarrow Rd ☎21785
*Set back off the road, 1m from Kendal
town centre. 7m from Lake Windermere
and surrounded by pleasant countryside.*
Etr–Oct 3hc (2fb) 🐾 TV 4P 240acres
mixed S% ✳B&bf5–£5.50 Wf35 Ⓜ

Mrs S. Beaty **Garnett House** *(SD500959)*
Burneside ☎24542
*A 15th-century stone-built farmhouse
standing in an elevated position
overlooking Howgill Fells. Close to both
Windermere and Kendal.*
4hc (2fb) 🐾 CTV 6P 270acres mixed
B&bf5 Bdif7.50 D4pm

Mr & Mrs J. Gardner **Natland Mill Beck**
(SD520907) ☎21122
*17th-century, local-stone farmhouse with
original beams, doors and cupboards. Large
well-furnished rooms. Attractive garden.*
Mar–Oct 3rm 2hc (1fb) 🐾 CTV 3P 🚲
100acres dairy S% B&bf5.50

KENNFORD Devon Map 3 SX98
Mrs R. Weeks **Holloway Barton**
(SX893855) ☎832302
*Well-appointed house retaining its old
charm situated 1 mile from the M5 and
1 mile from Haldon Racecourse. Well kept
garden and large lawn.*
4hc (1fb) 🐾 CTV 4P 2🏠 🚲 380acres beef
dairy S% B&bfr£6 Bdifr£9

Mrs G. J. Weeks **Lynwood** *(SX892859)*
☎832517
*Well-furnished farmhouse, about 5 miles
from Exeter. Rough shooting in grounds.
Views of Haldon Forest and Exe estuary.*
3hc (1fb) CTV 4P 350acres mixed S%
B&bfr£5 Bdifr£8 D6.30pm

KERRY Powys Map 6 SO19
Goitre *(SO176918)* ☎248
*Modernised farmhouse with comfortable
traditional furnishings in peaceful rural area.*
4rm 1hc 🐾 CTV P 2🏠 🚲 190acres mixed

KESWICK Cumbria *Map 11 NY22*
Low Nest *(NY291226)* ☎72378
Comfortable farmhouse with beamed ceiling in dining room. Clean and tidy decor.
May–Oct 5rm 4hc nc4 6P 120acres mixed D4pm

KILMACOLM Strathclyde *Renfrews Map 10 NS36*
Mrs M. M. Blair **Pennytersal** *(NS338714)* ☎2349
Well-maintained building and courtyard set in rolling farmland. Kilmacolm 2 miles.
May–Sep 3rm 2hc (1fb) ⊘ TV P 125acres mixed S% B&bfr£4.75

KILTARLITY Highland *Inverness-shire Map 14 NH54*
Mrs D. Fraser **Glebe** *(NH513415)* ☎252 ·
A comfortable, well-furnished farmhouse ½ mile off A833.
May–Sep 2rm (1fb) ⊘ nc8 CTV P 63acres arable beef S% B&b fr£4.50

KIMBOLTON Heref & Worcs *Map 3 SO56*
M. J. Lloyd **Menalls** *(SO528611)* ☎Leominster 2605
Delightful farmhouse set in Herefordshire valley scenery.
Mar–Oct 2hc (2fb) CTV P 40acres mixed S% B&b£6 Bdi£8 W£54 ⱥ

KING EDWARD Grampian *Aberdeens Map 15 NJ75*
Blackton *(NJ726583)* ☎205
A well run working farm catering for family holidays. Banff 6 miles.
May–Oct 5hc ♨ CTV 6P 113acres arable beef D6pm

KINGSCOTT Devon *Map 2 SS51*
Flavills *(SS538182)* St Giles
☎Torrington 3250
Well maintained,· large Elizabethan farmhouse, situated in the village of Kingscott. Torrington 3½ miles.
May–Oct 4rm TV 10P 125acres mixed D4pm

KINGSLAND Heref & Worcs *Map 3 SO46*
Mrs F. M. Hughes **Tremayne** *(SO447613)* ☎233
Deceptively large, two-storey building on one of main routes to Leominster.
Mar–Nov 3rm 1hc (1fb) CTV 4P ♨ 41acres mixed sheep S% ✳B&b£4.50

Westfield *(SO436622)* ☎348
Two-storey, 17th-century farmhouse with original oak beams and brasses. Trout fishing in River Pinsey which runs through farm.
Etr–Oct 2rm ⊘ nc TV 2P 1🏠 60acres mixed

KINGSWEAR Devon *Map 3 SX95*
Boohay *(SX899520)* ☎284
Large, comfortable farmhouse, well situated for touring the beaches of South Devon.
3hc (A 2rm) ⊘ CTV 6P 560acres mixed D6pm

KINGSWELLS Grampian *Aberdeens Map 15 NJ80*
M. Mann **Bellfield** *(NJ868055)* ☎Aberdeen 740239
Modernised and extended farm cottage on quiet road and set amid farmlands. 4m W of Aberdeen city centre off A944.

Closed 19 Dec–5 Jan 3hc (2fb) CTV 5P ♨ 200acres arable dairy S% B&b£4.50–£5 Bdi£8–£8.50 D6pm

KINGTON Heref & Worcs *Map 3 SO25*
Mrs E. E. Protheroe **School** *(SO266550)* Up Hergest ☎230453
Large farmhouse dating back to c1625 perched high on Hergest Ridge, overlooking valley of the River Arrow 2m SW of town.
4hc (A 2hc 1⌂🏠) (2fb) CTV 6P 290acres mixed S% B&b£5–£5.50 Bdi£9–£9.50 W£60–£63 ⱥ

KIPPEN Central *Stirlings Map 11 NS69*
Mrs J. Paterson **Powblack** *(NS670970)* ☎260
Pleasant farmhouse near the River Forth on the Kippen to Doune road.
May–Sep 2hc (1fb) CTV 4P ♨ 300acres mixed S% B&b£5–£5.25

KIRKCONNEL Dumfries & Galloway *Dumfriesshire Map 11 NS71*
Mrs E. A. Mcgarvie **Niviston** *(NS691135)* ☎346
Pleasant, well-maintained farm delightfully set in elevated position overlooking Nithsdale.
Jun–Sep 2rm (1fb) CTV P 1🏠 345acres mixed S% ✳B&b£3.50 Bdi£6.50 W£45 ⱥ D noon

KIRKHILL Highland *Inverness-shire Map 14 NH54*
Mrs C. Munro **Wester Moniack** *(NH551438)* ☎Drumchardine 237
Small, modern, two-storey house with a relaxing, tranquil atmosphere.
Apr–Nov 2hc (1fb) CTV 3P ♨ 600acres arable dairy S% B&b£4.50–£5 Bdi£6.50–£7.50 D5pm

KIRK IRETON Derbys *Map 8 SK25*
E. Brassington **Sitch** *(SK260515)* ☎Wirksworth 2454
Large sandstone farmhouse with extensive outbuildings standing in a fairly remote but picturesque area.
Closed Xmas 4hc (2fb) ♨ CTV 12P 2🏠 ♨ 327acres mixed S% B&b£7 Bdi£11 D8pm

KIRKTON OF DURRIS Grampian *Kincardines Map 15 NO79*
Mrs M. Leslie **Wester Durris Cottage** *(NO769962)* ☎Crathes 638
May–Oct 2rm (1fb) 4P 300acres arable S% B&b£4

KIRKWALL Orkney *Map 16 HY41*
Mrs M. Hourie **Heathfield** *(HY413108)* St Ola ☎2378
Two-storey, stone farmhouse on a gently sloping hill. There are distant views over Scapa Flow.
4hc (2fb) ⊘ 8P ♨ 500acres mixed B&b£4 Bdi£6.50 D5pm

KNAPTOFT Leics *Map 4 SP68*
A. M. Knight **Knaptoft House** *(SP619894)* Bruntingthorpe Rd ☎Peatling Magna 388
Modern building on site of Georgian farmhouse. Medieval fishponds restored and stocked with coarse fish. Off Shearsby–Bruntingthorpe rd, 1m W from its junction with A50. Or leave M1 at junc 20 then via Kimcote and Watton.
3hc (1fb) ♨ CTV 5P ♨ 145acres mixed S% ✳B&b fr£5 Bdi fr£8 Wfr£55 ⱥ D2pm

KNIGHTON Powys *Map 7 SO27*
R. Watkins **Heartsease** *(SO343725)*
☎Bucknell 220
*Large, mellow-stone residence over 300
years old. Country house atmosphere.
Large garden.*
3rm 2hc 1⇌🖼(1fb) ♨CTV 3🏠 600acres
mixed S% B&b£6.50–£7 Bdifr£12
D6.30pm

KNOWSTONE Devon *Map 3 SS82*
Mrs J. M. Millman **Eastacott** *(SS837231)*
☎Anstey Mills 215
*Isolated farmhouse in the heart of North
Devon. Large sun lounge at entrance.*
Mar–Nov 3rm ⊗TV 3P 1🏠 110acres dairy
B&b£4.50–£5 W£28–£35 Ⅿ (W only
during Summer Hols)

LADOCK Cornwall *Map 2 SW85*
Mrs P. M. Davies **Tregear** *(SW870506)*
☎Mitchell 214
*Attractive farmhouse set slightly back from
unclassified road. Lawn at front.*
Etr–Oct 3rm 1⇌🖼(1fb) ⊗TV P 250acres
dairy S% B&bfr£4.50

LAIRG Highland *Sutherland Map 14 NC50*
Mr A. MacKay **Alt-Na-Sorag** *(NC547123)*
14 Achnairn ☎2058
*Attractive farmhouse with good views of
Loch Shin. Lairg 5 miles.*
May–Sep 3rm CTV P 150acres mixed S%
B&bfr£4.60

Mrs V. Mackenzie **5 Tirryside** *(NC570110)*
☎2332 *(3½m N off A838)*
3rm ⊗CTV P lake 50acres mixed S%
B&bfr£4.60

Mrs M. Sinclair **Woodside** *(NC533147)*
☎2072
*Homely house surrounded by fields and
overlooking Loch Shin. Lairg about 7 miles.*
May–Sep 3rm ⊗ CTV 4P lake 360acres
mixed S% B&bfr£4.60

LAITY *(Nr Helston)* Cornwall *Map 2 SW63*
Crowgey *(SW698308)* ☎Constantine
40436
*Pleasantly situated farmhouse. Quiet but
not isolated. Off Falmouth–Helston rd
(A394), 3m NE of Helston.*
Etr–Sep 3hc ⊗CTV 3P 40acres mixed

LANGPORT Somerset *Map 3 ST42*
Woodstock *(ST442264)* Pibsbury
☎250394
*Small, well furnished and decorated
farmhouse with a pleasant garden.*

Apr–Sep 4hc nc8 CTV 8P 1🏠 river
60acres dairy D4pm

LANLIVERY Cornwall *Map 2 SX05*
Mr & Mrs J. Liwfoot **Treganoon**
(SX065589) ☎Bodmin 872205
*Farmhouse with small garden in fairly
isolated position and beautiful countryside.*
Etr–Oct 7rm 6hc (3fb) ♨CTV 8P 100acres
beef S% B&b£5–£6 Bdi£7–£8 W£42–£50
Ⅼ (W only Jul & Aug)

LATHERON Highland *Caithness
Map 15 ND13*
Mrs C. Sinclair **Upper Latheron**
(ND195352) ☎224
*Two-storey house in elevated position with
fine views out across North Sea. Farm also
incorporates a pony stud.*
May–Oct 2rm (2fb) ♨CTV P 200acres
mixed S% B&b£4.50–£5

LAUNCELLS Cornwall *Map 2 SS20*
Mrs A. Colwill **Moreton Mill** *(SS283085)*
☎Kilkhampton 306
*Pleasant, 15th-century, cottage-style
farmhouse with oak beams. Small,
attractive garden.*
Etr–mid Oct 5rm 3hc (3fb) ⊗TV 10P
52½acres mixed S% B&b£4.50–£4.75
W£46.90–£49 Ⅿ D4pm

LAWERS Tayside *Perths Map 11 NN63*
Croftintygan *(NN676389)* ☎Killin 534
*Secluded stone farmhouse standing on
hillside with dramatic views over Loch Tay.
Between A827 and Lochside.*
May–Sep 6rm 4hc TV lake 3,000acres
mixed

LEEK Staffs *Map 7 SJ95*
Mrs D Needham **Holly Dale** *(SK019556)*
Bradnop ☎383022
*Two-storey-stone-built farmhouse typical
of the area. 2m SE on an unclassified road
off A523.*
Apr–Oct 2rm ⊗TV 3P 72acres S% B&b£5
Bdi£8 W£55 Ⅼ D2pm

LEOMINSTER Heref & Worcs
Map 3 SO45
Mrs S. J. Davenport **Stagbatch**
(SO465584) ☎2673
*14th-century, half-timbered farmhouse
which is a listed building. Peaceful setting
2m W off A4112.*
Closed Xmas 3⇌🖼 nc10 CTV 10P 🍴
40acres beef sheep horse-stud B&b£6–£7
W£40–£45 Ⅿ W only Aug

Mrs H. C. Davies **Wharton Bank**
(SO508556) ☎2575
Extensively modernised farmhouse.
Comfortable pleasant atmosphere.
Closed Xmas 3hc 1⇨⌷ (1fb) ⊘ nc5 TV P
2🏠 ▦ 212acres dairy mixed S% B&b£6–£7
Bdi£9–£10 D5pm

LEW Oxon *Map 4 SP30*
M. J. Rouse **University** *(SP322059)*
☎Bampton Castle 850297
17th-century farmhouse, modernised
without losing traditional character. House
set back from road in secluded position
behind farm buildings. **See colour section.**
Closed Xmas & New Yr 4rm 1hc 3⇨⌷
(2fb) ⊘ nc6 CTV 8P ▦ 216acres mixed S%
B&b£7.18–£8.62 Bdi£12.35–£13.80
W£82.80–£92.57 ⱪ D4pm

LEWDOWN Devon *Map 2 SX48*
Mrs M. E. Horn **Venn Mill** *(SX484885)*
☎Bridestowe 288
Large modern bungalow set in attractive
countryside. Guests welcome to watch
farm activities.
Etr–Sep 4rm 3hc (1fb) ⊘ CTV 4P 2🏠
160acres dairy mixed S% B&b£6–£6.50
Bdi£9–£9.50 W£48–£55 ⱪ D4pm

LIFTON Devon *Map 2 SX38*
Markstone (SX429825) ☎289
Pleasant, well decorated house with small
attractive garden.
Etr–Sep 3rm 2hc TV 3P 48acres dairy

LINLITHGOW Lothian *W Lothian*
Map 11 NS97
Mr & Mrs W. Erskine **Woodcockdale**
(NS973760) ☎2088
Modern two-storey house lying about
50 yards from farmyard and outbuildings.
3rm 1⇨⌷ (1fb) ⚛ CTV 12P ▦ 300acres
dairy S% B&b£5 Bdi£7 Wfr£42 ⱪ D8pm

LISKEARD Cornwall *Map 2 SX26*
S. A. Kendall **Tencreek** *(SX265637)*
☎43379
A clean, well-decorated farmhouse set in
beautiful countryside. Liskeard 1 mile.
Mar–Sep 2hc ⊘ 2P 250acres mixed S%
B&b£4.50–£5 W£30–£33 Ⓜ

LITTLE EVERSDEN Cambs *Map 5 TL35*
Mrs F. Ellis **Five Gables** *(TL371535)*
Bucks Ln ☎Comberton 2236
Historic farmhouse of 15th and 17th
centuries. Oak beams and inglenook
fireplace. Listed as being worthy of
preservation.
May–Aug 3rm 2hc (1fb) ⊘ nc12 TV P
240acres arable S% B&b£6.50

LITTLEHEMPSTON Devon *Map 3 SX86*
Mrs E. P. Miller **Buckyette** *(SX812638)*
☎Staverton 638
19th-century stone farmhouse. Set in a
spacious garden, its position provides
excellent views of surrounding Devon.
Jun–Sep 7rm 6hc (4fb) ⊘ ⚛ TV 6P 51acres
S% B&b£8 Bdi£11 W£66–£75 ⱪ D6.30pm

LITTLE MILL Gwent *Map 3 SO30*
Mrs A. Bradley **Pentwyn** *(SO325035)*
(off A472, ½m E of junc with A4042) ☎249
3hc (1fb) ⚛ CTV 6P ▦ S% B&bfr£5.50
Bdifr£8.50 Wfr£59 Ⓜ D noon

LITTLE TORRINGTON Devon
Map 2 SS41
Mrs J. Watkins **Lower Hollam**

(SS501161) ☎Torrington 3253
Historic house in an unusually peaceful
position. Good play facilities for children.
May–Oct 4hc (2fb) ⊘ ⚛ CTV 4P 160acres
mixed S% B&b£4.50–£6 Bdi£6.50–£8
W£42–£50 ⱪ D5.30pm

LITTLE WALDEN Essex *Map 5 TL54*
Sadlers (TL558416) ☎Saffron Walden
23280
Small farmhouse, attractive interior with
exposed beams. Peacefully situated in
Essex countryside and has horses, ponies,
ducks and sheep.
3rm ⊛ nc2 CTV 6P ▦ 10acres
non-working

LITTON Derbys *Map 7 SK17*
Mr & Mrs H. Radford **Hall** *(SK159754)*
☎Tideswell 871124 Closed Xmas 3rm
1hc (2fb) ⊘ ⚛ TV 6P ▦ 10acres mixed
B&b£5.50 Bdi£8 W£55 ⱪ

LLANARTH Gwent *Map 3 SO31*
Mr & Mrs J. Morgan **Llwynderi**
(SO382130) ☎Llantilio 226
Secluded, stone-built farmhouse with many
period features, including a classical oak
staircase. Rooms larger than average.
Mar–Oct 4hc (2fb) ⊘ CTV 6P 120acres
mixed S% B&b£6

LLANARTHNEY Dyfed *Map 2 SN52*
Mrs W. M. Edwards **Glantowy**
(SN534206) ☎Dryslwyn 275
Spacious, well-maintained farmhouse near
River Tywi.
Etr–Sep 2hc (1fb) ⊘ TV 5P ▦ 140acres
dairy S% B&b£5

LLANDEGLA Clwyd *Map 7 SJ15*
Dol Ddu (SJ188503) ☎219
Modern, two-storey farmhouse.
2rm ⊛ nc10 CTV 4P 95acres mixed

Mr & Mrs H. Roberts **Graig** *(SJ202506)*
☎272
Recently-built (1974) farmhouse in
elevated position. 1m S of junc
A525/A5104.
Etr–Oct 2hc (1fb) ⊘ TV 2P ▦ mixed sheep
S% B&b£5 Bdi£7.50 Wfr£50 Ⓜ D6pm

B. C. Lightfoot **Pentre Isa** *(SJ195498)*
☎220
Pleasant, stone-built, two-storey
farmhouse in elevated position.
Etr–Nov 1rm (1fb) ⊘ TV P 128acres mixed
sheep S% B&bfr£4.50 Bdifr£6.50 Wfr£45
ⱪ

LLANDINAM Powys *Map 6 SO08*
Mrs G. F. Lloyd **Llandinam Hall**
(SO028903) ☎Caersws 234
Two-storey, half-timbered farmhouse
probably of late 17th-century, backing onto
River Seven. Fine views of the Cambrian
Mountains.
Mar–Oct 6rm 5hc (2fb) ⊘ CTV P 450acres
mixed S% ✳B&b£5.50–£6.50
Bdi£9.50–£10.50

Mrs M. C. Davis **Trewythen** *(SJ003901)*
☎Caersws 444
2m south-west of Caersws, on unclassified
road off B4569.
May–Oct 3rm 2hc (1fb) ⊘ CTV P ▦
200acres mixed S% B&b£5.75 Bdi£8.25
W£55 ⱪ D8pm

LLANDOVERY Dyfed *Map 3 SN73*
Glangwydderig (SN789347) ☎20381
Small farmhouse on the outskirts of

Llandovery/Llechwedd

*Llandovery alongside the Brecon Beacons
National Park. Fishing available in farm
grounds.*
May–mid Oct 2rm 3P 75acres sheep

LLANDRINDOD WELLS Powys
Map 3 SO06
Mrs M. A. Davies **Highbury** *(SO044623)*
Llanyre ☎2573
*Typical Welsh beef and sheep farm. Situated
2m W of Llandrindod Wells, ½m off A4081.*
Apr–Sep 4rm 3hc (1fb) TV 4P 184acres
beef sheep S% B&bfr£5.50 Bdi fr£9 Dnoon

LLANDYSSIL Powys *Map 7 SO19*
Mrs C. Parry **Gwern Yr Uchain** *(SO193960)*
☎ Montgomery 298
Etr–Nov 3hc (1fb) CTV 5P 190acres beef
sheep S% B&b£5.50 Bdi£8.50 W£56
⊁ D7pm

LLANEGRYN Gwynedd *Map 6 SH60*
E. Pughe **Argoed** *(SH604057)*
☎ Tywyn 710361
*Homely, comfortable farmhouse with
tasty country food.*
Etr–Sep 3hc TV 3P 7acres ✱B&bfr£5

LLANELIDAN Clwyd *Map 6 SJ15*
M. Mosford **Trewyn** *(SJ138515)*
Rhydymeudwy ☎ Clawddnewydd 676
*Homely farmhouse in valley of fields and
trees. Ruthin about 5 miles. 2m E of B5429.*
Mar–Nov 3rm 1hc (1fb) ✿ TV 6P ♨
80acres mixed B&b£4.50–£5.50
Bdi£6–£7 W£40–£43 ⊁ D5pm

LLANFACHRETH Gwynedd *Map 6 SH72*
Mrs C. T. Owen **Rhedyncochion**
(SH762222) ☎ Rhydymain 600
*100-year-old, stone-built farmhouse with
extensive views of surrounding countryside
and mountains.*
Etr–Oct 2rm 1hc (1fb) ✿ TV P ♨ 120acres
mixed S% B&b£5.25 Bdi£10

LLANFAIR DYFFRYN CLWYD Clwyd
Map 6 SJ15
Mrs E. Jones **Llanbenwch** *(SJ137533)*
☎ Ruthin 2340
*Modernised farmhouse with oak beams
situated on the A525, Wrexham to Ruthin
road.*
Feb–Nov 3hc (1fb) ✿ TV P ♨ 40acres mixed
S% Bdi£6.50 W£42 ⊁ D6pm

LLANFAIR TALHAIARN Clwyd
Map 6 SH96
Bodrochwyn *(SH938731)*
☎ Abergele 823525
*Large, brick-built, L-shaped farmhouse of
distinction.*
Etr–Oct 3rm 1hc TV 174acres

LLANFAIR WATERDINE Salop
Map 7 SJ27
Mrs J. M. Morgan **Selley Hall** *(SJ264766)*
Waterdine ☎ Knighton 528429
*Old stone-built three-storey house dating
back to 1780. Situated in rather remote but
very picturesque area. Offa's Dyke runs
within 200yds of farm. 5m NW of Knighton;
take A488 then unclassified road on N
side of River Teme.*
May–Sep 3rm 1hc (1fb) ✿ 4P 500acres
mixed S% B&b£4.50–£5.50 Bdi£7–£8.50
D4pm

LLANGERNYW Clwyd *Map 6 SH86*
Mr & Mrs E. Roberts **Tan-Y-Craig**
(SH875669) ☎249

*Large farmhouse on hillside. Situated 1 mile
north of village.*
Mar–Nov 3hc ✿ nc5 TV 3P 100acres
mixed S% B&bfr£5 Bdi fr£7.50 Wfr£54 ⊁

LLANGOLLEN Clwyd *Map 7 SJ24*
Mrs A. Kenrick **Rhydonnen Ucha Rhewl**
(SJ174429) ☎860153
*Large, stone-built, three-storey farmhouse.
Pleasantly situated. Shooting on farm.
Trout fishing in River Dee (permit).*
Etr–Nov 4rm 3hc (2fb) TV 6P river 115acres
dairy S% B&bfr£6 Bdifr£9 Wfr£55 ⊁ D5pm

LLANRHAEADR Clwyd *Map 6 SJ06*
C. Evans **Pen-Y-Waen** *(SJO74615)*
☎ Llanynys 234
*Positioned between sloping hills with
views of valleys.*
May–Oct 2rm 1(1fb) ✿ CTV P ♨ 100acres
mixed S% B&b£4.50–£5

LLANRWST Gwynedd *Map 6 SH86*
Mrs M. Owen **Bodrach** *(SH852629)*
☎640326
*Farm situated in remote position about
3½m E of Llanrwst, in a cul-de-sac on the
B5113 just off the A548.*
Apr–Dec 2rm (1fb) ✿ TV P ♨ 184acres
mixed S% ✱B&b£4–£4.50 Bdi£7–£7.50
W£49 ⊁ D6pm

LLANSANNAN Clwyd *Map 6 SH96*
Mrs G. James **Fferwd** *(SH933658)* ☎230
*Remote, brick-built farmhouse on the main
Denbigh to Llansannan road. Denbigh
about 7 miles.*
May–Oct 3rm 1hc (1fb) ✿ nc13 CTV 3P
270acres mixed D8pm

LLANSANTFFRAID-YM-MECHAIN
Powys *Map 7 SJ22*
D. B. & M. E. Jones **Glanvyrnwy**
(SJ229202) ☎258
*Two-storey, stone-built, detached
farmhouse set back from road behind
pleasant lawns and orchard.*
Mar–Oct 3hc (2fb) CTV 6P 43acres dairy S%
B&b£6–£7 D10pm

LLANUWCHLLYN Gwynedd *Map 6 SH83*
D. Bugby **Bryncaled** *(SH866314)* ☎270
*Farmhouse with beamed ceiling.
Overlooking Aran Mountains, has fishing
river running through grounds.*
Closed Xmas day 3rm 2hc ✿ CTV P ♨
500acres mixed sheep S% B&b£5–£6
Bdi£8–£9 D6pm

Bryn Gwyn *(SH862309)* ☎272
*80-year-old, stone-built farmhouse with
fine views of the Aran Mountains and Lake
Bala.*
Etr–Oct 2hc ✿ ⚘ TV 3P river 400acres
mixed

LLANWDDYN Powys *Map 6 SJ01*
H. A. Parry **Tyn-Y-Maes** *(SJ048183)*
☎216
*Farmhouse is on edge of the nature
reserve at Lake Vyrnwy.*
2hc (1fb) CTV 4P 420acres mixed S%
✱B&b£4.50–£5 Bdi£7–£8 Wfr£48 ⊁
D6pm

LLECHWEDD Gwynedd *Map 6 SH77*
Mrs C. Roberts **Henllys** *(SH779466)*
☎ Conwy 3269
*Large, stone-built farmhouse, signposted
from main road.*
May–Sep 2rm TV 3P 100acres mixed S%
B&b£4.50–£5.50 Bdi£7–£8

Mr & Mrs J. A. Jones **Llechan Ucha**
(SH755757) ☎ Conwy 2451
Modern farmhouse in isolated position.
High on mountainside with good views of
the surrounding area.
Etr–Oct 3rm (1fb) CTV 3P ⋘ river 102acres
beef sheep S% B&b£5.06–£5.75
Bdi£7.48–£8.63 W£48.30–£57.50 ⋎
D3pm

LLEDROD Dyfed *Map 6 SN67*
P. & G. Steiner **Brynarth** *(SN669698)*
☎ Crosswood 367
Etr–Oct & 25Dec–15Jan 2rm 1hc 1⇔⊞
(A 8⇔⊞) (1fb) ⊗ CTV 10P ⋘ 6¼acres
non-working S% Bdi£13 W£115 D8pm

LOCHGOILHEAD Strathclyde *Argyll*
Map 10 NN10
Mr J. Jackson **Pole** *(NN192044)* ☎221
Pleasant, well-kept farmhouse. Lochgoilhead
2 miles.
Etr–Oct 3rm (1fb) TV 4P ⋘ 7,500acres
sheep S% B&b£5–£6 Bdi£8–£9
W£50–£55 ⋎ D7pm

LOCHWINNOCH Strathclyde *Renfrews*
Map 10 NS35
Mrs M. Mackie **High Belltrees**
(NS377584) ☎842376
Situated 1 mile off the A737 1 mile S of
Howwood. Overlooks Castle Semple Loch
which has a R.S.P.B. Bird Sanctuary and
yachting facilities.
5rm 3hc (2fb) CTV 8P ⋘ lake 160acres
dairy mixed S% B&b£5–£5.50
Bdi£7–£7.50 Wfr£49 ⋎ D5pm

LODDISWELL Devon *Map 3 SX74*
E. N. Pethybridge **Reads** *(SX727489)*
☎317
Two-storey, stone-built farmhouse in
isolated position. Fine countryside views.
Full working farm using own produce.
Apr–Sep 2rm 1hc (1fb) 3P 100acres mixed
S% B&b£4–£5 W£28–£35 Ⓜ

LODDON Norfolk *Map 5 TM39*
Stubbs House *(TM358977)* ☎20231
Fine old farm with excellent kitchen
producing delicious, professional meals.
9hc ⊗ nc10 TV 20P ⋘ 300acres arable
(W only last 2 wks Sep–Jun except Bank
Hols)

LONGDOWN Devon *Map 3 SX89*
Steep Acres *(SX885912)* Bakers Hill
☎291
Modern, bungalow-style farmhouse
situated in an elevated position, with
views of the moors. Off B3212.
Apr–Oct 4hc 6P 10acres mixed

LONGDOWNS Cornwall *Map 2 SW73*
Mr E. J. Lavers **Calamankey** *(SW746343)*
☎Stithians 860314
Small farmhouse of Cornish granite; down
a short lane off A394.
Apr–Oct 3rm (3fb) ⊗ nc6 CTV 6P 55acres
arable beef dairy S% B&b£4.25–£5

LONGLEAT Wilts *Map 3 ST84*
J. Crossman **Stalls** *(ST806439)*
☎Maiden Bradley 323
Detached Bath stone house, originally the
home farm for Longleat House. Sun terrace
with trim lawns and garden to stream.
Access off A362 at Corsley Heath.
Apr–Nov 3hc CTV 6P ⋘ 304acres dairy
S% ✳B&b£5.50–£6 D7pm

LONGMORN Grampian *Moray*
Map 15 NJ25
Mrs M. Shanks **Cockmuir** *(NJ232571)*
☎227
Clean, pleasant farmhouse in attractive
position. Farm is set off main road down
farm track.
Jun–Sep 5rm TV 10P 1🏠 50acres mixed
S% B&b fr£5 Bdi fr£8 Wfr£55 ⋎

LOOE Cornwall *Map 2 SX25*
Mr & Mrs K. Hembrow **Tregoad**
(SX272560) ☎27186
Large, well built, stone farmhouse on high
ground with sea view over Looe.
Etr–Nov rs Etr–Whit 6hc (4fb) ⋩ CTV 20P
sea 60acres dairy S% ✳B&b£4.50–£6
Bdi£8–£9 W£50–£60 ⋎ D3pm

LOSTWITHIEL Cornwall *Map 2 SX15*
Mr & Mrs R. C. Dunn **Pelyn Barn** Pelyn
Cross *(SX091588)* ☎872451
Large farmhouse, formerly an old toll house,
with a well-kept lawn enclosure at rear.
4hc (1fb) ⊗ CTV 8P 1🏠 378acres mixed
S% B&b fr£7.50

LUSS Strathclyde *Dunbartons*
Map 10 NS39
Duchlage *(NS350872)*
Pleasant, homely house. Luss 4 miles, S off
B832.
Etr–Sep 3rm ⋩ nc12 TV 2P 1🏠 135acres
mixed

LYDBURY NORTH Salop *Map 7 SO38*
Brunslow *(SO366849)* ☎244
Old brick-built Georgian farmhouse in rural
setting.
Closed Xmas 4rm 3hc CTV 4P 150acres
dairy & sheep D5pm

LYDFORD Devon *Map 2 SX58*
Mrs J. Wild **Kirtonia** *(SX524862)* Vale
Down ☎331
Detached farmhouse adjacent to main
A386. Bedrooms enjoy scenic views of
Dartmoor and surrounding countryside.
Apr–Oct 5hc (3fb) ⋩ CTV 6P 6acres
mixed S% B&b£5.50 Bdi£7 W£46 ⋎

LYDHAM Salop *Map 7 SO39*
Pultheley *(SO324945)* ☎Linley 214
Pleasant farmhouse set amid picturesque
countryside. 2¾m N A488.
Apr–Oct 2rm ⋩ 3P 264acres mixed Ⓜ
D7pm

LYMPSHAM Somerset *Map 3 ST35*
Mr & Mrs D. J. Brown **Batch** *(ST330555)*
☎Edingworth 371
Large, attractive and well-equipped
farmhouse. Pleasant gardens and lawns.
Fishing available in River Axe on farm land.
Etr–Oct 10hc (4fb) ⋩ nc4 CTV 30P 2🏠
150acres beef S% B&b£7–£8 Bdi£9–£10
W£58–£65 ⋎ D6.30pm

LYONSHALL Heref & Worcs *Map 3 SO35*
Mrs M. A. Eckley **Holme** *(SO339553)*
☎216
Fully-modernised farmhouse standing on
outskirts of village.
Etr–Nov 4rm 3hc (1fb) ⋩ nc9 8P ⋘ mixed
S% B&b£5–£6 W£32–£35 Ⓜ
J. A. Layton **Park Gate** *(SO332575)* ☎243
Two-storey, stone-built farmhouse with land
overlooking Wales. Offa's Dyke runs through
part of farm.
Closed Xmas 2hc (1fb) ⊗ ⋩ CTV 6P ⋘

230acres mixed sheep S% B&b£6 Bdi£10 W£63 ⅄ D4pm

MABE Cornwall *Map 2 SW73*
Mrs E. Jelbert **Higher Halvosso** *(SW740335)* ☎Stithians 860430
Small farmhouse 3 miles from Penryn.
Etr–Sep 2rm 3P 44acres mixed S% B&b£4–£4.50 W£28–£31.50 M

MALPAS Cheshire *Map 7 SJ44*
Mrs N. Evans **Kidnal Grange** *(SJ473493)* ☎344
Clean and comfortable farmhouse. Attractive rural surroundings. Duck pond. Much home produce used in cooking.
Etr–Sep 5rm (2fb) TV 12P 120acres arable mixed pigs S% B&b£6.50–£7

MALVERN WELLS Heref & Worcs *Map 3 SO74*
J. L. Morris **Brick Barns** Hanley Pl *(SO783420)* ☎Malvern 61775
Imposing old farmhouse standing in its own grounds.
Etr–Sep rs Oct–Etr 2rm (1fb) CTV 4P 讍 200acres mixed S% B&b£4–£5.25

MANATON Devon *Map 3 SX78*
Mr & Mrs R. V. Hugo **Langstone** *(SY747823)* ☎266
Long, low granite farmhouse in traditional Dartmoor style. Lawn with children's swings. On edge of the Moor. Fine views.
Mar–Oct 3hc ⌘ nc5 TV 3P 130acres beef S% B&b£6 Bdi£9

MARDEN Heref & Worcs *Map 3 SO54*
Mrs M. Morris **Woodbine** *(SO520477)* ☎ Sutton St Nicholas 291

Two-storey, red brick, Georgian-style farmhouse. Large lawns at front. Situated on edge of small village.
Closed Xmas & New Year 1rm ⌘ nc TV 1P 讍 46acres mixed ✻B&b£6 Bdi£10 W£70 ⅄ D5pm

MARK CAUSEWAY Somerset *Map 3 ST34*
Mrs E. Puddy **Croft** *(ST355475)* ☎Markmoor 206
Comfortable and well-decorated farmhouse with traditional furnishings throughout.
4hc (1fb) ⌘ nc14 CTV TV 4P 130acres dairy S% B&bfr£5–£5.50 Bdi fr£6 Wfr£35 ⅄ D6pm

MARSHFIELD Avon *Map 3 ST77*
Mrs E. Saville **Motcombe** *(ST784718)* ☎201
Modernised, Cotswold-stone farmhouse in pastureland and woodland. Views across valley to Salisbury plain and Mendip Hills.
Apr–Sep 3hc (1fb) ⌘ nc6 10P 讍 40acres beef sheep S% B&b£9.20–£9.90 D4pm

MARSHGATE Cornwall *Map 2 SX19*
Mrs P. Bolt **Carleton** *(SX153918)* ☎ Otterham Station 252
Farmhouse is situated adjacent to the Boscastle road in Marshgate. Views over the surrounding farmlands.
Etr–Sep 3rm (1fb) ⌘ CTV 3P 120acres dairy S% B&b£5.75 Bdi£8.63 W£51.75 D8pm

MARSHWOOD Dorset *Map 3 SY39*
Mr & Mrs D. Edwards **Marshwood Manor** *(SY396993)* ☎ Broadwindsor 68442

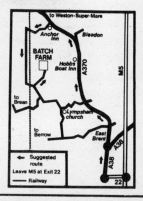

Set in the beauty and peace of Marshwood Vale five miles from Charmouth's unspoilt beach.
Closed Xmas day 8rm 4hc 2🛏(4fb) 🐕
CTV 25P 🐎 B&b£11.50–£12.65 Bdi£16.10–£17.25 W£74.75–£94.30 ⚓ D7pm

MATHON Heref & Worcs *Map 3 SO74*
Mrs Williams **Moorend Court** *(SO726454)*
☎ Ridgeway Cross 205
Beautiful 15th-century farmhouse in secluded position with panoramic views towards Malvern. Trout fishing on farm.
Closed Xmas 3hc (1fb) CTV P 🐎 120acres mixed S% B&b£6–£6.75 D10am

MATLOCK Derbys *Map 8 SK36*
M. Haynes **Packhorse** *(SK323617)* Matlock Moor ☎2781
Former inn on much-travelled Chesterfield to Manchester packhorse route. Tastefully furnished. Lawns and putting greens.
Closed Xmas 4hc (2fb) nc4 CTV P 🐎 40acres mixed S% B&b£5

Mrs J. Hole **Wayside** *(SK324630)*
Matlock Moor ☎2967
Pleasant, modernised, stone-built farmhouse adjacent to A632 Matlock–Chesterfield road.
Closed Xmas & New Years Day 6hc (2fb) nc3 TV 8P 🐎 30acres dairy S% B&bfr£5.50

MATTERDALE END Cumbria
Map 11 NY32
Mrs S. E. Hindson **Ivy House** *(NY396235)*
☎ Glenridding 227
Small stream runs close by farmhouse.
Etr–Oct 3rm 2hc (2fb) P 19½acres beef sheep S% ✳B&bfr£4 Bdifr£5.80 D6.30pm

MATTISHALL Norfolk *Map 9 TG01*
Mrs J. Faircloth **Moat** *(TG049111)*
☎ Dereham 850288
Period farmhouse standing back from road. Good friendly atmosphere.
Jun–Oct 2rm (1fb) 🐾nc4 TV 2P 50acres mixed S% B&b£5.50 Bdi£8.50 W£50 ⚓ D5.30pm

MAWNAN SMITH Cornwall *Map 2 SW72*
Mrs H. Mann **Penwarne Barton** *(SW773301)*
Interesting, well equipped farm with many animals. In very good position within sight of the sea
Etr–Nov 3rm (1fb) TV 3P sea 118acres mixed S% B&b£5–£6

MENDHAM Suffolk *Map 5 TM28*
G. Holden **Weston House** *(TM292828)*
☎ St Cross 206
Fine old house about 300 years old. Fishing nearby.
Mar–Oct 3hc nc12 CTV 4P 🐎 150acres mixed S% B&b£4.50 Bdi£6 W£30–£40 D8pm

MENHENIOT Cornwall *Map 2 SX26*
Mrs S. Rowe **Tregondale** *(SX294643)*
☎ Liskeard 42407
Farm situated 1½ miles north of A38 east of Liskeard.
Closed Xmas 3rm 🐾 🐕CTV 3P 330acres mixed S% B&b£4.50–£5.50 Bdi£6.50–£7.50 D8pm

MERRYMEET Cornwall *Map 2 SX26*
B. Cole **Merrymeet** *(SX279660)*
☎ Liskeard 43231

*Small two-storey, tile-hung farmhouse
with small front garden. Yard and buildings
at rear.*
End May–25Sep 3rm ⚘ TV 2P 40acres
mixed S% ✻B&b£4.50 Bdi£6 W£40 ⚲
D6.30pm

MIDDLETON ON THE HILL Heref &
Worcs *Map 3 SO56*
Mrs C. E. Moseley **Moor Abbey**
(SO545633) ☎ Leysters 226
*Former monastery about 400 years old.
Original oak staircase and upper floors.
Dining room in refectory with open log
fire. Access from A4112 1m SW of Leysters.*
Etr–Oct 3hc (2fb) ⚘ nc8 8P 246acres
mixed S% B&b£5 Bdi£7 D7pm

MIDDLETOWN Powys *Map 7 SJ21*
Mrs E. J. Bebb **Bank** *(SJ325137)*
☎ Trewern 260
*Traditional farmhouse with rear garden and
an attractive outlook.*
Apr–Oct 2hc (1fb) ⚘ CTV P ▥ 30acres
mixed S% B&bfr£4.50 Bdi fr£7.50 D7.30pm

MILBORNE PORT Somerset *Map 3 ST61*
Mrs M. J. Tizzard **Venn** *(ST684183)*
☎250208
*Modern, purpose-built farmhouse in
mellow stone. Situation amid rural scenery
on outskirts of village.*
Mar–Nov 3rm 2hc (2fb) ⚘ ♨ CTV 6P ▥
300acres mixed S% B&b£5.50

MILNGAVIE Strathclyde *Dunbartons
Map 11 NS57*
Mrs L. Fisken **High Craigton**
(NS525766) ☎041-956 1384
*Two-storey, stone-built farmhouse with
numerous outbuildings. Good access road.*
2hc ⚘ CTV 10P ▥ 1200acres S% B&b£4

MOLLAND Devon *Map 3 SS82*
Mrs P. England **Yeo** *(SS785266)*
☎ Bishops Nympton 312
*Well-maintained farmhouse with good
furnishings and décor. Set in large
garden.*
Apr–Oct 3hc (1fb) ⚘ CTV 4P 200acres
mixed S% B&b£5–£6 Bdi£9–£10
W£60–£65 ⚲ D7pm

MONEYDIE Tayside *Perths Map 11 NO02*
Mrs S. Walker **Moneydie Roger**
(NO054290) ☎ Almondbank 239
*A substantial, two-storey farmhouse
standing amid good arable land. Perth
7 miles.*
Apr–Sep ⚘ 2P 143acres arable mixed S%
B&bfr£4.50

MONKTON Devon *Map 3 ST10*
Pugh's *(ST186029)* ☎ Honiton 2860
*Well situated farmhouse on the A30 at
Monkton. Honiton about 1½ miles.*
Feb–Oct 3rm 2hc nc3 CTV 6P ▥ 8acres
mixed D5pm

MONTGOMERY Powys *Map 7 SO29*
Mrs S. M. Davies **East Penyllan**
(SO244941) ☎246
*Farmhouse is in England, 2m SE of
Montgomery on B4385.*
Closed 20Dec–1Jan 3rm (1fb) CTV 5P
195acres mixed S% B&b£4.50–£4.75
Bdi£6.50–£7 W£45–£49 ⚲ D6pm

MONTROSE Tayside *Angus Map 15
NO75*

Mrs A. Ruxton **Muirshade of Gallery**
(NO671634) ☎Northwater Bridge 209
*Situated in beautiful countryside facing the
Grampian Mountain range and only 5 miles
from the seaside.*
2rm (1fb) ⚘ TV 3P 110acres arable S%
B&b£4–£4.50 Bdi£7.50–£8
W£52.50–£56 ⚲ D6pm

MORNINGTHORPE Norfolk *Map 5 TM29*
Mrs O. K. Gowing **Hollies** *(TM212939)*
☎Long Stratton 30540
*Large Georgian property standing in own
grounds, in quiet rural area. ¾m E of A140.
Good atmosphere, plenty of amenities.*
Apr–Oct 9hc (4fb) ⚘ CTV 6P ▥ 350acres
arable B&b£6.50–£8.50 Bdi£8.50–£9.50
⚲ (W only end Jul–Aug) D6.30pm

MORVAH Cornwall *Map 2 SW33*
Mrs J. Mann **Merthyr** *(SW403355)*
☎Penzance 788464
*Well-appointed farmhouse on B3306
north west of Penzance.*
May–Oct 6hc (3fb) ⚘ CTV TV 6P sea
100acres beef S% B&b£6–£7.50
W£38.50–£49

MOUNT Cornwall *Map 2 SX16*
E. J. Beglan **Mount Pleasant** *(SX152680)*
☎Cardinham 342
*Farm 6 miles east of Bodmin in open
country on the edge of Bodmin Moor. Own
transport essential.*
Mar–Oct 5hc (A 2rm) (3fb) CTV 6P ▥
50acres arable S% ✻B&b£5–£5.75
Bdi£7.50–£8.75 W£49–£58 ⚲ D5pm

MOYLGROVE Dyfed *Map 2 SN14*
Mrs A. D. Fletcher **Penrallt Ceibwr**
(SN116454) ☎217
*A very pleasant farm off A487. ½m from
Ceibwr beach.*
6hc (4fb) ♨ CTV TV P ▥ sea 250acres
mixed B&b£8–£10 Bdi£13–£15
W£90–£100 ⚲ D7pm

MUSBURY Devon *Map 3 SY29*
Mrs S. L. Cligg **Higher Bruckland**
(SY284933) ☎Colyton 52371
*Farmhouse completely surrounded by
farmland. Seaton 4 miles.*
Etr–Oct 3hc (1fb) ⚘ CTV P 236acres mixed
S% B&b£4–£5 Bdi£6.50–£7.50 Wfr£49
⚲ (W only Aug) D4.30pm

NANTGAREDIG Dyfed *Map 2 SN42*
Mrs J. Willmott **Cwmtwrch** *(SN497220)*
☎238
*Early 19th-century Welsh-stone
farmhouse, carefully modernised and
furnished.*
3rm 2hc 1⟶▥ ⚘ TV 10P 30acres mixed S%
B&bfr£5.50 Bdifr£9 Wfr£60 ⚲ D8pm

NETHER COMPTON Dorset *Map 3 ST51*
Mrs C. D. Allard **Halfway House**
(ST603163) ☎Sherborne (Dorset) 2781
*Mellow, stone-built house in elevated
position. Well-kept gardens. Interesting
display of horseriding awards. On A30.*
Mar–Oct 3hc (1fb) CTV 8P ▥ 120acres
beef & horses S% B&bfr£6.50

NEWBOLD ON STOUR Warwicks
Map 4 SP24
Mrs J. Kerby **Berryfield** *(SP216483)*
☎Ilmington 248

245

A deceptively-large farmhouse in secluded position.
Apr–Oct 3hc (1fb) ⌾ P 100acres mixed S%
B&b£5–£6

NEWBRIDGE Lothian *Midlothian*
Map 11 NT17
Mr & Mrs W. Pollock **Easter Norton**
(NT157721) ☎031-333 1279
Small attractive farmhouse. Excellent position for motorway and Edinburgh Airport.
Apr–Sep 3rm (2fb) CTV P 🛏 5acres poultry
S% B&b fr£5

NEWBURGH Fife *Map 11 NO21*
Glen Duckie *(NO283188)* ☎352
A large farm set amid rolling hills with main farmhouse dating from 16th century.
May–Sep 2rm ⌾ TV 4P 358acres mixed

NEWCASTLE Salop *Map 7 SO28*
Mrs P. M. Reynolds **Newcastle Hall**
(SO246824) ☎Clun 350
Large stone-built Georgian farmhouse in peaceful setting surrounded by tree-clad hills.
Etr–Oct 4rm 3hc (1fb) P 278acres mixed
S% B&b£6–£7 Bdi£9–£10 D5pm

NEW CUMNOCK Strathclyde *Ayrs*
Map 11 NS61
Mr & Mrs A. Howat **Pollshill** *(NS652132)*
☎301
Pleasant, well-kept old mill house, parts of which date back 300 years.
Jun–Oct 2rm (2fb) ⌾ nc5 CTV 3P 230acres
arable beef S% B&b fr£4

NEWQUAY Cornwall *Map 2 SW86*
Legonna *(SW834594)* ☎2272
Granite farmhouse in beautiful wooded valley. Swimming pool, tennis court, private fishing lake, children's play area and pony riding. 2½m SE of Newquay.
May–Sep 10hc TV 10P 140acres mixed

Mr & Mrs A. R. E. Wilson **Manuels**
(SW839601) Lane ☎3577
17th-century farmhouse in sheltered, wooded valley 2 miles from Newquay on A392.
Closed Xmas 4rm (2fb) ⌂ CTV 4P 35acres
mixed S% B&b£5–£6.50 Bdi£8.20–£10.80
W£57–£75 ⚓ (W only May–Aug)

NEWTON (Nr Vowchurch) Heref & Worcs
Map 3 SO33
Mrs J. Powell **Little Green** *(SO335337)*
☎Michaelchurch 205

Modernised farmhouse which used to be an inn. Friendly atmosphere.
Closed Xmas 3hc (2fb) CTV 3P 50acres
mixed S% B&b fr£6.50 Bdi fr£8.50 ⚓

NEWTON ARLOSH Cumbria
Map 11 NY15
Oak Tree *(NY199553)* ☎Kirkbride 418
Clean, unpretentious farmhouse in rural surroundings ¾ mile from sea.
May–Oct 1rm ⌾ CTV 150acres arable & dairy D8.30pm

NEWTOWN Powys *Map 6 SO19*
L. Whitticase **Highgate** *(SJ111953)*
☎25981
Wonderful views over valley and hills.
3hc ⌾ ⌂ CTV P 🛏 300acres mixed S%
B&b fr£6 Bdi fr£9 Wfr£60 ⚓ D5pm

NOMANSLAND (nr Tiverton) Devon
Map 3 SS81
Mrs R. I. Pratt **Moor Barton** *(SS844134)*
☎Tiverton 860325
Farmhouse is well placed for touring North Devon and Exmoor. In peaceful surroundings. Friendly atmosphere.
9hc (4fb) CTV 12P 🛏 200acres mixed S%
B&b£7.50 Bdi£9.50 W£60.95 Ⓜ D7.30pm

NORMANBY N Yorks *Map 8 NZ90*
D. I. Smith **Heather View** *(NZ928062)*
☎Whitby 880451
Attractive, modern farmhouse. Well-appointed and comfortable. Conveniently situated for coastal visits.
20 Mar–Oct 5hc (2fb) ⌾ nc5 CTV 5P 🛏
40acres mixed S% B&b£5–£5.50
Bdi£7–£7.50 D5.30pm

NORTH CADBURY Somerset
Map 3 ST62
Mr R. Buxton **Ferngrove** *(ST637274)*
Woolston ☎40329
In a pleasant secluded locality. Lawn and produce garden adjoining house.
4rm (1fb) ⌾ CTV 6P 130acres arable
beef sheep S% B&b£5.50 Bdi£8.50 W£56
⚓

E. J. Keen **Hill** *(ST634279)* ☎40257
Two-storey, red-brick, double-fronted farmhouse with front garden and extensive outbuildings.
Etr–Sep 3rm 1hc (1fb) ⌾ nc TV P dairy S%
B&b fr£5 Bdi fr£7.50

NORTH WOOTTON Somerset
Map 3 ST54
Mrs M. White **Barrow** *(ST553416)*
☎Pilton 245

Stone-built farmhouse with beams. Garden
and concreted yard. ½ mile from village.
Mar–Oct 3hc (1fb) ⚘ CTV 3P 146acres
dairy B&b£5 Bdi£8

NORTON Notts *Map 8 SK57*
Norton Grange *(SK572733)* ☎ Warsop
2666
*A 200-year-old stone-built farmhouse
fronted by tidy gardens at edge of village.*
Etr–Sep 3rm 1hc CTV 6P 🍴 175acres
beef & mixed

NOTTER Cornwall *Map 2 SX36*
Notter *(SX390609)* ☎ Saltash 3593
*Quietly situated farmhouse a few yards off
the A38 overlooking the valley.*
3rm 32hc ⚘ TV 6P 🍴 200acres mixed M

ODDINGLEY Heref & Worcs *Map 3 SO95*
Mrs P. B. Wardle **Pear Tree's** *(SO909589)*
☎ Droitwich 8489
*Large modern farmhouse in quiet country
lane close to M5 motorway.*
Closed Dec & Jan rs Nov–Mar B&b 4rm 2hc
⚘ nc5 CTV P 🍴 17acres mixed S%
B&b£6.50 Bdi£8.50 W£45.50–£49 ⚡

OKEHAMPTON Devon *Map 2 SX59*
Mrs E. Maile **Agiestment** *(SX603979)*
☎ 2359
*Well-appointed farmhouse with extensive
moor and forest views.*
Mar–Oct 2rm ⚘ nc12 CTV 4P 150acres
mixed sea S% B&b£5–£6 Bdi£7–£8
W£47.50–£50 ⚡

Mrs M. Pennington **Hill Barton**
(SX594984) ☎ 2454
*Good working farm in peaceful setting in
the heart of beautiful, well-wooded
countryside.*
Mar–Nov 3rm 2hc ⚘ nc8 TV 4P 280acres
mixed S% B&b£6.50 Bdi£10.50

Mrs K. C. Heard **Hughslade** *(SX561932)*
☎ 2883
*Pleasant farmhouse on the edge of town.
Ideal base for exploring Dartmoor and
north and south Devon coasts.*
Closed Xmas 5hc CTV P 2🏠 500acres
mixed S% B&b£5.50–£7.50 Bdi fr£8
Wfr£55 ⚡ D5.30pm

OKEOVER Staffs *Map 7 SK14*
E. J. Harrison **Little Park** *(SK160490)*
☎ Thorpe Cloud 341
*Red brick and stone farmhouse, interior
abounds with oak beams.*
Apr–7Sep 3rm 2hc (2fb) ⚘ nc3 CTV 3P
130acres dairy S% W£45 ⚡

OLD DALBY Leics *Map 8 SK62*
Mrs V. Anderson **Home** *(SK673236)* Church
Lane ☎ Melton Mowbray 822622
*19th-century farmhouse, parts dating from
1730. Former bailiff's house when property
was part of estate.*
Closed Dec 3hc (1fb) TV 4P 🍴 3acres
non-working S% B&b£7 Bdi£10.50 Dnoon

ONICH Highland *Inverness-shire
Map 14 NN06*
Cuilcheanna House *(NN019617)* ☎ 226
*Large Victorian house with gardens set in
sloping fields leading to Loch Linnhe.
Excellent views over lochs and mountains.
Secluded.*
Etr–Sep 9rm 8hc ⚘ 8P 🍴 120acres arable
beef D7pm

ORKNEY *Map 16*
See Kirkwall, Orphir (below), **Rendall**

ORPHIR Orkney *Map 16 HY30*
Orakirk *(HY302047)* ☎ 328
*Pleasant farmhouse reached by a typical
farm road almost ½ mile long.*
2rm ⚘ nc10 CTV 2P 114acres arable
beef D7.30pm

OTTERBURN Northumb *Map 12 NY89*
Mr & Mrs G. F. Stephenson **Monkridge**
(NY913917) ☎ 20639
*Well-cared-for, comfortable farmhouse in
the attractive environment of the
Northumberland Moors.*
Closed Xmas 3rm (1fb) ⚘ CTV 3P 🍴
1,400acres sheep S% B&b£5–£6
Bdi£8–£8.50 W£56–£59.50 ⚡ D3pm

OXENHOPE W Yorks *Map 7 SE03*
Mrs A. Scholes **Lily Hall** *(SE023362)*
Uppermarsh Ln ☎ Howarth 43999
*Pleasant farmhouse in 9-acre smallholding
rearing turkeys and hens. Overlooking
pleasant valley in Brontë country. Horse
riding, golf, tennis and bathing 4 miles.*
Closed Xmas day 3hc ⚘ CTV 12P 🍴 9acres
beef poultry horses S% ✱B&b£5 Bdi£7–£8
D8pm

PADOG Gwynedd *Map 6 SH85*
M. L. Davis **Dylasau Isa** *(SH832157)*
☎ Betws-y-Coed 265
*Stone-built farmhouse ½ mile from A5,
east of town.*
Mar–Oct 3rm (1fb) ⚘ TV 6P 300acres
mixed S% B&b£4.50–£5.50 W£30–£32 M

Hughslade Farm Okehampton, Devon

The farm is ideally situated for touring Devon,
Cornwall, Dartmoor and Exmoor. Hughslade is a
large working farm with plenty of animals around.
The farmhouse is comfortably furnished. Lounge
with colour TV and central heating on the ground
floor. Meals served in the dining room, are mainly
made from home-produced vegetables and meat.
Bed, breakfast and evening meal or bed and
breakfast daily. Okehampton is just 2 miles from
the farm and has a superb golf course, tennis courts
and covered swimming pool. Horse riding
available at the farm. Happy holiday assured. SAE
please for terms to Mrs. K. C. Heard, Hughslade
Farm, Okehampton, Devon. Tel: Okehampton
2883.

Mrs D. O. Jones **Ty-Uchaf** *(SH830503)*
☎ Pentrefoelas 280
Stone-built farmhouse on hill farm.
Closed Dec 4hc (2fb) ⚭ CTV 20P 300acres
mixed sheep S% B&b£5−5.50
Bdi£7−£7.50 W£46−£50 ⚹ D5.30pm

PANCRASWEEK Devon *Map 2 SS20*
M. A. Brown **Higher Kingford** *(SS285061)*
☎ Bridgerule 281
Small working farm 6 miles from Bude.
5rm 2hc (4fb) ⚭ CTV 6P 84acres mixed

PANDY TUDUR Clwyd *Map 6 SH86*
Llywn Llydan *(SH851647)*
☎ Llangernyw 243
*Modernised farmhouse in an elevated
situation. Magnificent views.*
2rm 1hc ⚭ nc8 4P river 85acres mixed

PANTYGELLI *(Nr Abergavenny)* Gwent
Map 3 SO31
Mrs M. E. Smith **Lower House** *(SO3141599)*
Old Hereford Rd ☎ Abergavenny 3432
*Isolated, stone-built farmhouse. Well
situated 3 miles from Abergavenny.*
Etr−Oct 3hc (1fb) TV 6P 209acres beef
sheep S% B&b£5−£5.50

PEBWORTH Heref & Worcs *Map 4 SP14*
Mrs M. J. Jordan **Pebworth Fields**
(SP134459) ☎ Stratford-on-Avon 720318
*Unusual, colonial-style farmhouse. Trim
grounds fairly remote and ideal for local
tourist areas.*
May−Sep 3rm 1hc (1fb) ⚭ TV P 100acres
mixed S% B&bf6−£6.50 W£40−£43 M

PELYNT Cornwall *Map 2 SX25*
Mrs E. Tuckett **Trenderway** *(SX214533)*
☎ Polperro 72214
*Comfortable and well-maintained
farmhouse about 3 miles from Looe.*
3hc (1fb) ⚭ CTV P 400acres mixed S%
B&bf5−£6.25

PENMACHNO Gwynedd *Map 6 SH75*
Tyddyn Gethin *(SH799514)* ☎392
*Farm situated high on mountainside with
panoramic views of surrounding country.*
3hc ⚭ TV P 60acres beef, mixed and sheep

PENRUDDOCK Cumbria *Map 12 NY42*
Mrs S. M. Smith **Highgate** *(NY444275)*
☎ Greystoke 339
*250-year-old, stone-built farmhouse with
beamed ceilings; tastefully modernised.
Good base for touring and recreational
facilities. Children's playground. 2m E
on A66.*

Feb−Nov 4rm 2hc ⚭ nc10 CTV 4P 400acres
beef sheep S% B&bf5−£6 Bdi£8−£9
W£50−£56 ⚹ D6pm

PENTREFOELAS Clwyd *Map 6 SH85*
M. Thomas **Tai Hirion** *(SH839525)* ☎202
*Two-storey, stone-built house. Adjacent to
A5 Corwen to Betws-y-Coed road.*
2hc ⚭ TV 204acres mixed S%
B&bf4.50−£5 Bdi£6.50−£7 W£45.50 ⚹

PENYBONT Powys *Map 3 SO16*
Mrs J. R. Collard **Neuadd** *(SO092618)*
Cefnllys ☎ Llandrindod Wells 2571
*Two-storey, isolated farmhouse situated in
elevated position. Fine views.*
May−Oct 4rm 3hc (2fb) CTV 8P 🐎 river
329½acres mixed S% B&bf6 90 Bdi£9.20
W£63.25 ⚹ D5pm

PILSDON Dorset *Map 3 SY49*
Monkwood *(SY429986)*
☎ Broadwindsor 68723 2rm 3P 130acres
mixed ⚹

PITLOCHRY Tayside *Perths Map 14 NN95*
Mrs M. M. Hay **Faskally House**
(NN918601) ☎2007
*Pleasant 'U'-shaped farm with popular
caravan site attached. Set on west side of
A9 on northern outskirts of Pitlochry.
Sheltered from Loch Faskally by trees.*
Apr−Oct 7rm 6hc (2fb) P 100acres
non-working S% ✱B&bf4.50

PLAYING PLACE Cornwall *Map 2 SW84*
Halvarras *(SW814415)* ☎Devoran
862305
*Typical stone-built farmhouse about 1½
miles from A39.*
Apr−Sep 6hc ⚭ 6P 115acres arable & beef

PLYMOUTH Devon *Map 2 SX45*
Ford *(SX582554)* Plympton ☎336863
*Clean and well decorated farmhouse.
Ideal base for riding, golf, tennis. Near local
beaches. 4m E off A38.*
Closed Xmas 3rm 2hc ⚭ CTV 6P 2🏠
110acres dairy

PONSWORTHY Devon *Map 3 SX77*
Mr & Mrs Fursdon **Old Walls** *(SX697745)*
☎Poundsgate 222
*Farmhouse standing in its own small estate.
Isolated, near Dartmoor. Pleasant
atmosphere.*
3rm ♨ 6P 36acres beef mixed S%
B&bfr£6.32

PONTARDULAIS W Glam *Map 2 SN50*
Mr & Mrs G. Davies **The Croft** *(SN612015)*

Heol-y-Barna ☎883654
*Farmhouse has open aspect to the Gower
Peninsula and the Loughour Estuary.*
3rm 2hc 1⊣🛏 (1fb) nc5 TV 4P 1🏠 ∰ sea
5acres beef S% B&b£5.50—£7.50
Bdi£8.50—£10.50 W£55—£70 ⬩ D5pm

POOLEY BRIDGE Cumbria *Map 12 NY42*
Mrs A. Strong **Barton Hall** *(NY478251)*
☎275
*Attractive farmhouse, well furnished and
decorated. Large garden with lawn and
summer house. Boating, fishing and golf
nearby.*
Mar—Oct 3rm 2hc (1fb) ❀ nc8 3P 66acres
dairy S% B&b fr£6

PORT OF MENTEITH Central *Perths
Map 11 NN50*
Mrs J. Fotheringham **Collymoon**
(NN593966) ☎Buchlyvie 268
*Attractive white-painted farmhouse near
lane. Situated just off B8034.*
Etr—Oct 3rm 1hc (3fb) nc TV 3P ∰
350acres arable beef S% B&b£5—£6
Bdi£7—£8.50 (W only Etr—Oct) D6pm

PORTREE Isle of Skye, Highland
Inverness-shire Map 13 NG44
Mrs M. Bruce **Cruachanlea** *(NG513373)*
Braes ☎Sligachan 233
*Situated 6 miles SE of Portree on B883,
overlooking sea to the Isle of Raasay. Hill
views everywhere.*
3hc (2fb) CTV 8P ∰ sea 10acres sheep S%
B&b£5.50—£8 Bdi£7—£9 D7pm

No 1 Uigishadder (NG430463)
☎Skeabost Bridge 279
*Small crofting farm situated high on moor
in isolated position facing north west.
Portree about 4 miles.*
Apr—Sep 3rm ❀ 6P 6acres arable

Mrs S. MacDonald **Upper Ollach**
(NG518362) Braes ☎Sligachan 225
*Grey, stone crofting farm in 7 acres of hilly
farmland with gardens and trees screening
the house. Close to coastline 6½m SE of
Portree on B883.*
Apr—Oct 3rm ❀ TV 4P sea 7¾acres mixed
S% B&b fr£4.50 Bdi fr£8

POUNDSGATE Devon *Map 3 SX77*
Mrs G. Fursdon **Lowertown** *(SX712729)*
☎282
*Pleasantly-situated farmhouse with wooden
beams in entrance hall.*
Closed Xmas 3rm (1fb) 3P 120acres beef
S% B&b£5.50

PWLLHELI Gwynedd *Map 6 SH33*
M. E. Hughes **Bryn Crin** *(SH379358)*
☎2494
*Large, stone-built farmhouse in an elevated
position overlooking Cardigan Bay and
Snowdonia. Within easy reach of sandy
beaches.*
May—Oct 3rm 2hc (2fb) ❀ CTV 3P sea
70acres beef sheep S% ✱B&b£4.50—£5

REDMILE Leics *Map 8 SK73*
Mrs A. Barton **Olde Mill House**
(SK789358) ☎Bottesford 42460
*A beautiful house approximately 250 years
old, which has been considerably
modernised; set in peaceful Belvoir valley.*
4hc ❀ nc10 CTV 4P 2🏠 ∰ 5acres small
holding S% B&b£6.50—£7
Bdi£10.75—£11.25 W£71.75—£75.25 ⬩
D noon

Mr & Mrs Need **Peacock** *(SK791359)*
☎Bottesford 42475
*Modernised 250-year-old farmhouse.
Hunter stud farm with paddocks. Horse
riding available. In rural Vale of Belvoir
close to Castle.*
Closed Xmas 4rm 1hc (A 2rm) (2fb) ♨ CTV
P ∰ 5acres horses S% B&b£7.50 Bdi£11
W£76 ⬩ D8.30pm

RENDALL Orkney *Map 16 HY32*
Mrs H. R. Hargus **Lower Ellibister**
(HY386213) ☎Evie 224
*Farmhouse set amid beautiful countryside
with extensive views across the bay to
Kirkwall.*
3rm (1fb) CTV 3P sea 344acres arable beef
sheep S% B&b fr£4 Bdi fr£7 D6pm

RHANDIRMWYN Dyfed *Map 3 SN74*
G. A. Williams **Galltybere** *(SN772460)*
☎218
*Isolated farmhouse 9 miles north of
Llandovery amid splendid scenery. Ideal for
bird watching and hikers.*
Apr—Nov 1rm (A 2hc) (1fb) ❀ nc8 CTV P
river 325acres mixed B&b fr£6 W£35 Ⓜ
(W only Apr—Nov)

ROBOROUGH Devon *Map 2 SS51
Rapson Court (SS573179)*
☎High Bickington 246
*Typical small Devonshire farmhouse dating
from 17th century. Thatched roof, oak
beams, horse brasses. Good views of
surrounding countryside.*
Etr—mid Sep 2hc ❀ nc5 TV 2P 125acres
mixed

ROCHESTER Northumb *Map 12 NY89*
Mrs G. E. Wilson **Woolaw** *(NY821985)*
☎Otterburn 20686
*The farmhouse was built about 1800 and
overlooks the valley of the River Rede. It is
about 100 yards from A68.*
3rm (1fb) ❀ CTV 3P 800acres mixed S%
B&b£4.50—£5 W£35 Ⓜ

ROGART Highland *Sutherland
Map 14 NC70*
Mr & Mrs J. S. R. Moodie **Rovie**
(NC716023) ☎209
*Farmhouse situated in the Strathfleet
valley 4 miles from sea. Rabbit-shooting on
farm and fishing locally in River Fleet. S off
A839.* **See colour section.**
Apr—Oct 3hc ♨ CTV 4P 2120acres arable
beef sheep S% B&b£5.50 Bdi£9 W£70 ⬩
D6.30pm

ROSEDALE ABBEY N Yorks *Map 8 SE79*
Mrs D. J. Rawlings **High House**
(SE698974) ☎Lastingham 471
*18th-century modernised farmhouse,
stone-built and oak-beamed. Log fires.
Panoramic views over dale.*
3hc 3⊣🛏 6P ∰ 100acres beef sheep S%
B&b£6—£7 Bdi£10—£12 W£42—£49 ⬩

ROSTON Derbys *Map 7 SK14*
Mrs E. K. Prince **Roston Hall** *(SK133409)*
☎Ellastone 287
*Former Manor House, part Elizabethan and
part Georgian, in centre of quiet village.
Ideal centre for touring Peak District.*
May—Sep 2rm 1hc (1fb) ❀ nc14 TV 4P
100acres arable beef D10am

ROTHESAY Isle of Bute, Strathclyde
Bute Map 10 NS06

Birgidale Crieff *(NS073591)*
☎Kilchattan Bay 236
Well cared for, attractively furnished farmhouse on south end of island. Well maintained garden. 3m S off A845.
Apr–Oct 2rm nc4 TV 3P ✉ sea 300acres arable dairy

RUSHTON SPENCER Staffs *Map 7 SJ96*
Mr J. Brown **Barnswood** *(SJ945606)*
☎261
Large stone-built farmhouse. Grounds stretch to edge of Rudyard Lane. Splendid views across lake to distant hills.
3rm 2hc (2fb) ✗ CTV 4P lake 100acres dairy S% B&b£6 Bdi£9.50 W£63 ⱪ D noon

RUSKIE Central *Perths Map 11 NN60*
Mrs S. F. Bain **Lower Tarr** *(NN624008)*
☎Thornhill (Stirling) 202
Large, well-maintained farm over 200 years old, with partly-modernised interior. Good views over rolling hill land.
Apr–Oct 3rm 1hc (1fb) ✗ CTV 5P 161acres mixed S% B&b£4.50–£5 Bdi£7–£8 D4pm

RUTHIN Clwyd *Map 6 SJ15*
M. E. Jones **Pen-y-Coed** *(SJ107538)*
Pwllglas ☎Clawdd Newydd 251
Isolated farmhouse on high ground with extensive views. Stone-built with timbered ceilings.
3hc (3fb) TV P ✉ 160acres mixed S% ✱B&b fr£4.50 Bdi fr£6 Wfr£39 M

Mrs T. Francis **Plas-y-Ward** *(SJ118604)*
Rhewl ☎3822
Period farmhouse, dating back to 14th-century. 2m N A525.
Jun–Sep 2rm ✗ nc6 TV 10P 216acres mixed S% B&b£6.50 W£40 M

RUYTON-XI-TOWNS Salop *Map 7 SJ32*
Mrs V. Mason **Lower** *(SJ362261)*
Shotatton ☎Knockin 461
Smallholding with well-furnished accommodation. Well placed for touring. Two acres of private ground. Fishing and golf 3 miles.
4hc 1⇌ (1fb) CTV 6P ✉ 2acres non-working S% B&b£6–£8 Bdi£9–£12 W£55–£65 ⱪ D7pm

RYDE Isle of Wight *Map 4 SZ59*
Mrs C. Morey **Aldermoor** *(SZ582906)*
Upton Rd ☎64743
Two Victorian cottages situated in rural surroundings. 1½m from Ryde.
Etr–Oct 3hc (2fb) CTV 3⌂ 60acres dairy S% B&b£4.50 Bdi£6.50

ST AGNES Cornwall *Map 2 SW75*
W. R. & K. B. Blewett **Mount Pleasant** *(SW722508)* Rosemundy ☎2387
Spacious bungalow set in the farm meadows. Stands in its own large garden with beautiful views.
Etr–Oct 11hc (4fb) CTV 20P 40acres dairy S% B&b£5–£6 Bdi£8–£9

ST BURYAN Cornwall *Map 2 SW42*
Boskenna Home *(SW423237)* ☎250
Farmhouse situated in a convenient position. Beaches a few miles away. Pleasant spacious rooms with traditional furniture.
Etr–Sep 3rm 2hc ✗ ♧ CTV P 75acres dairy ⱪ D6pm

Mrs M. R. Pengelly **Burnew Hall** *(SW407236)* ☎200
Former 'gentleman's residence' with spacious rooms. Farm has its own coastline with safe bathing.
mid May–mid Oct 3hc (1fb) ✗ nc CTV 3P sea 150acres dairy B&b£4.50–£5 Bdi£8–£9 W£50–£55 ⱪ D4pm

ST DOGMAELS Dyfed *Map 2 SN14*
Mrs M. Cave **Granant Isaf** *(SN126473)*
Cipyn ☎Moylegrove 241
The Pembrokeshire Coastal Path runs along the boundary of this farm which enjoys spectacular views of the sea and cliffs.
Apr–Oct rs Nov–Mar 2rm (1fb) ♧ CTV 2P ✉ sea 400acres dairy S% B&b£4–£5 Bdi£7–£8 W£46.50–£52.50 ⱪ D6pm

ST ERME Cornwall *Map 2 SW85*
Pengelly *(SW856513)* Trispen
☎Mitchell 245
Attractive, well built farmhouse. Good central base for touring Cornwall.
Mar–Oct 4hc ✗ nc10 CTV 4P 230acres mixed

Mrs B. Dymond **Trevispian Vean** *(SW850502)* Trispen ☎Truro 79514
Extensively modernised farmhouse. Clean and well maintained. Large sun lounge at the front.
Etr & mid May–mid Sep 7rm 6hc (3fb) ✗ ♧ CTV P 430acres mixed S% B&b£5.50–£6 Bdi£7.50–£8 W£44 ⱪ (W only mid May–mid Sep D6.30pm

ST EWE Cornwall *Map 2 SW94*
J. G. Kent **Lanewa** *(SW983457)*
☎Mevagissey 3283
Comfortable farmhouse situated in the small village of St Ewe. St Austell about 6 miles.
mid May–Sep 3hc ✗ CTV 3P 60acres mixed S% ✱B&b fr£5 Bdi fr£7

ST JOHN'S IN THE VALE Cumbria *Map 11 NY32*
Mrs H. Harrison **Shundraw** *(NY308236)*
☎Threlkeld 227
Large, well maintained, stone-built farmhouse, parts dating from 1712. In elevated position with views across valley.
May–Oct 3rm (1fb) ✗ TV 4P 52acres sheep S% B&b£4

ST JUST-IN-ROSELAND Cornwall *Map 3 SW83*
Mrs W. Symons **Commerrans** *(SW842375)* ☎Portscatho 270
Pleasant modernised farmhouse, attractively decorated throughout. Large garden. Wonderful scenery in the area.
Etr–Nov 4rm 3hc (1fb) ✗ nc2 CTV 6P 61acres beef sheep ✱B&b£6 Bdi£7.50 W£50 ⱪ D am

ST KEW HIGHWAY Cornwall *Map 2 SX07*
Mrs N. Harris **Kelly Green** *(SX047758)*
☎Bodmin 850275
Old, two-storey farmhouse with lawn at the front.
5hc (4fb) ✗ CTV 5P 300acres mixed S% B&b£5–£6.50 Bdi£8 W£35 ⱪ

ST KEYNE Cornwall *Map 2 SX26*
V. R. Arthur **Killigorrick** *(SX228614)*
☎Dobwalls 20559
Farmhouse lies 3½ miles from Liskeard 1m W off Dulce–Dobwalls road.
4hc (2fb) ✗ nc5 TV 4P 1⌂ 20acres mixed S% ✱B&b£4.50–£5 Bdi£7–£7.50 D11am

We've got a lot of good things going for you . . .

...and they are all in our catalogues, packed full of useful and practical things for you, your family and your friends.

We cover the whole spectrum of leisure activities, including camping, travelling and do it yourself, a range of marvellous AA books and much more for the motorist.

To see our range, fill in the coupon below and our current catalogue will be on its way to you. So broaden your leisure outlook this year . . . with the AA, and remember as an AA member you have both 14 day approval and free credit facilities up to a value of £150.

Please send me a FREE copy of the latest AA Catalogue

Membership No. . . . .

Name Mr./Mrs./Miss. . . . .

Address. . . . .

. . . .

. . . .

Send to: The Automobile Association Mail Order Dept., P.O. Box 50, FREEPOST, Basingstoke, Hampshire RG21 2BR.

ST MARGARET, SOUTH ELMHAM
Suffolk *Map 5 TM38*
Mr H. B. Custerson **Elm House**
(TM310840) ☎St Cross 228
*Delightful period farmhouse in extremely
quiet location; friendly atmosphere.*
Apr–Oct 3hc ⊗ nc10 CTV 6P 📖 240acres
arable sheep S% B&b fr£7 Bdi fr£12
Wfr£72 ⠠ D5pm

SAMPFORD PEVERELL Devon
Map 3 ST01
Mrs M. H. Parkhouse **Higher Shutehanger**
(ST030133) ☎820569
*Secluded farmhouse adjacent to the Grand
Western Canal. Well situated for touring
Devon and the Dartmoor and Exmoor
National Parks.*
Etr–Oct 3hc (1fb) ⊗ CTV 3P 3🏠 📖
15acres mixed S% B&b£5.25–£5.50
W£33.50–£35 M

SAXELBY Leics *Map 8 SK62*
Mrs M. Morris **Manor House** *(SK701208)*
☎Melton Mowbray 812269
*Part 12th, part 15th-century farmhouse in
high Leicestershire village. Feature is
15th-century staircase.*
Etr–Oct 2hc (1fb) ⊗ ⠠ TV 6P 📖 125acres
dairy sheep S% B&b fr£6.50 Bdi fr£10.50
W£70 ⠠ D noon

SCANIPORT Highland *Inverness-shire
Map 14 NH63*
Mr D. A. Mackintosh **Antfield** *(NH616371)*
☎219
*Large, two-storey building, ½ mile off
B862.*
May–Sep 2rm (2fb) ⊗ nc4 CTV 10P
354acres mixed S% B&b£5

SCARISTA Isle of Harris, Western Isles
Inverness-shire Map 13 NG09
Mrs M. Macdonald **Croft** *(NG002926)*
1 Scarista Vore ☎201
*Small, well maintained croft which doubles
as local Post Office. Good position facing
west overlooking golden sands and ocean.*
Apr–Sep 2rm 2P 19acres mixed S%
B&b£5.50–£6 Bdi£9.50–£10

SEABOROUGH Dorset *Map 3 ST40*
Mrs C. R. Creed **West Swillets**
(ST428056) ☎ Broadwindsor 68264
*Modernised early-17th-century farmhouse
with oak beams and low ceilings, situated in
remote part of West Dorset.*
Mar–Sep 4hc (1fb) ⊗ TV 4P 200acres
arable & beef S% B&b£6–£7 W£42–£49
M

SEBERGHAM Cumbria *Map 11 NY34*
Mrs E. M. Johnston **Bustabeck**
(NY373419) ☎ Raughton Head 339
*Stone-built farmhouse dating from 1684.
Extensively modernised.*
Etr, May, Jun & Aug 3rm ⊗ nc TV 6P
72acres mixed S% B&b£4 Bdi£7 D6pm

SHAP Cumbria *Map 12 NY51*
Green *(NY551121)* ☎619
*Large farmhouse dating from 1705.
Countryside suitable for walking holidays.*
Etr–Sep 3rm 2hc ⊗ TV P 167acres mixed

S. J. Thompson **Southfield** *(NY561184)*
☎282
*Farmhouse set in pleasant area with good
views. Guests are welcome to interest
themselves in farm work.*

252

Mar–Oct 2rm 1hc ⊗ nc12 CTV 3P
110acres mixed S% B&b£4–£5
(W only during season)

SHAWBURY Salop *Map 7 SJ52*
Braggs Country Suppers *(SJ602228)*
Longley Farm, Stanton Heath
☎ Shawbury 289
*Originally dating back to 1710, this
attractive brick and tile cottage was named
after Paul C Bragg the world authority on
Natural Farming. 2½m NE off A53.*
Lic 3rm 1hc 8P 2🏠 📖 23acres mixed
D8.30pm

SHAWHEAD Dumfries & Galloway
Dumfriesshire Map 11 NX87
Mrs M. D. Riddet **Henderland** *(NX872746)*
☎ Lochfoot 270
*Small farmhouse about 5 miles from
Dumfries. Golf, fishing and tennis are
available.*
Jun–Oct 4rm (3fb) CTV 3P 210acres dairy
S% B&b£5 W£33 M

SHILLINGFORD Devon *Map 3 SS92*
J. R. Holloway **Zeal** *(SS998226)*
☎ Clayhanger 231
*Old farmhouse with low ceilings and oak-
beamed rooms.*
Etr–Nov 3rm 1hc (2fb) ⊗ 3P 283acres
mixed S% B&b£5–£10 Bdi£8–£12 D5pm

SHIPMEADOW Suffolk *Map 5 TM38*
Mrs M. Steward **Manor Farm** *(TM379903)*
☎ Beccles 715380 Closed Xmas 2rm 1hc
⊗ nc TV 4P 4🏠 📖 S% B&b fr£6.50
Bdi fr£10.50 Wfr£73.50 ⠠

SHIRWELL Devon *Map 2 SS53*
Mrs G. Huxtable **Higher Upcott**
(SS585384) ☎216
*Situated in a quiet picturesque area on the
foothills of Exmoor. The bedrooms overlook
the unspoilt Devon countryside.*
Etr–Oct 3rm (1fb) ⊗ ⠠ CTV 2P 105acres
beef sheep S% B&b£4.50–£5

SIMONSBATH Somerset *Map 3 SS73*
Gallon House *(SS810394)* ☎ Exford 283
*Small, detached farmhouse, formerly an
inn. Surrounded by grassland. Horse riding
facilities are available.*
Apr–Oct 4rm 2hc nc13 CTV 4P 📖 50acres
beef

SKELSMERGH Cumbria *Map 7 SD59*
E. Johnston **Hollin Root** *(SD526976)*
Garth Row ☎ Selside 638
*Clean and comfortable farmhouse situated
in attractive valley.*
Etr–Oct 4hc (1fb) ⊗ nc10 TV 4P 60acres
mixed B&b£5–£6

SKYE, ISLE OF Highland *Inverness-shire
Map 13* **See Clachan, Dunvegan, Portree,
Uig**

SLAGGYFORD Northumb *Map 12 NY65*
Mrs D. M. Staley **Crainlarich** *(NY680523)*
☎ Alston 329
*Attractive, modern farmhouse built of local
stone. Situated in rolling hill land.*
5hc (1fb) ⊗ CTV 5P river 1,950acres
stock rearing S% B&b fr£4 Bdi fr£6.50

SLAIDBURN Lancs *Map 7 SD75*
Mrs P. M. Holt **Parrock Head** *(SD697527)*
Woodhouse Ln ☎614

*Modernised farmhouse dating back to
1677, set in the Bowland Fells.*
See colour section.
Closed 21–30Dec 3⇆🍽 (A 4⇆🍽) (2fb)
CTV 10P 250acres mixed S% B&b£10
Bdifr£13 W£70 Ⓜ D7.45pm

SOUTH BRENT Devon *Map 3 SX66*
M. E. Slade **Great Aish** *(SX689603)* ☎2238
*Situated near Dartmoor National Park.
Extensive views of countryside from
farmhouse.*
Closed Dec 5rm 4hc (3fb) ⊗ CTV 6P
60acres mixed S% B&b£5.50 Bdi£7 D5pm

SOUTH MOLTON Devon *Map 3 SS72*
Mrs J. Richards **Hacche Barton**
(SS713278) ☎2112
*Modern, brick-built farmhouse of stylish
design.*
mid Apr–Sep 2hc (2fb) 4P 212acres dairy
S% ✳B&b£5.50–£6.60

SPARROWPIT Derbys *Map 7 SK08*
Mrs E. Vernon **Whitelee** *(SK099814)*
☎ Chapel-en-le-Frith 2928
*Modernised farmhouse, parts built in 1600.
In pleasant hillside setting. Good centre
for hill walking or touring.*
Etr–Oct 3rm 1hc nc12 TV 6P 🍽 42acres
mixed S% B&b£5–£5.50 Bdi£8.25–£8.75
W£57.75–£61.25 ⅄ D4.30pm

SPAXTON Somerset *Map 3 ST23*
Mrs B. M. Shelley **Parish Land** *(ST214353)*
Higher Merridge ☎391
*Small, pleasing farmhouse. Situated in
attractive countryside. Spaxton 1½ miles.*
Mar–Oct 2rm (1fb) ⊗ CTV 2P 4acres
sheep S% ✳B&bfr£5.50 Bdifr£9 W£63 ⅄
D2pm

STALBRIDGE Dorset *Map 3 ST71*
M. Selway **Thornhill** *(ST741149)* ☎62751
*Mellow-stone, modernised farmhouse with
gabled outbuildings in elevated position
offering open views across Dorset.*
Apr–Sep 1rm ⊗ nc8 CTV 4P 240acres
mixed S% ✳B&b£4.50 W£30 Ⓜ

STANTON Staffs *Map 7 SK14*
Shrewsbury *(SK127462)*
☎ Ellastone 310
Stone-built farmhouse in centre of village.
Apr–Sep 2hc (A 2rm 1hc) CTV 4P 🍽
100acres beef dairy

STAPLE FITZPAINE Somerset
Map 3 ST21
Mrs D. M. Jee **Rutters Leigh** *(ST261164)*

☎ Buckland St Mary 392
Small, very pleasant farmhouse off A303.
3rm (1fb) CTV 2P 69acres dairy S% Dnoon

STEWARTON Strathclyde *Ayrs*
Map 10 NS44
Low Gallowberry *(NS434494)*
☎ Dunlop 279
*Two-storey, stone farmhouse, comfortably
furnished. Secluded setting. 3m NE off
unclassified road.*
May–Sep 4rm TV 6P river 134acres beef
D8pm

STIRLING Central *Stirlings Map 11 NS79*
Mrs R. Johnston **King's Park** *(NS787936)*
Dunbarton Rd ☎4142
*Large, modernised farmhouse situated on
the outskirts of the town and offering
splendid views of Stirling Castle.*
Etr–mid Oct 3rm (2fb) ⊗ CTV 4P 🍽
230acres beef ✳B&b£5.50

Powis Mains *(NS819959)*
Causewayhead ☎3820
*Well sited, stone farmhouse dating from
1840. Stands in Forth Valley overlooked by
Wallace Monument and Ochill Hills.
3m NE A91.*
Jun–Sep 2rm ⊗ CTV 6P 250acres mixed

STOCKLEIGH POMEROY Devon
Map 3 SS80
Westwood *(SS869029)*
☎ Cheriton Fitzpaine 202
*Large, well equipped farmhouse 3 miles
from Crediton.*
4rm TV P 117acres

STOGUMBER Somerset *Map 3 ST03*
Mrs L. R. Watts **Manor House** *(ST082381)*
☎614
Farmhouse overlooking Quantock Hills.
Closed Xmas 6hc 1⇆🍽 (2fb) CTV P 🍽
300acres mixed S% B&bfr£5.25 Bdifr£8
D4pm

Mrs S. J. Watts **Rowdon** *(ST082381)*
☎280
*Solidly built stone farmhouse overlooking
Quantock Hills.*
4hc (1fb) ⊗ CTV 4P 🍽 150acres mixed
B&b£5.50–£6.50 Bdi£9–£10

STOKE HOLY CROSS Norfolk
Map 5 TG20
Mr & Mrs Harrold **Salamanca** *(TG235022)*
☎ Framingham Earl 2322
*Old house with large garden on city
outskirts. Simple but comfortable.*
Mar–Sep 3hc (A 1⇆🍽) (1fb) ⊗ nc6 CTV 6P
168acres arable dairy S% B&b£5–£6.50
Bdi£7.75–£9.25 D9am

STOKEINTEIGNHEAD Devon
Map 3 SX97
W. J. & E. A. Cluett **Rocombe House Hotel**
(SX910701) ☎ Shaldon 3367
*Large farmhouse situated in secluded
valley.*
12hc (10fb) ⊗ CTV 15P ⟡ 92acres beef
sheep S% B&b£6.95 Bdi£11.50
W£65.50–£75.50 M D6pm

STOKE PRIOR Heref & Worcs
Map 3 SO55
Mrs G. H. Pugh **Norman's** *(SX524555)*
☎ Steensbridge 221
*Secluded hilltop farm approached by rough
track, entrance of which is near the village
Post Office.*
Etr–Sep 3rm 1hc (1fb) ⊗ TV 2P 50acres
mixed S% ✳B&b£4.50–£5 Bdi£6–£6.50
W£40–£45 ⫽ D5pm

Wheelbarrow Castle *(SO516573)*
☎ Leominster 2219
*Large, imposing, brick-built manor house
overlooking River Luss. Four-poster bed
available. Numerous antiques.*
3rm ⊗ ⚐ TV 6P 2🏠 ⟡

STON EASTON Somerset *Map 3 ST65*
Mrs J. Doman **Manor** *(ST626533)*
☎ Chewton Mendip 266
*Well-kept and attractively-furnished
farmhouse. Lawn at the front, and fruit and
vegetable garden. Situated in quiet minor
road.*
Closed Dec 2hc (1fb) ⊗ CTV P ⟡
250acres mixed

STONE (in Oxney) Kent *Map 5 TQ92*
Tighe *(TQ937268)* Tighe ☎Appledore 251
May–Oct 3hc ⊗ nc8 TV 4P ⟡ S% B&b£6
W£40 M

STOWFORD Devon *Map 2 SX48*
Mrs S. M. Brown **Stowford Barton**
(SX434870) ☎ Lewdown 272
*Signposted from main road, north of the
A30.*
Apr–Nov 3rm (1fb) ⊗ CTV 4P 53acres
dairy S% B&b£4.50–£5.50 Bdi£6–£7
W£45–£55 D4pm

STRAITON Lothian *Midlothian*
Map 11 NT26
Mrs A. M. Milne **Straiton** *(NJ273667)*
Straiton Rd. ☎031-440 0298
*Georgian farmhouse with garden, situated
on southern outskirts of Edinburgh. Swing,
climbing frame and lots of pets for the
children.*
Mar–Nov 4hc (3fb) ⚐ CTV 10P 200acres
mixed B&b£6

STRATFORD-UPON-AVON Warwicks
Map 4 SP25
Mrs M. K. Meadows **Monk's Barn**
(SP206516) Shipston Rd ☎293714
*Well-appointed farm offering clean and tidy
accommodation. Adjacent to A34 Stratford–
Oxford Rd.*
Closed 25–26Dec 4rm 3hc (1fb) ⊗ CTV 4P
⟡ 75acres mixed S% B&b£4.50–£4.75

STRATHAVEN Strathclyde *Lanarks*
Map 11 NS74
E. Warnock **Laigh Bent** *(NS701413)*
☎20103
*Attractive, stone-built farmhouse with
out-buildings surrounding the courtyard.*
Jun–Sep 2rm (1fb) ⊗ nc8 TV P 1🏠 100acres
beef S% B&b£5 W£30 M

Tower of Udstonhead *(NS704469)*
Hamilton Rd ☎20907 2rm ⊗ CTV 6P
⟡ 5¾acres poultry

STREET Somerset *Map 3 ST43*
Mr N. Tucker **Marshalls Elm** *(ST485348)*
☎42878
*Old well-preserved farmhouse with back
and front gardens, set in country
surroundings. Street 1½ miles.*
Closed Xmas 3rm (1fb) TV 3P 200acres
mixed S% B&b£4.50–£5 Bdi£7.50–£8
D6.30pm

SUMMERCOURT Cornwall *Map 2 SW85*
W. E. Lutey **Trenithon** *(SW895553)*
☎ St Austell 860253
*Modern farmhouse situated in quiet location
in open countryside a few miles from the
coast.*
Jan–Nov 4hc (2fb) CTV 6P ⟡ 148acres
mixed S% B&b£4–£4.50 Bdi£6–£6.25
W£38–£40 ⫽ D3pm

SWINSCOE Staffs *Map 7 SK14*
Carlton Moor House *(SK115487)*
☎Waterhouses 221
Large, Georgian-style farmhouse.
Etr–Oct 3rm 2hc 1⇌🔥 nc5 CTV 4P ⟡
200acres dairy

TACOLNESTON Norfolk *Map 5 TM19*
Mrs R. F. Easton **White House** *(TM142940)*
24 Bently Rd ☎ Bunwell 220
*Small, well-kept property fairly close to
Norwich. Large rooms, comfortably
appointed.*
Mar–Oct 4rm 1hc nc3 4P 2🏠 ⟡ 1,200acres
mixed S% B&b£5.25–£7 Bdi£7.75–£10.10
W£36.75–£45.50 M D6pm

TALATON Devon *Map 3 SY09*
J. Buxton **Harris** *(SY068997)*
☎ Whimple 822327
*17th-century thatched cob farmhouse set
in quiet village. Large concrete yard.
Lawns and gardens.*
3rm 1hc (1fb) ⊗ CTV 5P 130acres dairy
S% B&b£5.50

TAUNTON Somerset *Map 3 ST22*
Mrs B. Cozens **Musgrave** *(ST269236)*
Henlade (3m E off A356) ☎Henlade
442346
*Oak-beamed farmhouse, comfortably
furnished. Side garden and orchard.
400yds from main road.*
Closed Xmas 2rm (1fb) ⊗ nc7 CTV 3P
107acres dairy S% B&bfr£4.50 Bdi fr£6.50
Wfr£40 ⫽ D am

TAVISTOCK Devon *Map 2 SX47*
Mrs E. G. Blatchford **Bungalow**
(SX464731) Parswell ☎2789
*Well-situated building on the Callington
road, commanding good views of
surrounding countryside.*
Etr–Nov 2rm (2fb) ⊗ TV P 106acres mixed
S% B&b£4.50–£5

TEMPLE CLOUD Avon *Map 3 ST65*
Mr J. Harris **Cameley Lodge** *(ST609575)*
Cameley (1m W unclass) ☎52423
*Newly-converted barn attractively designed
in keeping with the area, overlooking
13th century church and trout lakes.*
4hc (1fb) ⊗ CTV 4P ⟡ lake 200acres
mixed S% B&b£9 Bdi£14 W£98 D8pm

TEMPLECOMBE Somerset Map 3 ST72
Manor House (ST709221) ☎70560
3rm 2hc 6P

TEMPLE SOWERBY Cumbria
Map 12 NY62
Skygarth (NY612262) ☎Kirkby Thore 300
Attractive farmhouse with high standard of
facilities and furnishings. Large airy rooms.
Overlooks River Eden.
May–Oct 3rm ∅ CTV 6P river 220acres
mixed M

THORNCOMBE Dorset Map 3 ST30
P. J. Atyeo **Higher** (ST376034)
☎Winsham 340
Detached, two-storey, brick and stone
farmhouse. Milking parlour and farmland
adjacent. Large lawn.
3hc (2fb) 4P ⌑ 50acres dairy S% B&b£5
W£35 M

THORNHILL Dumfries & Galloway
Dumfriesshire Map 11 NX89
Mrs A. Mackie **Waterside Mains**
(NS870971) (SX353600)
Farmhouse set on banks of River Nith.
Fishing parties catered for.
Etr–Oct 3hc ∅ nc TV 3P ⌑ river 146acres
arable dairy S% B&b£5 Bdi£7.50

THROWLEIGH Devon Map 3 SX69
Mr & Mrs C. Mosse **East Ash Manor**
(SX680911) ☎Whiddon Down 244
17th-century thatched, oak-beamed
farmhouse situated in beautiful countryside.
1m E on Whiddon Down road.
3hc (1fb) ∅ ♨ TV 4P ⌑ 160acres dairy
mixed S% B&b£6.50–£7 Bdi£11–£11.50
D7pm

TIDEFORD Cornwall Map 2 SX35
Mrs B. A. Turner **Kilna House** (SX353600)
☎Landrake 236 Closed Xmas Lic 4hc
(3fb) CTV 6P S% B&b£5–£5.50 Bdi£8–£9
W£49–£56 ⌳

Trenance (SX340600) ☎Landrake 319
Large, stone-built farmhouse situated
north of the A38 west of Saltash.
Etr–Sep 3hc ∅ TV P 87acres dairy

TILLINGTON Heref & Worcs Map 3 SO44
Mrs J. Seaborn **Stone House** (SO443465)
☎Hereford 760631
Views of Herefordshire countryside.
3rm 2hc CTV 6P ⌑ 60acres mixed S%
B&b£7–£8 Bdi£10–£11 D7pm

TIVERTON Devon Map 3 SS91
R. Olive **Lower Collipriest** (SS953117)
☎2321
Modernised, scheduled building on the
banks of River Exe.
Mar–Oct 4hc 2⇥▥ nc14 CTV 6P 3🏠 ⌑
221acres dairy S% ✳B&b£7–£8
Bdi£8.50–£10 W£55–£59 ⌳ D noon

TODMORDEN W Yorks Map 7 SD92
Mrs R. Bayley **Todmorden Edge South**
(SD924246) Parkin Ln, Stourhall ☎3459
Converted 17th-century farmhouse on rural
hillside. Clean, comfortable rooms. Cosy
residents' lounge. Ample entertainments
nearby.
3hc (1fb) ∅ nc8 CTV 10P ⌑ ½acre
non-working S% B&b£6.25 Bdi fr£10.50
W£41.50 M D8pm

TOMDOUN Highland Inverness-shire
Map 14 NH10
Mrs H. Fraser **No 3 Greenfield** (NH201006)
☎221
Small modern bungalow set in isolated
position in rugged, hilly countryside. 3m E,
on S side of Loch Garry.
mid May–Oct 3rm (1fb) ∅ TV 6P
170acres mixed S% B&b£4.50–£5
Bdi£7.50–£8 W£50–£52 ⌳ D6pm

TOTNES Devon Map 3 SX86
Mrs G. J. Veale **Broomborough House**
(SX793601) ☎863134
Spacious, country-manor-style house in
hilly parkland. Games room. Views of
Dartmoor and surrounding countryside.
Local game fishing.
Apr–Nov 3hc (1fb) ∅ ♨ CTV P ⌑
600acres mixed S% B&b£7.30 Bdi£12.30
W£45 M

TREFEGLWYS Powys Map 6 SN99
Mrs J. Williams **Cefn-Gwyn** (SO993923)
☎648
Clean and homely farmhouse.
2hc (1fb) ∅ ♨ CTV 12P 3🏠 ⌑ 54acres
mixed B&b£5–£5.50 Bdi£7–£7.50
W£45–£49 ⌳ D7.30pm

TREFRIW Gwynedd Map 6 SH76
Mr & Mrs D. E. Roberts **Cae-Coch**
(SH779646) ☎Llanrwst 640380
Pleasant farmhouse in elevated position on
side of Conwy Valley.
Apr–Sep rs Oct–Mar 3rm (2fb) ∅ nc3 TV
4P 50acres mixed S% B&b£6 W£40 M

TRENEAR (Nr Helston) Cornwall

Map 2 SW63
Mrs G. Lawrance **Longstone** *(SW662319)*
☎Helston 2483
*Well appointed farmhouse set in beautiful
countryside. Facilities include a playroom
and sun lounge. From the Helston–Redruth
rd (B3297) take unclass rd SW–(Helston)
1½m; Trenear 1m)–thence via Coverack
Bridges.*
Closed Xmas 5hc (3fb) CTV 8P 62acres
dairy S% B&b£4.60–£5.75
Bdi£6.90–£8.62 W£48.30–£61.20 ⊬
D6pm

TRESPARRETT Cornwall *Map 2 SX19*
Tresparrett House *(SX146919)*
☎Otterham Station 272
*Situated in quiet surroundings in village.
Good approach road and parking area.*
2hc CTV 5P ∰ 30acres dairy

TRESPARRETT POSTS Cornwall
Map 2 SX19
Mrs C. Horwell **Wilslea** *(SX153934)*
☎St Gennys 231
*Typical Cornish farmhouse set in downland.
Adjacent to A39.*
May–Oct 3rm 1hc CTV 10P 183acres
mixed B&b£5

TREVALGA Cornwall *Map 2 SX08*
Reddivallen *(SX099887)* ☎Boscastle
361
*Comfortable house with garden in isolated
position off the B3266.*
Jun–Sep 2rm ⊛ CTV 2P 320acres arable,
dairy & sheep

TREVEIGHAN Cornwall *Map 2 SX07*
Mrs M. Jory **Treveighan** *(SX075795)*
☎Bodmin 850286
*Two-storey, stone built farmhouse with
farm buildings attached. Situated in
isolated village. Views over valley.*
Mar–Oct 3rm (2fb) ⊛ TV 3P 150acres
dairy S% B&b£5 Bdi£8–£8.50 W£56 ⊬
(W only out of season) D6.30pm

TREVENEN BAL *(Nr Helston)* Cornwall
Map 2 SW62
Mrs W. M. Dallas **Roselidden House**
(SW676297) ☎Helston 2118
*Approach from unclass rd off A394, ½m N of
Helston or from B3297 near Wendron.*
Etr–Sep 3hc ⊛ nc5 CTV 6P sea 17½acres
beef S% Bdi£10.92 W£68.42 ⊬

TROON Cornwall *Map 2 SW63*
Sea View *(SW671370)* ☎Praze 260
*Farmhouse has been modernised, yet still
retains atmosphere of family run farm.
Tastefully furnished with extensive pine
wood decor.*
Mar–Oct 11rm 10hc CTV 10P 5🏠∰ sea
8acres mixed ⊬ W only Jul & Aug D6pm

TROUTBECK *(Nr Penrith)* Cumbria
Map 11 NY32
R. Bird **Askew Rigg** *(NY371280)*
☎Threlkeld 638
*17th-century stone-built farmhouse.
Attractively modernised to retain original
character. Entrance to drive is situated only a
few yards from the A66.*
Closed Xmas 4rm 1hc (2fb) CTV 5P ∰
200acres mixed B&b£4.50–£5
Bdi£7–£7.50 D6pm

Mrs M. Dobson **Riverside** *(NY382253)*
☎Greystoke 220
*Stone-built house and buildings in quiet
rural setting. Fine views of surrounding
hills.*

Etr–Oct 3rm (2fb) ⊛ nc4 CTV 4P 87acres
mixed S% B&b£4–£4.50 Bdi£6–£6.50
W£42–£45.50 ⊬ D3pm

TYWARDREATH Cornwall *Map 2 SX05*
Great Pelean *(SX085563)* ☎Par 2106
*Situated near Pempillick with walled
garden to front entrance. Par beach 2 miles.
½m N towards A390.*
May–8Sep 6rm 5hc ⊛ TV P 140acres
mixed

TYWYN Gwynedd *Map 6 SH50*
Mrs A. E. Jones **Dolgoch** *(SH648049)*
☎Abergynolwyn 229
*Two-storey, brick farmhouse with stream
running by. Five minutes walk from the
Dolgoch Waterfalls.*
May–Oct 3hc (2fb) ⊛ 3P 356acres mixed
S% B&b£4.75–£5 Bdi£6.75–£7

Mrs Davies **Dyffryngwyn** *(SH632984)*
Happy Valley ☎710305
*Modern clean bungalow. Follow A493
south for 1¾m, then unclassified road east
(signposted Happy Valley) for 2½m. The
farmhouse is on the right.*
May–Oct 3rm (1fb) 3P 600acres beef
sheep B&b£5 Bdi£8.75 W£56 ⊬ D5.45pm

UFFCULME Devon *Map 3 ST01*
Mrs M. D. Farley **Houndaller** *(ST058138)*
☎Craddock 40246
*Very old. attractive farmhouse standing
in beautiful garden.*
Apr–Oct 2hc (2fb) ⊛ CTV 4P 1🏠 176acres
dairy mixed S% B&b£5.50–£6.50
Bdi£7.50–£8.50 Wfr£56 ⊬ D8pm

Mrs C. M. Baker **Woodrow** *(ST054107)*
☎Craddock 40362
*Farmhouse set in pleasant lawns and
gardens with meadowland stretching to
River Culm. Trout fishing available.*
1rm 3hc (2fb) ⊛ & CTV 10P 200acres
mixed S% B&b£6–£6.50 Bdi£9–£9.50
D9pm

UFFINGTON Salop *Map 7 SJ51*
Mr & Mrs D. Timmis **Preston** *(SJ530118)*
Preston-on-Severn ☎Upton Magna 240
*1½m S on unclassified road joining B5062
and A5.*
2rm 1hc (2fb) nc5 CTV 4P S% ✱B&b£5

UIG Isle of Skye, Highland
Inverness-shire Map 13 NG36
Mrs J. Macleod **No 11 Earlish** *(NG388614)*
☎319 mid May–Oct 4rm (1fb) CTV TV
12P sea 36acres sheep S% B&b£4.50–£5
W£30–£33 Ⓜ

ULEY Glos *Map 3 ST79*
Mrs N. Hill **Newbrook** *(ST775980)*
☎Dursley 860251
*Stone-built farmhouse with lawn, garden
and orchard. In attractive village below
western escarpment of Cotswolds.*
3rm 2hc (1fb) ⊛ nc5 CTV 6P ∰ 120acres
mixed S% B&b£6 Bdi£8.50

ULLINGSWICK Heref & Worcs
Map 3 SO54
Mrs P. A. Howland **'The Steppes' County
Guest House** *(SO586490)* ☎Burley Gate
424 Closed Xmas 3⊡🍴 (1fb) nc12 CTV 4P
∰ poultry S% ✱B&b£8 Bdi£12 W£75 ⊬

UPOTTERY Devon *Map 3 ST20*
Mr J. Gregory **Hoemoor** *(ST218104)*
☎Churchstanton 265

Well-kept, small, modern farmhouse. Rather isolated but with beautiful views.
Apr–Oct 3rm 1hc (1fb) nc11 P 3🏠 50acres mixed S% B&b£5.50–£6 B🍴£7–£7.50 (W only Apr)

Mrs M. M. Reed **Yarde** *(ST193045)* ☎318
17th-century farmhouse with interesting oak panelling and beams. Overlooks the Otter Valley. Near Monkton on the A30.
Mar–Nov 3rm 2hc (1fb) 🐾 CTV 3P 1🏠 94acres beef dairy S% B&b£5–£6 B🍴£8–£9 W£50 ⅃

UPPER ELKSTONE Staffs *Map 7 SK05*
Mrs C. R. Faulkner **Mount Pleasant** *(SK056588)* ☎Blackshaw 380
Stone building, parts of which date back 250 years. Situated on hillside with excellent views across Elstone Valley. Off B5053. Donkeys for children to ride.
Mar–Oct 3hc nc6 CTV 4P 🍴 2acres non-working S% ✳B&b£6.75 B🍴£10.50

UPTON PYNE Devon *Map 3 SX99*
Mrs Y. M. Taverner **Pierce's** *(SX910977)* ☎Stoke Canon 252
Large farmhouse about 1 mile north of A377 Exeter to Barnstaple road.
Etr–Sep 1hc (1fb) nc2 CTV 6P 🍴 300acres mixed S% B&b£5 W£32 M

USK Gwent *Map 3 SO30*
J. Arnett **Ty Gwyn** *(SO391045)* ☎2878
Large modernised farmhouse situated between Raglan and Usk at Gwehelog 3m NE off Raglan rd unclass.
Closed 25Dec 3rm 1⇔🖻(1fb) nc3 TV 3P 🍴 24acres beef sheep & horses S% B&b£6–£8 B🍴£9.50–£11 W£60–£63 ⅃ D4pm

UTTOXETER Staffs *Map 7 SK03*
P. J. Tunnicliffe **Moor House** *(SK102327)* Wood Ln ☎2384
Stone rendered farmhouse, about 200 years old, extensively modernised and renovated and containing antiques. Rural setting overlooking racecourse and fields.
4rm 3hc (1fb) CTV P 🍴 180acres dairy

WALL Cornwall *Map 2 SW63*
Mrs A. Rowe **Reawla** *(SW605363)* ☎Leedstown 320
Pleasant well-situated farmhouse close to beaches, with small, well-kept garden.
Etr–Sep 3hc (1fb) CTV P 40acres beef

WARCOP Cumbria *Map 12 NY71*
Mrs E. Collinson **Highwood Holme** *(NY760150)* Flitholme ☎Brough 304.

Modern bungalow of local stone adjacent to original farmhouse. Well decorated and comfortable.
Apr–Sep 2rm (2fb) CTV 2P 🍴 S% B&b£4

WAREHAM Dorset *Map 3 ST98*
N. I. Barnes **Redcliffe** *(SY932866)* ☎2225
Modern farmhouse in quiet, rural surroundings. Pleasant location adjacent to River Frome and overlooking hills and fields. ½ mile from Wareham.
5rm 3hc (1fb) 🐾 CTV 4P 1🏠 🍴 river 250acres beef

WATERPERRY Oxon *Map 4 SP60*
S. Fonge **Manor** *(SP628064)* ☎Ickford 263
Stone farmhouse standing in large garden.
3rm 2hc (1fb) 🐾 TV 4P 250acres mixed S% B&b£5–£6

WATERROW Somerset *Map 3 ST02*
Mr J. Bone **Hurstone** *(ST056252)* ☎Wiveliscombe 23441
Set on the edge of Brendon Hills overlooking the valley of the River Tone. Comfortably furnished with log fires during winter months and on chilly evenings.
5hc TV 8P river 65acres mixed S% B&b£7–£8.50 B🍴£12–£13.50 W£65–£85 ⅃

WEEDON LOIS Northants *Map 4 SP64*
Mrs B. Raven **Croft** *(SP600465)* Milthorpe ☎Blakesley 475
New detached house in rural surroundings.
Feb–Nov 2rm CTV P 🍴 25acres turkeys & pigs S% B&b£6.50 B🍴£9 W£63 ⅃ D7pm

WEETON Lancs *Map 7 SD33*
Mrs T. Colligan **High Moor** *(SD388365)* ☎273
Compact, homely farmhouse. Clean and tidy. Much farm produce used in cooking.
Closed Xmas 2rm (1fb) 🐾 CTV 20P 7 acres mixed S% B&b£5 W£31.50 M

WELSHPOOL Powys *Map 7 SJ20*
Mrs E. Jones **Gungrog House** *(SJ235089)* Rhallt ☎3381
300-year-old farmhouse in quiet situation high on hillside. Commanding superb views of the Severn Valley. 1m NE off A458.
Apr–Oct 2hc 🐾 🐾 CTV 4P 🍴 15acres beef S% B&b£6 B🍴£10 W£60 D8pm

Mr & Mrs W. Jones **Moat** *(SJ214042)* ☎3179
Situated in Severn Valley. Games room in house and tennis court in garden.
Etr–Sep 3rm 2hc (1fb) 🐾 TV P 250acres dairy S% ✳B&bfr£5 B🍴 fr£8 Wfr£49 ⅃ D5pm

Mr & Mrs J. H. Emberton **Tynllwyn**
(SJ215085) ☎3175
*Large brick-built farmhouse, dating from
1861, in peaceful surroundings with lovely
views. One mile from Welshpool.*
6hc (4fb) ⊗ CTV 10P 🔟 150acres mixed
S% B&b£5.50 Bdi£9 W£56 ⱡ D8pm

WESTBOURNE W Sussex *Map 4 SU70*
Mr & Mrs E. D. Edgell **Tibbalds Mead**
(SU750873) White Chimney Row
☎Emsworth 4786
*Elizabethan farmhouse with recent
addition, some beamed ceilings. Situated
on the south side of the village.*
Feb Nov 3rm (1fb) ⊗ nc2 TV 3P
70acres mixed S% B&b£7–£9

WEST CHILTINGTON W Sussex
Map 4 TQ01
A. M. Steele **New House** *(TQ091186)*
☎2215
*This is a listed 15th-century farmhouse
with oak-beamed rooms and Inglenook
fireplace. Situated in the heart of the
picturesque village of West Chiltington.*
Jan–Nov 3hc (2fb) ⊗ CTV P 150acres
mixed S% ✳B&b fr£7.50

WEST TAPHOUSE Cornwall *Map 2 SX16*
Mrs K. Bolitho **Penadlake** *(SX144636)*
Two Waters Foot ☎Bodmin 872271
*Old-world farmhouse with large garden set
in the picturesque Glynn Valley.*
2rm (1fb) TV 4P 2🏠 250acres arable mixed
S% ✳B&b£5–£6 Wfr£38.50 ⱡ

WETTON Staffs *Map 7 SK15*
J. G. Stubbs **Yew Tree** *(SK111553)*
☎Alstonefield 202
*Natural stone house with pleasant lawns
and rose gardens. In village in renowned
Manifold Valley, part of Peak District
National Park.*
4rm 2hc (1fb) TV 4P 178acres dairy &
sheep

WHATSTANDWELL Derbys *Map 8 SK35*
A. J. Clarke **Watergate** *(SK328545)*
☎Wirksworth 2135
*Stone house built in 1779. Set in quiet
surroundings.*
Closed Dec-Feb 2rm 1hc 1 ⇄▥ (1fb) TV 6P
🔟 120acres non-working S% B&b£7
Bdi£7

WHEDDON CROSS Somerset
Map 3 SS93
Triscombe *(SS921377)* ☎Winsford 227
Large, modernised, 17th century

*farmhouse on elevated site. Secluded from
main road. 1 mile from village.*
Etr–Oct 5hc CTV 16P 🔟 30acres mixed
ⱡ D7pm

WHIDDON DOWN Devon *Map 3 SX69*
Mrs J. S. Robinson **South Nethercott**
(SX688947) ☎276
*Brick-built farmhouse in mature gardens
1½ miles from Whiddon Down.*
3rm 1hc 1⇄⊗ nc12 CTV 4P 170acres
arable & dairy B&b£9.50–£10
Bdi£14.50–£15

WHIMPLE Devon *Map 3 SY09*
Mrs H. I. Pinn **Down House** *(SY056968)*
☎822475
*Spacious farmhouse with large garden of
lawns, attractive flower beds and shrubs.
Pleasant and homely atmosphere.*
6hc nc5 TV 8P 5acres mixed S%
B&b£5.50–£7 Bdi fr£7.50 Wfr£52.50 ⱡ

WHITE CROSS Cornwall *Map 2 SW97*
Torview *(SW966722)* ☎Wadebridge 2261
*Modern farmhouse on main A39.
Wadebridge 1½ miles.*
4hc CTV 6P 22acres mixed ⱡ D6pm

WHITE MILL Dyfed *Map 2 SN42*
Mr & Mrs J. F. Gant **Pencnwc** *(SN464232)*
☎Nantgaredig 325
*Two-storey, stone-built Victorian residence.
Large lawned and wooded garden adjacent.
1 mile from village.*
Apr–Oct 4rm 3hc (2fb) ⊗ CTV 6P 82acres
mixed S% ✳B&b£5 Bdi£7.25 W£47.25 ⱡ
D4.30pm

WHITESTONE Devon *Map 3 SX89*
Mrs S. Lee **Rowhorne House**
(SX880948) ☎Exeter 74675
*Farmhouse set in attractive gardens and
lawns. Exeter 6 miles.*
3hc (2fb) ⊗ CTV 6P 90acres dairy S%
✳B&b£4.50 Bdi£7 W£49 ⱡ D6pm

WHITLAND Dyfed *Map 2 SN21*
C. M. I. A. Lewis **Cilpost** *(SN191184)* ☎280
*Two-storey, 300-year-old farmhouse in an
elevated position. 1½ miles north of the
village amid extensive gardens.* **See colour
section.**
Apr–Sep 8rm 4⇄▥ (3fb) 12P 🔟 160acres
mixed ✳B&b£10 Bdi£14 Wfr£88 ⱡ
(W only School Hols).D6.30pm

WIDDINGTON Essex *Map 5 TL53*
Mrs L. Vernon **Thistley Hall** *(TL556311)*
☎Saffron Walden 40388

This historic farmhouse is pleasantly surrounded by gardens and pastureland with beautiful views of the countryside.
Closed Dec–mid Jan 3rm 2hc (1fb) nc5 TV 7P 🚪 30acres mixed S% ✳B&b£6.50 W£42 M

WIDECOMBE IN THE MOOR Devon
Map 3 SX77
Captain & Mrs R. E. Curnock **Scobitor** *(SX725750)* ☎254
Well-appointed, moorland farmhouse set in the heart of Dartmoor National Park.
Closed Xmas 6rm 5hc 3⇆🛏 ♨ CTV 6P 1🏠 🚪 50acres beef Bdi£22 D8pm

WIGHT, ISLE OF *Map 4* **See Ryde**

WIGTOWN Dumfries & Galloway
Wigtowns Map 10 NX45
Moorhead of Glenturk *(NX414569)*
☎3293
Isolated, homely farm, with attractive views over Solway Firth and surrounding countryside.
May–Oct rs Nov–Apr (1db rm open all yr –book 1swk advance) 2rm CTV 2P 62acres mixed

WILLAND Devon *Map 3 ST01*
Mrs J. M. Granger **Doctors** *(ST015117)*
Halberton Rd ☎Sampford Peverell 820525
Farmhouse situated in garden and farmland. Tiverton and Cullompton 4 miles.
Mar–Oct 3rm (1fb) ♨ CTV 6P 90acres mixed S% B&b£4.50 Bdi£7 W£45 ⩒ D3pm

WILLITON Somerset *Map 3 ST04*
Yarde *(ST059392)* Yarde ☎Washford 8848
Once a coaching inn, this Grade III listed farmhouse is surrounded by agricultural land and situated in Exmoor National Park. 2½m S off B3188.
Etr–Oct 3hc ♨ nc12 CTV 3P 🚪 6acres sheep ⩒ D7pm

WIMPSTONE Warwicks *Map 4 SP24*
Mrs J. E. James **Whitchurch** *(SP222485)*
☎Alderminster 275
Lovely Georgian farmhouse built 1750. Listed buildings set in park-like surroundings on edge of Cotswolds. 4½ miles from Stratford-upon-Avon.
3hc (2fb) ♨ TV 3P 🚪 500acres mixed S% B&b£4–£5

WINFRITH Dorset *Map 3 SY88*
G. W. Grout **Home** *(SY828860)* Dorchester Rd (A352) ☎Warmwell 852847
Modern, red-brick farmhouse in rural surroundings ¾ mile from village of Wool. Surrounded by rolling countryside.
Apr–Sep 3hc ♨ nc6 TV 3P 17acres Horse & Calf rearing S% B&b£5.50 W£37 M

WITHIEL Cornwall *Map 2 SW96*
Mr & Mrs P. U. G. Sharp **Tregawne** *(SX002662)* ☎Lanivet 303
Charming, carefully-modernised farmhouse furnished with antiques. Stands in Ruthern valley away from the farm. Heated outdoor swimming pool.
Closed Xmas 4rm 2hc 1⇆🛏 (1fb) 6P 🚪 160acres dairy S% B&b£8–£9.20 Bdi£10.80–£11.96 W£71.30–£79.35 ⩒

Display of Hotel Prices

All hotels, motels, inns and guest houses in Britain, with four bed-rooms or more (including self-catering accommodation) and offering accommodation to guests, are required to display notices showing minimum and maximum overnight charges. The notice must be displayed in a prominent position in the reception area, or at the entrance.

The prices shown must include any service charge, and may include Value Added Tax, and it must be made clear whether or not these items are included. If VAT is not included then it must be shown separately. If meals are provided with the accommodation, this must be made clear too. If prices are not standard for all rooms, then only the lowest and highest prices need be given.

WITHLEIGH Devon *Map 3 SS91*
Jurishayes *(SS913121)* ☎Tiverton 2984
*Warm and comfortable farmhouse with
pleasant atmosphere. Well positioned for
touring North and mid Devon.*
5rm 2hc ⊗ TV 100P 134acres mixed
D6pm

WIVELISCOMBE Somerset *Map 3 ST02*
Deepleigh *(ST079294)* Langley Marsh
☎23379
*16th century farmhouse, converted into
small hotel. Comfortable lounge with
original beams, panelling and log fire.
1m N unclass rd.*
6hc 1⇨柵凸 CTV 6P 幽 15acres mixed ⱔ
(W only Jul & Aug) D5.30pm

Hillacre *(ST104275)* ☎23355
*Traditional farmhouse set back about
200yds to the north of A361.*
3rm 2hc CTV P 1🏠 700acres mixed

WOODBURY SALTERTON Devon
Map 3 SY08
Mrs M. Hamilton **Stallcombe House**
(SY039891) Sanctuary Ln ☎32373
*Early 17th-century cottages converted into
fine farmhouse with oak beams. 3½ miles E
of Clyst St Mary.*
Closed Xmas 3rm 2hc (1fb) ⊗ CTV 3P 幽
55acres dairy S% B&b£5.50 Bdi£8

WOOKEY Somerset *Map 3 ST54*
Mr & Mrs Law **Honeycroft** *(ST509453)*
Worth ☎Wells (Somerset) 78971
*Large whitewashed cottage with lawns and
orchard, on B3139.*
Jan–mid Dec 3rm 1hc (1fb) ⊗ nc6 CTV P
幽 21acres beef poultry & pigs S% B&b£5

D. & A. Barnard **Manor** *(ST508454)* Worth
☎Wells (Somerset) 72838
Modernised old farmhouse.
4hc TV P 35acres dairy

WOOLFARDISWORTHY Devon
Map 2 SS32
Mrs B. Hancock **South View** *(SS335213)*
☎Clovelly 397
*Farmhouse set in very quiet and peaceful
surroundings.*
Etr–Sep 2rm 1hc (1fb) ⊗ CTV 2P 40acres
dairy S% B&b£5.25 W£49 ⱔD am

R. C. & C. M. Beck **Stroxworthy**
(SS341198) ☎Clovelly 333
*Tastefully decorated and set in beautiful
countryside offering a variety of farm
produce on menu. Herd of Guernsey cows.*
10rm 9hc (4fb) ⊗ CTV 20P 100acres dairy
S% Bdi£8.63–£9.49 W£57.50–£63.25 ⱔ
D9pm

Mrs P. I. Westaway **Westvilla** *(SS329215)*
☎Clovelly 309
*Well-decorated accommodation. Good
farmhouse meals served.*
Etr–Oct 3hc (1fb) ⊗ CTV P 22acres beef
sheep S% B&b£5.50–£6 Bdi£7.50–£8
Wfr£45 ⱔ

WOOLLEY Cornwall *Map 2 SS21*
G. Colwill **East Woolley** *(SS254167)*
☎Morwenstowe 274
*Farm set in undulating pastureland, close
to A39. Homely atmosphere. Play area with
swings, see-saw and pony for children.*
Etr–Oct 3rm (1fb) CTV 6P 190acres arable
beef S% B&b£5–£5.50 Bdi£9–£9.50
W£44–£46 ⱔ D6pm

WOOTTON COURTENAY Somerset
Map 3 SS94
Ford *(SS929426)* ☎Timberscombe 211
A genuine working farm.
5rm 4hc ⊗ TV 5P 150acres dairy D6.30pm

N. Gooding **Ranscombe** *(SS947433)*
☎Timberscombe 237
*Dark redstone house with gardens at front
and a duck pond to the side. Easy access
via M5.*
Etr–Oct 3hc 5P 120acres beef sheep S%
B&bfr£5.50

WORMBRIDGE Heref & Worcs
Map 3 SO43
Mrs M. Thomas **Wormbridge Court**
(SO429309) ☎239
*A 400-year-old manor house standing
adjacent to A465 Hereford–Abergavenny
road. Horse riding, with lessons available
from qualified instructor.*
See colour section.
Mar–Oct 5rm 4hc (3fb) 凸 CTV 8P 4🏠
250acres mixed S% ✳B&b£7.50 Bdi£11
W£70 ⱔ (W only Jun–Aug)

WORMELOW Heref & Worcs *Map 3 SO43*
Mrs E. Jones **Lyston Smithy** *(SO495292)*
☎Golden Valley 540368
*Old stone farmhouse, formerly blacksmith's
cottage, extensively renovated to a high
standard. South facing with views towards
Gloucester, Forest of Dean and Wye Valley.
Guests have use of lawns and recreation
area.*
Mar–Oct 3⇨柵 (1fb) nc6 TV P 幽 14acres
fruit S% B&b£6.50–£7 W£45.50–£49 ⱔ

YARCOMBE Devon *Map 3 ST20*
Mrs V. Rich **Broadley** *(ST239069)*
☎Upottery 274
*Traditional-style farmhouse in remote,
East Devon countryside. Good home
cooking.*
May–Sep 2rm ⊗ nc5 TV P 136acres dairy
sheep S% B&bfr£4

Crawley *(ST259079)* ☎Chard 2259
*Attractive stone building with a thatched
roof.*
Apr–Oct 3rm 2hc ⊗ CTV 1P 1🏠
200acres mixed

YEALMPTON Devon *Map 2 SX55*
Mrs A. German **Broadmoor** *(SX574498)*
☎Plymouth 880407
*Stone-built farmhouse and outbuildings,
situated in open countryside enjoying
distant views of Dartmoor.*
3hc ⊗ nc7 CTV P 207acres mixed S%
B&bfr£5.50

YEOVIL Somerset *Map 3 ST51*
G. M. Tucker **Carents** *(ST546188)*
Yeovil Marsh ☎6622
*Clean, pleasant traditional-style farmhouse
on the outskirts of Yeovil. 2m N of A37.*
Closed Xmas 3rm 1hc (1fb) ⊗ CTV P
350acres arable beef S% B&b£5.50–£6
Bdi£8.50–£9 W£59–£62 ⱔ D7pm

YSBYTY IFAN Gwynedd *Map 6 SH84*
Mrs F. G. Roberts **Ochr Cefn Isa**
(SH845495) ☎Pentrefoelas 602
*Farm set in elevated position with good
views high above A5.*
Mar–Oct 3rm 2hc (1fb) ⊗ TV 2P 123acres
mixed S% B&b£5–£5.25 Bdi£8–£8.50
Wfr£48 D5pm

ZELAH Cornwall *Map 2 SW85*
Honeycombe *(SW827527)* ☎411
*Detached house on smallholding. Lawned
garden at front. Fine views over unspoilt
countryside. ½m S of A30, 300yds E of
junction A30/B3285.*
May–mid Sep 3hc ⊗ nc12 TV 4P 13½acres
beef

ZENNOR Cornwall *Map 2 SW43*
M. C. Osborne **Osborne's** *(SW455385)*
Boswednack ☎ Penzance 796944
*Farmhouse offering own dairy produce
and vegetables. Wholesome country food.
Lands End about 5 miles. Bathing in nearby
coves.*
Mar–Oct 2hc CTV 4P sea 70acres beef
crops S% B&b£5 D7pm

NATURE TRAILS

Nature Trails are arranged to please and
instruct, covering distances from under a mile
to three miles or so, in locations from sand-
dunes to deep forests.

The AA has prepared a booklet giving full
details of Nature Trails throughout Great Britain.
It is available free to AA members.

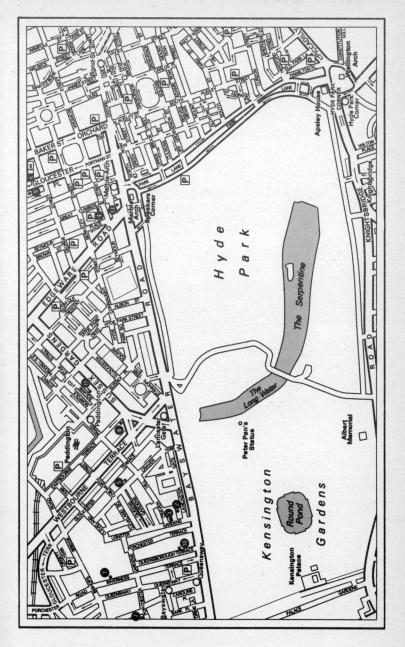

London Plan 2

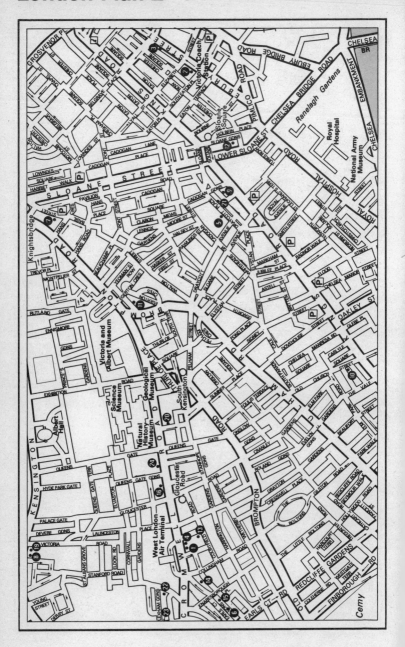

London Plan 3

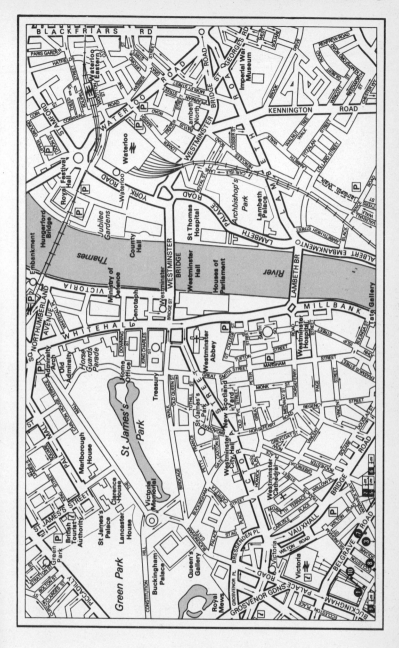

1 Arden House
2 Beverley Towers
Hotel
5 Corbigoe Hotel

6 Corona Hotel
7 Easton Hotel
8 Elizabeth Hotel
3 Tra terre Hotel

9 Hanover Hotel
10 Holly House

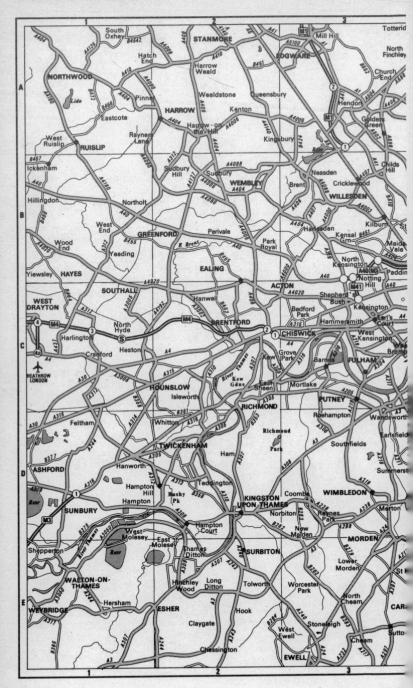

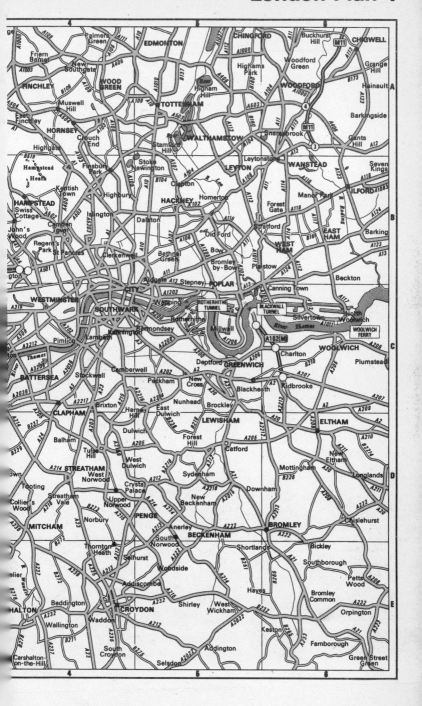

London Postal Districts and ways in & out of London

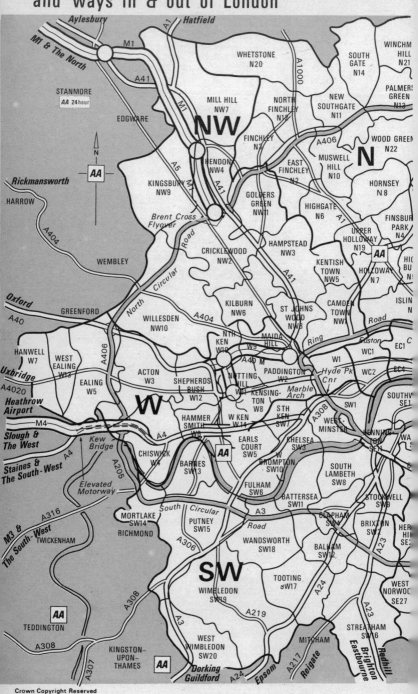

Crown Copyright Reserved

London Postal Area Boundary
London Postal District Boundaries
Main Roads into and out of London
Signposted North and South Circular
Roads & Ring Road
Other Main Roads

Service Centre **AA**

Scale of Miles

0   1   2   3   4

© The Automobile Association 1980

The National Grid

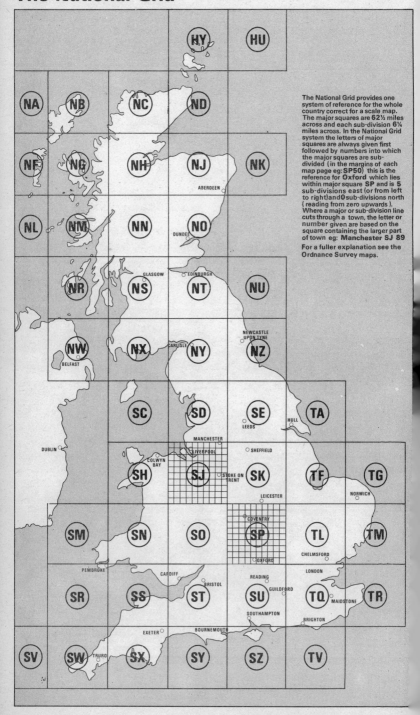

The National Grid provides one system of reference for the whole country correct for a scale map. The major squares are 62½ miles across and each sub-division 6¼ miles across. In the National Grid system the letters of major squares are always given first followed by numbers into which the major squares are sub-divided (in the margins of each map page eg: SP50) this is the reference for **Oxford** which lies within major square SP and is 5 sub-divisions east (or from left to right) and 0 sub-divisions north (reading from zero upwards). Where a major or sub-division line cuts through a town, the letter or number given are based on the square containing the larger part of town eg: **Manchester SJ 89**

For a fuller explanation see the Ordnance Survey maps.

Key to Atlas

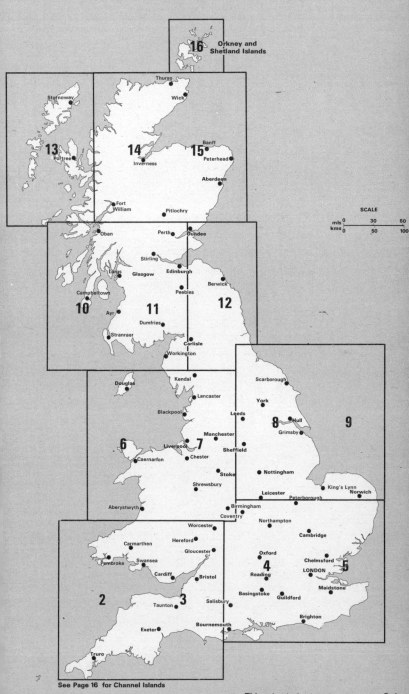

16 Orkney and Shetland Islands

Stornoway

Thurso
Wick

13 Portree
14 Inverness
Banff **15**
Peterhead

Aberdeen

Fort William
Pitlochry

Oban
Perth Dundee

Stirling
Largs
Glasgow Edinburgh
Campbeltown
Berwick

10
Ayr
11 Peebles
12
Dumfries

Stranraer

Carlisle
Workington

Kendal

Douglas
Scarborough

Lancaster

York
Blackpool

Leeds

Manchester
8 Hull
Liverpool
7 Grimsby
6
Chester
Sheffield
9
Caernarfon

Stoke
Nottingham
Shrewsbury

Leicester
King's Lynn
Aberystwyth
Birmingham
Peterborough
Norwich

Coventry
Worcester
Northampton

Hereford
Cambridge
Carmarthen
Gloucester

Oxford
Chelmsford
Pembroke Swansea
4 **5**
Cardiff
Bristol
Reading
LONDON

2
3
Basingstoke
Maidstone
Taunton
Salisbury
Guildford

Bournemouth
Brighton
Exeter

Truro

See Page 16 for Channel Islands

SCALE
mls 0   30   60
kms 0   50   100

Maps produced by
The AA Cartographic Department
(Publications Division), Fanum House,
Basingstoke, Hampshire RG21 2EA

Town with guesthouse or inn
Town with guesthouse or inn and farmhouse
Town with farmhouse only

IRISH SEA

CARDIGAN BAY

Scale
0   10   20 miles
0   10   20   30 kilometres

SC

SH

SN

DOUGLAS
Port Erin
Port St Mary

Eskda
Holmrook
B

Trearddur Bay
Bodedern
Benllech Bay
LLANDUDNO
CONWY
COLWYN BAY
PRESTATYN
RHYL
ABERGELE
Glan Conway
Llanfair Talhaiarn
Rhuallt
BEAUMARIS
Llechwedd
LLANFAIRFECHAN
Gaerwen
BANGOR
Rowen
Betws-yn Rhos
Llansannan
Tal-y-Bont
Llangernyw
Pandy Tudur
Llanrhaeadr
CAERNARFON
Dinorwic
Trefriw
RUTHIN
CLW
Bontnewydd
LLANRWST
Llanberis
Capel Garmon
Llansannan
Pontllyfni
BETWS-Y-COED
Pentrefoelas
L
Dolwyddelan
Padog
Clawddnewydd
Penmachno
Ysbyty Ifan
Gwyddelwern
Corwe
Beddgelert
Glan-yr-Afon
BLAENAU FFESTINIOG
GWYNEDD
Cynwy
FFESTINIOG
Llandderfel
Morfa Nefyn
Nefyn
CRICCIETH
BALA
Llanystumdwy
PORTHMADOG
PWLLHELI
Harlech
Llanuwchllyn
Llanbedrog
Abersoch
Llanfachreth
Bontddu
Llanwddyn
Llanaber
DOLGELLAU
BARMOUTH
Dinas Mawddwy
Fairbourne
Llwyngwril
Tal-y-Llyn
Cemmaes
Llanegryn
TYWYN
POWYS
Gar
Aberdovey
Aberhosan
Carno
Llar
Trefeglwys
NEWTOWN
Llandinan
ABERYSTWYTH
Capel Seion
DYFED
Capel Bangor
Lledrod
Abbey Cwmhir

6

Town with guesthouse or inn
Town with guesthouse or inn and farmhouse
Town with farmhouse only

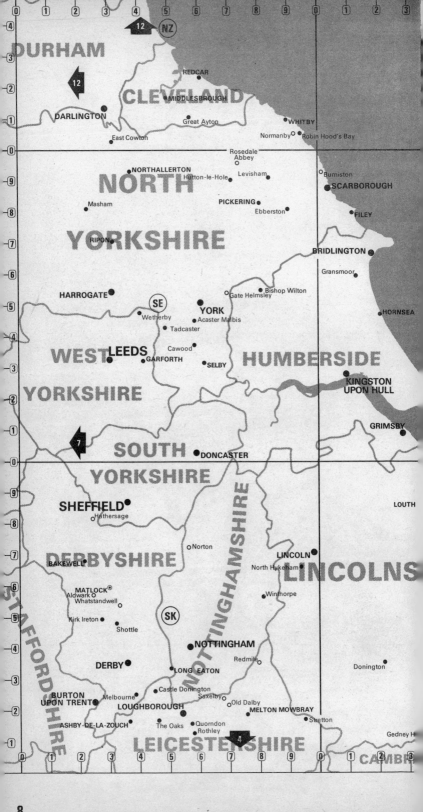

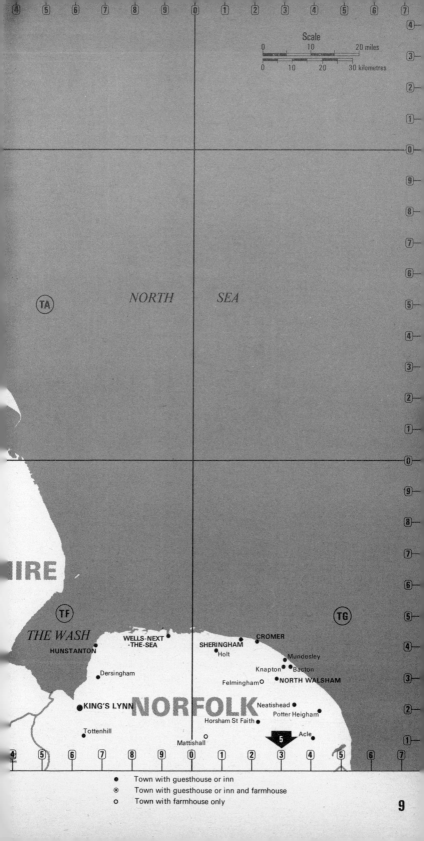

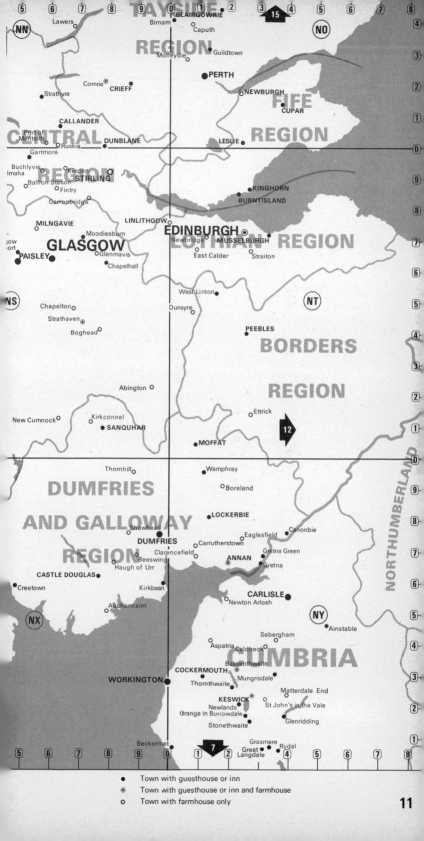

Town with guesthouse or inn
Town with guesthouse or inn and farmhouse
Town with farmhouse only

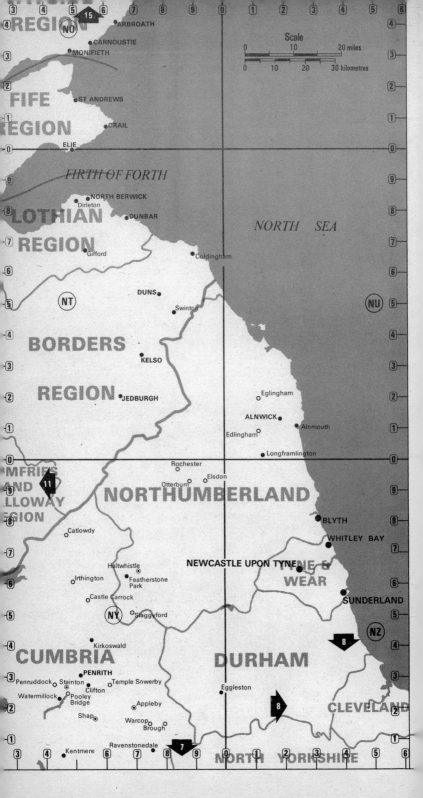

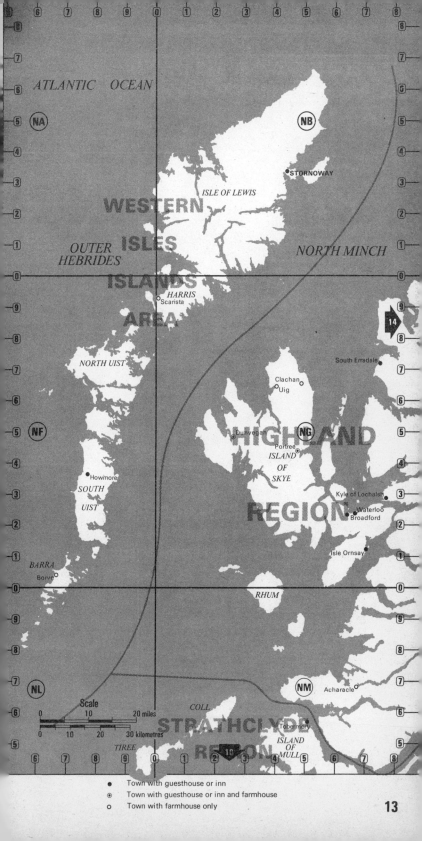

Scale

0	10	20 miles
0	10	20	30 kilometres

- ● Town with guesthouse or inn
- ◉ Town with guesthouse or inn and farmhouse
- ○ Town with farmhouse only

13

Town with guesthouse or inn
Town with guesthouse or inn and farmhouse
Town with farmhouse only

15

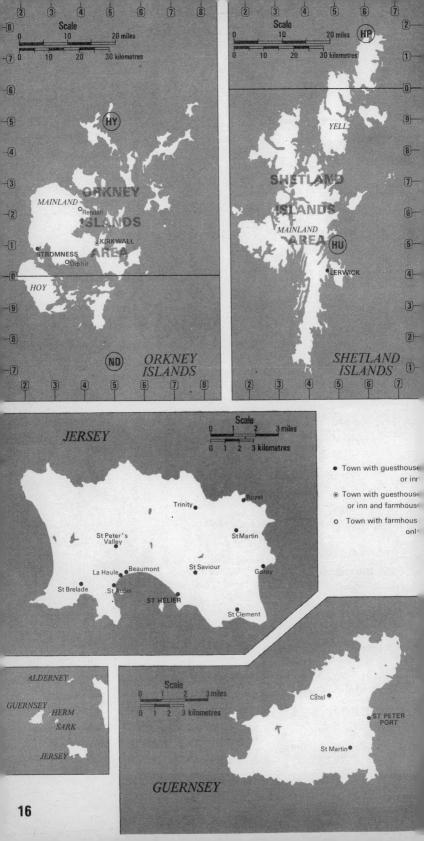

ORKNEY ISLANDS

HY

MAINLAND
Rendall
ORKNEY
ISLANDS
KIRKWALL
STROMNESS
AREA
Orphir

HOY

ND

Scale
0   10   20 miles
0   10   20   30 kilometres

SHETLAND ISLANDS

HP

YELL

SHETLAND
ISLANDS
MAINLAND
AREA
HU

LERWICK

Scale
0   10   20 miles
0   10   20   30 kilometres

JERSEY

Scale
0   1   2   3 miles
0 1 2 3 kilometres

Trinity
Rozel
St Peter's
Valley
St Martin
La Haule   Beaumont
St Saviour
St Brelade
St Aubin
Gorey
ST HELIER
St Clement

- ● Town with guesthouse
  or inn
- ◉ Town with guesthouse
  or inn and farmhouse
- ○ Town with farmhouse
  only

ALDERNEY
GUERNSEY   HERM
SARK
JERSEY

Scale
0   1   2   3 miles
0 1 2 3 kilometres

Câtel
ST PETER
PORT
St Martin

GUERNSEY

16

REPORT FORM

cut along here

To:
The Automobile Association,
Hotel and Information Services Department,
9th Floor,
Fanum House,
Basingstoke,
Hampshire
RG21 2EA

Name of establishment

Town	County

Date of visit

Did you find:	above expectation	satisfactory	below expectation
Service			
Accommodation			
Meals			

Do you agree with the classification or recommendation	YES	NO
May we quote your name when taking up any complaint with the hotel/restaurant?	YES	NO
Did you take up your complaint with the manager at the time of your visit?	YES	NO

Name

Address

Date	Membership no.

Signature

Further copies of this form can be obtained from any AA office

Additional remarks:

For office use:

Head office action	Regional office action
Acknowledged	Inspected by
Recorded	Date
Action	
File	
Inspect	